Martin Manley's

BASKETBALL
HEAVEN

1990

DOUBLEDAY
NEW YORK LONDON TORONTO SIDNEY AUCKLAND

PUBLISHED BY DOUBLEDAY

a division of Bantam Doubleday Dell Publishing Group, Inc.
666 Fifth Avenue, New York, New York 10103

DOUBLEDAY and the portrayal of an anchor with a dolphin are
trademarks of Doubleday, a division of Bantam Doubleday
Dell Publishing Group, Inc.

ISBN 0-385-26658-8

ACKNOWLEDGEMENTS

There are a number of people that deserve mention. In one way or another each of these people were important to the production of this book. My thanks to Lori Ince, Doug Birtell, Scott Ferguson, Bill James, Virginia Pruitt, David Gernert, Charles Schreiner, Alex Sachare, Kevin Maher, Liz Darhansoff and Chuck Verrill.

Perhaps a more essential individual is David Stern. His direction of the NBA has been nothing short of miraculous. If not for him, <u>Basketball Heaven</u> would not be possible.

Finally, I have to give credit to my wife - Chris. Her support has been unwavering and I'm lucky she's been willing to sacrifice so much of me to my other love - basketball.

"Uh,oh. Magic's not playing.
I'd better recalculate the odds of the Lakers winning.
Let's see. Hmm.... Here we go.... 312,911 to 1.
Wow! That really tightens it up!"

INTRODUCTION

DEXTER:

Last season I sent a copy of my book to Ted Green of "SportsLook" (ESPN). After a week or so I called him to get his opinion. When I told the receptionist that my name was Martin Manley, she put me on hold. After a few moments Ted came on and loudly greeted me, "Hello, Dexter". Well, we had a good chuckle over that one. But I thought it would be interesting to add an alter-ego to this year's edition. Thanks to Ted, I've named him Dexter, and he disputes various subjects with me in chapter 1. I've asked him to come back next year for a longer stay. It's funny, but I have the feeling he'll acquiesce to my wishes.

~~FOOTBALL~~ BASKETBALL:

One of the more interesting aspects of sports is that people tend to excel at what they're exposed to. Clearly, the best hockey players in the world (per capita) are in the Soviet Union and Canada, the best snow skiers are in Austria and Switzerland, the best tennis players are in Sweden and Germany, and, of course, the best golfers are in the United States. But there's no logical reason to believe that humans in any country couldn't be as good as humans in any other country at any sport given the same amount of national fervor, training, and facilities. But like everything else that varies from one country to the next, so do these phenomena. Consequently, America plays the best football, baseball, and basketball in the world, but lags far behind in rugby, ping pong, and soccer.

What's more, even within the United States, there is a clear preference by our youth for particular sports depending on the state. Volleyball is big in California, basketball in Indiana, football in Texas. In fact, each part of the country has become identified with certain sports. Collegiate baseball is big in the southwest, wrestling in the central states, and hockey in the north.

Here in the Big-8 we've always been known for our football - especially since 1971. In that year Nebraska defeated Oklahoma for the national title. Oh sure, they had to go on and play bowl games, but both teams demolished their opponents and finished 1-2 in the polls. Colorado had lost to both during the season, but to no one else. When they won their bowl game, it vaulted them to 3rd. Never before has it happened, nor likely will it ever happen again that a conference placed 1-2-3 in the final poll. From then on the Big-8 was "the football conference".

Obviously, with Oklahoma and Missouri's recent basketball success and KU's national championship, the Big-8 has become more respectable in basketball. In fact, as shocking as it will be to a lot of people, this non-North Carolina, non-Indiana, non-populous football hotbed has produced the most *basketball* 1st-round draft picks the last two years (8) of any conference in America. When you divide the total number of players by the number of teams in each conference, the achievement is even more remarkable. Oh, and by the way, in doing that, we've just discovered a "creative statistic".

TOP CONFERENCES FROM 1987-88 TO 1988-89

	RAW STATS		CREATIVE STAT
	Players	Teams	Players/Teams
BIG-8	**8**	**8**	**1.00**
BIG-10	7	10	.70
BIG EAST	6	10	.60
METRO	4	7	.57
SEC	4	10	.40
ACC	3	8	.38
PAC-10	3	10	.30

CREATIVE STATISTICS:

In last year's book, I defined a creative stat as a "...product of more than one raw statistic. Points *and* games are raw, but points *per* game is creative." That's certainly a true statement. For example, a creative baseball statistic which says that Pitcher A had a successful save ratio of 81.8% is much more meaningful than saying he had 27 saves or 41 appearances. Those are raw numbers. Even the statement that he had 33 save opportunities is raw - it's just a number. Without the benefit of preconceived ideas as to what's meaningful, raw numbers are useless. But since we know 100% is perfect, we can conclude a fair amount by knowing only that Pitcher A had a successful save ratio of 81.8% (27/33). If Pitcher B was 77.6%, then Pitcher A was better or more dependable. It's nearly irrelevant that Pitcher B had 38 saves because it took him 49 opportunities to achieve them. Creative statistics include ratios and percentages because raw stats never take into consideration how many chances a player had to achieve them.

You see, what makes a stat creative is that it is the product of more than one raw statistic. But it is also something else. If I say that the Denver Nuggets under 9 years of Doug Moe are 89-49 during the month of March, or if I tell you that they have won more games then they've lost every one of those months, then I haven't multiplied or divided anything, but I've still given you a "creative statistic". Therefore, my definition of a creative stat must be expanded to include any raw number (89 wins and 49 losses are indeed raw numbers) which is used in a unique or unusual manner. The previous example is a good one, but there are many others.

If I tell you that Clyde Drexler collected more offensive rebounds last season than any other NBA guard since this statistic was first kept in 1974, I'm saying something important and meaningful. On the other hand, if I tell you he had 289 offensive boards and leave it at that - so what? Does that mean anything to you? Here is a case where the raw statistic became creative - not by arithmetic manipulations, but by placing it in the context of an unusual category. Saying Kareem Abdul-Jabbar played at age 42 is one thing, but saying he's the oldest player who ever played in the NBA is something else. There are thousands of ways to make a "raw" statistic into a far more entertaining and enlightening "creative" statistic, but the endeavor always boils down to two methods - either by adding, subtracting, multiplying or dividing one or more raw statistics into one creative stat or by examining a raw stat within the context of a unique or unusual category.

SUGGESTIONS:

Each year I have taken this opportunity to tell the basketball world what I think needs to be done to improve the game. Although there are many changes which I can suggest, I'll narrow them down to a handful.

1) I'd be surprised to see this idea implemented before the year 2,000, but I would like to see two awards - one for the Most Productive and one for the Most Valuable. It's the old "Chamberlain vs Russell" issue revisited in recent years by Jordan vs Johnson or Jordan vs Bird. Oftentimes, the winner of each award would be the same person, but oftentimes not. In 1989, I can easily imagine Jordan winning one and Magic winning the other had both awards been given. The problem with the current manner of rewarding excellence is that none of us knows (And after all these years, when will we?) what we're really voting on.

2) Expand the All-Star teams from 2 to 4 (1 for each division) and play a 4-team tournament. Not only would this begin to give each division an identity which will become more and more important as the number of teams increases, but would also accomodate more and more good players. I suggest cutting the teams from 12 players to 10, however. Also, expand the activities to include exhibitions on rebounding and passing like I've suggested before. Finally expand the slam-dunk and 3-point shooting to two or three size categories. Let's see some 7 footers shoot 3-pointers or some 6'1 guards (Spud was an anomaly) stuffing it.

3A) It's past time to give the defender some rights in the NBA. Ninety percent of the time a player will "draw" the foul by jumping into a vertical or even backpeddling defender. Barely 1 of 10 times will he be charged with "creating" or "causing" the foul when in actuality he does just that probably half the time.

3B) There absolutely must be a new statistic called "turnovers created" (or some such label). In my opinion, this category could just be lumped under steals because that's what, in effect, they are. Dennis Rodman probably forces opposing teams into turning the ball over five times a game just by taking charges. It is exactly the same as a steal - only better. (The opposing player gets a foul.) How can that not be rewarded? I would go another step. When a player clearly forces an errant pass or causes his opponent to dribble out of bounds or was in any way the primary reason why the other team turned the ball over, he should be given a "turnover created" or a "steal". This statistic would diminish enormously the difficulty in measuring defensive value. An argument against it will be that it is too subjective, that all of the other basketball statistics are absolute and verifiable. That's incorrect in the first place, as steals and blocks and turnovers are sometimes able to be debated, but even if this allegation were true, other sports have their subjective scoring. In baseball, it's hits and errors. In football, it's tackles and yardage gained. Besides, no law says that a David Stern-led National Basketball Association can't lead the way here like they have done in so many other areas.

4A) How about the NBA asking each team to keep track of dunks and layups? Some teams already do, but the figures are not made public. Shooting percentages would be far more fascinating and meaningful if those could be tabulated separately.

4B) I hate to say it. I've hated to say it in the past. And I'll probably hate to say it in the future. But, if there is anything among these suggestions that I wish the NBA would accept, it's this one. Until they do, there will continue to be a major misunderstanding about shooting percentages. The mistake is that the league still combines the 2-pt and 3-pt shots when identifying a player's "field-goal-percentage". I hate that statistic with a passion. It is 100% meaningless and irrelevant! Before the introduction of the 3-pointer it was fine, but once that occurred, it was immediately outdated. Even so, it was an ongoing mistake that could be tolerated until more and more players started shooting more and more 3-pointers. As they did, their shooting percentages began dropping even if their effective shooting percentage (points made off field goals divided by field goals attempted - see page 217) was as good or better. What is the point in comparing two players' field goal percentages when one player's stats are obviously skewed by having shot a lot of 3-pointers. Michael Adams had a "poor" 43.3% shooting percentage, but his value as a shooter was very high because he shot 466 treys. Why can't we just say he shot 3-pointers at 35.6% (good), 2-pointers at 49.0% (average), and 1-pointers at 81.9% (good)? We already break up the other areas of his game (offensive vs defensive rebounds, for example) into statistics which evaluate where he excels and where he doesn't, why can't we break down something so obvious as shooting? To say that Adams shot 43.3% tells 100% of the population 0% of nothing! Dump it. Please.

5) No one will accept this, so I'll just make this award official in that my recognition is official. I am hereby declaring the first annual 1989 Special K **Coaching** Award goes to Chuck Daly (runners-up were Pat Riley and Lenny Wilkens), the 1989 Special K **Player** Award goes to Magic Johnson (runner-up to Michael Jordan), and the 1989 Special K **Team** Award goes to the Lakers (runner-up to the Celtics). As you computer wizards know, K means thousand. So my award is for the period of 1,000 days (3 years). Now, I suppose you want to know why I would give an award for a 3-year period. Well, I think it makes sense. In the case of Riley, he would have won it in 1988 which actually covered 1986-88. He might have won it before as well. This, despite the fact that he has never stood a ghost of a chance at Coach-of-the-Year and probably won't as long as there are 27 teams in the league, many of which will improve dramatically from one year to the next. Additionally, as long as any coach has a Magic Johnson, he won't get an annual coaching honor either.

CONTENTS

CONTENTS

LONELINESS
ISIAH THOMAS VS LOS ANGELES

CHAPTER 1

POINTS VS PRODUCTION

POINTS VS PRODUCTION

A Fan's Introduction to Production Rating

I've always found it puzzling, even mystifying, why every major American sport except basketball places so much more emphasis on portions of the game other than scoring. Not that they shouldn't. That's my point. For some reason basketball is viewed differently. The player who scores is the player who is widely remembered, not the player who stole the pass, or the player who made the assist, but rather the one who finished the play - he who stuffeth the ball. In most cases the act of scoring a bucket is far less demanding of skill than the ability required to resist two fakes, leap high into the air and swat away the shot of a determined scorer - all without fouling. Nevertheless, it's the shot that the shot-blocker missed, the one that went in, that gets the attention - and the headlines.

In hockey an assist is of equal value to a goal. A player's "points" are his assists *plus* his goals. It's never been disputed that a goal is nearly impossible to achieve without some great passing. Of course, in hockey that's especially true. In football, the quarterback's pass is generally regarded at least as highly as the receiver's catch even though it was not the quarterback who scored. And, it's as traditional as moms and apple pie that the batter who drives in the runner on base will get the lion's share of the credit in baseball. Willie Wilson can bunt for a single, steal second, go to third on a ground out and come home on George Brett's sacrifice fly, but it won't be Wilson's run that makes the All Star voters take notice nearly as much as Brett's RBI. That's OK because that's baseball. But isn't it interesting how baseball's hero is not so much the one who scores as the one who *helped* him score.

Certainly, there is nothing wrong with admiring all of basketball's great scorers. Let's face it. The game is won or lost based on the number of points on the scoreboard. Regardless of how "well" the team played, they lose if they don't outscore their opponents. It's that simple. Basketball, unlike life, has an absolute winner and an absolute loser. It all boils down to points. I guess then, I can understand why the temptation is so strong to reward the scorer with the publicity, but that doesn't mean I accept it.

Several years ago I developed a very simple formula for evaluating a player's overall contributions. As an, admittedly, insane basketball fan, I just couldn't stand to continue seeing players evaluated exclusively by points. I thought a simple, but comprehensive, formula could be used to evaluate a player's complete game performance. What I came up with was the Production Rating. Never again would I be in the dark about which player really deserved the headlines. My dream, of course, was, and is, that not only I could be enlightened, but so could basketball fans everywhere. That's why I originally wrote Basketball Heaven a couple years ago. It won't surprise anybody to know that basketball statistical data goes miles beyond Production Rating. I'll be delving deeply into Production Rating later and if you want to read on, great. But if you don't, just use the following formula every time you peruse a box score and you'll know which player won the game for his team - even if the newspaper doesn't tell you.

(PTS + REB + AST + BLK + STL) - (T.O. + MISSED FG + MISSED FT) = CREDITS
CREDITS FOR SEASON / GAMES = CREDITS PER GAME = PRODUCTION RATING

I grew up in rural Kansas 20 years ago. Let me tell you, the box scores in those days were abysmally deficient. They told only the halftime score, the final score, the total points each player had accumulated and if he fouled out. Can you believe that? Who cares if he fouled out? Even then, I was lucky if the player's points added up to the team's totals.

The box score is an invention of sports lovers to condense an entire game into a few moments of analysis. It works pretty well nowadays - especially considering what it used to be. Nevertheless, it has some weaknesses. In the introduction, I discuss additional areas where statistical data should be kept. Apart from that, however, everything you need to know is basically available in the boxscore. (I'm referring to the complete boxscores seen in USA Today and other major newspapers.) However, if the boxscore had just one more line for credits or Production Rating, it would make a world of difference. If a player's production were to become as commonplace as his scoring, it would greatly benefit the average fan's appreciation of the game.

As you can see by the formula, it only takes a few seconds to compute from a complete box score, but it is so unnecessary. If only the existing box score were modified to include Production Rating (PR) it would be beneficial since so few fans will calculate PR on their own. I believe that sooner or later a player's total game credits will be in the box score. I would think to the right of points would be a good place for it.

The mentality that we, as fans, exhibit while skimming the box score is the same as that of the writer who must give an account of a particular game. He or she thinks that the leading scorer is the one who "led" the team to victory. Or if he doesn't believe it himself, he believes the reader will. After all, who's going to take you seriously if you begin your story with "James Donaldson led the Dallas Mavericks to victory last night with 15 rebounds and 9 points." if Rolando Blackman led the team in scoring with 20 points. That is an example of two players who are better and worse than their scoring average indicates. Blackman averages 19.67 ppg while Donaldson averages only 9.08 ppg. Despite this seemingly insurmountable margin of superiority on Blackman's part, Donaldson has a higher Production Rating. His 17.70 credits-per-game (cpg) is more important to Dallas than Blackman's 16.74 cpg. A really astute fan already knows Donaldson's value, but Production Rating verifies it. So does the fact that Dallas has been 11-4 without Blackman the last two years while only 10-20 without Donaldson. Now I ask, who really leads Dallas to victory? In this case, the 9 point-per-game player, not the 20 point-per-game player.

On March 21 of last season, the Nuggets played the Rockets at Houston. And although I can cite many similar examples, this one should be adequate to make my point. The entire write-up in USA Today went like this: "Alex English scored 29 of his 37 points in the second half to boost Denver to a 112-110 victory against Houston, moving the Nuggets to within a half game of the Rockets in the NBA Midwest Division. English had 18 points in the third quarter and 11 in the fourth to give Denver its fourth consecutive victory and end a two-game Houston winning streak."

Now I certainly have no criticism of the highlighting of Alex English's 37 points. I do have a regret, however. I mourn the fact that not 10 individuals alive who read that write-up and who didn't see the game know English was no more valuable or productive against Houston than Fat Lever. Even if they glanced at the box score what they would have seen was only 16 points for Lever. How can that compete with 37? Fat had 2 more rebounds, 8 more assists, 5 more steals and 6 less field-goal-attempts $(2+8+5+6=21)$ $(21+16=37)$. As you can see, both players had equal games. As it turns out, both had 28 credits. Both deserved mention, but as is usually the case, the scorer got it.

To make matters worse, that exclusivity of recognition unfortunately goes beyond a given box score. Alex English has been an All-Star each of the last three years while Fat Lever has been snubbed twice. This, despite the fact that Lever has ranked in the Top-10 by production each year while English was out of the Top-20 twice. But in scoring, ah. That's different. English has outscored Lever by 8 ppg in that span of time. Several years ago, Alex was generous enough to offer to trade his position on the All-Star team to Fat. The league said "no, no", but why do you think he did it? He knew what the deal was. Lever was the most valuable player on the team then and has been ever since!

Production Rating is very simple and very meaningful. As a composite statistic, it incorporates various positive and negative values a player accumulates during a game. Tellingly, it follows very closely the parameters of scoring. 30+ per game is *super* star, while 25-30 is *all* star. 20-25 is *very* good, while 15-20 is *pretty* good. 10-15 is a *role* player, while below 10 is a *bench* player.

I felt it was obvious that whatever composite index the general public used, it would never be accepted unless it was 1) simple and 2) fit into the preconceived ideas of what we already know to be true. We already accept those scoring parameters above as *the* yardstick to measure value. I'm merely suggesting that we plug in Production instead of, or in conjunction with, points. 30 points-per-game is still excellent. It's just that points represents only part of production. 30 credits-per-game is what really matters. If a player has a Production Rating of 30, it says a lot more about his value than if a player scores 30.

One last example just to reinforce your understanding of Production Rating and its merit. Kelly Tripucka and Larry Nance are both Eastern Conference forwards recently traded by Western Conference teams. Who is the more productive of the two? No, I'm not going to shock you by telling you that Tripucka is the superior player. Nevertheless, his scoring average is 22.62 while Nance's average is a mere 17.25. On the flip side, Nance has a Production Rating of 22.66 vs Tripucka's 17.61. Nance produces at a greater rate than he scores, while Tripucka is just the opposite. Nance overcame a 5 point scoring *disadvantage* to take a 5 credit production *advantage*. He did it by averaging 3 less missed field goals, 4 more rebounds, 1 less assist, 1.5 fewer turnovers and 2.5 more blocks per game (3+4 - 1+1.5+2.5=10). That's how he gained 10 credits on Tripucka's scoring advantage and why he's a superior player.

Nance and Tripucka are two of the more "lopsided" players in the NBA. What I mean by that is that the differential between their scoring and production is fairly large (approximately 5). Magic Johnson, at 10.84, has the largest difference between Production Rating minus points-per-game. What this means is that although he scores well, he produces at a rate for a point guard that only Oscar Robertson has ever matched. Jeff Malone, at 6.46, leads all players in the differential between points-per-game minus Production Rating. Shown below are the top-10 in both categories. I've also shown a list on the following page of the ten players whose scoring and production are nearly equivalent. As you can see, Production Ratings averages are slightly higher than scoring averages. I explained all about that in last year's book so I won't go into it now. Even so, they are similar enough that it is fair to say that each point scored is, in effect, a credit which ultimately ends up in someone's Production Rating. In some cases, scoring and production vary a lot. In other cases, like that of Steve Johnson, it is virtually one and the same.

PRODUCTION RATING MINUS POINTS

PLAYER	TEAM	PR	PPG	MAR
E. Johnson	LA.L	33.31	22.47	10.84
Eaton	Utah	16.59	6.20	10.39
Stockton	Utah	27.40	17.07	10.33
McMillan	Seat	16.63	7.09	9.54
Donaldson	Dall	17.70	9.08	8.62
W. Cooper	Denv	14.43	6.58	7.85
Lever	Denv	27.48	19.85	7.63
Parish	Bost	26.10	18.57	7.53
Rodman	Detr	16.32	8.96	7.36
D. Walker	Wash	16.13	9.04	7.09

POINTS MINUS PRODUCTION RATING

PLAYER	TEAM	PPG	PR	MAR
J. Malone	Wash	21.72	15.26	6.46
Ellis	Seat	27.48	21.13	6.35
Chapman	Char	16.89	11.03	5.86
English	Denv	26.52	21.38	5.14
Tripucka	Char	22.62	17.61	5.01
McDaniel	Seat	20.45	16.29	4.16
Reid	Char	14.72	10.85	3.87
Dailey	LA.C	16.14	12.48	3.66
Ed Johnson	Phoe	21.49	17.93	3.56
McGee	N.J.	12.97	9.51	3.46

PRODUCTION RATING MINUS POINTS

PLAYER	TEAM	PR	PPG	(PR-PPG)
Sparrow	Miam	12.62	12.50	+.12
Cartwright	Chic	12.49	12.38	+.11
Ainge	Sacr	17.64	17.55	+.09
Dudley	Clev	3.08	3.03	+.05
S. Johnson	Port	10.04	10.01	+.03
Gilliam	Phoe	15.74	15.89	-.15
Schoene	Seat	5.03	5.19	-.16
Hodges	Chic	8.78	8.97	-.19
K. Smith	Sacr	17.04	17.32	-.28
J. Edwards	Detr	7.01	7.30	-.29

Although I'm pleased with how well Production Rating works out as a composite statistic, it seems to be true that basketball is not the ideal sport for this type of index. It is, however, better adapted to it than hockey or football for several reasons. Hockey has so few measurable statistics that trying to assess a player's performance apart from the obvious goals and assists would be impossible. It might be feasible to assess a quarterback in football - in fact, that's already being done - but even then it is only with respect to other quarterbacks. There is simply no adequate way to statistically measure linemen or cornerbacks or special teams players.

Baseball is different. The national pastime is extremely conducive to this type of stat. Total Average was created by Tom Boswell and is used commonly in baseball as a single stat to measure all players' offensive contributions. Baseball strategies can be classified offensively in hundreds of ways. Every pitch is thrown in a "situation". That situation can be evaluated by dozens of variables. Consequently, the opportunities to create composite formulas based on baseball stats are endless. Even so, what about pitchers and defense?

Basketball has one major advantage over the other sports. The NBA has statistical categories which cover most every phase of the game, both offensive and defensive. More importantly, every player has the opportunity to equally participate in every statistical category. Because of this unique characteristic, a composite statistic in basketball may even be more meaningful than a composite statistic in any of the other major sports - including baseball.

Before I go on, I should say that no statistical ranking can measure a clutch player's abilities in the closing seconds of a game. Nor can it measure a player's abilities to psych up his teammates or psych out his opponents. It can't measure flash, charisma, or intensity, ingredients which all go into the process of winning. Still, those categories which are statistically measurable constitute at least 90% of winning and losing.

A Fanatic's Technical Analysis of Production Rating

Michael Jordan was not only the league's leading scorer in 1989 but an excellent producer as well. He scored 32.51 points-per-game and 36.99 credits-per-game. Production Rating is derived simply by adding 5 positive values and subtracting 3 negative values. On the positive side, Jordan scored 2633 points, blocked 65 shots, stole the ball 234 times, corralled 652 rebounds, and dished out 650 assists. On the negative side, he missed 829 field goals, 119 free throws, and committed 290 turnovers. By applying the formula, he earned 2996 credits. Since he played in 81 games, he had a Production Rating of 36.99. As I've stated before, this means he earned 36.99 credits-per-game. As you might expect, Michael was the most productive player in the league for 1989. In fact, his PR is the highest since Kareem Abdul-Jabbar's in 1976 (39.65).

Formulas are a dime a dozen. You know it and so do I. Anyone who can add and subtract can create his or her version of Production Rating. That's not to say, however, that they don't have any validity. Perfectly legitimate arguments can be made for many of them. Nevertheless, I think I've seen and analyzed them all. And I continue to believe that taking everything into consideration, the version of Production Rating (PR) which I've spelled out here is the most desirable.

As I mentioned earlier, I wanted a formula which, when applied, yielded a result which had aesthetic meaning (30 is All-NBA, 25 is All-Star, 20 is good, etc.). Other formulas which end up with numbers that don't fit into preexisting categories in our thinking just cannot be expected to catch on with the general public. Who is going to remember that 902 is the best or that a .6124 led the league? But tell me that Michael Jordan ended the season with 36.99 credits-per-game, and I'll know that you're telling me that he was probably the league's most productive player - just as if you were to tell me that he scored 32.51 points-per-game, which would indicate by this that he was probably the league's top scorer too.

The second thing I wanted to accomplish with PR was to create something that could be calculated easily on a game-by-game basis. Five positive and three negative numbers are easy to add and subtract. The third priority when creating this ultimate formula was to make sure that it covered the four major aspects of the game - shooting, rebounding, passing, and defense. As I hope to show, Production Rating not only accomplishes these 3 goals, but is based on a very fundamental premise.

My theory is founded on that premise. In very general terms, each team's possession yields approximately 1 point (100 possessions = 100 points). This is not technically correct, but it is very close, and certainly it is accurate enough for the purposes of this discussion. I'll debate a slight variation on the principle of 1 possession = 1 point later, but for now it will more than do to understand the basics. This 100 = 100 = 100 could be proved valid if I were able to identify each CREDIT with either a point or a possession.

Having established my premise, the first step was to look at the statistical categories authorized by the NBA: games, minutes, 3-point FGA & FGM, 2-point FGA & FGM, FTA & FTM, offensive and defensive rebounds, assists, fouls, disqualifications, steals, turnovers, blocked shots, points, and scoring average. By analysis, I was able to eliminate various categories as too cumbersome, too insignificant, too irrelevant, or combinations of all three. Here is a breakdown of each statistical category and arguments for or against each category being included in the Production Rating formula.

The first statistic I want to look at is fouls. I decided to ignore fouls, since determining the value or lack of value a foul represents is very difficult. If your team has a one point lead and your opponent has the ball 75 feet from the basket with only two seconds left, obviously to foul would be foolish. Rarely, however, are fouls so clearly a negative statistic. Later in this chapter I'll discuss four possible variations to Production Rating. The addition of fouls as a negative credit will be one of them. For now, let's leave them out.

Disqualifications are a negative statistic, but the inability to play and contribute in other statistical categories already penalizes the player. Therefore, DQ's need not be considered. Scoring average is merely a reflection of points and games, both of which are already being considered in credits-per-game. Finally, minutes-played is used only in qualifying the player. This leaves thirteen categories which can be reduced to nine by simply combining some shooting groups.

I then tried to apply the remaining statistical categories to this principle of 1 point = 1 possession = 1 credit. Here, in a nutshell, is how I justify taking points, missed field goals, missed free throws, total rebounds, assists, steals, turnovers, and blocked shots and turning them into a consistent, meaningful number. Five (5) positive categories minus three (3) negative categories equals total credits. This statistic is then divided by the number of games played and the ultimate evaluation is by credits/games or Production Rating.

The important premise here is that 1 point = 1 rebound = 1 assist = 1 steal = 1 blocked shot. On the negative side, 1 missed field goal = 1 missed free throw = 1 turnover. By relating each category or credit to the concept of 1 point = 1 possession = 1 credit, it can be shown to be a valid theory.

To begin with, assessing the impact of a turnover is easy. It is a loss of a possession and thus a loss of a point. As a result, a turnover is 1 negative credit. A steal is just the opposite. It is the gaining of a possession and thus the gaining of a point. As a result, a steal is 1 positive credit. A rebound always represents the gaining of a possession - even an offensive rebound. The reason is that the alternative is to let your opponent get a defensive rebound and thus lose a possession. And yes, it's a fallacy to believe that an offensive rebound is more valuable than a defensive rebound, even though it seems like an offensive rebound is better. Dexter: "Aren't you more likely to get an easy basket after an offensive board?" Clearly you are. But that's irrelevant to the question. Let's take it to the extreme. Suppose an offensive stickback was worth 100 points. Which is more valuable, getting it and winning or stopping it and winning? Obviously, they are of equal value. Besides, in terms of possession, there can't even be an emotional argument against their equality. Consequently, a rebound - any rebound - equals 1 positive credit.

This still leaves 2-point FG's, 3-point FG's, free throws, assists, blocked shots, and points. Let's look at blocked shots first. A percentage of the time a blocked shot will result in a change of possession, but many times it will not. So how can one justify making it equal to a steal or rebound? I think it can be done this way. As I said earlier, certain qualities are not measurable. One of those is intimidation. How much worse do one's opponents shoot because of a particular defensive player? Probably the only measurable statistic which incorporates this intangible facet of the game is blocked shots. In fact, I've been tempted to make blocked shots equal to 2 credits. Not so much because they prevent 2 points from being scored (we can't always know that), but because Mark Eaton, for example, may block 4 shots per game, but he probably alters 20. (Read discussion on Defensive Player-of-the-Year on page 32.) As a result, I'm giving a blocked shot, just like a steal and a rebound, 1 positive credit - partly because of a change of possession, partly because of intimidation and defense, partly because most shots which are blocked are close to the basket and would likely have gone in, and partly because it takes time off the 24 second clock, which might prevent a team from scoring on its possession.

Next we examine assists. An assist does not affect possession in any way. It is not a point either. So how can it be a credit? It's not easy to explain, but here goes. Leadership, ball control, and passing comprise the largest group of intangible facets. Each of these facets are at least partially measurable by assists. The assist leader on a team is usually the player who brings the ball up court, dribbles against pressure, risks the most turnovers, sets up scoring opportunities, calls plays, and controls tempo. Most importantly, though, is the argument that an assist turns a possession (worth approximately 1 point) into 2 points. Of course, a few assists result in 3 point possessions, but that's quibbling for this basic formula. Therefore, an assist is worth 1 credit.

That leaves only scoring. As I said, a point is roughly equal to a possession which is roughly equal to a credit. However, what about missed shots? Every missed 2 or 3-point FGA as well as most missed FTAs are a loss of possession for the following reason. The team may retain possession with an offensive rebound, but that means the possession was, in effect, lost and then regained. If the missed shot was not a negative credit, the offensive rebound could not be a positive one. The only questionable area here is the missed first free throw of two attempts. There is no loss of possession, but there is an implied loss of a point or at least nearly a point since most free throws are made. A free throw is, as it says, free. To miss it is to lose something already, in effect, given to you. Finally, there is no chance to regain possession to compensate for it.

As a result of this interesting phenomenon that 1 possession = 1 point = 1 credit, it is possible to measure a player's performance by taking all facets of the game into consideration. To repeat, the formula says:

$$(\text{PTS} + \text{REB} + \text{AST} + \text{BLK} + \text{STL}) - (\text{T.O.} + \text{MISSED FG} + \text{MISSED FT}) = \text{CREDITS}$$

$$\text{CREDITS FOR SEASON / GAMES} = \text{CREDITS PER GAME} = \text{PRODUCTION RATING}$$

The Critic's Challenge to Production Rating

Now having made the case so strongly that Production Rating solves everything from war to famine, let me offer several more views. But before I do, let me preface it. I have, over the years, seen and heard many variations to Production Rating. Some have been published, some have been presented to me during radio talk shows, some have captured my attention by letter. I've examined each of them. In fact, in <u>Basketball Heaven 1987-88</u>, I did a similar study of several specific rating systems. At the time it verified the superiority of Production Rating. Hopefully, a more technical analysis of some of these variations will bear that out as well.

Variation One: Possession = .9275

Some may and have argued that since a possession does not exactly equal a point, that PR should be adjusted accordingly. Fine, let's do it. I discussed two formulas for defining possession last year and neither are the best. However, the one I accepted then is very simple and comes extremely close to what I would now choose as a more accurate version. Without going into all that, let's just accept that 1 possession = .9275 points or 100 possessions = 92.75 points, to think of it as a game. By that criterion, I should substitute into Production Rating .9275 wherever I previously had 1 possession. As you may remember, my justification for rebounds, steals, turnovers, and missed field goals were that they gained or lost 1 possession. I just added or subtracted 1. Well, rather than that, I will now add or subtract .9275. An assist is also affected because I came up with it by saying "2 points minus 1 possession = 1." Let's adjust that to 2 points minus .9275 = 1.0725. Finally, a more technically accurate argument regarding the missed free throw would be to say it costs the shooting team .7677 points (the average FT% in the NBA last season). Here again, I had just used a negative one in PR. I left blocks alone. Again, I believe blocks are under-valued, if anything. I sure can't see making them 7.25% less. And, of course, a point remains a point. The new and improved Production Rating would then look like this.

$$\text{PTS} + [(\text{REB}+\text{STL}-\text{T.O.}-\text{MISSED FG}) * .9275] + (\text{AST} * 1.0725) - (\text{MISSED FT} * .7677) + \text{BLK} = \text{CREDITS}$$

$$\text{CREDITS FOR SEASON / GAMES PLAYED} = \text{CREDITS PER GAME} = \text{PRODUCTION RATING}$$

The obvious question I would ask is, "Do we really need to complicate the formula this much?" After all, if we make these changes no one will waste time calculating this baby out when they read the morning's box score. And we can forget ever having total game credits listed to the right of points. Especially when it's not a whole number any longer. Bryant: "How many credits did Ewing get last night, Willard?" Willard: "Oh, let's see here. Looks like 27.143." Bryant "Say what?" Dexter: "That's a cute story, but at least you could use the more technically accurate version at year's end when ranking players, even if not on a game-by-game basis, couldn't you Manley?" I could, but then the game-by-game credits don't equal those at the end of the year. No, I can only justify it if there is a substantial difference between the two. I think by looking at the top-20 by both PR and Variation One, you can see that the variation has little effect.

PRODUCTION RATING				VARIATION ONE		
	NAME	TEAM	PR		NAME	TEAM	PR
1.	Jordan	Chic	36.99	1.	Jordan	Chic	38.12
2.	Ea. Johnson	LA.L	33.31	2.	Ea. Johnson	LA.L	34.51
3.	Barkley	Phil	32.68	3.	Barkley	Phil	33.24
4.	Olajuwan	Hous	31.02	4.	Olajuwon	Hous	31.74
5.	K. Malone	Utah	29.53	5.	K. Malone	Utah	30.38
6.	Drexler	Port	28.87	6.	Drexler	Port	29.86
7.	Lever	Denv	27.48	7.	Stockton	Utah	28.76
8.	Ewing	N.Y.	27.46	8.	K. Johnson	Phoe	28.51
9.	Stockton	Utah	27.40	9.	Lever	Denv	28.25
10.	K. Johnson	Phoe	27.06	10.	Ewing	N.Y.	27.96
11.	Parish	Bost	26.10	11.	Mullin	G.St	26.94
12.	Mullin	G.St	26.01	12.	Parish	Bost	26.21
13.	Chambers	Phoe	24.11	13.	Chambers	Phoe	24.87
14.	M. Malone	Atla	23.84	14.	McHale	Bost	24.21
15.	McHale	Bost	23.68	15.	M.Malone	Atla	24.16
16.	D. Wilkins	Atla	22.84	16.	D. Wilkins	Atla	23.68
17.	Nance	Clev	22.66	17.	Porter	Port	23.56
18.	Porter	Port	22.42	18.	Price	Clev	23.37
19.	Daugherty	Clev	22.37	19.	Daughtery	Clev	22.97
20.	Price	Clev	22.33	20.	Nance	Clev	22.93

The top-20 are the same players and the top-6 are in the exact same order. The variations are small and exist only where players are closely bunched. Does it really matter if Parish is #12 and Mullin #11 or if Mullin is #12 and Parish #11? I'm all for accuracy, but achieving it is useless and meaningless if it's not feasible to use. Production Rating is feasible, while Variation One, though more technically accurate, isn't.

Variation Two: Fouls

I earlier alluded to the notion of including fouls as a negative credit in Production Rating. As you remember, I dismissed this notion. To begin with, many fouls are considered "smart" ones - for example forcing out-of-bounds plays, sending a poor free throw shooter to the line, or preventing a breakaway layup. Moreover, many fouls do not have any real penalty associated with them at all since they occur prior to the penalty situation. What about all the fouls that come at game's-end in an effort to stop the clock? Would it make sense to penalize a player who was only trying to improve his team's chances of winning? Add to that the fact that an offensive foul *is* a negative credit and is already listed as a turnover on the stat sheets due to a change of possession. Since it is a negative statistic, it would be a mistake to deduct it again as a foul. Also, some loose-ball fouls are treated as some type of a turnover and hence should not be counted again as a foul.

What I intend to show next is what I believe to be the most accurate comprehensive statistical evaluation yet published regarding the negativity of fouls. New information has eliminated the guesswork for some of the most important parts of the formula. Consequently, I hope to show that an average foul technically represents a negative -.322 credits.

Hey Dexter, are you ready to plow through this with me? Dexter: "Well, if you haven't heard anything out of me by the time you're done, just give me a nudge." I'll admit that it is complicated, but not boring. Anyway, we know that there are three ways a player can go to the line. First of all, he can shoot a technical free throw. Second, he might be shooting a free throw to complete a three-point play. Last, of course, he might be going to the line to shoot two free throws. This would be any foul in the act of shooting or any foul in the penalty situation during a game. I will use the 1987-88 stats for this example. During that season there were 54,933 free throws attempted. Thanks to Harvey Pollack, we know that 1133 were as a result of a technical foul, while 5,206 were free throw attempts tacked onto a made field goal. That means 48,594 (54,933 - 5,206 - 1,133) free throw attempts were the result of half that many fouls since each foul yielded two attempts. Consequently, there were 24,297 (48594 / 2) two-shot fouls in 1988.

We also know that every one of the 45,461 fouls was either an offensive foul, a loose ball foul, a foul in the act of shooting, a two-shot foul, or a foul with no penalty (prior to the penalty situation). Four of those variables are known to begin with. We know that there were 3851 offensive fouls and 3977 loose-ball fouls. (Actually, these fouls are calculated by multiplying turnovers by 12.2% and 12.6% - variables which we know are very close to being accurate.) We also know, as previously stated, that there are 5,206 fouls committed during the process of a made field goal. That leaves us with 32,427 fouls (45,461 - 3,851 - 3,977 - 5,206) - some non-penalty, some two-shot. Well, we've already calculated that there were 24,297 two-shot fouls. Therefore, that leaves 8130 (32,427 - 24,297) non-penalty fouls. Ok?

Now, some fouls are smart fouls as I mentioned earlier. Some of them occur in the non-penalty column. In fact, I believe that a team, on an average, has 1/2 of a good foul for each game that is strictly due to preventing a breakaway. (Remember, this is assuming the penalty has not been reached yet.) That means there are 943 fouls that fit into this category and 7187 (8130 - 943) *other* non-penalty fouls. I also claim that some of the two-shot fouls are smart - for example, to prevent an easy layup. I estimate each team has one of these per game or 1,886. Finally, I argue that each team chalks up roughly one foul per game in an effort to stop the clock. This results in another 1,886. On the other hand, bad fouls are the 5,206 committed on a made field goal and 20,525 two-point shot fouls (24,297 - 1,886 - 1,886).

You may be confused, so let me mention each type of foul plus the number committed. Offensive fouls (3,851), loose-ball fouls (3,977), non-penalty fouls (7,187), smart non-penalty fouls (943), smart prevent lay-up fouls (1,886), smart stop clock fouls (1,886), attached to made-field-goal fouls (5,206), bad two-point shot fouls (20,525). Total fouls = 45,461.

The major remaining question is what values (positive or negative) to assign to each type of foul. Well, offensive fouls (3,851) are already deducted as a turnover. So are some loose-ball fouls (3,977). Therefore, they have been "neutralized". Dexter: "I don't think very many loose ball fouls are deducted as a turnover." (I didn't know you were listening. Unfortunately, you are right. I'm a little unsure as to the exact percentage of loose-ball fouls that are regarded as a turnover. For the sake of this discussion, I'll accept that none were - although it hurts my argument. Therefore, each loose ball represents a negative -.5 points. [(2 free throws = 1.5 points) vs (1 possession = 1 point)]. Also neutral is a non-penalty foul (7,187). The last neutral foul is the smart foul which stops the clock (1,886) - although you could argue that if it were smart, why not reward it? There are two reasons. First of all, it takes no real skill to do - anyone can be the designated fouler. The second reason is that it still gives the other team a likely advantage [(2 free throws = 1.5 points) vs (1 possession = 1 point)]. Nevertheless, the player needs to do it to improve his team's chances, so it certainly shouldn't be deducted from his positive stats.

The other two smart fouls I assign positive values to. As to the pre-penalty foul which prevents a breakaway (943), I argue it is worth a +.8 points. Why? Because a breakaway is probably worth 1.8 points, as layins are rarely missed. Since he saved 1.8 points, but the opponent retained possession (-1 point), he therefore had a net gain of +.8 points. The second smart foul that I reward is the foul that prevents a dunk or a layup (1,886) but sends a player to the line (the Bill Laimbeer foul). I'm assuming a player will score 1.5 points from the line, but would have scored an average of 1.9 points on the dunk or layup. That results in a saving of .4 points.

Finally, on the negative side, I submit that each foul in the act of shooting a made field-goal (5,206) costs the fouling team -.75 points. That just means that the player got an extra free throw, of which he is going to hit 75 of 100 (approximate league average). Last, I designate each remaining two-point shot foul (20,525) as a negative -.5 . Here again, by fouling, you gain a possession (+1), but you lose 1.5 points at the line. Thus, a negative -.5 .

Now that I've said all that, I arrive at -.322 (as the value for every foul) by calculating the following sequence: Total negative points = [two-point shot fouls (20,525) times -.50] + [foul in the act of shooting a made field goal (5,206) times -.75] + [loose ball foul (3,977) times -.50] + [smart foul prevent layup (1,886) times .40] + [smart foul prevent breakaway (943) times .80]. There is no need to include in the calculations the three types of neutral fouls since they're just multiplied times zero anyway.

$$(20,525 \times -.50) + (5,206 \times -.75) + (3,977 \times -.50) + (1,886 \times .40) + (943 \times .80) = -14,647$$

The value 14,647 is the total number of negative points created by 45,461 fouls. That means the average foul is a negative .322 (14,647/45,461). With a value that close to zero, I claim it makes no real sense to include it in Production Rating.

For some reason, this variation seems to be the one people get so hung up on. The more I've been asked about fouls, the more positive I am that it would be a mistake to consider them negative in any form. Although I am planning on charting fouls for a large number of games next season to evaluate the positive fouls' value, I doubt that the outcome will affect much the final negativity of a foul (-.322). Naturally, to the degree that a foul forces players to sit, it is harmful, but from the standpoint of production - what the player produced good and bad while *on* the court not what he missed by being *off* the court - fouls are basically meaningless. Therefore, they can be, and I believe should be, ignored in the formula. As you can see by listing the top-20 using this deduction, it doesn't greatly affect PR. Once again, both lists show the same 20 players slightly shuffled. Consequently, why use it?

	PRODUCTION RATING				VARIATION TWO		
	NAME	TEAM	PR		NAME	TEAM	PR
1.	Jordan	Chic	36.99	1.	Jordan	Chic	35.94
2.	Ea. Johnson	LA.L	33.31	2.	Ea. Johnson	LA.L	32.54
3.	Barkley	Phil	32.68	3.	Barkley	Phil	31.54
4.	Olajuwan	Hous	31.02	4.	Olajuwan	Hous	29.64
5.	K. Malone	Utah	29.53	5.	K. Malone	Utah	28.29
6.	Drexler	Port	28.87	6.	Drexler	Port	27.69
7.	Lever	Denv	27.48	7.	Lever	Denv	26.62
8.	Ewing	N.Y.	27.46	8.	Stockton	Utah	26.39
9.	Stockton	Utah	27.40	9.	Ewing	N.Y.	26.13
10.	K. Johnson	Phoe	27.06	10.	K. Johnson	Phoe	26.10
11.	Parish	Bost	26.10	11.	Mullin	G.St	25.26
12.	Mullin	G.St	26.01	12.	Parish	Bost	25.21
13.	Chambers	Phoe	24.11	13.	M. Malone	Atla	23.19
14.	M. Malone	Atla	23.84	14.	Chambers	Phoe	22.96
15.	McHale	Bost	23.68	15.	McHale	Bost	22.69
16.	D. Wilkins	Atla	22.84	16.	D. Wilkins	Atla	22.24
17.	Nance	Clev	22.66	17.	Price	Clev	21.88
18.	Porter	Port	22.42	18.	Nance	Clev	21.78
19.	Daugherty	Clev	22.37	19.	Porter	Port	21.63
20.	Price	Clev	22.33	20.	Daugherty	Clev	21.60

Variation Three: Game Pace

While I'm at it, another commonly argued variation of PR is to consider the pace of the team on which each player played. I can easily see the superficial rationale for this position, however I reject it categorically. In fact, I can no longer understand how anyone can even bother with the discussion. The facts are that a faster pace (meaning higher Production Ratings) means more wins and indicates more talented players. Far too often I've heard the old "Well, I wouldn't want to be rich anyway" justification when referring to team defense. What I mean is that those teams who can't run choose to justify their deficiency by saying they play better defense. Yeh, and if you're interested in buying a bridge or swampland ... The top teams by scoring won over twice as many games as the lowest scoring teams. Do we penalize the better players for making use of their quicker feet or their more accurate shot? That's pointless. Why have a rating system at all if you're going to do that?

Let's look at an example. Suppose TEAM A had a scoring average of 118.6 ppg and led the league. Let's say TEAM B scored only 97.8 ppg and was last among the 25 teams. I realize this argument is going to be simplistic, but it makes the point. Let's also say that our factoring process was to be calculated by saying that all players on TEAM B should multiply their PR by 121% (118.6/97.8 = 1.21) to be fairly evaluated with TEAM A's players. Let's go on to say that a player on TEAM B had a PR of 14.41 which, after being adjusted, was now 17.44. Imagine a player on TEAM A with a nearly identical PR as the now-adjusted player on TEAM B. Should they be equal? Well, let me ask you this. Should Grant Long of Miami and Eddie Johnson of Phoenix be equal? That's exactly who those hypothetical players are on TEAMS A & B. In effect, you are undoing the very positive things these player's did all year. If Phoenix defeated Miami on an average by the score of 119-98 (which they would), they will have approximately 21 more credits distributed among their players despite the same number of possessions (meaning that both teams had the same number of opportunities to create positive credits). Phoenix just did a lot better job of it. The attempt at factoring means either 21 free credits are given to Miami or 21 less credits are given to Phoenix. In either case it means a statistical lie! It means that this argument's supporter(s) must say to Mark West, "No, Mark, you didn't really get those blocks" and to Kevin Johnson, "Sorry, Kev, that just looked like an assist." Christmas comes early to Ron Seikaly when you tell him "We feel sorry for you. Here's a few more points on a few less shots." Come on! The reality is that Phoenix won this hypothetical game by 21 points because they do the 5 positive things in PR better and don't do the 3 negative things in PR as bad. If you factor out the credit advantage to the Phoenix players, the 119 and 98 averages would have been a lot closer than in actuality.

Besides that, 12 of the top 13 scoring teams all had winning records. More scoring means, on an average, more winning. Period. All teams in the NBA have effectively the same motive. They all want to score as many points as possible, they play by the same rules, and every team since 1955 has played with a 24 second shot clock. Of course, maybe it was the coach's decision to have Miami only score 97.8 ppg. (That's sarcasm, by the way.)

Variation Four: 48-Minute Projections

Dexter: "This is a variation which is one that you should really appreciate, Martin. It's the notion of measuring production on a 48 minute basis. After all, you do all your other rankings on a 48 minute basis (rebounds, assists, blocks, steals)." While I agree that it is more accurate to evaluate a player's production while in the game, I can only use the 48 minute rankings as an interesting list for this book, not the basis for ultimate rankings. Why?

To begin with, let me justify the 48 minute basis for the other categories. I think the notion of basing excellence on cumulative data is an old argument overcome years ago when the league quit giving awards based on total rebounds or points or assists etc. per *season* and went to the total per *game*. The rationale for this change was that a player might only play 2/3rds of the season. He should still qualify, but if he doesn't have an inordinately high number of (say) assists, he will lose the title to someone who played every game. Common sense says to go one step further and ask, what if he plays 2/3rds of the minutes (not games, but minutes) that another player plays? One plays 36 minutes per game, another 24. Assuming the 24 minutes would qualify him for the title, he still loses because he couldn't accomplish as much in so little time though his per-minute stats were better. I argue that he should, of course, get the title. Why? Simple. He's the best. Assuming reasonable qualification standards, when he's on the floor, he's the best. How do you argue with that?

I have decided, however, to use scoring <u>per game</u>, not per 48 minutes, as the criterion for the top scorer. Dexter: "Isn't this 100% inconsistent with (reb, ast, blk & stl)?" Yes, nevertheless, I do so because I have always believed that many scorers (shooters) do not help their team. If a player scores quickly while in the game, he may lead the league in points-per-48 minutes even though he's a gunner shooting 41% from the field. He's certainly not deserving of an award. That same player will never lead in pts/games, though, because no coach will play him enough minutes in every game since his shooting can be so costly. This player is most likely going to be used to try to come back from a big deficit. If he's cold, so what. You were going to lose anyway. If he's hot, he may pull the game out for you. Because a player can *choose* to shoot anytime, whereas the other 4 performance categories (reb, ast, blk & stl) happen only by the old-fashioned way, I have had to view scoring differently.

A second reason to use pts/games as opposed to pts-per-48 minutes is that it is *the* single statistic which is identified with basketball. Every NBA fan conjures up a meaning when he or she hears 30 ppg. On a 48 minute basis, 30 pts becomes confusing as to how good that is. Quick, tell me. Where does 30 pts based on 48 minutes rank? I'll tell you since you probably don't know. It ranks 25th depending on how you qualify players, whereas it ranks 2nd by pts/games. On the other hand, far fewer fans have preconceived ideas about rebounding-per-game or assists-per-game. So I can convert those to 48 minute numbers without confusing too many people.

Now that you see why I maintain 48 minute averages for (reb, ast, blk & stl) but not for points-per-game, you can surely understand my desire to use credits-per-game as opposed to credits-per-48 minutes. The main reason is to follow the same parameters of scoring - you know 30+ is All-NBA, 25+ is All-Star etc. The second reason, though, is because of my problem with scoring - which is that it is a sometimes selfish, sometimes misleading statistic. Since points are a big part of credits, PR would be adversely affected by some potential "bad" scoring if done on a 48 minute basis. Even so, PR/48 is relevant if only to see who might be a diamond in the rough. Two years ago John Stockton ranked in the top-15 by credits-per-48 minutes even though his PR rank was #80. After reading that, Frank Layden started playing him more and look what happened. He was #8 in 1988 and #9 in 1989. (Actually, I don't know if Frank was swayed by his credits-per-minute rank or not.) I thought it would be interesting to see the players whose rank increased the most by virtue of a 48 minute system. Maybe some of these are future John Stocktons. Take a look.

	NAME	TEAM	RANK BY CREDITS PER GAME (PRODUCTION RATING)	RANK BY CREDITS PER 48 MINUTES	POSITIONS GAINED IN RANK
1.	Corbin	Phoe	128	54	+74
2.	Threatt	Seat	142	68	+74
3.	W. Cooper	Denv	96	24	+72
4.	Hoppen	Char	156	87	+69
5.	O. Smith	G.St	146	82	+64
6.	Schayes	Denv	85	23	+62
7.	Bogues	Char	127	69	+58
8.	Higgins	G.St	115	58	+57
9.	Pinckney	Bost	99	43	+56

	NAME	TEAM	RANK BY CREDITS PER GAME (PRODUCTION RATING)	RANK BY CREDITS PER 48 MINUTES	POSITIONS GAINED IN RANK
10.	J. Williams	Clev	94	41	+53
11.	Koncak	Atla	144	92	+52
12.	Teagle	G.St	112	62	+50
13.	Rodman	Detr	77	29	+48
14.	W. Davis	Denv	123	75	+48
15.	L. Smith	G.St	114	72	+42

By now you have surely surmised that I am satisfied with Production Rating as I originally described it. Last year, I did some research on how to convert it to exactly 1 point = 1 possession = 1 credit. I still ended up with what I have. From this discussion you can see that I appreciate using .9275 instead of 1 for a possession and I appreciate 48 minute projections for PR. But I completely dismiss the idea of making fouls a negative credit or any part of a negative credit, and I have little appreciation for factoring based on game pace.

MVP (Most Valuable Player)

PD (Position Dominance)

WR (Winning Ratio)

$$MVP = PD + WR$$

As you remember from earlier in the chapter, Michael Jordan was the most productive player in the NBA - but was he the most valuable? I realized early on that there must be a statistical way to evaluate who had the most valid claim to MVP. The formula I came up with has served that purpose very well. Despite the subtleties of the mind, biases, early voting, etc., my statistical MVP has been the same one voted MVP roughly half of the time since the award was first presented in 1956. More impressively, with only a few exceptions, the league's MVP was always in the top 3 of my statistical list.

As widespread coast to coast exposure becomes more and more commonplace, I would expect my formula and the voters to be in closer and closer agreement. There will always be one distinction, however. Part of my MVP formula is based on playoff performance, while the league's is not. Most of the value of the MVP formula is not so much for a given season anyway. I primarily use it to help determine the greatest players ever. (See discussion of greatness beginning on page 16).

Let's use an example. By doing so the strengths of the formula should become clear. To begin with, we will look only at Position Dominance (PD). Later we will look at Winning Ratio (WR). As I have said previously, credits = points + rebounds + assists + blocked shots + steals - missed FG - missed FT - turnovers. Adding and subtracting these eight categories for a given year for a given player equals so many credits. Dividing the credits by games-played, establishes a player's Production Rating. Last year Michael Jordan amassed 2996 credits. He played in 81 games, so he had a Production Rating of 36.99 credits-per-game. It would be nice to compare straight across the board this 36.99 with the Production Ratings of Neil Johnston or Jerry Lucas or Julius Erving. The problem is that during each era, Production Ratings fluctuate due to rules, tradition, and coaching. Therefore, to be fair, Michael Jordan's 36.99 can only be compared to the ratings of other players in 1988-89. Even then, it can only be compared to other off guards, since there has been a consistent variance in Production Rating from one position to another over the years.

Now, if Michael Jordan's 1988-89 Production Rating of 36.99 can only be compared to other off guards in 1988-89, how should this be done? I finally chose to create a statistic which all off guards in 1988-89 could be evaluated against. (I'm calling Michael Jordan an off guard even though he played the point late in the season. Next year will be different if he plays point all year.) The statistic is called Comparative Index (CI). The same index can be applied to centers in 1955, small forwards in 1978, etc. Obviously, the CI will be different in each case, but it's still the same formula. After ranking all the off guards by Production Rating, I chose four - the first, second, fifth and median.

COMPARATIVE INDEX (CI) = (1st + 2nd + 5th + median)/4

Michael Jordan was first at 36.99, Clyde Drexler was second at 28.87, Ron Harper fifth at 21.09, and Terry Teagle was the median off guard at 12.85. With slight deviations due to rounding...

$$CI = (36.99 + 28.87 + 21.09 + 12.85) / 4 = 24.95$$

The Comparative Index (CI) for all off guards for 1988-89 was 24.95. To find out how productive any particular off guard was last year with respect to any other player at any other time in history, one need only to divide that guard's Production Rating by the CI. For Michael Jordan it would be 36.99/24.95 = 1.483

Position Dominance (PD) = Production Rating/CI = 1.483

The nice thing about PD is that it can be applied to any player in any year at any position and will objectively show how that player performed with respect to his peers and with respect to any player in any year in NBA history. Again, the MVP formula is equal to PD which we have just looked at, plus Winning Ratio (WR).

No matter how good or productive a player is, he will not be considered particularly valuable if his team loses. Value is more than just production. It has to be reflected in team success as well. The most valuable players make other players around them better and thus their teams will win most of the time. Of the top-20 all time greatest players, every one of them has a career Winning Ratio (WR) of over 50%. This means they won more games than they lost. They were not only top producers, but winners as well.

$$\frac{(\text{Regular season wins} + 3 \text{ times postseason wins})}{(\text{Regular season games played} + 3 \text{ times postseason games played})}$$

As you can see, I made each playoff game 3 times as valuable as a regular season game, whether it was a win or a loss. Much of what determines value comes from how a player does in the playoffs. To continue with Jordan...

$$WR = [47 + 3(9)] / [82 + 3(17)] = .556$$

A winning ratio of .556 is respectable though not exceptionally high, as it represents a 47-35 regular season record and 9-8 in the playoffs. The highest 10-year average WR in history was earned by Sam Jones at .706. Now we can complete the formula for Michael Jordan.

$$MVP = PD + WR$$

$$2.039 = 1.483 + .556$$

An MVP rating of 2.039 is extremely high. Jordan would become one of the greatest players ever if he could do that over a ten year period. Wilt Chamberlain has the highest 10-year *average* of 2.068.

Greatness

Whenever a discussion of the greatest or most valuable players in any sport comes up, controversy is sure to follow. The problem is one of definition. Unfortunately, it has never been settled whether "most valuable" means most indispensable or most productive. For that matter, it has never been settled whether the player deemed indispensable or productive could play for just any team or whether he must play for a winning or even a championship team. "Greatness" confuses the issue further. Simply put, that element is defined according to the criteria of the different eras that players perform in. Each era has different rules and standards, more or fewer opposing teams, etc. The question becomes obvious. Could Jesse Owens be greater than Carl Lewis? Could Babe Ruth be greater than Jose Canseco? In fact, could any player of yesteryear be greater than the top players today? After all, today's players are bigger, stronger, and faster. Presumably, they have better training techniques, better coaching, and better travel arrangements. How then can Bob Cousy be "greater" than Isiah Thomas? How can Bob Pettit be "greater" than Tom Chambers?

Greatness, it seems to me, must be measured in terms of four basic categories: dominance, winning, statistics, and endurance. I have created a formula which encompasses the subtleties of each of these categories, and as a result, claims to determine the greatest professional basketball players of all time.

The MVP rating has taken into consideration the era a player played in, other players at his position, his production, and the regular season and post-season team records. The only major category left is endurance. I decided that in order to be considered among the greatest all-time players a player must qualify (see page 240 for qualification requirements) for at least six years. Obviously, more players will qualify for six years than ten or fifteen years. I am of the opinion that a player should qualify at least ten years to be considered truly great; however, George Mikan only qualified eight years. Consequently, I have included two lists - the top-100 6-year and the top-100 10-year ratings. I have left it up to the reader to determine which requirement he or she feels should be met.

By the way, Mikan is a classic case of a player who couldn't begin to play with today's athletes. However, he was the most dominant big man ever in that dominance is defined as how well a player did against like opponents in his era. Here is a guy who was voted as the best basketball player for the first half of the century. He only played healthy 8 years in the NBA & NBL, but won 7 championships and was effectively the "MVP" 7 years.

It's reasonable to ask how a player who endures fifteen years benefits over a player who plays for ten years. I could, of course, have a list which allowed only fifteen-year qualifiers. However, that list would be meaningless since Russell, Robertson, Cousy, Chamberlain, etc. would not be on it. In fact, only a few players qualified sixteen years or more. Therefore, I decided that whether it be the six-year list or ten-year list, it would be based on the best six years or the best ten years of a player's career. This way a player qualifying fifteen years has an advantage over a player qualifying only ten or six. That is because his best years are the only ones considered. Since a fifteen-year player has more years to choose from, endurance becomes a major factor in appraising greatness.

In summation, (MVP = PD + WR) for any given year makes a statement about a player's ability to dominate by Production Rating. It also makes a statement about his team's winning percentage, both during the season and in the playoffs. "Greatness" then averages a player's best six years or ten years of MVP ratings, depending on whether you think a player should have to qualify at least ten years or not.

As I said earlier, every player in the top-20 all-time greatest players by Position Dominance (PD) only, has a career winning Ratio (WR) of over 50%. This is not an accident. What it says is that the most productive players are good enough to win - regardless of their teammates. On an average, the more productive an individual player is, the more wins - although exceptions exist. On the other hand, a player who ranked below #50 probably did not *lead* his team to success, but rather *participated* in it. For these players it would seem to be more valid to ignore WR and look only at Position Dominance (PD). Therefore, I have included two more lists - the top-100 six-year and the top-100 ten-year Position Dominance ratings. The only difference between the top-100 PD ratings and the top-100 MVP ratings is that Winning Ratio (WR) is not shown in the PD ratings. Again, remember the basic formula, MVP = PD + WR.

Finally, you as a reader have two choices to make. 1) Should a player be called the greatest ever if he only qualifies six years or should he have to qualify for at least ten? 2) Should a player's team's winning percentages be a determining factor in assessing how great a player is?

On the next four pages you will see the four lists which I previously discussed. Before you turn to them, I would like to make a few last points. Just as there are lists for 6-year and 10-year qualifiers, there are also 7-year, 8-year, 9-year, etc. Obviously, six and ten are arbitrary numbers. As a rule, there are no major differences from one list to the next one a year later except that a player who failed to qualify enough years might be on the first list and not on the second. In some cases two players will exchange positions from one list to another. An example of this would be Jerry Lucas and Jerry West. On both six-year lists Lucas is ranked higher than West. On both 10-year lists West ranks ahead of Lucas. What this means is that Lucas' "greatness" was more intensely packed into a fewer number of years, while West's "greatness" was more diffused.

Secondly, only 101 players have qualified ten years or more. It might be a bit much to say Tom Sanders (#100) is "greater" than George Mikan who failed to make the ten-year list because he only qualified eight years (Mikan ranks #4 in six-year ratings). Therefore, it would be more appropriate to look at six-year ratings when evaluating Mikan. No doubt the average fan will look up his favorite player and choose that list which ranks the player the highest. Thus the reason for the four lists.

Although many players have qualified for six years and not ten, few of the greatest players fit that mold. George Mikan (#4) is the most obvious exception. There are a few others who played in the 1950's who qualified for fewer than ten years. Neil Johnston (#26) and Tom Gola (#32) are two examples. And of course, there are present players who have not yet qualified ten years. Magic Johnson (#2) and Larry Bird (#5) would be the most conspicuous cases. Although there are two top-50 six-year MVP players who began their career after 1960 and who failed to qualify at least ten years (Billy Cunningham (#30) qualified nine years, while David Thompson (#42) qualified only seven years), they are, nevertheless, the exception and not the rule.

It should be clear by now that I enjoy ratings. In the chapters ahead you will see many more. Nevertheless, I can appreciate the fact that statistics are no substitution for watching a player night in and night out to determine his value. The reality, however, is that 99% of the readers of this book never saw Mikan or Johnston or Arizin play. Probably less than 50% of the readers saw Russell or Cousy or Baylor. Even those who were fortunate enough to do so, probably only saw them occasionally. What I have tried to do is to take the names that most basketball fans have somewhere in the back of their heads and enable them to place the player in history. Maybe the player is ranked a little too high or a little too low by some other standard, but at least the majority of NBA fans who are forty years old or less and who failed to see most of these players play, will now have the opportunity to rank them according to their quality. If a young reader can see that an Elgin Baylor ranks comparably with a Julius Erving, or a Wilt Chamberlain ranks with a Kareem Abdul-Jabbar, or that a Bob Cousy ranks favorably with a Magic Johnson, he or she can imagine how great those players were. At the very least, any fan will have a better appreciation for the history of the game as well as of those players who made it great.

6 -YEAR MVP RATING

1. Wilt Chamberlain	2.149	51. Paul Westphal	1.563
2. **Earvin Johnson**	**2.093**	52. Bob Lanier	1.561
3. Oscar Robertson	2.080	53. Dan Issel	1.554
4. George Mikan	2.078	54. Ed Macauley	1.554
5. **Larry Bird**	**2.046**	55. **James Worthy**	**1.547**
6. Kareem Abdul-Jabbar	2.018	56. Gus Williams	1.543
7. Bill Russell	1.955	57. Jim Pollard	1.543
8. Bob Cousy	1.923	58. Paul Silas	1.541
9. Julius Erving	1.889	59. **Dennis Johnson**	**1.540**
10. Dolph Schayes	1.875	60. Maurice Lucas	1.538
11. Elgin Baylor	1.863	61. Truck Robinson	1.538
12. Jerry Lucas	1.845	62. **Walter Davis**	**1.535**
13. **Moses Malone**	**1.832**	63. Pete Maravich	1.533
14. Bob Pettit	1.822	64. **Jack Sikma**	**1.528**
15. Jerry West	1.819	65. Jo Jo White	1.527
16. George Gervin	1.811	66. Jamaal Wilkes	1.524
17. **Kevin McHale**	**1.740**	67. **Terry Cummings**	**1.519**
18. Elvin Hayes	1.738	68. Bobby Wanzer	1.515
19. **Sidney Moncrief**	**1.732**	69. Happy Hairston	1.509
20. Rick Barry	1.728	70. Gail Goodrich	1.505
21. George McGinnis	1.727	71. Willis Reed	1.504
22. Walt Frazier	1.718	72. **Larry Nance**	**1.504**
23. **Robert Parish**	**1.700**	73. Nate Thurmond	1.502
24. Harry Gallatin	1.695	74. Dan Roundfield	1.501
25. John Havlicek	1.688	75. Connie Hawkins	1.499
26. Neil Johnston	1.664	76. Joe Fulks	1.496
27. Bill Sharman	1.646	77. **Dominique Wilkins**	**1.493**
28. **Isiah Thomas**	**1.640**	78. Wes Unseld	1.493
29. **Alex English**	**1.636**	79. Hal Greer	1.491
30. Billy Cunningham	1.631	80. Cedric Maxwell	1.485
31. Bob McAdoo	1.625	81. Dick McGuire	1.476
32. Tom Gola	1.623	82. Rudy Tomjanovich	1.476
33. Spencer Haywood	1.617	83. Randy Smith	1.473
34. Vern Mikkelsen	1.617	84. Bailey Howell	1.471
35. Larry Kenon	1.617	85. Bill Bridges	1.470
36. Artis Gilmore	1.614	86. Jack Coleman	1.467
37. Dave Cowens	1.612	87. Carl Braun	1.463
38. Marques Johnson	1.610	88. Clyde Lovellette	1.461
39. Nate Archibald	1.605	89. Sam Jones	1.460
40. **Bill Laimbeer**	**1.604**	90. Dave DeBusschere	1.457
41. Andy Phillip	1.601	91. **Fat Lever**	**1.456**
42. David Thompson	1.598	92. Cliff Hagan	1.456
43. **Maurice Cheeks**	**1.594**	93. Earl Monroe	1.453
44. Norm Nixon	1.587	94. Chet Walker	1.450
45. **Adrian Dantley**	**1.582**	95. Max Zaslofsky	1.450
46. Bobby Jones	1.577	96. Len Wilkens	1.449
47. Paul Arizin	1.576	97. Ray Williams	1.447
48. Bob Dandridge	1.572	98. **Mark Aguirre**	**1.447**
49. Arnold Risen	1.563	99. **Kiki Vandeweghe**	**1.445**
50. Bob Davies	1.563	100. World Free	1.438

10-YEAR MVP RATINGS

1. Wilt Chamberlain	2.068	
2. Oscar Robertson	1.997	
3. Kareem Abdul-Jabbar	1.963	
4. Bill Russell	1.881	
5. Bob Cousy	1.845	
6. Julius Erving	1.819	
7. Jerry West	1.776	
8. Dolph Schayes	1.775	
9. Bob Pettit	1.764	
10. Elgin Baylor	1.760	
11. Moses Malone	**1.735**	
12. George Gervin	1.706	
13. Jerry Lucas	1.678	
14. Rick Barry	1.657	
15. Elvin Hayes	1.651	
16. Walt Frazier	1.644	
17. Robert Parish	**1.619**	
18. John Havlicek	1.602	
19 Artis Gilmore	1.565	
20. Bill Sharman	1.546	
21. George McGinnis	1.542	
22. Alex English	**1.521**	
23. Adrian Dantley	**1.503**	
24. Dan Issel	1.501	
25. Dave Cowens	1.496	
26. Harry Gallatin	1.492	
27. Bob Dandridge	1.490	
28. Maurice Cheeks	**1.489**	
29. Bob Lanier	1.474	
30. Bobby Jones	1.472	
31. Dennis Johnson	**1.469**	
32. Paul Arizin	1.459	
33. Jack Sikma	**1.459**	
34. Jamaal Wilkes	1.458	
35. Arnold Risen	1.448	
36. Spencer Haywood	1.445	
37. Bob McAdoo	1.432	
38. Sam Jones	1.430	
39. Wes Unseld	1.427	
40. Vern Mikkelsen	1.422	
41. Maurice Lucas	1.418	
42. Hal Greer	1.414	
43. Andy Phillip	1.414	
44. Paul Silas	1.409	
45. Nate Archibald	1.408	
46. Chet Walker	1.404	
47. Gus Williams	1.397	
48. Bailey Howell	1.390	
49. Gail Goodrich	1.385	
50. Carl Braun	1.381	
51. Walter Davis	**1.381**	
52. Nate Thurmond	1.381	
53. Len Wilkens	1.374	
54. Dan Roundfield	1.372	
55. Bill Bridges	1.366	
56. Dave DeBusschere	1.361	
57. Earl Monroe	1.354	
58. World Free	1.346	
59. Walt Bellamy	1.341	
60. Dave Bing	1.333	
61. Dick McGuire	1.333	
62. Michael Cooper	**1.326**	
63. Mychal Thompson	**1.322**	
64. Jo Jo White	1.322	
65. Calvin Murphy	1.321	
66. Zelmo Beatty	1.302	
67. Cliff Hagan	1.296	
68. Ron Boone	1.291	
69. Richie Guerin	1.289	
70. Lou Hudson	1.286	
71. Alvan Adams	1.282	
72. Larry Foust	1.282	
73. Freddy Brown	1.279	
74. Randy Smith	1.278	
75. Billy Knight	1.273	
76. Slater Martin	1.273	
77. Reggie Theus	**1.267**	
78. John Kerr	1.264	
79. Louie Dampier	1.244	
80. Mickey Johnson	1.228	
81. Jack Twyman	1.206	
82. Guy Rodgers	1.203	
83. Dick Van Arsdale	1.191	
84. Sam Lacey	1.165	
85. Tom Sanders	1.153	
86. Billy Paultz	1.147	
87. Bob Boozer	1.146	
88. Mike Gale	1.146	
89. Dick Barnett	1.145	
90. Caldwell Jones	**1.140**	
91. Dick Snyder	1.109	
92. Mark Olberding	1.102	
93. Chris Ford	1.100	
94. Wayne Rollins	**1.100**	
95. John Johnson	1.098	
96. Joe Caldwell	1.089	
97. Tom Meschery	1.055	
98. Robert Reid	**.994**	
99. Tom Van Arsdale	.971	
100. Leroy Ellis	.957	

6-YEAR POSITION DOMINANCE

1. Oscar Robertson	1.562	51. Rudy Tomjanovich	1.007
2. Wilt Chamberlain	1.546	52. Randy Smith	1.007
3. George Mikan	1.385	53. Paul Westphal	1.006
4. **Earvin Johnson**	**1.378**	54. Joe Fulks	1.004
5. Kareem Abdul-Jabbar	1.349	55. Billy Knight	1.003
6. Bob Cousy	1.347	56. Truck Robinson	1.003
7. **Larry Bird**	**1.340**	57. **Bill Laimbeer**	**1.001**
8. Jerry Lucas	1.323	58. **Larry Nance**	**.995**
9. Dolph Schayes	1.297	59. Nate Thurmond	.989
10. Elgin Baylor	1.291	60. **Bernard King**	**.988**
11. Bob Pettit	1.278	61. Bailey Howell	.982
12. George Gervin	1.253	62. Dave Cowens	.981
13. Bill Russell	1.247	63. World Free	.979
14. Neil Johnston	1.225	64. Len Wilkens	.979
15. Julius Erving	1.218	65. Norm Nixon	.978
16. **Moses Malone**	**1.214**	66. **Reggie Theus**	**.978**
17. Jerry West	1.212	67. Maurice Lucas	.975
18. Elvin Hayes	1.192	68. Gail Goodrich	.970
19. George McGinnis	1.179	69. Willis Reed	.970
20. **Adrian Dantley**	**1.170**	70. Gus Williams	.966
21. Rick Barry	1.159	71. **Walter Davis**	**.966**
22. Walt Frazier	1.152	72. Vern Mikkelsen	.965
23. Spencer Haywood	1.142	73. Arnold Risen	.965
24. Bob McAdoo	1.140	74. Clyde Lovellette	.960
25. Harry Gallatin	1.133	75. Dan Issel	.958
26. **Alex English**	**1.119**	76. John Drew	.957
27. Billy Cunningham	1.118	77. Gus Johnson	.957
28. **Sidney Moncrief**	**1.111**	78. Bobby Jones	.955
29. Pete Maravich	1.101	79. Earl Monroe	.954
30. Nate Archibald	1.086	80. **Dominique Wilkins**	**.949**
31. Andy Phillip	1.080	81. Bill Bridges	.949
32. John Havlicek	1.079	82. **Buck Williams**	**.948**
33. Tom Gola	1.079	83. Bob Dandridge	.947
34. **Kevin McHale**	**1.067**	84. Wes Unseld	.945
35. Paul Arizin	1.066	85. Lou Hudson	.944
36. **Isiah Thomas**	**1.066**	86. Connie Hawkins	.944
37. Bill Sharman	1.065	87. **Kiki Vandeweghe**	**.944**
38. Bob Lanier	1.061	88. Ray Williams	.943
39. David Thompson	1.057	89. Calvin Murphy	.942
40. Artis Gilmore	1.047	90. Bobby Wanzer	.939
41. Larry Kenon	1.046	91. Larry Foust	.936
42. Marques Johnson	1.042	92. Bob Davies	.928
43. Richie Guerin	1.039	93. Happy Hairston	.925
44. Ed Macauley	1.027	94. Dave Bing	.924
45. Sidney Wicks	1.027	95. Dick McGuire	.924
46. Dan Roundfield	1.023	96. **Fat Lever**	**.923**
47. Walt Bellamy	1.021	97. Carl Braun	.922
48. **Jack Sikma**	**1.016**	98. **Maurice Cheeks**	**.915**
49. **Robert Parish**	**1.013**	99. Mike Newlin	.912
50. **Terry Cummings**	**1.009**	100. Freddy Brown	.905

10-YEAR POSITION DOMINANCE

1. Wilt Chamberlain	1.479	51. Carl Braun	.857
2. Oscar Robertson	1.469	52. Calvin Murphy	.857
3. Kareem Abdul-Jabbar	1.320	53. Dave Bing	.854
4. Bob Cousy	1.249	54. Bill Bridges	.849
5. Bob Pettit	1.236	55. Billy Knight	.849
6. Elgin Baylor	1.210	56. Hal Greer	.848
7. Dolph Schayes	1.199	57. Dave DeBusschere	.839
8. Bill Russell	1.180	58. Gus Williams	.838
9. Jerry West	1.178	59. Earl Monroe	.836
10. Julius Erving	1.161	60. Dick McGuire	.831
11. George Gervin	1.161	61. Bobby Jones	.826
12. **Moses Malone**	**1.157**	62. Jamaal Wilkes	.826
13. Jerry Lucas	1.156	63. Lou Hudson	.824
14. Elvin Hayes	1.129	64. Larry Foust	.819
15. Rick Barry	1.096	65. **Dennis Johnson**	**.814**
16. Walt Frazier	1.081	66. Chet Walker	.807
17. **Adrian Dantley**	**1.049**	67. Paul Silas	.794
18. **Alex English**	**1.045**	68. Mickey Johnson	.779
19. Artis Gilmore	1.015	69. Freddy Brown	.771
20. George McGinnis	1.002	70. Jack Twyman	.766
21. John Havlicek	.988	71. Alvan Adams	.761
22. Bob Lanier	.986	72. Jo Jo White	.760
23. **Robert Parish**	**.965**	73. Ron Boone	.758
24. Harry Gallatin	.957	74. Cliff Hagan	.755
25. Spencer Haywood	.955	75. Dick Van Arsdale	.745
26. Bob McAdoo	.953	76. John Kerr	.743
27. **Jack Sikma**	**.944**	77. **Mychal Thompson**	**.739**
28. Paul Arizin	.936	78. Guy Rodgers	.731
29. Walt Bellamy	.932	79. Sam Jones	.725
30. Bill Sharman	.928	80. Zelmo Beatty	.718
31. Dan Issel	.927	81. Sam Lacey	.711
32. Dave Cowens	.907	82. Bob Boozer	.688
33. Bailey Howell	.906	83. Slater Martin	.683
34. Maurice Lucas	.904	84. Louie Dampier	.663
35. Len Wilkens	.902	85. John Johnson	.655
36. Nate Thurmond	.898	86. Dick Snyder	.649
37. Dan Roundfield	.894	87. Tom Meschery	.628
38. Bob Dandridge	.892	88. **Caldwell Jones**	**.622**
39. Nate Archibald	.889	89. **Michael Cooper**	**.616**
40. World Free	.886	90. Billy Paultz	.615
41. **Reggie Theus**	**.881**	91. **Robert Reid**	**.612**
42. Gail Goodrich	.880	92. Dick Barnett	.610
43. Wes Unseld	.879	93. Tom Van Arsdale	.604
44. Andy Phillip	.878	94. Mark Olberding	.599
45. Arnold Risen	.877	95. Joe Caldwell	.584
46. Vern Mikkelsen	.868	96. **Wayne Rollins**	**.578**
47. Randy Smith	.867	97. Mike Gale	.553
48. **Walter Davis**	**.865**	98. Chris Ford	.551
49. **Maurice Cheeks**	**.862**	99. Leroy Ellis	.539
50. Richie Guerin	.861	100. Tom Sanders	.502

POETRY IN MOTION
AP/WIDE WORLD PHOTOS

HORACE GRANT VS JOHNNY NEWMAN

CHAPTER 2

DISCUSSION AND DEBATE

DISCUSSION AND DEBATE

Are the NBA analysts that bad?

During the playoffs, a nationally distributed article written by Norman Chad (<u>Washington Post</u>) argued that the NBA analysts were by far the worst among the major sports commentators. His main argument was that no "personalities" had developed. I'll agree that no Dick Vitales or John Maddens or Howard Cosells are found on national broadcasts of the NBA, but that's not all bad. Besides that, an NBA analyst, as opposed to those in other sports, has much more difficulty in being a factor during a broadcast. Both baseball and football games have dozens of substantial interruptions (their weakness, from my perspective). Because of these interludes, analysts have a great deal of time and opportunity to evaluate what has just happened as well as what will come next. Try doing that between plays in the NBA. The abilities of the play-by-play man, the analyst, and the production crews who handle the fast-paced NBA are, in my view, impressive.

NBC's Black Athletes: Was the show justified?

In my opinion, yes. As one of the scientists stated on the show, "Knowledge is the greatest safeguard against prejudice, whereas ignorance fosters prejudice." That is the single reason that I believe it is a valid subject to have addressed, and I hope the debate continues. There can never be enough enlightened discussion over matters of this magnitude. It is essential to realize that this discussion does occur, anyway. The only issue is, can it be discussed in the light of day where erroneous cause and effect relationships can be put to rest once and for all! Until then, we'll have to put up with foolishness on both sides of the argument.

How strange was this season really?

From 1988 to 1989 there were 11 teams that either gained 10+ wins or 10+ losses. This number is very high. With 23 teams qualifying, that represents a .478 ratio (11/23). With two expansion teams, the number of 10+ winners should have been higher than normal and the number of 10+ losers lower. Despite this, there were 6 teams that lost 10 or more games from the previous year - tying the most ever. Not surprisingly, Golden State was one of the 11 teams (+23 wins). The Warriors have increased or decreased by ten wins in 54% of their seasons - easily the most. Utah is the most consistent year-to-year at a low 21%. Incredibly, the Celtics hold the record for both the most consecutive seasons without varying +/- 10 wins (18, 1952-69) as well as the most consecutive seasons where they did vary that many (5, 1970-74). The fact that one pattern immediately followed the other is all the more interesting.

How have the old ABA teams done?

The ABA folded in 1976. Four teams merged into the NBA the next season. Critics scoffed, claiming the ABA was far weaker than the NBA and that these teams would get trounced. As it turns out, they averaged a very respectable 38-44 record that first year. What is perhaps strange is that these franchises were basically winning franchises. Therefore, logically, one would assume that these teams would win more games as time went by than during their first year in the league. At least they should have averaged 41 wins. But, nooooo. Though Denver has done its best to hold up the lot, last season was, by far, the worst yet for the group, as they averaged only 29.8 wins each. Nevertheless, I believe next year will be at least average (41 victories).

Once again I say, "If you don't like it, turn it off."

Maybe it's because I write part of this book during the NBA playoffs that this bugs me, but every year I hear the clamor that the playoffs are too long. I doubt that anyone reading this (other than some players, perhaps) would agree. As a fan, I say the more the better. Some argue that they cut too much into the baseball season. Well, that's just too bad. I can argue that baseball starts too early. Besides, baseball runs 2 months into football which runs 2 months into basketball which runs 2 months into baseball. For half the year we have the "pleasure" of watching two of the three major sports at once. Who gets hurt? As I see it, everyone benefits - except maybe a somewhat overworked sports staff (and I've never met a sportswriter who complained about too many sources for stories). If you don't like it, change the channel!

How many times is it OK to mispronounce a name?

You can tell when someone has been announcing in professional basketball for a long time when they say Xavier McDaniel(s) and Chris Mullin(s). Once and for all, they don't have S's on the ends of their name! Mel Daniels played 8 years in the ABA and 1 year in the NBA, but he hasn't played in a dozen years! Jeff Mullins played from 1964-1976. So it's been even longer since he played. It bugs me when names are mispronounced, but you can always excuse an occasional blunder of Krystkowiak (Krysto) or Stipanovich (Stipo) or Brickowski (Bricko). (I confess to using short cuts.) Maybe you can even excuse the Chris Mullin(s) announcers. After all, not only are the Mullin names closer, they are at least of the same race, and both Mullins (have) played in San Francisco virtually their whole pro career. But Xavier McDaniel(s)?

Will a 2-round draft hurt the NBA?

I don't see it making any real difference. That's not to say there aren't good players left to pick after #54, it's just that no one knows who they are. If they did, they would have picked them sooner and so would everyone else. Many 1st round players never play more than sparingly and many 2nd rounders don't even make the team. And most 3rd round players never even make an NBA roster. In some ways, their chances will improve since they can be looked at by any team. Nevertheless, of the 176 players who qualified last season, only 13 of them were picked after #54. Moreover, of those 13, four were on expansion teams.

Am I the only one who thinks so?

I guess if I had to estimate, I've probably watched 10,000 NBA instant replays per year for the last several years. I'm sure most sports fans would agree that the instant replay is the greatest invention since the wheel. Nevertheless, some of them can be improved. The majority of time when there is a replay shown of a winning shot or a shot of exceptional length, they freeze the picture just as the ball swishes the net. I suppose the argument is that 1) aesthetically, it looks bad to see the ball "loose", 2) the "event" is completed. I disagree. The "event" is not complete until the human mind perceives it to be complete. The replay is to see what happened. A major part of what happened was the realization by those watching of what just transpired. That happens in the first 1-2 seconds *after* the shot is made. The "perfect" frozen picture is the view of 99% of the fans with arms raised as high as they will go. That ever-so-slight variation would greatly improve the "meaning" of the instant replay. It would change it from being a static entity into a dynamic experience.

Is there too much violence in the NBA?

I always laugh a little when I hear contentions that there is. I don't advocate violence and if I could wave a wand, I would eliminate it completely. But to say there is too much violence - implying there is a serious problem with it - is a joke. Counting the playoffs, there were nearly 1100 games played last season. That's over 50,000 minutes. In every minute there are 10 guys with enormous size and strength moving at incredible speeds attempting to prove themselves as worthy of this season's million dollars, or perhaps more importantly, next season's million dollars. Despite this, how many fights were there? Maybe a dozen. Oh sure, there were a few shoving matches - big deal. All that means is that they continued playing basketball after the whistle blew. The purist will lament that the game has become so physical that it causes what fights there are. That may be, but I'm not bothered by a dozen little skirmishes that rarely ever have any long-term negative impact (injuries, hatred, etc.). The game that I love and the game that has come to be loved by record millions of fans is the game that we see - where strength matters. It is a game where Charles Barkley wins a rebounding battle with Brad Sellers because he's stronger, not because he's taller. The NBA used to be dominated by the big guy. There were few exceptions. If you still want to watch that, watch high school basketball.

Are NBA players overpaid?

I'm a firm believer in free enterprise. It seems to me that they're worth what they can get. NBA players are the highest paid in any sport. If the big money made them work any less hard it might be a problem, but I haven't seen evidence of that. Once the players have gotten paid to the point they are being paid, no additional amount will affect their work habits. I am concerned about one other possibility, however. It would seem possible, if not probable, that many NBA players would cut their careers short because their wealth permits it. I doubt that will happen much though. Obviously, these guys love the competition and the headlines. But more than that, they love the game.

How did the 3-official experiment work out?

I think it went very well. Yes, the rookie officials performed like rookies some of the time, but what do you expect? The bottom line is that the officiating is in place to be able to better call every NBA game for years. One of the fears coming into the season was that there would be a plethora of fouls called. Not so. Each team averaged 24.1 fouls in 1988. The number actually *decreased* in 1989 to 23.7

Could he have been serious when he recommended hitting the free throw?

I won't say who, but I actually heard an announcer suggest that a player should hit the second of two free throws when his team trailed by 2 points with 2 seconds left. His argument was that you should hit the free throw (cutting the deficit to one) and then attempt a steal since every team practices stealing the ball, but not missing free throws. His partner concurred, arguing that if he tries to miss, his teammates are more likely to rush into the lane for a violation.
Both arguments are completely off-base from a probability point of view. Practice or not, a team is much less likely to get a steal than an offensive rebound. Second, even if they get the steal, the odds of scoring an off-balance 70 footer (assuming the leading team uses common sense and throws the ball down court) are nil, whereas the odds of scoring after an offensive rebound are actually pretty reasonable.

The other argument is just as bad. Even if his team gets a lane violation, that just means his team is down by two instead of one while the other team has the ball out of bounds (the same position the announcers wanted in the first place). It doesn't matter whether the deficit is 2 or 1 since, if you steal, you're going to have to hit a 3-pointer to prevent a loss anyway.

When are they going to start fouling with a 3-point lead?

I looked at this question statistically in <u>Basketball Heaven 1987-88</u>, but it remains a mystery to me how any coach can let the opposing player shoot a 3-pointer when his team leads by 3 with just a few seconds to go. Yes, theoretically you could lose on an almost non-existant 4-point play. Nevertheless, if a player grabs an opponent and forces him to hit the first free throw, intentional miss the second, rebound, and get a stickback, the odds of overtime are overwhelmingly slimmer than if the coach let the player try to tie it up with a 3-pointer.

Did Isiah think of missing?

In game 2 of the championships, there was a classic game-ending strategy which called for Isiah Thomas to intentionally miss a free throw. The Pistons were leading by 2 points with only 1 second left on the clock, the Lakers had no time-outs remaining, and it was Isiah's 2nd free throw attempt. Had he missed it intentionally, it would have been deemed a brilliant tactic. From that day on he could have been thought of as the "Don Shula of basketball". (As you may remember, Shula became famous for calling an intentional safety many years ago. After the announcers recovered, they realized the soundness of the strategy. His reputation as a great revisionist was established. From that day on football has never been the same.) I'm disappointed to say that basketball is still played on such a conservative level.

You see, the problem is that a coach looks at the situation from the standpoint of how his team might lose, not how best to insure victory. Those are two different attitudes. If Thomas made the free throw (which he did) and the Lakers were unable to score a three pointer (which they were) to tie, then the coach wins - and no controversy. Even if LA ties the game, Detroit may still win in overtime. Anyway, even if the worst case scenario happens (LA hits the 3-pointer and goes on to win in overtime), Daly or Thomas will not be criticized for having hit the free throw.

To further understand the problem, you have to realize that, in sports, a coach or player will receive a lot more negative criticism from a "bad" decision than vocal support for a good decision. Because of that, the natural tendency is to remain somewhat passive and to avoid controversial decisions like the plague. I can't blame coaches for that, I just keep waiting for the next Don Shula to appear. That person might be Don Nelson. Nelson did a lot of very unorthodox things last season, risked a lot of criticism, but almost won Coach-of-the-Year for the third time.

Think about it. If Thomas misses the free throw, the opposing team not only has to get the rebound, but they have to get it cleanly, turn, and fire an 80 foot hook shot to win. How many of those have ever gone in in the history of the game??? Since the odds of losing are infinitesimal if you miss, why hit the free throw? The reason is, again, simple. If, by some miracle, a shot in this situation were to go in before the strategy had been proven to be successful 1,000 consecutive times, the coach would be crucified by a possibly ignorant viewer. A coach or player is never criticized in these "pre-Shula" days of NBA basketball when his team hits the free throw, but still loses. And what are the odds that that will happen? If a team gets to throw in a long pass, they could conceivably hit a 25' three-pointer to tie in one second. That can and does happen, you know. Now, assuming a 50-50 chance of winning in overtime, we see that it is, although slim, at least realistic that a team could lose in this situation. However, it is highly unlikely that a team will lose if the free throw is missed.

WHO'S BEST?

I am constantly asked who I think the best player or players are. Unquestionably, I am more likely to pick those whose production is the highest as opposed to some popular choices. Nevertheless, production is not the only criterion. I am going to go ahead and discuss who I think should have won the 1989 annual awards in a later section, but before I do that, I thought I'd list who I consider to be my top players. Actually, I have six groups that I put the top-87 players into. Naturally, there are many alternative classifications of players after the best-87, but most fans are primarily interested in those at the top.

Before I list them, I should qualify a couple of things. I honestly doubt if there are a handful of people in the world who watch more NBA games than I do. That doesn't mean I'm absolutely right about who's best, but I would argue that my lists are more realistic than the All-Star voting. Furthermore, I believe that I have a good idea as to the obscure skills a player possesses as well as the obvious ones. Finally, I think I can reasonably evaluate how each player benefits his team. Granted, on another team, perhaps a player's value would be different, but that's speculation. By the way, each group is in alphabetical order.

Group 1	Group 2	Group 3
Larry Bird	Charles Barkley	Tom Chambers
Magic Johnson	Pat Ewing	Brad Daugherty
Michael Jordan	Kevin Johnson	Clyde Drexler
	Karl Malone	Fat Lever
	Akeem Olajuwon	Moses Malone
	John Stockton	Kevin McHale
		Chris Mullin
		Larry Nance
		Robert Parish
		Mark Price
		Roy Tarpley
		James Worthy

Group 4	Group 5	Group 6
Terry Cummings	Michael Adams	Willie Anderson
James Donaldson	Mark Aguirre	Thurl Bailey
Joe Dumars	Danny Ainge	Manute Bol
Mark Eaton	Benoit Benjamin	Bill Cartwright
Dale Ellis	Rolando Blackman	Maurice Cheeks
Alex English	Joe Barry Carroll	Wayne Cooper
Mark Jackson	Kevin Duckworth	Adrian Dantley
Eddie Johnson	Eric Floyd	Vern Fleming
Bill Laimbeer	Mike Gminski	Derek Harper
Mitch Richmond	A.C. Green	Jeff Hornacek
Glenn Rivers	Ron Harper	Reggie Lewis
Alvin Robertson	Vinnie Johnson	Alton Lister
Dennis Rodman	Kareem Abdul-Jabbar	Nate McMillan
Jack Sikma	Jerome Kersey	Sam Perkins
Isiah Thomas	Bernard King	Chuck Person
Wayman Tisdale	Xavier McDaniel	Paul Pressey
Dominique Wilkins	Charles Oakley	Ralph Sampson
John S. Williams	Ricky Pierce	Danny Schayes

Group 5	Group 6
Terry Porter	Byron Scott
Rik Smits	Charles Smith
Steve Stipanovich	Mychal Thompson
Rod Strickland	Mark West
Otis Thorpe	Buck Williams
Kelly Tripucka	John Williams

HOME ADVANTAGE - PLAYOFFS

During one of the 1989 playoff broadcasts by WTBS, Rick Barry strongly made the case that the home-court advantage in the playoffs wasn't as significant as during the regular season. As I recall, his justification for this judgement was that each team had more time during the playoffs to prepare than they did during the season. I would add, as further support for his position, the fact that jet lag is nearly eliminated since road teams have several days to travel. Additionally, one of the assumptions as to why the home-court is such an advantage is that road teams don't have as good a concentration level (distractions, etc.). One could easily assume that, during the playoffs, the concentration levels would be virtually identical between the home and visiting teams.

I could accept all these arguments as reasonable. Therefore, going into this research, I assumed Barry was probably right. What I found out, though, was, if anything, just the opposite. Since the NBA officially began in 1950, the regular season home-court winning percentage is 64.45%. The playoff winning percentage is 66.77%. Now, that seems to settle the question, but an astute statistical buff might ask what it is recently - say since 1966 (Barry's first year in the NBA) or 1976 (the merger of the ABA and the NBA) or even just last season. Additionally, one might wonder if the regular season home-court winning percent between the same teams that met in the playoffs was comparable to the overall league home-court winning percentage. I think these stats are extremely interesting.

Incredibly, since the four ABA teams entered the NBA in 1976, the regular season home-court winning percentage (HCWP) has been 65.46%, the playoff home-court winning percentage (HCWP) has been virtually the same (65.42%) and the home-court regular season winning percentage between the same teams that would later meet in the playoffs is 65.68%. As you can see, there is virtually no difference whatsoever. In fact, before 1989, the playoff HCWP was actually higher than the regular season HCWP for four consecutive years.

I was curious, then, as to why Barry, who is usually so perceptive, believed something that is so clearly erroneous. After examining the data, I think I know 4 reasons why his thinking evolved the way it did.

1) As I said earlier, Barry's first year was 1966. That was an incredible year in regard to the subject of this discussion. Not only was the regular season HCWP the highest of any year from 1957 to 1989 (68.88%), but the playoff HCWP was the lowest ever (33.33%). As a rookie, such a radical introduction to the NBA would likely make an impression.

2) As I mentioned, the playoff HCWP in 1966 was 33.33%. That percentage was by far the lowest ever. But there was one other year that the road teams actually won more games than the home teams. The year was 1981, and the playoff HCWP was .4906. As you probably remember, Barry played for Golden State his entire NBA career until his last two seasons, which were played at Houston. Barry's last season was 1980, but his interest in the Rockets, no doubt, persisted at least to the next year. The fact that his old teammates made the finals in 1981 had to capture his attention. When you realize that the home team's record in Houston's games during that playoffs was 8-13 (amazingly low), you can see why he might have been impressed with the belief that the home court wasn't as valuable in the playoffs.

3) On April 21, 1973, Barry's Golden State Warriors hosted the Los Angeles Lakers. The Warriors had lost the first two games of the series at Los Angeles. Both games were close. After the teams returned to San Francisco, I'm sure most everyone expected the game to go to the Warriors or to at least be competitive. What happened was that the Lakers (the road team) won. And they won big. In fact, they won by 56 points (126-70). This 56 point home loss was the largest, playoffs or not, in NBA history until 1986 when, in a regular season game, Houston lost at home, also by 56 points (80-136), to Seattle. That debacle doubtlessly made an impression as well.

4) As I stated before, the playoff HCWP was *higher* than the regular season HCWP during the years 1985, 1986, 1987, and 1988. However, Barry made his contention during the 1989 playoffs, so the context should be at least partly based on the most recent year. In the 1989 regular season, the home-court winning percentage was a very high 67.71%. On the other hand, in the playoffs the percentage ended at only 56.67% for the home team. My point is that this seemingly radical difference could have affected his opinion, especially when it reinforced those impressions that were made in 1966, 1973 and 1981. Even so, apart from his personal experiences, there is simply no evidence to support his claim. Sorry, Rick. Next year, I'll pick on someone else.

AWARDS

As you just saw in the first section, I listed the players in groups according to how good I believe they are. I did not rank them one by one in order because there is so little difference between some players at certain levels. Nevertheless, the awards don't go to a group of people, except in the cases of All-Defensive team, All-Rookie team, or All-League teams. There are nine basic awards given out in addition to Executive-of-the-Year. That award was given to Jerry Colangelo of Phoenix for the third time. I agree with that choice.

ALL LEAGUE VOTING: 85 media members who cover the NBA

1st TEAM		2nd TEAM		3rd TEAM	
Karl Malone	425	Pat Ewing	267	Dominique Wilkins	116
Michael Jordan	423	John Stockton	224	Dale Ellis	83
Magic Johnson	423	Tom Chambers	174	Mark Price	75
Charles Barkley	412	Chris Mullin	137	Terry Cummings	70
Akeem Olajuwon	379	Kevin Johnson	131	Robert Parish	70

The interesting thing about this voting is that Karl Malone made every voter's first team while both Jordan and Johnson were picked on one second team. I guess in a way that's like saying either Malone was the top player or someone was an idiot. Anyway, as you can see from the previous discussion of who my top players are, I pretty well agree with these choices. My only real disagreements would come over the third team selections where I would pick Fat Lever or Clyde Drexler over Dale Ellis at guard. As for the third team center, I'll accept Robert Parish. However, if the pick had been Moses Malone or Brad Daugherty or even Mark Eaton, I could have lived with it. I disagree with both forward position selections on the third team. I would have chosen Kevin McHale and Larry Nance. There is simply no way that the average NBA team is better off with Dominique Wilkins or Terry Cummings as opposed to McHale or Nance. It's not that I don't think Cummings and Wilkins are good, maybe even outstanding players, but in the top-15? No way. At least not yet.

COACH-OF-THE-YEAR: 85 media members

Cotton Fitzsimmons	Phoenix	36.5
Don Nelson	Golden State	26.5
Lenny Wilkens	Cleveland	9
Chuck Daly	Detroit	5
Wes Unsled	Washington	4
Rick Pitino	New York	2
Del Harris	Milwaukee	1
Pat Riley	Los Angeles	1

I don't know about you, but I thought there were an exceptionally large number of possible candidates last season. Maybe we'll have to have an All-Coaches team. Mine would be, in sequence, Nelson, Fitzsimmons, Harris, Unseld, and Daly. I know, where's Riley? Despite all these candidates, it really boils down to the top-2. How can you ignore gaining 27 wins or 23 wins from the year before? I can't. But which coach? I vote for Don Nelson.

That doesn't mean that I don't think Fitzsimmons did a great, great job. I do, ... but I also recognize that Tom Chambers was brought to the team, Kevin Johnson turned into a superstar (yes, Cotton contributed to that), Eddie Johnson had an unbelievable year, etc. Everything went right for Phoenix.

As far as Golden State goes, when I think of creative coaching, what Nelson did this year may have been the most creative ever. He made incredibly tough decisions. His use of the "short" line-up was virtually unheard of before 1989 and now it is being talked about all over the league. What's even more impressive was his use of it when he had two of the tallest players in the league. His decision to bring in Manute Bol and to sit Ralph Sampson was gritty and elicited much criticism. Additionally, his drafting Mitch Richmond, when his only quality player had already played that position, was controversial, and as it turns out, brilliant. Beyond all that, Nellie only had two 1st round picks who qualified - less than any team in the league. Add to those accomplishments +23 victories over the previous season and how can you vote against him? It's a close call, but Nelson gets the nod.

ALL ROOKIE TEAM: NBA head coaches

1st Team			**2nd Team**		
Mitch Richmond	G.St	48	Brian Shaw	Bost	26
Willie Anderson	S.A.	45	Rex Chapman	Char	25
Hersey Hawkins	Phil	40	Chris Morris	N.J.	22
Rik Smits	Indi	38	Rod Strickland	N.Y.	18
Charles Smith	LA.C	31	Kevin Edwards	Miam	16

My only change here would be to substitute Grant Long of Miami on the second team for Rex Chapman. Chapman was more well-known and I believe that did it for him. Long had superior stats in almost every category, with the exception of scoring. One thing a team rarely needs is a scorer shooting 41% from the field. In fairness to Rex and Charlotte's coach (Dick Harter), they really had little choice, but that doesn't change Chapman's accomplishments - good or bad. I vote 2nd team Grant Long. Besides that major change, I would have given a slight nod to Gary Grant of the Clippers over Kevin Edwards of Miami. The reasons are subtle and debatable, so Edwards will do.

ROOKIE-OF-THE-YEAR: 85 media members

Mitch Richmond	Golden State	80
Willie Anderson	San Antonio	4
Chris Morris	New Jersey	1

Though the voting was overwhelmingly in favor of Richmond, it deserved to be closer. Anderson ranked ahead of Richmond in overall shooting, assists, blocks and steals. Mitch is the better scorer and rebounder, but it was the fact that Golden State gained 23 wins while San Antonio lost an additional 10 that most likely made the difference to the voters. Beyond that, Richmond played with a poise that few rookies possess. He gets my vote and not just because he played at Kansas State. (Remember, I chose Nelson over K-State's Cotton Fitzsimmons for Coach-of-the-Year.)

ALL DEFENSIVE TEAM: NBA head coaches

1ST TEAM				**2ND TEAM**		
F	Dennis Rodman	Detr	47	F	Kevin McHale	Bost	11
F	Larry Nance	Clev	28	F	A.C. Green	LA.L	10
C	Mark Eaton	Utah	29	C	Patrick Ewing	N.Y.	25
G	Michael Jordan	Chic	39	G	John Stockton	Utah	15
G	Joe Dumars	Detr	36	G	Alvin Robertson	S.A.	11

I only have one problem with this list. When you look at the next list you will see Akeem Olajuwon barely missing Defensive-Player-of-the-Year with 25 votes, while Pat Ewing had only 2. How then do the coaches justify voting Pat Ewing as the 2nd team center with 25 points and Olajuwon with only 15 points? My vote is for Olajuwon on the 2nd team for good reasons.

Let's look at the four measurable defensive categories - defensive rebounds, blocks, steals, and defensive FG%. Olajuwon had 767 defensive rebounds. Not only was that more than Ewing's defensive boards, it was even more than Ewing's total rebounds! Also, considering his blocks (trying to block a shot generally leaves one out of position for a rebound), that is a huge number of defensive boards. Olajuwon had slightly more blocks, twice as many steals, and a substantially lower defensive FG% (.468 to .494). You can argue that there are teammates involved in defensive FG%. True, but the center is the primary reason for low defensive FG%'s and no other player on either team is particularly noteworthy for his defense. Only Mark Jackson received any votes at all and he only got 1. None of Olajuwon's teammates received votes. I rest my case.

DEFENSIVE PLAYER-OF-THE-YEAR: 85 media members

Mark Eaton	Utah	26
Akeem Olajuwon	Houston	25
Dennis Rodman	Detroit	23
Manute Bol	Golden State	4
Michael Jordan	Chicago	3
Patrick Ewing	New York	2
Fat Lever	Denver	1
Buck Williams	New Jersey	1

As you can see, it was a close vote. In my opinion, the winner is absolutely correct. I vote for Mark Eaton for one simple reason. It was primarily because of Eaton that Utah had the stingiest defense in NBA history! That's quite a claim, but based on defensive FG% divided by the league average FG%, Utah's ratio was lower than any team - ever. That's very impressive. Even so, I'm not sure but what Manute Bol is more of a defensive factor when he plays; Akeem Olajuwon is probably a better defensive center - one on one; and Dennis Rodman is possibly the best defensive player man on *man* that I have ever seen. Nevertheless, Mark Eaton is a tremendous defensive player man on *team*. That counts most in my book.

SIXTH MAN: 85 media members

Eddie Johnson	Phoenix	33
Thurl Bailey	Utah	26
Dennis Rodman	Detroit	17
John Williams	Washington	4
Xavier McDaniel	Seattle	2
Ron Anderson	Philadelphia	1
Ricky Pierce	Milwaukee	1
John Williams	Cleveland	1

For the second year in a row, Thurl Bailey finished second in this category. Truthfully, it's a little bit of a misnomer to call Bailey a 6th man. Sure, he doesn't start, but his minutes were similar to a well-played starter. As a matter of fact, he had more minutes than any player of five whole teams! But you have to draw the line somewhere and he qualifies by not starting the minimum number of games, so he's eligible.

This is a difficult choice. John Williams of Washington is probably the most versatile player and he had the highest Production Rating of the bunch. On the other hand, Eddie Johnson and Thurl Bailey both provided essential scoring off the bench for very successful teams. Hum. I think I'll choose ..... Dennis Rodman. That's right. Rodman was the league's leading offensive rebounder on a per minute basis, he shot 60% from the field, he is the best one-on-one defender in the NBA. And, when he comes in, he provides an inspirational boost unlike any other player you can find. Those are qualities that make him absolutely irreplaceable. He is *a* major reason, if not *the* major reason that the Pistons were the league's best team in both the regular season and post season.

MOST IMPROVED: 85 media members

Kevin Johnson	Phoenix	48
Reggie Lewis	Boston	14
Chris Mullin	Golden State	12
Ron Anderson	Philadelphia	2
Ken Norman	LA Clippers	2
Kelly Tripucka	Charlotte	2
Patrick Ewing	New York	1
Larry Krystkowiak	Milwaukee	1
Derrick McKey	Seattle	1
Scottie Pippen	Chicago	1
Dennis Rodman	Detroit	1

There is a problem with this award as well, in that it is hard to determine what constitutes improvement. From my point of view, production on a 48-minute basis is about as good as anything. By that standard, Kevin Johnson gets my vote as well. He was +8.41. Ken Norman (+7.70) and Terry Teagle (+7.40) were next.

MOST VALUABLE PLAYER: 85 media members

Magic Johnson	LA Lakers	664.5
Michael Jordan	Chicago	598.8
Karl Malone	Utah	362.0
Patrick Ewing	New York	200.0
Akeem Olajuwon	Houston	179.3
Charles Barkley	Philadelphia	94.3
John Stockton	Utah	28.0
Kevin Johnson	Phoenix	22.0
Tom Chambers	Phoenix	20.0
Mark Price	Cleveland	18.0

This was the closest vote in many years. Magic Johnson also won the MVP by my rating system. As to whether I *think* he should have won, I'll say yes, but barely. Both players had the most productive years of their careers - though Jordan's rating was higher. On the other hand, Magic was the leader of a team that won 10 more games than Chicago. Of course Magic had better teammates, but he excelled in making them better. I'll predict that if Michael Jordan plays the point next year, and assuming no injuries, he will win the MVP for, not only 1990, but several years to come.

THREE - 20 PPG TEAMMATES

It is a fairly unusual occurance to have 3 teammates who score 20+ points per game. Despite this, there has now been one team per year three consecutive years and seven of the last nine who have had 3 teammates accomplish this feat. In case you're wondering, there has never been a team with four, although this season's Phoenix club has come the closest, with Armon Gilliam the 4th leading scorer (16 ppg). What is even more interesting is that he was scoring 19 ppg at the midway point of the season. Had he not found Cotton Fitzsimmons' dog house the second half of the season, he could have conceivably been the fourth player to score 20 ppg.

My criterion for a player to qualify is that he play in at least 60% of his team's games. If a high scoring player were traded near the end of the season to a club with two other 20 ppg scorers, this club would not qualify. It is probably obvious why not, but the basic reason is because the interesting thing about these (3-20ppg) teams is that they had high scorers on the floor at the same time. Racking up points with another club or even while your other high scoring teammates are injured isn't as impressive or interesting. Consequently, there are only fifteen teams to have three 20 ppg scorers the same year. What is perhaps most interesting about this is that there really seem to be two trends. There were no teams the first 10 years, eight teams in the next 13 seasons, no teams in the next 8 years, and finally seven teams in the last 10.

An obvious question would be whether any team has done it two years in a row. The answer is that three teams have: The 1960 and 1961 St. Louis Hawks, the 1982 and 1983 Denver Nuggets, and finally, the 1987 and 1988 Seattle SuperSonics. The Denver Nuggets actual-

did it three years in a row (1981-1983), however the 1981 team had a slightly different trio than the 1982 and 1983 teams. David Thompson was the team's leading scorer in 1981, but slipped due to injuries the following season. He was replaced in the group by Kiki Vandeweghe. The other two players who were part of this 3-year stretch were Alex English and Dan Issel.

Only one other player has done it three consecutive years. Moreover, he is the only player to have done it with two different clubs as well. The player is Tom Chambers. As you recall, he teamed with Dale Ellis and Xavier McDaniel in 1987 and 1988 at Seattle before combining with Kevin Johnson and Eddie Johnson last season at Phoenix.

Although I just suggested that English, Issel, and Chambers are the only players to have been part of this three years in a row, actually, the St. Louis trio of the early 1960's (Bob Pettit, Cliff Hagan, and Clyde Lovellette) accomplished virtually the same thing. The reason I don't count them is that, in the third year (1962), Clyde Lovellette played in only 40 of 80 games and thus did not qualify.

Only twice has more than one team done it in the same year - in 1969, both the San Francisco Warriors and the Los Angeles Lakers. Interestingly, the next year (1970), two completely different teams did it - the Phoenix Suns and the Chicago Bulls.

Only one time has a player been a part of one of these trios in different years with one or more years in between. Both Jeff Mullins and Nate Thurmond did it in 1969 with San Francisco (teaming with Rudy LaRusso) and then again in 1972 (teaming with Cazzie Russell).

The 1983 Denver Nuggets (English 28.4, Issel 26.7, and Vandeweghe 21.6) had the highest scoring group (76.7) while the 1970 Chicago Bulls (Chet Walker 21.5, Bob Love 21.0, and Clem Haskins 20.3) had the "lowest" scoring group (62.8).

It is commonly thought that teams with high scorers are high scoring teams and thus cannot win it all. I want to examine that assumption. The first premise is that these teams score a lot more points as opposed to teams that don't have at least three high scorers. The reason that we think this is probably because of the 1980's teams. I've already mentioned the 1981-83 Denver teams, the 1987 and 1988 Seattle teams, and the 1989 Phoenix team. The other 80's team was the 1984 Philadelphia 76ers. The average 1980's team has placed at a 84.4 percentile for team scoring, including 4 of the 7 as the highest scoring team of the year. So, based on our recent experience, this assumption that these teams are high scoring would be true. It is not true, however, based on the teams from 1960-1972 which averaged a 47.3 percentile and seems to indicate that it may not matter to overall team scoring if a team has three 20 ppg scorers. For all 15 teams, though, the average percentile was 64.6.

Let's assume then that there is a justifiable relationship between the probability of having three 20 ppg scorers and ranking high in terms of team scoring. Perhaps something changed in recent years or perhaps it's just coincidence. But at least, at this time, there appears to be a strong relationship. Besides that, it's logical that a relationship would exist.

Now, what about the statement that these teams cannot win it all. The truth is that they do win during the season. In fact, they averaged winning at a .574 clip. That's good, though not great. Since the 1969 Lakers, however, none of these teams has won a division. What's more often pointed out is that none of these teams has ever won a championship. I would add that only two of the fourteen teams even had a winning record in the playoffs (14 of the 15 made the playoffs). Only the 1969 Lakers (11-7) and last season's Suns (7-5 despite being swept by the Lakers) had winning playoff records.

Perhaps the strongest argument suggesting that those teams are unlikely to win it all, is provided by the 1967 Boston Celtics. This is the first time I've mentioned them, although I've had reason to discuss every other team. Boston is the eastern-most team of the fifteen. In fact, only three of the fifteen teams were east of the Mississippi. What is most interesting is that, although this was the only time the Celtics accomplished this feat, and they did have a 60-21 regular season record, it was the only year during an eleven year stretch that they did *not* win the NBA championship. So, maybe there is validity to the argument that says you may win with three 20 ppg scorers, or with a corresponding high scoring team, but you're unlikely to be as successful in the defense-oriented playoffs.

THE 1980's

The decade of the 1980's has been "bedy bedy guud" to the NBA. There are many reasons, not the least of which are the rivalries between Magic & Bird and the Lakers & Celtics. I thought it would be appropriate to look at the four most popular statistical categories (besides championships, of course). I listed all players who scored 10,000 points or more, the top-10 in rebounds and assists, and lastly, the 23 teams by regular season victories. (Since Dallas has only had a team for 9 years, I included a 10th year at the same rate.) Also, I should add that the 10 years extend from 1979-80 to 1988-89. As you can see, that means this period is not technically the 1980's. If it were, the stats would run from the middle of 1979-80 to the middle of this season (1989-90). Still, I consider last season as the final season of the decade because this season's championship will be decided in 1990.

TOP SCORERS OF THE 80's

	NAME	POINTS			NAME	POINTS
1	Alex English	21,018		20	World Free	12,662
2	Moses Malone	19,082		21	Terry Cummings	12,159
3	Adrian Dantley	18,157		22	Rolando Blackman	12,127
4	Larry Bird	17,899		23	Bernard King	12,100
5	Kareem Abdul-Jabbar	16,246		24	Eddie Johnson	11,825
6	Dominique Wilkins	14,557		25	Joe Barry Carroll	11,657
7	Mark Aguirre	14,488		26	Sidney Moncrief	11,594
8	Reggie Theus	14,429		27	Michael Jordan	11,263
9	George Gervin	14,216		28	Cliff Robinson	10,794
10	Robert Parish	14,043		29	Mychal Thompson	10,742
11	Magic Johnson	13,943		30	Buck Williams	10,440
12	Kiki Vandeweghe	13,775		31	Maurice Cheeks	10,429
13	Jack Sikma	13,342		32	Dennis Johnson	10,414
14	Julius Erving	13,263		33	Kelly Tripucka	10,369
15	Walter Davis	13,106		34	Bill Laimbeer	10,351
16	Tom Chambers	12,896		35	Marques Johnson	10,323
17	Isiah Thomas	12,862		36	Artis Gilmore	10,233
18	Kevin McHale	12,830		37	John Long	10,183
19	Purvis Short	12,740		38	Larry Nance	10,126

Notes: Few people would have guessed that Alex English was the decade's top scorer, probably because he scores his points so "quietly"... Only five of the 38 players had retired before last season... Both Boston and Detroit have 4 players on the list, Atlanta, Los Angeles, Milwaukee 3... Atlanta's three players were in the top-8... In case you're wondering, a few more superstars' point totals were, James Worthy (9,857), Clyde Drexler (9,484), Akeem Olajuwon (8,883), and Charles Barkley (8,616)... Larry Bird is the only player to show up on all three lists. His ranks are #4, #6, #6... Isn't it surprising that David Greenwood out-rebounded Kareem Abdul-Jabbar?

	REBOUNDS IN THE 80's	
	NAME	**REB**
1	Moses Malone	10,269
2	Robert Parish	8,195
3	Jack Sikma	8,192
4	Bill Laimbeer	7,957
5	Buck Williams	7,576
6	Larry Bird	7,319
7	Larry Smith	6,440
8	David Greenwood	6,238
9	Kareem Abdul-Jabbar	5,980
10	Artis Gilmore	5,977

	ASSISTS IN THE 80's	
	NAME	**AST**
1	Magic Johnson	8,025
2	Isiah Thomas	6,220
3	Maurice Cheeks	5,781
4	Reggie Theus	5,239
5	Norm Nixon	5,096
6	Larry Bird	5,396
7	Dennis Johnson	4,381
8	Rickey Green	4,369
9	John Lucas	4,223
10	John Stockton	3,941

As expected, the Lakers and Celtics led the decade in victories. Amazingly, Boston won by a scant single victory (592-591). Those two are by themselves. The next two (Philadelphia, Milwaukee) are also by themselves. Then come the rest of the teams with the Clippers buried in last. Gee, what a surprise.

REGULAR SEASON VICTORIES IN THE 80's

	TEAM	VICTORIES		TEAM	VICTORIES
1	Boston Celtics	592	13	Dallas Mavericks	398
2	Los Angeles Lakers	591	14	San Antonio Spurs	387
3	Philadelphia 76ers	535	15	Utah Jazz	377
4	Milwaukee Bucks	522	16	New York Knicks	374
5	Atlanta Hawks	449	17	Chicago Bulls	369
6	Portland Trail Blazers	442	18	Sacramento Kings	348
7	Phoenix Suns	439	19	New Jersey Nets	346
8	Denver Nuggets	430	20	Golden State Warriors	332
9	Seattle SuperSonics	424	21	Cleveland Cavaliers	326
10	Detroit Pistons	423	22	Indiana Pacers	317
11	Washington Bullets	417	23	Los Angeles Clippers	253
12	Houston Rockets	402			

ROOKIES - 1989

Last season was a particularly interesting one for rookies. It seemed to me that there were a surprisingly high number of rookies who made strong contributions to their teams. As justification for my position, I would like to point out that 19 rookies qualified using my qualification standards on page 240. This is the second highest number in a season. Also, 13 of these rookies had Production Ratings of 10 or more. That too is the second highest total. Interestingly, these groups do not include Danny Manning, Rod Strickland, or Jeff Grayer - all players that I am extremely confident will be successful in the NBA, but who failed to qualify in their rookie seasons.

I went ahead and evaluated 59 rookies last year and I discovered several mentionable items. You can see the rookies who qualified listed by Production Rating on page 243. Mitch Richmond led with a 19.44 rating, followed by Willie Anderson (18.99) and Charles Smith (16.66). Manning, who failed to qualify, had a 17.58 rating. What is sometimes more interesting, especially when looking at rookies, is to evaluate them by production based on 48 minutes. What this really determines are who the top rookies would be if they got to play more. Very interestingly, Rod Strickland ranked #1 (see the New York overview for discussion of the Jackson/Strickland dilemma).

PRODUCTION RATING (48 MINUTE BASIS)

1.	Rod Strickland	New York	27.99	DNQ
2.	Mitch Richmond	Golden State	27.14	
3.	Rik Smits	Indiana	27.12	
4.	Willie Anderson	San Antonio	27.12	
5.	Charles Smith	LA Clippers	26.96	
6.	Charles Shackleford	New Jersey	25.88	DNQ
7.	Andrew Lang	Phoenix	25.00	DNQ
8.	Jerome Lane	Denver	24.35	DNQ
9.	Gary Grant	LA Clippers	24.27	
10.	Tim Perry	Phoenix	23.69	DNQ
11.	Grant Long	Miami	23.30	
12.	Danny Manning	LA Clippers	23.09	DNQ
13.	Chris Morris	New Jersey	22.88	
14.	Eric Leckner	Utah	22.24	DNQ
15.	Brian Shaw	Boston	22.03	
16.	Ledell Eackles	Washington	21.38	
17.	Anthony Frederick	Indiana	21.16	DNQ
18.	Bill Jones	New Jersey	21.11	DNQ
19.	John Shasky	Miami	21.00	DNQ
20.	Ricky Berry	Sacramento	20.93	

Another interesting stat to look at for rookies is the largest change from the first half of the season to the second half. The presumption is that most rookies will improve throughout the year. Most do, though some rookies just fail to show any improvement at all. They may even show a decline. Listed below are the players who had the largest increases and decreases from the All-Star game to season's end.

LARGEST INCREASES			LARGEST DECREASES		
PR (48 Minute Basis)			**PR (48 Minute Basis)**		
1. Shackleford	N.J.	+12.45	59. Garrick	LA. C	-5.99
2. Perry	Phoe	+10.64	58. Del Negro	Sacr	-5.31
3. Lang	Phoe	+9.33	57. Lane	Denv	-4.01
4. Shasky	Miam	+6.38	56. Smits	Indi	-3.88
5. Edwards	Miam	+5.42	55. Berry	Sacr	-3.30
6. Upshaw	Bost	+4.59	54. Strickland	N.Y.	-3.18
7. Bryant	Port	+3.80	53. M.Anderson	S.A.	-2.34
8. Seikaly	Miam	+3.78	52. Eackles	Wash	-1.85
9. Morris	N.J.	+3.74	51. W.Anderson	S.A.	-1.45
10. Hawkins	Phil	+3.54	50. Chevious	Hous	- .84

The statistics on the previous page would indicate that Shackleford may be a big surprise next season or sometime in the near future. Shown below are the top-5 players by the six performance categories. * = Did not qualify

SCORING
(POINTS PER GAME)

1. Richmond	G.St	22.04
2. W. Anderson	S.A.	18.62
3. Chapman	Char	16.89
4. Manning	LA.C	16.69 *
5. Smith	LA.C	16.27

SHOOTING
(SEE PAGE 240 FOR DISCUSSION)

1. Leckner	Utah	1.037 *
2. Berry	Sacr	1.023
3. Kerr	Phoe	1.018 *
4. Perry	Phoe	1.016 *
5. Smits	Indi	1.016

REBOUNDS
(PER 48 MINUTES)

1. Ferreira	Port	18.35 *
2. Lane	Denv	17.45 *
3. Shackleford	N.J.	15.17 *
4. Seikaly	Miam	13.43
5. Lang	Phoe	13.41 *

ASSISTS
(PER 48 MINUTES)

1. Les	Port	13.21 *
2. Grant	LA.C	12.62
3. Johnson	Seat	12.04 *
4. Rivers	LA.L	11.56 *
5. Neal	Miam	11.33 *

BLOCKS
(PER 48 MINUTES)

1. Lang	Phoe	4.38 *
2. Smits	Indi	3.55
3. Horford	Milw	3.00 *
4. Perry	Phoe	2.50
5. Seikaly	Miam	2.35

STEALS
(PER 48 MINUTES)

1. Grant	LA.C	3.59
2. Johnson	Seat	3.46 *
3. Strickland	N.Y.	3.46 *
4. Wiley	Dall	2.94 *
5. M. Anderson	S.A.	2.89 *

Finally, here are a couple categories you might be interested in. The first one, Total Shooting Efficiency Points, indicates how many actual points a player made more than he should have made based on the number of shots he took and the league shooting averages (see page 224 for further explanation). Any positive number at all is excellent for a rookie.

Also shown is Fishing Buddy Rating. This is the ratio between free throw attempts and fouls. Since few rookies excel in either drawing fouls or avoiding them, this is an indicator of what players may be stars in the future. (The league leaders in this category, more than almost any other, are major NBA stars.) * = Did not qualify

TOTAL SHOOTING EFFICIENCY

1. Smits	Indi	+30
2. W. Anderson	S.A.	+27
3. Hawkins	Phil	+26
4. Berry	Sacr	+25
5. Leckner	Utah	+16 *

FISHING BUDDY RATING

1. Richmond	G.St	2.27
2. Eackles	Wash	2.22
3. Maxwell	S.A.	1.79
4. Shasky	Miam	1.78 *
5. Strickland	N.Y.	1.63 *

FORMER TEAMMATES
PAT EWING VS BILL CARTWRIGHT

CHAPTER 3

TEAM BY TEAM ANALYSIS

TEAM BY TEAM ANALYSIS

On the following 154 pages you will find an analysis of each of the 25 teams in the NBA. Each team has six pages dedicated to it (except for the two expansion teams, which have two). Each of the six pages lists specific information which is consistent from team to team.

It was my intention when developing this chapter to provide the most comprehensive analysis of each team in the NBA as possible. I have provided a thorough statistical analysis of each club, various overviews of the previous year, and a look into the future. Moreover, I've attempted to create and provide as much unique information regarding each of these areas as I could.

Page 1: On this page I try to show the subtleties of which players most influenced their team's winning and losing and how they did it. Some of the abbreviations may not be apparent. They are listed below.

SCR = Scoring	DNP = Did not play	SF = Small Forward
REB = Rebounds	PG = Point Guard	PF = Power Forward
AST = Assist	OG = Off Guard	C = Center

In the first section I show the record by the team when a player led in each category. Since there may be more than one leader in a game, a particular vertical column will usually add up to more than 41. (I break each column down by both home and away - 41 games each.) In the second section I broke the player's scoring into groups of 10. There are many cases where this does not tell the whole story, so I attempted to be more specific in the team overviews. In the third section I've broken the team's record down based on who started at what position. These can generally be determined from the boxscore. The first two entries in a box score are the starting forwards, then the center, then the guards. I use my experience to determine which player played which forward or guard position.

Finally, I chose only to analyze the top-10 players on the team because I believe that fringe players rarely ever offer anything interesting to look at statistically. In the extreme case that they did, I tried to refer to them in the overview section for the team.

Page 2: On the second page, I have given both the raw numbers from last year and the rankings for each player based on those numbers. About the only thing that might need clarification on this page is to explain the column headings and to make sure the reader understands that the shaded-in areas represent a player's rank. The second group shows his rank by all players who qualified (see pages 240 for qualification requirements). The 3rd group shows his rank by players at his position only. The abbreviations are listed on the following page.

MIN	= Minutes	TO	= Turnovers
PF	= Personal Fouls	G	= Games Played
DQ	= Disqualifications	GS	= Games Started
HI	= High Scoring Game Of The Year	PPG	= Points Per Game
PR	= Production Rating (see page 2 for explanation)		
SC	= Scoring Rank (per game basis)		
SH	= Shooting Rank (see page 240 for discussion)		
RB	= Above - Total Rebounds	Below - Rankings (48 min basis)	
AS	= Above - Total Assists	Below - Rankings (48 min basis)	
BL	= Above - Total Blocks	Below - Rankings (48 min basis)	
ST	= Above - Total Steals	Below - Rankings (48 min basis)	

Page 3: On the third page is a weekly power rating chart for each team as well as the value and rank of 32 categories. There are a couple of interesting things about the chart which separates it from other attempts at showing a team's running strength. First of all, I converted the power rating to a scale of 0 wins to 82 wins. The last thing of interest is that on any given week, the rating represents the level of play the team had been exhibiting for approximately the previous three weeks. This allows the chart to more graphically show hot and cold stretches. A true power rating would fluctuate very little past mid season. More often than not it would reach an equilibrium and appear more as a general trend up or down.

The 32 categories are mostly self-explanatory, however, I should explain that, under attendance, the notation K means thousand. Also key-man-games missed represent my determination of who is a critical player. The league keeps man-games missed due to injury. There are two problems with this. The first is, despite rumors to the contrary, all men are not created equal. If Magic Johnson misses 10 games, but James Edwards misses 20 - which team was hurt the worst? The other problem is that I don't distinguish as to why a player missed a game. Whether due to a family problem, or an injury or something else, the point is, he's not playing. Probably, the only other thing I need to mention on this page are the last four categories - rebounding, assists, FG%, & FTA's. These records are the times a particular team did better than their opponents vs those times they were not as good.

Page 4: The most important thing to note on this page is that the 10 former players shown are listed in order as to the greatest production while a member of that franchise only. Production is based on a player's total accumulated credits (CRD) (see chapter 1 for definition of CREDITS). Each of a player's credits are added up for every year he played with that club. This total is shown as CRD. Wilt Chamberlain is on the All-Time teams for three separate franchises (Warriors #1, 76ers #7, and Lakers #8). Bill Russell has the highest CRD for one team (Celtics, 30,533).

You may notice a discrepancy between certain player's spans and their years (Yrs) with the team. An example would be Mickey Johnson with the Chicago Bulls. He was with the team five years, but I only show four years. The reason is because he only played thirty-eight games his first year and failed to qualify. A second example is Rick Barry with the Warriors. Barry played with the club for thirteen years, but is only credited for eight years with the team. The reason is that, after beginning with the Warriors, Barry sat out one year and spent four more in the ABA. He then resumed his NBA career with the club.

J#   = Jersey Number
R#   = Round number in the draft the player was selected
D#   = Player's actual draft selection number
HT   = Height
WT   = Weight
Atla = Number of years with his club (in this case Atlanta)
NBA = Number of years played in NBA or ABA

Pages 5 & 6: Although I call these pages over*views*, they really represent re*views* of 1988/89 and pre*views* of 1989/90. However you look at it, I offer my *views* on strengths and weaknesses, good moves and bad. Mostly, I try to bring together the important statistical information on the proceeding pages. I hope the overviews are interesting to read. Here is the ultimate place in the book where the fun and excitement of creative statistics can be seen. I will have achieved that goal only if I create emotion - laughter, anticipation, controversy, anger, or fascination. Lastly, I resort to the traditional predictions. But even there, I vary from the mainstream by giving a best case and worst case scenario.

Atlanta Hawks . . . . Influence on Winning

TEAM RECORD BY

PLAYER	GAMES	... SCR Leader		... REB Leader		...AST Leader	
		HOME	ROAD	HOME	ROAD	HOME	ROAD
Moses Malone	81	7-1	5-2	24-5	16-17	0-1	0-0
Dominique Wilkins	80	23-6	12-12	3-3	1-2	1-0	0-1
Glenn Rivers	76	1-0	0-2	0-0	1-0	23-5	14-10
Reggie Theus	82	4-0	1-4	0-0	0-1	8-3	4-6
Cliff Levingston	80	1-0	1-0	5-0	2-1	0-0	0-0
Jon Koncak	74	0-0	0-1	3-0	1-3	0-0	0-0
Antoine Carr	78	0-0	0-1	0-0	0-0	0-0	0-0
John Battle	82	0-0	0-0	0-0	0-0	0-1	0-2
Spud Webb	81	0-1	0-0	0-0	0-0	5-2	2-4
Ray Tolbert	51	0-0	0-0	0-0	0-0	0-0	0-0

TEAM RECORD BY SCORING *

PLAYER	PLAY	DNP	0-9	10-19	20-29	30-39	40+
Moses Malone	52-29	0-1	0-6	16-15	33-7	3-1	0-0
Dominique Wilkins	51-29	1-1	0-2	6-5	23-16	21-5	1-1
Glenn Rivers	49-27	3-3	9-6	32-16	7-5	1-0	0-0
Reggie Theus	52-30	0-0	4-9	34-9	12-12	2-0	0-0
Cliff Levingston	52-28	0-2	30-20	18-7	4-1	0-0	0-0
Jon Koncak	46-28	6-2	43-24	3-4	0-0	0-0	0-0
Antoine Carr	50-28	2-2	37-23	13-4	0-1	0-0	0-0
John Battle	52-30	0-0	26-16	24-14	2-0	0-0	0-0
Spud Webb	51-30	1-0	48-27	3-2	0-1	0-0	0-0
Ray Tolbert	35-16	17-14	35-16	0-0	0-0	0-0	0-0

TEAM RECORD BY STARTING POSITION *

PLAYER	GAMES	STARTS	PG	OG	SF	PF	C
Moses Malone	81	80	0-0	0-0	0-0	0-1	51-28
Dominque Wilkins	80	80	0-0	0-0	51-29	0-0	0-0
Glenn Rivers	76	76	49-27	0-0	0-0	0-0	0-0
Reggie Theus	82	82	0-0	52-30	0-0	0-0	0-0
Cliff Levingston	80	52	0-0	0-0	1-0	32-19	0-0
Jon Koncak	74	22	0-0	0-0	0-0	14-5	1-2
Antoine Carr	78	12	0-0	0-0	0-1	6-5	0-0
John Battle	82	0	0-0	0-0	0-0	0-0	0-0
Spud Webb	81	6	3-3	0-0	0-0	0-0	0-0
Ray Tolbert	50	0	0-0	0-0	0-0	0-0	0-0

* For further definition of each category and column heading see pages 42 & 43.

Atlanta Hawks . . . . 1988-89 Statistics

RAW NUMBERS *

PLAYER	2pt%	3pt%	FT%	MIN	PF	DQ	HI	TO	RB	AS	BL	ST
Moses Malone	.496	0-12	.789	2878	154	0	37	**245**	**956**	112	**100**	79
Dominique Wilkins	.475	.276	.844	**2997**	138	0	**41**	181	553	211	52	117
Glenn Rivers	.474	**.347**	.861	2462	263	**6**	32	158	286	**525**	40	**181**
Reggie Theus	.476	.293	.851	2517	236	0	32	194	242	387	16	108
Cliff Levingston	**.531**	.200	.696	2184	**270**	4	23	105	498	75	70	97
Jon Koncak	.530	0-3	.553	1531	238	4	16	60	453	56	98	54
Antoine Carr	.481	0-1	.855	1488	221	0	22	82	274	91	62	31
John Battle	.465	.324	.815	1672	125	0	21	104	140	197	9	42
Spud Webb	.493	.045	**.867**	1219	104	0	21	83	123	284	6	70
Ray Tolbert	.426	0-0	.622	341	55	0	9	35	88	16	13	13

OVERALL RANKINGS *

PLAYER	G	GS	PPG	PR	RANK	SC	SH	RB	AS	BL	ST
Moses Malone	81	80	20.21	**23.84**	14	24	74	5	156	34	120
Dominique Wilkins	80	80	**26.24**	22.84	16	7	104	81	104	81	76
Glenn Rivers	76	76	13.58	**18.70**	41	86	73	128	17	85	4
Reggie Theus	**82**	**82**	15.80	**15.06**	91	65	96	148	41	135	57
Cliff Levingston	80	52	9.17	**13.04**	109	136	54	56	162	41	54
Jon Koncak	74	22	4.66	**10.36**	144	174	132	14	159	11	94
Antoine Carr	78	12	7.46	**8.86**	159	151	82	83	121	23	152
John Battle	**82**	0	9.50	**8.27**	167	132	116	162	56	141	128
Spud Webb	81	6	3.94	**6.84**	DNQ						
Ray Tolbert	50	0	2.06	**2.60**	DNQ						

POSITION RANKINGS *

PLAYER	POSITION	RANK	SC	SH	RB	AS	BL	ST
Moses Malone	Center	4	3	13	3	19	19	9
Dominique Wilkins	Small Forward	3	3	24	15	25	22	12
Glenn Rivers	Point Guard	10	14	12	13	17	3	3
Reggie Theus	Off Guard, PG	16	18	25	31	11	28	21
Cliff Levingston	Power Forward	24	25	10	23	24	13	4
Jon Koncak	Center, PF	26	29	21	6	21	9	5
Antoine Carr	Small Forward, PF	37	38	18	17	30	3	34
John Battle	Off Guard	41	36	28	39	19	32	41
Spud Webb	Point Guard	DNQ						
Ray Tolbert	Power Forward	DNQ						

*For further definition of each category and column heading see pages 42 & 43.

Atlanta Hawks .... Team Info

WEEKLY POWER RATING
41 WINS - AVERAGE (See page 43 for Team Power Rating discussion.)

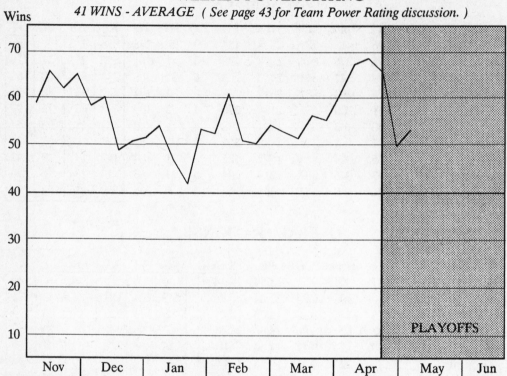

Miscellaneous Categories	Data	Rank
Attendance	644K	11
Key-Man Games Missed	106	19
Season Record	52-30	5
- Home	33-8	8
- Road	19-22	5
Eastern Conference	38-18	2
Western Conference	14-12	15
Overtime Record	2-3	17
Record 5 Pts. or Less	12-11	7
Record 10 Pts. or More	29-12	4
Games Won By Bench	3	16
Games Won By Starters	19	2
Winning Streak	9	2
Losing Streak	3	2
Home Winning Streak	8	15
Road Winning Streak	3	9
Home Losing Streak	2	5
Road Losing Streak	4	2

Performance Categories	Data	Rank
Offensive Scoring (per game)	111.0	9
Defensive Scoring (per game)	106.1	7
Scoring Margin (per game)	4.9	6
Defensive FG%	.472	10
Offensive 2-point%	.483	16
Offensive 3-point%	.277	21
Offensive Free Throw %	.800	3
Offensive Rebs ..... (Off REB/Opp Def REB)		2
Defensive Rebs .... (Def REB/Opp Off REB)		22
Offensive Assists .... (AST/FGMade)		20
Offensive Blocks .. (BLK/Opp FGAttempted)		7
Offensive Steals .... (STL/Game)		7
Turnover Margin .... (Def T.O. - Off T.O.)		3
Fouls Margin .... (Opp FOULS - FOULS)		4
Rebounding Record	42-37-3	7
Assists Record	43-37-2	10
Field Goal Pct. Record	44-38-0	11
Free Throw Att. Record	52-25-5	4

Atlanta Hawks . . . . .Team Roster

MOST PRODUCTIVE PLAYERS

Player	Span	Yrs	CRD
Bob Pettit	1955-65	11	24,638
Bill Bridges	1963-71	9	15,366
Lou Hudson	1967-77	11	13,870
Cliff Hagan	1957-66	10	13,558
Dominique Wilkins	1983-89	7	12,270
Wayne Rollins	1978-88	11	11,540
John Drew	1975-82	8	11,084
Dan Roundfield	1979-84	6	9,958
Lenny Wilkens	1961-68	8	9,442
Eddie Johnson Jr	1978-85	8	8,864

Atlanta Hawks

PRESENT PLAYERS*

J#	VETERANS	COLLEGE	POS	R#	D#	HT	WT	Atla	NBA
12	John Battle	Rutgers	G	4	84	6-2	175	4	4
22	Dudley Bradley	North Carolina	G	1	13	6-6	195	1	9
35	Antoine Carr	Wichita State	F	1	8	6-9	235	5	5
33	Duane Ferrell	Georgia Tech	F	X	X	6-7	209	1	1
32	Jon Koncak	SMU	C	1	5	7-0	260	4	4
53	Cliff Levingston	Wichita State	F	1	9	6-8	220	5	7
2	Moses Malone	None	C	3	22	6-10	255	1	15
25	Glenn Rivers	Marquette	G	2	31	6-4	185	6	6
44	Ray Tolbert	Indiana	F	1	18	6-9	225	1	5
4	Spud Webb	N. Carolina State	G	4	87	5-7	135	4	4
21	Dominique Wilkins	Georgia	F	1	3	6-8	200	7	7
42	Kevin Willis	Michigan State	F-C	1	11	7-0	235	4	4

FUTURE PLAYERS

ROOKIES	COLLEGE	POS	R#	D#	HT	WT
Roy Marble	Iowa	G	1	23	6-6	190
Haywoode Workman	Oral Roberts	G	2	49	6-3	180

* For further definition of category and column headings, see pages 42 & 43.

Atlanta Hawks .... Overview

As you may recall, Jack Tripper kept his "secret" from Mr. Roper for quite a few seasons. Unfortunately for Reggie Theus, he couldn't keep his from Mr. Fratello for even one. As a result, "Three's Company" lasted for years on network T.V., while "Three's A Crowd" quickly seccumbed to bad ratings in Atlanta and was cancelled after its first run.

From very early in the season, it was obvious that Fratello was not happy with Theus' play. There were cries from everywhere that he was too selfish, didn't fit into the team framework, etc. When the Hawks left him unprotected in the expansion draft, it was the ultimate humiliation. In effect they said, "Since you're not worth much as trade bait, we'll give you up... for nothing."

I've always kind of liked Reggie Theus. Given the right team situation, I think he could have been a much bigger star than he was. But clearly, in retrospect, Atlanta was not the situation in which to bring that about. Theus needs to have the ball - if not to shoot it, then to control the game. He's much like Jordan in the sense that he's not a true point guard, but still tends to control the offense. All his career he's either been miscast at point guard or miscast at the 2-guard. Heads they win, tails he loses.

In Atlanta he was in a hopeless situation. To begin with, it was Dominique Wilkins' team and had been for several years. Secondly, adding one of the greatest stars the game has ever known (Moses Malone) would make the job of spreading the wealth tough enough. Thirdly, Doc Rivers was a very steady, very confident point guard who wasn't about to give up offensive control. As a result Reggie was made to feel unwelcome and his play showed it.

What's ironic is that regarding the question of assists per field-goals-attempted (a measure of unselfishness), Theus ranked 7th among the 25 starting off-guards. Three of the six who ranked ahead of him are probably point guards in disguise (Lever, Dumars, and Hornacek). Still, his ratio of

.363 is substantially lower then his career ratio (.460). But that's why he was brought to Atlanta - to shoot. The team exhibits a severe lack of perimeter shooting and Theus was to be the answer. Well, anyway, it didn't work and the Orlando Magic picked him second in the expansion draft. He'll probably score 23 ppg next season (Kelly Tripucka revisited).

The question of selfishness has plagued Atlanta for some time. It was there before Malone and Theus came, that's for sure. There are many statistical ways to evaluate selfishness, but I want to look at only three. 1) First of all, the Hawks ranked #20 in assists (AST/FGMade). That indicates a lot of one-on-one play, a lot of shoot-first mentality and questionable chemistry. 2) They ranked #2 in offensive rebounds, but incredibly enough, #22 in defensive rebounds. What that tells me is that they have guys who are perfectly willing to crash the boards for a stickback on one end, but unwilling to get the "rewardless" defensive rebound at the other. Here again, that's selfishness. A defensive rebound is just as critical as an offensive one (contrary to some temporarily uninformed opinion) because it prevents the stickback at the other end. And 2 points *is* 2 points. 3) Inevitably, selfishness will rear its ugly head late in a game. One or more players wants to be the hero and so he shoots far too many foolish shots. If that were true, it would be logical to assume that the Hawks lost a lot of games in the fourth quarter. They did! In fact, although their combined first three quarters yielded a 142-92-12 record (#3), their 4th quarters were a shabby 37-38-7 (#15). And it mattered. As most Hawk fans painfully remember, Atlanta ranked dead last in the league in blown games (losses when leading after quarter #3).

Atlanta Hawks	**11**
Indiana Pacers	10
Houston Rockets	9
San Antonio Spurs	9
New Jersey Nets	8

Atlanta Hawks .... Overview

Whether Theus's departure will ameliorate the selfishness problem or team chemistry remains to be seen. What is as more true then ever is that the club needs a perimeter shooter. They ranked #16 in 2pt% and #21 in 3pt%. Considering the fact that Atlanta won 93% of their games when they won the field goal percentage battle, the need for a good shooter is obvious. What this team could do with Scott, Ainge, Blackman, or Pierce, to name a few.

I don't know about you, but I would have gone into draft-day looking for one thing - pure shooting ability. That's not what the Hawks did, however. No, they went after another pure athlete in the Wilkins/Jordan mold (Roy Marble). That's fine, but it's not what they needed. Not only is his range a question, but he ranked last among guards drafted by (assists/points). The last thing Atlanta needs is another "athlete" who craves the ball. In all seriousness, I wish the Hawks and Marble all the luck, but I think he was the wrong pick for this team at this time.

Among the bright spots for Atlanta was the late-season play of Jon Koncak. He was being wasted as a back-up center, but finally got to start at power forward for the last 16 regular season games. It worked out well for the Hawks, who went 13-3 during that span. It will be interesting to see what they do when Kevin Willis returns this season. Koncak provided the defensive element, long a team trademark, but missing since Rollins left. During that span, the club had a defensive FG% of .456 - a full 2% better than the rest of the season. That may not seem like much, but 2% is worth roughly 4 points and the Hawks lost 10 games by 4 points or less. If you don't think there is a magical point at which defensive FG% matters, consider that the team was 0-0 when their opponents shot 48%, but when they shot better then that Atlanta was 11-21. When the Hawks held them below 48%, they were 41-9!

Moses Malone continues to defy aging (although Kareem has set new standards). Malone is entering his 16th season without a noticeable drop-off the past few campaigns. As usual, he led in my Fishing Buddy Rating (FTA's/Fouls). Malone has always gone to the line a lot, but his immortality in the game may be his not having fouled out in 884 contests (#2). He should pass the existing record (1,045 - Wilt Chamberlain) around the last day of the 1990-91 season. Atlanta was 33-7 when Malone scored in the 20's and 26-7 when he went to the line at least 10 times.

It will probably never happen again, but last season was the first time the two career leaders in turnovers (at this time - Malone and Theus) played on the same team. What's most intriguing is that Atlanta was among the league's *best* in not turning the ball over. Actually, the club ranked #3 in turnover margin superiority (+177).

Notes: Atlanta was 38-18 (#2) vs the Eastern Conference, but only 14-12 (#15) vs the Western Conference... When Dominique Wilkins scored in the 30's, the team went 21-5... When Reggie Theus scored in the teens, they were 34-9... Doc Rivers was the most <u>consistent</u> scorer at home in the NBA (see page 215), but was #126 on the road... Atlanta signed 6'10" Alexander Volkov of the USSR late in the summer. Volkov was originally drafted by the Hawks in 1986, but another forward?

Prediction - best case: 55-27

Without an outside shooter, it's impossible to win more than 55 games, not to mention being in the same division as the Pistons, Cavaliers, and Jordanians. Nevertheless, if everyone remains healthy, 55 wins is indeed possible.

Prediction - worst case: 43-39

The pressure to win in Atlanta will be unbearable this season. With possible dissension among the forward contingency (5 players vying for the power slot) and no proven 2-guard, this team could unravel.

To order back issues of Basketball Heaven or to obtain the 1990 Mid-season Report, see page 324.

Boston Celtics . . . . Influence on Winning

TEAM RECORD BY

PLAYER	GAMES	... SCR Leader HOME	ROAD	... REB Leader HOME	ROAD	...AST Leader HOME	ROAD
Robert Parish	80	7-1	3-5	22-8	8-21	0-1	0-1
Kevin McHale	78	13-5	3-12	11-0	0-8	0-0	0-2
Reggie Lewis	81	7-1	4-11	1-0	2-0	1-0	0-1
Ed Pinckney	29	0-0	0-1	0-0	0-1	0-0	1-1
Brian Shaw	82	0-0	0-1	2-0	0-2	12-5	6-9
Dennis Johnson	72	0-0	0-0	0-0	0-0	17-5	3-15
Joe Kleine	28	0-0	0-0	2-0	0-0	0-0	0-0
Larry Bird	6	1-0	0-1	0-1	0-0	0-1	0-0
Kelvin Upshaw	23	0-0	0-0	0-0	0-0	2-0	0-2
Jim Paxson	57	0-0	0-0	0-0	0-0	0-0	0-0

TEAM RECORD BY SCORING *

PLAYER	PLAY	DNP	0-9	10-19	20-29	30-39	40+
Robert Parish	40-40	2-0	2-6	15-21	20-12	3-1	0-0
Kevin McHale	40-38	2-2	0-0	13-11	25-23	2-4	0-0
Reggie Lewis	42-39	0-1	2-8	18-16	19-10	3-5	0-0
Ed Pinckney	17-12	25-28	9-7	6-5	2-0	0-0	0-0
Brian Shaw	42-40	0-0	26-25	16-13	0-1	0-1	0-0
Dennis Johnson	37-35	5-5	16-18	18-15	3-2	0-0	0-0
Joe Kleine	16-12	26-28	12-11	4-1	0-0	0-0	0-0
Larry Bird	2-4	40-36	1-0	0-2	1-2	0-0	0-0
Kelvin Upshaw	13-10	29-30	12-6	1-4	0-0	0-0	0-0
Jim Paxson	31-26	11-14	17-20	12-5	2-1	0-0	0-0

TEAM RECORD BY STARTING POSITION *

PLAYER	GAMES	STARTS	PG	OG	SF	PF	C
Robert Parish	80	80	0-0	0-0	0-0	0-0	40-40
Kevin McHale	78	74	0-0	0-0	0-0	38-36	0-0
Reggie Lewis	81	57	0-0	0-2	30-25	0-0	0-0
Ed Pinckney	29	9	0-0	0-0	0-1	4-4	0-0
Brian Shaw	82	54	24-19	5-6	0-0	0-0	0-0
Dennis Johnson	72	72	15-18	22-17	0-0	0-0	0-0
Joe Kleine	28	2	0-0	0-0	0-0	0-0	2-0
Larry Bird	6	6	0-0	0-0	2-4	0-0	0-0
Kelvin Upshaw	23	0	0-0	0-0	0-0	0-0	0-0
Jim Paxson	57	7	0-0	1-1	3-2	0-0	0-0

* For further definition of each category and column heading see pages 42 & 43.

Boston Celtics . . . . 1988-89 Statistics

RAW NUMBERS *

PLAYER	2pt%	3pt%	FT%	MIN	PF	DQ	HI	TO	RB	AS	BL	ST
Robert Parish	**.570**	0-0	.719	2840	209	2	34	**200**	**996**	175	**116**	79
Kevin McHale	.548	0-4	.818	**2876**	223	2	36	196	637	172	97	26
Reggie Lewis	.493	.136	.787	2657	**258**	**5**	**39**	142	377	218	72	**124**
Ed Pinckney	.518	0-6	.800	2012	202	2	26	119	449	118	66	83
Brian Shaw	.441	0-13	.826	2301	211	1	31	188	376	**472**	27	78
Dennis Johnson	.459	.140	.821	2309	211	3	24	175	190	**472**	21	94
Joe Kleine	.407	0-2	.882	1411	192	2	19	104	378	67	23	33
Larry Bird	.471	0-0	**.947**	189	18	0	29	11	37	29	5	6
Kelvin Upshaw	.487	**.200**	.692	617	80	1	13	55	49	117	3	26
Jim Paxson	.470	.167	.816	1138	96	0	21	57	74	107	8	38

OVERALL RANKINGS *

PLAYER	G	GS	PPG	PR	RANK	SC	SH	RB	AS	BL	ST
Robert Parish	80	**80**	18.57	26.10	11	33	15	2	118	26	118
Kevin McHale	78	74	**22.54**	23.68	15	14	13	63	123	36	174
Reggie Lewis	81	57	18.46	**17.64**	54	36	97	108	86	50	45
Ed Pinckney	80	33	11.47	**14.27**	99	112	43	61	125	38	64
Brian Shaw	**82**	54	8.57	**12.88**	110	144	161	95	18	100	99
Dennis Johnson	72	72	10.01	**12.87**	111	127	149	165	19	116	69
Joe Kleine	75	13	6.45	**8.08**	170	165	160	28	148	84	137
Larry Bird	6	6	19.33	**21.00**	DNQ						
Kelvin Upshaw	32	0	6.84	**7.44**	DNQ						
Jim Paxson	57	7	8.63	**7.02**	DNQ						

POSITION RANKINGS *

PLAYER	POSITION	RANK	SC	SH	RB	AS	BL	ST
Robert Parish	Center	3	5	4	2	9	15	8
Kevin McHale	Power Forward, C	3	3	2	27	10	10	29
Reggie Lewis	Small Forward, OG	11	15	21	32	17	12	9
Ed Pinckney	Power Forward, SF	23	20	6	26	12	11	6
Brian Shaw	Point Guard	22	25	28	4	18	5	28
Dennis Johnson	Off Guard, PG	20	34	38	40	1	20	24
Joe Kleine	Center	29	24	27	14	16	28	12
Larry Bird	Small Forward	DNQ						
Kelvin Upshaw	Point Guard	DNQ						
Jim Paxson	Small Forward	DNQ						

*For further definition of each category and column heading see pages 42 & 43.

Boston Celtics .... Team Info

WEEKLY POWER RATING

41 WINS - AVERAGE (See page 43 for Team Power Rating discussion.)

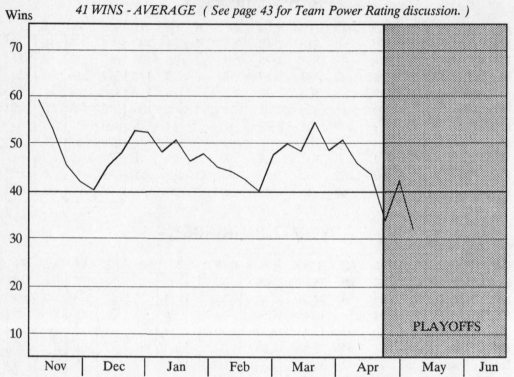

Miscellaneous Categories	Data	Rank
Attendance	612K	13
Key-Man Games Missed	125	21
Season Record	42-40	15
- Home	32-9	9
- Road	10-31	16
Eastern Conference	27-29	14
Western Conference	15-11	10
Overtime Record	2-2	8
Record 5 Pts. or Less	8-10	20
Record 10 Pts. or More	22-19	15
Games Won By Bench	3	16
Games Won By Starters	7	11
Winning Streak	4	17
Losing Streak	5	10
Home Winning Streak	14	9
Road Winning Streak	1	21
Home Losing Streak	2	5
Road Losing Streak	5	6

Performance Categories	Data	Rank
Offensive Scoring (per game)	109.2	10
Defensive Scoring (per game)	108.1	10
Scoring Margin (per game)	1.1	14
Defensive FG%	.484	14
Offensive 2-point%	.504	7
Offensive 3-point%	.252	22
Offensive Free Throw %	.783	11
Offensive Rebs ..... (Off REB/Opp Def REB)		6
Defensive Rebs .... (Def REB/Opp Off REB)		2
Offensive Assists .... (AST/FGMade)		7
Offensive Blocks .. (BLK/Opp FGAttempted)		14
Offensive Steals .... (STL/Game)		21
Turnover Margin .... (Def T.O. - Off T.O.)		21
Fouls Margin .... (Opp FOULS - FOULS)		9
Rebounding Record	57-23-2	2
Assists Record	42-39-1	13
Field Goal Pct. Record	44-38-0	11
Free Throw Att. Record	36-42-4	14

Boston Celtics . . . . Team Roster

MOST PRODUCTIVE PLAYERS

Player	Span	Yrs	CRD
Bill Russell	1957-69	13	30,533
John Havlicek	1963-78	16	25,310
Larry Bird	1980-89	10	21,817
Dave Cowens	1971-80	10	18,664
Bob Cousy	1951-63	13	17,251
Robert Parish	1981-89	9	16,535
Kevin McHale	1981-89	9	14,792
Sam Jones	1958-69	12	13,748
Jo Jo White	1970-79	10	11,761
Tommy Heinsohn	1957-65	9	11,542

PRESENT PLAYERS*

J#	VETERANS	COLLEGE	POS	R#	D#	HT	WT	Bost	NBA
33	Larry Bird	Indiana State	F	1	6	6-9	220	10	10
34	Kevin Gamble	Iowa	G	3	63	6-5	215	1	1
31	Ron Grandison	New Orleans	F	5	100	6-8	217	1	1
3	Dennis Johnson	Pepperdine	G	2	29	6-4	202	6	13
53	Joe Kleine	Arkansas	C-F	1	6	6-11	240	1	4
35	Reggie Lewis	Northeastern	G-F	1	22	6-7	195	2	2
32	Kevin McHale	Minnesota	F-C	1	3	6-10	225	9	9
00	Robert Parish	Centenary	C	1	8	7-0	230	9	13
4	Jim Paxson	Dayton	G	1	12	6-6	210	2	10
54	Ed Pinckney	Villanova	F	1	10	6-9	215	1	4
45	Ramon Rivas	Temple	C	X	X	6-10	260	1	1
20	Brian Shaw	Cal. Santa Barbara	G	1	24	6-6	190	1	1
7	Kelvin Upshaw	Utah	G	X	X	6-2	180	1	1

FUTURE PLAYERS

ROOKIES	COLLEGE	POS	R#	D#	HT	WT
Michael Smith	Brigham Young	F	1	13	6-10	225
Dino Radja	Yugoslavia	F	2	40	6-10	220

* For further definition of category and column headings, see pages 42 & 43.

Boston Celtics .... Overview

When Larry Bird struggled through his first 6 games last season, opponents were holding their breath. When he opted for surgery to remove bone spurs on both heels, foes sighed with relief. When he toyed with coming back for the playoffs, the perspiration again flowed. But when he decided not to play after all, there was collective relaxation. Now, after sitting out an entire year, anxious to take no prisoners, and scoring 33 points in his summer All-Star celebrity game, I think it's fair to say... He's Baaaack!

It's probably a bit much to assume he will step right in and play like he has in the past, but even 80% of his former self might be good enough to help Boston back into the top spot in the Atlantic Division. The Celtics were respectable in 1989 with a winning record and a playoff berth, but now that Lewis and Shaw have another year of experience and with the addition of Rookie Mike Smith as well as Bird, this club could be as good as we're used to seeing them.

Let's face it, Bird has been named the NBA MVP three times, was 1st-team All-League every year in the NBA prior to last season's injury, and his Celtics teams have averaged 61+ wins per season. And, although his feet may have slowed just a tad, he still has the quickest hands in Boston this side of Sam Malone. I see no evidence to indicate that he's over the hill or that the cumulative abilities of his teammates are less than what he's used to.

Mike Smith is a 6'10" forward from BYU who is kind of a cross between Tom Chambers and Kevin McHale. He's a high-scoring athletic big guy who loves to pop the jumper. He really is a good shooter (40%+ from 3pt range and 90%+ from the line for his career.) At 24 years of age, he has maturity and should offer immediate help to the front line. As team physician Dr. Arnold Scheller said, "We should change the team colors to black and blue and the symbol to the red cross."

Hold everything. Rigor mortis hasn't set in yet, but Robert Parish is 36, Kevin

McHale 31, and Bird 32, so I'd keep the respirator plugged in just in case. Despite picking up Joe Kleine (last in the NBA in 2pt%) and Ed Pinckney from Sacramento for Danny Ainge and Brad Lohaus, the front line can still use some young talent. Smith may be just what the doctor ordered. Interestingly, the Celtics had not played a single game without Bird, McHale, *and* Parish since they became teammates in 1980 (almost 1000 games ago). Last season, they all missed the same game and, perhaps surprisingly, the team beat Portland 106-97.

Though rumors had Kevin McHale being traded, it appears that he's safe for now. Occasionally, an inverse relationship exists where a team does better the fewer field goal attempts a player takes. In almost every case it's because they're not good shooters, which makes sense. Of course, Kevin McHale is one of the best shooters in NBA history, yet the Celtics were 13-2 when he shot *less* than 13 Field Goal Attempts. I don't quite understand why that was. Do you? Nevertheless, using a scoring consistency formula that I explain on page 215, McHale ranked numero uno in the NBA. As an example, he went one 8-game stretch where he scored 22, 25, 26, 23, 26, 22, 25, and 26.

1. Kevin McHale	**Boston**	**1.4119**
2. Winston Garland	Golden St.	1.4203
3. Terry Porter	Portland	1.4309
4. Thurl Bailey	Utah	1.4337
5. Vern Fleming	Indiana	1.4436

Robert Parish was simply amazing in 1989. The team revolved so much around the Chief that when he scored above his average (18.6 ppg) Boston was 29-16. When he was below it, they were only 11-24. More than anything else though, Parish had the highest Production Rating of his career in 1989 (26.10). His previous high was in 1982 when he was 24.58. What's most amazing is that, by achieving the highest Production Rating in his "lucky" 13th year, he is the only player in NBA his-

Boston Celtics .... Overview

tory to "peak" so late. Of the 59 players who have played that long, Don Nelson is the closest - having managed his 3rd best season by Production Rating in year #13. Over half of the 59 experienced their worst year up to that point in their careers.

Robert Parish	**Boston**	**1989**	**1st**
Don Nelson	Boston	1975	3rd
Lenny Wilkens	Cleveland	1973	4th
Dolph Schayes	Syracuse	1961	5th
Johnny Green	Cincinnati	1972	8th
Leroy Ellis	Philadelphia	1975	8th

With Dennis Johnson at 35 years of age and his lowest Production Rating in 10 years, and with Danny Ainge gone, a whole new group has taken up residence on the parquet floor. Celtic Guards: The Next Generation. Brian Shaw was picked #24 in the 1988 draft, but was impressive as an all-around player and received the most votes for the All-Rookie 2nd team. Though Reggie Lewis played small forward in 1989, he can, and will, play the 2-guard position. Lewis has turned into a strong offensive threat. By dividing the season into thirds you can see his scoring improvement: 1st third: 11.85 ppg, 2nd third: 20.89 ppg, last third: 22.63 ppg. Finally, Kevin Gamble came out of nowhere to start the last 6 games during which he was very impressive. His 23 points per game were good, but his 60%+ shooting, 5 rebounds, and 4 assists were the icing. If I were Dennis Johnson, I'd retire. Well, on second thought, if I was pulling in a cool mil every 360 days or so, I'd stick around till I was 60. And then they'd have to throw me out! Hey, D.J., scoot over.

Even though this guard crop was impressive, they do have one serious weakness. The combined 3pt% of Lewis, Shaw, and Gamble was a bottom-of-the-barrel bad 11%. What they need is a serious infusion of 3-point shooting by the 3-time winner of the 3-point shooting contest - Larry Bird. With Bird absent, the Celtics were a lowly 22nd in 3pt%. That's a radical change from the four previous seasons.

1989	**.252**	**22nd**
1988	.384	1st
1987	.366	2nd
1986	.351	1st
1985	.356	1st

If you look at the Celtics' Power Rating chart on page 52, you can see the decline when Bird left at the beginning of the season. It resulted in a 5-7 record during December, the first losing month after 61 consecutive winners. Though the team rebounded, struggled, then rebounded again, late-season injuries to both Parish and McHale caused the final slide. The Celtics limped into the playoffs and were easily handled by the Pistons in three games. When Bird criticized his teammates for not working hard enough, several voiced their lack of appreciation for his admonishment.

Notes: During one 50-game stretch, the Celtics won the battle of the boards 41 times... When the club scored 115+ at home they were a perfect 17-0... Boston was the only NBA team which failed to defeat a winning team on the road... When Jim Paxson scored 10+ points, the team was 14-6... When the Celts shot better than 50%, they were a sparkling 25-5. When they didn't, they fizzled (17-35).

Prediction - best case: 60-22

You bet! If this team can squeeze one more good year out of Parish and if Bird comes back strong, there is absolutely no reason why they won't come close to this figure. If Smith and the young guards really excel, then this could be the NBA's best team.

Prediction - worst case: 47-35

Even if Bird is never the same player as he was, this club is incapable of accruing anywhere near the number of losses as last year (40). If Larry were to get injured again... now that's a different story.

To order back issues of Basketball Heaven or to obtain the 1990 Midseason Report, see page 324.

Charlotte Hornets . . . . Influence on Winning

TEAM RECORD BY

PLAYER	GAMES	... SCR Leader		... REB Leader		...AST Leader	
		HOME	ROAD	HOME	ROAD	HOME	ROAD
Kurt Rambis	75	0-3	0-2	10-20	3-15	0-0	0-1
Kelly Tripucka	71	8-12	4-17	0-0	0-1	0-1	0-2
Tyrone Bogues	79	0-0	0-0	0-1	0-1	6-19	4-20
Rex Chapman	75	1-7	3-7	0-0	0-1	0-0	0-0
Michael Holton	67	0-1	0-0	0-0	0-0	7-11	2-9
Robert Reid	82	3-4	1-4	1-0	0-2	0-0	0-0
Earl Cureton	82	0-0	0-0	2-7	1-8	0-0	0-0
Dave Hoppen	77	0-0	0-0	0-2	2-6	0-0	0-0
Dell Curry	48	0-3	1-3	0-0	0-0	0-0	0-0
Tim Kempton	79	0-0	0-0	1-2	2-1	0-0	0-1

TEAM RECORD BY SCORING *

PLAYER	PLAY	DNP	0-9	10-19	20-29	30-39	40+
Kurt Rambis	18-57	2-5	6-25	11-30	1-2	0-0	0-0
Kelly Tripucka	17-54	3-8	0-2	3-24	5-21	6-7	3-0
Tyrone Bogues	19-60	1-2	13-51	6-9	0-0	0-0	0-0
Rex Chapman	19-56	1-6	2-9	8-25	9-21	0-1	0-0
Michael Holton	17-50	3-12	13-31	4-17	0-2	0-0	0-0
Robert Reid	20-62	0-0	2-17	13-30	5-15	0-0	0-0
Earl Cureton	20-62	0-0	14-43	6-19	0-0	0-0	0-0
Dave Hoppen	18-59	2-3	13-46	5-13	0-0	0-0	0-0
Dell Curry	8-40	12-22	2-19	3-17	2-4	1-0	0-0
Tim Kempton	19-60	1-2	17-48	1-12	1-0	0-0	0-0

TEAM RECORD BY STARTING POSITION *

PLAYER	GAMES	STARTS	PG	OG	SF	PF	C
Kurt Rambis	75	75	0-0	0-0	0-0	18-56	0-1
Kelly Tripucka	71	65	0-0	0-0	16-49	0-0	0-0
Tyrone Bogues	79	21	5-16	0-0	0-0	0-0	0-0
Rex Chapman	75	44	0-0	10-43	0-0	0-0	0-0
Michael Holton	67	60	14-45	1-0	0-0	0-0	0-0
Robert Reid	82	54	0-0	9-28	4-13	0-0	0-0
Earl Cureton	82	41	0-0	0-0	0-0	2-6	8-25
Dave Hoppen	77	36	0-0	0-0	0-0	0-0	9-27
Dell Curry	48	0	0-0	0-0	0-0	0-0	0-0
Tim Kempton	79	0	0-0	0-0	0-0	0-0	0-0

* For further definition of each category and column heading see pages 42 & 43.

Charlotte Hornets . . . . 1988-89 Statistics

RAW NUMBERS *

PLAYER	2pt%	3pt%	FT%	MIN	PF	DQ	HI	TO	RB	AS	BL	ST
Kurt Rambis	.521	0-3	.734	2233	208	**4**	23	148	**703**	159	57	100
Kelly Tripucka	.476	.357	.866	**2302**	196	0	**40**	236	267	224	16	88
Tyrone Bogues	.437	.077	.750	1755	141	1	14	124	165	**620**	7	**111**
Rex Chapman	.431	.314	.795	2219	167	1	37	113	187	176	25	70
Michael Holton	.433	.214	.839	1696	165	0	22	119	105	424	12	66
Robert Reid	.432	.327	.776	2152	235	2	28	106	302	153	20	53
Earl Cureton	.502	0-1	.537	2047	230	3	17	114	488	130	**61**	50
Dave Hoppen	**.564**	**.500**	.727	1419	**239**	4	16	77	384	57	21	25
Dell Curry	.509	.345	**.870**	813	68	0	31	44	104	50	4	42
Tim Kempton	.512	0-1	.686	1341	215	3	21	121	304	102	14	41

OVERALL RANKINGS *

PLAYER	G	GS	PPG	PR	RANK	SC	SH	RB	AS	BL	ST
Kurt Rambis	75	**75**	11.09	**17.80**	51	114	61	10	100	52	52
Kelly Tripucka	71	65	**22.62**	17.61	55	13	62	129	69	130	79
Tyrone Bogues	79	21	5.35	**11.90**	127	173	170	152	1	152	15
Rex Chapman	75	44	16.89	11.03	133	53	162	161	87	103	105
Michael Holton	67	60	8.25	10.88	134	148	155	175	8	129	77
Robert Reid	**82**	54	14.72	10.85	135	70	165	109	101	112	133
Earl Cureton	**82**	41	6.49	10.46	139	167	141	48	114	44	134
Dave Hoppen	77	36	6.49	9.32	156	166	17	26	155	89	163
Dell Curry	48	0	11.90	9.50	DNQ						
Tim Kempton	79	0	6.13	7.53	DNQ						

POSITION RANKINGS *

PLAYER	POSITION	RANK	SC	SH	RB	AS	BL	ST
Kurt Rambis	Power Forward	12	21	12	5	4	15	3
Kelly Tripucka	Small Forward	12	6	12	38	10	36	13
Tyrone Bogues	Point Guard	24	33	31	21	1	20	8
Rex Chapman	Off Guard	29	15	42	38	33	13	36
Michael Holton	Point Guard, OG	26	26	26	32	8	12	27
Robert Reid	Small Forward, OG	31	21	38	33	23	33	29
Earl Cureton	Center, PF	23	26	23	24	8	21	10
Dave Hoppen	Center	28	25	5	12	18	29	22
Dell Curry	Off Guard	DNQ						
Tim Kempton	Power Forward	DNQ						

*For further definition of each category and column heading see pages 42 & 43.

Charlotte Hornets .... Team Info

WEEKLY POWER RATING
41 WINS - AVERAGE (See page 43 for Team Power Rating discussion.)

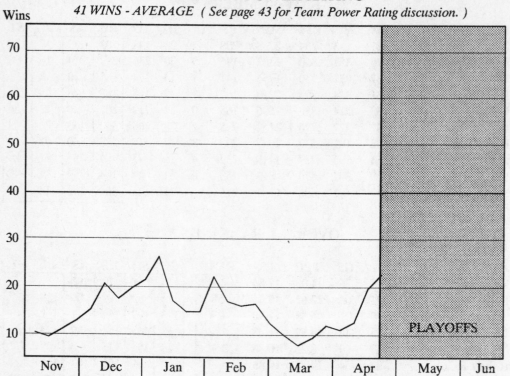

Miscellaneous Categories	Data	Rank
Attendance	950K	1
Key-Man Games Missed	67	15
Season Record	20-62	24
- Home	12-29	24
- Road	8-33	20
Eastern Conference	12-44	22
Western Conference	8-18	22
Overtime Record	1-3	22
Record 5 Pts. or Less	13-10	5
Record 10 Pts. or More	5-36	24
Games Won By Bench	4	13
Games Won By Starters	1	23
Winning Streak	2	24
Losing Streak	9	19
Home Winning Streak	4	22
Road Winning Streak	2	16
Home Losing Streak	13	25
Road Losing Streak	11	19

Performance Categories	Data	Rank
Offensive Scoring (per game)	104.5	22
Defensive Scoring (per game)	113.0	21
Scoring Margin (per game)	-8.5	23
Defensive FG%	.500	24
Offensive 2-point%	.470	23
Offensive 3-point%	.312	16
Offensive Free Throw %	.767	16
Offensive Rebs (Off REB/Opp Def REB)		23
Defensive Rebs (Def REB/Opp Off REB)		21
Offensive Assists (AST/FGMade)		1
Offensive Blocks (BLK/Opp FGAttempted)		25
Offensive Steals (STL/Game)		17
Turnover Margin (Def T.O. - Off T.O.)		7
Fouls Margin (Opp FOULS - FOULS)		24
Rebounding Record	23-56-3	25
Assists Record	57-21-4	1
Field Goal Pct. Record	23-58-1	25
Free Throw Att. Record	23-57-2	24

Charlotte Hornets . . . . Team Roster

MOST PRODUCTIVE PLAYERS

Player	Span	Yrs	CRD
Kurt Rambis	1989	1	1,335
Kelly Tripucka	1989	1	1,250
Tyrone Bogues	1989	1	940
Robert Reid	1989	1	890
Earl Cureton	1989	1	858
Rex Chapman	1989	1	827
Michael Holton	1989	1	729
Dave Hoppen	1989	1	718
Tim Kempton	1989	1	595
Dell Curry	1989	1	456

PRESENT PLAYERS*

J#	VETERANS	COLLEGE	POS	R#	D#	HT	WT	Char	NBA
1	Tyrone Bogues	Wake Forest	G	1	12	5-4	140	1	2
3	Rex Chapman	Kentucky	G	1	8	6-5	185	1	1
25	Earl Cureton	Detroit	F	3	58	6-9	215	1	9
30	Dell Curry	Virginia Tech	G	1	15	6-5	195	1	3
	Stuart Gray	UCLA	C	2	29	7-0	245	0	5
6	Michael Holton	UCLA	G	3	53	6-4	195	1	5
42	David Hoppen	Nebraska	C	3	65	6-11	235	1	2
41	Tim Kempton	Notre Dame	C	6	124	6-10	245	1	2
35	Sidney Lowe	N. Carolina State	G	2	25	6-0	195	1	3
32	Greg Kite	BYU	C	1	21	6-11	250	1	6
31	Kurt Rambis	Santa Clara	F	3	58	6-8	218	1	8
50	Robert Reid	St. Marys (Tx)	F-G	2	40	6-8	215	1	11
45	Brian Rowsom	N.C. (Wilmington)	F	2	34	6-9	220	1	2
7	Kelly Tripucka	Notre Dame	F	1	12	6-6	220	1	8

FUTURE PLAYERS

ROOKIES	COLLEGE	POS	R#	D#	HT	WT
J.R. Reid	North Carolina	F	1	5	6-9	250

* For further definition of category and column headings, see pages 42 & 43.

Charlotte Hornets . . . . Overview

I think the general perception by most NBA pundits a year ago was that Charlotte had done just about everthing right. What was there to criticize? They had a beautiful new arena, they'd generated great anticipation in the city, and they had an energetic owner (most of all, they had good-looking uniforms). They had all that, sure. But what they didn't have was a "big" man.

Because of that deficiency, there was wide-spread criticism for selecting Rex Chapman as opposed to someone up front in the 1988 draft. Most felt the Hornets would get demolished even worse than an expansion team had any business getting demolished. It's true that they ranked last in both height and weight among the 25 NBA teams. It is also true that their sister expansion team - Miami - averaged a #16 ranking in those two areas. And yes, it's true that, because of the size limitations, Charlotte ended up last in rebounding in the NBA, with a deficiency of -474 to their opponents while Miami nearly broke even at -34. But I guess it wasn't *that* big an issue as the Hornets won 20 games while the Heat managed to win but 15.

If there was any doubt left in anyone's mind that the NBA has changed, the Charlotte/Miami situation should erase it. It is simply no longer true that a team cannot win without a big, huge center. Obviously, there has to be a reasonable amount of height, but the most important single element is the point-guard. (Passing, leadership, tempo, chemistry, fast breaks, etc.) Those are the elements which make winning teams. Golden State won 43 games last season by starting a 6'8" power forward at center much of the time, and the first true center wasn't taken in last summer's draft until the last player of the first round - and he's not even an American. My point is that Charlotte wasn't compromising that much by going with a small (everything's relative) lineup.

Whereas it's true that they may have suffered in rebounding, they more than made up for it in assists. The club led the league in virtually every assist category. To begin with, they were 1st in assists-per-field goals made - registering an assist on 68% of their buckets. (That's great coaching, by the way, especially for a young team which hasn't played together. That required good discipline, unselfishness, and learning plays - all in a very short time.) They also ranked #1 in assist-to-turnover ratio, indicating their passes were smart. Finally, they were #1 in assist record as they won that battle 57 times, lost 21, and tied 4. As further evidence that the assists (and all that goes with them) was more important to Charlotte's wins than rebounding was to Miami's wins, consider this: Of the 20 Charlotte victories, the team was 19-0-1 in assists (#1). Of the 15 Miami victories, Miami was 8-5-2 in rebounding (#15). Now, how's this? Miami's most important ingredient in winning 15 games was... assists also, as they were 11-3-1 (#9) in their 15 wins. I hope I don't have to hear too much more about how a team is going to die if it doesn't get a "big" man.

Thank God Charlotte finally came to its senses and got a "big" man in this year's draft. When their turn (#5) came to choose, they went with a local hero, J.R. Reid. Management had already made it clear that they were going to pick Reid if he was still available. He was, and they did. In doing so, they passed over a better choice - Stacey King. I'm sure they probably believe it too, but what was their alternative? The fans wanted Reid and, at this point in franchise history, they owe them a lot. (Charlotte led the NBA in attendance - the only expansion team to do so.) Besides, as the club said, if they didn't choose Reid and he turned out to be great for someone else, they would never hear the end of it. J.R. will be trying to follow in the footsteps of three other Tar Heels who went into the NBA early: Michael Jordan and Bob McAdoo were both Rookies-of-the-Year and league MVP's. James Worthy was drafted #1 and has since won three world titles. What you have to remember, though,

Charlotte Hornets . . . . Overview

is that those player's teams had an average record the year before, of 35-47, as opposed to 20-62.

I have another concern about Reid. He's a massive 250 lbs, but only 6'9", so I expect him to eventually play power forward. Unfortunately, he'll need to play center initially. Some will argue that he is not that unlike Wes Unseld, who, at 6'8" and 245 lbs, manned the pivot. They'll tell you he won Rookie-of-the-Year honors and a world title. That's true, however although Kareem was around in those days, Olajuwon, Ewing, Robinson and monsters like Eaton and Bol weren't. I do not think he can be an offensive force, which is a little questionable anyway, against players of this kind. I do think he can be a very good power forward and I hope he eventually gets to play that position.

I thought it would be interesting to look at how Charlotte compared with other expansion teams in their first year. The group consisted of 13 teams. The club's 20 wins was right in the middle. The most victories were by the Chicago Bulls, with 33. The fewest were shared by four teams with 15 (Cleveland, Dallas, Houston, and Miami). Despite this level of success, there is one moderating point to make. Though most expansion teams improve in the second half of the season over the first half, Charlotte did not. They actually won 2 fewer games. Only one expansion team has declined farther - the San Diego Rockets (Houston) dropped 7 more games in the second half. Charlotte's slip was especially noticeable during two back-to-back 9-game losing streaks late in the year.

Kelly Tripucka was the star of the team last season. After being sentenced to two years in Utah (a state he refused to recognize), he was given a pardon by being left unprotected in the expansion draft. Tripucka had averaged 22 ppg in five seasons at Detroit, but was benched much of his two years in Utah. At Charlotte, he was back to his old scoring self - managing a 22.6 average (#13). Whereas his shooting

was labeled "selfish" in Utah, it was essential to this team which went 9-7 when he scored 30 or more points. Considering his being picked up for free, I thought I'd place him on my All-Reject team - meaning the best players who were acquired for little-to-nothing. PR = Production Rating.

	From	To	PR
Dale Ellis	Dall	Seat	21.13
Kelly Tripucka	**Utah**	**Char**	**17.61**
Bernard King	N.Y.	Wash	17.35
Winston Garland	Milw	G. St	16.76
Ron Anderson	Indi	Phil	14.93

Tyrone Bogues was the spark plug for the club. The league's shortest player was the tops in the NBA in both assist-to-turnover ratio as well as assists-per-48 minutes (16.96). If not for his extreme defensive short-comings, he could well be considered a point guard that Charlotte could depend on for a long time.

Notes: Dell Curry was #1 in the league in field goal attempts per 48 minutes... When Curry played, the team was only 8-40. When he didn't, they were a much better 12-22... Michael Holton ranked last in the league in defensive rebounding... Rex Chapman and Robert Reid ranked last in the NBA in 2-pt efficiency points (see page 225)... Charlotte was #1 in 3 point games or less (9-4)... But they were last in 20 point games or more (0-16).

Prediction - best case: 30-52

Assuming that J.R. Reid helps the team overcome their biggest weakness - rebounding - they should improve a little. I'm not sure fans should expect much more however.

Prediction - worst case: 20-62

A lot of people think Charlotte overachieved a little in their maiden year. Since their second half was disappointing, it's not inconceivable to envision a second verse, same as the first.

To order back issues of Basketball Heaven or to obtain the 1990 Midseason Report, see page 324.

Chicago Bulls . . . . Influence on Winning

TEAM RECORD BY

PLAYER	GAMES	... SCR Leader		... REB Leader		...AST Leader	
		HOME	ROAD	HOME	ROAD	HOME	ROAD
Michael Jordan	81	28-11	16-21	13-5	6-12	19-6	12-15
Horace Grant	79	0-0	0-0	10-4	7-9	0-0	0-0
Scottie Pippen	73	0-0	3-1	3-0	4-3	3-1	0-0
Bill Cartwright	78	1-0	0-0	9-2	3-2	0-0	0-1
Sam Vincent	70	0-0	0-1	1-0	0-0	7-2	4-8
John Paxson	78	1-0	0-0	0-0	0-0	3-2	1-3
Craig Hodges	49	0-0	1-0	0-0	0-0	0-1	1-0
Brad Sellers	80	0-0	0-1	0-0	0-0	0-0	0-0
Dave Corzine	81	0-0	0-0	1-1	1-0	0-0	0-0
Charles Davis	48	0-0	0-0	0-0	0-2	0-0	0-0

TEAM RECORD BY SCORING *

PLAYER	PLAY	DNP	0-9	10-19	20-29	30-39	40 +
Michael Jordan	47-34	0-1	0-0	1-2	14-14	25-10	7-8
Horace Grant	45-34	2-1	11-13	28-21	6-0	0-0	0-0
Scottie Pippen	43-30	4-5	4-12	31-16	6-2	2-0	0-0
Bill Cartwright	44-34	3-1	9-19	25-13	10-2	0-0	0-0
Sam Vincent	40-30	7-5	24-12	15-16	1-2	0-0	0-0
John Paxson	47-31	0-4	34-21	11-10	2-0	0-0	0-0
Craig Hodges	32-17	15-18	14-10	15-7	3-0	0-0	0-0
Brad Sellers	46-34	1-1	34-25	12-8	0-0	0-1	0-0
Dave Corzine	46-35	1-0	37-33	9-1	0-1	0-0	0-0
Charles Davis	27-22	20-13	24-19	2-3	0-0	0-0	0-0

TEAM RECORD BY STARTING POSITION *

PLAYER	GAMES	STARTS	PG	OG	SF	PF	C
Michael Jordan	81	81	13-11	34-23	0-0	0-0	0-0
Horace Grant	79	79	0-0	0-0	0-1	45-33	0-0
Scottie Pippen	73	56	0-0	0-0	32-22	1-1	0-0
Bill Cartwright	78	76	0-0	0-0	0-0	0-0	43-33
Sam Vincent	70	56	28-21	3-4	0-0	0-0	0-0
John Paxson	78	20	6-3	5-6	0-0	0-0	0-0
Craig Hodges	49	6	0-0	5-1	0-0	0-0	0-0
Brad Sellers	80	25	0-0	0-0	14-11	0-0	0-0
Dave Corzine	81	7	0-0	0-0	0-0	0-1	4-2
Charles Davis	49	3	0-0	0-1	1-1	0-0	0-0

* For further definition of each category and column heading see pages 42 & 43.

Chicago Bulls . . . . 1988-89 Statistics

RAW NUMBERS *

PLAYER	2pt%	3pt%	FT%	MIN	PF	DQ	HI	TO	RB	AS	BL	ST
Michael Jordan	.553	.276	.850	3255	247	2	53	290	652	650	65	234
Horace Grant	.522	0-5	.704	2809	251	1	25	128	681	168	62	86
Scottie Pippen	.496	.273	.668	2413	261	8	31	199	445	256	61	139
Bill Cartwright	.475	0-0	.766	2333	234	2	23	190	521	90	41	21
Sam Vincent	.495	.118	.822	1703	124	0	23	142	190	335	10	53
John Paxson	.532	.331	.861	1738	162	1	24	71	94	308	6	53
Craig Hodges	.512	.417	.842	1204	90	0	23	57	89	146	4	43
Brad Sellers	.485	.500	.851	1732	176	2	32	72	227	99	69	35
Dave Corzine	.465	.250	.740	1483	134	0	23	93	315	103	45	29
Charles Davis	.440	.267	.731	545	58	1	15	22	114	31	5	11

OVERALL RANKINGS *

PLAYER	G	GS	PPG	PR	RANK	SC	SH	RB	AS	BL	ST
Michael Jordan	81	81	32.51	36.99	1	1	9	74	22	69	5
Horace Grant	79	79	12.03	17.52	56	103	65	40	124	62	109
Scottie Pippen	73	56	14.36	16.38	75	72	134	82	62	54	23
Bill Cartwright	78	76	12.38	12.49	118	99	119	60	158	80	175
Sam Vincent	70	56	9.37	11.24	132	133	93	132	24	139	108
John Paxson	78	20	7.27	8.78	161	154	33	176	32	158	110
Craig Hodges	59	6	8.97	8.78	162	139	2	171	53	162	91
Brad Sellers	80	25	6.89	8.11	169	161	80	115	127	29	154
Dave Corzine	81	7	5.91	7.60	172	170	144	68	107	43	157
Charles Davis	49	3	3.78	4.24	DNQ						

POSITION RANKINGS *

PLAYER	POSITION	RANK	SC	SH	RB	AS	BL	ST
Michael Jordan	Off Guard, PG	1	1	3	5	3	5	2
Horace Grant	Power Forward	13	17	13	19	11	17	16
Scottie Pippen	Small Forward, OG	18	22	33	16	8	14	2
Bill Cartwright	Center	19	14	17	27	20	27	29
Sam Vincent	Point Guard	25	23	15	14	21	15	30
John Paxson	Point Guard, OG	30	28	5	33	27	24	31
Craig Hodges	Off Guard	38	38	1	43	17	39	33
Brad Sellers	Small Forward	38	39	17	35	31	5	36
Dave Corzine	Center	30	28	24	29	5	20	18
Charles Davis	Small Forward	DNQ						

*For further definition of each category and column heading see pages 42 & 43.

Chicago Bulls .... Team Info

WEEKLY POWER RATING

41 WINS - AVERAGE (See page 43 for Team Power Rating discussion.)

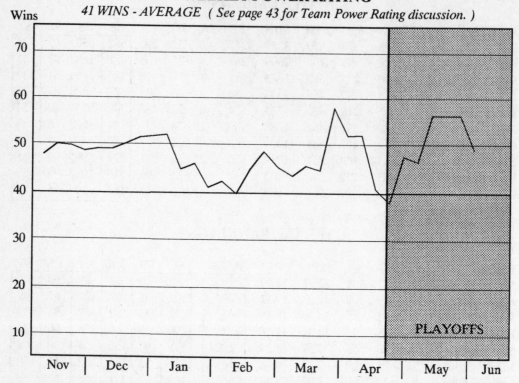

Miscellaneous Categories	Data	Rank
Attendance	737K	4
Key-Man Games Missed	42	8
Season Record	47-35	9
- Home	30-11	13
- Road	17-24	7
Eastern Conference	28-28	11
Western Conference	19-7	4
Overtime Record	2-2	8
Record 5 Pts. or Less	19-7	1
Record 10 Pts. or More	21-16	12
Games Won By Bench	3	16
Games Won By Starters	13	5
Winning Streak	6	9
Losing Streak	6	12
Home Winning Streak	6	18
Road Winning Streak	5	3
Home Losing Streak	1	1
Road Losing Streak	6	8

Performance Categories	Data	Rank
Offensive Scoring (per game)	106.4	17
Defensive Scoring (per game)	105.0	5
Scoring Margin (per game)	1.4	13
Defensive FG%	.474	11
Offensive 2-point%	.509	4
Offensive 3-point%	.328	10
Offensive Free Throw %	.786	10
Offensive Rebs .....(Off REB/Opp Def REB)		21
Defensive Rebs ....(Def REB/Opp Off REB)		3
Offensive Assists ....(AST/FGMade)		4
Offensive Blocks ..(BLK/Opp FGAttempted)		21
Offensive Steals.....................(STL/Game)		15
Turnover Margin........(Def T.O. - Off T.O.)		15
Fouls Margin ....(Opp FOULS - FOULS)		16
Rebounding Record	36-43-3	17
Assists Record	46-34-2	7
Field Goal Pct. Record	47-35-0	6
Free Throw Att. Record	32-47-3	19

Chicago Bulls ....Team Roster

MOST PRODUCTIVE PLAYERS

Player	Span	Yrs	CRD
Artis Gilmore	1977-87	7	12,076
Michael Jordan	1985-89	5	11,225
Jerry Sloan	1967-76	10	11,150
Bob Love	1969-76	8	9,914
Tom Boerwinkle	1969-78	10	9,522
Chet Walker	1970-75	6	9,227
Norm Van Lier	1972-78	7	8,278
David Greenwood	1980-85	6	8,108
Reggie Theus	1979-84	6	7,496
Dave Corzine	1983-89	7	7,275

PRESENT PLAYERS*

J#	VETERANS	COLLEGE	POS	R#	D#	HT	WT	Chic	NBA
24	Bill Cartwright	USF	C	1	3	7-1	245	1	9
22	Charles Davis	Vanderbilt	F	2	35	6-7	215	1	7
54	Horace Grant	Clemson	F	1	10	6-10	215	2	2
15	Jack Haley	UCLA	C	4	79	6-10	240	1	1
14	Craig Hodges	Long Beach	G	3	48	6-3	190	1	7
23	Michael Jordan	North Carolina	G	1	3	6-6	198	5	5
5	John Paxson	Notre Dame	G	1	19	6-2	185	4	6
32	Will Perdue	Vanderbilt	C	1	11	7-0	240	1	1
33	Scott Pippen	C. Arkansas	F	1	5	6-7	210	2	2

FUTURE PLAYERS

ROOKIES	COLLEGE	POS	R#	D#	HT	WT
Stacey King	Oklahoma	C-F	1	6	6-10	230
B.J. Armstrong	Iowa	G	1	18	6-2	170
Jeff Sanders	Georgia Southern	F	1	24	6-9	230

* For further definition of category and column headings, see pages 42 & 43.

Chicago Bulls . . . . Overview

Well, as usual, Michael Jordan had a great year. He ranked #1 in minutes played, #1 in scoring average, and #1 in Production Rating. Not only that, but he became the first player since 1972 to score 2,000+ points, 600+ rebounds, and 600+ assists. In fact, only three players have ever done it.

	Year	Pts.	Reb	Ast
Jordan	**1989**	**2633**	**652**	**650**
Havlicek	1972	2252	672	614
Havlicek	1971	2338	730	607
Robertson	1965	2279	674	861
Robertson	1964	2480	738	868
Robertson	1963	2264	835	758
Robertson	1962	2432	985	899
Robertson	1961	2165	716	690

Additionally, Jordan was the only player who ranked in the top-5 in all six performance categories at his position. In fact, he was the only player to rank in the top-10 of all six. IN FACT, it's not until you reach the top-15 that other players are included - and then just barely. Shown below are the closest players to Jordan, their *worst* rank, and the category.

Jordan	**Chic**	**# 5**	**Reb, Blk**
Parish	Bost	#15	Blocks
Johnson	LA.L	#15	Steals
Benjamin	LA.C	#15	Steals
Schayes	Denv	#16	Reb, Stl
Drexler	Port	#16	Shooting
Malone	Utah	#16	Blocks
Olajuwon	Hous	#16	Shooting

Not only does this reveal his great versatility, but it indicates that he has absolutely no weaknesses. Add to that his being selected for the All-Defensive first-team and you've got the definition of a superstar. What you don't have is the definition of the league MVP. That honor went to Magic Johnson. The voting was the closest in years because the reality is that there's about as much difference in value between MJ vs MJ as there is in Coke vs Pepsi.

What was most intriguing about Jordan last year was "the experiment". From mid-March on, Michael started at point guard. You can see the sharp increase in the team's power rating (page 64) shortly afterward. Unfortunately, the team then died before coming on strong in the playoffs. The obvious off-season question asked was, "Will Michael man the point in 1990?" Apparently not. At least Jordan is reportedly against the idea. If so, it's too bad.

What makes Magic so valuable to L.A. is the fact that he controls the offense. So does Jordan, but the difference is that, at the point, Magic is more able to include all four teammates - to make them better. By operating from the side much of the time, at least 1 or 2 players are left out of the typical Chicago play. There is an argument that says a player penetrating from the wing actually sees three players instead of two (depending on which way the point guard would be looking - left or right). That sounds good on paper, but in reality a symmetrical offense works the best. It always has and, as far as I can see, always will. With Jordan at the point, teams can't overload one side, the defense is more honest, he's more able to get an offensive rebound, and it involves more teammates.

And if the Bulls are to win, they must get more players involved. As evidence that Chicago can best accomplish that by Jordan playing the point, consider the following: 1) The fact that Jordan's last game at off-guard was game #57, he missed #58, and began playing the point in #59. In game #58, the Bulls didn't know what to do. So lethargic was their offense that they only had 6 free throw attempts for the entire game - one of the lowest totals in NBA history. 2) When Michael scored in the 30's and one or more of his teammates had 20 or more points, the team went 11-1. 3) When Michael played the point, both his production *and* that of the team went up. 4) One last point. Chicago was only 16-19 when Michael shot 24+ field goal attempts. When he shot less (thus the team more) the Bulls were 31-15. I think the concern is that an entire season at point guard

Chicago Bulls . . . . Overview

would be too draining on him. Maybe so, Maybe no. Unfortunately, we may never find out.

Chimes were sure ringing in the windy city on draft day. Chicago lucked out and picked up what may turn out to be the top player in the draft on pick #6! Chicago can thank Sacramento for picking Pervis Ellison over Stacey King #1 and Charlotte for going with hometown favorite J.R. Reid (#5). King is the perfect player for the club. Not only will he be able to eventually replace center Bill Cartwright, but he gives them a top-flight power forward for now. The most important benefit, however, is that he's a big-time scorer.

It will be very interesting to see how King performs in the NBA compared to Wayman Tisdale. Tisdale was unworthy of his #2 pick at Indiana, but may yet become a star at Sacramento. Both King and Tisdale are between 6-9 and 6-10. Both weigh 230-240 lbs. Both registered 25-26 points and 10 rebounds per game in their senior seasons. Both were black, 1st-Team All-American, left-handed shooters from Oklahoma University. If that's not a close comparison, then I don't know what is. If there's one difference, it might be that King is considered as a potentially better defensive player.

Also picked up in the draft was B.J. Armstrong. Presumably, Armstrong will be the heir-apparant to Jordan's vacated point-guard position. B.J. is a strong floor leader and, despite his passing ability, he might be more aptly named B.J. Floorstrong. As the all-time assist leader in Iowa history, he's just what a scorer like Jordan wants to see.

Chicago's third first-round pick was Jeff Sanders. Jeff will be used a lot up front now that Corzine and Sellers have been traded. Sanders averaged 23 points and 9 rebounds per game for Georgia Southern.

Chicago desperately needed outside shooting last season prior to picking up Craig Hodges. As the 3-point percentage king in 1988, Hodges helped a lot. In the 49 games he played in, Chicago was 32-17.

In the 33 he missed, they were only 15-18. Additionally, he started 6 games - during which the Bulls played their best ball. Though 5 of the 6 were on the road and 5 of the 6 were against teams with winning records, they won 5 of the 6 nonetheless! Hodges is a free agent as I write this, but it would behoove the Bulls to re-sign him.

The speculation in Chicago is that Doug Collins and Michael Jordan didn't get along as well as they claimed last season. Result? Collins took the first train to Clarksville. Jerry Reinsdorf contended that it was a dispute over the Jeff Sanders draft pick. Hey Jerry, we didn't just get off the boat. A more likely scenario is that the issue of Jordan playing the point was at the heart of the debate. Picked to replace Collins was his assistant coach and former Knick, Phil Jackson.

Notes: The club was 14-0 when they broke 115 points at Chicago Stadium... Two years ago, the franchise lost 13 of the last 14 games decided by 5 points or less. Last season, they were 1st in the NBA at 19-7... Remarkably, the team was 3rd in defensive rebounds, but a rather bad (#21) in offensive boards... When Chicago shot better than 47% from the field, they were 40-12. When they shot 47% or worse, they usually lost (7-23)... Sooner or later it's going to catch up with them, but the Bulls have had the fewest Key Man Games Missed the last three years (89).

Prediction - best case: 60-22

Holy cow! Can I be serious? That I am. If King and Armstrong fulfill the roles they are capable of, Chicago can finally climb the mountain they've been trying to get up during the Michael Jordan era.

Prediction - worst case 50-32

Assuming no debilitating injuries, Chicago cannot possibly help but win 50 games. Though we can dream up all kinds of scenarios, these guys are just too good.

To order back issues of Basketball Heaven or to obtain the 1990 Mid-season Report, see page 324.

Cleveland Cavaliers . . . . Influence on Winning

TEAM RECORD BY

PLAYER	GAMES	... SCR Leader		... REB Leader		...AST Leader	
		HOME	ROAD	HOME	ROAD	HOME	ROAD
Larry Nance	73	9-0	2-3	8-0	9-5	0-0	0-0
Brad Daugherty	78	7-2	3-4	23-2	6-13	2-0	2-1
Mark Price	75	7-1	7-7	0-0	0-0	28-4	14-12
Ron Harper	82	15-1	5-5	4-0	0-1	10-0	3-6
John Williams	2	1-0	3-1	1-2	3-5	0-0	0-0
Craig Ehlo	82	0-0	0-1	4-0	0-0	1-0	2-2
Mike Sanders	82	0-0	0-1	1-0	0-0	0-0	0-1
Darnell Valentine	77	0-0	0-0	0-0	0-0	3-0	1-1
Wayne Rollins	60	0-0	0-0	0-0	1-1	0-0	0-0
Chris Dudley	61	0-0	0-0	0-0	2-2	0-0	0-0

TEAM RECORD BY SCORING *

PLAYER	PLAY	DNP	0-9	10-19	20-29	30-39	40+
Larry Nance	51-22	6-3	4-3	29-12	17-7	1-0	0-0
Brad Daugherty	55-23	2-2	1-1	25-13	27-6	2-3	0-0
Mark Price	53-22	4-3	1-3	26-9	25-8	1-2	0-0
Ron Harper	57-25	0-0	2-3	23-14	28-7	4-1	0-0
John Williams	57-25	0-0	16-9	37-15	4-1	0-0	0-0
Craig Ehlo	57-25	0-0	39-15	17-9	1-1	0-0	0-0
Mike Sanders	57-25	0-0	34-14	23-9	0-1	0-1	0-0
Darnell Valentine	56-21	1-4	51-19	5-2	0-0	0-0	0-0
Wayne Rollins	40-20	17-5	40-20	0-0	0-0	0-0	0-0
Chris Dudley	46-15	11-10	44-14	2-1	0-0	0-0	0-0

TEAM RECORD BY STARTING POSITION *

PLAYER	GAMES	STARTS	PG	OG	SF	PF	C
Larry Nance	73	72	0-0	0-0	0-0	50-22	0-0
Brad Daugherty	78	78	0-0	0-0	0-0	0-0	55-23
Mark Price	75	74	53-21	0-0	0-0	0-0	0-0
Ron Harper	82	82	0-0	57-25	0-0	0-0	0-0
John Williams	82	10	0-0	0-0	0-0	7-3	0-0
Craig Ehlo	82	4	2-2	0-0	0-0	0-0	0-0
Mike Sanders	82	82	0-0	0-0	57-25	0-0	0-0
Darnell Valentine	77	4	2-2	0-0	0-0	0-0	0-0
Wayne Rollins	60	2	0-0	0-0	0-0	0-0	1-1
Chris Dudley	61	2	0-0	0-0	0-0	0-0	1-1

* For further definition of each category and column heading see pages 42 & 43.

Cleveland Cavaliers . . . . 1988-89 Statistics

RAW NUMBERS *

PLAYER	2pt%	3pt%	FT%	MIN	PF	DQ	HI	TO	RB	AS	BL	ST
Larry Nance	.541	0-4	.799	2526	186	0	33	117	581	159	**206**	57
Brad Daugherty	.538	.333	.737	2821	175	1	36	**230**	**718**	285	40	63
Mark Price	**.548**	**.441**	**.901**	2728	98	0	**37**	212	226	**631**	7	115
Ron Harper	.540	.250	.751	**2851**	224	1	32	**230**	409	434	74	**185**
John Williams	.510	.250	.748	2125	188	1	27	102	477	108	134	77
Craig Ehlo	.495	.390	.607	1867	161	0	25	116	295	266	19	110
Mike Sanders	.455	.300	.719	2102	**230**	2	30	104	307	133	32	89
Darnell Valentine	.436	.214	.813	1086	88	0	15	83	103	174	7	57
Wayne Rollins	.453	0-1	.632	583	89	0	8	22	139	19	38	11
Chris Dudley	.437	0-1	.364	544	82	0	14	44	157	21	23	9

OVERALL RANKINGS *

PLAYER	G	GS	PPG	PR	RANK	SC	SH	RB	AS	BL	ST
Larry Nance	73	72	17.25	**22.66**	17	49	18	54	116	9	140
Brad Daugherty	78	78	**18.91**	22.37	19	30	40	33	66	93	142
Mark Price	75	74	18.85	22.33	20	31	1	163	15	170	61
Ron Harper	**82**	**82**	18.61	21.09	26	34	48	107	42	51	13
John Williams	82	10	11.56	**14.87**	94	109	69	58	139	12	89
Craig Ehlo	**82**	4	7.41	**10.50**	137	152	103	97	47	109	20
Mike Sanders	**82**	**82**	9.32	9.54	152	134	154	106	115	88	60
Darnell Valentine	77	4	4.75	**5.45**	DNQ						
Wayne Rollins	60	2	2.27	**3.97**	DNQ						
Chris Dudley	61	2	3.03	**3.08**	DNQ						

POSITION RANKINGS *

PLAYER	POSITION	RANK	SC	SH	RB	AS	BL	ST
Larry Nance	Power Forward, SF	4	6	3	21	7	2	24
Brad Daugherty	Center	5	4	10	18	2	30	14
Mark Price	Point Guard	5	3	1	25	15	28	22
Ron Harper	Off Guard	5	10	14	13	12	2	6
John Williams	Power Forward	20	19	15	24	15	3	12
Craig Ehlo	Off Guard SF	30	41	26	11	15	16	9
Mike Sanders	Small Forward	34	32	36	31	29	25	11
Darnell Valentine	Point Guard	DNQ						
Wayne Rollins	Center	DNQ						
Chris Dudley	Center	DNQ						

*For further definition of each category and column heading see pages 42 & 43.

Cleveland Cavaliers .... Team Info

WEEKLY POWER RATING
41 WINS - AVERAGE (See page 43 for Team Power Rating discussion.)

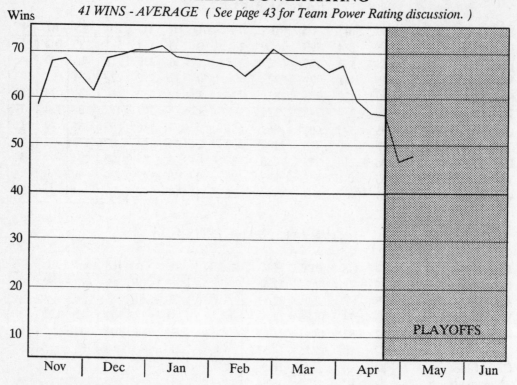

Miscellaneous Categories	Data	Rank
Attendance	731K	5
Key-Man Games Missed	24	2
Season Record	57-25	2
- Home	37-4	1
- Road	20-21	3
Eastern Conference	38-18	2
Western Conference	19-7	4
Overtime Record	1-2	18
Record 5 Pts. or Less	8-9	18
Record 10 Pts. or More	39-9	1
Games Won By Bench	6	9
Games Won By Starters	23	1
Winning Streak	11	1
Losing Streak	2	1
Home Winning Streak	22	3
Road Winning Streak	4	6
Home Losing Streak	1	1
Road Losing Streak	4	2

Performance Categories	Data	Rank
Offensive Scoring (per game)	108.8	12
Defensive Scoring (per game)	101.2	3
Scoring Margin (per game)	7.6	2
Defensive FG%	.461	3
Offensive 2-point%	.513	2
Offensive 3-point%	.359	3
Offensive Free Throw %	.747	19
Offensive Rebs ..... (Off REB/Opp Def REB)		19
Defensive Rebs .... (Def REB/Opp Off REB)		15
Offensive Assists .... (AST/FGMade)		3
Offensive Blocks .. (BLK/Opp FGAttempted)		3
Offensive Steals .... (STL/Game)		10
Turnover Margin .... (Def T.O. - Off T.O.)		8
Fouls Margin .... (Opp FOULS - FOULS)		1
Rebounding Record	39-37-6	11
Assists Record	48-31-3	4
Field Goal Pct. Record	57-25-0	2
Free Throw Att. Record	71-9-2	1

Cleveland Cavaliers ....Team Roster

MOST PRODUCTIVE PLAYERS

Player	Span	Yrs	CRD
Bingo Smith	1971-80	10	8,614
Austin Carr	1972-80	9	8,341
World Free	1983-86	4	6,918
Jim Chones	1975-79	5	6,784
Jim Brewer	1974-79	6	5,641
John Johnson	1971-73	3	5,184
Phil Hubbard	1982-88	7	5,021
Brad Daugherty	1987-89	3	4,908
Foots Walker	1975-80	6	4,724
John Bagley	1983-87	5	4,524

PRESENT PLAYERS*

J#	VETERANS	COLLEGE	POS	R#	D#	HT	WT	Clev	NBA
43	Brad Daugherty	North Carolina	C	1	1	7-0	245	3	3
22	Chris Dudley	Yale	C	4	75	6-11	235	2	2
3	Craig Ehlo	Washington State	G	3	48	6-7	185	3	6
4	Ron Harper	Miami (Ohio)	G	1	8	6-6	205	3	3
35	Phil Hubbard	Michigan	F	1	15	6-8	225	8	10
31	Randolph Keys	Southern Mississippi	F	1	22	6-9	195	1	1
22	Larry Nance	Clemson	F	1	20	6-10	217	2	8
25	Mark Price	Georgia Tech	G	2	25	6-1	174	3	3
30	Wayne Rollins	Clemson	C	1	14	7-1	240	1	12
11	Michael Sanders	UCLA	F	4	74	6-6	210	2	7
18	John Williams	Tulane	F	2	45	6-11	230	3	3

FUTURE PLAYERS

ROOKIES	COLLEGE	POS	R#	D#	HT	WT
John Morton	Seton Hall	G	1	25	6-3	180
Chucky Brown	N. Carolina St.	F	2	43	6-8	211

* For further definition of category and column headings, see pages 42 & 43.

Cleveland Cavaliers .... Overview

It's been a long time since basketball fans in Cleveland have had anything good to say about their team. It started bad (15 wins in their first year tying the all-time low for an expansion team) and has stayed that way almost without exception. Well, there was a 3-year period during the mid-70's when they won a few more games than they lost. But any fond memories of that era more than dissipated when Ted Stepien took over the club in 1980. The "Cadavers", as they came to be called, were so bad that the league actually voted to give them an extra draft pick in 1983! But that was then.

Finally, in 1986, it all began to pay off. Four of their top players were rookies in the 86-87 season. Three of them made the All-Rookie team. Had more been expected from Mark Price, and had he subsequently been given more playing time, they very well could have had four players on the team - something that's never been done. In fact, only one other time has it been true that three teammates were on the All-Rookie team. In 1965, the New York. Knicks placed three members on the team led by Willis Reed. It kind of happened again to the Knicks in 1968. That group included Walt Frazier and Phil Jackson. It also included a player who would later join New York - Earl Monroe. As you will recall, the Knicks won the NBA championships twice - exactly five years after each group's rookie season (1970 & 1973). If history is any indicator, Cleveland might rightfully expect that they will win it all in 1992. When you think about it, that's a good possibility. Considering the progress they've made and what playoff experience they've gained, they could even win it sooner. After all, it took New York five years to reach 54 wins while Cleveland won a franchise record 57 games in just year #3. Of course, this is sheer speculation. They may win it all each of the next four years or they may never win it. Who knows?

Another point of speculation is what the results of the 1987 injury to Ron Harper were. As bizarre as it sounds, I honestly believe it may have been a blessing in disguise. Harper had finished 2nd in the Rookie-of-the-Year voting the previous season. Then, in game #2 of the 1987-88 campaign, he suffered a severely sprained ankle. It ended up costing him 24 games. My belief is that Harper had come into the 1987-88 season with the intentions of living up to the "Michael Jordan" label which had been thrust upon him. That could be interpreted as meaning he should shoot... a lot. In fact, he did average 17.5 field goal attempts in less than 2 games. A persistence on his part to continue shooting that often would have been costly to the team-oriented Cavs. As it was, Price was developed and the team played very good ball. When Harper came back, it was *his* responsibility to fit into a greatly improved team. He did, averaging less than 13 field goal attempts the rest of the season. And, although he appears to have become a team player (43-10 when he shot 13+ fga's in 1989, but 14-15 when he shot less than 13), he was still mentioned in numerous trade rumors last summer.

The Cavaliers had a marvelous 37-4 home record, which tied Detroit for the best in the league. Since Cleveland came into the NBA in 1971, only two teams have had more success in their natural surroundings.

Boston	1986	40-1	.976
Milwaukee	1971	34-2	.944
Cleveland	**1989**	**37-4**	**.902**
Detroit	1989	37-4	.902
LA Lakers	1987	37-4	.902
Philadelphia	1981	37-4	.902
LA Lakers	1980	37-4	.902
Philadelphia	1978	37-4	.902
LA Lakers	1977	37-4	.902

One of the primary reasons Cleveland was so good in 1989 was balance. The Cavs had very good production at four positions. No other team can claim to have as good a balance between their top players. Truthfully, it is seldom that a good team achieves it. Most of the time it is poor teams. I believe the reason is good clubs have good players

Cleveland Cavaliers .... Overview

and good players want the ball. Consequently, four "good" players are rarely bunched at the top because there aren't that many balls. Because of this phenomenon, Lenny Wilkens deserves enormous credit for keeping his stars' egos in check enough to maintain the balance. Whether he can continue to do so or not is another subject. You can see what I mean that poor teams dominate this category by the list below. Shown is the differential between the #1 scorer (Brad Daugherty - 18.91) and the #4 scorer (Larry Nance - 17.25) by points-per-game.

		Diff	Wins
1.	Cleveland	1.66	57
2.	LA Clippers	1.98	21
3.	Miami	2.98	15
4.	New Jersey	2.98	26
5.	Dallas	4.65	38
6.	San Antonio	4.95	21
7.	Sacramento	4.99	27

Cleveland won all 8 preseason games and the first 4 games of the regular season. They went on to win 32 games by mid-year - a feat only 20 clubs in league history have accomplished. Notwithstanding this brilliant beginning and a 43-12 record thru March 2nd, the Cavs finished the season by going 16-16 (including the playoffs). The winds of March and the rains of April cancelled their divisional victory parade. Detroit finally passed the slumping Cavaliers on March 26th and never looked back. (See Cleveland's power rating chart on page 70.) Ironically, the slide began against Detroit, in a hard-fought game lost by the Cavs 90-96 in which 5 technicals were called. It is also true that, although Mark Price missed only 6 games all year, the slump began when he was injured and continued through the post-season when he played hurt against Chicago.

For that reason, as well as several others, Price was probably the most indispensable Cavalier. He ranked #1 in shooting - an index which covers all three types of shots (see page 240). He shot 55% from 2-point range, 44% from 3-point country and 90% from the line. In fact, by shooting 53% from the combined 2-point and 3-point range (a ludicrous and outdated statistic, by the way), he ranks as only the third player in NBA history to shoot 50%+ from the field and 90%+ from the line. Only Larry Bird, who has done it twice (1987 & 1988), and Magic Johnson (1989) have done it as well. Is that fraternizing with the big boys or what? Price also ranked first in fewest fouls per minutes-played. Largely because of him, the team was #1 in foul differential (advantage of 378) and actually went to the line more than their opponents in 35 of 37 games during one stretch.

Notes: No other North Carolina great, including Jordan, McAdoo, Ford, Worthy, Perkins, Davis or Reid has ever managed to score 20.2 ppg under Dean Smith. But Brad Daugherty did... Rookie John "Mr. Smooth" Morton scored 35 points in the NCAA championship game for Seton Hall vs Michigan... Cleveland ranked #2 in Key Man Games Missed... Only the Cavaliers and the Lakers played with the same 12 players all season... Cleveland's starters won 23 games (#1) by my formula. Atlanta's were second at 19... When the club shot 50% or better, they were nearly unbeatable (36-4). When their shooting was below 50%, they merely broke even (21-21).

Prediction - best case: 62-20
Though the sky's the limit, I'm concerned about that 16-16 late-season finish. Nevertheless, all the pieces are there for a great record.

Prediction - worst case: 49-33
History doesn't like teams who have gained as many wins as Cleveland has in back-to-back years (see New York prediction). Because of that and the March/April decline, this relatively low number is not as impossible as it might seem.

To order back issues of Basketball Heaven or to obtain the 1990 Midseason Report, see page 324.

Dallas Mavericks . . . . Influence on Winning

TEAM RECORD BY

PLAYER	GAMES	... SCR Leader		... REB Leader		...AST Leader	
		HOME	ROAD	HOME	ROAD	HOME	ROAD
Derek Harper	81	6-2	3-3	0-0	0-0	16-13	11-17
Sam Perkins	78	1-0	4-3	8-6	6-11	0-0	1-1
James Donaldson	53	0-0	0-0	9-7	4-9	0-0	0-0
Rolando Blackman	78	4-5	4-11	0-0	0-0	3-1	0-5
Adrian Dantley	31	3-4	2-5	0-0	0-1	0-0	0-1
Herb Williams	30	0-0	0-0	1-1	3-3	0-0	0-0
Roy Tarpley	19	1-1	0-1	4-2	2-3	0-0	0-0
Brad Davis	78	0-0	0-0	0-0	0-0	2-3	1-1
Bill Wennington	65	0-1	0-0	1-0	0-1	0-0	0-0
Terry Tyler	70	0-0	0-0	0-1	0-0	0-0	0-0

TEAM RECORD BY SCORING *

PLAYER	PLAY	DNP	0-9	10-19	20-29	30-39	40+
Derek Harper	38-43	0-1	3-3	19-29	14-10	2-1	0-0
Sam Perkins	35-43	3-1	5-7	22-31	7-5	1-0	0-0
James Donaldson	29-24	9-20	17-14	11-9	1-1	0-0	0-0
Rolando Blackman	36-42	2-2	3-4	14-14	17-21	2-3	0-0
Adrian Dantley	11-20	27-24	1-4	2-5	6-9	2-2	0-0
Herb Williams	10-20	28-24	8-14	2-6	0-0	0-0	0-0
Roy Tarpley	12-7	26-37	1-1	8-3	2-2	1-1	0-0
Brad Davis	37-41	1-3	24-36	13-5	0-0	0-0	0-0
Bill Wennington	30-35	8-9	28-32	2-2	0-1	0-0	0-0
Terry Tyler	32-38	6-6	25-29	6-9	1-0	0-0	0-0

TEAM RECORD BY STARTING POSITION *

PLAYER	GAMES	STARTS	PG	OG	SF	PF	C
Derek Harper	81	81	38-43	0-0	0-0	0-0	0-0
Sam Perkins	78	77	0-0	0-0	0-1	33-42	1-0
James Donaldson	53	53	0-0	0-0	0-0	0-0	29-24
Rolando Blackman	78	78	0-0	36-42	0-0	0-0	0-0
Adrian Dantley	31	25	0-0	0-0	9-16	0-0	0-0
Herb Williams	30	20	0-0	0-0	0-0	1-0	5-14
Roy Tarpley	19	6	0-0	0-0	0-0	4-2	0-0
Brad Davis	78	4	0-0	2-2	0-0	0-0	0-0
Bill Wennington	78	4	0-0	2-2	0-0	0-0	0-0
Terry Tyler	70	11	0-0	0-0	4-7	0-0	0-0

* For further definition of each category and column heading see pages 42 & 43.

Dallas Mavericks . . . . 1988-89 Statistics

RAW NUMBERS *

PLAYER	2pt%	3pt%	FT%	MIN	PF	DQ	HI	TO	RB	AS	BL	ST
Derek Harper	.517	.356	.806	2968	219	3	38	205	228	570	41	172
Sam Perkins	.476	.184	.833	2860	224	1	30	141	688	127	92	76
James Donaldson	.573	0-0	.766	1746	111	0	21	83	570	38	81	24
Rolando Blackman	.485	.353	.854	2946	137	0	37	165	273	288	20	65
Adrian Dantley	.493	0-1	.810	2422	186	1	35	163	317	171	13	43
Herb Williams	.439	0-5	.686	2470	236	5	25	149	593	124	134	46
Roy Tarpley	.544	0-1	.688	591	70	2	35	45	218	17	30	28
Brad Davis	.545	.314	.805	1395	151	0	17	92	108	242	18	48
Bill Wennington	.444	.111	.744	1074	211	3	21	54	286	46	35	16
Terry Tyler	.479	.111	.758	1057	90	0	20	51	209	40	39	24

OVERALL RANKINGS *

PLAYER	G	GS	PPG	PR	RANK	SC	SH	RB	AS	BL	ST
Derek Harper	81	81	17.33	19.33	36	46	34	169	28	95	22
Sam Perkins	78	77	15.01	18.51	43	69	112	44	150	40	123
James Donaldson	53	53	9.08	17.70	52	138	7	8	174	18	170
Rolando Blackman	78	78	19.67	16.74	67	26	68	155	68	133	147
Adrian Dantley	73	67	19.18	16.29	79	29	60	116	103	143	162
Herb Williams	76	66	10.22	13.78	103	123	167	46	141	13	160
Roy Tarpley	19	6	17.26	22.89	DNQ						
Brad Davis	78	4	6.37	7.71	DNQ						
Bill Wennington	65	9	4.62	6.95	DNQ						
Terry Tyler	70	11	5.51	6.30	DNQ						

POSITION RANKINGS *

PLAYER	POSITION	RANK	SC	SH	RB	AS	BL	ST
Derek Harper	Point Guard	8	7	6	29	24	4	11
Sam Perkins	Power Forward, C	8	10	23	20	18	12	19
James Donaldson	Center	10	21	1	4	28	13	26
Rolando Blackman	Off Guard	12	8	19	35	23	27	43
Adrian Dantley	Small Forward	21	12	11	36	24	38	38
Herb Williams	Center, PF	17	17	28	22	14	10	20
Roy Tarpley	Power Forward, C	DNQ						
Brad Davis	Off Guard, PG	DNQ						
Bill Wennington	Center	DNQ						
Terry Tyler	Small Forward	DNQ						

*For further definition of each category and column heading see pages 42 & 43.

Dallas Mavericks .... Team Info

WEEKLY POWER RATING

41 WINS - AVERAGE (See page 43 for Team Power Rating discussion.)

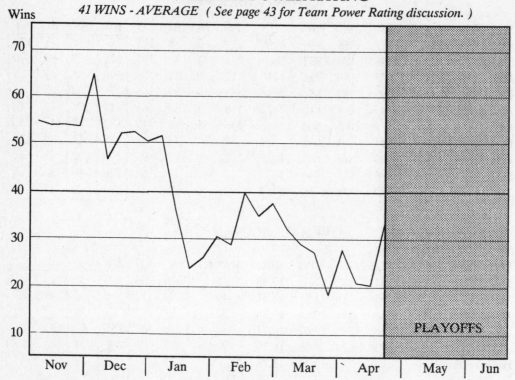

Miscellaneous Categories	Data	Rank
Attendance	695K	8
Key-Man Games Missed	134	22
Season Record	38-44	18
- Home	24-17	18
- Road	14-27	12
Eastern Conference	8-16	18
Western Conference	30-28	16
Overtime Record	2-2	8
Record 5 Pts. or Less	11-11	9
Record 10 Pts. or More	17-26	17
Games Won By Bench	4	13
Games Won By Starters	16	4
Winning Streak	5	13
Losing Streak	12	21
Home Winning Streak	4	22
Road Winning Streak	5	3
Home Losing Streak	4	16
Road Losing Streak	12	20

Performance Categories	Data	Rank
Offensive Scoring (per game)	103.5	24
Defensive Scoring (per game)	104.7	4
Scoring Margin (per game)	-1.2	17
Defensive FG%	.469	8
Offensive 2-point%	.486	15
Offensive 3-point%	.310	17
Offensive Free Throw %	.789	6
Offensive Rebs (Off REB/Opp Def REB)		25
Defensive Rebs (Def REB/Opp Off REB)		16
Offensive Assists (AST/FGMade)		22
Offensive Blocks (BLK/Opp FGAttempted)		8
Offensive Steals (STL/Game)		23
Turnover Margin (Def T.O. - Off T.O.)		14
Fouls Margin (Opp FOULS - FOULS)		7
Rebounding Record	27-52-3	24
Assists Record	24-54-4	23
Field Goal Pct. Record	44-37-1	9
Free Throw Att. Record	47-31-4	7

Dallas Mavericks ....Team Roster

MOST PRODUCTIVE PLAYERS

PLAYER	Span	Yrs	CRD
Mark Aguirre	1982-89	8	11,720
Rolando Blackman	1982-89	8	10,646
Brad Davis	1981-89	9	9,059
Derek Harper	1984-89	6	7,561
Sam Perkins	1985-89	5	6,960
Jay Vincent	1982-86	5	6,270
James Donaldson	1986-89	4	4,912
Kurt Nimphius	1982-85	5	3,413
Roy Tarpley	1987-89	3	2,943
Pat Cummings	1983-84	2	2,553

PRESENT PLAYERS*

J#	VETERANS	COLLEGE	POS	R#	D#	HT	WT	Dall	NBA
33	Uwe Blab	Indiana	C	1	17	7-1	252	3	3
22	Rolando Blackman	Kansas State	G	1	9	6-6	194	8	8
4	Adrian Dantley	Notre Dame	F	1	6	6-5	210	1	13
15	Brad Davis	Maryland	G	1	15	6-3	180	9	12
40	James Donaldson	Washington State	C	4	73	7-2	277	4	8
12	Derek Harper	Illinois	G	1	11	6-4	203	6	6
21	Anthony Jones	UNLV	G	1	21	6-6	195	1	2
44	Sam Perkins	North Carolina	F	1	4	6-9	238	5	5
42	Roy Tarpley	Michigan	F-C	1	7	7-0	244	3	3
41	Terry Tyler	Detroit	F	2	23	6-7	220	1	11
23	Bill Wennington	St. Johns	C	1	16	7-0	240	4	4
32	Herb Williams	Ohio State	F-C	1	14	6-11	240	1	8

FUTURE PLAYERS

ROOKIES	COLLEGE	POS	R#	D#	HT	WT
Randy White	Louisiana Tech	F	1	8	6-9	250
Pat Durham	Colorado State	F	2	35	6-8	210
Jeff Hodge	South Alabama	G	2	53	6-3	165

* For further definition of category and column headings, see pages 42 & 43.

Dallas Mavericks .... Overview

Maverick fans debated all last season about the exact contribution of Blackman and Perkins and Harper and Dantley and Aguirre. They argued that these are good players and they therefore should be able to right a sinking ship. The truth is, folks, they're mid-cities. That's all. The pillars at either end are all that hold them up and they're named Tarpley and Donaldson. You take away one and you get major problems. You take away both and you get a losing record.

Dallas ranked 22nd in Key Man Games Missed, but to local partisans, it must have seemed like 26th on a scale of 25. What a year. There was the torn cartilage in the knee of Roy Tarpley and the drug relapse, the annual Mark Aguirre distractions, the rumored firing of John MacLeod, THE TRADE, the holdout, the Donaldson injury, Schrempf for Williams, etc. It was a messy, unproductive year - the first for the team after seasons of success. Only time will tell if anything of value comes from it.

When it comes to being invaluable, no player as yet qualifies on this team more than James Donaldson. As the starting center, Donaldson provides not only the obvious rebounding and sure-shooting when he's open, but the big, immovable body on defense. Before Donaldson was injured, the club had a 1.5% shooting *advantage* over their opposition. In the final 29 games without the big guy, they suffered a 2.6% *disadvantage* in shooting. Before you reach for your calculators, that's a 4.1% differential, which is worth roughly 8 points per game! Dallas lost 8 games by 8 points or less in Donaldson's absence and it would not be unreasonable to assume that if he were not injured, they would have gone 46-36 instead of 38-44. Additionally, when you realize that the team was 29-24 when he played and 9-20 when he didn't, it's easy to see how much he was missed. If we apply the team's winning percentage when he played (.547) to the 29 games he didn't, we see that Dallas very well might have won 16 instead of 9. So, no matter how you look at

it, they need the big fella. The worst part is that he was playing his best ball just prior to the injury. In his last six games he was scoring 17.5 points per game and rebounding at an 18.5 clip. Unfortunately, his status won't be determined until shortly before the season begins.

Roy Tarpley has truly awesome potential. He only played in 19 games, but led the Mavs to a 12-7 record when he did get to contribute. In starting the last 5 games, he managed an outstanding 25.5 Production Rating which is very good. Had he qualified, he would have won the rebounding crown on a 48-minute basis. As it was, he yanked down the boards at 17.71 (per 48 minutes) compared to the actual winner - Akeem Olajuwon (17.54).

You can view Donaldson and Tarpley's influence on the team's power rating chart on page 76. Donaldson was injured when the team reached its second peak in late February. Tarpley's return corresponded to the club's last rise in mid-April. Finally, if any doubt lingers about how important they both are, take a look at the club's rebounding rank during the last six years.

1984	21st	
1985	21st	
1986	15th	Donaldson acquired
1987	4th	Tarpley drafted
1988	1st	
1989	**23rd**	**Both injured**

What was especially frustrating to fans was the Mavericks' oftentimes terrible play at Reunion Arena. In recent years the team had been nearly unbeatable at home. Last season, however, Dallas actually recorded a longer winning streak on the road (5, #3) than they did at home (4, #22). You have to go back to Dallas' second year (1981-82) to find a season with a shorter home winning streak.

In a desperate search for answers, the Mavericks' front office decided to do some house-cleaning. Mark Aguirre had continually been a thorn in both Dick Motta and John MacLeod's side. Anxious to get

Dallas Mavericks .... Overview

rid of him, the club made a seemingly hasty deal with Detroit which shipped out Aguirre and brought in Adrian Dantley. It is easy to argue that the Pistons got the better end of it. Though both scored rather modestly (by their standards) after the move, the Pistons were nearly unbeatable with Aguirre aboard while Dallas will show a substantially worse record with Dantley than with Aguirre. In fact, the combined team's record for Aguirre during the season was 55-25 (.688) while Dantley, despite being with the better team longer, had a combined record of 41-32 (.562). Let's go ahead and add that Adrian is 3.5 years older than Aguirre and it doesn't look like a good trade at all. Even A.D. disliked it so much he refused to play for the first four games. Yes, it's true that Dallas picked up Detroit's 1991 first round pick in the deal, but so what? It's not like it's Miami's #1.

The simple reality is that Dantley can't have a whole lot left. He's a one-dimensional post-up player who excels only in a half-court offense in his 14th year. Admittedly, Aguirre had to go, but I can't believe Dantley was the best the club could get for a former #1 pick in the draft, a player in his prime with a career scoring average of nearly 25 ppg. So they had to compromise because he's got a "reputation", but it's not like they brought in Mahatma Gandhi. Dantley's had problems with other clubs as well. In fact, of all the players who have ever scored 30+ ppg for a season, only two have been with more teams then Adrian (World Free and Bob McAdoo).

Dallas also traded Detlef Schrempf plus a second rounder to Indiana for Herb Williams. That's a fair trade. Detlef is younger with more potential, but Herb has proven his ability over a longer time. Nevertheless, Williams lost his last 10 games with Indiana and went 4-17 in his first 21 with Dallas. Not a good sign!

With Donaldson, Tarpley, Perkins and Williams all jammed into two positions, I was a little surprised to see the team draft a power forward last summer. Either they 1) are very worried about Donaldson and/or Tarpley's future (which is reasonable if they are), 2) were left without the ideal swingman pick when Indiana inexplicably chose George McCloud, 3) were unwilling to take a chance on passing up Karl Malone II. As you may recall, Dallas has taken an unfair amount of heat for selecting Detlef Schrempf over Karl Malone in the 1985 draft. I hate to tell you, but 13 teams made that mistake (he was picked #14). Still, with the chance to take a near carbon-copy player from the same school, it was too good an opportunity to pass up. What it all means, however, is that Dallas is the weakest non-expansion team in the NBA for guard help off the bench. Other than 13-year veteran Brad Davis, they have almost nothing. I believe they will pick up a free agent prior to opening day.

Notes: Rolando Blackman has never fouled out of a game. He now ranks third on the all-time list with 630 games (Chamberlain 1,045, Buse 648)... When Sam Perkins took 7 field goal attempts or less, Dallas was 9-0... When Brad Davis shot the ball 9 or more times, the club was 16-7... Dallas went 0-7 to start off the calendar year of 1989. The average losing margin was 18 ppg... In games decided by 8 points or less, the Mavericks were 19-14. In games of 9 or more they were 19-30.

Prediction - best case: 55-27

If this team can stay injury-free, they'll come very close to this lofty level. Roy Tarpley could well become All-NBA in 1990. He's capable of carrying the team.

Prediction - worst case: 38-44

If Donaldson and Tarpley are unable to compete, and if anything happens to Blackman or Harper, then even 38 wins will be tough to come by. That's a long shot, however, and no team should be that unlucky two years in a row.

To order back issues of Basketball Heaven or to obtain the 1990 Midseason Report, see page 324.

Denver Nuggets . . . . Influence on Winning

TEAM RECORD BY

PLAYER	GAMES	... SCR Leader		... REB Leader		...AST Leader	
		HOME	ROAD	HOME	ROAD	HOME	ROAD
Fat Lever	71	5-2	0-2	12-2	3-12	19-3	6-22
Alex English	82	19-4	6-23	0-0	0-2	2-3	0-6
Michael Adams	77	4-0	3-2	0-0	0-0	14-0	4-11
Danny Schayes	76	3-0	0-2	7-1	1-6	0-0	0-0
Wayne Cooper	79	0-0	0-0	15-3	3-8	1-0	0-0
Walter Davis	81	3-0	0-4	0-0	0-0	0-0	0-2
Elston Turner	78	0-0	0-0	0-0	0-1	0-0	0-0
Blair Rasmussen	77	1-0	0-0	2-0	1-2	0-0	0-0
Bill Hanzlik	41	0-0	0-0	0-0	0-0	0-0	0-0
Jerome Lane	54	0-0	0-0	1-0	0-3	0-0	0-0

TEAM RECORD BY SCORING *

PLAYER	PLAY	DNP	0-9	10-19	20-29	30-39	40+
Fat Lever	38-33	6-5	0-1	20-17	15-13	3-2	0-0
Alex English	44-38	0-0	0-0	7-13	21-12	15-10	1-3
Michael Adams	42-35	2-3	2-6	14-19	24-9	2-1	0-0
Danny Schayes	40-36	4-2	12-14	22-15	4-7	2-0	0-0
Wayne Cooper	43-36	1-2	33-26	9-10	1-0	0-0	0-0
Walter Davis	44-37	0-1	8-8	23-17	12-11	1-1	0-0
Elston Turner	42-36	2-2	38-33	4-3	0-0	0-0	0-0
Blair Rasmussen	42-35	2-3	24-26	15-9	3-0	0-0	0-0
Bill Hanzlik	24-17	20-21	19-17	4-0	1-0	0-0	0-0
Jerome Lane	26-28	18-10	20-27	6-1	0-0	0-0	0-0

TEAM RECORD BY STARTING POSITION *

PLAYER	GAMES	STARTS	PG	OG	SF	PF	C
Fat Lever	71	71	2-3	36-30	0-0	0-0	0-0
Alex English	82	82	0-0	0-0	43-37	1-1	0-0
Michael Adams	77	77	42-35	0-0	0-0	0-0	0-0
Danny Schayes	76	64	0-0	0-0	0-0	2-2	33-27
Wayne Cooper	79	72	0-0	0-0	0-0	30-24	9-9
Walter Davis	81	0	0-0	0-0	0-0	0-0	0-0
Elston Turner	78	12	0-0	5-5	1-1	0-0	0-0
Blair Rasmussen	77	22	0-0	0-0	0-0	10-8	2-2
Bill Hanzlik	41	0	0-0	0-0	0-0	0-0	0-0
Jerome Lane	54	1	0-0	1-0	0-0	0-0	0-0

* For further definition of each category and column heading see pages 42 & 43.

Denver Nuggets . . . . 1988-89 Statistics

RAW NUMBERS *

PLAYER	2pt%	3pt%	FT%	MIN	PF	DQ	HI	TO	RB	AS	BL	ST
Fat Lever	.463	.348	.785	2745	178	1	38	157	**662**	**559**	20	**195**
Alex English	.492	.250	.858	**2990**	174	0	**51**	198	326	383	12	66
Michael Adams	.490	**.356**	.819	2787	149	0	35	180	283	490	11	166
Danny Schayes	**.525**	.333	.826	1918	**320**	8	37	160	500	105	81	42
Wayne Cooper	.498	.250	.745	1864	302	7	20	73	619	78	**211**	36
Walter Davis	.512	.290	**.879**	1857	187	1	33	132	151	190	5	72
Elston Turner	.431	.286	.589	1746	209	2	15	60	287	144	8	90
Blair Rasmussen	.445	0-0	.852	1308	194	2	24	49	287	49	41	29
Bill Hanzlik	.445	.200	.782	701	82	1	22	53	93	86	5	25
Jerome Lane	.438	0-7	.384	550	105	1	18	50	200	60	4	20

OVERALL RANKINGS *

PLAYER	G	GS	PPG	PR	RANK	SC	SH	RB	AS	BL	ST
Fat Lever	71	71	19.85	**27.48**	7	25	130	42	20	127	7
Alex English	**82**	**82**	**26.52**	21.38	23	5	72	136	51	151	145
Michael Adams	77	77	18.49	19.60	34	37	46	143	33	153	18
Danny Schayes	76	64	12.75	15.49	85	94	21	30	132	22	149
Wayne Cooper	79	72	6.58	14.43	96	164	94	6	153	2	159
Walter Davis	81	0	15.64	12.21	123	66	44	166	65	168	78
Elston Turner	78	12	4.32	7.45	173	175	173	94	85	149	33
Blair Rasmussen	77	22	7.57	7.90	DNQ						
Bill Hanzlik	41	0	4.90	6.17	DNQ						
Jerome Lane	54	1	4.83	5.17	DNQ						

POSITION RANKINGS *

PLAYER	POSITION	RANK	SC	SH	RB	AS	BL	ST
Fat Lever	Off Guard, PG	3	7	32	1	2	24	3
Alex English	Small Forward	6	1	14	39	4	40	31
Michael Adams	Point Guard	7	4	9	18	28	21	10
Danny Schayes	Center, PF	14	13	6	16	11	14	16
Wayne Cooper	Power Forward, C	21	28	21	2	20	1	27
Walter Davis	Off Guard, SF	26	19	13	41	22	43	28
Elston Turner	Off Guard	43	44	44	10	32	34	14
Blair Rasmussen	Power Forward, C	DNQ						
Bill Hanzlik	Off Guard, SF	DNQ						
Jerome Lane	Small Forward, PF	DNQ						

*For further definition of each category and column heading see pages 42 & 43.

Denver Nuggets .... Team Info

WEEKLY POWER RATING

41 WINS - AVERAGE (See page 43 for Team Power Rating discussion.)

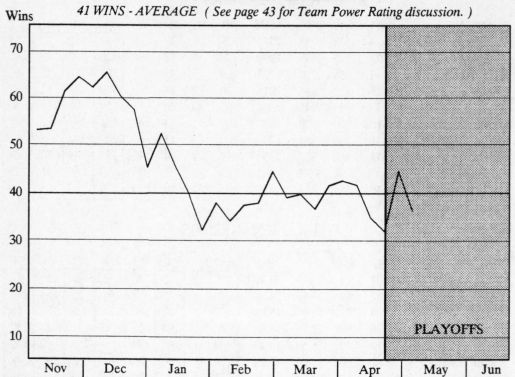

Miscellaneous Categories	Data	Rank
Attendance	556K	16
Key-Man Games Missed	65	13
Season Record	44-38	13
- Home	35-6	3
- Road	9-32	18
Eastern Conference	12-12	11
Western Conference	32-26	14
Overtime Record	2-4	18
Record 5 Pts. or Less	11-11	9
Record 10 Pts. or More	25-20	14
Games Won By Bench	8	6
Games Won By Starters	6	14
Winning Streak	5	13
Losing Streak	5	10
Home Winning Streak	19	5
Road Winning Streak	2	16
Home Losing Streak	2	5
Road Losing Streak	9	14

Performance Categories	Data	Rank
Offensive Scoring (per game)	118.0	2
Defensive Scoring (per game)	116.3	4
Scoring Margin (per game)	1.7	10
Defensive FG%	.495	22
Offensive 2-point%	.480	19
Offensive 3-point%	.337	6
Offensive Free Throw %	.787	8
Offensive Rebs ..... (Off REB/Opp Def REB)		24
Defensive Rebs .... (Def REB/Opp Off REB)		7
Offensive Assists .... (AST/FGMade)		13
Offensive Blocks .. (BLK/Opp FGAttempted)		13
Offensive Steals .... (STL/Game)		9
Turnover Margin ....(Def T.O. - Off T.O.)		1
Fouls Margin .... (Opp FOULS - FOULS)		18
Rebounding Record	28-49-5	22
Assists Record	44-35-3	9
Field Goal Pct. Record	33-49-0	19
Free Throw Att. Record	23-53-4	22

Denver Nuggets . . . . Team Roster

MOST PRODUCTIVE PLAYERS

Player	Span	Yrs	CRD
Alex English	1980-89	10	18,887
Dan Issel	1976-85	10	17,910
David Thompson	1976-82	7	10,434
Byron Beck	1968-77	10	10,284
Lafayette Lever	1985-89	5	9,188
Ralph Simpson	1971-78	7	7,872
Bobby Jones	1975-78	4	7,627
Dave Robisch	1972-83	8	7,259
Kiki Vandeweghe	1981-84	4	6,376
T.R. Dunn	1981-88	8	6,210

PRESENT PLAYERS*

J#	VETERANS	COLLEGE	POS	R#	D#	HT	WT	Denv	NBA
14	Michael Adams	Boston College	G	3	66	5-11	165	2	4
6	Walter Davis	North Carolina	G	1	5	6-6	200	1	12
2	Alex English	South Carolina	F	2	23	6-7	190	10	13
24	Bill Hanzlik	Notre Dame	F-G	1	20	6-7	200	7	9
35	Jerome Lane	Denver	F	1	23	6-6	230	1	1
12	Lafayette Lever	Arizona State	G	1	11	6-3	175	5	7
41	Blair Rasmussen	Oregon	C	1	15	7-0	250	4	4
34	Danny Schayes	Syracuse	C	1	13	6-11	245	7	8
20	Elston Turner	Mississippi	G	2	43	6-5	220	1	8

FUTURE PLAYERS

ROOKIES	COLLEGE	POS	R#	D#	HT	WT
Todd Lichti	Stanford	G	1	15	6-4	205
Michael Cutwright	McNeese State	G	2	42	6-4	220
Reggie Turner	Alabama-Birmingham	F	2	47	6-8	215

* For further definition of category and column headings, see pages 42 & 43.

Denver Nuggets .... Overview

Coming into last season, the Denver Nuggets had to overcome two major obstacles. The first was that Doug Moe had been named Coach-of-the-Year the season before and the second was that the club had won the Midwest Division crown in 1988. "Why's that a problem?", you say.

Well, because 20 of the 25 teams whose coach has won C.O.Y. honors lost more games (-5.7) the following year than the year he won it. Compounding the problem was the fact that every Midwest Division champion since the division came into existence in 1971 has declined in wins (-6.1) the following year except two - and one of them did it by changing to another division. Those are long odds. By adding them together, you get a situation that spells trouble. Not surprisingly, Denver dropped 10 games, from 54 wins to 44 wins. And it wasn't Doug Moe's fault. It was destiny!

What Moe will say is that the club could have been as good as the year before if not for the mystifyingly bad play on the road. That brings up an interesting question which I am going to solve one of these days. How does anyone say a particular team played worse on the road than they should have? In Denver's case there is, unquestionably, a huge difference between how good they seem to be in McNichols Arena versus foreign soil, but which is the "real" Denver team? Maybe they just played above their heads at home.

Nevertheless, last season Denver won 35 games at home and only 9 on the road for a net difference of 26 (35-9 = 26). That, my friends, is the largest such difference in NBA history. What's more, the home team won 70% of the games Denver was involved in during the past decade. That too is higher than any other franchise. What it means is that the Nuggets consistently seem to play inordinately better at home vs on the road.

My theory is that Denver's quality of play is less the issue then that of their opponents. The real factor is oxygen. The Nuggets should be helped, if anything, by traveling to a place where there is plenty of oxygen. It's exactly the opposite for their opponents. When a team visits Denver, they are far more susceptible to wearing down late in a game and succumbing to Denver's fast break. To justify the argument, the club was the best in the NBA when they led at home after three quarters. How good were they? How's 30-0? But no matter how you look at it - great at home (#3), horrible on the road (#18), or both - the club has some things to take care of.

First and foremost is the question of rebounding. Denver, as you may recall, drafted Jerome Lane in the 1988 draft. Lane was the leading rebounder in college the season before at Pittsburg. The concern by some in the NBA was that he might be too short (6'6") to be effective. Yes and No. Yes: He only had 200 boards in his rookie year, or 5.4% of all the rebounds collected by the team. No: Had he qualified, he would have led the league in offensive rebounds on a 48-minute basis (7.59). Dennis Rodman actually was first at 7.11. Since Denver ranked next to last in offensive rebounding as a percentage of all rebounds available at that end of the floor, why didn't Moe play Lane more often? Well, he clearly has massive shooting problems. That's why. Even with all those potentially easy stickbacks, he shot a miserable 42.6% from the field and an even worse percentage from the line (38.4%). And here's gall for you. He had enough guts to actually shoot seven 3-pointers. How many do you think he hit?

The problem Denver has is that Schayes (500), Cooper (619), and Rasmussen (287) don't collect the number of rebounds they should - given their size and the team's style of play. And as long as your 7-footers are being beaten by a 6'3" guard (Fat Lever -662), as they have been for 4 consecutive years, the need for a strong rebounder will continue. Interestingly, the last time a Denver team outrebounded its opponents for the season was in 1980 - the year before Doug Moe took over, and, as I'm sure

Denver Nuggets .... Overview

Doug would point out, the worst year (30 wins) in franchise history.

In an attempt to solve their rebounding woes, the Nuggets offered Larry Smith of Golden State a 2-year deal. That went nowhere. To make matters worse, they then lost Wayne Cooper (free agent) to Portland. Barring a deal after this has gone to print, they're in deep trouble up front.

Alex English continues to astonish me. I guess his ability to keep his body from wearing down is related to the non-physical style he plays, but one would think that running the court as much as he does in Moe's system would wear a player out quicker than anything else. Whatever the case, Alex scored 2,175 points last season. That moved him past the two statistically greatest players ever. Both Wilt Chamberlain and Oscar Robertson accomplished that feat a *mere* 7 consecutive seasons. What is even more impressive to me is that English's point totals are overwhelmingly better than any other NBA player in his 13th year.

1. Alex English	**2,175**	**1989**
2. Dolph Schayes	1,868	1961
3. Kareem Abdul Jabbar	1,818	1982
4. Moses Malone	1,760	1987
5. Julius Erving	1,727	1984

Now, if he can just score 2,000 points for *another* 8 years, he'll barely nip Abdul-Jabbar on the all-time scoring list. (Does that put Kareem's scoring in perspective or what?) Despite English's success, I would be remiss if I didn't point out that his Production Rating has dropped 6 consecutive years. He told me at the All-Star game that 2 years will be it. We'll see.

Whereas Dolph Schayes was as consistent a player as we've seen in the NBA, his son, Danny isn't. In one 3 game stretch, he scored 3, 37, and 10 points. In another 12 game period, he averaged 23 ppg for the first 6 games and 9 ppg for the last half dozen. In addition, he was #1 in the NBA in fouls per game (4.21) despite playing only 25 minutes per contest.

Fat Lever is, without a doubt, *the* most underrated player in the NBA (see page 28). I've said it before, but I guess I'll just keep having to. Not only does he have great offensive stats - and I mean great - but he's actually a very tough defensive player, he is one of only three people in the NBA with more steals than turnovers (+38, Rivers +23, Hornacek +18), and he leads the league in having played the most consecutive games without a technical (557 games). His not being selected to the All-Star game last season was blindness beyond comprehension!

The Nuggets picked up a winner in the draft when they got Todd Lichti. I honestly believe that he will cure their draft-pick-woes. As a schoolboy track star, Lichti has the ability to play Denver's tempo. As a 53% 3-point shooter, he has the ability to play Denver's style. He's also ambidextrous, an asset in the NBA for a player who likes to take it to the hoop.

Notes: Denver was ahead of only Miami and Charlotte in free throw differential... Miami and Charlotte are the only two road teams the club beat in one 21 road-game period... Michael Adams led the league in both 3-pt attempts and 3-pt goals... Doug Moe is 9-0 in the months of March during his tenure in Denver. The team's record during those 9 months is 89-49... Walter Davis played the most minutes with no starts of any player in the league.

Prediction - best case: 48-34

Denver may rebound in 1990 if they get a rebounder and if Lichti comes through. Challenging for the division title will be tough, but in this division, it always is.

Prediction - worst case: 38-44

This is possible if they fail to get another good board man. In addition, if anything happens to Lever or English, then it will be the Nuggets who are gasping for breath - not their opponents.

To order back issues of Basketball Heaven or to obtain the 1990 Midseason Report, see page 324.

Detroit Pistons . . . . Influence on Winning

TEAM RECORD BY

PLAYER	GAMES	... SCR Leader		... REB Leader		...AST Leader	
		HOME	ROAD	HOME	ROAD	HOME	ROAD
Bill Laimbeer	81	6-1	3-3	19-2	8-4	2-0	0-1
Isiah Thomas	80	9-1	6-6	0-0	0-0	26-4	18-10
Joe Dumars	69	7-0	12-1	0-0	0-0	11-0	10-3
Dennis Rodman	82	1-0	0-2	14-3	7-10	0-0	0-0
Mark Aguirre	36	3-0	1-2	2-0	0-0	0-0	0-0
Vinnie Johnson	82	7-1	3-3	0-0	1-0	1-0	1-0
Rick Mahorn	72	0-0	0-0	6-0	10-1	0-0	0-0
John Salley	67	0-0	0-0	0-0	1-0	0-0	0-1
James Edwards	76	0-0	0-0	0-0	1-0	0-0	0-0
John Long	24	0-0	0-0	0-0	0-0	0-0	0-0

TEAM RECORD BY SCORING *

PLAYER	PLAY	DNP	0-9	10-19	20-29	30-39	40+
Bill Laimbeer	62-19	1-0	19-5	30-10	13-3	0-1	0-0
Isiah Thomas	61-19	2-0	7-3	28-8	20-7	6-1	0-0
Joe Dumars	54-15	9-4	7-4	20-10	22-1	4-0	1-0
Dennis Rodman	63-19	0-0	41-10	21-8	1-0	0-1	0-0
Mark Aguirre	30-6	33-13	2-3	20-2	7-1	1-0	0-0
Vinnie Johnson	63-19	0-0	19-6	27-9	13-4	4-0	0-0
Rick Mahorn	5715	6-4	40-12	17-3	0-0	0-0	0-0
John Salley	50-17	13-2	39-10	11-7	0-0	0-0	0-0
James Edwards	59-17	4-2	37-13	22-4	0-0	0-0	0-0
John Long	22-2	41-17	21-2	1-0	0-0	0-0	0-0

TEAM RECORD BY STARTING POSITION *

PLAYER	GAMES	STARTS	PG	OG	SF	PF	C
Bill Laimbeer	81	81	0-0	0-0	0-0	0-0	62-19
Isiah Thomas	80	76	58-18	0-0	0-0	0-0	0-0
Joe Dumars	69	67	5-1	47-14	0-0	0-0	0-0
Dennis Rodman	82	8	0-0	0-0	5-3	0-0	0-0
Mark Aguirre	36	32	0-0	0-0	28-4	0-0	0-0
Vinnie Johnson	82	21	0-0	16-5	0-0	0-0	0-0
Rick Mahorn	72	61	0-0	0-0	0-0	49-12	0-0
John Salley	67	21	0-0	0-0	0-0	14-7	0-0
James Edwards	76	1	0-0	0-0	0-0	0-0	1-0
John Long	24	0	0-0	0-0	0-0	0-0	0-0

* For further definition of each category and column heading see pages 42 & 43.

Detroit Pistons . . . . 1988-89 Statistics

RAW NUMBERS *

PLAYER	2pt%	3pt%	FT%	MIN	PF	DQ	HI	TO	RB	AS	BL	ST
Bill Laimbeer	.515	.349	.840	2640	259	2	32	129	776	177	100	51
Isiah Thomas	.485	.273	.818	2924	209	0	37	298	273	663	20	133
Joe Dumars	.506	.483	.850	2408	103	1	42	178	172	390	5	63
Dennis Rodman	.614	.231	.626	2208	292	4	32	126	772	99	76	55
Mark Aguirre	.488	.293	.733	2597	229	2	41	208	386	278	36	45
Vinnie Johnson	.472	.295	.734	2073	155	0	34	105	255	242	17	74
Rick Mahorn	.519	0-2	.748	1795	206	1	19	97	496	59	66	40
John Salley	.502	0-2	.692	1458	197	3	19	100	335	75	72	40
James Edwards	.502	0-2	.686	1254	226	1	18	72	231	49	31	11
John Long	.410	.400	.921	919	84	1	25	57	77	80	3	29

OVERALL RANKINGS *

PLAYER	G	GS	PPG	PR	RANK	SC	SH	RB	AS	BL	ST
Bill Laimbeer	81	81	13.65	19.70	33	82	36	16	110	31	158
Isiah Thomas	80	76	18.22	19.09	37	38	106	153	16	132	50
Joe Dumars	69	67	17.19	16.59	72	50	31	173	38	173	125
Dennis Rodman	82	8	8.96	16.32	77	140	3	3	149	35	131
Mark Aguirre	80	76	18.89	15.74	83	32	124	105	61	94	165
Vinnie Johnson	82	21	13.78	12.30	121	79	136	123	57	120	92
Rick Mahorn	72	61	7.25	11.90	126	155	56	22	164	32	143
John Salley	67	21	6.97	9.88	150	160	120	55	137	15	121
James Edwards	76	1	7.30	7.01	DNQ						
John Long	68	1	5.47	4.21	DNQ						

POSITION RANKINGS *

PLAYER	POSITION	RANK	SC	SH	RB	AS	BL	ST
Bill Laimbeer	Center	8	10	9	7	6	18	19
Isiah Thomas	Point Guard	9	5	19	22	16	13	18
Joe Dumars	Off Guard, PG	13	14	10	44	9	44	40
Dennis Rodman	Small Forward	19	33	1	1	39	7	27
Mark Aguirre	Small Forward	22	13	29	30	7	27	39
Vinnie Johnson	Off Guard, PG	25	23	34	18	20	21	34
Rick Mahorn	Power Forward	27	26	11	11	25	9	25
John Salley	Power Forward, SF	29	27	26	22	14	4	18
James Edwards	Center	DNQ						
John Long	Off Guard	DNQ						

*For further definition of each category and column heading see pages 42 & 43.

Detroit Pistons .... Team Info

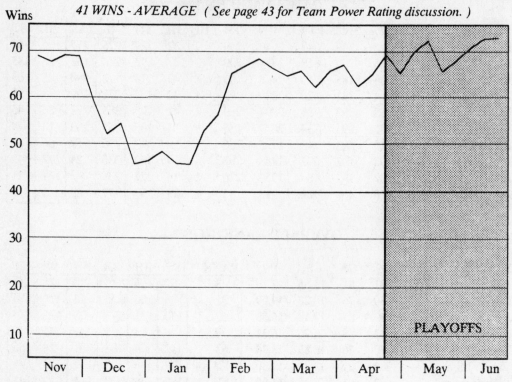

WEEKLY POWER RATING

41 WINS - AVERAGE (See page 43 for Team Power Rating discussion.)

Miscellaneous Categories	Data	Rank
Attendance	880K	2
Key-Man Games Missed	37	6
Season Record	63-19	1
- Home	37-4	1
- Road	26-15	1
Eastern Conference	41-15	1
Western Conference	22-4	1
Overtime Record	4-1	2
Record 5 Pts. or Less	8-5	3
Record 10 Pts. or More	33-10	3
Games Won By Bench	7	7
Games Won By Starters	12	7
Winning Streak	9	2
Losing Streak	2	1
Home Winning Streak	21	4
Road Winning Streak	6	1
Home Losing Streak	1	1
Road Losing Streak	6	8

Performance Categories	Data	Rank
Offensive Scoring (per game)	106.6	16
Defensive Scoring (per game)	100.8	2
Scoring Margin (per game)	5.8	4
Defensive FG%	.447	2
Offensive 2-point%	.505	6
Offensive 3-point%	.300	19
Offensive Free Throw %	.769	15
Offensive Rebs .....(Off REB/Opp Def REB)		7
Defensive Rebs ....(Def REB/Opp Off REB)		4
Offensive Assists ....(AST/FGMade)		14
Offensive Blocks ..(BLK/Opp FGAttempted)		15
Offensive Steals.....................(STL/Game)		25
Turnover Margin........(Def T.O. - Off T.O.)		19
Fouls Margin ....(Opp FOULS - FOULS)		6
Rebounding Record	56-22-4	1
Assists Record	46-35-1	8
Field Goal Pct. Record	65-17-0	1
Free Throw Att. Record	43-34-5	9

Detroit Pistons ....Team Roster

MOST PRODUCTIVE PLAYERS

Player	Span	Yrs	CRD
Bob Lanier	1971-80	10	18,822
Isiah Thomas	1982-89	8	13,939
Dave Bing	1967-75	9	13,582
Bill Laimbeer	1982-89	8	13,489
Bailey Howell	1960-64	5	9,754
Larry Foust	1951-57	7	8,803
Dave DeBusschere	1963-69	7	8,721
Terry Tyler	1979-85	7	8,427
Ray Scott	1962-67	6	7,806
Vinnie Johnson	1982-89	8	7,761

PRESENT PLAYERS*

J#	VETERANS	COLLEGE	POS	R#	D#	HT	WT	Detr	NBA
24	Mark Aguirre	DePaul	F	1	1	6-6	235	1	8
50	William Bedford	Memphis State	C	1	6	7-1	235	1	2
34	Fennis Dembo	Wyoming	F	2	30	6-5	215	1	1
4	Joe Dumars	McNeese State	G	1	18	6-3	190	4	4
53	James Edwards	Washington	C	3	46	7-1	252	2	12
	Scott Hastings	Arkansas	F-C	2	29	6-10	235	0	7
15	Vinnie Johnson	Baylor	G	1	7	6-2	200	8	10
40	Bill Laimbeer	Notre Dame	C	3	65	6-11	260	8	9
25	John Long	Detroit	G	2	29	6-5	195	9	11
10	Dennis Rodman	S.E. Oklahoma	F	2	27	6-8	210	3	3
22	John Salley	Georgia Tech	F-C	1	11	6-11	231	3	3
11	Isiah Thomas	Indiana	G	1	2	6-1	185	8	8

FUTURE PLAYERS

ROOKIES	COLLEGE	POS	R#	D#	HT	WT
Anthony Cook	Arizona	F	1	24	6-9	206

* For further definition of category and column headings, see pages 42 & 43.

Detroit Pistons . . . . Overview

"We bad. We bad." That's the way the season began (8-0) and the way it ended (7-0). Somewhere along the line "bad" became "good" and boy, were the Pistons bad last year.

There are many reasons why, but the "bad boy" image and all that went with it is as much responsible as anything. Led by the baddest bad boy among them, Rick Mahorn ($11,000), the club was first in the league in total fines ($27,500) for fighting. (Had Mahorn just done it with the gloves on like Detroit native, Tommy Hearns, he could have collected $11 million.) Bill Laimbeer ($6,000) and Isiah Thomas ($5,000) joined in. Once Mahorn was left unprotected and chosen by Minnesota in the expansion draft, the "bad boy" image was officially retired. Presumably, they'll all be a bunch of pussycats now.

Regardless of what anyone says, that rough style of playing worked for Detroit in 1989. It worked during the season (63-19 #1) and it worked in the playoffs (world championship). It served to both keep their opponents off guard, as well as to psyche themselves up. After Detroit won their first 8 games, they then went through a stretch where they were 18-13. In the final game of that rather uneventful period, Laimbeer was ejected for fighting. After the contest, he was suspended for one game. This was a severe blow to Billy-boy because it broke his consecutive games-played streak at 685. Only Randy Smith (906), Johnny Kerr (804) and Dolph Schayes (706) were ahead of him. The team's outrage was apparant as they blistered Sacramento in Laimbeer's absence. The win began a 37-6 streak to end the season.

That same physical style of play worked mainly as an effective defensive mechanism. Very few opponents drove the lane without thinking about what was waiting for them. Because of the altered shots via intimidation, Detroit ranked #2 in defensive scoring and #2 in defensive fg%. In fact, they held their opponents below 48% in 66 games. Of those, they won 56.

Without any doubt, defense was the primary factor in Detroit's winning the NBA title. In truth, it is for most champions, but never more so then for this club. By holding their playoff opponents to just 92.9 ppg, the team ranks as the stingiest champion in the post shot-clock (1955) era.

Detroit	**1989**	**92.9**
Milwaukee	1971	94.6
Golden State	1975	94.9
Syracuse	1955	94.9
Boston	1974	96.8

So tough was their defense that the Pistons actually held their opponents to below 100 points in 15 of the 17 post-season games, including a playoff record 14 consecutive. I don't know whether it was the desire by Thomas and Aguirre to beat out their best friend - Magic Johnson - or whether it was the self-imposed ban on alcohol that did it, but something sure motivated this club. And, as a result, turned 1988's close-but-no-cigar playoff loss vs the Lakers into 1989's I'll-never-go-thirsty-again victory party. And before it was over, every 1962 Chevy Impala in working class Detroit was honking its horn.

The biggest reason, bar none, for Detroit's defensive success throughout the season was Dennis Rodman. The "worm" was voted onto the All-Defensive first team, and, largely due to this honor, was *my* Sixth-Man-of-the-Year (see page 33). There is no better one-on-one defensive player in the league today, and I'm not sure there ever has been, given his size and speed. In addition to his great defensive abilities, Rodman was unstoppable on the offensive boards - leading the league with a 48-minute projection of 7.11 offensive rebounds. During the playoffs, he actually averaged 10 rebounds per game in only 24 minutes of action. His efforts were so spectacular that had it not been for the truly special performance by Joe Dumars, he would have won the MVP.

As it was, that award was unanimously given to Dumars. Not only did he con-

Detroit Pistons . . . . Overview

tribute mightily on defense, but he showed the world what an offensive force he can be if unleashed. Dumars set a Detroit record earlier in the playoffs with a 30 point second half explosion against Cleveland, but it was the often-times unconscious shooting (58%) versus the Lakers in the finals that had the basketball world buzzing in the off-season.

The questions will begin to arise as to whose team this is going to be in the future - Dumars' or Thomas'? I'm sure Joe would quickly say Isiah's, but if that's true, Thomas is going to have to turn over the scoring to J.D. When Dumars broke 20 points, Detroit was 27-1. When Thomas did it, they were 26-8. When Joe shot 16+ field goal attempts they were 16-0. When Isiah did the same, the team didn't (28-13). Finally, when Dumars took 10+ free throw attempts, the Pistons were 8-0. The club was only 6-3 when Thomas went to the line that often. There was nothing wrong with Isiah's stats, but Dumars may now be one of the very best players in the NBA. He needs to be cut loose as he was against L.A.

Speaking of being cut loose, Adrian Dantley (Dumar's best friend) was sent packing at mid-season. In his stead came Thomas' best friend (Mark Aguirre). At least, on that score, Isiah won. But it was also in the best interest of the team. Dantley was too one-dimensional for Detroit. Aguirre fits in perfectly - assuming he's willing to only score 15 points per outing. His story is really quite similar to Mychal Thompson's at L.A. Both were #1 picks in their drafts. Both played 7 years prior to being sent to Detroit and L.A. respectively. Both came from Texas and both were the perfect piece to each club's championship puzzle. L.A. was 43-8 (including playoffs) after Thompson arrived. Detroit cruised along at 45-8 (including playoffs) from Aguirre's first game. The final irony will be if Aguirre can win the title two years in a row as Thompson did.

The Pistons were so hot at the tail end of the season that they won 30 of their last 34.

During the 1980's only one other team has done as well in their final 34 contests.

Detroit	**1989**	**30-4**
Los Angeles	1985	30-4
Los Angeles	1987	29-5
Boston	1986	28-6
Boston	1982	28-6

Detroit picked up Anthony Cook in the draft. The similarities to Rodman are compelling. Both are 6'8" to 6'9", 205 to 210 lbs. Both shot 63% from the field and 63% from the line in college. Both are excellent leapers and shot blockers. Finally, both play the game very enthusiastically. He may have a start on it, but Cook still has a long way to go to equal Rodman's value.

Notes: Detroit won their last 21 home games... The Pistons won the field goal percentage battle in every one of their 26 road victories... In games decided by exactly 6 points, Detroit was curiously 10-0... Despite their quickness, the club was last in the NBA in steals... After 11 consecutive years of scoring between 10.5 and 16.7 ppg, James Edwards averaged just 7.3... The highest scorer on the team was Adrian Dantley at 18.4 ppg. Since 1955 every single NBA championship team and every single club with the league's best record has had a player average higher than Dantley's 18.4.

Prediction - best case: 65-17

Though it's extremely hard to improve on 63 victories, the club has a chance to do it. If they decide that one championship isn't enough, perhaps they'll find the necessary motivation.

Prediction - worst case: 54-28

Clearly, this team has enough talent and depth to avoid this modest record. But it requires something from deep within to maintain intensity after winning a championship. It's that attribute that signals greatness.

To order back issues of Basketball Heaven or to obtain the 1990 Midseason Report, see page 324.

Golden State Warriors . . . . . . Influence on Winning

TEAM RECORD BY

PLAYER	GAMES	... SCR Leader		... REB Leader		...AST Leader	
		HOME	ROAD	HOME	ROAD	HOME	ROAD
Chris Mullin	82	20-7	10-17	4-2	4-3	10-2	4-6
Mitch Richmond	79	7-2	3-4	4-2	2-3	6-4	3-7
Winston Garland	79	1-0	0-1	2-0	2-1	19-6	8-12
Terry Teagle	66	1-2	1-3	2-1	0-1	0-0	0-1
Larry Smith	80	0-0	0-1	16-4	4-7	1-0	0-1
Rod Higgins	81	1-1	0-1	0-1	2-1	0-0	1-0
Manute Bol	80	0-0	0-0	3-1	0-5	0-0	0-0
Otis Smith	80	0-0	0-0	0-1	1-4	0-0	0-1
Ralph Sampson	61	0-0	0-0	3-3	2-6	0-1	0-1
Steve Alford	57	0-0	0-0	0-0	0-0	1-1	0-1

TEAM RECORD BY SCORING *

PLAYER	PLAY	DNP	0-9	10-19	20-29	30-39	40+
Chris Mullin	43-39	0-0	0-2	2-12	21-20	18-4	2-1
Mitch Richmond	43-36	0-3	1-1	12-18	22-16	7-1	1-0
Winston Garland	42-37	1-2	4-7	29-29	8-1	1-0	0-0
Terry Teagle	35-31	8-8	7-10	17-12	10-6	1-3	0-0
Larry Smith	41-39	2-0	28-33	13-6	0-0	0-0	0-0
Rod Higgins	43-38	0-1	14-19	24-16	4-3	1-0	0-0
Manute Bol	41-39	2-0	40-36	1-3	0-0	0-0	0-0
Otis Smith	41-39	2-0	20-17	19-21	2-1	0-0	0-0
Ralph Sampson	31-30	12-9	25-20	6-10	0-0	0-0	0-0
Steve Alford	35-25	11-14	25-19	7-6	0-0	0-0	0-0

TEAM RECORD BY STARTING POSITION *

PLAYER	GAMES	STARTS	PG	OG	SF	PF	C
Chris Mullin	82	82	0-0	0-0	19-22	24-17	0-0
Mitch Richmond	79	79	1-2	41-33	1-1	0-0	0-0
Winston Garland	79	79	42-37	0-0	0-0	0-0	0-0
Terry Teagle	66	41	0-0	0-1	22-16	0-0	0-2
Larry Smith	80	78	0-0	0-0	0-0	19-22	20-17
Rod Higgins	81	1	0-0	0-0	0-0	0-0	0-1
Manute Bol	80	4	0-0	0-0	0-0	0-0	4-0
Otis Smith	80	5	0-0	1-3	1-0	0-0	0-0
Ralph Sampson	61	36	0-0	0-0	0-0	0-0	18-18
Steve Alford	57	3	0-0	1-2	0-0	0-0	0-0

* For further definition of each category and column heading see pages 42 & 43.

Golden State Warriors . . . . 1988-89 Statistics

RAW NUMBERS *

PLAYER	2pt%	3pt%	FT%	MIN	PF	DQ	HI	TO	RB	AS	BL	ST
Chris Mullin	.527	.230	**.892**	3093	178	1	**47**	296	483	415	39	**176**
Mitch Richmond	.475	.367	.810	2717	223	**5**	**47**	269	468	334	13	82
Winston Garland	.442	.233	.809	2661	216	2	31	187	328	**505**	14	175
Terry Teagle	.481	.167	.809	1569	173	2	36	116	263	96	17	79
Larry Smith	**.552**	0-0	.310	1897	**248**	2	18	110	**652**	118	54	61
Rod Higgins	.505	**.393**	.821	1887	172	2	30	76	376	160	42	39
Manute Bol	.423	.220	.606	1769	226	2	13	79	462	27	**345**	11
Otis Smith	.448	.189	.798	1597	165	1	24	129	330	140	40	88
Ralph Sampson	.451	.375	.653	1086	170	3	17	90	307	77	65	31
Steve Alford	.476	.364	.820	906	57	0	17	45	72	92	3	45

OVERALL RANKINGS *

PLAYER	G	GS	PPG	PR	RANK	SC	SH	RB	AS	BL	ST
Chris Mullin	**82**	**82**	**26.54**	**26.01**	12	6	19	98	49	97	24
Mitch Richmond	79	79	22.04	**19.44**	35	16	95	86	52	146	111
Winston Garland	79	79	14.49	**16.76**	66	71	156	122	29	144	12
Terry Teagle	66	41	15.18	**12.85**	112	67	111	89	119	105	35
Larry Smith	80	78	5.70	**12.66**	114	172	67	4	117	49	104
Rod Higgins	81	1	10.57	**12.64**	115	118	26	75	83	60	153
Manute Bol	80	4	3.92	**10.46**	140	176	176	29	176	1	176
Otis Smith	80	5	10.04	**10.30**	146	128	151	71	82	55	27
Ralph Sampson	61	36	6.44	**9.00**	DNQ						
Steve Alford	66	3	5.55	**5.24**	DNQ						

POSITION RANKINGS *

PLAYER	POSITION	RANK	SC	SH	RB	AS	BL	ST
Chris Mullin	Small Forward, OG	1	2	3	24	3	28	3
Mitch Richmond	Off Guard, SF	7	4	24	6	16	33	38
Winston Garland	Point Guard	15	11	27	9	25	16	6
Terry Teagle	Off Guard, SF	21	20	27	8	40	14	15
Larry Smith	Power Forward	25	29	14	1	8	14	15
Rod Higgins	Small Forward	28	29	5	11	16	17	35
Manute Bol	Center	24	30	30	15	30	1	30
Otis Smith	Off Guard, SF	34	35	40	3	30	3	10
Ralph Sampson	Center	DNQ						
Steve Alford	Off Guard	DNQ						

*For further definition of each category and column heading see pages 42 & 43.

Golden State Warriors . . . . Team Info

WEEKLY POWER RATING

41 WINS - AVERAGE (See page 43 for Team Power Rating discussion.)

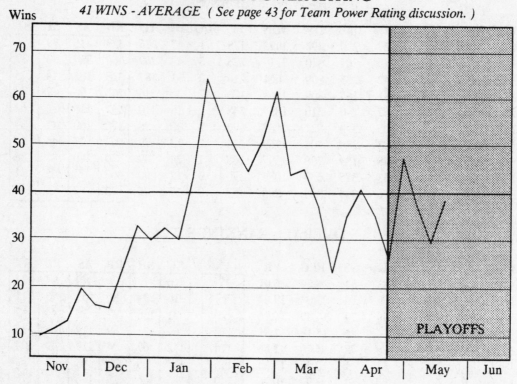

Miscellaneous Categories	Data	Rank
Attendance	588K	14
Key-Man Games Missed	25	3
Season Record	43-39	14
- Home	29-12	16
- Road	14-27	12
Eastern Conference	14-10	5
Western Conference	29-29	18
Overtime Record	4-4	8
Record 5 Pts. or Less	8-11	21
Record 10 Pts. or More	20-21	16
Games Won By Bench	3	16
Games Won By Starters	11	9
Winning Streak	8	5
Losing Streak	6	12
Home Winning Streak	11	12
Road Winning Streak	3	9
Home Losing Streak	3	14
Road Losing Streak	7	11

Performance Categories	Data	Rank
Offensive Scoring (per game)	116.6	4
Defensive Scoring (per game)	116.9	25
Scoring Margin (per game)	-0.3	16
Defensive FG%	.462	4
Offensive 2-point%	.481	18
Offensive 3-point%	.308	18
Offensive Free Throw %	.799	4
Offensive Rebs ..... (Off REB/Opp Def REB)		9
Defensive Rebs ....(Def REB/Opp Off REB)		23
Offensive Assists .... (AST/FGMade)		24
Offensive Blocks .. (BLK/Opp FGAttempted)		2
Offensive Steals .... (STL/Game)		4
Turnover Margin........(Def T.O. - Off T.O.)		11
Fouls Margin .... (Opp FOULS - FOULS)		10
Rebounding Record	35-45-2	19
Assists Record	30-47-5	20
Field Goal Pct. Record	45-35-2	7
Free Throw Att. Record	37-44-1	15

Golden State Warriors . . . . Team Roster

MOST PRODUCTIVE PLAYERS

Player	Span	Yrs	CRD
Wilt Chamberlain	1960-65	6	20,024
Nate Thurmond	1964-74	11	19,745
Paul Arizin	1951-62	10	15,209
Rick Barry	1966-78	8	13,759
Jeff Mullins	1967-76	10	12,148
Neil Johnston	1952-59	8	11,386
Purvis Short	1979-87	9	10,271
J.B. Carroll	1981-88	7	9,893
Larry Smith	1981-89	9	9,697
Guy Rodgers	1959-66	8	9,681

PRESENT PLAYERS*

J#	VETERANS	COLLEGE	POS	R#	D#	HT	WT	G.St	NBA
10	Manute Bol	Bridgeport	C	2	31	7-6	225	1	4
32	Tellis Frank	W. Kentucky	F	1	14	6-10	240	2	2
12	Winston Garland	S.W. Missouri St.	G	2	40	6-2	170	2	2
40	Rod Higgins	Fresno State	F	2	31	6-7	205	3	7
17	Chris Mullin	St. Johns	G	1	7	6-7	220	4	4
23	Mitch Richmond	Kansas State	G	1	5	6-5	215	1	1
50	Ralph Sampson	Virginia	C	1	1	7-4	230	2	6
20	Terry Teagle	Baylor	G	1	16	6-5	195	5	7

FUTURE PLAYERS

ROOKIES	COLLEGE	POS	R#	D#	HT	WT	
Tim Hardaway	Texas-El Paso	G	1	14	5-11	180	
Sarunas Marciulionis	Soviet Union	G	6	127	6-3	195	(87'-Draft)
Leonard Taylor	California	F	X	X	6-8	225	

* For further definition of category and column headings, see pages 42 & 43.

Golden State Warriors . . . . Overview

The big experiment of bringing Don Nelson out of retirement and back into coaching obviously worked. Not only did the Warriors improve their wins by a whopping +23 (4th best in NBA history), but they did it with a young group of players - setting attendance records all the while.

As a player, Nelson was on a winning team 12 of 14 seasons. As a coach, he has been a winner 10 of 12. Throughout his career, Nelson has proven that he has a very creative mind and that he understands the game's nuances. And perhaps his success story is best demonstrated by realizing that, of all the people ever associated with the game, Nellie has participated as coach or player in more playoff games than any other.

Don Nelson	**246**
K.C. Jones	238
K. Abdul-Jabbar	237
Bill Russell	226
Tommy Heinsohn	184

Among the many innovative or controversial decisions Nelson made last season, the smartest was surely the drafting of Mitch Richmond. Though he was only the #5 pick overall, Richmond was nearly a unanimous choice for Rookie-of-the-Year honors. Mitch was a brilliant scorer for a first-year player. His 47 points in one game were the 3rd-most for a rookie in the 1980's, behind only Bird (49) and Tripucka (49). In addition, the team was 17-4 when he hit for 27 points or more. That represented the kind of leadership that he brought to the team.

What made his drafting controversial was that the club's best player (Chris Mullin) was fixed at the position Richmond was slated to play. It meant Mullin would have to move to forward. If you look around the league you'll find very few 6'7" players who can't run or jump playing at forward. Nevertheless, Nelson knew what he was doing. Not only did Mullin excel, but he became an All-Star for the first time in his career, averaging 26.5 ppg and ranking #12

in the league by Production Rating. As you know, Mullin is a recovering alcoholic. Rebportedly, Nelson had a lot to do with his turning his life around. Because of it, Mullin, like Richmond, was pivotal to the team's success. When he scored 29+ points, they were outstanding (24-5).

The second most impressive decision Nelson made was the acquiring of Maute Bol. Some will scoff that Bol is clumsy and one-dimensional. They'll point out that of the 176 qualifiers, he was last by my shooting index, assists per minute, steals per minute, and scoring per game. Although I nearly talked myself out of saying it - all that may be true, but he's still extremely valuable to this club. The reason is really very simple. It's called defense. Now, I'm sure some of you defensive-minded readers from the Eastern Conference are laughing. You're wondering how any team which ranked last in the league in defensive scoring can even have the word "defense" uttered in the same sentence as Golden State. Here's how.

What Manute enabled the team to do was to run to their heart's content without paying for it defensively. Golden State only had 283 blocked shots in 1988, but increased that to 643 last season. The 283 were the lowest in the decade of the 1980's, except for Dallas' expansion year, while the 683 was the 9th most ever by a club! That's as stunning a turn around as you'll ever see. And it was directly due to Manute Bol, whose 9.36 blocks per 48 minutes represented an all-time high.

Because of all those blocks, the Warriors ranked #4 in defensive fg% (.462). When you consider all the fast breaks the club is involved in, that's excellent. What's most important to realize is that the Warriors were next to last in 1988 in defensive fg% at .501. Considering the pace they played in 1989, while reducing the defensive fg% from 50.1% to 46.2%, the team actually gained 7.8 points defensively per game over the previous year. Given the fact that they lost 27 games by 8 points or less in 1988, you can see in a nutshell why they gained

Golden State Warriors . . . . **Overview**

23 wins. Field goal percentage, both offensive and defensive, is the single most important stat affecting team success.

When Manute makes a mistake, his Sudanese dialect leads him to say, "my bad", and he does have to say it occasionally. Unfortunately, he got on a 3-point shooting binge late in the season. His 22% is not atrocious, but it's not worthy of a disciplined offense either. Nevertheless, his two 3-pt FGA's per game over the last 31 games cost the team 27 points or .4 points per game. That hardly compares with the 7.8 points he gains defensively, if that's all it takes to keep him happy. I'm sure there were many nights when Nelson was saying to himself, "my good" regarding his decision to get Bol.

The third best move Nelson made was to sit Ralph Sampson. Yea, sure, it was because of his knee. That was an excuse. But it was the right decision, nonetheless. I've been critical of Ralph in the past, so I won't say much here other than that immediately after he was sidelined, the club went 10-2 and when he shot 7+ FGA's, they were 10-16, while 21-14 when he shot less. There may not be a coach alive who can make Ralph be what he is - a world-class defensive center and stickback artist. If Nelson can just make him accept that...

The fourth good decision is one that will have to be modified. Nelson went out and got Winston Garland off waivers in 1987. And, although he has played very well for being free, the time has come to replace him. Garland has two problems. The first is that he's not a good shooter. His 44.2% from 2-point land and 23% from 3-point range demonstrate that. The second concern is that he's not the ideal playmaker they need. It's true that he had 505 assists, but of all the point guards who played 2,000 minutes or more, he ranked ahead of only Michael Adams and Rory Sparrow in assists divided by team fga's. When you consider that Adams splits PG duties with Lever and that Sparrow didn't have many scorers to give the ball to, his ranking is all

the more distressing - especially in light of the scoring machines he had on his own team (Mullin, Richmond, Teagle).

Because of Garland's weaknesses, Nellie got Tim Hardaway in the draft. Rated as the #1 point guard available, Hardaway is an excellent penetrator and passer who can shoot from the perimeter. The Warriors also picked up Sarunas Marciulionis from the Soviet Union (I hope someone coins a nickname for this guy like "Marcy"). I'm very impressed with him. His moves and ball-handling capabilities are more "Americanized" than that of any other foreign player I've seen. There still remains big off-the-court question marks, however. What about communication, culture, loneliness, politics?

Notes: Terry Teagle sat out 13 games during trade talks, but is apparently there to stay... Larry Smith isn't. As a free agent, he was lost to Houston... By breaking 50 points in a quarter, the Warriors were the first to do it in 4 years. They did it 3 times in March, including a record 57 points in quarter #3... The club's volatility was shown in one 8-game winning streak where they averaged winning by 15 ppg. In a later 4-game losing streak, they lost by 23 ppg... Prior to Golden State over Utah, the last team without the home-court advantage to sweep its foe in round one was in 1966.

Prediction - best case: 55-27

Assuming no major injuries, if Hardaway steps right in, if the team figures out how to replace Larry Smith, and if, by some miracle, Ralph becomes what he's capable of, then 55 wins and a divisional title are possible.

Prediction - worst case: 43-39

I really believe that with Nelson, Mullin, Richmond, and the Sudanese Warrior, this club has to do at least as well as last season. But you never know. That's the beauty of the NBA.

To order back issues of Basketball Heaven or to obtain the 1990 Midseason Report, see page 324.

Houston Rockets . . . . Influence on Winning

TEAM RECORD BY

PLAYER	GAMES	... SCR Leader		... REB Leader		...AST Leader	
		HOME	ROAD	HOME	ROAD	HOME	ROAD
Akeem Olajuwon	82	19-7	9-15	25-9	8-21	1-1	1-1
Otis Thorpe	82	4-1	0-6	7-1	6-6	1-0	0-0
Eric Floyd	82	4-1	2-3	0-0	0-0	28-10	12-21
Buck Johnson	67	2-1	0-0	0-0	0-1	1-0	1-2
Mike Woodson	81	3-0	1-3	0-0	0-0	0-0	0-1
Walter Berry	40	0-0	0-0	0-0	0-0	0-0	0-0
Derrick Chevious	81	0-0	2-1	0-0	0-0	0-0	0-0
Purvis Short	65	1-0	0-0	0-0	1-0	2-1	0-0
Tim McCormick	81	0-0	0-1	0-0	0-0	0-0	0-0
Frank Johnson	67	0-0	0-0	0-0	0-0	2-0	1-1

TEAM RECORD BY SCORING *

PLAYER	PLAY	DNP	0-9	10-19	20-29	30-39	40+
Akeem Olajuwon	45-37	0-0	0-1	11-12	23-13	11-9	0-2
Otis Thorpe	45-37	0-0	4-6	32-16	9-12	0-3	0-0
Eric Floyd	45-37	0-0	9-17	25-14	11-4	0-2	0-0
Buck Johnson	36-31	9-6	11-22	21-9	4-0	0-0	0-0
Mike Woodson	45-36	0-1	14-17	20-15	11-4	0-0	0-0
Walter Berry	20-20	25-17	10-13	10-7	0-0	0-0	0-0
Derrick Chevious	45-36	0-1	25-20	14-16	6-0	0-0	0-0
Purvis Short	34-31	11-6	21-24	11-6	2-1	0-0	0-0
Tim McCormick	44-37	1-0	37-31	7-5	0-1	0-0	0-0
Frank Johnson	38-29	7-8	32-28	6-1	0-0	0-0	0-0

TEAM RECORD BY STARTING POSITION *

PLAYER	GAMES	STARTS	PG	OG	SF	PF	C
Akeem Olajuwon	82	82	0-0	0-0	0-0	0-0	45-37
Otis Thorpe	82	82	0-0	0-0	0-0	45-37	0-0
Eric Floyd	82	82	44-35	1-2	0-0	0-0	0-0
Buck Johnson	67	51	0-0	0-0	27-24	0-0	0-0
Mike Woodson	81	79	0-0	44-35	0-0	0-0	0-0
Walter Berry	40	14	0-0	0-0	7-7	0-0	0-0
Derrick Chevious	81	1	0-0	0-0	1-0	0-0	0-0
Purvis Short	65	16	0-0	0-0	10-6	0-0	0-0
Tim McCormick	81	0	0-0	0-0	0-0	0-0	0-0
Frank Johnson	67	0	0-0	0-0	0-0	0-0	0-0

* For further definition of each category and column heading see pages 42 & 43.

Houston Rockets . . . . 1988-89 Statistics

RAW NUMBERS *

PLAYER	2pt%	3pt%	FT%	MIN	PF	DQ	HI	TO	RB	AS	BL	ST
Akeem Olajuwon	.511	0-10	.696	3024	**329**	10	43	275	1105	149	282	213
Otis Thorpe	**.543**	0-2	.729	3135	259	6	37	225	787	202	37	82
Eric Floyd	.478	.373	.845	2788	196	1	37	253	306	**709**	11	124
Buck Johnson	.532	.111	.754	1850	213	4	24	110	286	126	35	64
Mike Woodson	.447	.348	.823	2259	195	1	29	136	194	206	18	89
Walter Berry	.507	**.500**	.699	1355	183	1	26	89	267	77	48	29
Derrick Chevious	.446	.208	.783	1539	161	1	27	136	256	77	11	48
Purvis Short	.423	.273	**.865**	1157	116	1	26	70	179	107	13	44
Tim McCormick	.487	0-4	.674	1257	193	0	23	68	261	54	24	18
Frank Johnson	.450	.167	.806	879	91	0	17	102	79	181	0	42

OVERALL RANKINGS *

PLAYER	G	GS	PPG	PR	RANK	SC	SH	RB	AS	BL	ST
Akeem Olajuwon	82	82	24.80	31.02	4	10	102	1	146	6	8
Otis Thorpe	82	82	16.71	20.62	27	55	35	36	113	99	126
Eric Floyd	82	82	14.17	18.46	45	75	45	135	7	154	53
Buck Johnson	67	51	9.58	11.42	131	131	42	100	109	73	97
Mike Woodson	81	79	12.91	10.48	138	92	137	159	76	122	74
Walter Berry	69	31	8.83	9.43	154	142	89	77	129	33	150
Derrick Chevious	81	1	9.26	7.36	174	135	150	90	142	128	107
Purvis Short	65	16	7.42	7.09	DNQ						
Tim McCormick	81	0	5.25	6.05	DNQ						
Frank Johnson	67	0	4.39	5.06	DNQ						

POSITION RANKINGS *

PLAYER	POSITION	RANK	SC	SH	RB	AS	BL	ST
Akeem Olajuwon	Center	1	1	16	1	15	5	1
Otis Thorpe	Power Forward	5	7	5	16	6	27	20
Eric Floyd	Point Guard	11	13	8	16	7	22	19
Buck Johnson	Small Forward	30	31	8	26	28	18	18
Mike Woodson	Off Guard	31	28	35	37	25	23	26
Walter Berry	Small Forward	35	34	20	12	33	6	33
Derrick Chevious	Off Guard, SF	44	37	39	9	44	25	37
Purvis Short	Small Forward, OF	DNQ						
Tim McCormick	Center, PF	DNQ						
Frank Johnson	Point Guard	DNQ						

*For further definition of each category and column heading see pages 42 & 43.

Houston Rockets .... Team Info

WEEKLY POWER RATING

41 WINS - AVERAGE (See page 43 for Team Power Rating discussion.)

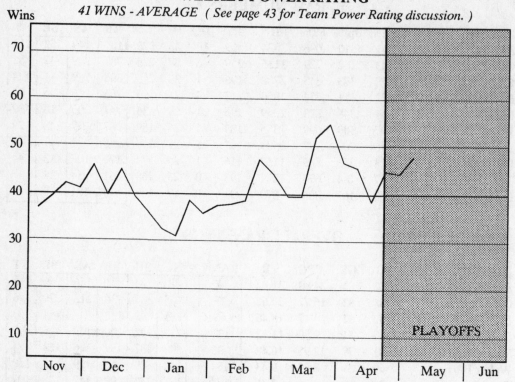

Miscellaneous Categories	Data	Rank
Attendance	681K	9
Key-Man Games Missed	36	5
Season Record	45-37	12
- Home	31-10	10
- Road	14-27	12
Eastern Conference	12-12	11
Western Conference	33-25	13
Overtime Record	3-3	8
Record 5 Pts. or Less	14-14	9
Record 10 Pts. or More	22-17	13
Games Won By Bench	4	13
Games Won By Starters	12	7
Winning Streak	6	9
Losing Streak	7	15
Home Winning Streak	8	15
Road Winning Streak	3	9
Home Losing Streak	2	5
Road Losing Streak	9	14

Performance Categories	Data	Rank
Offensive Scoring (per game)	108.5	13
Defensive Scoring (per game)	107.5	9
Scoring Margin (per game)	1.0	15
Defensive FG%	.468	7
Offensive 2-point%	.487	13
Offensive 3-point%	.314	15
Offensive Free Throw %	.755	17
Offensive Rebs (Off REB/Opp Def REB)		10
Defensive Rebs (Def REB/Opp Off REB)		5
Offensive Assists (AST/FGMade)		16
Offensive Blocks (BLK/Opp FGAttempted)		5
Offensive Steals (STL/Game)		11
Turnover Margin (Def T.O. - Off T.O.)		20
Fouls Margin (Opp FOULS - FOULS)		11
Rebounding Record	39-39-4	13
Assists Record	39-39-4	16
Field Goal Pct. Record	44-37-1	9
Free Throw Att. Record	45-34-3	8

Houston Rockets . . . . Team Roster

MOST PRODUCTIVE PLAYERS

Player	Span	Yrs	CRD
Calvin Murphy	1971-83	13	15,626
Rudy Tomjanovich	1971-81	11	14,133
Moses Malone	1977-82	6	13,340
Elvin Hayes	1969-84	7	12,612
Akeem Olajuwon	1985-89	5	10,937
Robert Reid	1978-88	10	10,121
Mike Newlin	1972-79	8	8,262
Allen Leavell	1980-89	10	7,504
Rodney McCray	1984-88	5	7,001
Ralph Sampson	1984-88	5	6,794

PRESENT PLAYERS*

J#	VETERANS	COLLEGE	POS	R#	D#	HT	WT	Hous	NBA
6	Walter Berry	St. Johns	F	1	14	6-8	215	1	3
3	Derrick Chievous	Missouri	F	1	16	6-7	195	1	1
21	Eric Floyd	Georgetown	G	1	13	6-3	175	2	7
1	Buck Johnson	Alabama	F	1	20	6-7	190	3	3
30	Allen Leavell	Oklahoma City	G	5	104	6-2	190	10	10
40	Tim McCormick	Michigan	C	1	12	7-0	240	1	5
52	Chuck Nevitt	N. Carolina State	C	3	63	7-5	237	1	6
34	Akeem Olajuwon	Houston	C	1	1	7-0	250	5	5
13	Larry Smith	Alcorn State	F	2	24	6-8	235	0	9
33	Otis Thorpe	Providence	F	1	9	6-10	235	1	5
42	Mike Woodson	Indiana	G	1	12	6-5	198	1	9

FUTURE PLAYERS

ROOKIES	COLLEGE	POS	R#	D#	HT	WT

---

* For further definition of category and column headings, see pages 42 & 43.

Houston Rockets . . . . Overview

"We want Calvin. We want Calvin." After Murphy hit the game-winning 3-pointer at the Legend's Classic in Houston last season, the chant was not only loud and long, but symbolic of the Rocket's needs. Murphy, of course, is Houston's all-time leading scorer and one of the most accurate free throw shooters in NBA history. His shot was ironic in that it came before the home crowd and because he had just been hired by the team to teach shooting fundamentals. What's really noteworthy is that shooting is *the* very problem the club has, and when the crowd was chanting "We want Calvin", they weren't kidding!

Though he's been out of the NBA since 1983, there was actually some serious debate as to whether he should rejoin his former team. Naturally, that will never happen, but with the 2-guard position in desperate straits, it would be entertaining to watch Murph give it a go for a couple of games.

The Rockets entered the 1988-89 season with very high hopes. There were two primary reasons - the additions of Otis Thorpe and Mike Woodson. A career 15 ppg scorer, Woodson appeared to be the ideal player to man the shooting guard spot. That was superficial thinking, though. A closer look revealed a player who had shot only 44% from the field the previous two seasons, a career 25% shooter from 3-point range, and one who had generally started with four clubs in eight years, but had done nothing to help them win. Find me one other player with 8 years' experience, nearly 10,000 points, but only 109 in playoff competition. Of all the active players with that many regular season points, only one (Eddie Johnson) had fewer playoff points before last season (107) - and even he has more now, 320-156. Houston made a mistake. It's that simple. Perhaps they just couldn't get anyone else, but as it turns out, Allen Leavell would have done as good a job.

Woodson ranked #31 at off-guard last year. His best position ranking in any of the 6 performance categories was #23 (blocks). Every one of the 41 off-guards who qualified had a better ranking in at least one of the the 6 categories. The biggest concern remained shooting. Only three other 2-guards had more negative 2-point efficiency points (see page 225) than Woodson in 1989. Two of them played for expansion clubs (Edwards, Miami and Chapman, Charlotte) and the other one was Dennis Hopson of New Jersey. The average of those 3 teams was 20-62. It's not a good sign when your shooting guard can't shoot.

The reason that Woodson's accuracy was so important was because the club didn't have any other shooting guards. Leavell and Johnson are both point-guards and besides, they're not great shooters. Rookie, Derrick Chevious, is a converted small forward who, after a good start (Production Rating of 14 thru 8 games), was at times wretched (Production Rating of 8.7 in his last 71 games). Purvis Short, who is on his last possible leg, shot as if he were playing with only one. Besides, he's a small forward too. That only leaves Sleepy Floyd and he can't play two positions at once.

What made it so crucial was that every team in the NBA cheated on Houston after it became clear that they weren't going to get beat by the Rockets' perimeter shooters. The collapsing down on Olajuwon and Thorpe only made their jobs more difficult. In fact, when the team was able to include other players, or to say it another way, when Otis Thorpe scored in the teens and Akeem in the twenties they were 18-4. On the other hand, when Otis scored 19+, the Rockets were only 9-17 and when Akeem scored 30+, they were a mere 11-11. Why? Well, it's simple really. When the perimeter game was not clicking, the burden fell on the big guys. They just couldn't do it alone regardless of their talent.

The perfect statistics to prove the point are found in the 22 games in which Akeem broke 30 points. His scoring average for

Houston Rockets .... Overview

those games was 35 while he hauled in 16 boards. Those are mammoth numbers. One would think that when the league's best center produces that well, his team should win the game. Like I said earlier, they were only 11-11. When he scored less than 30, his points average was 21.3 and his rebounding average was 12.7, but the team was pretty fair (34-26). The simple truth is, if they don't get some perimeter shooting, the Rockets will <u>never</u> get any better.

Because of the constant attention being paid to Akeem and Otis, Buck Johnson was able to roam rather freely at small forward. Maybe it's unfair to compare him with Rodney McCray because McCray played with a different cast, but Buck has already proven a certain indispensability. When he scored 15 points or more, the team was 9-1 and when he took 9+ field goal attempts they were 21-7. What's more, when he was injured, they slumped badly, but came on respectably after he returned. During his absence, Houston picked up Walter "my game does not consist of fundamentals" Berry from New Jersey. His value, as has been the case at each of his four NBA stops, was more than questionable as the Rockets went 25-17 without him, but were only .500 when he took the court.

Even with the constant double-teaming, Akeem Olajuwon is a super-star. Last season he became the first player to score 2,000+ points and 1,000+ rebounds since Moses Malone (1982, Houston). He became the first player in NBA history to record 200+ blocks and 200+ steals in the same season. The 200+ steals were the first ever by a center. He was the only player in the league to rank first at his position in three different categories (scoring, rebounding, steals); he was #1 in the league in defensive rebounding; he made the NBA's all-league 1st team; and was runner-up for Defensive Player-of-the-Year.

To the degree that Houston bombed out on Ralph Sampson, they've overachieved with Olajuwon. Akeem was in his 5th year

during the 1988-89 season. On an average, year #5 is a player's most productive, though not by much. Of all the #1 draft picks over the years, Akeem ranks #2 by Production Rating in his 5th year.

K. Abdul-Jabbar	1974	35.91
Akeem Olajuwon	**1989**	**31.02**
Bob Lanier	1975	30.36
Magic Johnson	1984	30.30
Elvin Hayes	1973	24.49

What is interesting in looking at the rest of this list is that of the 19 #1 picks who have played 5 years or more (pre 1985), I consider only the five above to have lived up to the expectations afforded a #1. Possibly you could argue that James Worthy has succeeded that well, but even assuming that, many of the others were no better than "good" players. Some weren't even average. If Houston had not drafted Akeem, it's hard to say where they'd be.

Notes: The Rockets signed monster rebounder Larry Smith to a 3-year deal... Houston became the first team in NBA history not to get a single draft pick last summer... Chuck Nevitt had the season's best line after being kissed by Morganna. "We laughed, we cried, and she became a part of me."... When Sleepy Floyd shot in the narrow area of 9-12 field goal attempts, the team was 24-6... Olajuwon was #2 in fines at $7,000, trailing Rick Mahorn ($11,000).

Prediction - best case: 51-31

This would tie the club's best season ever, but it assumes they get someone substantial at guard. If they do get an outstanding shooter, then the "sky's the limit".

Prediction - worst case: 42-40

If Akeem is healthy, it is impossible for the team not to win more games than they lose. Even so, the chemistry is bad on this club, they could sure use a true point guard, more NASA budget cuts, and "the sky is falling".

To order back issues of Basketball Heaven or to obtain the 1990 Mid-season Report, see page 324.

Indiana Pacers . . . . Influence on Winning

TEAM RECORD BY

PLAYER	GAMES	... SCR Leader		... REB Leader		...AST Leader	
		HOME	ROAD	HOME	ROAD	HOME	ROAD
Chuck Person	80	11-10	4-15	0-10	3-6	1-4	1-2
LaSalle Thompson	33	1-0	0-0	6-3	5-5	0-0	0-0
Vern Fleming	76	1-3	0-1	1-1	0-0	14-11	5-17
Reggie Miller	74	3-5	4-8	0-0	1-1	0-2	1-7
Rik Smits	82	1-3	0-6	1-3	0-11	0-0	0-0
Detlef Schrempf	32	1-0	0-1	3-1	0-1	0-0	0-1
Scott Skiles	80	0-0	0-1	0-0	0-2	7-7	1-11
Stuart Gray	72	0-0	0-0	2-1	0-2	0-0	0-0
Randy Wittman	33	0-0	0-0	0-0	0-0	0-0	0-1
Anthony Frederick	46	0-0	0-1	0-0	0-0	0-0	0-0

TEAM RECORD BY SCORING *

PLAYER	PLAY	DNP	0-9	10-19	20-29	30-39	40+
Chuck Person	27-53	1-1	1-2	6-22	13-24	6-3	1-2
LaSalle Thompson	17-16	11-38	7-6	6-7	4-3	0-0	0-0
Vern Fleming	26-50	2-4	3-8	17-34	6-8	0-0	0-0
Reggie Miller	23-51	5-3	2-14	11-23	9-13	1-1	0-0
Rik Smits	28-54	0-0	8-20	17-26	3-8	0-0	0-0
Detlef Shrempf	17-15	11-39	2-4	9-9	6-2	0-0	0-0
Scott Skiles	27-53	1-1	21-38	6-14	0-1	0-0	0-0
Stuart Gray	24-48	4-6	23-47	1-1	0-0	0-0	0-0
Randy Wittman	17-16	11-38	15-11	2-5	0-0	0-0	0-0
Anthony Frederick	14-32	14-22	13-29	1-3	0-0	0-0	0-0

TEAM RECORD BY STARTING POSITION *

PLAYER	GAMES	STARTS	PG	OG	SF	PF	C
Chuck Person	80	79	0-0	0-1	26-52	0-0	0-0
LaSalle Thompson	33	29	0-0	0-0	0-0	11-12	3-3
Vern Fleming	76	69	24-45	0-0	0-0	0-0	0-0
Reggie Miller	74	70	0-0	23-46	0-1	0-0	0-0
Rik Smits	82	71	0-0	0-0	0-0	0-0	25-46
Detlef Schrempf	32	12	0-0	0-0	1-1	6-4	0-0
Scott Skiles	80	13	4-9	0-0	0-0	0-0	0-0
Stuart Gray	72	0	0-0	0-0	0-0	0-0	0-0
Randy Wittman	33	11	0-0	5-6	0-0	0-0	0-0
Anthony Frederick	46	0	0-0	0-0	0-0	0-0	0-0

* For further definition of each category and column heading see pages 42 & 43.

Indiana Pacers . . . . 1988-89 Statistics

RAW NUMBERS *

PLAYER	2pt%	3pt%	FT%	MIN	PF	DQ	HI	TO	RB	AS	BL	ST
Chuck Person	.519	.307	.792	**3012**	280	12	**47**	308	516	289	18	83
LaSalle Thompson	.490	0-1	.808	2329	285	12	31	179	**718**	81	94	79
Vern Fleming	**.526**	.130	.799	2552	212	4	26	192	310	**494**	12	77
Reggie Miller	.511	.402	.844	2536	170	2	36	143	292	227	29	**93**
Rik Smits	.518	0-1	.722	2041	**310**	**14**	27	130	500	70	**151**	37
Detlef Schrempf	.492	.200	.780	1850	220	3	24	133	395	179	19	53
Scott Skiles	.485	.267	**.903**	1571	151	1	20	177	149	390	2	64
Stuart Gray	.474	0-1	.688	783	128	0	14	48	245	29	21	11
Randy Wittman	.454	**.500**	.683	1120	43	0	17	32	80	111	2	23
Anthony Frederick	.508	.400	.706	313	59	0	19	34	52	20	6	14

OVERALL RANKINGS *

PLAYER	G	GS	PPG	PR	RANK	SC	SH	RB	AS	BL	ST
Chuck Person	80	**79**	21.60	19.00	38	18	53	87	73	137	119
LaSalle Thompson	76	71	13.93	17.95	48	78	83	11	161	28	98
Vern Fleming	76	69	14.26	17.49	57	73	41	124	26	147	112
Reggie Miller	74	70	15.96	16.12	81	60	14	131	78	102	86
Rik Smits	**82**	71	11.66	14.06	101	107	66	39	163	10	161
Detlef Schrempf	69	13	12.00	13.91	102	104	99	67	71	108	116
Scott Skiles	80	13	6.82	8.95	158	162	78	150	10	175	68
Stuart Gray	72	0	2.61	4.79	DNQ						
Randy Wittman	64	13	4.55	4.78	DNQ						
Anthony Frederick	46	0	3.30	3.00	DNQ						

POSITION RANKINGS *

PLAYER	POSITION	RANK	SC	SH	RB	AS	BL	ST
Chuck Person	Small Forward	8	7	9	20	14	37	23
LaSalle Thompson	Power Forward, C	11	11	17	6	23	8	14
Vern Fleming	Point Guard	12	12	7	10	22	17	32
Reggie Miller	Off Guard	14	17	5	21	27	12	31
Rik Smits	Center	16	15	12	19	22	8	21
Detlef Schrempf	Small Forward	25	26	22	9	12	31	22
Scott Skiles	Point Guard	29	31	13	20	10	32	25
Stuart Gray	Center	DNQ						
Randy Wittman	Off Guard	DNQ						
Anthony Frederick	Small Forward	DNQ						

*For further definition of each category and column heading see pages 42 & 43.

Indiana Pacers . . . . Team Info

WEEKLY POWER RATING

41 WINS - AVERAGE (See page 43 for Team Power Rating discussion.)

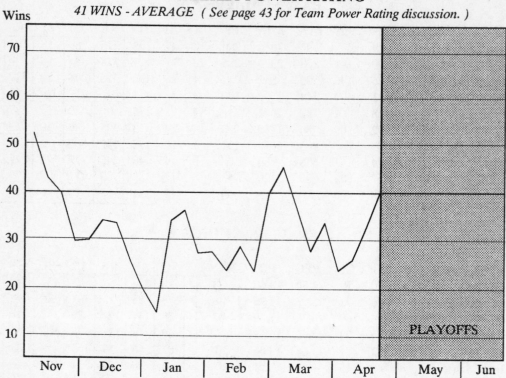

Miscellaneous Categories	Data	Rank
Attendance	469K	22
Key-Man Games Missed	101	18
Season Record	28-54	19
- Home	20-21	20
- Road	8-33	20
Eastern Conference	15-41	20
Western Conference	13-13	18
Overtime Record	3-3	8
Record 5 Pts. or Less	9-13	22
Record 10 Pts. or More	11-25	19
Games Won By Bench	3	16
Games Won By Starters	5	16
Winning Streak	4	17
Losing Streak	12	21
Home Winning Streak	4	22
Road Winning Streak	2	16
Home Losing Streak	4	16
Road Losing Streak	15	21

Performance Categories	Data	Rank
Offensive Scoring (per game)	106.9	15
Defensive Scoring (per game)	111.1	18
Scoring Margin (per game)	-4.2	19
Defensive FG%	.467	6
Offensive 2-point%	.503	8
Offensive 3-point%	.328	10
Offensive Free Throw %	.789	6
Offensive Rebs (Off REB/Opp Def REB)		17
Defensive Rebs (Def REB/Opp Off REB)		17
Offensive Assists (AST/FGMade)		15
Offensive Blocks (BLK/Opp FGAttempted)		16
Offensive Steals (STL/Game)		24
Turnover Margin (Def T.O. - Off T.O.)		25
Fouls Margin (Opp FOULS - FOULS)		17
Rebounding Record	31-50-1	21
Assists Record	41-36-5	11
Field Goal Pct. Record	46-36-0	8
Free Throw Att. Record	24-54-4	23

Indiana Pacers . . . . Team Roster

MOST PRODUCTIVE PLAYERS

Player	Span	Yrs	CRD
Mel Daniels	1969-74	6	12,835
George McGinnis	1972-82	7	11,154
Billy Knight	1975-83	8	10,324
Roger Brown	1968-74	8	10,059
Herb Williams	1982-87	6	9,312
Bob Netolicky	1968-75	8	9,062
Fred Lewis	1968-77	8	8,640
Billy Keller	1970-76	7	8,421
Don Buse	1973-82	7	7,096
Darnell Hillman	1972-77	6	7,070

PRESENT PLAYERS*

J#	VETERANS	COLLEGE	POS	R#	D#	HT	WT	Indi	NBA
54	Greg Dreiling	Kansas	C	2	26	7-1	250	3	3
10	Vern Fleming	Georgia	G	1	18	6-5	195	5	5
22	Anthony Frederick	Pepperdine	F	6	133	6-7	205	1	1
31	Reggie Miller	UCLA	G-F	1	11	6-7	190	2	2
45	Chuck Person	Auburn	F	1	4	6-8	225	3	3
11	Detlef Schrempf	Washington	F-G	1	8	6-10	214	1	4
24	Rick Smits	Marist	C	1	2	7-4	250	1	1
21	Everette Stephens	Purdue	G	2	31	6-3	180	1	1
40	Steve Stipanovich	Missouri	C-F	1	2	7-0	250	5	5
41	LaSalle Thompson	Texas	C-F	1	5	6-10	250	1	7
14	Randy Wittman	Indiana	G	1	22	6-6	210	1	6

FUTURE PLAYERS

ROOKIES	COLLEGE	POS	R#	D#	HT	WT
George McCloud	Florida State	G	1	7	6-6	205
Dyron Nix	Tennessee	F	2	29	6-7	205

* For further definition of category and column headings, see pages 42 & 43.

Indiana Pacers . . . . Overview

Prior to last summer's draft, I was getting all ready to start thinking about what I would write on Indiana when I did this book. I was going to be very encouraging, analyze how they had turned it around, and talk about their new point guard (pg) - the one that would lead them into the 1990's. The best laid plans...

It's not that I have anything against George McCloud (Indiana's first round pick), but he's not a pg and that's what this team needs most! In case anyone has yet to figure it out, the pg has become the single most important position in the NBA, surpassing even the center. But the off-guard position is 4th. Granted, McCloud can play either of the 2-guard or small forward, but either way, Indiana is stocked.

What's bothered me for some time about this club is that they can't seem to balance out their personnel. In 1985, they already had Herb Williams, Clark Kellogg, and Steve Stipanovich. Those are all NBA power forwards - and at the time, pretty good ones. Who did they draft? Wayman Tisdale, of course. What happened? They were last in their division the following season and Tisdale suffocated. The same thing is happening now at the swing position area (shooting guard, small forward). This team already has Chuck Person, Reggie Miller, Detlef Schrempf, and Randy Wittman. What's more, they just traded for Schrempf and Wittman and, believe me, they weren't free. So what's going on?

If the Pacers were being led by John Stockton or Kevin Johnson then I could understand it (of course, if they were, they wouldn't have been picking #7), but Vern Fleming is not the future pg of a good team. In fact, Fleming is more of a 2-guard than a true pg anyway.

Though there are a variety of ways to evaluate what a player's "true" position is (see page 201), the ability to accumulate assists is a major telling statistic for a pg. Fleming ranks #22 in assists per minute among pg's. What's more interesting, however, is that 14 pg's played 2552

minutes (the amount Fleming played) or more last season. The average record of the teams the pg's played on who were in the top-7 in assists of this group was 52-26. The average record of those clubs whose pg's were in the bottom-7 of assists was 33-49. Now, if that's too obscure an analysis for you, let me just summarize by saying that no team is going to win a lot of games with a pg (similar to Fleming) who lacks such basic pg necessities. If you add to this discussion the realities that this draft was the best for pg's in a long time and that Fleming's lone back-up pg, Scott Skiles, was lost in the expansion draft, then it confuses the mind as to why they chose George McCloud instead of Blaylock, Hardaway, Armstrong, or Richardson. Keep your eyes on those pg's in the future.

Now, I guess I'll have to find some other reason to hope for success. We can start with the return of Steve Stipanovich. Stipo has been a very consistent center in the NBA, but like most of the team's players, miscast. He is a true NBA power forward in the Bill Laimbeer mold. He faces the basket well and has a good perimeter jumper. With the opportunity to play the forward position, now that Rik Smits is on board, Stipo could flourish. With monster rebounder (LaSalle Thompson #11) roaming the baseline, Indiana's front line could be pretty decent. Finally, there is some real diversity there which allows for utilizing different strengths for different situations.

Rik Smits had a good rookie season. He led the group in blocked shots, averaged 12 ppg, and was named to the All-Rookie 1st team. Even so, he only led the club in boards 14 times in 82 games - the second lowest ratio among starting centers. Only 42 year-old Kareem Abdul-Jabbar was worse.

Abdul-Jabbar	L.A.L	6/74	.081
Smits	**Indi**	**14/82**	**.171**
Carroll	N.J.	12/64	.188
Cartwright	Chic	16/78	.205
Lister	Seat	18/82	.220

Indiana Pacers . . . . Overview

Indiana's season was rather unusual last year. They began with an abysmal 9-game losing streak and proceeded to ride a roller-coaster from there on out. After their 0-9 start, they actually went 5-5, 0-9, 4-0, 0-5, 2-0, 0-12, 17-14. That adds up to 28-54. If they could have only eliminated those losing streaks!

There was one moment early in the season when it looked as though the club might have finally jelled. During their 4-0 run listed above, they defeated the Hawks, Clippers, Pistons, and Celtics all by an average of 18 ppg. Their next two games were against New Jersey and Miami. If they could have defeated those two - thus winning 6 in a row - then have played 6 of 10 at home, well, who knows? What happened, however, was that the Pacers, though playing in Market Square Arena and leading by 10 at the half, lost to the lowly Nets. The next day, Indiana raced to a staggering 29 point lead over the even lowlier Heat, but managed to lose a heartbreaker in double O.T. Those were devastating losses which initiated a period where the Pacers won only 2 of 19 games. It wasn't until after the trades were made that things changed, but change they did.

In late February, the team sent Wayman Tisdale to Sacramento for LaSalle Thompson and Randy Wittman. At the same time, they traded Herb Williams to Dallas for Detlef Schrempf. Whereas the talent level seemingly improved very little, the club's record improved greatly. Indiana won 17 of their last 31. That's more impressive than you might realize. A total of 41 teams in the 1980's have won 28 or fewer games. Indiana is the only team of the bunch to have a winning record in their last 31 contests. Last year's Sacramento club was second, but a full 5 games below .500.

Indiana	1989	17-14
Sacramento	1989	13-18
Indiana	1984	12-19
Phoenix	1988	12-19
New Jersey	1987	12-19

Because of the radical ups and downs of the season, the club actually had 5 coaches. Only twice has a team even had 4 in the same year. In 1947 (the only year of the franchise), Toronto did it as did Cleveland in 1982. The records of Indiana's coaches were Jack Ramsay (0-7), Mel Daniels/Dave Twardzik (0-2), George Irvine (6-14), and Dick Versace (22-31).

Further complicating matters for Indiana is that they play in the rugged Central Division. The expansion Orlando Magic will be joining the Central this season, so that should offer some relief, but it didn't help last year, as the division won over 60% of its games - 4th best in history.

Midwest	1971	.640
Atlantic	1983	.624
Midwest	1974	.604
Central	**1989**	**.602**
Midwest	1972	.595

Notes: The Pacers ranked last in the NBA in turnover margin (341)... Track star, Florence Joyner, is responsible for the new Pacer uniform design... Indiana tied with Portland for #2 in most fines levied by the league last season at $10,500. Detroit was #1... Though it seems odd as to why, when Chuck Person led the team in rebounding at home, they were 0-10. When anyone else did it, they were 20-11... Indiana ranked a healthy #6 in both ft% and defensive fg%.

Prediction - best case: 44-38

A 17-14 finish, getting Stipanovich back, another year of maturity by a young team, and the addition of the top big guard in the draft, should mean an even bigger increase, however...

Prediction - worst case: 34-48

...Indiana hasn't passed 44 wins in 13 NBA seasons, they don't have a point guard, they play in the league's toughest division, and Bobby Knight wasn't available.

To order back issues of Basketball Heaven or to obtain the 1990 Midseason Report, see page 324.

Los Angeles Clippers . . . . Influence on Winning

TEAM RECORD BY

PLAYER	GAMES	... SCR Leader		... REB Leader		...AST Leader	
		HOME	ROAD	HOME	ROAD	HOME	ROAD
Benoit Benjamin	79	4-5	1-5	10-11	1-7	0-0	0-1
Ken Norman	80	4-7	1-10	6-7	1-14	0-2	2-1
Charles Smith	71	2-5	1-6	1-6	1-4	0-0	1-1
Gary Grant	71	1-2	0-3	0-0	0-0	8-11	1-17
Quintin Dailey	69	5-5	0-7	0-0	0-1	1-0	0-3
Reggie Williams	63	0-0	1-3	0-0	0-0	0-0	0-2
Tom Garrick	71	0-0	0-0	0-0	0-0	3-4	2-6
Joe Wolf	66	0-0	0-0	0-2	1-5	1-0	1-0
Danny Manning	26	1-1	0-5	1-1	1-3	1-2	0-1
Eric White	37	0-0	0-1	0-0	0-0	0-0	0-0

TEAM RECORD BY SCORING *

PLAYER	PLAY	DNP	0-9	10-19	20-29	30-39	40+
Benoit Benjamin	21-58	0-3	1-10	9-35	11-12	0-1	0-0
Ken Norman	21-59	0-2	2-9	7-31	9-15	3-4	0-0
Charles Smith	20-51	1-10	3-10	12-27	4-12	1-2	0-0
Gary Grant	19-52	2-9	7-21	7-24	4-6	1-1	0-0
Quintin Dailey	16-53	5-8	1-15	8-22	6-14	1-2	0-0
Reggie Williams	14-49	7-12	9-24	2-22	3-3	0-0	0-0
Tom Garrick	20-51	1-10	15-36	5-15	0-0	0-0	0-0
Joe Wolf	14-52	7-9	12-42	2-10	0-0	0-0	0-0
Danny Manning	9-17	12-44	2-2	4-7	3-8	0-0	0-0
Eric White	10-27	11-34	10-23	0-3	0-1	0-0	0-0

TEAM RECORD BY STARTING POSITION *

PLAYER	GAMES	STARTS	PG	OG	SF	PF	C
Benoit Benjamin	79	62	0-0	0-0	0-0	0-0	16-46
Ken Norman	80	79	0-0	0-0	1-3	20-55	0-0
Charles Smith	71	56	0-0	0-0	16-37	0-1	1-1
Gary Grant	71	48	13-31	0-4	0-0	0-0	0-0
Quintin Dailey	69	51	0-0	12-38	0-1	0-0	0-0
Reggie Williams	63	17	0-0	5-12	0-0	0-0	0-0
Tom Garrick	71	20	0-8	4-7	0-1	0-0	0-0
Joe Wolf	66	15	0-0	0-0	0-5	1-5	1-3
Danny Manning	26	18	0-0	0-0	4-14	0-0	0-0
Eric White	37	0	0-0	0-0	0-0	0-0	0-0

* For further definition of each category and column heading see pages 42 & 43.

Los Angeles Clippers . . . . 1988-89 Statistics

RAW NUMBERS *

PLAYER	2pt%	3pt%	FT%	MIN	PF	DQ	HI	TO	RB	AS	BL	ST
Benoit Benjamin	**.543**	0-2	.744	2585	221	4	34	237	**696**	157	**221**	57
Ken Norman	.507	.190	.630	**3020**	223	2	**38**	206	667	277	66	106
Charles Smith	.497	0-3	.725	2161	**273**	**6**	33	146	465	103	89	68
Gary Grant	.441	.227	.735	1924	170	1	31	**258**	238	**506**	9	**144**
Quintin Dailey	.468	.111	.759	1722	152	0	36	122	204	154	6	90
Reggie Williams	.469	**.288**	.754	1303	181	1	29	114	179	103	29	81
Tom Garrick	.509	0-13	.803	1499	141	1	17	116	156	243	9	78
Joe Wolf	.433	.143	.688	1450	152	1	17	94	271	113	16	32
Danny Manning	.499	.200	.767	950	89	1	29	93	171	81	25	44
Eric White	.517	0-0	**.810**	436	40	0	24	26	70	17	1	10

OVERALL RANKINGS *

PLAYER	G	GS	PPG	PR	RANK	SC	SH	RB	AS	BL	ST
Benoit Benjamin	79	62	16.44	**21.11**	25	56	30	27	122	8	148
Ken Norman	**80**	**79**	**18.13**	20.34	31	39	114	64	75	64	96
Charles Smith	71	56	16.27	**16.66**	69	57	107	65	147	25	106
Gary Grant	71	48	11.92	**13.70**	104	105	164	120	6	148	3
Quintin Dailey	69	51	16.14	**12.48**	119	59	135	126	80	157	30
Reggie Williams	63	17	10.19	**8.83**	160	124	142	114	89	61	16
Tom Garrick	71	20	6.39	**8.68**	163	168	81	142	37	136	31
Joe Wolf	66	15	5.85	**7.15**	176	171	172	80	91	104	146
Danny Manning	26	18	16.69	**17.58**	DNQ						
Eric White	38	0	4.16	**4.32**	DNQ						

POSITION RANKINGS *

PLAYER	POSITION	RANK	SC	SH	RB	AS	BL	ST
Benoit Benjamin	Center	6	8	7	13	10	7	15
Ken Norman	Power Forward, SF	6	4	24	28	2	19	13
Charles Smith	Small Forward, PF	16	17	25	8	38	4	20
Gary Grant	Point Guard	21	17	29	8	6	18	2
Quintin Dailey	Off Guard	24	16	33	19	28	35	11
Reggie Williams	Off Guard, SF	37	33	36	15	35	4	7
Tom Garrick	Off Guard, PG	39	43	21	27	8	29	12
Joe Wolf	Small Forward, PF	40	40	40	14	19	29	32
Danny Manning	Small Forward, PF	DNQ						
Eric White	Small Forward	DNQ						

*For further definition of each category and column heading see pages 42 & 43.

Los Angeles Clippers .... Team Info

WEEKLY POWER RATING
41 WINS - AVERAGE (See page 43 for Team Power Rating discussion.)

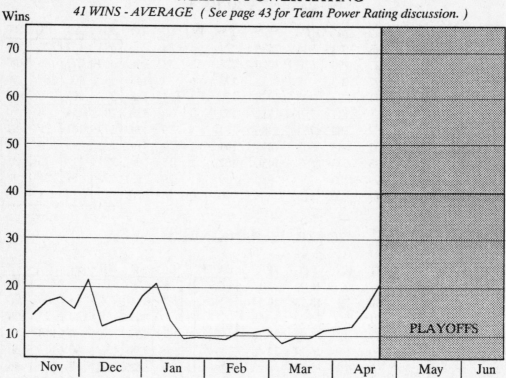

Miscellaneous Categories	Data	Rank
Attendance	451K	24
Key-Man Games Missed	142	23
Season Record	21-61	22
- Home	17-24	22
- Road	4-37	23
Eastern Conference	4-20	24
Western Conference	17-41	23
Overtime Record	2-5	21
Record 5 Pts. or Less	11-11	9
Record 10 Pts. or More	6-39	23
Games Won By Bench	0	25
Games Won By Starters	6	14
Winning Streak	3	20
Losing Streak	19	5
Home Winning Streak	5	20
Road Winning Streak	1	21
Home Losing Streak	8	23
Road Losing Streak	20	24

Performance Categories	Data	Rank
Offensive Scoring (per game)	106.2	18
Defensive Scoring (per game)	116.2	23
Scoring Margin (per game)	-10.0	24
Defensive FG%	.484	14
Offensive 2-point%	.483	16
Offensive 3-point%	.231	23
Offensive Free Throw %	.723	23
Offensive Rebs .....(Off REB/Opp Def REB)		18
Defensive Rebs ....(Def REB/Opp Off REB)		24
Offensive Assists ....(AST/FGMade)		6
Offensive Blocks ..(BLK/Opp FGAttempted)		6
Offensive Steals ....(STL/Game)		8
Turnover Margin........(Def T.O. - Off T.O.)		24
Fouls Margin ....(Opp FOULS - FOULS)		13
Rebounding Record	29-51-2	23
Assists Record	31-49-2	21
Field Goal Pct. Record	37-44-1	14
Free Throw Att. Record	36-41-5	13

Los Angeles Clippers ....Team Roster

MOST PRODUCTIVE PLAYERS

Player	Span	Yrs	CRD
Randy Smith	1972-83	9	12,072
Bob McAdoo	1973-76	5	9,951
Swen Nater	1978-82	6	7,233
Benoit Benjamin	1986-89	4	5,265
Michael Cage	1985-88	4	4,761
Garfield Heard	1974-81	4	4,326
Norm Nixon	1984-89	4	4,101
Jim McMillian	1974-76	3	3,917
Terry Cummings	1983-84	2	3,622
Elmore Smith	1972-73	2	3,515

PRESENT PLAYERS*

J#	VETERANS	COLLEGE	POS	R#	D#	HT	WT	LA.C	NBA
	Ken Bannister	Indiana State	F	7	156	6-9	235	1	3
00	Benoit Benjamin	Creighton	C	1	3	7-0	245	4	4
4	Tom Garrick	Rhode Island	G	2	45	6-2	185	1	1
23	Gary Grant	Michigan	G	1	15	6-3	195	1	1
25	Danny Manning	Kansas	F	1	1	6-10	230	1	1
33	Ken Norman	Illinois	F	1	19	6-8	225	2	2
54	Charles Smith	Pittsburgh	F	1	3	6-10	230	1	1
34	Reggie Williams	Georgetown	G-F	1	4	6-7	180	2	2
24	Joe Wolf	North Carolina	F-C	1	13	6-11	230	2	2

FUTURE PLAYERS

ROOKIES	COLLEGE	POS	R#	D#	HT	WT
Danny Ferry	Duke	F	1	2	6-10	230
Jeff Martin	Murray State	F	2	31	6-6	205
Jay Edwards	Indiana	G	2	33	6-4	180

* For further definition of category and column headings, see pages 42 & 43.

Los Angeles Clippers .... Overview

Whenever I write these team overviews, I always try to reveal as many subtle, yet meaningful, insights into a team's performance as I can. I'm trying to find out why they succeeded or failed as well as predict how they might do in the future. There's rarely a club so inept that almost nothing of statistical interest can be derived from its previous season. If ever a team pushed my creative limit, it's got to be the Clippers.

One of the primary problems with LA is that the team is just loaded with young players. In fact, it's interesting to note that, heading into last season, the club with the least pro experience was not the expansion Heat or Hornets, but rather the Clippers. Because of this, the players on the team had very little history in the league. That forces anyone talking about this group to concentrate on college careers and college statistics. So, it's probably an appropriate time to make the point that college stats don't mean diddly squat to me. Oh, sure, they are important to evaluate a player prior to drafting him, but even then you better know the level of his competition and the style of ball his team played. But once the Star Spangled Banner is sung and his first pro game has tipped off, whatever he did in college is meaningless.

A perfect example on the Clippers is Reggie Williams. Here is a guy who played on two final-four teams, averaged 24 ppg as a senior at Georgetown, played under a tough coach noted for teaching defense and mental intensity, was runner-up as national Player-of-the-Year, and was drafted #4. Considered a "can't miss" player, he all but has. After two years in the big leagues, Williams has a career scoring average of just 10.3 ppg while shooting a mere 40.4% from the field. His attitude was so bad that he was suspended the final 3 contests for refusing to enter the game when called upon. Maybe he'll turn it around. I hope so. But either I have to say that what he did in college is irrelevant to the NBA or else I have to conclude - as I suggested in last season's worst-case prediction - that

Memorial Arena has something in the air which just kills good players. That latter option is a real possibility also.

After Danny Manning, Memorial Arena's latest victim, tore up his knee early in the season, the frustration on the club hit an all-time high. Manning, who had the third best Production Rating among rookies, was just beginning to contribute. Danny missed the first 4 games of the season, but played well in the 26 which followed. In fact, in the 9 games prior to his injury, he was scoring 21 points per outing. It's true that the team was only 10-19 when he went down, but compare that to 11-42 when he didn't get up.

It's difficult to say what needs to happen to turn the franchise around. Last year's rookies Manning, Charles Smith, and Gary Grant are not used to losing and shouldn't take it casually. Neither is Danny Ferry - the closest thing to Bird since Larry and the #2 choice in the draft. Ferry split most Player-of-the-Year awards with Sean Elliott and is considered by most experts as a franchise player. But so was Manning, and, although he played well, the team was still a relatively poor club when he was out there.

Now, for the annual pathetic news that usually greets this organization. In early August, Ferry decided to spend his first year in Europe. This is obviously a power play on his part as he doesn't want to play with the Clippers. As fans, we got screwed. As for the Clippers, they probably deserved it. Choosing Ferry (forward) in the draft when they desperately needed a replacement for Williams at off-guard, was rediculous - unless they planned on trading him. Ferry left because he was convinced no trade was imminent. I would have taken Elliott in the draft. That's easy to say now, but I said it before he left the country too. My guess is that LA will have to trade Ferry to get the 2-guard they need. Theoretically, they could trade him to another team who could buy out his foreign contract allowing him to play now.

Los Angeles Clippers .... Overview

What I recommend is that they trade Ferry and Williams for a proven NBA shooting guard plus something in the draft. In fact, I'm going to go ahead and reveal (for free) my idea of what the Clippers should do. Remember, I think they should move Ferry and Williams for one of the following.

Team	Player	Draft Picks
Dallas	Blackman	#1-1990, #1-1991
Denver	Lever	#1-1990, #2-1991
Milwaukee	Robertson	#1-1990, #2-1991
Sacramento	Ainge	#1-1990, #2-1991
Washington	Malone	#1-1990, #2-1991

Any of those trades would seem reasonable to me. In each case the Clippers would be acquiring a proven NBA off-guard, though each possesses different skills. In terms of leadership, Blackman would be superior, range - Ainge, pure shooting - Malone, defense - Robertson, and versatility - Lever. LA would also have a couple future draft picks. The teams in question could all use another Larry Bird and a player with Williams' potential to help fill the void left by their star guard's departure. On the other hand, the Clippers could just keep Williams and the rights to Ferry and let the chips fall where they may. The problem with this franchise is that the chips have been falling for a long time.

The club's other 2-guard is Quintin Dailey, who started 51 games. Dailey's 46.5% "shoot first, ask questions later" approach didn't win too many games. Add to that his very limited range and you can see why they need someone else.

At point guard, Gary Grant came along well as a playmaker, but his shooting was, at times, suspect. A lot will be learned this season about his ability to lead the team.

I probably should mention Jay Edwards of Indiana - the Clippers' second pick. It's true that he is a shooting guard. And yes, it's true that he was a top player in the Big-10 last season as well. But it's not true that he's going to step in and help. Not only is he coming out of school early, but he's had

academic problems, drug problems, and law problems. If he contributes at all, it will likely be several years from now.

Beyond everything else on this team, it has one of the potentially best centers (from the neck down) in the league. If Benoit Benjamin can continue to play the rest of his career like he did the final 19 games of the season (and if a bird dog could fly), this team will be NBA Champs. Shown below are his stats with respect to the league's top-5 centers from March 13th on. You'll notice that he was #3 with a very high Production Rating, and an even better #2 in rebounding per game, blocks per game, and field goal percentage.

	PR	RPG	BPG	FG%
Olajuwon	34.1	13.9	4.3	.512
Ewing	30.5	10.9	3.7	.579
Benjamin	**29.7**	**11.7**	**3.9**	**.575**
Malone	23.6	11.4	1.7	.477
Parish	23.2	11.6	1.5	.565
Daugherty	23.1	9.7	.5	.521

Notes: the Clippers were 11-7 in games decided by 4 points or less, but 1-33 in games with a margin of 15 or more... Gary Grant led all rookies in steals and assists on a per-minute basis... Los Angeles ended up last in victories during the 1980's, averaging 25 per season - 6 fewer than Indiana.

Prediction - best case: 38-44

The talent on this club is embarrassingly good. If Manning is healthy, with or without a Ferry trade, and in spite of themselves, they just about have to improve.

Prediction - worst case: 25-57

Don't ask me to explain how they would manage to be this bad, but I've long since learned not to underestimate this team's ability to lose. If they do only win 25 games next season, the league office should remove their license and everyone from Elgin Baylor on down should be fired!

To order back issues of Basketball Heaven or to obtain the 1990 Mid-season Report, see page 324.

Los Angeles Lakers . . . . Influence on Winning

TEAM RECORD BY

PLAYER	GAMES	... SCR Leader		... REB Leader		...AST Leader	
		HOME	ROAD	HOME	ROAD	HOME	ROAD
Earvin Johnson	77	17-4	7-10	10-2	8-4	34-5	20-18
James Worthy	81	4-4	5-7	2-2	2-2	0-0	1-0
A.C. Green	82	2-0	3-1	19-2	10-10	0-0	0-0
Byron Scott	74	10-0	5-3	0-0	0-0	0-0	0-0
Mychal Thompson	80	1-0	0-0	4-0	4-3	0-0	0-0
K. Abdul-Jabbar	74	1-0	0-0	4-0	1-1	0-0	0-0
Michael Cooper	80	1-0	0-0	0-0	0-0	2-1	2-1
Orlando Woolridge	74	1-0	1-0	0-1	0-0	0-0	0-0
Tony Campbell	63	1-0	1-0	0-0	1-0	0-0	0-0
David Rivers	47	0-0	0-0	0-0	0-0	0-0	0-0

TEAM RECORD BY SCORING *

PLAYER	PLAY	DNP	0-9	10-19	20-29	30-39	40+
Earvin Johnson	54-23	3-2	2-0	16-8	27-12	8-3	1-0
James Worthy	56-25	1-0	4-1	21-10	29-11	2-3	0-0
A.C. Green	57-25	0-0	15-9	33-13	8-3	1-0	0-0
Byron Scott	51-23	6-2	0-6	19-13	24-4	8-0	0-0
Mychal Thompson	56-24	1-1	33-15	20-8	3-1	0-0	0-0
K. Abdul-Jabbar	50-24	7-1	21-13	28-10	1-1	0-0	0-0
Michael Cooper	55-25	2-0	33-23	22-22	0-0	0-0	0-0
Orlando Woolridge	52-22	5-3	24-15	24-7	4-0	0-0	0-0
Tony Campbell	44-19	13-6	32-15	12-4	0-0	0-0	0-0
David Rivers	38-9	19-16	36-9	2-0	0-0	0-0	0-0

TEAM RECORD BY STARTING POSITION *

PLAYER	GAMES	STARTS	PG	OG	SF	PF	C
Earvin Johnson	77	77	54-23	0-0	0-0	0-0	0-0
James Worthy	81	81	0-0	0-0	56-25	0-0	0-0
A.C. Green	82	82	0-0	0-0	0-0	57-25	0-0
Byron Scott	74	73	0-0	51-22	0-0	0-0	0-0
Mychal Thompson	80	8	0-0	0-0	0-0	0-0	7-1
K. Abdul-Jabbar	74	74	0-0	0-0	0-0	0-0	50-24
Michael Cooper	80	13	3-2	5-2	1-0	0-0	0-0
Orlando Woolridge	74	0	0-0	0-0	0-0	0-0	0-0
Tony Campbell	63	2	0-0	1-1	0-0	0-0	0-0
David Rivers	47	0	0-0	0-0	0-0	0-0	0-0

* For further definition of each category and column heading see pages 42 & 43.

Los Angeles Lakers . . . . 1988-89 Statistics

RAW NUMBERS *

PLAYER	2pt%	3pt%	FT%	MIN	PF	DQ	HI	TO	RB	AS	BL	ST
Earvin Johnson	.548	.314	**.911**	2886	172	0	**40**	312	607	**988**	22	**138**
James Worthy	.556	.087	.782	**2960**	175	0	38	182	489	288	56	108
A.C. Green	.536	.235	.786	2510	172	0	33	119	**739**	103	55	94
Byron Scott	.508	**.399**	.863	2605	181	1	35	157	302	231	27	114
Mychal Thompson	**.560**	0-1	.678	1994	**224**	0	27	97	467	48	59	58
K. Abdul-Jabbar	.477	0-3	.739	1695	196	1	21	95	334	74	**85**	38
Michael Cooper	.468	.381	.871	1943	186	0	18	94	191	314	32	72
Orlando Woolridge	.469	0-1	.738	1491	130	0	29	103	270	58	65	30
Tony Campbell	.481	.095	.843	787	108	0	19	62	130	47	6	37
David Rivers	.414	.167	.833	440	50	0	10	61	43	106	9	23

OVERALL RANKINGS *

PLAYER	G	GS	PPG	PR	RANK	SC	SH	RB	AS	BL	ST
Earvin Johnson	77	77	**22.47**	33.31	2	15	4	70	3	124	41
James Worthy	81	81	20.46	**21.80**	21	21	16	93	70	74	87
A.C. Green	**82**	**82**	13.27	18.61	42	89	29	15	154	63	82
Byron Scott	74	73	19.57	17.89	50	27	27	130	81	106	56
Mychal Thompson	80	8	9.22	12.11	124	137	32	51	172	46	113
K. Abdul-Jabbar	74	74	10.11	10.74	136	126	131	78	151	14	141
Michael Cooper	80	13	7.34	10.11	147	156	37	145	39	83	84
Orlando Woolridge	74	0	9.66	9.22	157	130	133	85	157	20	156
Tony Campbell	63	2	6.16	5.49	DNQ						
David Rivers	47	0	2.85	3.70	DNQ						

POSITION RANKINGS *

PLAYER	POSITION	RANK	SC	SH	RB	AS	BL	ST
Earvin Johnson	Point Guard	1	1	2	1	3	9	15
James Worthy	Small Forward	4	9	2	22	11	19	16
A.C. Green	Power Forward	7	13	4	8	21	18	10
Byron Scott	Off Guard	9	9	9	20	29	15	20
Mychal Thompson	Center, PF	21	20	8	26	26	23	7
K. Abdul-Jabbar	Center	22	18	20	30	17	11	13
Michael Cooper	Off Guard, PG	35	42	11	29	10	8	29
Orlando Woolridge	Small Forward	36	30	32	19	40	2	37
Tony Campbell	Small Forward, OG	DNQ						
David Rivers	Point Guard	DNQ						

*For further definition of each category and column heading see pages 42 & 43.

Los Angeles Lakers .... Team Info

WEEKLY POWER RATING
41 WINS - AVERAGE (See page 43 for Team Power Rating discussion.)

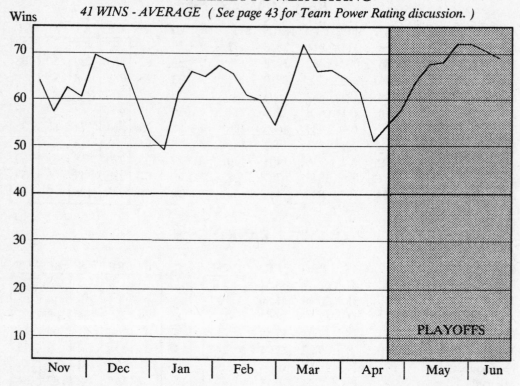

Miscellaneous Categories	Data	Rank
Attendance	717K	6
Key-Man Games Missed	26	4
Season Record	57-25	2
- Home	35-6	3
- Road	22-19	2
Eastern Conference	14-10	5
Western Conference	43-15	3
Overtime Record	2-2	8
Record 5 Pts. or Less	13-11	6
Record 10 Pts. or More	35-10	2
Games Won By Bench	6	9
Games Won By Starters	17	3
Winning Streak	7	7
Losing Streak	4	7
Home Winning Streak	17	6
Road Winning Streak	5	3
Home Losing Streak	2	5
Road Losing Streak	8	12

Performance Categories	Data	Rank
Offensive Scoring (per game)	114.7	5
Defensive Scoring (per game)	107.5	8
Scoring Margin (per game)	7.2	3
Defensive FG%	.470	9
Offensive 2-point%	.518	1
Offensive 3-point%	.340	5
Offensive Free Throw %	.802	2
Offensive Rebs ..... (Off REB/Opp Def REB)		12
Defensive Rebs .... (Def REB/Opp Off REB)		6
Offensive Assists .... (AST/FGMade)		5
Offensive Blocks .. (BLK/Opp FGAttempted)		17
Offensive Steals .... (STL/Game)		14
Turnover Margin .... (Def T.O. - Off T.O.)		17
Fouls Margin .... (Opp FOULS - FOULS)		2
Rebounding Record	48-31-3	5
Assists Record	47-29-6	3
Field Goal Pct. Record	53-28-1	3
Free Throw Att. Record	59-22-1	2

Los Angeles Lakers ....Team Roster

MOST PRODUCTIVE PLAYERS

Player	Span	Yrs	CRD
Kareem Abdul-Jabbar.....	1976-89	14	29,626
Elgin Baylor......................	1959-72	14	25,156
Jerry West	1961-73	13	25,149
Earvin Johnson.................	1980-89	10	21,027
George Mikan	1948-56	9	12,796
Vern Mikkelsen................	1950-59	10	12,044
Gail Goodrich	1966-76	9	11,368
Wilt Chamberlain.............	1969-73	5	11,031
James Worthy...................	1983-89	7	10,614
Rudy LaRusso..................	1960-67	8	10,319

PRESENT PLAYERS*

J#	VETERANS	COLLEGE	POS	R#	D#	HT	WT	LA.L	NBA
19	Tony Campbell	Ohio State........................	F	1	20	6-7	215	2	5
21	Michael Cooper.............	New Mexico State	G-F	3	60	6-7	176	11	11
45	A.C. Green.....................	Oregon State	F	1	23	6-9	224	4	4
32	Earvin Johnson	Michigan State	G	1	1	6-9	220	10	10
3	Jeff Lamp	Virginia	G	1	15	6-6	205	2	6
31	Mark McNamara...........	California	C	1	22	6-11	235	1	6
4	Byron Scott	Arizona State	G	1	4	6-4	193	6	6
43	Mychal Thompson	Minnesota	F-C	1	1	6-10	235	3	10
0	Orlando Woolridge.......	Notre Dame	F	1	6	6-9	215	1	8
42	James Worthy	North Carolina..............	F	1	1	6-9	235	7	7

FUTURE PLAYERS

ROOKIES	COLLEGE	POS	R#	D#	HT	WT
Vlade Divac	Yugoslavia	F-C	1	26	6-11	243

* For further definition of category and column headings, see pages 42 & 43.

Los Angeles Lakers . . . . Overview

Though Pat Riley was gagged after the Lakers' 1988 championship - symbolically preventing him from guaranteeing a third in a row - he was able to set the theme for the 1988-89 season as "we've only just begun". Supposedly, what was to come was the swan song for 42-year old Kareem Abdul-Jabbar, to "threepeat", to establish a place in immortality with 6 championships in the decade and to enter the 1990's with new goals and new visions. Call it luck, fate, mother nature or father time, but whatever you call it, the Lakers became just another good team when Byron Scott and Magic Johnson fell to injuries in the finals against the Pistons. When just days before all of tinseltown, nay all the world, had waited in anticipation of Kareem's final act, we now watched painfully as the gun sounded and a new king was crowned. There was no escaping the irony that such a spectacular career in the NBA had ended in such a commonplace and uneventful manner. The "white lace and promises" quietly turned brown and broken.

What was left behind, however, was a list of accomplishments far too long to print. Most importantly, Kareem was voted league MVP 6 times and won 6 championships. His pairing with Magic Johnson will long be remembered as one of the great 1-2 punches of all-time. Together they won 5 titles in the 1980's and led this team to a place in history which puts it among the greatest dynasties in any sport.

Boston Celtics	9	1960's	Basketball
New York Yankees	6	1950's	Baseball
Montreal Canadians	6	1970's	Hockey
Green Bay Packers	6	1960's	Football
Los Angeles Lakers	**5**	**1980's**	**Basketball**

Though there will surely be other dynasties - even in the NBA - it's hard to imagine any team again winning 5 championships in a decade. The fact that the Lakers did it against so many teams is all the more impressive and why, as there is more and more competition, the feat will become harder and harder.

Now that Methuselah has walked into the sunset and we've all gotten over feeling a little bit older, it's time to look at LA's lineup. Even without Jabbar, the Lakers are among the top-5 oldest clubs. Based on the most likely top-7 players, the average age of the Lakers as the season tips off will be closing in on 29 years. Only Denver, Milwaukee, Boston, and yes, Detroit will be older.

The most urgent need on draft day was a center to replace Kareem. LA was very fortunate to obtain Vlade Divak from Yugoslavia. Picking 26th, Divac was still available to L.A. As the best center in the draft, that is unheard of. Doubtless, his lack of skill in the English language and unfamiliarity with American customs made him a riskier proposition then most, but if any team can make him feel at home, it's the Lakers. There's everything else in southern California, surely there's a "little Yugoslavia". Divac is still only 21, capable of getting better, and fortunate enough to play with the master at making players better - Magic Johnson.

Johnson became the first guard in history to win two regular season MVP's as he took the crown from Michael Jordan last season. Magic became the second player to shoot 90%+ from the line and 50%+ from the field. Larry Bird had done it twice before and Mark Price also did it in 1989. His accuracy from the line resulted in his winning the free throw shooting crown (91.8%). That, as well as his leadership offensively, helped the team rank #1 in overall shooting. Additionally, Johnson ranked #2 in assists/games, #2 in Production Rating and ranked first among point guards in both scoring and rebounding. Who could ask for anything more?

There really is no reason to think the Lakers can't challenge again. Besides Magic playing at MVP levels, the rest of the remaining starters all experienced highs last season. Both A.C. Green and James Worthy had career high Production Ratings, while Byron Scott and Worthy

Los Angeles Lakers . . . . Overview

both had playoff scoring highs. Even the 34-year old Mychal Thompson, who is likely to be the team's starting center, has helped LA to a regular-season winning percentage of 74% during his brief two and one half years. And in case you think the Lakers are slipping, LA *only* won 71% of their games in the 1980's *before* Thompson arrived.

There is no doubt that the keys to another championship (beyond the obvious - Magic's knees) lie with Byron Scott and James Worthy. If those two consistently play the style of ball that fits with Magic, they'll win again. But that's not as easy as it sounds. What it will require is more participation by Scott and perhaps (as strange as it sounds) less by Worthy. When the team depended too heavily on James, it meant other parts of the game were not working well. When Worthy took 15+ field goal attempts, they were 26-21, but when he shot less, they were an astonishing 30-4. The same principle was true in the playoffs where they went 4-4 when he put it up 18 or more times, but 7-0 when he didn't. Oddly, however, Scott's legacy was just the opposite. When he scored 18 or more points, the club was 39-5!

From a statistical point of view, Scott may be more isolated by virtue of the fact that he's the only returning Laker who fouled out of a game last season. His lone disqualification and the one Kareem received were a combined lower total than any team has ever had.

Los Angeles	1989	2
Washington	1987	5
Los Angeles	1972	7
Los Angeles	1985	7
Los Angeles	1986	8
Houston	1981	8

The bench will primarily consist of Divac, Michael Cooper, and Orlando Woolridge. Cooper is entering his 11th year, but played well as Magic's replacement in the finals. Incredibly, he only had 2 turnovers in 4 games while playing over 40 minutes per contest and racking up 27 assists.

Woolridge also showed signs of being valuable in last season's playoff sweep of Phoenix. He averaged 11 points, 6 rebounds, and 2 blocks. Additionally, he was #1 in the league in the ratio of free throw attempts to field goal attempts, meaning he likes to take it to the hole. Nevertheless, he's oftentimes inconsistent and holds the dubious distinction of seeing each team he's been traded to drop in wins the year he arrived.

Pat Riley continues to be the winningest coach in history despite not coming close to being named Coach-of-the-Year. Furthermore, he never will win it with Magic on the team. However, he would win Coach-of-the-Decade hands down - at least if the criterion were wins during the 1980's.

Pat Riley	527
Don Nelson	474
Bill Fitch	458
John MacLeod	433
Doug Moe	389

Notes: The Lakers were a record 11-0 in the playoffs before the finals... The club ranked a relatively low #17 in blocks and turnover margin... When Los Angeles shot 50% or better, they almost never lost (42-2)... LA was 61-19-2 in quarter #1. That was tops in the NBA and well ahead of #2 Detroit (53-26-3).

Prediction - best case: 62-20

There's no doubt about it. It will take a perfect season by everyone and a real contribution by Divac, but the talent and experience are there. Maybe Riley will call this season "Five more in the 90's."

Prediction - worst case: 52-20

Magic will not let this team slip to 52 wins unless, for some reason, he's unable to play. The worst case depends on how many games he misses. It's easy to figure. When he plays they win 75% of the time and when he doesn't, they win half.

To order back issues of Basketball Heaven or to obtain the 1990 Midseason Report, see page 324.

Miami Heat . . . . Influence on Winning

TEAM RECORD BY

PLAYER	GAMES	... SCR Leader		... REB Leader		...AST Leader	
		HOME	ROAD	HOME	ROAD	HOME	ROAD
Billy Thompson	79	0-6	1-2	3-14	0-8	0-3	0-2
Grant Long	82	2-3	2-8	6-2	2-12	0-0	0-0
Rory Sparrow	80	3-4	1-7	0-1	0-1	5-13	3-20
Kevin Edwards	79	2-4	1-10	1-1	0-1	4-5	0-13
Ron Seikaly	78	0-5	0-6	2-10	1-10	0-0	0-0
Jon Sundvold	68	3-5	0-1	0-0	0-0	0-2	0-2
Sylvester Gray	55	0-0	0-3	1-3	0-4	0-4	0-1
Dwayne Washington	54	1-2	0-1	0-1	0-1	3-6	0-5
Scott Hastings	75	0-1	0-0	0-2	0-3	0-0	0-0
John Shasky	65	0-1	0-0	1-1	0-2	0-0	0-0

TEAM RECORD BY SCORING *

PLAYER	PLAY	DNP	0-9	10-19	20-29	30-39	40+
Billy Thompson	14-65	1-2	6-29	8-32	0-3	0-1	0-0
Grant Long	15-67	0-0	4-26	7-37	2-4	2-0	0-0
Rory Sparrow	16-66	1-1	4-23	5-36	5-7	0-0	0-0
Kevin Edwards	14-65	1-2	2-21	7-31	5-12	0-1	0-0
Ron Seikaly	15-63	0-4	7-29	8-26	0-7	0-1	0-0
Jon Sundvold	13-55	2-12	5-29	5-22	3-4	0-0	0-0
Sylvester Gray	10-45	5-22	7-30	3-14	0-1	0-0	0-0
Dwayne Washington	12-42	3-25	9-28	2-14	1-0	0-0	0-0
Scott Hastings	14-61	1-6	11-50	3-11	0-0	0-0	0-0
John Shasky	11-54	4-13	10-45	1-9	0-0	0-0	0-0

TEAM RECORD BY STARTING POSITION *

PLAYER	GAMES	STARTS	PG	OG	SF	PF	C
Billy Thompson	79	58	0-0	0-0	11-47	0-0	0-0
Grant Long	82	73	0-0	0-0	3-6	12-52	0-0
Rory Sparrow	80	79	13-58	1-7	0-0	0-0	0-0
Kevin Edwards	79	62	0-0	14-48	0-0	0-0	0-0
Ron Seikaly	78	62	0-0	0-0	0-0	0-0	10-52
Jon Sundvold	68	8	1-7	0-0	0-0	0-0	0-0
Sylvester Gray	55	15	0-0	0-0	1-14	0-0	0-0
Dwayne Washington	54	8	1-2	0-5	0-0	0-0	0-0
Scott Hastings	75	6	0-0	0-0	0-0	0-0	1-5
John Shasky	65	4	0-0	0-0	0-0	1-2	0-1

* For further definition of each category and column heading see pages 42 & 43.

Miami Heat .... 1988-89 Statistics

RAW NUMBERS *

PLAYER	2pt%	3pt%	FT%	MIN	PF	DQ	HI	TO	RB	AS	BL	ST
Billy Thompson	.490	0-4	.696	2273	260	8	30	189	**572**	176	**105**	56
Grant Long	.489	0-5	.749	2435	**337**	**13**	30	201	546	149	48	122
Rory Sparrow	.469	.243	**.879**	**2613**	168	0	29	204	216	**429**	17	103
Kevin Edwards	.431	.270	.746	2349	154	0	**34**	**246**	262	349	27	**139**
Ron Seikaly	.449	.250	.511	1962	258	8	30	200	549	55	96	46
Jon Sundvold	.444	**.522**	.825	1338	78	0	28	87	87	137	1	27
Sylvester Gray	.421	.250	.673	1220	144	1	25	102	286	117	25	36
Dwayne Washington	.437	.071	.788	1065	101	0	21	122	123	226	4	73
Scott Hastings	.447	.321	.850	1206	203	5	17	68	231	59	42	32
John Shasky	**.492**	0-2	.689	944	94	0	19	46	232	22	13	14

OVERALL RANKINGS *

PLAYER	G	GS	PPG	PR	RANK	SC	SH	RB	AS	BL	ST
Billy Thompson	79	58	10.81	**14.42**	97	117	126	35	92	19	132
Grant Long	**82**	73	11.90	**14.41**	98	106	110	59	120	70	36
Rory Sparrow	80	**79**	12.50	**12.62**	117	98	138	164	36	134	73
Kevin Edwards	79	62	**13.85**	**11.91**	125	80	169	133	43	101	19
Ron Seikaly	78	62	10.87	**10.38**	141	116	175	21	168	16	135
Jon Sundvold	68	8	10.43	**7.29**	175	119	101	174	64	176	155
Sylvester Gray	55	15	8.00	**9.45**	DNQ						
Dwayne Washington	54	8	7.61	**8.70**	DNQ						
Scott Hastings	75	6	5.15	**6.41**	DNQ						
John Shasky	65	4	5.49	**6.35**	DNQ						

POSITION RANKINGS *

PLAYER	POSITION	RANK	SC	SH	RB	AS	BL	ST
Billy Thompson	Small Forward, PF	24	28	30	2	20	1	28
Grant Long	Power Forward, SF	22	18	22	25	9	23	1
Rory Sparrow	Point Guard, OG	23	15	23	26	29	14	26
Kevin Edwards	Off Guard	27	24	43	22	13	11	8
Ron Seikaly	Center	25	16	29	10	25	12	11
Jon Sundvold	Point Guard, OG	33	21	17	31	33	33	33
Sylvester Gray	Small Forward	DNQ						
Dwayne Washington	Off Guard, PG	DNQ						
Scott Hastings	Center	DNQ						
John Shasky	Center	DNQ						

*For further definition of each category and column heading see pages 42 & 43.

Miami Heat .... Team Info

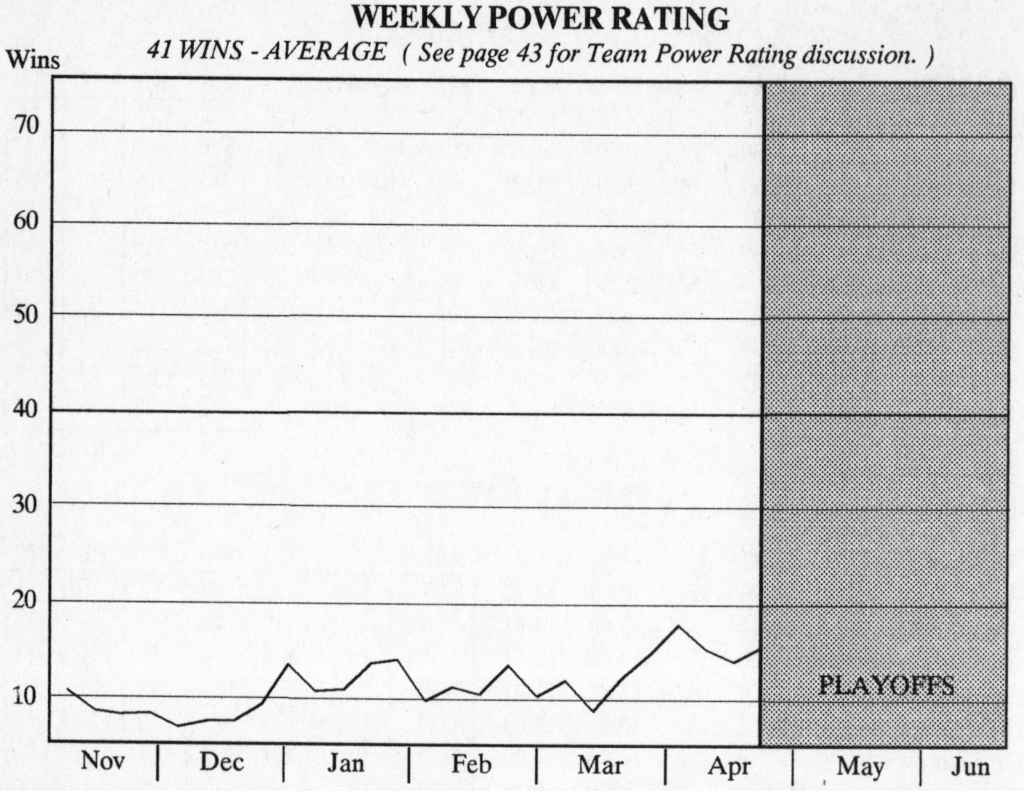
WEEKLY POWER RATING
41 WINS - AVERAGE (See page 43 for Team Power Rating discussion.)
Wins
70
60
50
40
30
20
10
PLAYOFFS
Nov
Dec
Jan
Feb
Mar
Apr
May
Jun

Miscellaneous Categories	Data	Rank
Attendance	613K	12
Key-Man Games Missed	107	20
Season Record	15-67	25
- Home	12-29	24
- Road	3-38	24
Eastern Conference	5-19	23
Western Conference	10-48	25
Overtime Record	3-2	7
Record 5 Pts. or Less	10-11	16
Record 10 Pts. or More	3-39	25
Games Won By Bench	2	23
Games Won By Starters	1	23
Winning Streak	3	20
Losing Streak	17	24
Home Winning Streak	3	25
Road Winning Streak	1	21
Home Losing Streak	11	24
Road Losing Streak	18	23

Performance Categories	Data	Rank
Offensive Scoring (per game)	97.8	25
Defensive Scoring (per game)	109.0	11
Scoring Margin (per game)	-11.2	25
Defensive FG%	.488	18
Offensive 2-point%	.458	25
Offensive 3-point%	.326	12
Offensive Free Throw %	.702	24
Offensive Rebs (Off REB/Opp Def REB)		5
Defensive Rebs (Def REB/Opp Off REB)		20
Offensive Assists (AST/FGMade)		9
Offensive Blocks (BLK/Opp FGAttempted)		12
Offensive Steals (STL/Game)		13
Turnover Margin (Def T.O. - Off T.O.)		22
Fouls Margin (Opp FOULS - FOULS)		25
Rebounding Record	39-40-3	15
Assists Record	34-45-3	19
Field Goal Pct. Record	30-52-0	23
Free Throw Att. Record	21-60-1	25

Miami Heat ....Team Roster

MOST PRODUCTIVE PLAYERS

Player	Span	Yrs	CRD
Grant Long	1989	1	1,182
Billy Thompson	1989	1	1,139
Rory Sparrow	1989	1	1,010
Kevin Edwards	1989	1	941
Ron Seikaly	1989	1	810
Sylvester Gray	1989	1	520
Jon Sundvold	1989	1	496
Scott Hastings	1989	1	481
Dwayne Washington	1989	1	470
John Shasky	1989	1	413

PRESENT PLAYERS*

J#	VETERANS	COLLEGE	POS	R#	D#	HT	WT	Miam	NBA
42	Pat Cummings	Cincinnati	F	3	59	6-9	245	1	10
21	Kevin Edwards	DePaul	G	1	20	6-3	190	1	1
40	Sylvester Gray	Memphis State	F	2	35	6-6	240	1	1
43	Grant Long	Eastern Michigan	F	2	33	6-8	230	1	1
11	Craig Neal	Georgia Tech	G	3	71	6-5	180	1	1
41	Dave Popson	North Carolina	C-F	4	87	6-10	220	1	1
4	Ron Seikaly	Syracuse	C-F	1	9	6-11	240	1	1
45	John Shasky	Minnesota	C	3	61	6-11	240	1	1
2	Rory Sparrow	Villanova	G	4	75	6-2	175	1	9
20	Jon Sundvold	Missouri	G	1	16	6-2	170	1	6
55	Billy Thompson	Louisville	F	1	19	6-7	210	1	3

FUTURE PLAYERS

ROOKIES	COLLEGE	POS	R#	D#	HT	WT
Glen Rice	Michigan	G	1	4	6-7	215
Sherman Douglas	Syracuse	G	2	28	6-0	180
Scott Haffner	Evansville	G	2	45	6-4	180

* For further definition of category and column headings, see pages 42 & 43.

Miami Heat .... Overview

What can you say about a team that only shot 45.3% from the field (last), scored but 97.8 points per game (last), and got beat by over 11 points per contest (last)? Where is the silver lining in losing the first 17 outings of the season or ending up winning a mere 15 games? Ron Rothstein may have felt a little like Paul "HELP - I need somebody" McCartney when draft day came.

Glen Rice was "not just anybody" either. Fortunately for Miami, the Heat were able to get a player that any team in the NBA would love to have. Rice is a big-time scorer who is also a winner. Quite often, you'll see a gunner who can fill it up, but for whatever reason, the team suffers. On the other hand, there are scorers that score within the framework of the system and thus contribute to their to club's success. Those players are like gold, and Rice appears to be the man with the golden gun.

Not only did he lead the Big-10 with a 25.6 point per game average last season, but he set an all-time NCAA record of 184 points in the post-season tournament. Every one of them mattered, as his Michigan club barely nipped Seton Hall in the championship game. Rice shot an astonishing 58% from the field - including 52% from 3-point range. He's truly a great shooter who, just for good measure, will dazzle you with his spectacular dunks. Though you never can tell with rookies, he should be a lock as an All-Rookie first-teamer and, along with Stacey King, appears to be the most likely Rookie-of-the-Year. That wouldn't be unheard of as 3 of the previous 11 expansion teams have had the Rookie-of-the-Year in year #2.

Also part of the calvary is Sherman Douglass. After replacing Pearl Washington at Syracuse, he may do the same at Miami. Despite becoming the NCAA's all-time assist leader, accumulating huge numbers, Douglas scored 18+ points per contest as well for the Orangemen. And even though there are similarities to Washington, Douglas plays a smarter floor game and should be a better pro.

The final knight in shining armor is Scott Haffner of Evansville. The first thing fans are going to want to know about this guy is that he scored 65 points in one game last season versus Dayton. Furthermore, he hit his 3-pointers at a very respectable 46% clip as well as making over 90% of his freebies. He's not real quick, but he's smart (Academic All-American) and he knows when to take the shot.

Miami did a pretty good job with this draft, and should improve their record next season. Three of the 11 previous expansion clubs won 15 games - the same as Miami. It's true that those four are the lowest of the 13 (including Charlotte), but it's also true that the previous three gained over 14 victories in year #2. Perhaps the same will happen to the Heat.

That should be good news to Rothstein. But what else should be good to hear is that the average stay for the beginning coach of an expansion team is 3.32 years. Now, that may not seem very long, but compared to the NBA as a whole, it is. Over 40 years, the average length of a coaching stay is only 2.25 seasons. The best news of all, though, is that the average tenure for the first coach for the 3 previous 15-win clubs is 6.3 years. Finally! The formula for holding on to one's job in the NBA coaching ranks has been found. Take over an expansion club and lose big in year #1 while you take your time building. Actually, that's not a bad formula for coach *or* team.

As I mentioned earlier, Miami ranked last in scoring during the 1988-89 season. Since 1957, only the 1977 Nets (95.9) and the 1983 Cavaliers (97.1) have scored lower. This, despite the fact that the club ranked a very good #5 in offensive boards. The problem was that, although three players had over 200 offensive rebounds (only Portland had as many), they couldn't put the ball back into the hole. Consequently, their FG% ranked last too. In fact, so anemic was their scoring, that the highest average on the team was owned by Kevin Edwards at a rather paltry 13.8 points per

Miami Heat .... Overview

game. Only one time since the shot clock was introduced, has a team not had at least one player score more. In 1955, Bobby Wanzer was the high man for Rochester (now Sacramento). His average was 13.1 points per game.

With bad scoring comes getting beat badly. Miami averaged losing by 11.2 points per game, but there have been some teams that have actually been hammered worse.

Philadelphia	1973	-12.1
Houston	1983	-11.6
LA. Clippers	1987	-11.4
Denver	1950	-11.4
Miami	**1989**	**-11.2**

I don't want to leave the impression that it was all bad last year. Actually, the franchise has to consider the first year as a success. Other than the "game postponed due to riot" episode, everything seemed to go smoothly. Ticket sales were up and the team ranked in the upper half among all NBA clubs in attendance. Though I'm sure a lot of fans couldn't stand the *heat*, they stayed in the kitchen anyway. This season, they'll open a couple of windows and air it out. And who knows? Maybe they'll be fun to watch.

Miami won 11 games in the second half of the season. That's 7 more than in the first half. And that's noteworthy because only one previous expansion team has ever improved more in the second half. The New Orleans Jazz increased their victories by 13 in the second half during their inaugural year (1975). Two other teams as well as the Heat improved 7 wins. Cleveland did it in 1971 as did Milwaukee in 1969.

Several players on the team had remarkable seasons. During one six game stretch as a starter, Scott Hastings scored 15 points and 7 rebounds per game while shooting 55% from the field. Nevertheless, he's a free agent at press time. Ron Seikaly, like most rookies, had an up and down year. He was last in the league in total

shooting efficiency (Kevin Edwards was next to last. See page 225), but he was first among rookies in rebounding. Grant Long was last in the league in total fouls, but was #4 by Production Rating among rookies.

1. Mitch Richmond	Golden State	19.44
2. Willie Anderson	San Antonio	18.99
3. Charles Smith	LA. Clippers	16.66
4. Grant Long	**Miami**	**14.41**
5. Rik Smits	Indiana	14.06

Jon Sundvold was last in the league in blocks per minute, but was first with the fewest fouls per game. Additionally, he set an NBA record by connecting on 52.2% of his 3-pointers. Shown are the all-time top-5.

Sundvold	**Miami**	**1989**	**.522**
Hodges	Milwaukee	1988	.491
Price	Cleveland	1988	.486
Vandeweghe	Portland	1987	.481
Ellis	Seattle	1989	.478

Notes: Miami was 3-2 in overtime games (#7)... Even better was their record in margins of 3 points or less (8-4)... When they allowed 105+ on the road, their record was slightly different (0-29)... The Heat move from the Central to the Atlantic division this season... No expansion team ever outrebounded their opponents, though Miami came the closest (3520-3554, -34).

Prediction - best case: 29-53

I'll give them a 14 win improvement for two reasons. 1) That was the average of the other 15-win expansion clubs and 2) they gained 7 wins from the first half to the second half last season. If they can do it both halves, they might be competitive.

Prediction - worst case: 20-62

They are certainly going to improve. (Although, three expansion teams failed to improve in year #2.) However, considering there will be four other "expansion" clubs to compete against (counting the Clippers), I will be disappointed if they only win 20.

To order back issues of Basketball Heaven or to obtain the 1990 Mid-season Report, see page 324.

Milwaukee Bucks . . . . Influence on Winning

TEAM RECORD BY

PLAYER	GAMES	... SCR Leader		... REB Leader		...AST Leader	
		HOME	ROAD	HOME	ROAD	HOME	ROAD
Terry Cummings	80	20-6	7-12	11-4	7-9	0-0	1-0
Jack Sikma	80	0-2	1-4	11-6	8-6	3-2	4-3
Paul Pressey	67	1-0	0-2	3-0	0-0	12-3	8-11
Larry Krystkowiak	80	3-0	2-1	11-4	4-8	0-0	0-0
Ricky Pierce	75	4-2	7-7	0-0	0-0	0-2	1-1
Jay Humphries	73	1-0	2-0	1-0	0-0	12-3	6-7
Sidney Moncrief	62	1-0	0-1	0-0	0-0	4-0	0-3
Fred Roberts	71	0-0	0-0	0-0	1-1	0-1	0-0
Rickey Green	30	0-0	0-0	0-0	1-0	2-0	1-3
Randy Breuer	48	0-0	0-1	0-0	0-0	0-0	0-0

TEAM RECORD BY SCORING *

PLAYER	PLAY	DNP	0-9	10-19	20-29	30-39	40+
Terry Cummings	48-32	1-1	0-0	14-12	23-17	11-3	0-0
Jack Sikma	48-32	1-1	7-10	38-15	3-6	0-1	0-0
Paul Pressey	43-24	6-9	14-7	26-14	3-3	0-0	0-0
Larry Krystkowiak	47-33	2-0	15-12	21-18	10-3	1-0	0-0
Ricky Pierce	45-30	4-3	6-6	18-12	21-12	0-0	0-0
Jay Humphries	44-29	5-4	12-15	27-14	5-0	0-0	0-0
Sidney Moncrief	35-27	14-6	14-6	17-19	4-2	0-0	0-0
Fred Roberts	43-28	6-5	34-24	9-4	0-0	0-0	0-0
Rickey Green	15-15	34-58	12-11	3-4	0-0	0-0	0-0
Randy Breuer	29-19	20-14	27-17	2-1	0-1	0-0	0-0

TEAM RECORD BY STARTING POSITION *

PLAYER	GAMES	STARTS	PG	OG	SF	PF	C
Terry Cummings	80	78	0-0	0-0	47-31	0-0	0-0
Jack Sikma	80	80	0-0	0-0	0-0	2-1	46-31
Paul Pressey	67	62	21-11	20-10	0-0	0-0	0-0
Larry Krystkowiak	80	77	0-0	0-0	0-0	45-32	0-0
Ricky Pierce	75	4	0-0	0-0	2-2	0-0	0-0
Jay Humphries	73	50	28-22	0-0	0-0	0-0	0-0
Sidney Moncrief	62	50	0-0	27-23	0-0	0-0	0-0
Fred Roberts	71	3	0-0	0-0	0-0	2-0	1-0
Rickey Green	30	0	0-0	0-0	0-0	0-0	0-0
Randy Breuer	48	4	0-0	0-0	0-0	0-0	2-2

* For further definition of each category and column heading see pages 42 & 43.

Milwaukee Bucks . . . . 1988-89 Statistics

RAW NUMBERS *

PLAYER	2pt%	3pt%	FT%	MIN	PF	DQ	HI	TO	RB	AS	BL	ST
Terry Cummings	.467	**.467**	.787	**2824**	265	5	**38**	201	**650**	198	**72**	106
Jack Sikma	.449	.380	**.905**	2587	**300**	6	30	145	623	289	61	85
Paul Pressey	.497	.218	.776	2170	221	2	25	184	262	**439**	44	119
Larry Krystkowiak	.475	.333	.823	2472	219	0	31	147	610	107	9	93
Ricky Pierce	**.529**	.222	.859	2078	193	1	29	112	197	156	19	77
Jay Humphries	.516	.266	.816	2220	187	1	24	160	189	405	5	**142**
Sidney Moncrief	.514	.342	.865	1594	114	1	25	94	172	188	13	65
Fred Roberts	.498	.214	.806	1251	126	0	19	80	209	66	23	36
Rickey Green	.498	.273	.909	871	35	0	14	61	69	187	2	40
Randy Breuer	.480	0-0	.549	513	59	0	20	29	135	22	37	9

OVERALL RANKINGS *

PLAYER	G	GS	PPG	PR	RANK	SC	SH	RB	AS	BL	ST
Terry Cummings	**80**	78	**22.86**	**21.54**	22	11	127	53	105	53	81
Jack Sikma	**80**	80	13.35	**18.47**	44	88	55	43	60	57	102
Paul Pressey	67	62	12.13	**16.39**	74	101	105	125	21	68	28
Larry Krystkowiak	**80**	77	12.71	**15.29**	88	95	91	38	152	156	80
Ricky Pierce	75	4	17.56	**14.95**	92	42	25	151	95	114	85
Jay Humphries	73	50	11.56	**14.07**	100	110	63	160	31	171	14
Sidney Moncrief	62	50	12.13	**12.79**	113	102	24	137	55	121	67
Fred Roberts	71	3	5.87	**6.79**	DNQ						
Rickey Green	63	2	4.62	**6.19**	DNQ						
Randy Breuer	48	4	4.17	**5.38**	DNQ						

POSITION RANKINGS *

PLAYER	POSITION	RANK	SC	SH	RB	AS	BL	ST
Terry Cummings	Small Forward, PF	5	5	31	6	26	13	14
Jack Sikma	Center, PF	9	12	11	21	1	24	6
Paul Pressey	Point Guard, OG, SF	17	16	18	11	19	1	13
Larry Krystkowiak	Power Forward	18	16	19	18	19	29	9
Ricky Pierce	Off Guard	17	11	8	33	37	18	30
Jay Humphries	Point Guard OG	20	19	11	24	26	29	7
Sidney Moncrief	Off Guard	22	31	7	23	18	22	23
Fred Roberts	Power Forward SF	DNQ						
Rickey Green	Point Guard	DNQ						
Randy Breuer	Center	DNQ						

*For further definition of each category and column heading see pages 42 & 43.

Milwaukee Bucks . . . . Team Info

WEEKLY POWER RATING
41 WINS - AVERAGE (See page 43 for Team Power Rating discussion.)

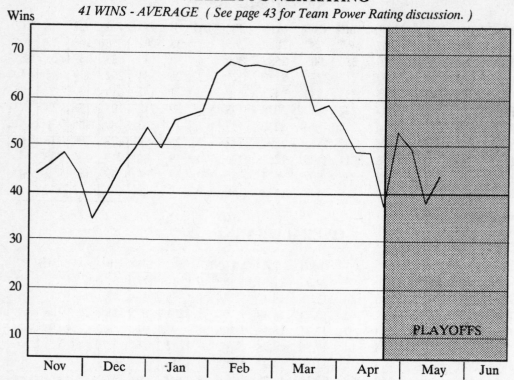

Miscellaneous Categories	Data	Rank
Attendance	701K	7
Key-Man Games Missed	66	14
Season Record	49-33	8
- Home	31-10	10
- Road	18-23	6
Eastern Conference	29-27	10
Western Conference	20-6	2
Overtime Record	2-0	1
Record 5 Pts. or Less	5-11	24
Record 10 Pts. or More	31-15	8
Games Won By Bench	10	4
Games Won By Starters	3	19
Winning Streak	6	9
Losing Streak	3	3
Home Winning Streak	11	12
Road Winning Streak	4	6
Home Losing Streak	2	5
Road Losing Streak	6	8

Performance Categories	Data	Rank
Offensive Scoring (per game)	108.9	11
Defensive Scoring (per game)	105.3	6
Scoring Margin (per game)	3.6	8
Defensive FG%	.478	12
Offensive 2-point%	.488	11
Offensive 3-point%	.316	13
Offensive Free Throw %	.821	1
Offensive Rebs (Off REB/Opp Def REB)		14
Defensive Rebs (Def REB/Opp Off REB)		12
Offensive Assists (AST/FGMade)		8
Offensive Blocks (BLK/Opp FGAttempted)		23
Offensive Steals (STL/Game)		6
Turnover Margin (Def T.O. - Off T.O.)		2
Fouls Margin (Opp FOULS - FOULS)		12
Rebounding Record	37-40-5	16
Assists Record	40-39-3	14
Field Goal Pct. Record	42-40-0	13
Free Throw Att. Record	38-41-3	12

Milwaukee Bucks ....Team Roster

MOST PRODUCTIVE PLAYERS

Player	Span	Yrs	CRD
Kareem Abdul-Jabbar	1970-75	6	17,608
Sidney Moncrief	1980-89	10	12,671
Bob Dandridge	1970-81	9	12,035
Marques Johnson	1978-84	7	12,023
Junior Bridgeman	1976-87	10	8,994
Terry Cummings	1983-89	7	8,647
Paul Pressey	1983-89	7	8,483
Brian Winters	1976-83	8	8,378
Jon McGlocklin	1969-76	8	7,256
Oscar Robertson	1971-74	4	5,967

PRESENT PLAYERS*

J#	VETERANS	COLLEGE	POS	R#	D#	HT	WT	Milw	NBA
	Greg Anderson	Houston	C-F	1	23	6-10	230	0	2
45	Randy Breuer	Minnesota	C	1	18	7-3	230	6	6
35	Tony Brown	Arkansas	G	4	82	6-6	195	1	4
20	Jeff Grayer	Iowa State	G	1	13	6-5	200	1	1
11	Rickey Green	Michigan	G	1	16	6-0	172	1	11
50	Tito Horford	Miami	C	2	39	7-1	245	1	1
24	Jay Humphries	Colorado	G	1	13	6-3	182	2	5
42	Larry Krystkowiak	Montana	F	2	28	6-10	245	2	3
44	Paul Mokeski	Kansas	C	2	42	7-1	255	7	10
22	Ricky Pierce	Rice	G-F	1	18	6-4	220	5	7
25	Paul Pressey	Tulsa	F-G	1	20	6-5	201	7	7
31	Fred Roberts	BYU	F	2	27	6-10	220	1	6
	Alvin Robertson	Arkansas	G	1	7	6-4	190	0	5
43	Jack Sikma	Ill. Wesleyan	C	1	8	6-11	250	3	12

FUTURE PLAYERS

ROOKIES	COLLEGE	POS	R#	D#	HT	WT
Frank Kornet	Vanderbilt	F	2	30	6-9	225

* For further definition of category and column headings, see pages 42 & 43.

Milwaukee Bucks .... Overview

The Milwaukee Bucks were expected by most "knowlegeable" people to drop out of sight last season. They were old, they had dropped 8 games from 1988 to 1989, they had lost 13 of their last 14 road games and their 42 wins were the fewest since the 1970's. I'm still not quite sure how, but this group, led by Del Harris, put on a marvelous show and, if not for a late-season slump, would have broken the 50-win barrier - reminiscent of the Nelson glory days.

In spite of their final tally, the Bucks were a disappointing 3-11 in games decided by 4 points or less during 1988-89. That's bad, to be sure. It even ranks last. But what is so significant about it is that it continues a very disturbing trend which appears to reflect a deficiency in the players, not the coaches. Let me explain.

Though I could go back farther, Milwaukee is a rather lousy 48-67 (.417) in games decided by 4 points or less over the past 6 years. If you remove the 48-67 record from Milwaukee's complete totals, you'll see that they won 259 while losing only 118 over the 6-year period. That's a tremendous 68.7 winning percentage and would have translated into 56 wins a year instead of the 51 they actually got.

This is interesting enough, but what I wanted to find out was whether it was due to the team or the coaches. (As you remember, Nelson coached 4 of the 6 seasons while Harris has coached the last 2.) What I thought I should do would be to look at 4 point margins or less for these coaches while coaching other teams. That meant taking a look at Del Harris in 4 years with Houston and Don Nelson in 1 year with Golden State. What I discovered was revealing. Although the average winning percentage for those 5 years in games decided by 5 points or more was only 40.8%, the winning percentage for *close* games was substantially better (54.5%). This leads to the conclusion that these coaches are capable of winning tight battles, but that the Bucks (for some reason) aren't. With Moncrief and Cummings, the two primary players on the team during this period, now gone, I will be very curious to see how the team does this season in close games.

Sidney Moncrief will be missed. As a five-time All-NBA performer, he ranks as the 19th greatest player ever (see page 18). Nevertheless, he's been hobbled for the last three years and has not been the same player as he was in his prime.

Justifiably, the club decided it needed to replace him. If you are going to do it, why not go out and get a near carbon copy? That's not to say Alvin Robertson is as good as Moncrief was, but he ain't no Swiss cheese either. Robertson and Moncrief were the 2nd-team All-NBA guards in 1986, both have been named Defensive Players-of-the-Year, both are 6'4" - 185 lbs, and both attended the University of Arkansas. There's one big difference, though. Robertson is 5 years younger... and healthy.

Like most things, you get what you pay for and Milwaukee paid a lot for Alvin. The Bucks sent Terry Cummings to San Antonio and, in addition to Robertson, the Spurs packaged Greg Anderson. I think Harris was absolutely right when he defended the trade by saying they got 2 bodies for 1. With Larry Krystkowiak likely to miss all of 1990 with major knee damage, this killed two birds with one stone.

The obvious question is, where will the front-court scoring come from? Greg Anderson had a 13.7 ppg average last season while Jack Sikma managed at 13.4. Those are so-so averages, but even then, Anderson is a wretched free throw shooter and Sikma is entering his 13th season. Besides, if next year is anything like this one, the club will want to keep Jack in the 13 ppg scoring range. In 1988-89, when he scored from 11-16 points, the team was 33-9. When he drifted outside of that narrow area - either up or down - they were substandard (15-23). Now that Krysto and Cummings are gone and with no first round draft pick, the Bucks are desperate.

Milwaukee Bucks .... Overview

There appear to me to be only a few possibilities. The first would be to have Paul Pressey start at small forward - a position he's occasionally started at. Based on that, Jay Humphries could then take over the point guard responsibilities. Humphries' contributions were valuable last season, as the team was 22-6 when he scored 13+ points. So, getting him in the lineup would seem to be a good idea.

The second alternative might be to see if Fred Roberts can match the effort he put forth in the final playoff game vs Detroit when he scored 33 points. I was astonished, as I'm sure were others. Whether he can do anything approaching that on a consistent basis remains to be seen.

The third possibility is that often-injured Jeff Grayer can play at small forward. He was projected as a 2-guard and only got in 11 games as a rookie, so it's doubtful.

Milwaukee not only won the free throw percentage battle in the NBA last season, but they set the all-time record (.8207) in the process. What can be safely wagered against, however, are the odds that they will do as well this season. Newcomers Greg Anderson, Alvin Robertson, and Frank Kornet combined to shoot 59.8% from the stripe last year.

Milwaukee	1989	.8207
Kansas City	1975	.8205
Denver	1984	.818
Houston	1974	.812
Utah	1980	.809

Besides free throw shooting, Milwaukee had three other reasons to take pride in last season. 1) A look at their power rating chart on page 130 reveals the success they had from mid-December to mid-March. In fact, from game #17 to game #59, the Bucks were a fabulous 32-11, which tied Cleveland for the best record during that period. Unfortunately, they were 17-22 at the beginning and end of the year.

2) Milwaukee's game-five victory over Atlanta will be remembered in my book as one of the gutsiest and most courageous victories ever. The Bucks had lost all 6 meetings with the Hawks during the regular season, were forced to play the final game of the series at Atlanta, and had lost Cummings the game before - a game which would have closed out the series 3 to 1, but a game which saw Atlanta come back and win in overtime, thus capturing momentum and, presumably, breaking Milwaukee's spirit. During the contest, I kept expecting the Bucks to fold. They never did. For that they deserve commendation.

3) Just as Milwaukee was helpless vs Atlanta, they were giants against Detroit. The Bucks beat the Pistons 4 of 6 games during the regular season. What's especially notable about that is that since the NBA/ABA merger, only three times has a team beaten what would later become the NBA champion during the regular season series (6 games). In 1980, Portland defeated the Lakers 4-2 and in 1984, Philadelphia knocked off Boston also by a 4-2 count.

Notes: Milwaukee ranked #2 in the NBA with a 20-6 record versus the Western Conference... When the team scored 115+ points at home, they were outstanding (17-0)... When the club shot 48% or better, they were great (31-4), and an even better 32-3 when they held their opponents to 46% or less... Mike Dunleavy played 2 games in 1989 - 5 years after he retired. Only Kermit Washington (6 years) and Bob Cousy (7 years) have ever come back after so long an absence.

Prediction - best case: 49-33

I can't see how the team can do better than last season. Even 49 wins will seem like Mount Everest if the small forward situation is not resolved.

Prediction - worst cast: 39-43

Though the Bucks benefitted for a long time playing in the weak Central Division, they're now paying the piper.

To order back issues of Basketball Heaven or to obtain the 1990 Mid-season Report, see page 324.

Minnesota Timberwolves .... Team Roster

ADMINISTRATIVE INFORMATION

TEAM OFFICES: Minnesota Timberwolves
500 City Place
730 Hennepin Ave
Minneapolis, Minnesota
55403

TELEPHONE: 1-612-337-3865
HEAD COACH: Bill Musselman
HOME ARENA: Minneapolis Metrodome
CAPACITY: 23,000

PRESENT PLAYERS*

J#	VETERANS	COLLEGE	POS	R#	D#	HT	WT	Char	NBA
	Tyrone Corbin	DePaul	F	2	35	6-6	222	0	4
	Mark Davis	Old Dominion	G	4	79	6-5	195	0	1
	Steve Johnson	Oregon State	C-F	1	7	6-10	235	0	8
	Shelton Jones	St. Johns	F	2	27	6-9	210	0	1
	Brad Lohaus	Iowa	F	2	45	7-0	235	0	2
	Rick Mahorn	Hampton Va.	F	2	35	6-10	255	0	9
	Maurice Martin	St. Joseph's	G	1	16	6-6	200	0	2
	David Rivers	Notre Dame	G	1	25	6-0	170	0	1
	Scott Roth	Wisconsin	F	4	82	6-8	212	0	2
	Eric White	Pepperdine	G	3	65	6-0	180	0	2

FUTURE PLAYERS

ROOKIES	COLLEGE	POS	R#	D#	HT	WT
Pooh Richardson	UCLA	G	1	10	6-1	180
Gary Leonard	Missouri	C	2	34	7-1	250
Doug West	Villanova	G	2	38	6-6	205

* For further definition of category and column headings, see pages 42 & 43.

Minnesota Timberwolves . . . . Overview

Talk about a lobbying effort. This town has wanted an NBA franchise since 1960 when the Lakers packed up and headed west. Well, they finally got it. No, they don't have a George Mikan around, but they did make a good start at acquiring a representative club from the expansion draft and the regular draft.

It will be interesting to see how this region responds to the Timberwolves. Remember, when the Lakers were here, they weren't just good, they were great! The team won the NBL championship in 1948, the BAA title in 1949, and NBA crowns in 1950, 52, 53, and 54. I know it's been a long time, but the Laker mystique has never left. Whereas in most expansion cities the fans are content just to have a team (winning is a bonus) - this city might be different. On the other hand, any town that's waited for 39 years just to have a team can wait a few more for a winner.

One other interested party that may have a hard time being patient with losing will be coach Bill Musselman. Although he had a few difficulties winning in the ABA and NBA, his overall coaching record for college and pro is 471-260 (.644). He gained prominence when he won 4 titles with the Albany Patroons of the CBA.

His skeleton in the closet is that he was coach and VP for the Cleveland Cavaliers during the Ted Stepien era. Stepien is widely regarded as the worst owner in recent NBA history. Several horrible draft decisions came during this period. No doubt Musselman would prefer to forget that. Though I don't know the specific reason why 8 season ticket-holders threatened to cancel to protest the hiring of Musselman, I've got to think his involvement with Cleveland had a lot to do with it. Apparently, Bill met with the disgruntled fans and persuaded each not to cancel. Fifty years from now, when the club has overcome 100 crises, that will be regarded as pretty small potatoes.

In looking at the players Minnesota picked up in the drafts, I noticed that their free throw shooting was especially weak. Out of curiosity, I tallied up the combined free throw percentage of all the players and got 68.3%. What is interesting about this is that if it were to hold true next season, it would be the lowest for an NBA team in 20 years.

Minnesota should have a starting lineup of Rick Mahorn and Tyrone Corbin at forwards, Steve Johnson at center, and Pooh Richardson and Mark Davis or Doug West at guards. What is noticeably absent among the Timberwolves' players is anyone who can distribute the ball. Other than David Rivers, no other player in the team's expansion draft is a ball handler. Of course, that's why they drafted Richardson.

Although I might have chosen one of the other highly-rated point guards, there's nothing wrong with Richardson and it shows a lot of foresight to go after a point guard right away. If you're going to build, then build around the person with the ball!

The Wolves (I assume they'll become known as that - like the Sixers, Sonics, and Blazers) were also extremely fortunate to pick up Gary Leonard in the 2nd round. His stats aren't extremely impressive until you realize he only played 21 minutes per game. Here in the Big-8, I've had a chance to see Leonard (he's from Missouri). He's a very mobile big man. He's also very strong, with a decent touch. I believe he may be able to start in place of Johnson or Lohaus at some point in the near future. The rap on Leonard is his bad work ethic.

Prediction - best case: 23-59

This team has as much talent as Charlotte had last season, and more expansion teams to play against than the Hornets had, so it could well exceed Charlotte's 20 wins.

Prediction - worst case: 15-67

Four previous expansion teams have won 15 games - including Miami last season. None of them have won fewer. Why should Minnesota?

To order back issues of Basketball Heaven or to obtain the 1990 Mid-season Report, see page 324.

New Jersey Nets . . . . Influence on Winning

TEAM RECORD BY

PLAYER	GAMES	... SCR Leader		... REB Leader		...AST Leader	
		HOME	ROAD	HOME	ROAD	HOME	ROAD
Buck Williams	74	3-3	0-2	9-12	6-12	0-0	0-0
Lester Conner	82	0-2	1-0	2-0	1-2	14-14	3-20
Joe Barry Carroll	64	1-2	1-6	5-2	1-4	0-0	0-0
Roy Hinson	82	6-6	3-5	1-9	1-7	0-0	0-0
Chris Morris	76	3-4	1-10	1-2	0-5	0-0	0-2
Dennis Hopson	62	2-2	1-6	0-0	0-1	0-0	0-0
Mike McGee	80	5-5	3-5	0-1	0-0	0-0	0-0
John Bagley	68	0-0	0-0	0-0	0-0	3-13	6-11
Keith Lee	57	0-0	0-0	1-1	0-5	0-0	0-0
Charles Shackleford	60	2-2	1-6	0-0	0-1	0-0	0-0

TEAM RECORD BY SCORING *

PLAYER	PLAY	DNP	0-9	10-19	20-29	30-39	40+
Buck Williams	23-51	3-5	3-13	16-35	4-3	0-0	0-0
Lester Conner	26-56	0-0	6-29	19-27	1-0	0-0	0-0
Joe Barry Carroll	20-44	6-12	2-12	14-26	4-6	0-0	0-0
Roy Hinson	26-56	0-0	3-9	10-36	11-10	2-1	0-0
Chris Morris	24-52	2-4	9-15	9-26	5-9	1-2	0-0
Dennis Hopson	19-43	7-13	5-15	10-21	3-7	1-0	0-0
Mike McGee	25-55	1-1	8-23	10-23	7-7	0-2	0-0
John Bagley	21-47	5-9	13-35	8-12	0-0	0-0	0-0
Keith Lee	17-40	9-16	16-34	1-6	0-0	0-0	0-0
Charles Shackleford	17-43	9-13	16-41	1-2	0-0	0-0	0-0

TEAM RECORD BY STARTING POSITION *

PLAYER	GAMES	STARTS	PG	OG	SF	PF	C
Buck Williams	74	72	0-0	0-0	6-8	16-42	0-0
Lester Conner	82	63	19-43	0-1	0-0	0-0	0-0
Joe Barry Carroll	64	62	0-0	0-0	0-0	0-0	19-43
Roy Hinson	82	39	0-0	0-0	0-0	10-13	5-11
Chris Morris	76	48	0-0	0-0	13-34	0-1	0-0
Dennis Hopson	62	36	0-0	10-26	0-0	0-0	0-0
Mike McGee	80	49	0-0	16-29	0-4	0-0	0-0
John Bagley	68	20	7-13	0-0	0-0	0-0	0-0
Keith Lee	57	4	0-0	0-0	0-0	0-0	2-2
Charles Shackleford	60	0	0-0	0-0	0-0	0-0	0-0

* For further definition of each category and column heading see pages 42 & 43.

New Jersey Nets . . . . 1988-89 Statistics

RAW NUMBERS *

PLAYER	2pt%	3pt%	FT%	MIN	PF	DQ	HI	TO	RB	AS	BL	ST
Buck Williams	.534	0-3	.666	2446	223	0	27	142	**696**	78	36	61
Lester Conner	.463	.351	.788	2532	132	1	20	181	355	**604**	5	**181**
Joe Barry Carroll	.448	0-0	.800	1996	193	2	26	143	473	105	81	71
Roy Hinson	.483	0-2	.757	**2542**	**298**	3	**35**	165	522	71	**121**	34
Chris Morris	.479	**.366**	.717	2096	250	**4**	31	**190**	397	119	60	102
Dennis Hopson	.429	.148	**.849**	1551	150	0	32	102	202	103	30	70
Mike McGee	.515	.365	.535	2027	184	1	33	124	189	116	12	80
John Bagley	.443	.204	.724	1642	117	0	17	159	144	391	5	72
Keith Lee	.426	0-2	.746	840	138	1	16	53	259	42	33	20
Charles Shackleford	.497	0-1	.500	484	71	0	13	27	153	21	18	15

OVERALL RANKINGS *

PLAYER	G	GS	PPG	PR	RANK	SC	SH	RB	AS	BL	ST
Buck Williams	74	**72**	12.96	**16.92**	62	91	75	18	165	91	130
Lester Conner	**82**	63	10.28	**16.87**	64	121	123	110	13	174	6
Joe Barry Carroll	64	62	14.09	**15.59**	84	77	148	50	135	27	93
Roy Hinson	**82**	39	**15.95**	15.33	87	61	115	72	169	17	173
Chris Morris	76	48	14.13	**13.14**	108	76	113	79	130	48	38
Dennis Hopson	62	36	12.71	10.37	143	96	157	117	111	71	51
Mike McGee	80	49	12.97	9.51	153	90	84	154	126	138	72
John Bagley	68	20	7.35	9.38	155	153	171	157	14	166	55
Keith Lee	57	4	4.75	7.11	DNQ						
Charles Shackleford	60	0	3.12	4.35	DNQ						

POSITION RANKINGS *

PLAYER	POSITION	RANK	SC	SH	RB	AS	BL	ST
Buck Williams	Power Forward	14	14	16	9	26	24	22
Lester Conner	Point Guard, OG	14	22	22	5	13	31	4
Joe Barry Carroll	Center	13	9	25	25	12	16	4
Roy Hinson	Power Forward, C	17	8	25	29	27	5	28
Chris Morris	Small Forward	27	23	27	13	34	11	7
Dennis Hopson	Off Guard	33	29	41	16	39	6	19
Mike McGee	Off Guard	36	27	22	34	41	30	25
John Bagley	Point Guard	28	27	32	23	14	25	20
Keith Lee	Power Forward, C	DNQ						
Charles Shackleford	Center	DNQ						

*For further definition of each category and column heading see pages 42 & 43.

New Jersey Nets .... Team Info

WEEKLY POWER RATING

41 WINS - AVERAGE   (See page 43 for Team Power Rating discussion.)

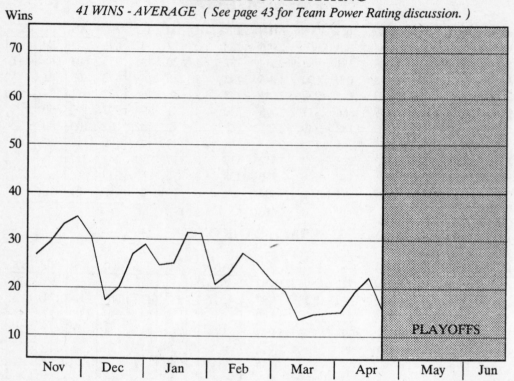

Miscellaneous Categories	Data	Rank
Attendance	520K	19
Key-Man Games Missed	68	16
Season Record	26-56	21
- Home	17-24	22
- Road	9-32	18
Eastern Conference	16-40	19
Western Conference	10-16	21
Overtime Record	4-1	2
Record 5 Pts. or Less	10-12	19
Record 10 Pts. or More	7-32	22
Games Won By Bench	0	25
Games Won By Starters	3	19
Winning Streak	2	24
Losing Streak	10	20
Home Winning Streak	3	25
Road Winning Streak	2	16
Home Losing Streak	6	20
Road Losing Streak	16	22

Performance Categories	Data	Rank
Offensive Scoring (per game)	103.7	23
Defensive Scoring (per game)	110.1	13
Scoring Margin (per game)	-6.4	21
Defensive FG%	.497	23
Offensive 2-point%	.473	21
Offensive 3-point%	.329	9
Offensive Free Throw %	.731	22
Offensive Rebs .....(Off REB/Opp Def REB)		13
Defensive Rebs ....(Def REB/Opp Off REB)		1
Offensive Assists ....(AST/FGMade)		25
Offensive Blocks ..(BLK/Opp FGAttempted)		10
Offensive Steals ....(STL/Game)		12
Turnover Margin........(Def T.O. - Off T.O.)		16
Fouls Margin ....(Opp FOULS - FOULS)		19
Rebounding Record	42-38-2	8
Assists Record	18-60-4	25
Field Goal Pct. Record	31-51-0	22
Free Throw Att. Record	36-37-9	11

New Jersey Nets ....Team Roster

MOST PRODUCTIVE PLAYERS

Player	Span	Yrs	CRD
Buck Williams	1982-89	8	13,881
Billy Paultz	1971-75	5	8,640
Julius Erving	1974-76	3	8,082
Mike Gminski	1981-88	8	7,167
John Williamson	1974-79	6	6,348
Albert King	1982-87	6	5,270
Darwin Cook	1981-86	6	5,249
Otis Birdsong	1982-88	7	4,877
M.R. Richardson	1983-86	4	4,593
Jan van Breda Kolff	1977-83	7	3,897

PRESENT PLAYERS*

J#	VETERANS	COLLEGE	POS	R#	D#	HT	WT	N.J.	NBA
5	John Bagley	Boston College	G	1	12	6-0	192	2	7
	Sam Bowie	Kentucky	C	1	2	7-1	240	0	4
11	Joe Barry Carroll	Purdue	C	1	1	7-1	255	1	8
35	Lester Conner	Oregon State	G	1	14	6-4	185	1	6
12	Cory Gaines	Loyola Marymount	G	3	65	6-3	195	1	1
23	Roy Hinson	Rutgers	F-C	1	20	6-10	215	2	6
2	Dennis Hopson	Ohio State	G	1	3	6-5	200	2	2
20	Bill Jones	Iowa	G-F	X	X	6-7	175	1	1
25	Mike McGee	Michigan	G	1	19	6-5	207	1	8
34	Chris Morris	Auburn	F	1	4	6-8	210	1	1
33	Charles Shackleford	N.C. State	F	2	32	6-10	245	1	1

FUTURE PLAYERS

ROOKIES	COLLEGE	POS	R#	D#	HT	WT
Mookie Blayock	Oklahoma	G	1	12	6-1	185
Stanley Brundy	DePaul	F	2	32	6-7	210

* For further definition of category and column headings, see pages 42 & 43.

New Jersey Nets . . . . Overview

The Nets are another one of those teams with so little going for them, you kind of wish they could play a season or two in the CBA just to get acclimated to winning. Of course, there's always the possibility that that wouldn't... Well, I think you know what I mean.

All kinds of phrases have been used to describe New Jersey the last few years. I don't know about you, but I'm not sure what paper bags, broad side of the barn, ocean, or hands being tied behind the back have to do with basketball. Still, I kept reading those phrases when I read about the Nets.

One good thing can be said about last season's 26-win club, however. That was that they stopped their downward spiral. The franchise had lost more games than the season before for 5 consecutive years - tying an NBA high.

New Jersey	5	1983-88
Denver	5	1975-80
Indiana	5	1973-78
Boston	4	1975-79
Detroit	4	1955-59
Golden State	4	1976-80

What's facinating is that as bad as New Jersey has been - "peaking" on the downside with only 19 victories last year - they have won more games every one of those seasons than the Clippers and have beaten them in head-to-head competition 70% of the time.

So what do you do when your club reeks and you have the only franchise in a state that allows gambling? You roll the dice. That's what. And if you're lucky, you hit the jackpot. Amazingly, I think the Nets may have done just that when they traded Buck Williams to Portland for Sam Bowie and a #12 pick. I have argued for two years that the Nets should trade Williams. If they had waited one more year, they wouldn't have gotten half what they got this time. The simple fact is that a power forward in the Buck Williams' mold is just not going to make the team a winner. He can't.

He primarily comes into play when the team fails. In other words, when the ball is brought down court, the play is called, the picks are set, the ball is passed, the shot is taken, then and, usually, only then, does a power forward contribute. He is not controlling the game or any part of it. Power forwards like Charles Barkley or Karl Malone or Kevin McHale or Larry Nance are different because of the other things they do. But a traditional power forward like Buck Williams, Otis Thorpe, Michael Cage, or Charles Oakley will never make a team into a winner. They can only contribute to the process of winning. On the other hand, a point guard or a small forward (someone who regularly handles the ball) can turn a team around. Even though Williams had successful seasons, one after another, the club was miserable. With his Production Rating sliding to 16.92 (easily a career low) and his having missed 8 games (20 in two seasons), it was time to get while the gettin' was good.

What the Nets got was far more than they should have. I argue the statistical merits of this deal in the Portland overview so I won't here. Suffice it to say that if New Jersey gets two to three decent years out of Bowie, that alone will make the gamble worth it. He's a better perimeter shooter and defensive player, and he's younger. Not only that, he's 7'1", can run and jump, and has a feathery shot. He's an excellent passer and was picked #2 in the draft. I'd take a chance on that even though I realize he could drop tomorrow. But even if he does, the stats suggest that Williams will only moderately produce for four more years in the NBA, while the #12 pick has a potentially long career ahead of him. Make no mistake about it, this was a situation where the Nets doubled down and came up big. It might take a year or two to collect on their investment, but I'm betting that they will.

Mookie Blaylock was the #12 pick. Several basketball rags picked him 1st-team All-American so he's a good one.

New Jersey Nets . . . . Overview

Blaylock was the perfect choice for the Nets because they have not had a decent point guard since Michael Ray Richardson in 1985 and they have ranked last in the league in assists two consecutive years. Remember what I said earlier. A good point guard can make a club into a winner. Blaylock knows a lot about winning and a lot of it was *because* of him. He's a fairly good shooter with decent range - something New Jersey desperately needs. But he's also a brilliant ball handler with the quickest hands you'll ever see. Mookie was the first player in NCAA history to compile 100+ steals and 200+ assists two years in a row. He's also an outstanding defensive player - which for a collegian is unusual. (He reminds me a lot of Mo Cheeks.) Given that the Nets had no first round pick, being able to get Blaylock and Bowie for a declining Williams was very fortunate.

Now that the Buck has passed, the final piece towards completely rebuilding this club has been placed. Incredibly, not a single player on the 1987 team (just 2 years ago) is still around. No other club can say that. Probably, no other club wants to.

With all the new faces, it would be nice, if not appropriate, for New Jersey to have its luck changed on injuries. The franchise has had an astonishing 463 key-man games missed over the last 3 years. Wouldn't it be ironic if Sam Bowie was healthy for a half a dozen years while the rest of the team took a quick trip to Lourdes themselves.

23.	New Jersey	463
22.	LA. Clippers	447
21.	Philadelphia	421
20.	Portland	419
19.	San Antonio	373

Earlier, I stated that the club has not had a decent point guard since 1985. Actually, I think Lester Conner is a respectable player (he even had 2 triple doubles in a 4 game period last year), but he's no star and, after 6 years, he's sure not going to improve beyond where he's at. Still, when he led the team in assists at home, they were 14-14, but when his teammate (John Bagley) did it, they were only 3-11.

Roy Hinson has never come through like I once thought he might. Nevertheless, he is a defensive asset in the middle. The hope is that with Blaylock, Bowie, and Hinson, the Nets might actually frustrate their opponents for a change - possibly even reminding Willis Reed of the good old days back when he was playing in the big apple. New Jersey was 6-7 on the road when Hinson started at power forward, but 3-25 when he didn't. I'd start him. Furthermore, when he got involved and scored 19+ points, they were 14-12 vs 12-44 when he didn't. I'd involve him. Isn't life simple?

After being horribly disappointing his first year and a half, Dennis Hopson showed signs of becoming a fair player in the latter part of last season. His scoring average thru 41 games was an inexcusable 9 ppg (especially for the #4 pick who was billed as a "scorer"), but his average was a much better 17 in the second half.

Notes: Buck Williams' 72 starts were the lowest high of any club... New Jersey lost their last 16 road games and ended the season as the second lowest power-rated club... When the team shot worse than 46%, they were 2-37... The Nets were first in the league in defensive rebounding... The club's 4-1 overtime record ranked #2.

Prediction - best case: 33-49

Though I actually have a little hope for this team, you need to realize that they have not played together much and there are so many unknowns. They gained 7 wins last season, and 33 in 1990 would be 7 more. They've never gained that many in successive seasons yet.

Prediction - worst case: 24-58

Bowie might not play, Blaylock might follow in Hopson or Pearl Washington's footsteps, J. B. Carroll might be J. B. Carroll, and the Nets might be the Nets.

To order back issues of Basketball Heaven or to obtain the 1990 Mid-season Report, see page 324.

New York Knicks . . . . Influence on Winning

TEAM RECORD BY

| PLAYER | GAMES | ... SCR Leader | | ... REB Leader | | ...AST Leader | |
		HOME	ROAD	HOME	ROAD	HOME	ROAD
Pat Ewing	80	12-4	11-15	12-4	9-9	1-0	0-0
Mark Jackson	72	12-0	2-3	2-0	0-0	25-4	14-19
Charles Oakley	82	4-0	1-1	20-4	10-15	0-0	0-1
Johnny Newman	81	6-1	1-3	1-0	0-0	1-0	0-2
Gerald Wilkins	81	2-1	3-2	0-0	1-0	3-2	2-1
Trent Tucker	81	1-0	0-0	0-0	0-0	0-0	0-0
Rod Strickland	81	0-0	0-0	0-0	0-0	8-0	1-4
Kiki Vandeweghe	27	2-0	0-1	0-0	0-0	0-0	0-0
Sidney Green	82	0-0	0-0	4-0	0-0	0-0	0-0
Kenny Walker	79	0-0	0-0	0-0	0-0	0-0	0-0

TEAM RECORD BY SCORING *

PLAYER	PLAY	DNP	0-9	10-19	20-29	30-39	40+
Pat Ewing	50-30	2-0	2-0	17-9	23-15	6-5	2-1
Mark Jackson	46-26	6-4	2-4	25-17	18-4	1-1	0-0
Charles Oakley	52-30	0-0	14-6	32-21	6-3	0-0	0-0
Johnny Newman	52-29	0-1	11-5	28-15	11-8	2-1	0-0
Gerald Wilkins	51-30	1-0	9-10	30-14	11-6	1-0	0-0
Trent Tucker	51-30	1-0	31-20	17-10	3-0	0-0	0-0
Rod Strickland	51-30	1-0	29-17	19-13	3-0	0-0	0-0
Kiki Vandeweghe	15-12	37-18	9-8	3-3	3-1	0-0	0-0
Sidney Green	52-30	0-0	37-30	15-0	0-0	0-0	0-0
Kenny Walker	49-30	3-0	39-27	10-3	0-0	0-0	0-0

TEAM RECORD BY STARTING POSITION *

PLAYER	GAMES	STARTS	PG	OG	SF	PF	C
Pat Ewing	80	80	0-0	0-0	0-0	0-0	50-30
Mark Jackson	72	72	46-26	0-0	0-0	0-0	0-0
Charles Oakley	82	82	0-0	0-0	0-0	52-30	0-0
Johnny Newman	81	80	0-0	0-0	51-29	0-0	0-0
Gerald Wilkins	81	58	0-0	34-24	0-0	0-0	0-0
Trent Tucker	81	24	0-0	18-6	0-0	0-0	0-0
Rod Strickland	81	10	6-4	0-0	0-0	0-0	0-0
Kiki Vandeweghe	27	0	0-0	0-0	0-0	0-0	0-0
Sidney Green	82	0	0-0	0-0	0-0	0-0	0-0
Kenny Walker	79	2	0-0	0-0	1-1	0-0	0-0

* For further definition of each category and column heading see pages 42 & 43.

New York Knicks . . . . 1988-89 Statistics

RAW NUMBERS *

PLAYER	2pt%	3pt%	FT%	MIN	PF	DQ	HI	TO	RB	AS	BL	ST
Pat Ewing	**.570**	0-6	.746	**2896**	311	**5**	45	266	740	188	**281**	117
Mark Jackson	.507	.337	.698	2477	163	1	34	226	341	**619**	7	**139**
Charles Oakley	.526	.250	.773	2604	270	1	27	248	**861**	187	14	104
Johnny Newman	.534	.338	.815	2336	259	4	35	153	206	162	23	111
Gerald Wilkins	.482	.297	.756	2414	166	1	30	169	244	274	22	115
Trent Tucker	.512	**.399**	.782	1824	163	0	25	59	176	132	6	88
Rod Strickland	.484	.322	.745	1358	142	2	22	148	160	319	3	98
Kiki Vandeweghe	.479	.396	**.899**	934	78	0	28	41	71	69	11	19
Sidney Green	.463	0-3	.759	1277	172	0	15	125	394	76	18	47
Kenny Walker	.503	.250	.776	1163	190	1	19	44	230	36	45	41

OVERALL RANKINGS *

PLAYER	G	GS	PPG	PR	RANK	SC	SH	RB	AS	BL	ST
Pat Ewing	80	80	**22.69**	27.46	8	12	11	31	112	5	70
Mark Jackson	72	72	16.93	**20.49**	30	54	90	113	9	167	25
Charles Oakley	**82**	**82**	12.94	**18.44**	46	93	50	7	98	142	71
Johnny Newman	81	80	15.96	**13.27**	106	62	28	156	108	110	43
Gerald Wilkins	81	58	14.33	**12.64**	116	74	129	144	59	115	42
Trent Tucker	81	24	8.48	8.67	164	147	8	147	96	163	40
Rod Strickland	81	10	8.90	9.78	DNQ						
Kiki Vandeweghe	45	1	11.09	**8.73**	DNQ						
Sidney Green	82	0	6.30	8.02	DNQ						
Kenny Walker	79	2	5.30	6.66	DNQ						

POSITION RANKINGS *

PLAYER	POSITION	RANK	SC	SH	RB	AS	BL	ST
Pat Ewing	Center	2	2	3	17	7	4	3
Mark Jackson	Point Guard	6	10	14	6	9	26	12
Charles Oakley	Power Forward	9	15	7	3	3	28	8
Johnny Newman	Small Forward, OG	26	19	6	40	27	32	8
Gerald Wilkins	Off Guard, SF	23	22	31	28	21	19	17
Trent Tucker	Off Guard	40	40	2	30	38	40	16
Rod Strickland	Point Guard	DNQ						
Kiki Vandeweghe	Small Forward	DNQ						
Sidney Green	Power Forward	DNQ						
Kenny Walker	Small Forward	DNQ						

*For further definition of each category and column heading see pages 42 & 43.

New York Knicks .... Team Info

WEEKLY POWER RATING

41 WINS - AVERAGE (See page 43 for Team Power Rating discussion.)

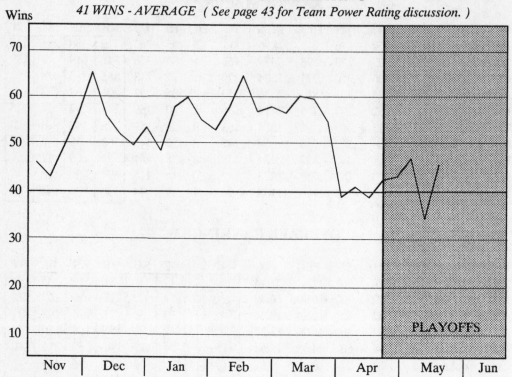

Miscellaneous Categories	Data	Rank
Attendance	747K	3
Key-Man Games Missed	19	1
Season Record	52-30	5
- Home	35-6	3
- Road	17-24	7
Eastern Conference	36-20	4
Western Conference	16-10	9
Overtime Record	4-1	2
Record 5 Pts. or Less	16-12	4
Record 10 Pts. or More	27-13	7
Games Won By Bench	7	7
Games Won By Starters	11	9
Winning Streak	6	9
Losing Streak	3	3
Home Winning Streak	26	2
Road Winning Streak	3	9
Home Losing Streak	3	14
Road Losing Streak	5	6

Performance Categories	Data	Rank
Offensive Scoring (per game)	116.7	3
Defensive Scoring (per game)	112.9	20
Scoring Margin (per game)	3.8	7
Defensive FG%	.494	21
Offensive 2-point%	.513	2
Offensive 3-point%	.337	6
Offensive Free Throw %	.752	18
Offensive Rebs ..... (Off REB/Opp Def REB)		4
Defensive Rebs .... (Def REB/Opp Off REB)		19
Offensive Assists .... (AST/FGMade)		23
Offensive Blocks .. (BLK/Opp FGAttempted)		9
Offensive Steals .... (STL/Game)		2
Turnover Margin .... (Def T.O. - Off T.O.)		6
Fouls Margin .... (Opp FOULS - FOULS)		22
Rebounding Record	42-39-1	10
Assists Record	24-55-3	24
Field Goal Pct. Record	32-50-0	20
Free Throw Att. Record	37-44-1	15

New York Knicks ....Team Roster

MOST PRODUCTIVE PLAYERS

Player	Span	Yrs	CRD
Walt Frazier	1968-77	10	17,100
Willis Reed	1965-74	10	15,607
Harry Gallatin	1949-57	9	11,701
Richie Guerin	1957-63	8	10,350
Bill Cartwright	1980-88	8	10,344
Dave DeBusschere	1969-74	6	8,733
Willie Naulls	1957-63	7	8,597
Earl Monroe	1972-80	9	8,335
Carl Braun	1948-60	12	8,297
Bill Bradley	1968-77	10	8,264

PRESENT PLAYERS*

J#	VETERANS	COLLEGE	POS	R#	D#	HT	WT	N.Y.	NBA
54	Greg Butler	Stanford	F-C	2	37	6-11	240	1	1
33	Patrick Ewing	Georgetown	C	1	1	7-0	240	4	4
13	Mark Jackson	St. Johns	G	1	18	6-3	205	2	2
8	Pete Myers	Arkansas L. R.	G	6	120	6-6	180	1	3
4	Johnny Newman	Richmond	G-F	2	29	6-7	190	2	3
34	Charles Oakley	Virginia Union	F	1	9	6-9	245	1	4
11	Rod Strickland	DePaul	G	1	19	6-3	175	1	1
6	Trent Tucker	Minnesota	G	1	6	6-5	190	7	7
55	Kiki Vandeweghe	UCLA	F	1	11	6-8	220	1	9
7	Kenny Walker	Kentucky	F	1	5	6-8	210	3	3
45	Eddie Wilkins	Gardner-Webb	F	6	133	6-10	220	3	3
21	Gerald Wilkins	Tennessee-Chatt.	F	2	47	6-6	195	4	4

FUTURE PLAYERS

ROOKIES	COLLEGE	POS	R#	D#	HT	WT
Brian Quinnett	Washington State	F	2	50	6-9	236
Steve Babiarz	Potsdam State	G	X	X	6-0	165

* For further definition of category and column headings, see pages 42 & 43.

New York Knicks . . . . Overview

The last twelve months in New York have been nothing short of sensational. It all began in a cooperative blockbuster trade with Chicago and it all ended with the principals of the trade contesting each other for survival in the playoffs. The rest of the story revolved around the Pitino departure, the Vandeweghe trade, a record 3-pt shooting exhibition, and a mammoth home-court winning streak. If that much activity had happened in Salt Lake City or Sacramento or Milwaukee, they'd call out the national guard, but in Metropolis, it's just another day at the office.

Starring as Superman for the Knicks in 1989 was Patrick Ewing. Though he was a little tall for the role (as well as missing certain other characteristics), he performed admirably. For starters, Ewing was voted 2nd-team All-NBA and 2nd-team All-Defense. Additionally, he placed among the league leaders in scoring, shooting and shot blocking. His rankings among centers in the 6 performance categories were also quite impressive (2, 3, 3, 4, 7, 17).

The #17 ranking was in rebounding - clearly his biggest weakness. Part of the reason why Ewing fails to get more boards is because he shoots so often. On the surface that wouldn't seem particularly harmful (after all, he shot 57% from the field), but the argument is that when he shot *less*, the team won *more*. The stats bear this conclusion out. When Ewing fired the ball up 15+ times a game, the club was a rather mediocre 25-22. When he shot less than 15 times, they were very tough (25-8). When a center or power forward shoots the ball, it normally is riskier than if a guard or small forward were to do it. The reason is that the shooter is always less likely to get the offensive board. By removing the center from proper rebounding position, the team can get hurt. Of course, that doesn't explain why they were a very good 4th in offensive boards. What does explain it is Sidney Green and Charles Oakley.

Green was among the top board men in the NBA per minutes played - just like always. But also, just as in the past, he couldn't shoot if he had to. And on a shooting team like the Knicks, that's an issue. Consequently, he was left unprotected in the expansion draft and claimed by Orlando on their first pick. Maybe the fact that the Knicks were 15-0 when Green scored in double figures had something to do with their taking him so quickly.

As for Oakley, his first season, since being traded for Bill Cartwright, was a success. His 343 offensive boards were easily the most ever by a Knick. But what fans want to know is, was he worth more than Cartwright. Well, even before looking at the stats you have to say yes, if for no other reason than that he's 6 years younger. Add to that that New York already had a center, and it was a great move for the Knicks. Statistically, it proved out, as Oakley had a Production Rating of 18.44 to Cartwright's 12.49. Oakley ranked 9th at his position, Cartwright 19th. And, although Cartwright played well in Chicago's playoff victory over New York, Oakley still had a superior post-season 16.0 to 13.0. Most importantly, the Knicks improved 14 wins in 1989, while the Bulls dropped 3. In the future, this trade will seem more and more lopsided.

Despite the team's success, Rick "Larry Brown with training wheels" Pitino decided to move on - preferring to go to Kentucky of the semi-pro league. Replacing him is Stu Jackson, his former assistant. One concern to fans is whether Jackson will maintain the same style of play. The presumption is that, as "Pitino players", this group may not function well in another system. Of course, Pitino was famous for using a constant 48-minute pressure defense. Supposedly that wouldn't work in the NBA, but he proved it could. New York came from behind in quarter #4 better than any other team in the league - winning 13 times. A big reason why was because the Knicks had 10 guys who played at least 70 games - more than any other team. Consequently, they didn't tire, though their opponents obviously did. Nevertheless, it

New York Knicks . . . . Overview

should be pointed out that the Knicks only went 10-11 in the last 21 games of the season and were marginal in the playoffs.

COMEBACKS

New York Knicks	**13**
Philadelphia 76ers	12
Washington Bullets	12
Houston Rockets	11
Chicago Bulls	10
Seattle SuperSonics	10

Another trademark of Pitino was his insistence on shooting the trey. That's good coaching. If a player can shoot 3-pointers at a rate of anything approaching 38% or more, he should shoot every time he can. The large number of them the Knicks took, while still hitting a good percentage, forced their opponents away from the basket. As a result, New York was #2 in 2-pt fg% and set NBA records for 3-pt goals and 3-pt attempts. As the game "evolves", Pitino will be seen as a man ahead of his time.

Attendance in the big apple was at a near record high last season. Only the golden years of the early 1970's were higher - and then just barely. It could well be the reason why the club had a 26-game home winning streak which ranks as the 5th longest in NBA history.

Boston	38	1985-86,	1986-87
Philadelphia	36	1965-66,	1966-67
Portland	34	1976-77,	1977-78
Seattle	29	1975-76,	1976-77
New York	**26**	**1988-89**	

New York has the enviable problem of one too many outstanding point guards. Mark "I've made that shot before" Jackson was Rookie-of-the-Year in 1988, but had an almost identical second season. Where he excelled, however was in leadership. Though he's not a great shooter (#14 among point guards), when he did score well, the team responded. As a rookie, Jackson scored 18+ points per game 21 times. The team was only 11-10. Last season, he scored 18+ on 31 occasions, during which N.Y. was a very good 25-6.

His excellent play makes the situation with Rod Strickland all the more difficult. I believe Strickland has more talent than Jackson, but that doesn't mean he'll be a better player. What it does mean is that he has more potential. In the 10 games Rod started for Mark, he averaged 14 points and 7 assists. The team went 7-3 with losses by only 4, 4, and 5 points. He subsequently ended the season with a Production Rating (based on 48 minutes) of 27.99, higher than any of the other 59 rookies last year (see page 38), and even higher than Jackson's rookie season (25.05).

I liken this situation to Cleveland's a couple of years ago when Kevin Johnson, as a rookie, backed up 2nd-year guard Mark Price. KJ was too talented to waste so Cleveland traded him. Based on his rookie season, Strickland is not a back-up point guard. He may be a potential star. The Knicks should play him or trade him.

Notes: New York's record with Kiki Vandeweghe was 15-12. Without him, they were 37-18... Kenny Walker is the new Slam Dunk Champion... The Knicks ranked #1 by going 12-0 when holding opponents under 100 points... The club ranked a poor 21st in defensive fg%, but when they held their opponents below 49%, they were a sparkling 31-6.

Prediction - best case: 57-25

If Kiki becomes a star again and the team lucks out on injuries like last season (fewest in league), then 55 wins is obviously possible. Most will ask, "Why not more?"

Prediction - worst case: 47-35

The Vandeweghe/Newman conflict, Jackson/Strickland debate, a new coach, and unreasonable expectations are bad enough. Add to this that of the 13 previous teams to improve 10+ games in back-to-back seasons, 9 declined in year three while only 4 improved. And if you need a really pessimistic reason, read page 223.

To order back issues of Basketball Heaven or to obtain the 1990 Midseason Report, see page 324.

Orlando Magic . . . . Team Roster

ADMINISTRATIVE INFORMATION

TEAM OFFICES: Orlando Magic
P.O. Box 76
Orlando, Florida
32802

TELEPHONE: 1-407-649-3200

HEAD COACH: Matt Guokas

HOME ARENA: Orlando Arena

CAPACITY: 15,500

PRESENT PLAYERS*

J#	VETERANS	COLLEGE	POS	R#	D#	HT	WT	Orla	NBA
	Mark Acres	Oral Roberts	F-C	2	40	6-11	220	0	2
	Terry Catledge	South Alabama	F	1	21	6-8	230	0	4
	Jim Farmer	Alabama	G	1	20	6-4	190	0	2
	Sidney Green	UNLV	F	1	5	6-9	220	0	6
	Frank Johnson	Wake Forest	G	1	11	6-3	185	0	8
	Keith Lee	Memphis State	C	1	11	6-10	220	0	3
	Jerry Reynolds	LSU	F	1	22	6-8	198	0	4
	Scott Skiles	Michigan State	G	1	22	6-1	190	0	3
	Otis Smith	Jacksonville	G	2	41	6-5	210	0	3
	Reggie Theus	UNLV	G	1	9	6-7	205	0	11
	Sam Vincent	Michigan State	G	1	20	6-2	185	0	4
	Morlon Wiley	Long Beach	G	2	46	6-4	185	0	1

FUTURE PLAYERS

ROOKIES	COLLEGE	POS	R#	D#	HT	WT
Nick Anderson	Illinois	G-F	1	11	6-6	215
Michael Ansley	Alabama	F	2	37	6-7	225

* For further definition of category and column headings, see pages 42 & 43.

Orlando Magic .... Overview

I'm not quite sure why, but I really like this club. It seems like everything has been so... well, I don't know. Should I say... magical? The Magic are located in one of the nicest areas in the world - central Florida; they've got unlimited access to entertainment (Disney World, Sea World, the Atlantic, the Gulf of Mexico, etc.) and they even won the coin flip with Minnesota for choosing whether to go first in the expansion draft or the regular draft. They correctly chose the expansion draft, making them 1 of 1 in managerial decisions.

The reason I say they chose correctly is because the number of players in the expansion draft are so few, hence the choices are far less. Also, each team is starting with a blank slate. Because of this, the odds of two teams wanting to go after the same player first are relatively high. Besides, what it really means is that Orlando got to pick ahead of Minnesota on all 11 rounds, plus getting a 12th player (there were 23 teams to pick from). By the time that's been done, both teams likely have different needs. So when the regular draft comes, the odds of going after the same player are slim. If that's the case, it doesn't matter if you pick 10th or 11th, you're going to get who you want anyway.

Orlando did get who they wanted in the draft. Their #11 pick was Nick Anderson who is an underclassman from Illinois. I think it's a good idea for an expansion club to take an underclassman. The reason is that you don't want him reaching his peak before the team has been developed enough to help him win. Anderson is a swing player with great leaping ability. He could become another Clyde Drexler.

The second pick by Orlando was Michael Ansley. Magic must have assumed that going after the first two players in the alphabet would bring luck. What's more likely is that they assumed Ansley would be able to play with the intensity he displayed in college. He was a ferocious rebounder and may play either forward spot. Physically, he's similar to Chuck Person. Both are

from Alabama and Person was Rookie-of-the-Year in 1987, so who knows?

This team's lineup does not look like an expansion club's lineup. Four of Orlando's players scored in double figures last season. Of the three other expansion teams, they *combined* to get only two.

Reggie Theus was a starting guard on a team that won 52 games. His average was 15.8 ppg last season. Sam Vincent was a starting guard on another 52-win team. His average was also in double figures at 12.0. The way I see it, everything else is gravy. Otis Smith averaged 10 ppg despite playing less than 20 minutes per outing with another winning team. Terry Catledge started 77 games at forward for a 40-win club and averaged 10.4 ppg. Dave Corzine is an experienced NBA center. He's here via a trade. And Sidney Green, a powerful rebounder, was the #1 pick in the expansion draft. Interestingly, four of those 6 players have played in Chicago. In fact, in 1983-84, Corzine, Green and Theus all played together.

I assume the starting lineup will be Vincent at point guard, Theus at off-guard, Corzine at center, Green at the power forward position, and Nick Anderson at small forward. With Otis Smith and Scott Skiles backing up the guards and Terry Catledge and Jerry Reynolds backing up the forwards - that ain't bad! If I had to start a club from scratch, I could live with it.

Prediction - best case: 33-48

The all-time best by an expansion team was, ironically, Chicago in 1967. They won 33 games. There will be a lot of players on this team determined to prove that their clubs made mistakes when they left them unprotected.

Prediction - worst case: 20-62

With Matt Guokas as coach and the distractions tempting visiting teams, I don't see Orlando losing more than 62.

To order back issues of Basketball Heaven or to obtain the 1990 Midseason Report, see page 324.

Philadelphia 76ers . . . . Influence on Winning

TEAM RECORD BY

PLAYER	GAMES	... SCR Leader		... REB Leader		...AST Leader	
		HOME	ROAD	HOME	ROAD	HOME	ROAD
Charles Barkley	79	21-8	8-15	20-8	12-13	1-0	6-7
Mike Gminski	82	5-1	1-4	11-3	3-9	0-0	1-2
Maurice Cheeks	71	1-1	0-0	0-0	0-0	22-10	6-12
Ron Anderson	82	1-1	3-5	1-0	1-2	0-0	0-0
Hersey Hawkins	79	2-0	3-5	0-0	0-0	0-0	0-1
Derek Smith	36	0-0	0-0	0-0	0-0	0-0	1-0
Cliff Robinson	14	1-0	0-2	1-0	0-1	0-0	1-0
Scott Brooks	82	0-0	1-0	0-0	0-0	6-1	3-3
Gerald Henderson	65	0-0	0-0	0-0	0-0	1-0	0-0
Chris Welp	72	0-0	0-0	0-0	0-0	0-0	0-0

TEAM RECORD BY SCORING *

PLAYER	PLAY	DNP	0-9	10-19	20-29	30-39	40+
Charles Barkley	44-35	2-1	0-0	6-7	21-19	14-9	3-0
Mike Gminski	46-36	0-0	4-4	25-22	17-10	0-0	0-0
Maurice Cheeks	39-32	7-4	12-12	23-17	4-3	0-0	0-0
Ron Anderson	46-36	0-0	7-6	28-24	7-5	4-1	0-0
Hersey Hawkins	44-35	2-1	13-9	17-18	12-8	2-0	0-0
Derek Smith	20-16	26-20	12-13	8-3	0-0	0-0	0-0
Cliff Robinson	9-5	37-31	3-1	3-2	3-2	0-0	0-0
Scott Brooks	46-36	0-0	39-30	7-6	0-0	0-0	0-0
Gerald Henderson	46-36	0-0	7-6	28-24	7-5	4-1	0-0
Chris Welp	41-31	5-5	39-31	2-0	0-0	0-0	0-0

TEAM RECORD BY STARTING POSITION *

PLAYER	GAMES	STARTS	PG	OG	SF	PF	C
Charles Barkley	79	79	0-0	0-0	20-9	24-26	0-0
Mike Gminski	82	82	0-0	0-0	0-0	0-0	46-36
Maurice Cheeks	71	70	39-31	0-0	0-0	0-0	0-0
Ron Anderson	82	12	0-0	0-0	3-9	0-0	0-0
Hersey Hawkins	79	79	3-1	41-43	0-0	0-0	0-0
Derek Smith	36	18	0-0	2-1	9-6	0-0	0-0
Cliff Robinson	14	13	0-0	0-0	0-0	9-4	0-0
Scott Brooks	82	6	4-2	0-0	0-0	0-0	0-0
Gerald Henderson	65	0	0-0	0-0	0-0	0-0	0-0
Chris Welp	72	0	0-0	0-0	0-0	0-0	0-0

* For further definition of each category and column heading see pages 42 & 43.

Philadelphia 76ers . . . . **1988-89 Statistics**

RAW NUMBERS *

PLAYER	2pt%	3pt%	FT%	MIN	PF	DQ	HI	TO	RB	AS	BL	ST
Charles Barkley	**.636**	.216	.753	**3088**	262	3	**43**	254	986	325	67	**126**
Mike Gminski	.479	0-6	.871	2739	142	0	29	129	769	138	**106**	46
Maurice Cheeks	.490	.077	.774	2298	114	0	24	116	183	**554**	17	105
Ron Anderson	.494	.182	.856	2618	166	1	36	126	406	139	23	71
Hersey Hawkins	.461	**.428**	.831	2577	184	0	32	158	225	239	37	120
Derek Smith	.449	.226	.686	1295	164	**4**	27	88	167	128	23	43
Cliff Robinson	.484	0-1	.727	416	37	0	26	34	75	32	2	17
Scott Brooks	.463	.359	**.884**	1372	116	0	18	65	94	306	3	69
Gerald Henderson	.461	.308	.819	986	121	1	20	73	68	140	3	42
Chris Welp	.448	0-1	.658	843	176	0	12	42	193	29	41	23

OVERALL RANKINGS *

PLAYER	G	GS	PPG	PR	RANK	SC	SH	RB	AS	BL	ST
Charles Barkley	79	79	**25.78**	**32.68**	3	8	5	9	63	65	66
Mike Gminski	**82**	**82**	17.18	20.55	28	51	87	20	140	30	167
Maurice Cheeks	71	70	11.61	16.38	76	111	109	167	12	126	49
Ron Anderson	**82**	12	16.22	14.93	93	58	71	99	134	119	122
Hersey Hawkins	79	79	15.14	13.68	105	68	70	158	74	92	46
Derek Smith	65	38	8.74	7.72	171	143	163	118	67	78	101
Cliff Robinson	14	13	15.14	13.93	DNQ						
Scott Brooks	**82**	6	5.22	7.46	DNQ						
Gerald Henderson	65	0	6.54	5.82	DNQ						
Chris Welp	72	0	3.42	4.75	DNQ						

POSITION RANKINGS *

PLAYER	POSITION	RANK	SC	SH	RB	AS	BL	ST
Charles Barkley	Power Forward, SF	1	2	1	4	1	20	7
Mike Gminski	Center	7	7	15	9	13	17	24
Maurice Cheeks	Point Guard	18	20	20	27	12	11	17
Ron Anderson	Small Forward, OG	23	18	13	25	36	34	24
Hersey Hawkins	Off Guard	19	21	20	36	24	10	18
Derek Smith	Small Forward, OG	39	35	37	37	9	21	19
Cliff Robinson	Power Forward, SF	DNQ						
Scott Brooks	Off Guard	DNQ						
Gerald Henderson	Point Guard, OG	DNQ						
Chris Welp	Center	DNQ						

*For further definition of each category and column heading see pages 42 & 43.

Philadelphia 76ers . . . . Team Info

WEEKLY POWER RATING

41 WINS - AVERAGE   (See page 43 for Team Power Rating discussion.)

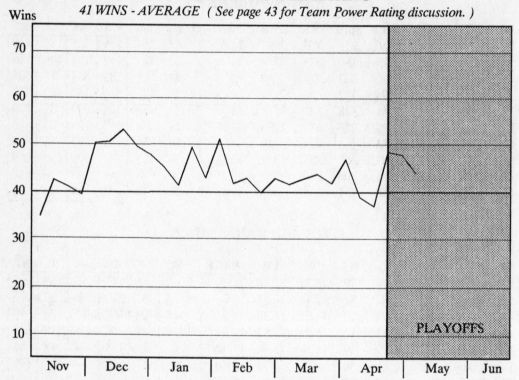

Miscellaneous Categories	Data	Rank	Performance Categories	Data	Rank
Attendance	558K	15	Offensive Scoring (per game)	111.9	8
Key-Man Games Missed	95	17	Defensive Scoring (per game)	110.4	14
Season Record	46-36	11	Scoring Margin (per game)	1.5	11
- Home	30-11	13	Defensive FG%	.501	25
- Road	16-25	10	Offensive 2-point%	.503	8
Eastern Conference	31-25	9	Offensive 3-point%	.316	13
Western Conference	15-11	10	Offensive Free Throw %	.787	8
Overtime Record	2-2	8	Offensive Rebs .....(Off REB/Opp Def REB)		15
Record 5 Pts. or Less	12-11	7	Defensive Rebs ....(Def REB/Opp Off REB)		14
Record 10 Pts. or More	23-14	9	Offensive Assists ....(AST/FGMade)		11
Games Won By Bench	5	11	Offensive Blocks ..(BLK/Opp FGAttempted)		22
Games Won By Starters	7	11	Offensive Steals.....................(STL/Game)		20
Winning Streak	5	13	Turnover Margin........(Def T.O. - Off T.O.)		12
Losing Streak	4	7	Fouls Margin ....(Opp FOULS - FOULS)		3
Home Winning Streak	6	18	Rebounding Record	40-38-4	12
Road Winning Streak	3	9	Assists Record	27-49-6	22
Home Losing Streak	2	5	Field Goal Pct. Record	35-47-0	16
Road Losing Streak	4	2	Free Throw Att. Record	58-23-1	3

Philadelphia 76ers ....Team Roster

MOST PRODUCTIVE PLAYERS

Player	Span	Yrs	CRD
Dolph Schayes	1949-64	16	22,991
Hal Greer	1959-73	15	20,345
Julius Erving	1977-87	11	19,237
John Kerr	1955-65	11	15,603
Maurice Cheeks	1979-89	11	15,143
Billy Cunningham	1966-76	9	15,085
Wilt Chamberlain	1965-68	4	12,220
Charles Barkley	1985-89	5	11,228
Chet Walker	1963-69	7	9,704
Larry Costello	1958-68	10	9,216

PRESENT PLAYERS*

J#	VETERANS	COLLEGE	POS	R#	D#	HT	WT	Phil	NBA
20	Ron Anderson	Fresno State	F	2	27	6-7	215	1	5
34	Charles Barkley	Auburn	F	1	5	6-6	253	5	5
1	Scott Brooks	California Irvine	G	X	X	5-11	165	1	1
10	Maurice Cheeks	West Texas State	G	2	36	6-1	181	11	11
54	Ben Coleman	Maryland	F	2	37	6-9	235	2	3
42	Mike Gminski	Duke	C	1	7	6-11	260	2	9
33	Hersey Hawkins	Bradley	G	1	6	6-3	190	1	1
12	Gerald Henderson	VCU	G	3	64	6-2	175	2	10
4	Cliff Robinson	USC	F	1	11	6-9	240	3	10
11	Jim Rowinski	Purdue	F	4	86	6-8	255	1	1
21	Derek Smith	Louisville	G	2	35	6-7	225	1	7
23	Bob Thornton	California Irvine	F	4	87	6-10	225	1	4
44	Chris Welp	Washington	C	1	16	7-0	245	2	2
25	David Wingate	Georgetown	G-F	2	44	6-5	185	3	3

FUTURE PLAYERS

ROOKIES	COLLEGE	POS	R#	D#	HT	WT
Kenny Payne	Louisville	F	1	19	6-8	200
Reggie Cross	Hawaii	F	2	44	6-8	243
Toney Mack	Georgia	G	2	54	6-5	215

* For further definition of category and column headings, see pages 42 & 43.

Philadelphia 76ers . . . . Overview

You remember, don't you? The 1988 playoffs, Charles Barkley on national television proclaiming to the world that he wouldn't be back in Philly for the 1988-89 season? You remember him talking about not getting along with management, that they didn't want him. Don't you? Well, the writers and broadcasters do. They were the ones green with envy, wishing just once in their life some superstar like Charles would walk up to them and publicly announce that he was hitting the road. Not surprisingly, Barkley easily got the most votes for the All-Interview team.

Charles Barkley	**37**
Karl Malone	27
Michael Jordan	23
Magic Johnson	22
Doc Rivers	21
Coach - Doug Moe	24

Interestingly, four of the five players were on the All-NBA 1st-team. But, before you jump to the conclusion that the media members only voted for players they liked to interview, you should realize that of the 25 players receiving votes for All-Interviewee, not one was named Akeem Olajuwon (5th member of All-NBA team).

Well, as you also remember, Charles Barkley did return to the Sixers and subsequently led them to 46 wins - an increase of 10 over the previous season. Now that things are apparently patched up, Charles may be able to keep raising the team's fortunes.

Barkley was one of only a few players to lead his position in more than one category. Among power forwards, he ranked first in both shooting (combined index) and assists per minute. Beyond that, he was 2nd in scoring, 4th in rebounding, and 7th in assists. In fact, the only category in which he shows any real weakness at all is blocks, where he was 20th among power forwards. Clearly, he is one of the most versatile players in the game today. In truth, he's one of the more gifted athletes in NBA history - perhaps world history.

By looking at the same 6 performance categories, we can see that his lowest *league* ranking was #66 in steals. Every player in the NBA had a lower ranking in some category - even Michael Jordan. Shown are the players who came the closest to claiming the Mr. Versatility award.

Charles Barkley	**#66**	**Steals**
Michael Jordan	#74	Rebounds
Clyde Drexler	#79	Blocks
Derrick McKey	#92	Rebounds
James Worthy	#93	Rebounds
Frank Brickowski	#97	Assists
Chris Mullin	#98	Rebounds

Of course, the big issue with Barkley is the question of whether he's too dominant within his own team. That's a question that has puzzled basketball fans for decades - going back to Wilt Chamberlain and before. I would argue that a player can be as dominant as Sir Charles while still leading the team to the crown. If we take Barkley's points + rebounds + assists and divide them by the team's totals, he was responsible for about 23% last season. That's a figure that other, possibly "too dominant" players (Jordan, Olajuwon), are familiar with. But it's also a figure that the top winners in the game (Bird, Johnson) have floated around. So the issue is not whether it's OK for him to be so dominant, but whether it's OK for *him* to be so dominant?

I've maintained for some time that the game is becoming more and more dependent upon the small positions (contrary to the bozos who want to raise the basket to 11 feet). By that, I mean those players who totally dominate from the perimeter will almost always lead their team to more victories than the player who equally dominates inside. The reason is basic. It's called teamwork.

Charles and Akeem will have major problems ever "leading" their team(s) to 55+ wins because their method of dominance doesn't include the rest of the

Philadelphia 76ers .... Overview

team. Magic and Larry are the consummate team players (though also as statistically dominant) while Michael is somewhere in between. An easy way to tell is to just count dunks. In a twisted sort of way, the less they get, the better the team's chances of winning (assuming equal dominance otherwise, of course).

Finally, I should point out that the team was 17-9 when Charles scored 30+ points - up from 1988 when they were only 18-15. He also ranked first in 2-pt efficiency points, but last in 3-pt efficiency points. Hey Charles, either read pages 223-225 or read my lips. Quit shooting threes!

Maurice Cheeks has been almost completely overshadowed by Barkley. He's obviously on the decline, and I hope he quits, like Dr. J, while he's still respectable. Even so, he did have a decent season in 1989. Among other things, he became the all-time steals leader with 1,942. Projecting his pace, I figure he should break 1,990 shortly after January 1st, 1990 and he could well steal our hearts by going over 2,000 on Valentine's Day. Cheeks also is among the leaders in most consecutive years (ongoing) with the same team.

Cheeks	Philadelphia	11
Cooper	Los Angeles	11
Bird	Boston	10
Magic	Los Angeles	10
English	Denver	10

The 76ers closed out the 1980's as the third winningest team in the decade. Their 535 wins was slightly ahead of Milwaukee's 522. And though there was a certain amount of *consistency* in their winning, there was sure a lot of *inconsistency* in a couple other areas - defensive field goal percentage and turnover margin.

In 1980, the Sixers were the best defensive fg% team in the league. Of course, they had Bobby Jones, a young Maurice Cheeks, Julius Erving, Caldwell Jones, etc. You get the point. In the first 5 years of the decade they had 11 entries on the All-Defensive 1st-team. That's truly remarkable. However, in the last 5 years they have only had 4 players on either the first *or* the second team. Another more amazing revelation of this defensive deterioration is that they were #1 in defensive fg% in 1981, #4 by 1983, #9 by 1985, #18 by 1987 and, as the decade ended, #25 (last) in 1989. Just because you can't get any lower than last doesn't mean it can't get any worse.

Another unusual statistic in the 80's was turnover margin. In 1980, the club was next to last. The difference in this stat vs defensive fg% is that it didn't reverse itself right away. It just stayed bad. The team was between 15th and 23rd every year from 1980-88. But then, out of nowhere, Philly ranked #1 last season. It was the first time they have had a positive margin since 1975.

Notes: By reaching the playoffs in 1989, Derek Smith broke out of an (0 for 6 season) slump - the longest among active players... Ron Anderson for Everette Stephens?... Kenny Payne may help the club's perimeter shooting, but he won't touch their defensive problems... When Philadelphia held their opponents to less than 50%, they were 36-9... Toney Mack (pick #54) was the NBA's version of Mr. Irrelevant (the last person chosen in the NFL draft). Only one #54 pick since 1977 has played in the NBA - Bobby Hansen, 6 years, Utah... Cliff Robinson and Mike Gminski were free agents at press time.

Prediction - best case: 49-33

It's hard for me to see the team improving that much. Charles can't get any better. The only reason a gain in wins is feasible at all is that Hawkins will be a year older and he still has superstar potential.

Prediction - worst case: 41-41

It's very difficult to imagine Chuck's team slipping below .500 - although they did just that in 1988. But with Robinson, Smith, Gminski and Cheeks all on the decline, they could come close.

To order back issues of Basketball Heaven or to obtain the 1990 Mid-season Report, see page 324.

Phoenix Suns . . . . Influence on Winning

TEAM RECORD BY

PLAYER	GAMES	... SCR Leader		... REB Leader		...AST Leader	
		HOME	ROAD	HOME	ROAD	HOME	ROAD
Kevin Johnson	81	5-1	4-5	0-0	2-1	31-6	18-19
Tom Chambers	81	16-5	10-12	10-4	6-12	0-0	0-0
Eddie Johnson	70	8-0	3-7	1-1	1-1	0-0	0-0
Jeff Hornacek	78	0-0	3-0	1-0	1-0	6-0	2-2
Armon Gilliam	74	6-1	1-0	10-1	3-4	0-0	0-0
Mark West	82	0-0	0-0	13-0	6-2	0-0	0-0
Tyrone Corbin	77	0-0	0-1	3-0	3-2	0-0	1-0
Dan Majerle	54	0-0	0-0	3-0	0-2	1-0	0-1
Tim Perry	62	0-0	0-0	0-0	0-0	0-0	0-0
Andrew Lang	62	0-0	0-0	0-0	1-0	0-0	0-0

TEAM RECORD BY SCORING *

PLAYER	PLAY	DNP	0-9	10-19	20-29	30-39	40+
Kevin Johnson	54-27	1-0	1-2	31-8	17-12	4-5	1-0
Tom Chambers	54-27	1-0	0-1	9-4	28-14	16-7	1-1
Eddie Johnson	48-22	7-5	2-3	13-9	26-9	7-0	0-1
Jeff Hornacek	52-26	3-1	13-8	30-15	8-3	1-0	0-0
Armon Gilliam	49-25	6-2	13-5	18-16	16-3	1-1	1-0
Mark West	55-27	0-0	37-24	17-3	1-0	0-0	0-0
Tyrone Corbin	51-26	4-1	35-16	12-9	4-0	0-1	0-0
Dan Majerle	34-20	21-7	1814	14-6	2-0	0-0	0-0
Tim Perry	42-20	13-7	33-19	9-1	0-0	0-0	0-0
Andrew Lang	44-18	11-9	43-17	0-1	1-0	0-0	0-0

TEAM RECORD BY STARTING POSITION *

PLAYER	GAMES	STARTS	PG	OG	SF	PF	C
Kevin Johnson	81	81	54-27	0-0	0-0	0-0	0-0
Tom Chambers	81	81	0-0	0-0	25-13	16-5	13-9
Eddie Johnson	70	7	0-0	0-0	3-4	0-0	0-0
Jeff Hornacek	78	73	1-0	48-24	0-0	0-0	0-0
Armon Gilliam	74	60	0-0	0-0	0-0	37-22	1-0
Mark West	82	32	0-0	0-0	0-0	0-0	23-9
Tyrone Corbin	77	30	0-0	4-1	18-6	1-0	0-0
Dan Majerle	54	5	0-0	2-2	0-1	0-0	0-0
Tim Perry	62	15	0-0	0-0	9-3	1-0	1-1
Andrew Lang	62	25	0-0	0-0	0-0	0-0	17-8

* For further definition of each category and column heading see pages 42 & 43.

Phoenix Suns . . . . 1988-89 Statistics

RAW NUMBERS *

PLAYER	2pt%	3pt%	FT%	MIN	PF	DQ	HI	TO	RB	AS	BL	ST
Kevin Johnson	.514	.091	**.882**	3179	226	1	41	**322**	340	991	24	135
Tom Chambers	.479	.326	.851	3002	271	2	42	231	**684**	231	55	87
Eddie Johnson	.510	**.413**	.868	2043	198	0	**45**	122	306	162	7	47
Jeff Hornacek	.511	.333	.826	2487	188	0	32	111	266	465	8	129
Armon Gilliam	.503	0-0	.743	2120	176	2	41	140	541	52	27	54
Mark West	**.653**	0-0	.535	2019	**273**	4	24	103	551	39	**187**	35
Tyrone Corbin	.542	0-2	.788	1655	222	2	30	92	398	118	13	82
Dan Majerle	.440	.329	.614	1354	139	1	25	48	209	130	14	63
Tim Perrry	.543	.250	.615	614	47	0	19	37	132	18	32	19
Andrew Lang	.513	0-0	.650	526	112	1	21	28	147	9	48	17

OVERALL RANKINGS *

PLAYER	G	GS	PPG	PR	RANK	SC	SH	RB	AS	BL	ST
Kevin Johnson	81	**81**	20.37	27.06	10	23	23	141	4	125	59
Tom Chambers	81	**81**	25.74	24.11	13	9	77	57	94	76	114
Eddie Johnson	70	7	21.49	17.93	49	19	22	104	88	159	138
Jeff Hornacek	78	73	13.51	17.06	60	87	49	140	30	165	32
Armon Gilliam	74	60	15.89	15.74	82	63	85	32	171	96	127
Mark West	**82**	32	7.24	13.17	107	157	10	24	175	7	164
Tyrone Corbin	77	30	8.19	11.73	128	149	20	45	99	123	37
Dan Majerle	54	5	8.65	9.91	149	145	166	101	72	107	47
Tim Perry	62	15	4.15	4.89	DNQ						
Andrew Lang	62	25	2.56	4.42	DNQ						

POSITION RANKINGS *

PLAYER	POSITION	RANK	SC	SH	RB	AS	BL	ST
Kevin Johnson	Point Guard	3	2	4	17	4	10	21
Tom Chambers	Small Forward, PF	2	4	15	7	21	20	21
Eddie Johnson	Off Guard, SF	8	6	6	12	34	36	42
Jeff Hornacek	Off Guard	11	26	15	26	5	42	13
Armon Gilliam	Power Forward	16	9	18	14	29	25	21
Mark West	Center	18	23	2	11	29	6	23
Tyrone Corbin	Small Forward	29	37	4	3	22	35	6
Dan Majerle	Small Forward, OG	32	36	39	27	13	30	10
Tim Perry	Small Forward	DNQ						
Andrew Lang	Center	DNQ						

*For further definition of each category and column heading see pages 42 & 43.

Phoenix Suns . . . . Team Info

WEEKLY POWER RATING

41 WINS - AVERAGE (See page 43 for Team Power Rating discussion.)

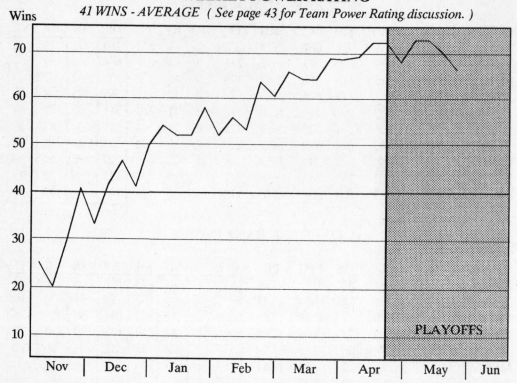

Miscellaneous Categories	Data	Rank
Attendance	511K	20
Key-Man Games Missed	59	11
Season Record	55-27	4
- Home	35-6	3
- Road	20-21	3
Eastern Conference	14-10	5
Western Conference	41-17	6
Overtime Record	1-2	18
Record 5 Pts. or Less	9-10	17
Record 10 Pts. or More	33-14	6
Games Won By Bench	5	11
Games Won By Starters	13	5
Winning Streak	9	2
Losing Streak	3	3
Home Winning Streak	11	12
Road Winning Streak	6	1
Home Losing Streak	2	5
Road Losing Streak	3	1

Performance Categories	Data	Rank
Offensive Scoring (per game)	118.6	1
Defensive Scoring (per game)	110.9	16
Scoring Margin (per game)	7.7	1
Defensive FG%	.464	5
Offensive 2-point%	.508	5
Offensive 3-point%	.349	4
Offensive Free Throw %	.791	5
Offensive Rebs (Off REB/Opp Def REB)		20
Defensive Rebs (Def REB/Opp Off REB)		10
Offensive Assists (AST/FGMade)		10
Offensive Blocks (BLK/Opp FGAttempted)		19
Offensive Steals (STL/Game)		19
Turnover Margin (Def T.O. - Off T.O.)		10
Fouls Margin (Opp FOULS - FOULS)		8
Rebounding Record	40-37-5	9
Assists Record	41-36-5	11
Field Goal Pct. Record	51-30-1	4
Free Throw Att. Record	49-26-7	5

Phoenix Suns . . . . Team Roster

MOST PRODUCTIVE PLAYERS

Player	Span	Yrs	CRD
Alvan Adams	1976-88	13	17,397
Walter Davis	1978-88	11	16,424
Dick Van Arsdale	1969-77	9	10,805
Larry Nance	1982-88	7	10,551
Paul Westphal	1976-84	6	8,535
Connie Hawkins	1970-73	5	7,436
Paul Silas	1970-72	3	5,202
Truck Robinson	1979-82	4	5,055
Kyle Macy	1981-85	5	4,882
Maurice Lucas	1983-85	3	4,210

PRESENT PLAYERS*

J#	VETERANS	COLLEGE	POS	R#	D#	HT	WT	Phoe	NBA
24	Tom Chambers	Utah	F	1	8	6-10	230	1	8
25	T.R. Dunn	Alabama	G	2	41	6-4	193	1	12
	Dean Garrett	Indiana	F	2	38	6-9	220	1	1
35	Armon Gilliam	UNLV	F	1	2	6-9	245	2	2
14	Jeff Hornacek	Iowa State	G	2	46	6-4	191	3	3
8	Eddie A. Johnson	Illinois	F	2	29	6-7	210	2	8
10	Kevin Johnson	California	G	1	7	6-1	180	2	2
4	Steve Kerr	Arizona	G	2	50	6-3	175	1	1
28	Andrew Lang	Arkansas	C	2	28	6-11	245	1	1
9	Dan Majerle	Central Michigan	F	1	14	6-6	220	1	1
45	Ed Nealy	Kansas State	F	8	166	6-7	238	1	6
34	Tim Perry	Temple	F	1	7	6-9	219	1	1
41	Mark West	Old Dominion	F-C	2	30	6-10	226	2	6
	Michael Williams	Baylor	G	2	48	6-2	175	0	1

FUTURE PLAYERS

ROOKIES	COLLEGE	POS	R#	D#	HT	WT
Kenny Battle	Illinois	F	1	27	6-6	211
Ricky Blanton	Louisiana State	F	2	46	6-7	215
Mike Morrison	Loyola (Md)	G	2	51	6-4	195
Greg Grant	Trenton State	G	2	52	5-6	140

* For further definition of category and column headings, see pages 42 & 43.

Phoenix Suns .... Overview

You've surely heard the phrases a hundred times by now - "land of the rising sun, phoenix rising from the ashes, etc." Well, regardless of how many times they've been said, they couldn't be more appropriate. The Phoenix Suns *did* rise from the ashes in 1989. After being consumed by the fire of drugs, defeats, death, and dismissal, this team, valiantly and courageously, transformed itself into an NBA power overnight (+27 wins). In fact, only two other teams in NBA history have had greater single-season turnarounds (Bird's rookie year with Boston, +32 wins, and Abdul-Jabbar's rookie season with Milwaukee, +29 wins) and I'm not sure there's ever been a bigger surprise than Phoenix.

Not only did the Suns win 55 games in 1989 and finish 2nd in the Western Conference behind the Lakers, but they did it despite a mediocre 11-10 start. From that beginning the club went 44-17 to LA's 41-20. The Suns played the final three-fourths of the season at a 60 win rate. In fact, so incredible was their momentum that a late-season 9-game winning streak showed an average victory margin of 23 points per outing. Their power rating chart on page 158 is impressive, to say the least.

What makes it even more impressive is that the average age of last season's top-10 players was only 25 years. With that kind of youth, the club could well improve yet more and their running game shouldn't miss a step.

Phoenix ranked #1 in scoring last season, having broken the 100-point barrier 79 of 82 games. Additionally, they had 4 players who scored 40+ points in a game and 3 who averaged 20+ ppg, both league highs. With such a potent offense, they seemed to be, at times, invincible. But what can happen to high scoring teams is that they are much less successful in the playoffs. Since the ABA joined the NBA in 1976, the league's highest scoring teams have won 59% of their regular-season games, but only 48% of their playoff encounters. The Suns reflected this pattern. Though they won 67% of their games, they went 7-5 (58%) in the playoffs and were swept in the Western Conference finals vs LA.

Though they deserved all the accolades they got, it is nonetheless true that if they want to go the next step to the finals or to the championship, they must improve their defense. When the Suns scored more than 115 points they were 34-15. That's fine and dandy. But when the club held their opponents to *less* than 115, they were 10 games better (44-5). With a little tougher defense, this will be the best team in the NBA and may well be anyway.

After a full year it's probably appropriate to evaluate the big trade with Cleveland. It is correctly regarded as a trade which helped both teams. The Cavs tied for 2nd, with 57 victories - up 15, while Phoenix was 4th with 55 - up 27. Whereas Nance and Sanders were the missing pieces to Cleveland's puzzle, Kevin Johnson, Mark West, Tyrone Corbin, and Dan Majerle were all instrumental in Phoenix's recovery. The Cleveland three (including Randolph Keys) contributed 24% of the team's production while the Phoenix four were even more significant contributors to their club's production (37%).

Whereas it's also true that West (#1 in the league in fg%), Majerle (14.3 ppg playoff average), and Corbin (11.7 Production Rating) were important to the team, the player who seemed to dwarf them all was Kevin Johnson. Though a year ago KJ was a virtual unknown, I predicted he would be an All-Star in the 1990 season. He will be.

Johnson possesses lightning-quick moves and because of his ability to penetrate, he got a lot of lay-ups and drew a lot of fouls. This talent was especially profitable since he hit a spectacular 88% from the line. In addition to that, Johnson became only the 5th player in league history to average 20+ points and 10+ assists in the same season. Oscar Robertson did it 5 times, Isiah Thomas 4, Magic Johnson 2, and Tiny Ar-

Phoenix Suns .... Overview

chibald 1. At only 23 years of age, Johnson might someday challenge the Big O. For these reasons, it's no surprise to anybody that he was named Most-Improved Player-of-the-Year in the NBA.

Tom Chambers also had a strong season - easily his highest year in overall production. Not only that, but his 25.7 scoring average was the highest in franchise history. As good as he was, he still worries me. Chambers is the quintessential offensive-minded player (#4 in scoring at small forward). But his defense is very questionable as he ranked #21 at his position in steals and #20 in blocks. Beyond that, he was 21st in assists indicating a lack of desire to pass the ball despite being a somewhat average shooter (15th).

It's not that I mean to be particularly critical of Tom (I'm sure some of you are saying, "Get off his back."), but unless he becomes a more conscientious shooter and a decent defensive player (I don't think he'll ever be either one), this team will always have a weakness that other teams can exploit. And, although he was voted 2nd-team All-NBA the same as Kevin Johnson, my contention is that ten years from now when the final chapter on this team has been written, it will have long since been decided that the primary reason (by far) that they were so good was KJ, not TC.

By singling out those two, I don't mean to dismiss Eddie Johnson. EJ was so explosive coming off the bench that he was voted 6th-Man-of-the-Year. His ability to score in bunches was displayed vividly in an early season game vs the Clippers. In that contest, he scored an unbelievable 43 points in the second half! He even improved on that by adding 3-point bombs to his arsenal late in the year. In his last 13 games, Johnson hit 27/54 (.500) which would have put him at the top of the league had he done it all season. Perhaps this year, he will.

Like everybody else on this team, Cotton Fitzsimmons won his award - Coach-of-the-Year - by beating out Don Nelson in a rela-

tively close vote. In so doing, Fitz tied with Nelson, Bill Fitch, and Gene Shue as the only two-time winners. Despite the company, the 55 wins last season represented the first time in 16 years of coaching that one of Cotton's teams has broken the 50 win barrier.

For whatever reason, Armon Gilliam found Cotton's dog house around mid-season. His playing time in the second half of the year was substantially reduced as Corbin started most of the time. The club failed to protect Tyrone in the expansion draft, however, so it would appear that Gilliam has a chance to work back into Fitz's good graces. He can start by passing more, as he ranked #2 in Black Hole rating (assists/fga's). Additionally, he was the 3rd-highest fined player in the NBA so he needs to learn how to control his temper. Still, when he played well (19+ points), so did the team (22-4).

Notes: Phoenix was 28-0 at home vs Western Conference foes until their last attempt - a loss to Houston... The Suns were #1 in percentage of comebacks in Q4 (5) vs blown games in Q4 (1) = .833... In one playoff game Phoenix was 28/28 from the line... Fitzsimmons' personal losing streak in LA is now at 39 games... Jerry Colangelo was named Executive-of-the-Year... When KJ scored in the teens, Phoenix was 31-8... When Mark West scored 9+ points, the club went 21-4... Amazingly, only Jeff Hornacek remains from the 1987 club.

Prediction - best case: 65-17

Who knows where the limits are? Even so, 65 wins is huge. Any team that gets that is up among the all-time best.

Prediction - worst case: 52-30

When you gain 27 wins in one season, over-confidence can block continued success extremely easily. I really don't think it will in this case though, so *only* 52 wins would surprise me a lot.

To order back issues of Basketball Heaven or to obtain the 1990 Mid-season Report, see page 324.

Portland Trail Blazers . . . . . . Influence on Winning

TEAM RECORD BY

PLAYER	GAMES	... SCR Leader		... REB Leader		...AST Leader	
		HOME	ROAD	HOME	ROAD	HOME	ROAD
Clyde Drexler	78	17-8	6-18	5-3	2-12	6-3	3-9
Terry Porter	81	2-3	2-2	1-0	0-2	23-11	9-23
Jerome Kersey	76	3-3	1-5	12-7	1-10	1-0	0-1
Kevin Duckworth	79	6-0	2-6	11-3	5-10	0-0	0-0
Steve Johnson	72	0-0	0-1	3-0	0-1	0-0	0-0
Danny Young	48	0-0	0-0	0-0	0-0	0-0	0-0
Richard Anderson	72	0-0	0-0	1-1	2-0	0-0	0-0
Caldwell Jones	72	0-0	0-0	1-0	2-0	0-0	0-0
Adrian Branch	67	1-0	0-0	0-0	0-1	0-0	0-0
Mark Bryant	56	0-0	0-0	1-1	0-0	0-0	0-0

TEAM RECORD BY SCORING *

PLAYER	PLAY	DNP	0-9	10-19	20-29	30-39	40+
Clyde Drexler	38-40	1-3	0-0	3-8	24-19	7-10	4-3
Terry Porter	38-43	1-0	0-3	25-27	12-13	1-0	0-0
Jerome Kersey	36-40	3-3	3-2	20-23	11-13	2-2	0-0
Kevin Duckworth	39-40	0-3	5-4	16-22	16-13	2-1	0-0
Steve Johnson	34-38	5-5	15-21	17-15	2-2	0-0	0-0
Danny Young	25-23	14-20	21-19	4-4	0-0	0-0	0-0
Richard Anderson	37-35	2-8	30-29	7-5	0-1	0-0	0-0
Caldwell Jones	35-37	4-6	34-36	1-1	0-0	0-0	0-0
Adrian Branch	32-35	7-8	19-23	11-10	2-2	0-0	0-0
Mark Bryant	26-30	13-13	23-24	3-6	0-0	0-0	0-0

TEAM RECORD BY STARTING POSITION *

PLAYER	GAMES	STARTS	PG	OG	SF	PF	C
Clyde Drexler	78	78	0-0	37-39	1-1	0-0	0-0
Terry Porter	81	81	38-43	0-0	0-0	0-0	0-0
Jerome Kersey	76	76	0-0	0-0	35-39	1-1	0-0
Kevin Duckworth	79	79	0-0	0-0	0-0	0-0	39-40
Steve Johnson	72	11	0-0	0-0	0-0	5-3	0-3
Danny Young	48	2	1-0	1-0	0-0	0-0	0-0
Richard Anderson	72	3	0-0	0-0	2-1	0-0	0-0
Caldwell Jones	72	40	0-0	0-0	0-0	18-22	0-0
Adrian Branch	67	4	0-0	0-2	1-1	0-0	0-0
Mark Bryant	56	32	0-0	0-0	0-0	15-17	0-0

* For further definition of each category and column heading see pages 42 & 43.

Portland Trail Blazers . . . . 1988-89 Statistics

RAW NUMBERS *

PLAYER	2pt%	3pt%	FT%	MIN	PF	DQ	HI	TO	RB	AS	BL	ST
Clyde Drexler	.511	.260	.799	3064	269	2	**50**	250	615	450	54	**213**
Terry Porter	.497	**.361**	.840	**3102**	187	1	34	248	367	**770**	8	146
Jerome Kersey	.472	.286	.694	2716	277	**6**	33	167	629	243	84	137
Kevin Duckworth	.478	0-2	.757	2662	**300**	**6**	32	200	**635**	60	49	56
Steve Johnson	**.524**	0-0	.527	1477	254	3	27	140	358	105	44	20
Danny Young	.490	.340	.781	952	50	0	19	45	74	123	3	55
Richard Anderson	.464	.348	**.842**	1082	100	1	20	54	231	98	12	44
Caldwell Jones	.423	0-1	.787	1279	166	0	11	83	300	59	**85**	24
Adrian Branch	.481	.226	.725	811	99	0	28	64	132	60	3	45
Mark Bryant	.486	0-0	.580	803	144	3	17	41	179	33	7	20

OVERALL RANKINGS *

PLAYER	G	GS	PPG	PR	RANK	SC	SH	RB	AS	BL	ST
Clyde Drexler	78	78	**27.22**	28.87	6	4	58	73	45	79	9
Terry Porter	**81**	**81**	17.67	22.42	18	41	47	127	11	169	44
Jerome Kersey	76	76	17.50	20.24	32	43	143	52	79	42	34
Kevin Duckworth	79	79	18.13	16.72	68	40	121	47	173	75	151
Steve Johnson	72	11	10.01	10.04	148	129	140	41	102	45	172
Danny Young	48	2	6.19	7.46	DNQ						
Richard Anderson	72	3	5.15	6.85	DNQ						
Caldwell Jones	72	40	2.81	6.50	DNQ						
Adrian Branch	67	4	7.43	6.07	DNQ						
Mark Bryant	56	32	5.00	5.75	DNQ						

POSITION RANKINGS *

PLAYER	POSITION	RANK	SC	SH	RB	AS	BL	ST
Clyde Drexler	Off Guard, SF	2	3	16	4	14	7	4
Terry Porter	Point Guard	4	6	10	12	11	27	16
Jerome Kersey	Small Forward	7	16	35	5	15	9	5
Kevin Duckworth	Center	11	6	18	23	27	26	17
Steve Johnson	Center, PF	27	19	22	20	4	22	28
Danny Young	Point Guard	DNQ						
Richard Anderson	Small Forward	DNQ						
Caldwell Jones	Power Forward	DNQ						
Adrian Branch	Off Guard	DNQ						
Mark Bryant	Power Forward	DNQ						

*For further definition of each category and column heading see pages 42 & 43.

Portland Trail Blazers .... Team Info

WEEKLY POWER RATING

41 WINS - AVERAGE (See page 43 for Team Power Rating discussion.)

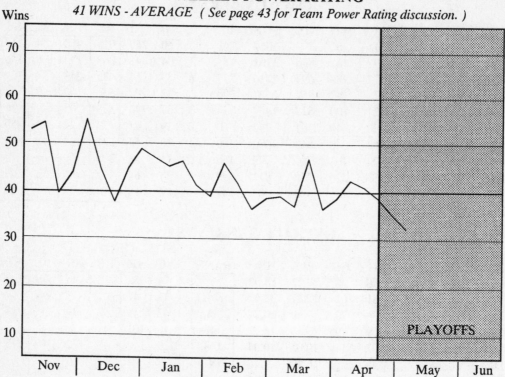

Miscellaneous Categories	Data	Rank
Attendance	527K	18
Key-Man Games Missed	151	25
Season Record	39-43	17
- Home	28-13	17
- Road	11-30	15
Eastern Conference	9-15	17
Western Conference	30-28	16
Overtime Record	4-1	2
Record 5 Pts. or Less	11-17	23
Record 10 Pts. or More	22-15	10
Games Won By Bench	3	16
Games Won By Starters	7	11
Winning Streak	4	17
Losing Streak	6	12
Home Winning Streak	12	10
Road Winning Streak	3	9
Home Losing Streak	4	16
Road Losing Streak	9	14

Performance Categories	Data	Rank
Offensive Scoring (per game)	114.6	6
Defensive Scoring (per game)	113.1	22
Scoring Margin (per game)	1.5	12
Defensive FG%	.488	18
Offensive 2-point%	.487	13
Offensive 3-point%	.335	8
Offensive Free Throw %	.740	21
Offensive Rebs .....(Off REB/Opp Def REB)		3
Defensive Rebs ....(Def REB/Opp Off REB)		13
Offensive Assists ....(AST/FGMade)		12
Offensive Blocks ..(BLK/Opp FGAttempted)		20
Offensive Steals.....................(STL/Game)		5
Turnover Margin........(Def T.O. - Off T.O.)		5
Fouls Margin ....(Opp FOULS - FOULS)		15
Rebounding Record	47-33-2	6
Assists Record	46-33-3	6
Field Goal Pct. Record	34-47-1	17
Free Throw Att. Record	35-44-3	17

Portland Trail Blazers . . . . Team Roster

MOST PRODUCTIVE PLAYERS

Player	Span	Yrs	CRD
Mychal Thompson	1979-86	7	10,945
Clyde Drexler	1984-89	6	10,605
Sidney Wicks	1972-76	5	9,382
Jim Paxson	1980-88	9	8,897
Geoff Petrie	1971-76	6	7,333
Calvin Natt	1980-84	5	6,188
Lloyd Neal	1973-78	7	6,148
Bob Gross	1976-82	7	6,061
Terry Porter	1986-89	4	5,841
Jerome Kersey	1985-89	5	5,808

portland trailblazers ™

PRESENT PLAYERS*

J#	VETERANS	COLLEGE	POS	R#	D#	HT	WT	Port	NBA
35	Richard Anderson	U.C. Santa Barbara	F	2	32	6-10	240	2	5
24	Adrian Branch	Maryland	G-F	2	46	6-8	185	1	3
2	Mark Bryant	Seton Hall	F	1	21	6-9	245	1	1
	Wayne Cooper	New Orleans	C	2	40	6-10	220	0	11
22	Clyde Drexler	Houston	G-F	1	13	6-7	215	6	6
00	Kevin Duckworth	Eastern Illinois	C	2	33	7-0	280	3	3
32	Rolando Ferreira	Houston	C	2	26	7-1	240	1	1
25	Jerome Kersey	Longwood	F	2	46	6-7	222	5	5
30	Terry Porter	Wisc. St. Point	G	1	24	6-3	195	4	4
	Buck Williams	Maryland	F	1	3	6-8	225	0	8
21	Danny Young	Wake Forest	G	2	39	6-4	175	1	5

FUTURE PLAYERS

ROOKIES	COLLEGE	POS	R#	D#	HT	WT
Byron Irvin	Missouri	G	1	22	6-6	191
Cliff Robinson	Connecticut	F-C	2	36	6-11	223

* For further definition of category and column headings, see pages 42 & 43.

Portland Trail Blazers . . . . Overview

This was a franchise that I had very high hopes for last season. In fact, it seemed inconceivable to me that they would win fewer than 50 games - probably closer to 60. The Blazers were a team with youth, speed, good coaching, good management and they hadn't won less than 40 games since 1980. Well, as you know by now, they didn't win 60. They didn't win 50. They didn't win 40. In fact, 1989 has to be viewed as the club's worst showing in the league since their expansion years of the early 1970's. What happened?

Ironically enough, I think what happened was too much of a good thing - talent. Shortly after being selected to the NBA All-Star team in 1988, Steve Johnson was injured. In came Kevin Duckworth. He played so well the second half of the season that Johnson was unable to get his job back. If you're an all-star and you can't start on your own team, you're not happy. Consequently, SJ was left unprotected and chosen by Minnesota in the expansion draft.

Nearly an identical story for Kiki Vandeweghe and Jerome Kersey. Remember, Vandeweghe averaged 27ppg in 1987. When Kersey replaced him as a starter for much of 1988, Kiki was less than pleased. It is no surprise that it came to a head last season. Result - Vandeweghe traded.

Throw in having to use a 38 year old as your starting power forward and Clyde Drexler's personality conflict with Mike Schuler... Well, you get the picture. Because the club had arguably the worst chemistry in the league, Schuler was let go at mid-season and replaced by Rick Adelman. Though Mike had been named NBA-Coach-of-the-Year in 1987 and was 3rd in the voting in 1988, he was easier to fire than the players. Portland was 25-22 when he left, yet finished 14-21.

With Caldwell Jones creaking around at power forward, Blazer management rightfully determined they needed a replacement. Obviously, Mark Bryant wasn't the next Karl Malone, so that left two choices - either hope to get a solid power forward in the draft or make a trade. Portland had long sought New Jersey forward Buck Williams. He seemed perfect. He was durable, had a good attitude, and played the position Portland needed the most. So the Blazers packed Sam Bowie's bags, stuck the #12 pick in his pocket and sent him to the Nets in exchange for Williams. Was it a good decision? I'm going to argue that it was not.

First of all, *the* job of the power forward is to rebound, yet the Blazers were already very strong in that area - having corralled more rebounds the last two seasons than any team in the league. And it wasn't because of Kiki or Steve or Sam - all of whom are gone. If rebounding wasn't the most important need to fill, what was? Leadership and setting a good example? Both Bowie and Williams were capable of that. Perimeter shooting? Other than Porter, who is average, they have only 6'10" Richard Anderson as a reasonable long-range shooter. Bowie is a much better outside shooter than Williams. Defense? Portland's was lousy - mostly because of the lack of a defensive anchor in the middle. Bowie may be among the league's best as a defensive center while Buck Williams is no better than average, defensively, at this stage of his career.

Despite all those reasons, though, I chose to decide this case on it's statistical merits. I looked at every power forward in recent NBA history and chose the four who most closely resembled Buck's career for his first 8 years. The four were Truck Robinson, Maurice Lucas, Dan Roundfield, and George McGinnis (RLRM). Shown below is that group and Williams side by side.

	HT	WT	PR/48	OR	PS
RLRM	6'8"	222	29.97	22.13	5.03
Williams	6'8"	225	29.92	22.98	5.25

Ht = Height, Wt = Weight, PR/48 = Production Rating on a 48-minute basis, OR = Overall League Rank (average per year), PS = League rank at power forward (average per year). As you can see, these

Portland Trail Blazers .... Overview

players are very similar. Next, I developed the average remainder of these player's careers. Here it is.

	G	MIN	PR	OR	PS
Year 9	75	2450	18.00	55	14
Year 10	68	1950	15.00	70	18
Year 11	62	1500	12.00	95	24
Year 12	55	1050	9.00	140	35

If that's what Portland can expect in the next four years from Williams, then they made a huge mistake. Some will argue that Buck has been indestructible and will play much longer. Sure, he *used* to be, but he has missed 20 games the past two years. History shows that the body starts breaking down after year 8, especially in the rugged power forward position. Last year his scoring and rebounding dropped to easily the lowest levels of his career.

With Bowie's injury history, though, this might seem like a feasible trade if not for the attached #12 pick. Are four declining years from a power forward (when you're an excellent rebounding team anyway) worth the entire careers of players like Mookie Blaylock or John Williams or Mike Woodson or Kelly Tripucka (all #12's)? Or, to bring it closer to home, Jim Paxson?

Speaking of rebounding, Clyde Drexler is clearly the best offensive rebounder since 1974 (when offensive rebounds were first kept) for a guard.

Drexler	1989	289
Drexler	1988	261
Magic	1982	252
Dunn	1983	231
Drexler	1987	227
Moncrief	1982	221
Drexler	1985	217

Despite his obvious skills at crashing the boards and getting stick-backs, or should I say slam-backs, it sometimes meant the club didn't get back on defense. As a result, often his highest scoring games resulted in a loss. Interestingly, the club was only 11-13 when Drexler scored 30+ points. Of the 18 NBA players who broke 30 at least 10 times, Clyde's 11-13 was the only losing record. What's more, those 18 players included Tripucka (Charlotte) and Person (Indiana). Clearly, his scoring was not always best for the team. Another point: When Clyde shot less than 22 field goal attempts, they were 24-17. When he shot 22+, they were only 14-23.

Kevin Duckworth had a poor season. After coming on like gang-busters in 1988, he was given a shocking $16 million contract. Perhaps the pressure of living up to it caused his decline or perhaps the league just figured out how to stop him. Either way, the results were that he ranked #17 or worse among centers in 5 of the 6 major statistical categories. His #6 rank in scoring prevented him from being Johnson's back-up. Unfortunately, his desire to score (like Drexler's) is a problem too. He easily led the league in the undesirable category "Black Hole" (FGA's/Assists).

Notes: Portland was 1-7 in 1 or 2 point contests. They are now 18-40 in the last 8 years in super close games... The club ranked last in key-man games missed... Jerome Kersey was shooting over 50% from the field prior to his December injury. After he came back, he only hit 45%... Richard Anderson made nearly 40% of his 3-pointers in the latter part of the year... Byron Irvin may turn out to be an excellent pro, but his outside shot is suspect...

Prediction - best case: 54-28

Even though the trade was a mistake, the Blazers should benefit for a year or two. With the late-summer acquisition of Wayne Cooper (defensive stopper), good things should prevail in the city of roses.

Prediction - worst case 44-38

If Portland only wins 44 games in 1990, Clyde Drexler will be history. It's hard to imagine how these players could only be average, but then that was true last season as well.

To order back issues of Basketball Heaven or to obtain the 1990 Mid-season Report, see page 324.

Sacramento Kings . . . . Influence on Winning

TEAM RECORD BY

PLAYER	GAMES	... SCR Leader		... REB Leader		...AST Leader	
		HOME	ROAD	HOME	ROAD	HOME	ROAD
Wayman Tisdale	31	1-2	1-7	7-2	1-8	0-0	0-0
Danny Ainge	28	3-3	1-3	0-0	0-0	3-2	2-2
Kenny Smith	81	6-6	3-10	0-0	0-0	16-13	2-26
Rodney McCray	68	0-4	0-2	3-7	2-9	2-3	2-5
Harold Pressley	80	2-1	0-3	2-4	1-6	1-1	0-1
Jim Petersen	66	1-0	0-1	3-3	1-4	0-0	0-0
Ricky Berry	64	4-1	0-5	0-0	0-1	0-0	0-1
Vinnie Del Negro	80	0-2	0-1	0-0	0-0	2-1	0-4
Brad Lohaus	29	1-0	0-0	2-1	0-0	0-0	0-0
Ben Gillery	24	0-0	0-0	0-0	0-0	0-0	0-0

TEAM RECORD BY SCORING *

PLAYER	PLAY	DNP	0-9	10-19	20-29	30-39	40+
Wayman Tisdale	13-18	14-37	0-1	8-9	5-6	0-2	0-0
Danny Ainge	12-16	15-39	1-1	5-8	5-5	1-1	0-1
Kenny Smith	27-54	0-1	1-8	12-30	14-14	0-2	0-0
Rodney McCray	21-47	6-8	7-14	13-28	1-5	0-0	0-0
Harold Pressley	27-53	0-2	8-19	14-29	5-5	0-0	0-0
Jim Petersen	23-43	4-12	8-22	13-20	2-1	0-0	0-0
Ricky Berry	21-43	6-12	10-22	5-17	4-4	2-0	0-0
Vinnie Del Negro	26-54	1-1	20-38	4-14	2-2	0-0	0-0
Brad Lohaus	12-17	15-38	7-11	3-6	2-0	0-0	0-0
Ben Gillery	6-18	21-37	6-18	0-0	0-0	0-0	0-0

TEAM RECORD BY STARTING POSITION *

PLAYER	GAMES	STARTS	PG	OG	SF	PF	C
Wayman Tisdale	31	30	0-0	0-0	0-0	13-17	0-0
Danny Ainge	28	26	0-0	10-16	0-0	0-0	0-0
Kenny Smith	81	81	27-54	0-0	0-0	0-0	0-0
Rodney McCray	68	65	0-0	0-0	18-40	1-6	0-0
Harold Pressley	80	36	0-0	12-20	1-3	0-0	0-0
Jim Petersen	66	40	0-0	0-0	0-0	6-11	8-15
Ricky Berry	64	21	0-0	0-5	7-9	0-0	0-0
Vinnie Del Negro	80	2	0-1	1-0	0-0	0-0	0-0
Brad Lohaus	29	10	0-0	0-0	0-0	0-0	5-5
Ben Gillery	24	0	0-0	0-0	0-0	0-0	0-0

* For further definition of each category and column heading see pages 42 & 43.

Sacramento Kings . . . . 1988-89 Statistics

RAW NUMBERS *

PLAYER	2pt%	3pt%	FT%	MIN	PF	DQ	HI	TO	RB	AS	BL	ST
Wayman Tisdale	**.516**	0-4	.773	2434	**290**	7	39	172	**609**	128	52	55
Danny Ainge	.488	.380	**.854**	2377	186	1	**45**	145	255	402	8	93
Kenny Smith	.475	.359	.737	**3145**	173	0	33	**249**	226	**621**	7	**102**
Rodney McCray	.474	.227	.722	2435	121	0	29	168	514	293	36	57
Harold Pressley	.457	.403	.780	2257	215	1	26	124	485	174	**76**	93
Jim Petersen	.465	0-8	.747	1633	236	**8**	25	147	413	81	68	47
Ricky Berry	.467	**.406**	.789	1406	197	4	34	82	197	80	22	37
Vinnie Del Negro	.482	.300	.850	1556	160	2	28	77	171	206	14	65
Brad Lohaus	.440	.091	.786	1214	161	1	29	77	256	66	56	30
Ben Gillery	.316	0-0	.565	84	29	0	5	5	23	2	4	2

OVERALL RANKINGS *

PLAYER	G	GS	PPG	PR	RANK	SC	SH	RB	AS	BL	ST
Wayman Tisdale	79	35	17.48	**18.43**	47	45	52	37	136	66	139
Danny Ainge	73	54	**17.55**	17.64	53	44	38	138	35	161	75
Kenny Smith	**81**	**81**	17.32	17.04	61	47	122	172	23	172	103
Rodney McCray	68	65	12.56	**16.65**	70	97	139	69	54	90	136
Harold Pressley	80	36	12.26	14.60	95	100	64	66	93	37	65
Jim Petersen	66	40	10.17	**11.61**	129	125	147	34	145	24	115
Ricky Berry	64	21	11.03	9.58	151	115	57	111	128	87	124
Vinne Del Negro	80	2	7.11	**8.36**	165	158	98	134	50	117	62
Brad Lohaus	77	25	6.52	6.95	DNQ						
Ben Gillery	24	0	1.04	**1.17**	DNQ						

POSITION RANKINGS *

PLAYER	POSITION	RANK	SC	SH	RB	AS	BL	ST
Wayman Tisdale	Power Forward	10	5	9	17	13	21	23
Danny Ainge	Off Guard	10	12	12	24	7	38	27
Kenny Smith	Point Guard	13	8	21	30	20	30	29
Rodney McCray	Small Forward	17	25	34	10	5	26	30
Harold Pressley	Off Guard	18	30	18	2	36	1	22
Jim Petersen	Power Forward, C	28	24	28	15	17	7	17
Ricky Berry	Small Forward	33	27	10	34	32	24	25
Vinnie Del Negro	Point Guard	31	29	16	15	32	7	23
Brad Lohaus	Center, PF	DNQ						
Ben Gillery	Center	DNQ						

*For further definition of each category and column heading see pages 42 & 43.

Sacramento Kings . . . . Team Info

WEEKLY POWER RATING
41 WINS - AVERAGE (See page 43 for Team Power Rating discussion.)

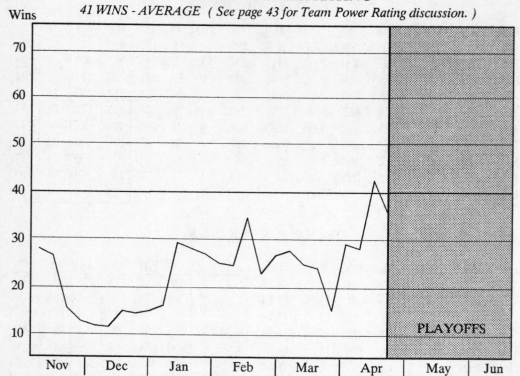

Miscellaneous Categories	Data	Rank
Attendance	677K	10
Key-Man Games Missed	49	9
Season Record	27-55	20
- Home	21-20	19
- Road	6-35	22
Eastern Conference	4-20	24
Western Conference	23-35	20
Overtime Record	0-3	24
Record 5 Pts. or Less	10-10	9
Record 10 Pts. or More	13-34	20
Games Won By Bench	2	23
Games Won By Starters	5	16
Winning Streak	3	20
Losing Streak	7	15
Home Winning Streak	7	17
Road Winning Streak	1	21
Home Losing Streak	7	22
Road Losing Streak	9	14

Performance Categories	Data	Rank
Offensive Scoring (per game)	105.5	20
Defensive Scoring (per game)	111.0	17
Scoring Margin (per game)	-5.5	20
Defensive FG%	.484	14
Offensive 2-point%	.468	24
Offensive 3-point%	.373	2
Offensive Free Throw %	.770	13
Offensive Rebs ..... (Off REB/Opp Def REB)		22
Defensive Rebs .... (Def REB/Opp Off REB)		9
Offensive Assists .... (AST/FGMade)		18
Offensive Blocks .. (BLK/Opp FGAttempted)		18
Offensive Steals .... (STL/Game)		22
Turnover Margin .... (Def T.O. - Off T.O.)		18
Fouls Margin .... (Opp FOULS - FOULS)		14
Rebounding Record	36-44-2	18
Assists Record	35-44-3	18
Field Goal Pct. Record	31-49-2	21
Free Throw Att. Record	33-47-2	18

Sacramento Kings . . . . Team Roster

MOST PRODUCTIVE PLAYERS

Player	Span	Yrs	CRD
Oscar Robertson	1961-70	10	26,764
Sam Lacey	1971-81	12	17,277
Jerry Lucas	1964-69	7	15,204
Jack Twyman	1956-66	11	14,530
Wayne Embry	1959-66	8	10,556
Nate Archibald	1971-76	6	10,042
Scott Wedman	1975-81	7	9,013
Arnie Risen	1948-55	8	8,334
LaSalle Thompson	1983-89	7	7,803
Bobby Wanzer	1948-57	10	7,231

PRESENT PLAYERS*

J#	VETERANS	COLLEGE	POS	R#	D#	HT	WT	Sacr	NBA
7	Danny Ainge	BYU	G	2	31	6-5	185	1	8
53	Randy Allen	Florida State	F	X	X	6-8	220	1	1
34	Ricky Berry	San Jose State	G	1	18	6-8	207	1	1
15	Vinny Del Negro	N.C. State	G	2	29	6-5	185	1	1
50	Ben Gillery	Georgetown	C	X	X	7-0	235	1	1
2	Michael Jackson	Georgetown	G	2	47	6-2	185	2	2
22	Rodney McCray	Louisville	F	1	3	6-8	235	1	6
44	Jawann Oldham	Seattle	C	2	41	7-1	245	1	8
9	Jim Petersen	Minnesota	F-C	3	51	6-10	236	1	5
21	Harold Pressley	Villanova	F	1	17	6-7	210	3	3
30	Kenny Smith	North Carolina	G	1	6	6-3	170	2	2
23	Wayman Tisdale	Oklahoma	F-C	1	2	6-9	240	1	4

FUTURE PLAYERS

ROOKIES	COLLEGE	POS	R#	D#	HT	WT
Pervis Ellison	Louisville	C-F	1	1	6-9	215

* For further definition of category and column headings, see pages 42 & 43.

Sacramento Kings . . . . Overview

One of my better friends always gets excited about the Kansas City Chiefs during the offseason. He manages to find one new reason to believe "this season will be different". He was the same way when the Kings were in K.C. (Thank God for the Royals). I used to always tell him that he was only making himself look foolish because the Kings are losers. It's that simple. The sun rises in the east and the Kings are losers. Well, that was before 1990 and (here goes) "this season will be different".

Oh sure, Sacramento will be doing good to break even, but that's a major step forward. With only brighter days ahead, it would be a real shame if fans lost interest before this team becomes a winner. With a push to get major league baseball and the NFL in Sacramento, that could happen. It happened in Kansas City, it could happen there too. Being partial toward the NBA, I hope they don't get another major sport for as long as possible.

This is a completely overhauled team. In fact, not one single player remains from the Kings who played their first season in Sacramento only 4 years ago. And only one player on the present team was there even 3 years ago. Most of the moves have been successful and Sacramento has a good blend of people. Who knows? They might even snap their 33-game road losing streak to the Lakers.

When Pervis Ellison was first announced as the Kings selection, I was disappointed for them. In my opinion, he was certainly not the best player available and his lack of emotional intensity, even now, has me concerned. My thinking is, when you can go for any player in the draft, why not take the most proven sure-bet player you can? Why take a risk? There were several players that I believe are better individually than Ellison. Even so, Sacramento needed a big man and Ellison or Stacey King were their only real choices. I guess they just didn't want a King of Kings.

Looking at Sacramento's expected starting line-up in 1990, Ellison may fit in better than King anyway. Some would argue that that only means you've got the wrong starting line-up. Nevertheless, Ellison is probably a better defensive player and shouldn't need to be relied upon that heavily for scoring with Tisdale, Ainge and Smith around. Ellison was the choice simply because he was more capable of becoming a Bill Russell clone. His long arms and shot-blocking ability give him the necessary power tools. Now all he needs is the electricity. (Havlicek, Cousy, Sharman, Jones, etc.)

It is so seldom that a franchise gets the overall #1 pick that there is a temptation to assume the player will make like Moses and lead the poor souls to the promised land. Jerry Reynolds, who is no fool, paved the way for a possible let-down when he said "If we're lucky enough, we'll get a guy who can win us five or six games on his ability." That's probably about what a player like Ellison is worth. It should be noted that, although surprising, only three number 1 picks in the draft went on to become Rookie-of-the-Year. Ellison certainly has a chance to play on a team that could make one of the bigger turnarounds, but I have to predict that either Glen Rice or Stacey King are most likely pre-season choices to get that honor.

As you recall, Danny Ainge came to Sacramento from Boston with Brad Lohaus while the Celtics received former Kings - Kleine and Pinckney. The Ainge/Lohaus duo outscored Kleine/Pinckney after the trade 28.52 to 22.16, so it was good in that respect. Unfortunately, each team could only protect eight players from the expansion clubs and Lohaus was eaten up by the Timberwolves. Ainge was a crucial ingredient to Sacramento's late-season success. (I still find it impressive that they went 11-11 in the last quarter of the season.) There can be little doubt that his knowledge of how to win (2 NBA championship rings) and his intensity were major factors in the turnaround.

As it looks now, Sacramento stole Wayman Tisdale from Indiana. Though

Sacramento Kings . . . . Overview

they gave up LaSalle Thompson and Randy Wittman, neither figured in any long-term plans for the Kings. What they gained was a 3-time 1st-Team All-American and the low post scorer they so desperately needed. As a King, Tisdale averaged 20 ppg. In four years as a Pacer, the most he ever scored was 16 ppg. With Ellison, McCray, Ainge, and Smith, who are all good passers, in the lineup, I expect Tisdale to score upwards of 23 ppg next season.

Sacramento experienced a strange year shooting the ball - ranking next to the top in 3-point percentage, but next to the bottom in 2-point percentage. In fact, the difference between the two percentages was only 9.5%, the smallest in history. Overwhelmingly, most good 3-point shooting teams are good shooting teams in general. This club was the exception.

I can remember more games than I care to count (and for me that's saying something) where one of the players (McCray, Petersen, Pressley, K.Smith, etc.) went 0-10 or 1-14 or 0-15 from the field. You can forget winning a game when you shoot that bad. The reality is that they lost a lot of games because they only shot 2-pointers at a 46.8% rate. Ainge and Tisdale shot collectively over 50% after they arrived, so hopefully, the team as a whole will put together a good shooting season in 1990 from 2-point range to go with the 3-point proficiency.

Ricky Berry set a new 3-point record for a rookie - hitting 65 treys. Harold Pressley ranked third, while Danny Ainge was 5th in most 3-pointers made for the season. In fact, Sacramento became so satisfied with the bomb that they pumped in 16 in one game! That destroyed the previous record of 11 set by New York earlier in the season.

Rodney McCray remains somewhat of a disappointment. He was brought in with Jim Petersen for Otis Thorpe. Although Thorpe had an excellent year for Houston, he didn't really help the Rockets win more games - exactly the point I made while he was at Sacramento. Unfortunately, McCray

and Petersen weren't of much more value to the Kings. Jim Petersen was a 3rd round draft choice, so whatever he offers is gravy, but Rodney McCray was picked #3 in the draft. His production for a #3 pick is well below average. I looked at the #3 picks from 1980 to 1985, which was the period in which he was drafted, and found that the average Production Rating of the other five was 24.31 last season. McCray's was a relatively mediocre 16.65. Maybe he'll excel more with the type of players he's around now. Whereas, Houston had the market on selfish players during McCray's stay, this group appears to be more team-oriented.

Notes: Vinnie Del Negro was protected over Brad Lohaus because he scored 28 points and looked like superman in the final game... Sacramento was 13-38 when Kenny Smith took less than 20 field goals per game, but 14-16 when he took 20+... When the Kings' opponents shot 49% or better from the field, it was bad news (1-41)... Danny Ainge was the only player in the NBA to score 40+ points for two different teams last season... When the bench outscored the starters, Sacramento's record was 20-19. When the starters scored more, they stunk (7-36)... The Kings allowed 57 third quarter points vs Golden State - 1 point short of an NBA record for a quarter.

Prediction - best case: 41-41

I figure if they went 11-11 without Ellison, they can sure go 30-30 with him. I can't quite put my finger on it, but I really see good things for this team. Maybe it's the ghosts of Red Auerbach or Dean Smith or Denny Crum that are floating around, with just a sprinkling of Billy Tubbs to keep them honest.

Prediction - worst case: 33-49

Thirty-three wins is a six game improvement, which is so-so. Unfortunately, it's not good enough and if it comes to pass, there will be heads a rollin'.

To order back issues of Basketball Heaven or to obtain the 1990 Mid-season Report, see page 324.

San Antonio Spurs . . . . Influence on Winning

TEAM RECORD BY

| PLAYER | GAMES | ... SCR Leader | | ... REB Leader | | ...AST Leader | |
		HOME	ROAD	HOME	ROAD	HOME	ROAD
Alvin Robertson	65	6-5	1-4	5-3	1-2	6-10	0-15
Willie Anderson	81	10-8	1-12	1-4	0-3	5-3	0-12
Frank Brickowski	64	1-4	0-8	1-2	1-11	0-1	0-1
Greg Anderson	82	2-3	0-7	10-11	1-22	0-1	0-0
Vernon Maxwell	79	2-4	1-2	0-0	0-0	2-7	1-13
Johnny Dawkins	32	0-3	0-4	1-0	0-1	6-5	1-7
Michael Anderson	36	0-0	0-1	0-0	0-0	0-2	1-10
Dallas Comegys	67	0-0	0-1	1-1	0-1	0-0	0-0
Jay Vincent	24	0-0	0-1	0-0	0-1	0-0	0-0
Mike Smrek	43	0-0	0-0	0-0	0-2	0-0	0-0

TEAM RECORD BY SCORING *

PLAYER	PLAY	DNP	0-9	10-19	20-29	30-39	40+
Alvin Robertson	19-46	2-15	2-6	7-27	8-12	2-1	0-0
Willie Anderson	21-60	0-1	2-5	6-36	10-17	3-2	0-0
Frank Brickowski	18-46	3-15	5-14	10-21	3-11	0-0	0-0
Greg Anderson	21-61	0-0	4-18	13-33	4-10	0-0	0-0
Vernon Maxwll	21-58	0-3	5-28	11-24	5-6	0-0	0-0
Johnny Dawkins	10-22	11-39	2-7	5-9	3-5	0-1	0-0
Michael Anderson	8-28	13-33	6-21	2-6	0-1	0-0	0-0
Dallas Comegys	19-48	2-13	14-35	5-12	0-1	0-0	0-0
Jay Vincent	7-17	14-44	5-10	2-5	0-2	0-0	0-0
Mike Smrek	11-32	10-29	11-27	0-5	0-0	0-0	0-0

TEAM RECORD BY STARTING POSITION *

PLAYER	GAMES	STARTS	PG	OG	SF	PF	C
Alvin Robertson	65	65	0-5	19-41	0-0	0-0	0-0
Willie Anderson	81	79	0-0	2-13	19-45	0-0	0-0
Frank Brickowski	64	60	0-0	0-0	0-0	5-12	11-32
Greg Anderson	82	56	0-0	0-0	0-0	8-34	5-9
Vernon Maxwell	79	36	8-27	0-1	0-0	0-0	0-0
Johnny Dawkins	32	30	10-20	0-0	0-0	0-0	0-0
Michael Anderson	36	12	3-9	0-0	0-0	0-0	0-0
Dallas Comegys	67	10	0-0	0-0	0-5	3-2	0-0
Jay Vincent	24	3	0-0	0-0	0-0	0-3	0-0
Mike Smrek	43	18	0-0	0-0	0-0	0-0	4-14

* For further definition of each category and column heading see pages 42 & 43.

San Antonio Spurs . . . . 1988-89 Statistics

RAW NUMBERS *

PLAYER	2pt%	3pt%	FT%	MIN	PF	DQ	HI	TO	RB	AS	BL	ST
Alvin Robertson	.497	.200	.723	2287	259	6	34	231	384	393	36	197
Willie Anderson	.503	.190	.775	**2738**	**295**	8	**36**	261	417	372	62	150
Frank Brickowski	**.517**	0-2	.715	1822	252	**10**	27	165	406	131	35	102
Greg Anderson	.505	0-3	.514	2401	221	2	29	180	**676**	61	**103**	102
Vernon Maxwell	.466	.248	.745	2065	136	0	29	178	202	301	8	86
Johnny Dawkins	.447	0-4	**.893**	1083	64	0	30	111	101	224	0	55
Michael Anderson	.429	.143	.695	730	64	0	21	84	89	153	3	44
Dallas Comegys	.490	0-2	.658	1119	160	2	21	85	234	30	63	42
Jay Vincent	.406	**.333**	.667	646	63	0	21	42	110	27	4	6
Mike Smrek	.471	0-0	.645	623	102	2	15	48	129	12	58	13

OVERALL RANKINGS *

PLAYER	G	GS	PPG	PR	RANK	SC	SH	RB	AS	BL	ST
Alvin Robertson	65	65	17.26	**20.52**	29	48	117	88	34	86	1
Willie Anderson	81	**79**	**18.62**	**18.99**	39	35	79	102	48	58	29
Frank Brickowski	64	60	13.67	**15.42**	86	84	76	62	97	72	26
Greg Anderson	**82**	56	13.74	**15.11**	90	83	159	19	170	21	58
Vernon Maxwell	79	36	11.73	**10.30**	145	108	152	146	46	155	63
Johnny Dawkins	32	30	14.19	**15.25**	DNQ						
Michael Anderson	36	12	5.67	**7.83**	DNQ						
Dallas Comegys	67	10	6.54	**7.34**	DNQ						
Jay Vincent	29	4	8.59	**6.24**	DNQ						
Mike Smrek	43	18	4.49	**5.79**	DNQ						

POSITION RANKINGS *

PLAYER	POSITION	RANK	SC	SH	RB	AS	BL	ST
Alvin Robertson	Off Guard	6	13	29	7	6	9	1
Willie Anderson	Small Forward, OG	9	14	16	28	2	16	4
Frank Brickowski	Center, PF	15	11	14	28	3	25	2
Greg Anderson	Power Forward, C	19	12	29	10	28	6	5
Vernon Maxwell	Point Guard	27	18	24	19	31	23	24
Johnny Dawkins	Point Guard	DNQ						
Michael Anderson	Point Guard	DNQ						
Dallas Comegys	Small Forward	DNQ						
Jay Vincent	Power Forward	DNQ						
Mike Smrek	Center	DNQ						

*For further definition of each category and column heading see pages 42 & 43.

San Antonio Spurs .... Team Info

WEEKLY POWER RATING

41 WINS - AVERAGE (See page 43 for Team Power Rating discussion.)

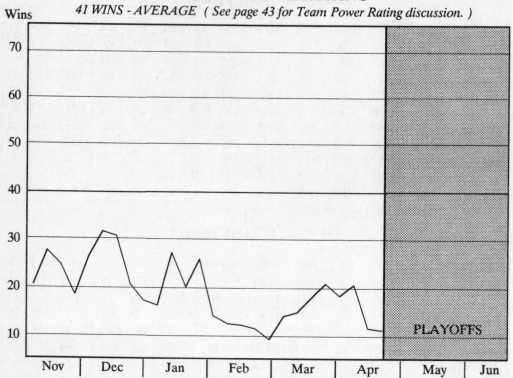

Wins

PLAYOFFS

Nov | Dec | Jan | Feb | Mar | Apr | May | Jun

Miscellaneous Categories	Data	Rank
Attendance	460K	23
Key-Man Games Missed	142	23
Season Record	21-61	22
- Home	18-23	21
- Road	3-38	24
Eastern Conference	6-18	21
Western Conference	15-43	24
Overtime Record	0-3	24
Record 5 Pts. or Less	4-14	25
Record 10 Pts. or More	14-38	21
Games Won By Bench	3	16
Games Won By Starters	2	22
Winning Streak	3	20
Losing Streak	13	23
Home Winning Streak	5	20
Road Winning Streak	1	21
Home Losing Streak	6	20
Road Losing Streak	20	24

Performance Categories	Data	Rank
Offensive Scoring (per game)	105.5	19
Defensive Scoring (per game)	112.8	19
Scoring Margin (per game)	-7.3	22
Defensive FG%	.488	18
Offensive 2-point%	.479	20
Offensive 3-point%	.215	24
Offensive Free Throw %	.698	25
Offensive Rebs (Off REB/Opp Def REB)		8
Defensive Rebs (Def REB/Opp Off REB)		25
Offensive Assists (AST/FGMade)		17
Offensive Blocks (BLK/Opp FGAttempted)		11
Offensive Steals (STL/Game)		1
Turnover Margin (Def T.O. - Off T.O.)		13
Fouls Margin (Opp FOULS - FOULS)		23
Rebounding Record	33-45-4	20
Assists Record	40-39-3	14
Field Goal Pct. Record	29-53-0	24
Free Throw Att. Record	26-49-7	21

San Antonio Spurs ....Team Roster

MOST PRODUCTIVE PLAYERS

Player	Span	Yrs	CRD
George Gervin	1974-85	12	20,394
Larry Kenon	1976-80	5	9,271
James Silas	1973-81	9	8,853
Artis Gilmore	1983-87	5	8,250
Johnny Moore	1981-87	8	7,755
Mike Mitchell	1982-88	7	7,574
Alvin Robertson	1985-89	5	7,539
Mark Olberding	1976-82	7	7,177
Rich Jones	1970-75	6	7,031
Billy Paultz	1976-83	4	6,431

PRESENT PLAYERS*

J#	VETERANS	COLLEGE	POS	R#	D#	HT	WT	S.A.	NBA
40	Willie Anderson	Georgia	G	1	10	6-7	190	1	1
25	Anthony Bowie	Oklahoma	G	3	66	6-6	190	1	1
43	Frank Brickowski	Penn State	F	3	57	6-10	240	3	5
22	Dallas Comegys	DePaul	F	1	21	6-9	205	1	2
34	Terry Cummings	DePaul	F	1	2	6-10	220	0	7
24	Johnny Dawkins	Duke	G	1	10	6-2	165	3	3
	Jens-uwe Gordon	Santa Clara	F	X	X	6-9	220	0	0
27	Caldwell Jones	Albany State	C	2	32	6-11	225	0	15
11	Vernon Maxwell	Florida	G	2	47	6-5	188	1	1
52	Mike Smrek	Canasius	C	2	25	7-0	263	1	4
31	Jay Vincent	Michigan State	F	2	24	6-7	220	1	8
6	Jerome Whitehead	Marquette	C-F	2	44	6-10	240	1	11

FUTURE PLAYERS

ROOKIES	COLLEGE	POS	R#	D#	HT	WT
David Robinson	Navy	C	1	1	7-1	235
Sean Elliott	Arizona	F	1	3	6-8	205

* For further definition of category and column headings, see pages 42 & 43.

San Antonio Spurs .... Overview

When Larry Brown was at Kansas University I discovered three things about him. 1) He couldn't make up his mind. 2) He couldn't win until he did. 3) You better hope that when he makes up his mind about you, it's good.

When Brown first came to KU he inherited a bunch of players left over from the Ted Owens' era. They were bigger and slower and just not his "type" of athletes. When he finally accepted what he had, he molded them into a great group and went to the final four in his third year. Two years later, KU was struggling along at 12-8 and a player named Milt Newton wasn't getting much playing time. Brown accepted what he had, played him, and the season turned on a dime. KU went on to go 15-3 and won the national championship.

It's been that type of a career for Brown. Lots of controversy, lots of decisions, lots of personality clashes. Oh, and did I say, lots of wins? Until last season Larry Brown had never finished the year at below .500. He went 16 consecutive seasons as head coach, winning every one of them, but confusing players, writers, and fans along the way.

When he decided to go to San Antonio, it seemed like a situation where he would excel quickly. The club was young, had managed to make the playoffs the year before, and was adding a budding star - Willie Anderson. What could keep this "Wizard from Oz" from improving the Spurs and possibly even having a winning record - his 17th?

The answer is simple. Larry Brown. But that's not necessarily bad. When he set up school and started teaching Brown 101 to his students, he realized some were wearing shorts and chewing gum in class. When he tried to get them expelled, the principal refused. The result was that Brown sulked and the team deteriorated to the lowest level possible - last - below even Miami and Charlotte by Power Rating. Though the honeymoon between Brown and the Spurs ended quickly, they got marriage counseling and lasted the season (though there were the usual rumors of Brown leaving). When the dust settled, the Spurs ended at 21-61. Not only was it Brown's worst record and his only losing one, it was the worst record in Spurs history! What were the odds of that before the season began? Take a look at Brown's worst five years as coach.

17.	1989	San Antonio	21-61	.256
16.	1979	Denver	28-25	.528
15.	1982	New Jersey	44-38	.537
14.	1974	Carolina	47-37	.560
13.	1978	Denver	48-34	.585

Once Brown got the green light, he traded Greg Anderson and Alvin Robertson to Milwaukee for Terry Cummings. This is a difficult trade to assess. Cummings is perhaps the best player of the three, although Robertson is close. Alvin has placed on the All-Defensive first or second team four consecutive years and is a 3-time All-Star. Not only that, but he's been named Defensive Player-of-the-Year and Most-Improved Player-of-the-Year.

Anderson is a rebounder and shot-blocker, but an abysmal free throw shooter - something which drove Brown up the wall. In fact, Anderson was the least efficient free throw shooter in the NBA last season, costing his team 102 points from the line (see discussion page 225).

Cummings is coming off one of his best years as a professional. He's a low post scorer, a phenomenon which was non-existent for the Spurs last season, and he's a respectable rebounder. His 22 ppg average and 700 rebounds per year will come in mighty handy. The problem with Cummings is that he's a little small for power forward, but unless he's with the right club that's where he has to play. With Anderson gone, he may end up there again.

Of course the big news is that the Spurs will be getting David Robinson for next season. Robinson was probably the most coveted player coming out of college since Lew Alcindor (28 points and 12 rebounds

San Antonio Spurs .... Overview

per game as well as 60% shooting and leading the country in blocks will do that), but his naval commitment has had everyone holding their breath for two years. Fortunately, nothing has gone wrong and he should be there to anchor the middle next season. The question will be how much has he lost by sitting out this long? Certainly, he has lost some and recovering it will take some time. Stamina, especially, could be a problem. But soon enough he will be in a position to challenge Ewing and Olajuwon as the top center in the league.

Frank Brickowski will play the power positions on the front line. He was the most-improved in the NBA in terms of production from 1987 to 1988, but slipped a little last season. He's ranked 1st and 3rd in assists at his position the last two years so he should be capable of unselfishly filling the void when Cummings or Robinson have to sit.

Presumably, Willie Anderson will now take over Robertson's spot at 2-guard while #3 pick in the draft (Sean Elliott) will play small forward. Willie Anderson finished second in the voting for Rookie-of-the-Year, but finished in the rookie top-10 in all six performance categories - the only one to do so. This indicates his versatility - something that will be a trademark with this team.

Elliott was considered by many as the most complete player in college last season, so how can you complain? Nevertheless, the Spurs reportedly wanted Danny Ferry. Ferry probably would have been a little better for the team since they lack outside shooting, but the talent is there to win 81 games. What's 1 more?

Nevertheless, outside shooting is a problem that needs to be dealt with. The Spurs only hit 63 3-pointers last season. Though the league average is 32.3%, the highest percentage accrued by one of the 15 players who took shots was only 25% by Albert King - and he's gone. Elliott hit 44% of his 3-pointers in college, but remember, that's kiddy distance.

One of the more interesting stats last season was San Antonio's 3rd quarters at home. Their record was a very good 27-13 and their rank was #4. What makes this unique is that they got beat badly in every other quarter both home and away.

	HOME		ROAD	
	Record	Rank	Record	Rank
Q1	19-21	22	11-29	19
Q2	17-19	21	9-28	25
Q3	**27-13**	**4**	13-25	20
Q4	17-23	23	10-28	25

Many of those third quarter victories ended up as losses, however, as the Spurs ranked last in blown games (games lost after leading through 3 quarters).

San Antonio	**2-9**	**.182**
Indiana	4-10	.286
Sacramento	3-7	.300
Dallas	3-7	.300
Atlanta	5-11	.313

Notes: When the Spurs' opponents scored 105+ points on the road, San Antonio could not win a single time (0-37)... In margins of 6 points or less on the road, the Spurs were nearly as anemic (0-32)... The club ranked last (#25) in FT%, but first in steals... Anthony Bowie was named CBA Player-of-the-Year in 1989.

Prediction - best case: 53-29

Well, I got shot out of the saddle on this one last season, but adding two collegiate Players-of-the-Year plus Terry Cummings may enable the Spurs to challenge the all-time mark for best turnarounds (+32 victories - Boston, 1980) in NBA history.

Prediction - worst case: 41-41

It is impossible for this team not to win 41 games. Well, nothing's impossible, but there's a better chance of the city council voting to tear down La Villita and putting up a McDonalds than Larry Brown having two losing seasons in a row.

To order back issues of Basketball Heaven or to obtain the 1990 Midseason Report, see page 324.

Seattle SuperSonics . . . . Influence on Winning

TEAM RECORD BY

PLAYER	GAMES	... SCR Leader		... REB Leader		...AST Leader	
		HOME	ROAD	HOME	ROAD	HOME	ROAD
Dale Ellis	82	20-6	11-19	0-0	2-1	2-0	0-1
Derrick McKey	82	4-1	3-1	4-1	2-3	0-1	0-0
Michael Cage	80	0-0	0-1	19-6	10-15	0-0	0-0
Nate McMillan	75	0-0	0-0	5-1	1-1	27-6	13-19
Xavier McDaniel	82	11-3	3-4	1-2	2-2	1-1	0-0
Alton Lister	82	0-0	0-0	5-2	3-8	0-0	0-0
Sedale Threatt	63	0-0	0-0	0-0	0-0	3-0	0-4
John Lucas	74	0-1	0-0	0-0	0-0	2-2	3-5
Russ Schoene	69	0-0	0-1	0-0	0-0	0-0	0-0
Olden Polynice	80	0-0	0-0	0-1	0-0	0-0	0-0

TEAM RECORD BY SCORING *

PLAYER	PLAY	DNP	0-9	10-19	20-29	30-39	40+
Dale Ellis	47-35	0-0	0-0	5-7	21-18	18-10	3-0
Derrick McKey	47-35	0-0	8-7	25-21	12-7	2-0	0-0
Michael Cage	47-35	2-0	18-20	25-13	2-2	0-0	0-0
Nate McMillan	45-30	2-5	32-25	13-5	0-0	0-0	0-0
Xavier McDaniel	47-35	0-0	2-4	15-19	23-8	7-4	0-0
Alton Lister	47-35	0-0	24-23	22-12	1-0	0-0	0-0
Sedale Threatt	37-26	10-9	25-14	12-10	0-2	0-0	0-0
John Lucas	40-34	7-1	36-30	4-3	0-1	0-0	0-0
Russ Schoene	35-34	12-1	28-28	5-6	2-0	0-0	0-0
Olden Polynice	46-34	1-1	43-32	3-2	0-0	0-0	0-0

TEAM RECORD BY STARTING POSITION *

PLAYER	GAMES	STARTS	PG	OG	SF	PF	C
Dale Ellis	82	82	0-0	47-35	0-0	0-0	0-0
Derrick McKey	82	82	0-0	0-0	47-35	0-0	0-0
Michael Cage	80	71	0-0	0-0	0-0	38-33	0-0
Nate McMillan	75	74	45-29	0-0	0-0	0-0	0-0
Xavier McDaniel	82	10	0-0	0-0	0-0	8-2	0-0
Alton Lister	82	82	0-0	0-0	0-0	0-0	47-35
Sedale Threatt	63	0	0-0	0-0	0-0	0-0	0-0
John Lucas	74	8	2-6	0-0	0-0	0-0	0-0
Russ Schoene	69	1	0-0	0-0	0-0	1-0	0-0
Olden Polynice	80	0	0-0	0-0	0-0	0-0	0-0

* For further definition of each category and column heading see pages 42 & 43.

Seattle Supersonics . . . . 1988-89 Statistics

RAW NUMBERS *

PLAYER	2pt%	3pt%	FT%	MIN	PF	DQ	HI	TO	RB	AS	BL	ST
Dale Ellis	.507	**.478**	.816	**3190**	197	0	**49**	218	342	164	22	108
Derrick McKey	**.519**	.337	.803	2804	264	**4**	34	188	464	219	70	105
Michael Cage	.502	0-4	.743	2536	184	1	24	124	**765**	126	52	92
Nate McMillan	.443	.214	.630	2341	236	3	16	211	388	**696**	42	**156**
Xavier McDaniel	.494	.306	.732	2385	231	0	39	210	433	134	40	84
Alton Lister	.499	0-0	.646	1806	**310**	3	20	117	545	54	**180**	28
Sedale Threatt	.502	.367	**.818**	1220	155	0	21	77	117	238	4	83
John Lucas	.437	.265	.701	842	53	0	25	66	79	260	1	60
Russ Schoene	.389	.382	.807	774	136	1	20	48	165	36	24	37
Olden Polynice	.511	0-2	.593	835	164	0	12	46	206	21	30	37

OVERALL RANKINGS *

PLAYER	G	GS	PPG	PR	RANK	SC	SH	RB	AS	BL	ST
Dale Ellis	**82**	**82**	**27.48**	**21.13**	24	3	12	139	138	131	100
Derrick McKey	**82**	**82**	15.91	**17.29**	59	64	39	92	90	56	83
Michael Cage	80	71	10.31	**16.90**	63	122	92	13	144	67	88
Nate McMillan	75	74	7.09	**16.63**	71	159	174	91	5	77	11
Xavier McDaniel	**82**	10	20.45	**16.29**	78	22	108	84	131	82	95
Alton Lister	**82**	**82**	8.01	**12.34**	120	150	125	12	166	4	169
Sedale Threatt	63	0	8.63	**10.38**	142	146	59	149	25	164	10
John Lucas	74	8	4.19	**5.96**	DNQ						
Russ Schoene	69	1	5.19	**5.03**	DNQ						
Olden Polynice	80	0	2.91	**4.46**	DNQ						

POSITION RANKINGS *

PLAYER	POSITION	RANK	SC	SH	RB	AS	BL	ST
Dale Ellis	Off Guard, SF	4	2	4	25	43	26	35
Derrick McKey	Small Forward	14	20	7	21	18	15	15
Michael Cage	Power Forward	15	23	20	7	16	22	11
Nate McMillan	Point Guard	16	30	33	3	5	2	5
Xavier McDaniel	Small Forward, PF	20	10	26	18	35	23	17
Alton Lister	Center	20	22	19	5	23	3	25
Sedale Threatt	Off Guard	32	39	17	32	4	41	5
John Lucas	Point Guard	DNQ						
Russ Schoene	Power Forward	DNQ						
Olden Polynice	Center	DNQ						

*For further definition of each category and column heading see pages 42 & 43.

Seattle SuperSonics .... Team Info

WEEKLY POWER RATING
41 WINS - AVERAGE (See page 43 for Team Power Rating discussion.)

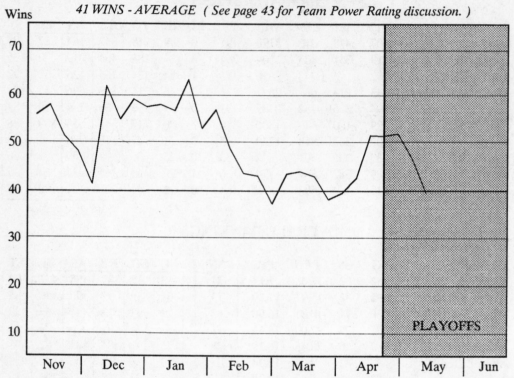

Miscellaneous Categories	Data	Rank
Attendance	530K	17
Key-Man Games Missed	38	7
Season Record	47-35	9
- Home	31-10	10
- Road	16-25	10
Eastern Conference	10-14	16
Western Conference	37-21	7
Overtime Record	3-1	6
Record 5 Pts. or Less	14-14	9
Record 10 Pts. or More	21-15	11
Games Won By Bench	9	5
Games Won By Starters	4	18
Winning Streak	8	5
Losing Streak	7	15
Home Winning Streak	17	6
Road Winning Streak	4	6
Home Losing Streak	4	16
Road Losing Streak	9	14

Performance Categories	Data	Rank
Offensive Scoring (per game)	112.1	7
Defensive Scoring (per game)	109.2	12
Scoring Margin (per game)	2.9	9
Defensive FG%	.486	17
Offensive 2-point%	.488	11
Offensive 3-point%	.379	1
Offensive Free Throw %	.746	20
Offensive Rebs ..... (Off REB/Opp Def REB)		1
Defensive Rebs .... (Def REB/Opp Off REB)		18
Offensive Assists .... (AST/FGMade)		19
Offensive Blocks .. (BLK/Opp FGAttempted)		4
Offensive Steals .... (STL/Game)		3
Turnover Margin........ (Def T.O. - Off T.O.)		4
Fouls Margin .... (Opp FOULS - FOULS)		21
Rebounding Record	51-30-1	4
Assists Record	46-31-5	5
Field Goal Pct. Record	34-48-0	18
Free Throw Att. Record	40-40-2	10

Seattle SuperSonics ....Team Roster

MOST PRODUCTIVE PLAYERS

Player	Span	Yrs	CRD
Jack Sikma	1978-86	9	15,370
Fred Brown	1972-84	13	12,617
Gus Williams	1978-84	6	9,117
Spencer Haywood	1971-75	5	8,640
Tom Chambers	1984-88	5	7,284
Lenny Wilkens	1969-72	4	7,161
Dick Snyder	1970-79	6	6,744
Xavier McDaniel	1986-89	4	6,145
Tom Meschery	1968-71	4	5,383
Dale Ellis	1987-89	3	5,059

SEATTLE
SUPERSONICS
®

PRESENT PLAYERS*

J#	VETERANS	COLLEGE	POS	R#	D#	HT	WT	Seat	NBA
44	Michael Cage	San Diego State	F	1	14	6-9	235	1	5
3	Dale Ellis	Tennessee	G	1	9	6-7	215	3	6
5	Avery Johnson	Southern	G	X	X	5-10	175	1	1
53	Alton Lister	Arizona State	C	1	21	7-0	240	3	8
34	Xavier McDaniel	Wichita State	F	1	4	6-7	205	4	4
31	Derrick McKey	Alabama	F	1	9	6-9	210	2	2
10	Nate McMillan	N.Carolina State	G	2	30	6-5	197	3	3
23	Olden Polynice	Virginia	C	1	8	6-11	245	2	2
40	Russ Schoene	Tennessee-Chatt.	F	2	45	6-10	215	3	4
	Brad Sellers	Ohio State	F	1	9	7-0	212	0	3
3	Sedale Threatt	W. Virginia Tech	G	6	139	6-2	177	2	6

FUTURE PLAYERS

ROOKIES	COLLEGE	POS	R#	D#	HT	WT
Dana Barros	Boston College	G	1	16	5-11	175
Shawn Kemp	Did Not Play College	F	1	17	6-10	220

* For further definition of category and column headings, see pages 42 & 43.

Seattle SuperSonics .... Overview

It seems hard to believe, but it was only two short years ago that the Sonics were the talk of the basketball world. Entering the 1988 season, they had high expectations. After all, the club had improved 8 wins from the year before, had reached the conference finals against the Lakers, had 3-20 ppg scorers on the team, had 5 first round draft picks coming up, and the average age of their starters was only 25. With most players reaching their primes in years 27 to 29, the future looked great, to say the least.

It's not really my intention to look disparagingly upon the success the club has had (I should point out that they've gained 5 wins and 3 wins the past two seasons), but I guess I expected quite a bit more. I would have guessed that two years later they would have won 55+ games and really challenged the Lakers for the conference championship. Instead, their playoff record is 5-8, and when they did face the Lakers, it was in the semifinals last year and they got swept.

It wasn't New York (+29), Cleveland (+26), or Phoenix (+19) that most prognosticators were salivating over 2 years ago, it was Seattle. No, the Sonics are no longer the media darlings. Words like "future" and "potential" and "dynasty" are labels being attached to teams like the Clippers and the Spurs. So, rather than saying "What went wrong?", I'll ask "What didn't happen?"

Well, to begin with, Seattle had overachieved in the playoffs in 1987, upsetting two heavily favored opponents. Because of the high profile the playoffs have, the question became more "How did they only win 39 games during the regular season?" rather than "How did they defeat Dallas and Houston?" With the perspective warped, expectations got out of hand. Secondly, the belief that 3-20 ppg scorers were an invaluable weapon was incorrect as I discuss on page 34. Thirdly, the team failed to re-sign Tom Chambers, lost him to Phoenix, and got nothing in return.

The fourth thing that hasn't happened is that the draft picks haven't showered the team with blessings. Derrick McKey has been OK, but I think most fans hoped for more from a player considered as "can't miss". Olden Polynice has been a huge disappointment for a #8 pick. In fact, only one other #8 pick in recent memory has been anything other than very good, and that was Lancaster Gordon. But he was drafted by the Clippers so you expect to be disappointed. Seattle traded their third 1st round pick to the Clippers for Michael Cage. Frankly, Cage was a disappointment last season before losing his starting job.

Of the two remaining 1st rounders, both are risky. Dana Barros was drafted #16. He's a point guard, so presumably, he'll be groomed to either back up McMillan or take his job. At 5-11, most scouts projected him to go in the middle of the 2nd round. His size will present defensive problems, but his scoring could well overcome that. He's compared favorably with Michael Adams. Both are the same size and both went to Boston College, but Barros was a better NCAA scorer. Shawn Kemp was picked #17, but he's got "Chris Washburn" written all over him. He was a consensus high school All-American, but was a Prop. 48 victim as a Kentucky freshman. He was kicked out of school for theft and went to Trinity Valley Community College in Texas. He got there too late to play, however, and thus will be entering the NBA as only the 4th player never have gone to college (Moses Malone, Darryl Dawkins, and Bill Willoughby are the others). The worst thing about Kemp is that he's got Sampsonitis (That's the disease some big players get when they want to dribble the ball too much.) Since he's 1) Only 20 years old with a long potential future, 2) The second first round pick the Sonics had, and 3) Not the #3 pick in the draft (Washburn was picked #3), the risk is probably reasonable - though I wouldn't have done it. Now, when he turns out to be a superstar you can read this back to me.

Seattle SuperSonics .... Overview

Seattle also picked up Brad Sellers from Chicago to back up McKey. Sellers is a good perimeter shooter, but is among the most fragile forwards in the NBA. Although he played over 20 minutes per game, the seven footer averaged a shockingly low 2.8 rebounds per outing.

The power forward position is a little unsettling. The Sonics gave up their #15 pick, which turned out to be Gary Grant, for Michael Cage. Cage's scoring dropped from 14.5 to 10.3, his rebounding per minute rank dropped from #3 to #13, and he lost his starting job to Xavier McDaniel the last 10 games of the season. His play declined so much that he averaged only 5 points and 6 rebounds per outing during those 10 games, and scored 0 points, 0-4 from the line, and 3 rebounds in the last game of the year.

McDaniel, who reluctantly agreed to come off the bench when Cage arrived, is the team's brightest hope. Seattle went 8-2 during McDaniel's starts, in large part because of his tremendous play. As a 6th man, his Production Rating was half of what it was as a starter. In fact, his scoring, at 30 ppg, was so good that, coupled with Dale Ellis, the two outscored any other duo (577 pts) for any other 10 game stretch.

McDaniel/Ellis	Seattle	577
Richmond/Mullin	Golden St.	568
Chambers/E.Johnson	Phoenix	535
Chambers/K.Johnson	Phoenix	531
English/Lever	Denver	507

Dale Ellis is a prolific scorer. His 27.5 average was a career high. Now in three years with Seattle, he has scored 26+ ppg while his 3-year average at Dallas was only 8. Ellis leads all NBA players for career 3-pointers with 472 (Larry Bird is second, 455). Furthermore, Ellis won the 3-point shooting crown during All-Star festivities last season and was easily #1 in 3-point efficiency points in 1989 at +159 - totally destroying the previous best by Danny Ainge of +112 in 1988 (see discussion, page 224).

Nate McMillan has continued to be the unsung hero on this team, ranking in the top-5 in the league by assists per minute each of his three years. As amazing as I'm sure it will sound, that's a feat no other present player has done - not Magic, not Isiah, not Stockton. Nevertheless, distributing the ball isn't the only thing McMillan can do. It's true that he's not much of a scorer or shooter, but he ranked in the top five among point guards in rebounds, steals, and blocks in addition to assists. In fact, he actually had two triple doubles in one three-day period last year. And if that wasn't enough evidence of his value, then the fact that Seattle was only 2-5 when he didn't play should be.

Misc: Seattle led both the championship contestants (Lakers and Pistons) in late-season games by 29 and 25 points respectively. They lost each... Seattle was 21-10 when Ellis scored 30+ and 30-12 when McDaniel scored 20+... When Alton Lister took 9+ field goal attempts, the Sonics were 18-4... Only Houston also had three players with 82 starts... When Seattle held their opponents to 100 points or less on the road, they were 10-0... The Sonics were #1 in offensive rebounds... When the club shot 50% or less from the field, they were (27-35). When they shot 51%, they were (20-0).

Prediction - best case: 55-27

I can and do expect some improvement, but after two years they're not going to suddenly start going crazy. Fifty-five wins could compete with L.A. and Phoenix in a division where nearly every team should get better.

Prediction - worst case: 47-35

I don't think the team is likely to lose more games than last season unless McDaniel gets injured. If he does, players like Polynice and Sellers and Kemp will be relied upon - and that prospect's scary!

To order back issues of Basketball Heaven or to obtain the 1990 Midseason Report, see page 324.

Utah Jazz . . . . Influence on Winning

TEAM RECORD BY

PLAYER	GAMES	... SCR Leader		... REB Leader		...AST Leader	
		HOME	ROAD	HOME	ROAD	HOME	ROAD
Karl Malone	80	28-5	12-18	17-4	8-13	0-0	0-0
John Stockton	82	0-0	4-3	0-0	0-0	34-7	16-23
Thurl Bailey	82	2-2	1-3	4-0	0-1	0-0	0-0
Mark Eaton	82	0-0	0-0	21-3	9-9	0-0	0-0
Darrell Griffith	82	4-0	1-1	1-0	0-1	0-0	0-1
Bobby Hansen	46	0-0	1-0	0-0	0-1	0-0	0-0
Mike Brown	66	0-0	0-0	1-0	0-0	0-0	0-0
Eric Leckner	75	0-0	0-0	0-0	0-0	0-0	0-0
Jim Les	82	0-0	0-0	0-0	0-0	0-1	1-1
Marc Iavaroni	77	0-0	0-0	0-0	0-0	0-0	0-0

TEAM RECORD BY SCORING *

PLAYER	PLAY	DNP	0-9	10-19	20-29	30-39	40+
Karl Malone	50-30	1-1	0-0	3-3	19-17	25-8	3-2
John Stockton	51-31	0-0	3-4	27-17	20-10	1-0	0-0
Thurl Bailey	51-31	0-0	1-2	24-14	24-13	2-2	0-0
Mark Eaton	51-31	0-0	38-30	13-1	0-0	0-0	0-0
Darrell Griffith	51-31	0-0	12-11	32-13	5-7	1-0	1-0
Bobby Hansen	28-18	23-13	15-16	12-2	1-0	0-0	0-0
Mike Brown	39-27	12-4	37-22	2-5	0-0	0-0	0-0
Eric Leckner	45-30	6-1	38-27	6-3	1-0	0-0	0-0
Jim Les	51-31	0-0	50-31	1-0	0-0	0-0	0-0
Marc Iavaroni	48-29	3-2	47-28	1-1	0-0	0-0	0-0

TEAM RECORD BY STARTING POSITION *

PLAYER	GAMES	STARTS	PG	OG	SF	PF	C
Karl Malone	80	80	0-0	0-0	9-5	41-25	0-0
John Stockton	82	82	51-31	0-0	0-0	0-0	0-0
Thurl Bailey	82	3	0-0	0-0	1-2	0-0	0-0
Mark Eaton	82	82	0-0	0-0	0-0	0-0	51-31
Darrell Griffith	82	73	0-0	45-28	0-0	0-0	0-0
Bobby Hansen	46	9	0-0	6-3	0-0	0-0	0-0
Mike Brown	66	16	0-0	0-0	0-0	10-6	0-0
Eric Leckner	75	0	0-0	0-0	0-0	0-0	0-0
Jim Les	82	0	0-0	0-0	0-0	0-0	0-0
Marc Iavaroni	77	50	0-0	0-0	31-19	0-0	0-0

* For further definition of each category and column heading see pages 42 & 43.

Utah Jazz . . . . 1988-89 Statistics

RAW NUMBERS *

PLAYER	2pt%	3pt%	FT%	MIN	PF	DQ	HI	TO	RB	AS	BL	ST
Karl Malone	.521	.313	.766	3126	286	3	**44**	285	**853**	219	70	144
John Stockton	**.561**	.242	**.863**	**3171**	241	3	30	**308**	248	**1118**	14	**263**
Thurl Bailey	.484	**.400**	.825	2777	185	0	33	208	447	138	91	48
Mark Eaton	.462	0-0	.660	2914	**290**	**6**	15	142	843	83	**315**	40
Darrell Griffith	.477	.311	.780	2382	175	0	40	141	330	130	22	86
Bobby Hansen	.492	.352	.560	964	105	0	20	43	128	50	6	37
Mike Brown	.419	0-0	.708	1051	133	0	16	77	258	41	17	25
Eric Leckner	.545	0-0	.699	779	174	1	21	69	199	16	22	8
Jim Les	.328	.071	.781	781	88	0	10	88	87	215	5	27
Marc Iavaroni	.444	0-1	.818	796	99	0	10	52	132	32	13	11

OVERALL RANKINGS *

PLAYER	G	GS	PPG	PR	RANK	SC	SH	RB	AS	BL	ST
Karl Malone	80	80	**29.07**	29.52	5	2	51	25	106	59	48
John Stockton	**82**	**82**	17.07	27.40	9	52	6	168	2	150	2
Thurl Bailey	**82**	3	19.45	16.79	65	28	86	96	143	39	166
Mark Eaton	**82**	**82**	6.20	16.59	73	169	158	17	167	3	171
Darrell Griffith	**82**	73	13.84	11.50	130	81	128	112	133	113	90
Bobby Hansen	46	9	7.41	7.09	DNQ						
Mike Brown	66	16	4.55	5.79	DNQ						
Eric Leckner	75	0	4.25	4.81	DNQ						
Jim Les	**82**	0	1.68	3.35	DNQ						
Marc Iavaroni	77	50	2.34	2.82	DNQ						

POSITION RANKINGS *

PLAYER	POSITION	RANK	SC	SH	RB	AS	BL	ST
Karl Malone	Power Forward	2	1	8	13	5	16	2
John Stockton	Point Guard	2	9	3	28	2	19	1
Thurl Bailey	Small Forward	15	11	19	23	37	8	40
Mark Eaton	Center	12	27	26	8	24	2	27
Darrell Griffith	Off Guard	28	25	30	14	42	17	32
Bobby Hansen	Off Guard	DNQ						
Mike Brown	Power Forward	DNQ						
Eric Leckner	Center	DNQ						
Jim Les	Point Guard	DNQ						
Marc Iavaroni	Small Forward	DNQ						

*For further definition of each category and column heading see pages 42 & 43.

Utah Jazz .... Team Info

WEEKLY POWER RATING

41 WINS - AVERAGE   (See page 43 for Team Power Rating discussion.)

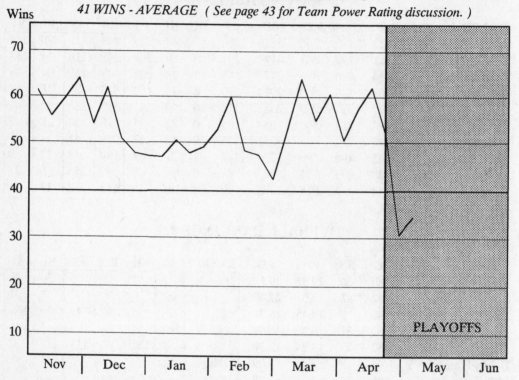

Miscellaneous Categories	Data	Rank
Attendance	510K	21
Key-Man Games Missed	61	12
Season Record	51-31	7
- Home	34-7	7
- Road	17-24	7
Eastern Conference	14-10	5
Western Conference	37-21	7
Overtime Record	0-1	23
Record 5 Pts. or Less	10-10	9
Record 10 Pts. or More	36-15	5
Games Won By Bench	12	2
Games Won By Starters	3	19
Winning Streak	7	7
Losing Streak	4	7
Home Winning Streak	12	10
Road Winning Streak	3	9
Home Losing Streak	1	1
Road Losing Streak	4	2

Performance Categories	Data	Rank
Offensive Scoring (per game)	104.7	21
Defensive Scoring (per game)	99.7	1
Scoring Margin (per game)	5.0	5
Defensive FG%	.434	1
Offensive 2-point%	.494	10
Offensive 3-point%	.300	19
Offensive Free Throw %	.770	13
Offensive Rebs .....(Off REB/Opp Def REB)		16
Defensive Rebs ....(Def REB/Opp Off REB)		8
Offensive Assists ....(AST/FGMade)		2
Offensive Blocks ..(BLK/Opp FGAttempted)		1
Offensive Steals ....(STL/Game)		16
Turnover Margin........(Def T.O. - Off T.O.)		23
Fouls Margin .... (Opp FOULS - FOULS)		5
Rebounding Record	50-28-4	3
Assists Record	56-24-2	2
Field Goal Pct. Record	51-30-1	4
Free Throw Att. Record	49-30-3	6

Utah Jazz . . . . Team Roster

MOST PRODUCTIVE PLAYERS

Player	Span	Yrs	CRD
Adrian Dantley	1980-86	7	12,419
Rickey Green	1981-88	8	9,075
Darrell Griffith	1981-89	8	8,515
Mark Eaton	1983-89	7	8,069
Karl Malone	1986-89	4	7,741
Thurl Bailey	1984-89	6	7,512
John Stockton	1985-89	5	7,495
Rich Kelley	1976-85	7	7,262
Pete Maravich	1975-79	5	7,140
Jeff Wilkins	1981-85	5	4,215

PRESENT PLAYERS*

J#	VETERANS	COLLEGE	POS	R#	D#	HT	WT	Utah	NBA
41	Thurl Bailey	N. Carolina State	F	1	7	6-11	222	6	6
40	Mike Brown	G. Washington	F	3	69	6-9	250	1	3
53	Mark Eaton	UCLA	C	4	72	7-4	290	7	7
35	Darrell Griffith	Louisville	G	1	2	6-4	190	8	8
20	Bob Hansen	Iowa	G-F	3	54	6-6	195	6	6
43	Marc Iavaroni	Virginia	F	3	55	6-10	225	4	7
45	Eric Leckner	Wyoming	C	1	17	6-11	265	1	1
25	Jim Les	Bradley	G	3	70	5-11	175	1	1
32	Karl Malone	Louisiana Tech	F	1	13	6-9	256	4	4
44	Jose Ortiz	Utah Jazz	F	1	15	6-10	225	1	1
12	John Stockton	Gonzaga	G	1	16	6-1	175	5	5

FUTURE PLAYERS

ROOKIES	COLLEGE	POS	R#	D#	HT	WT
Theodore Edwards	East Carolina	G	1	21	6-5	200
Junie Lewis	South Alabama	G	2	48	6-3	180

* For further definition of category and column headings, see pages 42 & 43.

Utah Jazz .... Overview

By far and away the biggest news of the year in Utah was the playoff loss to Golden State. And, unlike most playoff losses where the heavily favored team loses, you can't blame it on a freak injury or a lucky shot. In those cases, you're likely to hear fans of the *better* team lamenting that "if they could only replay the series..." Well, not in this case. Golden State beat Utah, they beat them soundly, and they beat them in all three games - two of which were at Salt Lake City - a place where Utah had not lost two in a row all season. NBA experts everywhere are scratching their heads trying to figure out how Golden State did it, as it had been 23 years since a team with the home-court advantage got swept in the first round.

Of course, the conventional wisdom is that Don Nelson is a coaching genius, that somehow he not only led his troops to 23 wins more than the previous year, but brilliantly figured out how to rip through powerful Utah in the playoffs. There may be some truth to that. In fact, I think there is. But I also think it's an oversimplified explanation. What really explains the upset more than anything else is that Utah matches up very poorly against Golden State. The Warriors actually outscored the Jazz during the regular season too, and it wasn't because Golden State was the better team. It really boils down to two people - Manute Bol and Mark Eaton.

Utah won a lot of games because of Mark "Defensive Player of the Year" Eaton's defense, but a team like Golden State minimizes his impact. The reason is simple - they just shoot from the perimeter. With Richmond (61%), Mullin (55%), Higgins (69%) and Teagle (50%) all popping jump shots from 2-point distance while adding more than their share of 3's, Eaton was neutralized defensively.

However, just the opposite was true for Manute Bol. Utah is a team that plays primarily a half-court offense. Unfortunately, their all-too-common offensive play is to have John Stockton and Karl Malone clear out one side and play 2 on 2. Normally, that's fine, however, against Bol, Malone is just not tall enough to take it to the hole (Who is?). When forced to shoot fall-away 12 footers, his value is substantially reduced. Since Eaton presented no offensive threat, Bol could concentrate almost exclusively on Malone and Bailey.

There is an offensive answer to this puzzle for Utah. The way to beat Golden State is by perimeter shooting. Yes, John Stockton is a tremendous perimeter shooter (1st among guards in 2-pt% .561), but not if he's guarded. He's just disciplined enough only to take the shot when he's open. The answer has to come from the 2-guard spot. Hansen and Griffith combined to shoot 39.3% from 2-point range in the series and that, more than anything else, cost Utah a chance to challenge the Suns and Lakers.

Well, when you've got a hole that needs to be filled, you go out on draft day and fill it. Subsequently, Utah picked up Theodore Edwards from East Carolina. Edwards was the nation's fifth-leading scorer last season at 27 ppg. As a 6'5" shooting guard, he could be the answer to the club's needs. And to add a little insurance to the backcourt, the Jazz grabbed a back-up point-guard from South Alabama - Junie Lewis. At 6'3", Lewis is smart, unselfish, and a strong rebounder in the Fat Lever mold.

As I said earlier, Utah won a lot of games because of their defense. But just how good was it? As I mention on page 33, it was among the best in NBA history! I arrive at that by dividing their defensive FG% (.434, lowest since 1972) by the league average defensive FG% for that year (.477). By that standard, the Utah Jazz of 1989 had the lowest ever.

	Team FG%	NBA FG%	% of NBA	Pts Saved
Utah 1989	.434	.477	.910	8.6
Milw 1984	.456	.499	.914	8.6
Utah 1988	.449	.490	.916	8.2
Phil 1981	.451	.491	.919	8.0
Atla 1987	.451	.490	.920	7.8

Utah Jazz .... Overview

One last thing: if you accept that each percentage point saved is worth 2 points - as Pat Lafferty does on page 220 - then Utah's great defense made them 8.6 points per game. Since their actual scoring margin was only 5 points per game, then it is reasonable to say their offense was somewhat substandard - a valid belief, but something that Theodore Edwards might correct.

Another way to look at the defense is to divide the defensive points allowed by the league average for that year. By that standard, Utah was 4th best (.913277) - behind, interestingly enough, three New York teams. The 1983 Knicks were first at .899, then the Championship Knicks of 1970 (.907) and 1973 (.913249).

One of Utah's problems is that, because of no strong off-guard, its offense is too narrowly defined. Teams don't wonder what they are going to do. A couple statistical oddities here: 1) They play primarily the same guys more than any other team. As evidence, their 6th most played man, Mike Brown, played only 1,051 minutes. Every other NBA team had at least one player with more. Secondly, Karl Malone was #2 on the team in assists, at 219. Here again, every other NBA team had at least two people with more. By adding Edwards, the Jazz will hopefully diversify their offense.

John Stockton had another magnificent year. Amazingly, he hasn't missed a single game (410 consecutive) in 5 years, thus leading the league. In the last two seasons he has amassed a record 2,246 assists to become the first person to break 1,000 twice. Stockton holds the NBA record for career assists per minute as well. Last season he was not only 1st in assists per *game* (trailing Bogues on a per-*minute* basis), but was also 1st in steals per game. In so doing, he becomes only the 3rd person to accomplish that feat (Michael Ray Richardson - 1980 and Don Buse - 1977 are the others). When Magic Johnson could not play in the All-Star game, John Stockton proudly took control and led the West to victory. John had a record 9 assists in the first quarter, 17 for the game, went 5-6 from the field and had 5 steals to end as the runner-up in the MVP voting.

The winner of the MVP trophy was Stockton's teammate, Karl Malone. Malone came into his own in 1989 as *the* prototype power forward in the NBA. His 28 points and 9 rebounds in the All-Star game left an impression that was still there when the All-NBA voting took place at season's end. Malone was the only player to be a unanimous selection to the 1st team. Not even Magic or Jordan received that honor. Additionally, he led the league with 918 FTA's.

Notes: Utah went 25-7 when Malone scored 29+.... The team was 19-6 when Bobby Hansen took 7+ field goal attempts... Layden was 11-6 while Sloan was 40-25 as coach... By breaking Darrell Griffith's season into sixths, his scoring averages were, in order, 20.5, 15.1, 14.4, 12.7, 10.6, and 9.6... Eric Leckner averaged 10.5 ppg the last 6 games... Utah was 26-0 when they scored 105+ points at home and 29-0 when the margin at home was 10+... When the Jazz shot 46% or better, their record was 42-8. When they shot 45% or worse, they suffered (9-32)... Mark Eaton had the NBA high of 14 blocks in a game last season... Thurl Bailey won the J. Walter Kennedy Citizenship Award.

Prediction - best case: 58-24

This is based on two essential ingredients: 1) The Jazz must continue to remain injury-free. 2) Edwards has to become a serious offensive threat. Otherwise, the team can't do much better than they have.

Prediction - worst case: 44-38

Make no mistake about it. If Malone or Stockton or Eaton get injured for a sustained period of time, this team will be ugly to watch and they'll lose a lot of games. And remember, no Midwest Division champion has repeated since 1983.

To order back issues of Basketball Heaven or to obtain the 1990 Mid-season Report, see page 324.

Washington Bullets . . . . Influence on Winning

TEAM RECORD BY

PLAYER	GAMES	... SCR Leader		... REB Leader		...AST Leader	
		HOME	ROAD	HOME	ROAD	HOME	ROAD
John Williams	82	1-0	1-4	7-3	2-6	6-2	1-5
Bernard King	81	14-3	3-9	5-1	1-5	1-2	3-7
Darrell Walker	79	0-1	0-2	9-4	3-4	19-9	6-12
Jeff Malone	76	14-3	5-13	0-0	0-1	3-1	0-3
Terry Catledge	79	1-2	1-2	11-4	5-11	0-0	0-0
Steve Colter	80	0-0	0-1	0-0	0-0	1-0	1-5
Ledell Eackles	80	2-2	1-1	0-0	0-0	0-0	0-0
Charles Jones	53	0-0	0-0	2-0	1-3	0-0	0-0
Mark Alarie	74	0-0	0-0	0-0	0-1	1-0	0-0
Harvey Grant	71	0-0	0-0	1-0	0-0	0-0	0-0

TEAM RECORD BY SCORING *

PLAYER	PLAY	DNP	0-9	10-19	20-29	30-39	40+
John Williams	40-42	0-0	10-9	19-27	1-5	0-1	0-0
Bernard King	4041	0-1	1-6	13-19	15-12	10-4	1-0
Darrell Walker	40-39	0-3	24-21	14-15	2-3	0-0	0-0
Jeff Malone	36-40	4-2	1-1	10-19	17-14	8-6	0-0
Terry Catledge	38-41	2-1	21-18	16-18	1-5	0-0	0-0
Steve Colter	39-41	1-1	27-31	11-9	1-1	0-0	0-0
Ledell Eackles	38-42	2-0	13-18	22-20	3-4	0-0	0-0
Charles Jones	26-27	14-15	26-27	0-0	0-0	0-0	0-0
Mark Alarie	35-39	5-3	19-34	15-5	1-0	0-0	0-0
Harvey Grant	38-33	2-9	30-28	8-5	0-0	0-0	0-0

TEAM RECORD BY STARTING POSITION *

PLAYER	GAMES	STARTS	PG	OG	SF	PF	C
John Williams	82	1	0-0	0-0	0-0	0-0	0-1
Bernard King	81	81	0-0	0-0	40-41	0-0	0-0
Darrell Walker	79	78	38-39	1-0	0-0	0-0	0-0
Jeff Malone	76	75	0-0	35-40	0-0	0-0	0-0
Terry Catledge	79	77	0-0	0-0	0-0	38-39	0-0
Steve Colter	80	5	2-3	0-0	0-0	0-0	0-0
Ledell Eackles	80	6	0-0	4-2	0-0	0-0	0-0
Charles Jones	53	45	0-0	0-0	0-0	0-0	25-20
Mark Alarie	74	5	0-0	0-0	0-0	2-3	0-0
Harvey Grant	71	1	0-0	0-0	0-1	0-0	0-0

* For further definition of each category and column heading see pages 42 & 43.

Washington Bullets . . . . 1988-89 Statistics

RAW NUMBERS *

PLAYER	2pt%	3pt%	FT%	MIN	PF	DQ	HI	TO	RB	AS	BL	ST
John Williams	.482	.268	.776	2413	213	1	30	157	573	356	70	142
Bernard King	.484	.167	.819	2559	219	1	43	227	384	294	13	64
Darrell Walker	.426	0-9	.772	2565	215	2	23	184	507	496	23	155
Jeff Malone	.486	.053	.871	2418	155	0	38	165	179	219	14	39
Terry Catledge	.493	.200	.602	2077	250	5	26	120	572	75	25	46
Steve Colter	.463	.120	.749	1425	158	0	27	64	182	225	14	69
Ledell Eackles	.447	.225	.786	1459	156	1	28	128	180	123	5	41
Charles Jones	.484	0-1	.640	1154	187	4	9	39	257	42	76	39
Mark Alarie	.491	.342	.839	1141	160	1	22	62	255	63	22	25
Harvey Grant	.465	0-1	.596	1193	147	2	14	28	163	79	29	35

OVERALL RANKINGS *

PLAYER	G	GS	PPG	PR	RANK	SC	SH	RB	AS	BL	ST
John Williams	82	1	13.66	18.74	40	85	118	49	44	47	21
Bernard King	81	81	20.67	17.35	58	20	100	103	58	145	129
Darrell Walker	79	78	9.04	16.13	80	141	168	76	27	118	17
Jeff Malone	76	75	21.72	15.26	89	17	88	170	77	140	168
Terry Catledge	79	77	10.41	12.30	122	120	146	23	160	98	144
Steve Colter	80	5	6.67	8.30	166	163	153	119	40	111	39
Ledell Eackles	80	6	11.46	8.13	168	113	145	121	84	160	117
Charles Jones	53	45	2.57	8.25	DNQ						
Mark Alarie	74	5	6.73	7.59	DNQ						
Harvey Grant	71	1	5.58	6.23	DNQ						

POSITION RANKINGS *

PLAYER	POSITION	RANK	SC	SH	RB	AS	BL	ST
John Williams	Small Forward, PF	10	24	28	4	1	10	1
Bernard King	Small Forward	13	8	23	29	6	39	26
Darrell Walker	Point Guard, OG	19	24	30	2	23	8	9
Jeff Malone	Off Guard	15	5	23	42	26	31	44
Terry Catledge	Power Forward	26	22	27	12	22	26	26
Steve Colter	Point Guard	32	32	25	7	30	6	14
Ledell Eackles	Off Guard	42	32	37	17	31	37	39
Charles Jones	Center	DNQ						
Mark Alarie	Small Forward	DNQ						
Harvey Grant	Power Forward	DNQ						

*For further definition of each category and column heading see pages 42 & 43.

Washington Bullets . . . . Team Info

WEEKLY POWER RATING

41 WINS - AVERAGE (See page 43 for Team Power Rating discussion.)

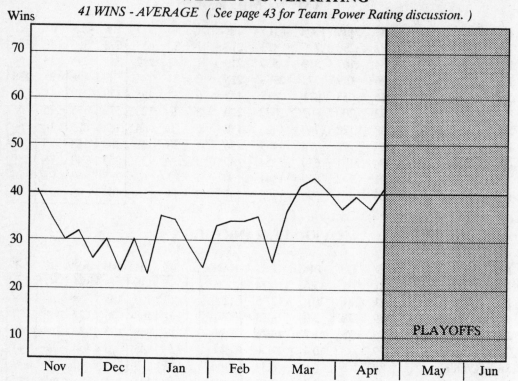

Miscellaneous Categories	Data	Rank
Attendance	402K	25
Key-Man Games Missed	58	10
Season Record	40-42	16
- Home	30-11	13
- Road	10-31	16
Eastern Conference	25-31	15
Western Conference	15-11	10
Overtime Record	3-3	8
Record 5 Pts. or Less	16-6	2
Record 10 Pts. or More	12-23	18
Games Won By Bench	12	2
Games Won By Starters	0	25
Winning Streak	5	13
Losing Streak	7	15
Home Winning Streak	15	8
Road Winning Streak	2	16
Home Losing Streak	2	5
Road Losing Streak	8	12

Performance Categories	Data	Rank
Offensive Scoring (per game)	108.3	14
Defensive Scoring (per game)	110.4	15
Scoring Margin (per game)	-2.1	18
Defensive FG%	.482	13
Offensive 2-point%	.472	22
Offensive 3-point%	.214	25
Offensive Free Throw %	.772	12
Offensive Rebs (Off REB/Opp Def REB)		11
Defensive Rebs (Def REB/Opp Off REB)		11
Offensive Assists (AST/FGMade)		21
Offensive Blocks (BLK/Opp FGAttempted)		24
Offensive Steals (STL/Game)		18
Turnover Margin (Def T.O. - Off T.O.)		9
Fouls Margin (Opp FOULS - FOULS)		20
Rebounding Record	40-40-2	13
Assists Record	36-40-6	17
Field Goal Pct. Record	37-45-0	15
Free Throw Att. Record	31-49-2	20

Washington Bullets ....Team Roster

MOST PRODUCTIVE PLAYERS

Player	Span	Yrs	CRD
Wes Unseld	1969-81	13	22,572
Elvin Hayes	1973-81	9	17,612
Gus Johnson	1964-72	9	12,694
Walt Bellamy	1962-65	4	10,908
Greg Ballard	1978-85	8	9,964
Kevin Loughery	1964-71	9	8,132
Jack Marin	1967-72	6	8,054
Phil Chenier	1972-79	9	7,795
Jeff Ruland	1982-86	5	7,086
Jeff Malone	1984-89	6	6,849

PRESENT PLAYERS*

J#	VETERANS	COLLEGE	POS	R#	D#	HT	WT	Wash	NBA
31	Mark Alarie	Duke	F	1	18	6-8	217	2	3
14	Steve Colter	New Mexico State	G	2	33	6-3	175	2	5
21	Ledell Eackles	New Orleans	G	2	36	6-5	220	1	1
44	Harvey Grant	Oklahoma	F	1	12	6-9	195	1	1
23	Charles Jones	Albany State	F	8	165	6-9	215	5	6
30	Bernard King	Tennessee	F	1	7	6-7	205	2	11
24	Jeff Malone	Mississippi State	G	1	10	6-4	205	6	6
5	Darrell Walker	Arkansas	G	1	12	6-4	180	2	6
34	John Williams	LSU	F	1	12	6-9	237	3	3

FUTURE PLAYERS

ROOKIES	COLLEGE	POS	R#	D#	HT	WT
Tom Hammonds	Georgia Tech	F	1	9	6-9	217
Ed Horton	Iowa	F	2	39	6-8	230
Doug Roth	Tennessee	C	2	41	6-11	255

* For further definition of category and column headings, see pages 42 & 43.

Washington Bullets . . . . Overview

During the All-Star festivities, I was invited to be on "Inside the NBA" with Fred Hickman - my good buddy. Before the show, we had gone over each of the teams and had graded them A-F. As I recall, we slapped the Bullets with a D-. That was about as bad as we could go. In retrospect, however, I'm not sure that we were totally fair. Granted, they were only 17-28, tied with New Jersey and ahead of only expansion Charlotte in the division. While that's true, it is also the case that the club did not have what most of us call a center. What can you expect with no center? And the bottom line is that a large part of each team's grade was based on what the expectations were before the season began (as it should be). Heck, we had even given the Hornets a "B" because, for an expansion team, they had already won 13 games. Actually, considering Washington's center woes and the fact that 2 of their top 8 players were rookies, their 17 wins wasn't that bad either. If I had to do it over again, I'd probably rate them a "C-".

Here now, for the first time, I can give them a grade for the second half of the season. Are you ready? How about an "A". That's right. No team in the NBA played better with what they had the second half of the season - although with Detroit's 32-6 record, I would have to give them an "A" as well. No, the Bullets weren't 32-6, but they were 23-14. When you look closely at their talent (or lack thereof), it's tough to figure out how they did that well. In fact, as hard to believe as it is, Washington won more games in the second half than did Eastern Conference heavy-weights Cleveland, Chicago, Atlanta, or New York.

Detroit	32-6	.842	
Washington	**23-14**	**.622**	**-8.5**
Cleveland	22-14	.611	-9.0
Chicago	21-14	.600	-9.5
Atlanta	22-15	.595	-9.5
New York	20-14	.588	-10.0

By season's end, the Bullets were playing so well that they actually had the 11th best Power Rating in the league. But despite this great play, the first half of the season was too much to overcome and they just couldn't catch the Celtics (falling 2 games short) for the last playoff spot.

What is especially interesting about last season was its similarity to the season before. In 1987-88, Washington began by going 19-32 before turning it around and winning 19-12. Last season they went 19-30 and then 21-12. A reasonable person might wonder if something is built into the system that caused it. I don't know about that, but I can say, without reservation, that the reason they lost so many games early is because of the team's poor first quarters. In 1987-88, they won the first quarter only once in the first 22 games. They barely improved that last season by winning quarter one just three times over the same period. Being behind so much gave the club a chance for a lot of comebacks. Interestingly, they tied for first in comebacks (wins when trailing after Q3) minus blown games (losses when leading after Q3).

Comebacks Minus Blown Games

1. **Washington**	12-3	= 9
2. Philadelphia	12-3	= 9
3. New York	13-4	= 9
4. Chicago	10-4	= 6
5. Seattle	10-7	= 3

The most intriguing things happened to the club after the season was over. To begin with, they chose not to protect Terry Catledge in the expansion draft. Catledge missed being the team's leading rebounder by only 1 board (572 to 573 - Williams) and ranked 5th on the team by Production Rating. Only one unprotected player ranked higher on his team, that being Reggie Theus of Atlanta (4th). Though who was or wasn't protected was not made public, it appears to me that Mark Alarie was protected. Who knows, though - the team has so many marginal players. If it did come down to Alarie vs Catledge, I can understand the front office's decision.

Washington Bullets .... Overview

Though Alarie's stats don't seem to compare with Catledge's, what matters is wins and losses. When Catledge scored 8 or more points, Washington was -11 in wins. When Alarie did it, they were +12. Moreover, when Catledge scored less than 8 points, the Bullets were +8 wins vs -16 when Alarie failed to score 8 points. Since the team desperately needs more scoring, Alarie is who you have to go with.

The second interesting happening after the season ended was the draft. Thankfully, the Bullets got the 9th position instead of the 12th as they had for the last four years. Clearly, with such a serious weakness up front, further depeleted by Catledge's departure, and with few decent centers available in the draft, the team went for a power forward. They got a very good one in Tom Hammonds. Hammonds looks like Orlando Woolridge, but his attitude is good and, unlike Woolridge, he loves to mix it up underneath. Washington also drafted forward Ed Horton. He's a ferocious rebounder, but a player that will have to be helped to develop discipline.

The Bullets would love to have drafted Danny Ferry (son of G.M. Bob Ferry), but as of the writing of this book, were unable to swing a deal with the Clippers. Since it's hard for me to believe the Clippers are going to stay with four of the best young small forwards in the game, some deal is possible. Jeff Malone (plus...) would be the likely offering on Washington's part, but L.A. needs a 2-guard with experience who is more of a leader.

Ledell Eackles was a pleasant surprise as a rookie and would be a good choice to replace Malone if he were to leave. Although he was drafted 36th, he nearly made the All-Rookie second team. (I would have to say that, along with Brian Shaw of Boston and Grant Long of Miami, he was among the best bargains in the 1988 draft). Eackles holds the distinction of being the only player to qualify in the NBA who had more offensive rebounds than defensive boards (100-80).

Bernard King has continued to come back strong from a nearly career-ending injury in 1985. King, who also missed most of the 1980 season and has had more comebacks then Sugar Ray Leonard, scored 25 ppg in a late-season 25 game stretch. Not bad. Especially when you realize this scoring machine's career average before the injury was "only" 24 ppg.

We can talk about King & Malone & Eackles, but the best player on this team is John Williams. Though JW has 3 years of NBA ball under his belt, he'll start the preseason only 22 years of age. Despite the team's ranking last in 3-point shooting, Williams hit 7 of his final 17, indicating his enormous versatility. His Production Rating has increased each year and was the league high in 1989 among 6th-men.

John Williams	**Wash**	**18.74**
Wayman Tisdale	Sacr	18.43
Eddie Johnson	Phoe	17.93
Thurl Bailey	Utah	16.79
Dennis Rodman	Detr	16.32

Notes: Charles Jones and his brother (Caldwell) are the two lowest scorers per minute in the NBA... Washington ranked 3rd in games decided by 10 points or less (28-19)... Attendance at the Cap Center was the lowest in the NBA... The Bullets are the only team in the league without a single 50% field goal shooter.

Prediction - best case: 48-34

If Hammonds is a force, Eackles and Grant improve, and Williams becomes a star... and if a deal for someone resembling a center emerges, then they actually could be good - something that hasn't been the case since the 1970's.

Prediction - worst case: 32-50

Watching this team's first quarters of games and first halves of the season will lead you to say "There *is* no worst case." Maybe, but I've got to go with something.

To order back issues of Basketball Heaven or to obtain the 1990 Midseason Report, see page 324.

BEST FRIENDS

ISIAH THOMAS VS MAGIC JOHNSON

AP/WIDE WORLD PHOTOS

CHAPTER 4

PLAYERS POSITIONS

PLAYERS POSITIONS

Any discussion of positions in the NBA needs to be prefaced with a disclaimer or two. Basketball, unlike baseball, has less definabled qualities which make up each position. Many times a player plays more than one position throughout the season. In fact, half the time a player plays more than one position in a given game. A team such as Denver makes little distinction between Adams and Lever at point or off guard. For that matter, Schayes and Rasmussen interchange regularly between center and power forward. The point is that some players play out of position because of the team's needs.

Then too, are there only five positions? What about a power center (Malone) vs a perimeter center (Laimbeer) or a finesse center (Jabbar) vs a defensive center (Eaton)? I call them all one thing - a center. A small forward is also a finesse forward, a quick forward or even a shooting forward; an off-guard is often referred to as a shooting guard or a two-guard; a point guard is called a lead guard; and a power forward is synonymous with a rebounding forward.

Despite the multitude of names associated with the five positions, it is generally accepted that only five positions exist. Although point forward (Pressey), swingman (McCray), and power guard (Jordan) are terms which have gained popularity. Nevertheless, until the NBA offices pick the All-NBA team by parameters other than guards, forwards and center, I will accept what is traditional.

POSITION AVERAGES

Certainly, some players can reasonably be listed at either of several positions, however, I generally chose the position they played at most often during the 1988-89 season. To help me determine what position a player "really" was, I developed a formula which identified the average center, power forward, etc. Once that was accomplished, I evaluated each player by those averages to determine how closely each was to his position.

I decided that to the degree a player came closer to one position than another on a scale of 100, he was most like the average player at that position. More precisely, I chose to compare each player to the average of each position by twelve categories - 2-pt %, FT%, 3-pt FGA's per minute, Pts/min, Reb/min, Ast/min, Blk/min, Stl/min, T.O./min, Fouls/min, height, and weight. When you think about it, some categories are more likely to indicate whether a player is of one position or another. For example, if a player shoots 2 pointers at 48.3% or 50.3% which is he? Is he a point guard or a center? That's not too easy to say. On the other hand if a player is 7'0" or 6'2", is he most likely a point guard or a center? That's easy. Therefore, I gave different values to the twelve categories. These values are not for the purpose of deciding which category is most *important*, but rather which is most *telling* about what position a player plays. Shown below are the averages for the twelve categories.

	2pt%	FT%	3-pt* FGA	*PPG	*RB	*AS	*BK	*ST	*T.O.	*FL	HT	WT
Center	50.1	71.8	.3	19.6	12.7	2.3	2.5	1.2	3.2	5.8	7'0"	248
Power Forward	50.9	74.0	.3	20.8	12.4	2.6	1.4	1.5	3.1	5.0	6'9"	232
Small Forward	49.0	78.0	1.2	24.4	8.6	3.9	1.0	1.6	3.3	4.7	6'8"	218
Off Guard	48.6	80.7	2.4	24.6	6.0	5.7	.5	2.1	3.2	4.0	6'5"	197
Point Guard	48.3	81.3	2.0	19.5	5.2	10.8	.3	2.5	3.9	3.7	6'2"	182
Values	**1**	**2**	**13**	**3**	**11**	**12**	**13**	**11**	**1**	**5**	**14**	**14**

*based on 48 minute averages.

The trends are obvious and unmistakable. Since they are, it is reasonable to say that a player who is very close to the average small forward and quite a ways from the other four positions is, in fact, a small forward - regardless of what position he plays.

As I mentioned earlier, I gave a possible 100 points to each player. These points were distributed according to the chart on the opposite page. Suppose a power player were more like a center in the first ten categories (up to fouls), but more like a power forward in height and weight. He would rate a 72 center 28 power forward.

The reason the twelve categories have different values is because of what I said earlier. Some categories are far more telling than others [height (14) vs FG% (1) or weight (14) vs T.O. (1)]. Therefore, the telling categories must carry the most weight.

Lets use an example. Johnny Dawkins of San Antonio is a point guard. He always has been. He plays that position virtually exclusively. However, should he? Maybe he's more of an off-guard. Here's a look at his twelve stats. * based on 48 minute averages.

	2pt%	FT%	3-pt* FGA	* PPG	* RB	* AS	* BK	* ST	* T.O.	* FL	HT	WT
Johnny Dawkins	44.7	89.3	.2	20.12	4.5	9.9	.0	2.4	4.9	2.8	6"2	165

If you care to work it out, you will see that Dawkins is closer to the average point guard vs off-guard in every single category. That means his rating is 100 point guard vs 0 (zero) off-guard. Therefore, the answer is "yes, he should definitely be playing the point".

I thought it would be interesting to see which players are most *like* the positions they play. Of course, even more interesting are the players who are most *unlike* the positions they play. Shown below are the top-10 at each position and their rating (100 scale) vs the two closest positions. Where two choices are given, the cumulative total was used as the basis.

Center	PF	Power Forward	C	SF	Small Forward	PF	OG	Off Guard	SF	PG	Point Guard	OG
Dudley	87	McHale	76	87	McKey	82	97	G. Wilkins	94	83	Dawkins	100
Breuer	86	Thorpe	88	81	Short	96	83	Scott	87	82	Stockton	99
Wennington	84	Pinckney	100	68	D. Wilkins	99	74	Griffith	72	94	Humphries	93
Eaton	81	L. Smith	79	86	K. Walker	65	99	Woodson	85	73	Webb	93
Donaldson	78	Tisdale	83	81	D. Smith	90	74	Curry	87	74	Bogues	92
Smrek	76	Petersen	65	98	B. Johnson	75	85	McGee	80	76	S. Vincent	88
Welp	75	Ho. Grant	79	86	Campbell	83	73	Ehlo	69	86	K. Smith	87
Koncak	74	Tolbert	76	87	Frederick	80	75	R. Harper	83	70	Thomas	85
Bol	74	Ha. Grant	89	61	Pippen	77	77	Hawkins	85	67	Cheeks	85
Lang	74	J. Williams	73	84	Higgins	84	70	Hansen	66	84	K. Johnson	85

Some players are miscast at their positions. Usually this is just because the team has unique needs. Shown below are the top players who are out of position and the reason why.

	PP	RT	AP	
Brickowski	C	8	PF	David Robinson will cure this.
Sellers	SF	14	PF	Too wimpy to play power forward.
C. Smith	SF	16	PF	If Smith is the PF, Norman (670 reb) is the SF.
Cureton	C	17	PF	Expansion teams lack traditional centers.
Lever	OG	17	PG	1988-89 was Michael Adams' best year at point guard.
M. Thompson	C	17	PF	With Kareem declining, someone had (has) to play center.
S. Johnson	C	19	PF	Will continue to play center for expansion Timberwolves.
Washington	OG	21	PG	Pearl's inconsistency keeps him from playing any position.
Bailey	SF	23	PF	Karl Malone is all the power forward any team needs.

Carr	SF	27	PF	With Levingston, Koncak & Willis, Carr plays out of position.
Battle	OG	27	PG	Doc Rivers and Spud Webb man the point for Atlanta.
Iavaroni	SF	27	PF	Karl Malone is all the power forward any team needs.
Rodman	SF	28	PF	No small forward rebounds like Rodman.
O. Smith	OG	28	SF	Who wasn't a small forward on Golden State last season.
Chevious	OG	28	SF	Chevious will never be great at the 2-guard spot.
Barkley	PF	28	SF	Some argue that Charles really is a small forward anyway.
Aguirre	SF	29	OG	His 3-pointers have increased every year.

PP = Present Position
RT = Rating
AP = Appropriate Position

POSITION VALUE

Once in a while a discussion comes up as to which position is the most important. There was a time (as in every year in the NBA until the early '80s) that the answer was "the center". However, many changes have taken place in the game. Johnson, Bird, Jordan, Drexler, Wilkens, Barkley and others have proven beyond question that the center is not necessarily the most critical position.

I decided to try to determine what position was the most valuable. To do this I evaluated the relationship between the best players at each position and the number of games their team's won. The long and the short of it is that the point guard (.593) is the most critical position in the 1980's. The small forward (.578), center (.569), off guard (.524) and power forward (.508) are next.

If you want the quick answer to position value, I've just given it. If you want to see how I came up with it, here goes. What I did was to look at the top-10 players at each position for every year in the 1980's. I then looked at that player's team's wins and losses. What I did was multiply the best player's team's wins times 10 and losses times 10, the second best player's team's wins times 9 and losses times 9, etc. As you can see, this gave more weight to the top players and less to those at the bottom. I then determined the winning percentage for each position for each year.

Next, I followed the same principle again. Because there were (profoundly enough) 10 years in the 1980's, I took the most recent winning percentage times 10, the second most recent winning percentage times 9, etc. This gave more weight to recent years. Subsequently, I came up with the winning percentages I mentioned earlier for each of the five positions.

What does it mean? Well, lets look at 1988-89 only. Last year, seven of the top-10 point-guards played on teams with 50+ wins, but only three of the top-10 off-guards played on teams that good. Coincidence? I don't think so. The facts are that off guards are normally at the end of a play - meaning they don't create action. Because of this, a great off-guard may not necessarily be able to pull his team along with him (witness Michael Jordan).

A similar situation exists with power forwards. The truth is that power forwards are good or great (excellent stats) largely because of the inadequacies of their team. The more a team misses from the field, the more chances the power forward has to get a rebound (1 positive credit) and a stick back (2 positive credits). Simply s'ated, the *better* the team, the less for the power forward to "achieve", while the *worse* the team, the more "potential" for the power forward.

Because of the wide open style so prevalent in the NBA, the point guard has become essential. A team without a very good point guard has almost no chance to be the league's best, whereas a team can win with just a banger at power forward. The other three positions fall somewhere in between.

COMPARISONS

Statistical comparisons have always been made between players and probably always will be. What makes them fascinating is to look at them side by side, stripping them bare of the subjective elements which go into evaluations. I won't try to kid anyone and argue that they tell the whole story, but they do provide a unique look at where one excels over another.

I've explained what Production Rating (PR) is in great detail in chapter 1. I also explained why I chose to use the 48-minute ratings (*) for rebounds, assists, blocks and steals in the first chapter. SH stands for shooting index. It is explained on page 240.

Some interesting comparisons are the top Tar Heels of the 80's, the "lucky" 13th-year players, the top off-guards (excluding Jordan) who could be point guards, and four sets of brothers as well as a close comparison of the Malones.

TOP TAR HEELS OF THE 80's

Although this is a fine group of players, Michael Jordan totally dominates. Maybe I'll be able to do a quartet of non-Jordan players in the future by adding J. R. Reid. Quiz: What year did these four players play together? The answer is spelled backwards. (.t'ndid yehT)

	PR	2pt%	3pt%	FT%	SC	* SH	* RB	* AS	* BK	* ST
M. Jordan	**36.99**	.553	.276	**.850**	**32.51**	**1.104**	9.59	**9.59**	**.96**	**3.45**
J. Worthy	21.80	**.556**	.087	.782	20.46	1.086	7.93	4.67	.91	1.75
B. Daugherty	22.37	.538	**.333**	.737	18.91	1.044	**12.22**	4.85	.68	1.07
S. Perkins	18.51	.476	.184	.833	15.01	.980	11.55	2.13	1.54	1.28

13th-YEAR PLAYERS

Not very many players survive 13 years in the NBA. It would appear that each of these players could play another couple years anyway. Parish leads the group, ranking as the 17th greatest player in league history by my 10-year MVP ratings (see page 19). Not far behind are the others. English ranks 22nd, Dantley 23rd, and Johnson 31st.

	PR	2pt%	3pt%	FT%	SC	* SH	* RB	* AS	* BK	* ST
R. Parish	**26.10**	**.570**	.000	.719	18.58	**1.089**	**16.83**	2.96	**1.96**	1.34
A. English	21.38	.492	**.250**	**.858**	**26.52**	1.010	5.23	6.15	.19	1.06
A. Dantley	16.29	.493	.000	.810	19.18	1.021	6.28	3.39	.26	.85
D. Johnson	12.87	.459	.140	.821	10.01	.930	3.95	**9.81**	.44	**1.95**

OFF GUARDS THAT COULD BE POINT GUARDS

Many guards could play either position. Vinnie Johnson, Jay Humphries, Sleepy Floyd, and Vern Fleming are among them. Nevertheless, there are four guards that are classified as off-guards simply because they play along side some of the best point guards in the NBA. Because of that, they fit into a unique category.

	PR	2pt%	3pt%	FT%	SC	* SH	* RB	* AS	* BK	* ST
L. Lever	**27.48**	.463	.348	.785	**19.85**	.958	**11.58**	**9.78**	**.35**	**3.41**
J. Dumars	16.59	.505	**.483**	.850	17.19	**1.053**	3.43	7.78	.10	1.26
J. Hornacek	17.06	**.511**	.333	.826	13.51	1.034	5.13	8.97	.15	2.49
R. Theus	15.06	.476	.293	**.851**	15.80	.992	4.62	7.38	.31	2.06

THE WILKINS BROTHERS

A lot of people have said that Gerald Wilkins is just a mini version of his better-known brother Dominique. Actually, there is more diversity between them than many might imagine. Gerald appears to be slightly more well-rounded, though inferior overall.

	PR	2pt%	3pt%	FT%	SC	* SH	* RB	* AS	* BK	* ST
D. Wilkins	22.84	.475	.276	.844	26.24	.985	8.86	3.38	.83	1.87
G. Wilkins	12.64	.482	.297	.756	14.33	.962	4.85	5.44	.44	2.29

THE GRANT BROTHERS

I probably should point out from the beginning that this comparison is a little unfair to Harvey. There is no doubt that having spent two years in the NBA has helped Horace's stats, while Harvey was only a rookie last season. Still, they are twins, so their stats shouldn't vary much - especially in the upcoming years.

	PR	2pt%	3pt%	FT%	SC	* SH	* RB	* AS	* BK	* ST
Ho. Grant	17.52	.522	.000	.704	12.03	1.017	11.64	2.87	1.06	1.47
Ha. Grant	6.23	.465	.000	.596	5.58	.911	6.56	3.18	1.17	1.41

THE PAXSON BROTHERS

Though Jim Paxson has clearly been the star between the two as an NBA player, John has virtually pulled even by 1990. Actually, it's more a case of Jim slipping in recent years. Either way, they are fairly close overall as you can see.

	PR	2pt%	3pt%	FT%	SC	* SH	* RB	* AS	* BK	* ST
Ji. Paxson	7.02	.470	.167	.816	8.63	.949	3.12	4.51	.34	1.60
Jo. Paxson	8.78	.532	.331	.861	7.27	1.052	2.60	8.51	.17	1.46

THE JONES BROTHERS

These are the last two of a very famous family. All six brothers went to Albany State and all were drafted by the NBA. Both Wilbert Jones and Major Jones played in the league. Caldwell is entering his 17th season in 1990 - tying him for #2 in longevity with Artis Gilmore.

	PR	2pt%	3pt%	FT%	SC	* SH	* RB	* AS	* BK	* ST
Ca. Jones	6.50	.423	.000	.787	2.81	.893	11.26	2.21	3.19	.90
Ch. Jones	8.25	.484	.000	.640	2.57	.942	10.69	1.75	3.16	1.62

THE MALONES

These three are unrelated, but possess both the same last name and the ability to play the game extremely well. Moses is one of all-time greats, while Karl looks to become one himself.

	PR	2pt%	3pt%	FT%	SC	* SH	* RB	* AS	* BK	* ST
K. Malone	29.52	.521	.313	.766	29.08	1.034	13.10	3.36	1.07	2.21
M. Malone	23.84	.496	.000	.789	20.21	1.009	15.94	1.87	1.67	1.32
J. Malone	15.26	.486	.053	.871	21.72	1.000	3.55	4.35	.28	.77

RANKINGS AMONG CENTERS *

RK	PLAYER	TEAM	PR	PPG	2pt%	3pt%	FT%	SC	SH	RB	AS	BL	ST
1.	A. Olajuwon	Hous	**31.02**	**24.80**	.511	0-10	.696	**1**	16	**1**	15	5	**1**
2.	Patrick Ewing	N.Y.	27.46	22.69	.570	0-6	.746	2	3	17	7	4	3
3.	Robert Parish	Bost	26.10	18.57	.570	0-0	.719	5	4	2	9	15	8
4.	Moses Malone	Atla	23.84	20.21	.496	0-12	.789	3	13	3	19	19	9
5.	Brad Daugherty	Clev	22.37	18.91	.538	.333	.737	4	10	18	2	30	14
6.	B. Benjamin	LA.C	21.11	16.44	.543	0-2	.744	8	7	13	10	7	15
7.	Mike Gminski	Phil	20.55	17.18	.479	0-6	.871	7	15	9	13	17	24
8.	Bill Laimbeer	Detr	19.70	13.65	.515	.349	.840	10	9	7	6	18	19
9.	Jack Sikma	Milw	18.47	13.35	.449	.380	**.905**	12	11	21	**1**	24	6
10.	J. Donaldson	Dall	17.70	9.08	.573	0-0	.766	21	**1**	4	28	13	26
11.	K. Duckworth	Port	16.72	18.13	.478	0-2	.757	6	18	23	27	26	17
12.	Mark Eaton	Utah	16.59	6.20	.462	0-0	.660	27	26	8	24	2	27
13.	Joe B. Carroll	N.J.	15.59	14.09	.448	0-0	.800	9	25	25	12	16	4
14.	Danny Schayes	Denv	15.49	12.75	.525	.333	.826	13	6	16	11	14	16
15.	F. Brickowski	S.A.	15.42	13.67	.517	0-2	.715	11	14	28	3	25	2
16	Rik Smits	Indi	14.06	11.66	.518	0-1	.722	15	12	19	22	8	21
17.	Herb Williams	Dall	13.78	10.22	.439	0-5	.686	17	28	22	14	10	20
18.	Mark West	Phoe	13.17	7.24	**.653**	0-0	.535	23	2	11	29	6	23
19.	Bill Cartwright	Chic	12.49	12.38	.475	0-0	.766	14	17	27	20	27	29
20.	Alton Lister	Seat	12.34	8.01	.499	0-0	.646	22	19	5	23	3	25
21.	M.Thompson	LA.L	12.11	9.22	.560	0-1	.678	20	8	26	26	23	7
22.	K.Abdul-Jabbar	LA.L	10.74	10.11	.477	0-3	.739	18	20	30	17	11	13
23.	Earl Cureton	Char	10.46	6.49	.502	0-1	.537	26	23	24	8	21	10
24.	Manute Bol	G.St	10.46	3.92	.423	.220	.606	30	30	15	30	**1**	30
25.	Ron Seikaly	Miam	10.38	10.87	.449	.250	.511	16	29	10	25	12	11
26.	Jon Koncak	Atla	10.36	4.66	.530	0-3	.553	29	21	6	21	9	5
27.	Steve Johnson	Port	10.04	10.01	.524	0-0	.527	19	22	20	4	22	28
28.	Dave Hoppen	Char	9.32	6.49	.564	**.500**	.727	25	5	12	18	29	22
29.	Joe Kleine	Bost	8.08	6.45	.407	0-2	.882	24	27	14	16	28	12
30.	Dave Corzine	Chic	7.60	5.91	.465	.250	.740	28	24	29	5	20	18

* Only players who qualify. See qualification requirements on page 240.

* Numbers in **bold** are the best for each category.

RK = Rank by Production Rating
PR = Production Rating (see page 2)
PPG = Points Per Game
SC = Rank for scoring (points per game)
SH = Rank for shooting (composite shooting formula - see page 240 for explanation)

RB = Rank for rebounds per 48 minutes
AS = Rank for assists per 48 minutes
BL = Rank for blocks per 48 minutes
ST = Rank for steals per 48 minutes

RANKINGS AMONG POWER FORWARDS *

RK	PLAYER	TEAM	PR	PPG	2pt%	3pt%	FT%	SC	SH	RB	AS	BL	ST
1.	Charles Barkley	Phil	**32.68**	25.78	**.636**	.216	.753	2	**1**	4	1	20	7
2.	Karl Malone	Utah	29.52	**29.07**	.521	.313	.766	1	8	13	5	16	2
3.	Kevin McHale	Bost	23.68	22.54	.548	0-4	.818	3	2	27	10	10	29
4.	Larry Nance	Clev	22.66	17.25	.541	0-4	.799	6	3	21	7	2	24
5.	Otis Thorpe	Hous	20.62	16.71	.543	0-2	.729	7	5	16	6	27	20
6.	Ken Norman	LA.C	20.34	18.13	.507	.190	.630	4	24	28	2	19	13
7.	A.C. Green	LA.L	18.61	13.27	.536	.235	.786	13	4	8	21	18	10
8.	Sam Perkins	Dall	18.51	15.01	.476	.184	**.833**	10	23	20	18	12	19
9.	Charles Oakley	N.Y.	18.44	12.94	.526	.250	.773	15	7	3	3	28	8
10.	Wayman Tisdale	Sacr	18.43	17.48	.516	0-4	.773	5	9	17	13	21	23
11.	L. Thompson	Indi	17.95	13.93	.490	0-1	.808	11	17	6	23	8	14
12.	Kurt Rambis	Char	17.80	11.09	.521	0-3	.734	21	12	5	4	15	3
13.	Horace Grant	Chic	17.52	12.03	.522	0-5	.704	17	13	19	11	17	16
14.	Buck Williams	N.J.	16.92	12.96	.534	0-3	.666	14	16	9	26	24	22
15.	Michael Cage	Seat	16.90	10.31	.502	0-4	.743	23	20	7	16	22	11
16.	Armon Gilliam	Phoe	15.74	15.89	.503	0-0	.743	9	18	14	29	25	21
17.	Roy Hinson	N.J.	15.33	15.95	.483	0-2	.757	8	25	29	27	5	28
18.	L. Krystkowiak	Milw	15.29	12.71	.475	**.333**	.823	16	19	18	19	29	9
19.	Greg Anderson	S.A.	15.11	13.74	.505	0-3	.514	12	29	10	28	6	5
20.	John Williams	Clev	14.87	11.56	.510	.250	.748	19	15	24	15	3	12
21.	Wayne Cooper	Denv	14.43	6.58	.498	.250	.745	28	21	2	20	**1**	27
22.	Grant Long	Miam	14.41	11.90	.489	0-5	.749	18	22	25	9	23	**1**
23.	Ed Pinckney	Bost	14.27	11.47	.518	0-6	.800	20	6	26	12	11	6
24.	Cliff Levingston	Atla	13.04	9.17	.531	.200	.696	25	10	23	24	13	4
25.	Larry Smith	G.St	12.66	5.70	.552	0-0	.310	29	14	**1**	8	14	15
26.	Terry Catledge	Wash	12.30	10.41	.493	.200	.602	22	27	12	22	26	26
27.	Rick Mahorn	Detr	11.90	7.25	.519	0-2	.748	26	11	11	25	9	25
28.	Jim Petersen	Sacr	11.61	10.17	.465	0-8	.747	24	28	15	17	7	17
29.	John Salley	Detr	9.88	6.97	.502	0-2	.692	27	26	22	14	4	18

* Only players who qualify.   See qualification requirements on page 240.

* Numbers in **bold** are the best for each category.

RK = Rank by Production Rating
PR = Production Rating (see page 2)
PPG = Points Per Game
SC = Rank for scoring (points per game)
SH = Rank for shooting (composite shooting formula - see page 240 for explanation)

RB = Rank for rebounds per 48 minutes
AS = Rank for assists per 48 minutes
BL = Rank for blocks per 48 minutes
ST = Rank for steals per 48 minutes

RANKINGS AMONG SMALL FORWARDS *

RK	PLAYER	TEAM	PR	PPG	2pt%	3pt%	FT%	SC	SH	RB	AS	BL	ST
1.	Chris Mullin	G.St	**26.01**	**26.54**	.527	.230	**.892**	2	3	24	3	28	3
2.	Tom Chambers	Phoe	24.11	25.74	.479	.326	.851	4	15	7	21	20	21
3.	D. Wilkins	Atla	22.84	26.24	.475	.276	.844	3	24	15	25	22	12
4.	James Worthy	LA.L	21.80	20.46	.556	.087	.782	9	2	22	11	19	16
5.	T. Cummings	Milw	21.54	22.86	.467	.467	.787	5	31	6	26	13	14
6.	Alex English	Denv	21.38	26.52	.492	.250	.858	1	14	39	4	40	31
7.	Jerome Kersey	Port	20.24	17.50	.472	.286	.694	16	35	5	15	9	5
8.	Chuck Person	Indi	19.00	21.60	.519	.307	.792	7	9	20	14	37	23
9.	W. Anderson	S.A.	18.99	18.62	.503	.190	.775	14	16	28	2	16	4
10.	J.S. Williams	Wash	18.74	13.66	.482	.268	.776	24	28	4	1	10	1
11.	Reggie Lewis	Bost	17.64	18.46	.493	.136	.787	15	21	32	17	12	9
12.	Kelly Tripucka	Char	17.61	22.62	.476	.357	.866	6	12	38	10	36	13
13.	Bernard King	Wash	17.35	20.67	.484	.167	.819	8	23	29	6	39	26
14.	Derrick McKey	Seat	17.29	15.91	.519	.337	.803	20	7	21	18	15	15
15.	Thurl Bailey	Utah	16.79	19.45	.484	.400	.825	11	19	23	37	8	40
16.	Charles Smith	LA.C	16.66	16.27	.497	0-3	.725	17	25	8	38	4	20
17.	Rodney McCray	Sacr	16.65	12.56	.474	.227	.722	25	34	10	5	26	30
18.	Scottie Pippen	Chic	16.38	14.36	.496	.273	.668	22	33	16	8	14	2
19.	Dennis Rodman	Detr	16.32	8.96	**.614**	.231	.626	33	1	1	39	7	27
20.	X. McDaniel	Seat	16.29	20.45	.494	.306	.732	10	26	18	35	23	17
21.	Adrian Dantley	Dall	16.29	19.18	.493	0-1	.810	12	11	36	24	38	38
22.	Mark Aguirre	Detr	15.74	18.89	.488	.293	.733	13	29	30	7	27	39
23.	Ron Anderson	Phil	14.93	16.22	.494	.182	.856	18	13	25	36	34	24
24.	Billy Thompson	Miam	14.42	10.81	.490	0-4	.696	28	30	2	20	1	28
25.	D. Schrempf	Indi	13.91	12.00	.492	.200	.780	26	22	9	12	31	22
26.	Johnny Newman	N.Y.	13.27	15.96	.534	.338	.815	19	6	40	27	32	8
27.	Chris Morris	N.J.	13.14	14.13	.479	.366	.717	23	27	13	34	11	7
28.	Rod Higgins	G.St	12.64	10.57	.505	.393	.821	29	5	11	16	17	35
29.	Tyrone Corbin	Phoe	11.73	8.19	.542	0-2	.788	37	4	3	22	35	6
30.	Buck Johnson	Hous	11.42	9.58	.532	.111	.754	31	8	26	28	18	18
31.	Robert Reid	Char	10.85	14.72	.432	.327	.776	21	38	33	23	33	29
32.	Dan Majerle	Phoe	9.91	8.65	.440	.329	.614	36	39	27	13	30	10
33.	Ricky Berry	Sacr	9.58	11.03	.467	.406	.789	27	10	34	32	24	25
34.	Mike Sanders	Clev	9.54	9.32	.455	.300	.719	32	36	31	29	25	11
35.	Walter Berry	Hous	9.43	8.83	.507	**.500**	.699	34	20	12	33	6	33

* Only players who qualify. See qualification requirements on page 240.

* Numbers in **bold** are the best for each category.

RK = Rank by Production Rating	**RB** = Rank for rebounds per 48 minutes
PR = Production Rating (see page 2)	**AS** = Rank for assists per 48 minutes
PPG = Points Per Game	**BL** = Rank for blocks per 48 minutes
SC = Rank for scoring (points per game)	**ST** = Rank for steals per 48 minutes
SH = Rank for shooting (composite shooting formula - see page 240 for explanation)	

RANKINGS AMONG OFF GUARDS *

RK	PLAYER	TEAM	PR	PPG	2pt%	3pt%	FT%	SC	SH	RB	AS	BL	ST
1.	Michael Jordan	Chic	**36.99**	**32.51**	**.553**	.276	.850	1	3	5	3	5	2
2.	Clyde Drexler	Port	28.87	27.22	.511	.260	.799	3	16	4	14	7	4
3.	Fat Lever	Denv	27.48	19.85	.463	.348	.785	7	32	1	2	24	3
4.	Dale Ellis	Seat	21.13	27.48	.507	.478	.816	2	4	25	43	26	35
5.	Ron Harper	Clev	21.09	18.61	.540	.250	.751	10	14	13	12	2	6
6.	Alvin Robertson	S.A.	20.52	17.26	.497	.200	.723	13	29	7	6	9	1
7.	M. Richmond	G.St	19.44	22.04	.475	.367	.810	4	24	6	16	33	38
8.	Eddie Johnson	Phoe	17.93	21.49	.510	.413	.868	6	6	12	34	36	42
9.	Byron Scott	LA.L	17.89	19.57	.508	.399	.863	9	9	20	29	15	20
10.	Danny Ainge	Sacr	17.64	17.55	.488	.380	.854	12	12	24	7	38	27
11.	Jeff Hornacek	Phoe	17.06	13.51	.511	.333	.826	26	15	26	5	42	13
12.	R. Blackman	Dall	16.74	19.67	.485	.353	.854	8	19	35	23	27	43
13.	Joe Dumars	Detr	16.59	17.19	.506	**.483**	.850	14	10	44	9	44	40
14.	Reggie Miller	Indi	16.12	15.96	.511	.402	.844	17	5	21	27	12	31
15.	Jeff Malone	Wash	15.26	21.72	.486	.053	.871	5	23	42	26	31	44
16.	Reggie Theus	Atla	15.06	15.80	.476	.293	.851	18	25	31	11	28	21
17.	Ricky Pierce	Milw	14.95	17.56	.529	.222	.859	11	8	33	37	18	30
18.	H. Pressley	Sacr	14.60	12.26	.457	.403	.780	30	18	2	36	1	22
19.	H. Hawkins	Phil	13.68	15.14	.461	.428	.831	21	20	36	24	10	18
20.	Dennis Johnson	Bost	12.87	10.01	.459	.140	.821	34	38	40	1	20	24
21.	Terry Teagle	G.St	12.85	15.18	.481	.167	.809	20	27	8	40	14	15
22.	Sidney Moncrief	Milw	12.79	12.13	.514	.342	.865	31	7	23	18	22	23
23.	Gerald Wilkins	N.Y.	12.64	14.33	.482	.297	.756	22	31	28	21	19	17
24.	Quintin Dailey	LA.C	12.48	16.14	.468	.111	.759	16	33	19	28	35	11
25.	Vinnie Johnson	Detr	12.30	13.78	.472	.295	.734	23	34	18	20	21	34
26.	Walter Davis	Denv	12.21	15.64	.512	.290	**.879**	19	13	41	22	43	28
27.	Kevin Edwards	Miam	11.91	13.85	.431	.270	.746	24	43	22	13	11	8
28.	Darrell Griffith	Utah	11.50	13.84	.477	.311	.780	25	30	14	42	17	32
29.	Rex Chapman	Char	11.03	16.89	.431	.314	.795	15	42	38	33	13	36
30.	Craig Ehlo	Clev	10.50	7.41	.495	.390	.607	41	26	11	15	16	9
31.	Mike Woodson	Hous	10.48	12.91	.447	.348	.823	28	35	37	25	23	26
32.	Sedale Threatt	Seat	10.38	8.63	.502	.367	.818	39	17	32	4	41	5
33.	Dennis Hopson	N.J.	10.37	12.71	.429	.148	.849	29	41	16	39	6	19
34.	Otis Smith	G.St	10.30	10.04	.448	.189	.798	35	40	3	30	3	10
35.	Michael Cooper	LA.L	10.11	7.34	.468	.381	.871	42	11	29	10	8	29

* Only players who qualify. See qualification requirements on page 240.

* Numbers in **bold** are the best for each category.

RK = Rank by Production Rating

PR = Production Rating (see page 2)

PPG = Points Per Game

SC = Rank for scoring (points per game)

SH = Rank for shooting (composite shooting formula - see page 240 for explanation)

RB = Rank for rebounds per 48 minutes

AS = Rank for assists per 48 minutes

BL = Rank for blocks per 48 minutes

ST = Rank for steals per 48 minutes

RANKINGS AMONG POINT GUARDS *

RK	PLAYER	TEAM	PR	PPG	2pt%	3pt%	FT%	SC	SH	RB	AS	BL	ST
1.	Earvin Johnson	LA.L	**33.31**	**22.47**	.548	.314	**.911**	1	2	1	3	9	15
2.	John Stockton	Utah	27.40	17.07	**.561**	.242	.863	9	3	28	2	19	1
3.	Kevin Johnson	Phoe	27.06	20.37	.514	.091	.882	2	4	17	4	10	21
4.	Terry Porter	Port	22.42	17.67	.497	.361	.840	6	10	12	11	27	16
5.	Mark Price	Clev	22.33	18.85	.548	.441	.901	3	1	25	15	28	22
6.	Mark Jackson	N.Y.	20.49	16.93	.507	.337	.698	10	14	6	9	26	12
7.	Michael Adams	Denv	19.60	18.49	.490	.356	.819	4	9	18	28	21	10
8.	Derek Harper	Dall	19.33	17.33	.517	.356	.806	7	6	29	24	4	11
9.	Isiah Thomas	Detr	19.09	18.22	.485	.273	.818	5	19	22	16	13	18
10.	Glenn Rivers	Atla	18.70	13.58	.474	.347	.861	14	12	13	17	3	3
11.	Eric Floyd	Hous	18.46	14.17	.478	.373	.845	13	8	16	7	22	19
12.	Vern Fleming	Indi	17.49	14.26	.526	.130	.799	12	7	10	22	17	32
13.	Kenny Smith	Sacr	17.04	17.32	.475	.359	.737	8	21	30	20	30	29
14.	Lester Conner	N.J.	16.87	10.28	.463	.351	.788	22	22	5	13	31	4
15.	W. Garland	G.St	16.76	14.49	.442	.233	.809	11	27	9	25	16	6
16.	Nate McMillan	Seat	16.63	7.09	.443	.214	.630	30	33	3	5	2	5
17.	Paul Pressey	Milw	16.39	12.13	.497	.218	.776	16	18	11	19	1	13
18.	Maurice Cheeks	Phil	16.38	11.61	.490	.077	.774	20	20	27	12	11	17
19.	Darrell Walker	Wash	16.13	9.04	.426	0-9	.772	24	30	2	23	8	9
20.	Jay Humphries	Milw	14.07	11.56	.516	.266	.816	19	11	24	26	29	7
21.	Gary Grant	LA.C	13.70	11.92	.441	.227	.735	17	29	8	6	18	2
22.	Brian Shaw	Bost	12.88	8.57	.441	0-13	.826	25	28	4	18	5	28
23.	Rory Sparrow	Miam	12.62	12.50	.469	.243	.879	15	23	26	29	14	26
24.	Tyrone Bogues	Char	11.90	5.35	.437	.077	.750	33	31	21	1	20	8
25.	Sam Vincent	Chic	11.24	9.37	.495	.118	.822	23	15	14	21	15	30
26.	Michael Holton	Chic	10.88	8.25	.433	.214	.839	26	26	32	8	12	27
27.	V. Maxwell	S.A.	10.30	11.73	.466	.248	.745	18	24	19	31	23	24
28.	John Bagley	N.J.	9.38	7.35	.443	.204	.724	27	32	23	14	25	20
29.	Scott Skiles	Indi	8.95	6.82	.485	.267	.903	31	13	20	10	32	25
30.	John Paxson	Chic	8.78	7.27	.532	.331	.861	28	5	33	27	24	31
31.	V. Del Negro	Sacr	8.36	7.11	.482	.300	.850	29	16	15	32	7	23
32.	Steve Colter	Wash	8.30	6.67	.463	.120	.749	32	25	7	30	6	14
33.	Jon Sundvold	Miam	7.29	10.43	.444	**.522**	.825	21	17	31	33	33	33

* Only players who qualify. See qualification requirements on page 240.

* Numbers in **bold** are the best for each category.

RK	= Rank by Production Rating	**RB**	= Rank for rebounds per 48 minutes
PR	= Production Rating (see page 2)	**AS**	= Rank for assists per 48 minutes
PPG	= Points Per Game	**BL**	= Rank for blocks per 48 minutes
SC	= Rank for scoring (points per game)	**ST**	= Rank for steals per 48 minutes
SH	= Rank for shooting (composite shooting formula - see page 240 for explanation)		

RANKINGS AMONG 6TH MEN *

RK	PLAYER	TEAM	PR	PPG	2pt%	3pt%	FT%	SC	SH	RB	AS	BL	ST
1.	J. S. Williams	Wash	**18.74**	13.66	.482	.268	.776	10	34	10	9	18	5
2.	Wayman Tisdale	Sacr	18.43	17.48	.516	0-4	.773	5	15	7	40	22	39
3.	Eddie Johnson	Phoe	17.93	**21.49**	.510	.413	.868	1	7	32	24	45	38
4.	Thurl Bailey	Utah	16.79	19.45	.484	.400	.825	3	25	28	44	14	50
5.	Dennis Rodman	Detr	16.32	8.96	.614	.231	.626	28	2	**1**	46	11	36
6.	X. McDaniel	Seat	16.29	20.45	.494	.306	.732	2	31	24	38	23	26
7.	Roy Hinson	N.J.	15.33	15.95	.483	0-2	.757	7	32	19	50	6	52
8.	Ricky Pierce	Milw	14.95	17.56	.529	.222	.859	4	8	46	28	33	21
9.	Ron Anderson	Phil	14.93	16.22	.494	.182	.856	6	20	30	39	35	33
10.	John Williams	Clev	14.87	11.56	.510	.250	.748	14	19	13	42	4	22
11.	H. Pressley	Sacr	14.60	12.26	.457	.403	.780	11	18	15	27	12	17
12.	Ed Pinckney	Bost	14.27	11.47	.518	0-6	.800	15	13	14	34	13	16
13.	D. Schrempf	Indi	13.91	12.00	.492	.200	.780	12	28	16	18	30	30
14.	Mark West	Phoe	13.17	7.24	**.653**	0-0	.535	39	4	3	52	2	49
15.	Rod Higgins	G.St	12.64	10.57	.505	.393	.821	18	9	20	21	20	43
16.	Vinnie Johnson	Detr	12.30	13.78	.472	.295	.734	9	38	38	15	36	24
17.	Walter Davis	Denv	12.21	15.64	.512	.290	**.879**	8	14	50	17	51	19
18.	M. Thompson	LA.L	12.11	9.22	.560	0-1	.678	26	10	11	51	17	29
19.	Tyrone Bogues	Char	11.90	5.35	.437	.077	.750	50	49	47	**1**	42	2
20.	Tyrone Corbin	Phoe	11.73	8.19	.542	0-2	.788	33	6	9	30	37	9
21.	Craig Ehlo	Clev	10.50	7.41	.495	.390	.607	35	30	29	11	31	4
22.	Manute Bol	G.St	10.46	3.92	.423	.220	.606	53	53	6	53	**1**	53
23.	Sedale Threatt	Seat	10.38	8.63	.502	.367	.818	31	17	44	4	49	**1**
24.	Jon Koncak	Atla	10.36	4.66	.530	0-3	.553	51	36	2	49	3	25
25.	V. Maxwell	S.A.	10.30	11.73	.466	.248	.745	13	45	42	10	43	15
26.	Otis Smith	G.St	10.30	10.04	.448	.189	.798	21	44	18	20	19	6
27.	M. Cooper	LA.L	10.11	7.34	.468	.381	.871	38	12	41	7	24	20
28.	Steve Johnson	Port	10.04	10.01	.524	0-0	.527	22	39	8	31	16	51
29.	Dan Majerle	Phoe	9.91	8.65	.440	.329	.614	30	48	31	19	29	12
30.	John Salley	Detr	9.88	6.97	.502	0-2	.692	41	35	12	41	5	32
31.	Ricky Berry	Sacr	9.58	11.03	.467	.406	.789	17	16	33	36	26	34
32.	Walter Berry	Hous	9.43	8.83	.507	**.500**	.699	29	26	21	37	10	41
33.	John Bagley	N.J.	9.38	7.35	.443	.204	.724	36	50	48	3	50	13
34.	Dave Hoppen	Char	9.32	6.49	.564	**.500**	.727	46	5	4	47	27	48
35.	O. Woolridge	LA.L	9.22	9.66	.469	0-1	.738	23	37	25	48	7	46

* Only players who qualify. See qualification requirements on page 240.
* Numbers in **bold** are the best for each category.

RK	= Rank by Production Rating	**RB**	= Rank for rebounds per 48 minutes
PR	= Production Rating (see page 2)	**AS**	= Rank for assists per 48 minutes
PPG	= Points Per Game	**BL**	= Rank for blocks per 48 minutes
SC	= Rank for scoring (points per game)	**ST**	= Rank for steals per 48 minutes
SH	= Rank for shooting (composite shooting formula - see page 240 for explanation)		

RANKINGS AMONG ROOKIES *

RK	PLAYER	TEAM	PR	PPG	2pt%	3pt%	FT%	SC	SH	RB	AS	BL	ST
1.	M. Richmond	G.St	**19.44**	**22.04**	.475	.367	.810	**1**	6	6	8	16	15
2.	W. Anderson	S.A.	18.99	18.62	.503	190	.775	2	4	10	6	5	3
3.	Charles Smith	LA.C	16.66	16.27	.497	0-3	.725	4	8	4	17	3	12
4.	Grant Long	Miam	14.41	11.90	.489	0-5	.749	9	9	3	13	6	5
5.	Rik Smits	Indi	14.06	11.66	**.518**	0-1	.722	11	2	2	18	**1**	19
6.	Gary Grant	LA.C	13.70	11.92	.441	.227	.735	8	16	12	**1**	17	**1**
7.	H. Hawkins	Phil	13.68	15.14	.461	**.428**	.831	5	3	18	10	8	7
8.	Chris Morris	N.J.	13.14	14.13	.479	.366	.717	6	10	5	15	4	6
9.	Brian Shaw	Bost	12.88	8.57	.441	0-13	.826	17	14	8	2	9	11
10.	Kevin Edwards	Miam	11.91	13.85	.431	.270	.746	7	18	14	4	10	2
11.	Rex Chapman	Char	11.03	16.89	.431	.314	.795	3	15	19	12	11	13
12.	Ron Seikaly	Miam	10.38	10.87	.449	.250	.511	14	19	**1**	19	2	18
13.	V. Maxwell	S.A.	10.30	11.73	.466	.248	.745	10	13	17	5	18	10
14.	Dan Majerle	Phoe	9.91	8.65	.440	.329	.614	16	17	9	9	12	8
15.	Ricky Berry	Sacr	9.58	11.03	.467	.406	.789	13	**1**	11	14	7	17
16.	Tom Garrick	LA.C	8.68	6.39	.509	0-13	.803	19	5	16	3	15	4
17.	V. Del Negro	Sacr	8.36	7.11	.482	.300	**.850**	18	7	15	7	13	9
18.	Ledell Eackles	Wash	8.13	11.46	.447	.225	.786	12	11	13	11	19	16
19.	D. Chevious	Hous	7.36	9.26	.446	.208	.783	15	12	7	16	14	14

* Only players who qualify.   See qualification requirements on page 240.
* Numbers in **bold** are the best for each category.

RK	= Rank by Production Rating	**RB**	= Rank for rebounds per 48 minutes
PR	= Production Rating (see page 2)	**AS**	= Rank for assists per 48 minutes
PPG	= Points Per Game	**BL**	= Rank for blocks per 48 minutes
SC	= Rank for scoring (points per game)	**ST**	= Rank for steals per 48 minutes
SH	= Rank for shooting (composite shooting formula - see page 240 for explanation)		

TYPICAL HUSTLE

AP/WIDE WORLD PHOTOS

LARRY BIRD VS THE BENCH

CHAPTER 5

FANCY FORMULAS

DEVIATIONS

One area which has perennially fascinated all sports fans is the question of consistency. In sports, it seems easy to measure. If Player A scores 3, 22, 9 and then 18 points, he's called inconsistent. On the other hand, if Player B scores 11, 14, 13 and then 14 points, he's about the most consistent player you could ask for. Only a few close observers will recognize levels of inconsistency between players over the course of a season. Since both Player A and Player B averaged 13 points per game, how can you distinguish consistency levels between these players or any players for that matter without charting points on a game-by-game basis. Not surprisingly, I survey every box score in the NBA and watch hundreds of games. Even so, without crunching numbers through my computer, I couldn't begin to tell you who were the most consistent and least consistent players by scoring last season.

Since computers are not subjective (big news), I had to derive a formula to evaluate consistency. No problem, I thought. I'll use a very basic formula taught in every freshman statistics course in college - Standard Deviation (SD). It didn't take long to realize, however, that SD was worthless for my purposes. It has what I consider to me two fundamental problems.

Problem 1: Let's suppose Player A played 6 games and Player B played 8 games. Let's also assume that Player A scored 15, 17, 15, 17, 15, 17 in his games. His SD would be 1.095445. Now, let's make the assumption that Player B's 8 games were 15, 17, 15, 17, 15, 17, 15, 17. I just added two more of the same scores. To my way of thinking, the two players should reflect the same deviation, but they don't. Player B has a lower rating (1.069045 - In the case of SD, lower means more consistent). Perhaps an argument could be made that Player B is more consistent because he maintained the same level of consistency over a longer period of time. Although I appreciate that argument, I lean away from accepting it because I want to know who was the most consistent while he played. If one player played 70 games and was injured 12 while another played all 82, I want to see that they were equally consistent if they were. I don't want a formula that camouflages inconsistency by volume of games played.

Problem 2: Standard Deviation has another flaw for my purposes. Suppose Player A played 4 games where his scoring went 10, 5, 10, 5 and Player B registered point totals of 30, 25, 30, 25. Standard Deviation will show the same rating for both (2.886752). My argument against that is that I want Player B to show a lower deviation rating (meaning he's more consistent) because otherwise the players that score the least will dominate this category. After all, Player A doubled his point total from game 1 to game 2 and game 3 to game 4 whereas player B was only 20% higher in games 2 and 4 - though the differential (5) was the same.

My mission then, once I decided to accept it, was to derive a formula which compensated for these problems. I decided I liked the concept which Standard Deviation used, so I adopted it as a starting point. To better understand SD, let's use an example: Assume a player scores the following point totals: 2, 5, 5, 1, 2. The way to calculate SD is to establish the average (mean) which in this case is 3 ($2+5+5+1+2=15$, $15/5=3$). The next step is to establish the difference between each variable and the mean. Those totals would be -1 (2 minus 3), 2 (5-3=2), 2 (5-3), -2 (1-3) and -1 (2-3). You then square each of these new totals (-1, 2, 2, -2, -1). The totals now read (1, 4, 4, 4, 1). Add those up ($1+4+4+4+1=14$). Now divide by N-1 or 4 (5-1=4) in this case. That equals 3.5 ($14/4=3.5$). Finally, take the square root of 3.5 which equals 1.87. That is Standard Deviation in a nutshell.

Both problems can be solved simply. Problem 1 can be eliminated just by dividing by N instead of N-1. That merely means you find the mean (average) again the second time you divide. This eliminates the advantage obtained by playing more games.

Problem 2 is eliminated by evaluating the distance the original point totals are away from the mean based on what percent that distance is with respect to the points scored. Therefore, 30, 25, 30, 25 is more consistent (lower deviation rating) than 10, 5, 10, 5 because I'm not using the difference from the mean as 2.5, I'm using points as a percent of the means (7.5 and 27.5). In the first case this new deviation is 1.09 (30/27.5). In the second case it is 1.33 (10/7.5). (As you may realize, your deviations will be less than 1 when you use the smaller point totals in the series (25 & 5). You will need to subtract them from 2 so that your number will be greater than 1 before you square.)

Now, after I solved both problems, I then evaluated every player. Guess what? I had a new problem. The players that scored the most points-per-game were clustered at the top (most consistent) which, after thinking about it, made sense. After all, players who score the least probably vary quite a bit in time played from one game to the next (affecting points). So, of course their rating would be worse, but through no fault of their own. After playing around with this some more, I decided to handicap the higher scoring players by dividing each player's scoring average by 100 and then adding it to their deviation. This produced several lists that I feel very good about. Shown below are the 20 most consistent and the 20 least consistent players (among players who played 1500 minutes or more).

	MOST CONSISTENT				LEAST CONSISTENT		
	NAME	TEAM	DEVIATION		NAME	TEAM	DEVIATION
1.	McHale	Bost	1.4119	159.	Skiles	Indi	1.7739
2.	Garland	G. St	1.4203	158.	Turner	Denv	1.7633
3.	Porter	Port	1.4309	157.	Del Negro	Sacr	1.7519
4.	Bailey	Utah	1.4337	156.	Corbin	Phoe	1.7236
5.	Fleming	Indi	1.4436	155.	Cureton	Char	1.7144
6.	Gminski	Phil	1.4442	154.	Smith	G.St	1.7130
7.	Malone	Atla	1.4514	153.	Paxson	Chic	1.7028
8.	Perkins	Dall	1.4521	152.	Koncak	Atla	1.7008
9.	Parish	Bost	1.4527	151.	Ehlo	Clev	1.6975
10.	Carroll	N.J.	1.4533	150.	Sellers	Chic	1.6851
11.	Daugherty	Clev	1.4630	149.	Maxwell	S.A.	1.6824
12.	Tisdale	Sacr	1.4634	148.	Chevious	Hous	1.6815
13.	Jackson	N.Y.	1.4641	147.	Bogues	Wash	1.6714
14.	Worthy	LA.L	1.4666	146.	Cooper	Denv	1.6669
15.	Williams	N.J.	1.4691	145.	Catledge	Wash	1.6560
16.	Oakley	N.Y.	1.4709	144.	McGee	N.J.	1.6535
17.	Ho. Grant	Chic	1.4723	143.	Walker	Wash	1.6523
18.	Price	Clev	1.4731	142.	Hopson	N.J.	1.6511
19.	Malone	Utah	1.4761	141.	Johnson	Detr	1.6407
20.	Cummings	Milw	1.4765	140.	Grant	LA.C	1.6367

Most player's home deviations and road deviations are quite similar. Why shouldn't they be? Amazingly, however, Doc Rivers ranks #1 at home, but #126 on the road, while Cliff Robinson was #1 on the road, but #179 at home. This wide variation is more understandable for Robinson. He only played in 14 games before being injured. And only 4 of those games were on the road, where he scored 26, 18, 14, and 22. That's pretty consistent. At home he went 16, 25, 22, 12, 4, 7, 14, 23, 8, and 1. That's what I call inconsistent!

Rivers' home and road rankings are harder to understand. He played in 76 games, so any inconsistency due to his not having played in enough games to establish a valid sample is ruled out. The quickest way to evaluate his inconsistency on the road would be to say that 10 of his 12 highest scoring games were played away from home, indicating that the variance in his point totals was quite diverse. At home, he was more consistent than any other player.

Kevin McHale was the most consistent player overall (home and road). Except for 2 games (13 points and 34 points), he scored between 14 and 31 points in every other game. In one 8-game stretch, he scored 22, 25, 26, 23, 26, 22, 25 and 26. That's why he is number 1 in consistency. Scott Skiles was the least consistent. His scoring average for the first 6 games was 8 ppg, the next 17 games - 4 ppg, the following 14 games - 10 ppg, the next 9 games - 2 ppg, then in 15 games - 10 ppg, and finally in his last 17 games 6 ppg. Well, actually, in his last 2 he averaged 18.5 ppg. Anyway, you get the picture.

Clearly, the same formula can be used for the teams. Shown below are two lists. The first is a list ranked according to order by the deviation formula I just outlined. The second list represents the order of consistency based on scoring per quarters. All I did to arrive at this list was to divide the points a team scored in a given game by four. I then took the difference between each of the quarter scores and the average. The values shown are the totals of all four deviations per game for all 82 games divided by 328 so that the deviation shown is the average amount of points a team deviates from the average quarter score in a game. Basically, this list shows a team's consistency during a game as opposed to consistency from one game to the next..

REVISED STANDARD DEVIATION

	TEAM	DEVIATION
1.	Washington	1.0715
2.	Boston	1.0763
3.	Phoenix	1.0771
4.	Chicago	1.0774
5.	Milwaukee	1.0787
6.	Detroit	1.0789
7.	Charlotte	1.0804
8.	Indiana	1.0813
9.	New York	1.0836
10.	Philadelphia	1.0839
11.	LA. Clippers	1.0846
12.	San Antonio	1.0850
13.	New Jersey	1.0851
14.	Cleveland	1.0854
15.	Houston	1.0859
16.	Portland	1.0870
17.	Utah	1.0892
18.	Dallas	1.0918
19.	Miami	1.0921
20.	Golden State	1.0923
21.	LA. Lakers	1.0934
22.	Denver	1.0947
23.	Seattle	1.0952
24.	Atlanta	1.0954
25.	Sacramento	1.1063

QUARTER DEVIATION

	TEAM	DEVIATION
1.	Detroit	3.28
2.	New Jersey	3.47
3.	Washington	3.53
4.	Boston	3.54
5.	LA. Clippers	3.58
6.	Utah	3.61
7.	LA. Lakers	3.65
8.	Chicago	3.69
9.	Charlotte	3.72
10.	Milwaukee	3.79
11.	Atlanta	3.80
12.	New York	3.83
13.	Seattle	3.83
14.	Houston	3.85
15.	Dallas	3.87
16.	Sacramento	3.88
17.	Indiana	3.91
18.	Miami	3.95
19.	Portland	3.96
20.	Denver	3.97
21.	Phoenix	3.98
22.	Philadelphia	3.99
23.	Cleveland	4.04
24.	San Antonio	4.07
25.	Golden State	4.13

By adding the ranks together, Washington (4), Boston (6), and Detroit (7) are the most consistent scoring teams. Golden State (45), Denver (42), and Sacramento (41) are the least consistent. Interestingly, the most consistent teams are from the "defensive" Eastern Conference, while the least consistent are from the "offensive" Western Conference.

OK, now it's time for a test. I'm going to ask you a few questions about what you just read. And just so you don't cheat, close your eyes.

POWER INDEX: By Pat Lafferty

There are no crystal balls in the NBA - only leather ones, objects of affection and obsession for the world's greatest athletes, their coaches and their fans. Yet our ability to succeed in the future depends in large part on our skill in analyzing the past, to understand why teams win or lose and the factors that separate success and failure. The Basketball Power Index was designed to help accomplish this goal.

Using the Power Index formula, an observer before the 1988-89 season could have forecast big years for Utah and Cleveland and likely declines for Denver and Indiana. Six weeks into the season, you could have known that the Lakers and Pistons had a chance to repeat as Division Champions, that the Cavaliers and Jazz could be the best teams in franchise history, and, despite a 10-8 record at the time, that Phoenix was playing at a level which predicted a stunning turnaround.

To be sure, hindsight is 20-10, and the primary purpose of developing the Power Index was not to be visionary. A formula which evaluates historical data cannot predict the impact of injuries, trades or draft choices. It cannot measure "heart", team chemistry, or coaching contributions, but it does show the results of those factors. The Power Index also measures the components of on-court play which show why teams win or lose, and its historical ability to do this over more than a decade leaves little doubt of its accuracy as a performance barometer.

What was the chief objective in developing the Power Index? Simply to find the key factors in a team's play which, when combined, would come as close as possible to explaining that team's won-loss ranking. In the perfect formula, team rankings would correlate exactly with won-loss rankings. Such an equation has never been developed for any sport, but the Power Index has correlated well with won-loss rankings. In both 1986-87 and 1987-88, the Power Index ratings for 15 of the NBA's 23 teams were within one position of their won-loss ranking. In 1988-89, 15 of 25 teams were within one position; five more teams were off by only two.

What ingredients go into our basketball recipe? Just four. But all are portrayals of performance that blend to show us the fine balance between winning and losing. Our four components are the MARGINS in field goal accuracy, ball handling efficiency, free throws made per game, and scoring opportunity points. Let's look at them individually.

EFFECTIVE FIELD GOAL PERCENTAGE MARGIN:

Unless we look at margins - what a team does against its collective opponents - we're wasting our time. One should not assume that the team that yields the fewest points is necessarily the NBA's best defensive team. That figure may actually reflect more a slow or deliberate style of play than defensive excellence. In fact, more often than not, it does. The team that gives up only 105 points a game will be vying for a ticket on the "lottery express" if it scores but 100. The keys are to reduce the number of points your opponents score per possession (regardless of tempo) and not allow extra possessions through turnovers or failure to protect the defensive boards. With the object to score more points other than your opponent, the margin becomes the critical factor.

No margin is more relevant to basketball success than field goal percentage. Almost 80% of all points are scored on field goals. And the average NBA team has about 90 field goal attempts per game. Before the advent of the 3-point field goal, calculating the impact of field goal percent margin was easy. A difference of 10 points in field goal percent (.500 vs .490) is worth 2 points per game. The value is the same whether the respective percentage figures are .530 vs .520 or .470 vs .460. The formula is valid as long as the number of attempts per team averages from 90 - 100.

The introduction and increasing use of the 3-point field goal now requires us to look at a new index - Effective Field Goal Percentage - to accurately measure the impact of both individual and team field goal shooting. For purposes of illustration, let's compare three starting point guards: Michael Adams, Winston Garland and Kevin Johnson.

	FG/FGA	%	2FG/2FGA	%	3FG/3FGA	%	TOTAL PTS	FT - PTS	=	FG PTS
Adams	468/1082	.433	302/616	.490	166/466	.356	1424	- 322	=	1102
Garland	466/1074	.434	456/1031	.442	10/43	.233	1145	- 203	=	942
Johnson	570/1128	.505	568/1106	.514	2/22	.091	1650	- 508	=	1142

For those who rely on the old basketball yardstick of simple field goal percentage, the accuracy of Michael Adams and Winston Garland appear to be almost identical and far below the accuracy of Kevin Johnson. In fact, Adams' and Johnson's field goal shooting is actually very close (and well above league average) while that of Garland is among the poorest of all NBA regulars.

The key is understanding that a player shooting .500 from 2-point range and a player shooting .333 from 3-point range will generate the same number of points for a team. For a player like Michael Adams, who took more than 43% of his shots beyond the 3-point line, merely looking at his .433 FG% does not begin to measure his offensive effectiveness. To accurately measure efficiency, we need to know how many points a player made from his field goal attempts, not just how many field goals he made. We caluate this by taking a player's total points, subtracting free throws made and dividing those field goal points by total field goal attempts. This gives us the average production for each player per shot, an index we refer to as points/fga. (Last season's NBA average was .978 or 97.8 points for every 100 shots. This is equivalent to .489 shooting if every shot was a 2-point attempt.) Let's look at our three players again.

	FG ATTEMPTS	FG POINTS	PTS/FGA'S	EFFECTIVE FG%
Adams	1082	1102	1.018	.509
Garland	1074	942	.877	.439
Johnson	1128	1142	1.012	.506

These numbers show that Michael Adams and Kevin Johnson were able to generate between 101 and 102 points for every 100 shots they took from the field, (50.9 X 2 or 50.6 X 2) while Winston Garland produced fewer than 88 points (43.9 X 2). And Adams' ".433 FG%" was every bit as accurate from the field as the ".508 FG%" of Akeem Olajuwon, who failed to make a 3-point FG all year.

The same principles apply to team evaluation, and there's no better example than the New York Knicks. If you look at New York's published stats, you'll find they were outshot from the field by 8 points (.486 to .494). This would be a loss of 1.6 points per game. In fact, the Knicks Effective FG% was 7 points (.0071) *better* than that of their opponents (.5116 to .5045) and an *advantage* of + 1.4 points per game.

	FG/FGA	%	3FG/3FGA	%	TOTAL PTS	FT - PTS	=	FG PTS	PTS/FGA's	EFF. FG%
N.Y.	3701/7611	.486	386/1147	.337	9567	- 1779	=	7788	1.023	.5116
OPP.	3636/7358	.494	152/534	.285	9258	- 1834	=	7424	1.009	.5045

Like the professional teams, college and prep teams have incorporated into their games the 3-point field goal, so simple field goal percentage is no longer the most accurate barometer to measure the production of teams and individual players. The use of points/fga and Effective FG% address the realities of today's game and are used in compiling the Power Index.

BALL HANDLING EFFICIENCY:

Basketball's best teams, the NBA Champions, rely on the pass as the chief weapon of attack. This was as true for Auerbach's great Boston teams of the 50's and 60's as it has been for the NBA's best teams of the last 20 years: the Knicks of the early 70's, the Trail Blazers of 1976-77 and '77-78, and the Larry Bird Celtics and Magic Johnson Lakers of the 80's.

The subject is addressed in the Bob Ryan-Terry Pluto book, Forty-eight Minutes ... A night in the life of the N.B.A. In his scouting report on Boston, Cleveland assistant coach Dick Helm says, "The Celtics have been playing the same way since Red Auerbach was coach. On offense, they pass the ball so much. Guys just don't take bad shots, and, if they do, their butts are on the bench." Helms adds, "I don't think any team dribbles as little as Boston. They understand that it is much easier to move the ball around with a pass than by a dribble. They keep swinging the ball from one side of the court to the other, waiting and probing the defense, looking for a breakdown. Whenever I watch Boston, I'm always impressed by how often they pass and how little dribbling goes on." The belief in the value of the pass - playing unselfishly, finding the open man, good judgment in shot selection - is central to this part of the Power Index formula and to what many believe is the key to effective offensive basketball.

My assumptions in evaluating Ball Handling Efficiency (BHE) were: 1) The best pass is an assist because it produces a basket. 2) The worst thing you can do with the ball is have an opponent steal it as a steal is more harmful to a team than another type of turnover - traveling, offensive foul, 3-second violation or a pass out-of-bounds. 3) An effective way to measure ball handling could be identified. 4) This statistical measure would correlate to a team's won-loss record. In reviewing the last 13 NBA seasons, these assumptions have proved valid.

Ball Handling Efficiency is measured by taking your assists and subtracting your opponents' steals. If Detroit has 28 assists in a game and yields 8 steals, their BHE is 20. If their opponent has 30 assists and the Pistons have 12 steals, the opponent's BHE would be 18. Detroit's BHE margin would be +2 (20 - 18 = 2) and they would probably win. The surprise in this research was discovering that, for most teams, Ball Handling Efficiency was almost as accurate as Field Goal Percentage in analyzing who won. In any game, the team with the highest field goal percentage wins about 75% of the time. The team with the highest BHE wins almost as often.

Combining margins for Effective FG% and BHE gives us a fairly reliable index for evaluating team performance, but our equation is not complete. In researching games where the team with the better BHE lost, I discovered that the winner often had an advantage of 10 or more free throws made. In addition, we know that a team may pass the ball well without generating assists if that production comes through free throws. For some teams - the Lakers, Philadelphia, and Cleveland - the ability to get to the line is vital to their success.

FREE THROWS MADE PER GAME:

With free throws producing approximately 20% of all points, the margin of free throws made per game must be factored into an equation that seeks accuracy. Research shows that the NBA's best teams usually have a superiority in this category. Because the average team makes nearly 75% of its free throws (and has for years), getting to the line more than your opponent increases your scoring efficiency. For the Los Angeles Lakers, the margin of free throws made per game is a cornerstone of their success. In 1987-88, the Lakers outscored their opponents by almost 500 points, yet made only 25 more field goals than the teams they played. 418 of those points came at the free throw line, a margin of +5.10 points per game.

In 1988-89, the Lakers' proficiency at the line was even greater (+5.72 points per game). Cleveland, Atlanta, Utah and Philadelphia joined Los Angeles in the NBA's "top 5" in this category. A superior margin in free throws made can often explain why a team with a mediocre FG% margin and/or BHE can still have a very good record.

SCORING OPPORTUNITY POINTS:

Extra scoring opportunities are created in two ways: making fewer turnovers than your opponents or building an advantage in offensive rebounds. A superiority in one can be cancelled by a weakness in the other. To evaluate impact, our search was for the overall effect; specifically to determine how those opportunities were turned into advantages (or disadvantages) in field goal and free throw attempts.

In the Power Index formula, each field goal attempt is worth 1 point since the average NBA team shoots just under 50%. Each additional free throw attempt is worth .75 points since the average NBA team shoots about 75% from the line. To get a complete picture, the two numbers must be combined. As an example, let's look at Denver. Last season the Nuggets had 656 more field goal attempts than their opponents, but 369 fewer free throws.

Our equation: (1 X 656) - (.75 X 369) = Scoring opportunity points   [656 - 277 = 379]

Dividing 379 by Denver's 82 games, we find the Nuggets per-game advantage from additional scoring opportunities was +4.62, third best in the NBA. The rest of the league's top 5 were Portland, Atlanta, Seattle and Milwaukee.

Historically, the margin of Scoring Opportunity Points is the least relevant of the four we use when juxtaposing team rankings with won-loss rankings; however, no coach needs to be convinced of the value of protecting the defensive boards and "taking care" of the basketball.

It is possible to have a poor ranking in this category and still be a premier team. In 1986-87, Boston forced the fewest turnovers in the NBA and had the league's lowest offensive rebounding percentage. Their weakness here was more than offset by a tremendous .054 advantage in FG% (.517 to .463) and high ranking in both Ball Handling Efficiency and Free Throws Made per game. The Power Index formula encompassed these strengths and weaknesses, balanced them, and reflected the Celtics' position among the league's elite teams.

Power Index: A team's Power Index is achieved by simply adding or subtracting the margins in our four key categories. Margins for Ball Handling Efficiency, Free Throws Made per game and Scoring Opportunity Points are treated at face value. The margin in Effective Field Goal Percentage must be converted into points per game.

This conversion is a simple procedure. If one team had an Effective FG% of 50.0% and the other shot 45.0%, the margin is 5.0 . By doubling the margin, you obtain the number of points that difference is actually worth. (2 X 5.0 equals 10 points). That is, in fact, the margin obtained if one team made 50 of 100 2-point shots (100 points) and the other, shooting 45%, made 45 of 100 (90 points). And remember, we have already allowed for the effect of 3-point field goals in our conversion to an Effective FG% for teams and their opponents.

The Power Index formula was developed to help gain a better understanding of TEAM PERFORMANCE. The concept has been based on providing equal weight to offense and defense. Additionally, the validity of the formula has been tested in regard to its ability to match Power Index rankings against won-loss rankings.

My survey period began with the 1976-77 season, the first following the merger between the NBA and ABA. The formula has been extremely accurate when compared to both won-loss records and scoring margins. It allows an observer to guage a team's level and quality of performance, and to gain an understanding of why teams win or lose and the direction they must take to improve their fortunes.

TEAM	W-L	RANK	EFG% MARG	RANK	BHE MARG	RANK	FTM/GM MARG	RANK	±FGA	±FTA	SCOR OPP	SC.OPP MARG	RANK	POWER INDEX	RANK	DIF	SCOR MARG	RANK
Detr	63-19	1	+.44	2	+0.59	12	+0.05	11	-143	+54	-103	-1.26	16	8.18	6	+5	+5.8	4
Clev	57-25	2t	+.42	3	+3.94	1	+5.65	2	-442	+690	+75	+0.91	9	18.90	1	-1	+7.6	2
LA.L	57-25	2t	+.35	4	+1.18	9	+5.72	1	-397	+457	-54	-0.66	15	13.24	2	0	+7.2	3
Phoe	55-27	4	+.31	5	+2.22	7	+3.83	6	-191	+286	+23	+0.28	11	12.53	4	0	+7.7	1
Atla	52-30	5t	-.03	14	+1.01	10	+4.17	5	+106	+380	+391	+4.77	2	9.35	5	0	+4.9	6
N.Y.	52-30	5t	+.07	8	-1.06	17	-0.67	14	+253	-24	+235	+2.87	7	2.54	12	+7	+3.8	7
Utah	51-31	7	+.44	1	+2.89	5	+4.21	4	-575	+400	-275	-3.35	23	12.55	3	-4	+5.0	5
Milw	49-33	8	-.06	15	+0.93	11	+1.43	8	+266	+13	+276	+3.37	5	4.53	8	0	+3.6	8
Seat	47-35	9t	-.02	13	+3.89	2	-1.71	17t	+411	-110	+329	+4.01	4	5.79	7	-2	+2.9	9
Chic	47-35	9t	+.20	7	+1.83	8	-0.45	13	-130	-84	-193	-2.35	19	3.02	11	+2	+1.4	13
Phil	46-36	11	-.13	16	-1.49	18	+5.06	3	-95	+481	+266	+3.24	6	4.21	9	-2	+1.5	11t
Hous	45-37	12	+.04	10	-0.12	14	+1.26	9	-94	+155	+22	+0.27	12	2.21	13	+1	+1.0	15
Denv	44-38	13	-.23	20	+3.56	3	-1.90	20	+656	-369	+379	+4.62	3	1.68	14	+1	+1.7	10
G.St	43-39	14	+.01	12	-2.88	19	-0.15	12	-23	-117	-111	-1.35	18	-4.18	18	+4	-0.3	16
Bost	42-40	15	+.05	9	-0.71	16	+0.73	10	-40	+55	+1	+0.01	13t	1.03	15	0	+1.1	14
Wash	40-42	16	-.25	21	+0.06	13	-1.71	17t	+356	-192	+212	+2.59	8	-4.06	17	+1	-2.1	18
Port	39-43	17	-.13	17	+2.79	6	-1.76	19	+473	-88	+407	+4.96	1	3.39	10	-7	+1.5	11t
Dall	38-44	18	+.04	11	-4.23	25	+2.59	7	-387	+173	-257	-3.13	22	-3.97	16	-2	-1.2	17
Indi	28-54	19	+.24	6	-3.60	23	-2.94	22	-455	-331	-703	-8.57	25	-10.31	19	0	-4.2	19
Sacr	27-55	20	-.18	18	-3.32	20	-1.55	16	-69	-197	-217	-2.65	21	-11.12	20	0	-5.5	20
N.J.	26-56	21	-.34	23	-3.80	24	-1.17	15	+64	-26	+45	+0.55	10	-11.22	22	+1	-6.4	21
S.A.	21-61	22t	-.27	22	-0.26	15	-5.54	23	+261	-347	+1	+0.01	13t	-11.19	21	-1	-7.3	22
L.A.C.	21-61	22t	-.19	19	-3.59	22	-2.78	21	-310	-180	-445	-5.43	24	-15.60	24	+2	-10.0	24
Char	20-62	24	-.38	24	+3.13	4	-5.61	24	+317	-569	-110	-1.34	17	-11.42	23	-1	-8.5	23
Miam	15-67	25	-.40	25	-3.49	21	-6.63	25	+188	-510	-194	-2.37	20	-20.49	25	0	-11.2	25

Difference In Rank Points Between Won-Lost and EFG% Margin: 90
Difference In Rank Points Between Won-Lost and BHE Margin: 136
Difference In Rank Points Between Won-Lost and FTM/GM Margin: 91
Difference In Rank Points Between Won-Lost and Score Opp. Margin: 171

Difference In Rank Points Between Won-Lost and Power Index: 44

Difference In Rank Points Between Won-Lost and Scoring Margin: 37
Difference In Rank Points Between Power Index and Scoring Margin: 35

EFG% = Effective Field Goal Percentage based on formula: (PTS-FTM)/FGA
BHE = Ball Handling Efficiency based on formula comparing Assists + Steals vs. totals of opponents

PREDICTIVE FORMULAS

Last season I introduced several formulas designed to predict how well a team would do in the upcoming season based on how they had done in the previous season or previous seasons. I won't go into all the explanations underlying each formula (you can get last season's book if you want), but I will restate a couple of them.

Formula 1

First, I introduced two terms, overwins and underwins. I arrived at these by first calculating what a team should have won based on the points a team scored and the points they allowed. According to that formula, teams either won more than they should have (overwins) or lost more than they should have (underwins). Probably the most accurate of the predictive formulas says that during the 1980's if a team overwins 4 games or more in a given year, it will lose more games the following year than it did in the present year. Between 1985 and 1989, ten times a team overwon 4+ games in year 1. All ten times the team proceeded to lose more actual games in year 2. The formula is shown below.

$$\text{Year 2 projected wins} = (\text{year 1 actual wins}) + [(\text{year 1 overwins})^2/-4)]$$

Only one team qualified for this prediction last season. In 1988, the Los Angeles Lakers overwon 4.45 games. Therefore, I predicted they would win 5 fewer games in 1989. If you plug in 62 wins (the number LA won in 1988) and 4.45 overwins you will get year 2 projected wins of 57.05. As you may remember, LA actually won 57 games last season. Ok, so I was off .05 wins.

There were three teams that overwon 4+ games in 1989. They were Washington (+5.46), LA Clippers (+5.25), and Detroit (+4.67). Using my formula, the Bullets should win 7.45 games less, the Clippers should have 6.89 fewer wins, and the Pistons 5.45 fewer victories. I can accept the possibility that the Bullets and Pistons might win less games than last year, but I'll be very surprised if the Clippers do also. Maybe I should have my head examined for dreaming of Clipper respectability in the upcoming season, but I have to give them one more chance. After all, as a Kansas Jayhawk fan, I hope Danny Manning gets to star next year.

Formula 2

I also determined that, in the 1980's, 19 of 24 times a team loses over 10 games more from year 1 to year 2, they rebounded the following year to win back, on an average, half of what they lost.

$$\text{Projected wins in year 3} = [(\text{year 2 wins minus year 1 wins})/-2] + \text{year 2 wins}$$

Coming into last year only one team fit this criterion. In 1987, the Warriors won 42 games. In 1988, they only won 20. That was a 22 win drop (for all you math majors). By my formula then, they should have won back 11 games last season. Well, they did that alright. They increased their wins by a whopping 23.

Amazingly, there were six teams who qualified in 1989. (Boston -15 wins, Dallas -15, Portland -14, Denver -10, Indiana -10, and San Antonio -10). This outcome is even more surprising given the inclusion of two expansion teams. That should have meant a fewer-than-average number of teams who dropped in wins. It will be very interesting to see if all these teams recover to win more games than last season. I will be surprised if any of them fail to improve. In fact, although the formula says they will cumulatively win 37 more games (-74/2), I will be surprised if they don't win at least 50.

Formula 3: Lafferty's Offshoot

As an offshoot to Lafferty's Power Index, I did a little study on what predictive capabilities it had. As you can see from the chart on page 221, the total difference in rank points between won-lost and Power Index was 44. This is the total of all of the differences of all 25 teams. For example, Cleveland ranked #1 in Power Index and #2 by won-loss record. Therefore, there is a differential of 1. Eight teams had the same rank in both categories. What that means is that they had a differential of zero. Portland and New York had the largest differentials (7). The Knicks, for example, ranked 12th by Power Index, but 5th by won-loss record. Cleveland's 1 plus New York's 7 plus Portland's 7 equals 15 for those three teams. The other 23 teams combined to add up to 29 (44-15).

It seemed reasonable to me that if a team had a much better record rank than Power Index rank, it probably meant that they overachieved - that their record was a reflection of a best possible scenario. Since the odds were the next year, or any year for that matter, would be a more normal reflection of the team's true ability, I decided to try to discover if these overachieving teams would decline in wins in year 2. I have only researched back to 1978 (the first year turnovers were kept), but there is a clear and unmistakable pattern which suggests that teams which rank 4+ notches higher by won-loss record as opposed to Power Index are destined to come back to earth the next year. Of the 24 teams who overachieved four positions or more since 1978, 19 declined the following season, 4 gained, and 1 stayed the same. In 1989, three teams (Golden State +4, Detroit +5 and New York +7) fit into this category. That means odds are each will decline in actual wins from 1989 to 1990.

Most fans would probably question this judgement since all three teams are considered up-and-coming. When I looked at the previous 24 teams, I realized that they were generally considered up-and-coming as well. Of the 27 teams (including the three in 1989) 20 had better records the year they "overachieved" than the previous year. Generally speaking, when a team improves its record, we, as fans, assume they are getting better and will subsequently improve further. Therefore, it is only reasonable to think of any team which fits into this category as up-and-coming. These three teams are not much different than the other 24, so it shouldn't come as a surprise if each team drops in wins next season - especially New York (+7). Overachieving by 7 wins is enormous and reality (when it comes) can be cruel. Only 1 team of 12, that has overachieved by 6 or more, has ever won more games the next year, and no team which has overachieved by 7 wins has done so. Who knows though, maybe there is a first time. Even so, the best formula I can come up with says...

Year 2 Projected wins = Year 1 wins minus 5 minus [(Overachieving Wins minus 4) X 1.5]

By plugging in the numbers, we can predict that New York will drop from 52 wins to 42.5, Golden State -5 wins (43 to 38), and Detroit -6.5 wins (63 to 56.5). Despite the track record, I'll be surprised, nay shocked, if the Warriors only win 38 games next season. The other two outcomes seem possible, however.

SHOOTING EFFICIENCY

A lot of interest has been expressed in my shooting efficiency formula. It's really quite a simple premise and I like the idea a lot. I want to modify it somewhat, however, so let me state what I previously devised as a formula. Let's use 2-point shooting as an example.

2-point efficiency points = (2pt FGMade times 1/z) minus 2-pt FGAttempted

...where z = the league 2-pt field-goal percentage. Now, let's make up a player's stats to understand it better. Suppose the league average is 49%, but a particular player hit 600 of 1000.

Using the formula shown shown on the previous page he had 224 efficiency points [(600 X (1/.49)) - 1000)]. In other words, what I've argued is that he scored 224 more points than he should have based on the league average, but is that right? Well, technically, no. It's close, but not quite accurate. What this formula really says is that it should have taken 1224 field goal attempts to score 600 2-pt baskets (assuming 49%). Since it only took this player 1000, then he was 224 less *field goal attempts* better than he should have been. But how many *points* was he better than he should have been? Yes, in every edition of Basketball Heaven you will read that a possession is worth roughly a point, but the points gained can be calculated very easily just by modifying the formula.

NEW 2-point efficiency points = [2-pt FGMade minus (FGAttempted times z)] times 2

...where z = the league 2-pt field-goal percentage. Based on this formula, this same player actually had 220 efficiency points - not 224 [600 - (1000 times .49)] times 2. Granted, the difference is minimal and will not change the order much, but according to this formula he should have hit 490 field goals in 1000 attempts (49%). Since he hit 600 he was +110. As each good 2-pt field goal is worth (drum roll) 2 points, he had a net gain of 220 efficiency points.

To convert the formula to 3-point efficiency points, just use a new (z) and change the 2 to a 3. Obviously, to use it for free throws, either change (z) to 1 or remove it altogether. The league averages in the NBA last year were 2-point FG% (48.96%), 3-point FG% (32.22%), and FT% (76.77%). (I might also mention that I figure 2-pt FG% by first removing the 3-pt field-goal-attempts and field-goals-made).

If you've read <u>Basketball Heaven</u> before, you will realize that I'm not measuring who the most accurate shooters are by this formula - only who created the most points based on the number of shots they took. Clearly, a player who went 450/1000 on 3-point shots would be much more valuable than a player who hit 50/100. Though the second player had a higher percentage (50% to 45%), he had only +53.34 3-point efficiency points while the first player had +383.40 efficiency points. Simply put, if you have a 3-pt FG% advantage and really exploit it, it will benefit you more than if your 3-pt FG% is slightly more, but rarely used. As you might expect, this principle holds true for poor shooters. A player who hits 20%, but never shoots doesn't hurt nearly as much as a gunner shooting 23%. Therefore, the 23% shooter has more negative efficiency points.

Shown on the opposite page are eight lists. Each one shows either the top or bottom players at each of the three shooting categories (3-pt, 2-pt, & free throws) during the 1988-89 season. The final two lists are the top and bottom players who earned the most total positive or negative efficiency points. Charles Barkley had the most 2-pt efficiency points for the third year in four while Dale Ellis had a mammoth 159 3-pt efficiency points. The next best ever was Danny Ainge in 1988, at 112. Magic Johnson not only led in FT%, but went to the line often enough to make it pay. He led in free-throw efficiency points for the first time in his career at +81.

Interestingly, for the first time in 20 years, two players from the same team are last in 2-point efficiency points. Both Robert Reid and Rex Chapman play for the expansion Charlotte Hornets and really had no alternative except to keep shooting. Also, for the first time in 20 years, since Wilt Chamberlain led in 2-pt efficiency points, but was dead last in free-throw efficiency points, a player has led a league in one category while trailing in another: As I already mentioned, Charles Barkley led in 2-pt efficiency points, but was last among 3-pt shooters. If he had shot a lot fewer treys last season, he would have won the total shooting efficiency crown. As it was, he was nipped by Michael Jordan, 266-244. On the opposite end of the scale, the two expansion teams had the four lowest ranked players overall. That should come as no surprise to anyone.

2-PT FG EFFICIENCY POINTS

	TOP 10					BOTTOM 10		
1.	Barkley	Phil	+306		1.	Reid	Char	-134
2.	Jordan	Chic	+216		2.	Chapman	Char	-126
3.	Ewing	N.Y.	+204		3.	Edwards	Miam	-126
4.	Worthy	LA.L	+168		4.	Garland	G.St	-98
5.	Parish	Bost	+140		5.	Walker	Wash	-96
6.	McHale	Bost	+140		6.	Hopson	N.J.	-82
7.	Rodman	Detr	+126		7.	Grant	LA.C	-80
8.	Stockton	Utah	+122		8.	Williams	Dall	-74
9.	West	Phoe	+122		9.	Kleine	Bost	-72
10.	Mullin	G.St	+116		10.	Woodson	Hous	-72

3-PT FG EFFICIENCY POINTS

	TOP 10					BOTTOM 10		
1.	Ellis	Seat	+159		1.	Barkley	Phil	-51
2.	Price	Clev	+75		2.	Maxwell	S.A.	-30
3.	Pressley	Sacr	+72		3.	Johnson	Bost	-27
4.	Tucker	N.Y.	+69		4.	Mullin	G.St	-27
5.	Miller	Indi	+57		5.	Bol	G.St	-27
6.	Ainge	Sacr	+54		6.	Harper	Clev	-27
7.	Hawkins	Phil	+54		7.	McMillan	Seat	-24
8.	Sundvold	Miam	+54		8.	Drexler	Port	-21
9.	Hodges	Chic	+51		9.	Webb	Atla	-18
10.	Ed. Johnson	Phoe	+48		10.	Thomas	Detr	-18

FT EFFICIENCY POINTS

	TOP 10					BOTTOM 10		
1.	Johnson	LA.L	+81		1.	G. Anderson	S.A.	-102
2.	Mullin	G.St	+68		2.	Seikaly	Miam	-91
3.	K. Johnson	Phoe	+66		3.	Johnson	Port	-59
4.	Jordan	Chic	+65		4.	Olajuwon	Hous	-47
5.	Chambers	Seat	+50		5.	West	Phoe	-47
6.	Tripucka	Char	+50		6.	Dudley	Clev	-43
7.	Stockton	Utah	+43		7.	Lane	Denv	-43
8.	Sikma	Milw	+40		8.	Catledge	Wash	-42
9.	Wilkins	Atla	+40		9.	Norman	LA.C	-37
10.	Price	Clev	+39		10.	McGee	N.J.	-34

TOTAL SHOOTING EFFICIENCY

	TOP 10					BOTTOM 10		
1.	Jordan	Chic	+266		1.	Seikaly	Miam	-151
2.	Barkley	Phil	+244		2.	Edwards	Miam	-136
3.	Ellis	Seat	+229		3.	Reid	Char	-132
4.	Price	Clev	+208		4.	Chapman	Char	-127
5.	Ewing	N.Y.	+187		5.	Garland	G.St	-100
6.	Johnson	LA.L	+185		6.	Williams	Dall	-96
7.	McHale	Bost	+164		7.	Walker	Wash	-94
8.	Worthy	LA.L	+158		8.	Grant	LA.C	-91
9.	Mullin	G.St	+157		9.	McMillan	Seat	-88
10.	Stockton	Utah	+150		10.	Hopson	N.J.	-79

SUPERSTARS

PAT EWING VS MICHAEL JORDAN

AP/WIDE WORLD PHOTOS

CHAPTER 6

THE TRENDS

OFFENSIVE TRENDS

On the opposite page are the annual averages for the NBA by various offensive categories since 1950. Just as society has changed in 40 years - so has the game of basketball. In 1950, the game was much slower, more methodical, less stylized and much less sophisticated. A lot has happened in the intervening years to change the game. Statistical information such as that on the next page merely reflects the development of the game. In most cases the trends that have developed are obvious. There are some surprises, however.

In the early years, the lane was 6 feet wide, there was no shot clock, goal tending was legal, and there was no limit on fouls per quarter. Because of these rules and others, the game varied from one decade to another. Later on, of course, the 3-point shot was added which also significantly affected the game.

By observing free throw and field goal percentages, it's clear that both have risen since 1950. It is also understandable. Players have grown up playing basketball, have had excellent coaching in grade school, high school and college, and have developed better training techniques. Since 1950, field goal percentage has risen continually, from 34% to 49%, while free throw percentage has been more volatile. In the most extreme scenario, free throw percentage has barely risen since 1959 when it was 75.6%. Since then it has been as low as 71.4% in 1969 and as high as 77.1% in 1974.

Virtually every category rose when the 24 second clock was introduced in 1955. Even free throw percentage rose sharply. The reason why is because fouling became less selective. Before the shot clock, primarily only *poor* free throw shooters were fouled to stop the clock. After 1955, fouls became evenly distributed. Field goal percentage also rose in 1955, proving those wrong who said the shot clock would force bad shots.

Somewhat surprisingly, scoring actually reached its peak in the early 1960's at over ten points per game more than today. Perhaps today's defenses are more sophisticated, or perhaps the offenses are more structured to take advantage of an opponent's weaknesses. In either event the result is more additional time off the clock and less scoring.

Assists have continually increased while rebounds have continually declined. Both patterns can be attributed to better field goal percentages. Since a good pass only becomes an assist if the other player scores, he will clearly register less assists when his teammate shoots field goals at 37% as opposed to 49% like he might do today. Furthermore, the reason more successful shots were not the result of an assist was largely because of stick-backs. The more misses, the more offensive rebounds and the less assists. Obviously, rebounds, both offensive and defensive, would be greater with lower field goal percentages as well. As a result, assists and rebounds are inversely proportionate.

Three point percentages have risen sharply since they were introduced in 1980. The trey has gone from an occasional event (1 attempt per team per game in 1980) to a regular part of the offense (6+ attempts per team per game in 1989). It has become commonplace for players to go long periods of time where they hit at least one 3-pointer in each game. New individual records were set for both 3-point attempts and accuracy last season.

The NBA began distinguishing between offensive and defensive rebounds in 1974. Although they have varied and no clear trend exists, offensive rebounds have constituted from 30% to 33% of all rebounds.

I have explained why the trends exist, but it is also noteworthy that not that much has changed since 1980. Take a look at the stats for the decade's first year. Compare them with 1989. You'll see very little difference other than 3-point FG%. Clearly the league has reached a certain equilibrium.

OFFENSIVE TRENDS

YEAR	SCORING	ASSISTS	REBOUNDS	2-PT FG%	3-PT FG%	FT%
1950	80.0	19.6	---	34.0	---	71.4
1951	84.1	21.0	46.8	35.7	---	73.2
1952	83.7	21.9	51.8	36.7	---	73.5
1953	82.7	21.0	48.9	37.0	---	71.6
1954	79.5	20.3	48.4	37.2	---	70.9
1955	93.9	23.6	53.1	38.5	---	73.8
1956	99.0	24.3	56.5	38.7	---	74.5
1957	99.6	18.9	58.0	38.0	---	75.1
1958	106.6	19.6	65.9	38.3	---	74.6
1959	108.2	19.6	62.3	39.5	---	75.6
1960	115.3	22.6	66.2	40.9	---	73.5
1961	118.1	24.2	66.0	41.5	---	73.3
1962	118.8	23.9	64.3	42.6	---	72.7
1963	115.3	22.7	60.1	44.1	---	72.7
1964	111.0	21.4	59.3	43.3	---	72.2
1965	110.6	21.0	60.5	42.6	---	72.1
1966	115.5	22.9	61.4	43.3	---	72.7
1967	117.4	22.4	60.6	44.1	---	73.2
1968	116.6	22.8	59.6	44.6	---	72.0
1969	112.3	23.1	56.9	44.1	---	71.4
1970	116.7	24.7	52.9	46.0	---	75.1
1971	112.4	24.3	53.1	44.9	---	74.5
1972	110.2	24.1	51.1	45.5	---	74.8
1973	107.6	25.2	50.3	45.6	---	75.8
1974	105.7	24.6	48.2	45.9	---	77.1
1975	102.6	23.8	47.1	45.7	---	76.5
1976	104.5	23.0	47.4	45.8	---	75.1
1977	106.6	22.8	47.1	46.5	---	75.1
1978	108.5	25.0	47.1	46.9	---	75.2
1979	110.3	25.8	45.2	48.5	---	75.2
1980	109.3	25.8	44.9	48.8	28.0	76.4
1981	110.1	25.5	43.5	49.1	24.5	75.1
1982	108.6	25.2	43.5	49.7	26.2	74.6
1983	108.5	25.9	42.6	49.2	23.8	74.0
1984	110.3	26.2	41.2	49.9	25.0	76.0
1985	110.8	26.3	43.5	49.9	28.2	76.4
1986	110.2	26.0	43.6	49.5	28.2	75.6
1987	109.9	26.0	44.0	49.0	30.1	76.3
1988	108.2	25.8	43.4	49.0	31.6	76.6
1989	109.2	25.6	43.9	49.0	32.3	76.8

MISCELLANEOUS TRENDS

On the opposite page are six miscellaneous trends in the NBA since 1950. As the NBA has grown and developed over the years, these numbers have also inflated. There are few surprises, but some explanation is necessary.

You will see that there are seventeen teams listed in 1950, but only eleven in 1951. There is a logical explanation. The National Basketball League (NBL) began back in 1937. The league, along with the American Basketball League, the negro leagues, and amateur leagues set the stage for a post World War II unification.

The Basketball Association of America (BAA) began in 1946-47. During the next three years, the NBL and BAA battled for the same players and franchises. In 1949 (1949-50 season) the two leagues finally merged to form the NBA.

Seventeen of the twenty clubs survived the merger to play in the 1950 season. Unfortunately for six of them, the first season in the NBA did not prove profitable. Their disbanding made the new league much stronger. Over the next five years three more teams would fold. Since 1955, no NBA team has gone under and the league has tripled in size.

DISBANDED TEAMS (1950-55)

1950	Anderson Packers
1950	Chicago Stags
1950	Denver Nuggets
1950	St. Louis Bombers
1950	Sheboygan Redskins
1950	Waterloo Hawks
1951	Washington Capitols
1953	Indianapolis Olympians
1955	Baltimore Bullets

It's no surprise that players' heights have increased consistently over the years. What is strange is that players' weights have not substantially risen since 1969. Strangely, the weights dropped during the 1970's to bottom out in 1979. Once again, they began rising in the 1980's to reach an all time high 216 pounds - only 2 more than in 1969.

The average players' salary has doubled the last four years. At the current rate, the 1990 average annual salary in the league could be over 700 thousand dollars.

Also rising at a rapid pace is the NBA's popularity. Average game attendance has increased substantially the last five years to record levels. In fact, last season was overwhelmingly the most successful from the standpoint of overall attendance.

TOP YEARS
INCREASED ATTENDANCE

YEAR	GAIN PER GAME	PCT
1989	**+1,669**	**12.44%**
1956	+1,153	34.47%
1970	+1,079	16.64%
1975	+960	10.14%
1987	**+902**	**7.58%**
1976	+840	8.99%
1977	+795	7.81%
1986	**+752**	**6.75%**
1988	**+624**	**4.88%**

This is all the more impressive considering capacity levels. Clearly, at some point the average per-game attendance cannot continue to rise. When every arena is sold out, increases will no longer happen. In 1989 the NBA sold out at 88.5% capacity. In 1988 it was 82.3% of capacity. In 1987 it was 78.6% of capacity and in 1986 - 73.1%. By dividing the change in capacity levels by the amount available to grow, [Example: (88.5 - 82.3) / (100 - 82.3) = 35.0%] 1989 was the most impressive year ever in attendance ahead of 1987. In 1987, attendance rose at 20.5% its available capacity to grow. The years 1989 and 1987, as well as 1988 (17.3% availability), are the top three years in history.

I believe the attendance levels are representative of the popularity of the sport. I see basketball as the sport of the future simply because player identification is easy, it's fast paced, it's indoors and under ideal conditions, it's conducive to statistical analysis, and its easy for anyone to play - even by themselves.

MISCELLANEOUS TRENDS

YEAR	TEAM	GAMES	HEIGHT	WEIGHT	ATTEN.	SALARY
1950	17	68	6'4"	197	U/A	U/A
1951	11	68	6'4"	198	U/A	U/A
1952	10	66	6'4.5"	198	U/A	U/A
1953	10	71	6'4.5"	200	3,210	U/A
1954	9	72	6'5"	205	3,583	U/A
1955	8	72	6'5"	203	3,345	U/A
1956	8	72	6'5"	206	4,498	U/A
1957	8	72	6'5"	207	4,895	U/A
1958	8	72	6'5"	205	4,824	U/A
1959	8	72	6'5"	208	5,077	U/A
1960	8	75	6'5.5"	206	5,008	U/A
1961	8	79	6'5.5"	207	5,494	U/A
1962	9	80	6'5.5"	208	4,566	U/A
1963	9	80	6'5.5"	208	5,054	U/A
1964	9	80	6'6"	211	5,266	U/A
1965	9	80	6'6"	213	5,371	U/A
1966	9	80	6'6"	211	6,019	U/A
1967	10	81	6'6"	210	6,631	U/A
1968	12	82	6'6"	211	5,967	U/A
1969	14	82	6'6"	214	6,484	U/A
1970	14	82	6'6"	211	7,563	U/A
1971	17	82	6'6"	210	7,648	U/A
1972	17	82	6'6"	211	8,061	U/A
1973	17	82	6'6"	211	8,396	U/A
1974	17	82	6'6"	210	8,479	U/A
1975	18	82	6'6"	208	9,339	U/A
1976	18	82	6'6.5"	209	10,179	U/A
1977	22	82	6'6.5"	208	10,974	130K
1978	22	82	6'6.5"	207	10,947	139K
1979	22	82	6'6.5"	206	10,822	148K
1980	22	82	6'6.5"	208	11,017	170K
1981	23	82	6'6.5"	209	10,021	171K
1982	23	82	6'6.5"	210	10,567	212K
1983	23	82	6'7"	211	10,220	249K
1984	23	82	6'7"	211	10,620	275K
1985	23	82	6'7"	212	11,141	325K
1986	23	82	6'7.5"	214	11,893	375K
1987	23	82	6'7.62"	215.46	12,795	440K
1988	23	82	6'7.38"	215.61	13,419	550K
1989	25	82	6'7.31"	215.58	15,088	603K

POSITION LEADERS

Listed below are the annual Production Ratings leaders regardless of position and the annual Production Ratings leaders at the forward position. I began making a distinction between small forwards with power forwards in 1974. A lack of statistical information makes Production Ratings prior to 1950 highly suspect.

PRODUCTION LEADER			FORWARD	
1950	G. Mikan	28.13	D. Schayes	25.20
1951	G. Mikan	30.16	D. Schayes	25.80
1952	P. Arizin	27.06	P. Arizin	27.06
1953	N. Johnston	26.99	D. Schayes	23.31
1954	N. Johnston	25.53	H. Gallatin	23.61
1955	N. Johnston	29.00	B. Pettit	24.85
1956	B. Pettit	29.74	B. Pettit	29.74
1957	D. Schayes	27.44	D. Schayes	27.44
1958	B. Russell	30.71	D. Schayes	29.07
1959	B. Pettit	32.99	B. Pettit	32.99
1960	W. Chamberlain	43.83	B. Pettit	32.29
1961	W. Chamberlain	45.58	E. Baylor	40.19
1962	W. Chamberlain	52.29	E. Baylor	39.31
1963	W. Chamberlain	50.59	E. Baylor	35.98
1964	W. Chamberlain	44.60	B. Pettit	32.41
1965	W. Chamberlain	40.62	J. Lucas	34.26
1966	W. Chamberlain	45.76	J. Lucas	33.66
1967	W. Chamberlain	45.54	R. Barry	31.32
1968	W. Chamberlain	42.80	J. Lucas	34.37
1969	W. Chamberlain	34.68	J. Lucas	33.66
1970	K. Abdul-Jabbar	33.63	B. Cunningham	30.48
1971	K. Abdul-Jabbar	38.88	J. Havlicek	30.40
1972	K. Abdul-Jabbar	42.63	J. Havlicek	29.11
1973	K. Abdul-Jabbar	39.12	S. Haywood	30.81

PRODUCTION LEADER			SMALL FORWARD		POWER FORWARD	
1974	K. Abdul-Jabbar	35.91	R. Tomjanovich	25.73	S. Haywood	26.92
1975	K. Abdul-Jabbar	35.62	R. Barry	26.26	E. Hayes	25.70
1976	K. Abdul-Jabbar	39.65	J. Drew	22.14	G. McGinnis	25.05
1977	K. Abdul-Jabbar	35.16	L. Kenon	25.17	E. Hayes	26.87
1978	K. Abdul-Jabbar	34.39	M. Johnson	24.13	T. Robinson	24.77
1979	K. Abdul-Jabbar	34.68	M. Johnson	26.64	E. Hayes	24.56
1980	K. Abdul-Jabbar	32.87	J. Erving	27.78	L. Bird	25.26
1981	M. Malone	31.67	A. Dantley	28.23	L. Bird	26.74
1982	M. Malone	33.12	A. Dantley	27.81	L. Bird	29.16
1983	M. Malone	30.08	A. English	28.30	L. Bird	30.04
1984	E. Johnson	30.30	L. Bird	29.99	J. Ruland	27.67
1985	L. Bird	34.39	L. Bird	34.39	T. Cummings	24.39
1986	L. Bird	31.30	L. Bird	31.30	C. Barkley	28.26
1987	L. Bird	34.28	L. Bird	34.28	C. Barkley	33.46
1988	M. Jordan	35.05	L. Bird	34.01	C. Barkley	32.51
1989	M. Jordan	36.99	C. Mullin	26.01	C. Barkley	32.68

POSITION LEADERS

Listed below are the annual Production Ratings leaders at the center and guard positions. I began making a distinction between off guards and point guards in 1974. A lack of statistical information makes Production Ratings prior to 1950 highly suspect. ABA ratings are not shown.

	CENTER			GUARD	
1950	G. Mikan	28.13		A. Phillip	14.83
1951	G. Mikan	30.16		A. Phillip	17.00
1952	G. Mikan	24.88		B. Cousy	20.03
1953	N. Johnston	26.99		B. Cousy	20.27
1954	N. Johnston	25.53		B. Cousy	19.56
1955	N. Johnston	29.00		B. Cousy	22.27
1956	N. Johnston	27.36		B. Cousy	22.49
1957	N. Johnston	27.20		B. Cousy	19.39
1958	B. Russell	30.71		T. Gola	21.81
1959	B. Russell	32.70		B. Cousy	21.25
1960	W. Chamberlain	43.83		T. Gola	22.44
1961	W. Chamberlain	45.58		O. Robertson	36.42
1962	W. Chamberlain	52.29		O. Robertson	40.51
1963	W. Chamberlain	50.59		O. Robertson	36.81
1964	W. Chamberlain	44.60		O. Robertson	39.15
1965	W. Chamberlain	40.62		O. Robertson	37.49
1966	W. Chamberlain	45.76		O. Robertson	36.41
1967	W. Chamberlain	45.54		O. Robertson	35.13
1968	W. Chamberlain	42.80		O. Robertson	33.46
1969	W. Chamberlain	34.68		O. Robertson	30.51
1970	K. Abdul-Jabbar	33.63		J. West	30.01
1971	K. Abdul-Jabbar	38.88		J. West	29.62
1972	K. Abdul-Jabbar	42.63		N. Archibald	28.21
1973	K. Abdul-Jabbar	39.12		N. Archibald	33.18

	CENTER		OFF GUARD		POINT GUARD	
1974	K. Abdul-Jabbar	35.91	P. Maravich	20.62	W. Frazier	23.46
1975	K. Abdul-Jabbar	35.62	G. Goodrich	18.11	W. Frazier	23.56
1976	K. Abdul-Jabbar	39.65	P. Maravich	20.39	W. Frazier	22.15
1977	K. Abdul-Jabbar	35.16	G. Gervin	21.68	P. Westphal	18.86
1978	K. Abdul-Jabbar	34.39	G. Gervin	24.93	P. Westphal	20.67
1979	K. Abdul-Jabbar	34.68	G. Gervin	25.31	P. Westphal	21.89
1980	K. Abdul-Jabbar	32.87	G. Gervin	27.19	E. Johnson	25.13
1981	M. Malone	31.67	G. Gervin	22.10	M. Richardson	21.81
1982	M. Malone	33.12	G. Gervin	24.82	E. Johnson	29.65
1983	M. Malone	30.08	S. Moncrief	22.80	E. Johnson	28.63
1984	M. Malone	25.85	S. Moncrief	22.76	E. Johnson	30.30
1985	M. Malone	27.30	M. Jordan	29.24	E. Johnson	28.77
1986	A. Olajuwon	28.40	A. Robertson	22.48	E. Johnson	28.50
1987	A. Olajuwon	28.99	M. Jordan	31.91	E. Johnson	31.79
1988	A. Olajuwon	28.10	M. Jordan	35.05	E. Johnson	27.71
1989	A. Olajuwon	31.02	M. Jordan	36.99	E. Johnson	33.31

CATEGORY LEADERS

Listed below are the annual leaders in three different categories. Scoring is based on points-per-game. Shooting is based on equally analyzing 2 pt. FG%, 3 pt. FG% and FT%. A rating of 1.000 means average shooting (50% - 2 pt FG%, 33% - 3pt FG%, 75% - FT%). The formula for shooting is equal to (points + 1/3 FTs made) / shots attempted. The third category is rebounds based on 48 minutes per game.

	SCORING		SHOOTING		REBOUNDS	
1950	G. Mikan	27.43	A. Groza	.962	Unavailable	
1951	G. Mikan	28.41	A. Groza	.978	D. Schayes	16.36
1952	P. Arizin	25.36	B. Wanzer	.974	D. Schayes	18.51
1953	N. Johnston	22.34	B. Sharman	.951	H. Gallatin	18.85
1954	N. Johnston	24.43	E. Macauley	.987	G. Mikan	20.89
1955	N. Johnston	22.65	L. Foust	.992	C. Share	19.48
1956	B. Pettit	25.68	N. Johnston	.974	M. Stokes	22.61
1957	P. Arizin	25.59	N. Johnston	.968	B. Russell	26.70
1958	G. Yardley	27.79	K. Sears	.954	B. Russell	28.44
1959	B. Pettit	29.24	K. Sears	1.042	B. Russell	25.97
1960	W. Chamberlain	37.60	K. Sears	1.021	W. Chamberlain	27.91
1961	W. Chamberlain	38.39	O. Robertson	.995	W. Chamberlain	27.34
1962	W. Chamberlain	50.36	O. Robertson	.994	W. Chamberlain	25.37
1963	W. Chamberlain	44.83	O. Robertson	1.050	B. Russell	25.28
1964	W. Chamberlain	36.85	J. Lucas	1.049	B. Russell	26.61
1965	W. Chamberlain	34.71	J. West	1.026	B. Russell	26.01
1966	W. Chamberlain	33.53	J. West	1.018	B. Russell	25.22
1967	R. Barry	35.58	O. Robertson	1.045	W. Chamberlain	25.21
1968	O. Robertson	29.17	O. Robertson	1.054	W. Chamberlain	24.43
1969	E. Hayes	28.38	J. Lucas	1.079	W. Unseld	24.10
1970	J. West	31.20	J. McGlocklin	1.071	T. Boerwinkle	20.89
1971	K. Abdul-Jabbar	31.66	K. Abdul-Jabbar	1.091	T. Boerwinkle	22.95
1972	K. Abdul-Jabbar	34.84	K. Abdul-Jabbar	1.087	C. Ray	22.68
1973	N. Archibald	33.99	M. Guokas	1.134	W. Chamberlain	20.68
1974	B. McAdoo	30.55	R. Tomjanovich	1.086	E. Hayes	19.50
1975	B. McAdoo	34.52	L. Steele	1.099	H. Hairston	19.89
1976	B. McAdoo	31.12	J. McMillian	1.086	K. Abdul-Jabbar	19.65
1977	P. Maravich	31.14	D. Twardzik	1.183	S. Nater	21.18
1978	G. Gervin	27.22	D. Twardzik	1.132	M. Malone	20.18
1979	G. Gervin	29.56	S. Nater	1.124	M. Malone	20.45
1980	G. Gervin	33.14	K. Abdul-Jabbar	1.159	S. Nater	20.41
1981	A. Dantley	30.65	A. Gilmore	1.182	L. Smith	18.51
1982	G. Gervin	32.29	A. Gilmore	1.194	L. Smith	17.63
1983	A. English	28.37	A. Gilmore	1.157	M. Malone	19.61
1984	A. Dantley	30.61	C. Natt	1.139	L. Thompson	17.77
1985	B. King	32.89	J. Donaldson	1.176	B. Walton	17.49
1986	D. Wilkins	30.33	J. Sichting	1.166	C. Oakley	17.99
1987	M. Jordan	37.09	K. McHale	1.182	L. Smith	18.54
1988	M. Jordan	34.98	J. Stockton	1.161	R. Tarpley	19.95
1989	M. Jordan	32.51	M. Price	1.157	A. Olajuwon	17.54

CATEGORY LEADERS

Listed below are the annual leaders in three different categories. All three are based on 48 minutes per game. The purpose of using this statistic, as opposed to a per-game-only statistic, is that it reveals those players who really excel in a particular area. For role players, a statistic based on 48 minutes is much more meaningful. Steals and blocks were not kept by the NBA until 1974.

	ASSISTS		BLOCKS		STEALS	
1950	A. Phillip	5.80	Unavailable		Unavailable	
1951	A. Phillip	6.27	Unavailable		Unavailable	
1952	D. McGuire	9.23	Unavailable		Unavailable	
1953	B. Cousy	8.92	Unavailable		Unavailable	
1954	B. Cousy	8.70	Unavailable		Unavailable	
1955	D. McGuire	11.26	Unavailable		Unavailable	
1956	B. Cousy	11.14	Unavailable		Unavailable	
1957	B. Cousy	9.71	Unavailable		Unavailable	
1958	B. Cousy	10.00	Unavailable		Unavailable	
1959	B. Cousy	11.13	Unavailable		Unavailable	
1960	B. Cousy	13.26	Unavailable		Unavailable	
1961	B. Cousy	11.42	Unavailable		Unavailable	
1962	B. Cousy	13.26	Unavailable		Unavailable	
1963	B. Cousy	12.52	Unavailable		Unavailable	
1964	O. Robertson	11.71	Unavailable		Unavailable	
1965	O. Robertson	12.08	Unavailable		Unavailable	
1966	G. Rodgers	13.99	Unavailable		Unavailable	
1967	G. Rodgers	14.23	Unavailable		Unavailable	
1968	G. Rodgers	11.80	Unavailable		Unavailable	
1969	A Williams	12.66	Unavailable		Unavailable	
1970	A. Williams	15.63	Unavailable		Unavailable	
1971	N. Van Lier	12.01	Unavailable		Unavailable	
1972	L. Wilkens	12.30	Unavailable		Unavailable	
1973	N. Archibald	11.87	Unavailable		Unavailable	
1974	S. Watts	11.83	E. Smith	6.46	L. Steele	3.93
1975	K. Porter	12.05	E. Smith	4.43	S. Watts	4.44
1976	S. Watts	11.43	K. Abdul-Jabbar	4.80	S. Watts	4.51
1977	K. Porter	13.42	G. Johnson	5.14	D. Buse	4.58
1978	K. Porter	14.28	W. Rollins	5.83	R. Lee	5.60
1979	K. Porter	17.22	W. Rollins	6.42	E. Jordan	4.27
1980	K. Porter	14.68	G. Johnson	5.84	D. Bradley	5.00
1981	K. Porter	13.67	G. Johnson	6.90	D. Bradley	4.78
1982	J. Moore	15.94	G. Johnson	7.12	M. Cheeks	4.02
1983	J. Moore	14.16	W. Rollins	6.66	M. Richardson	4.21
1984	J. Lucas	17.88	M. Eaton	7.88	D. Cook	4.21
1985	I. Thomas	17.45	M. Eaton	7.78	J. Moore	4.09
1986	E. Johnson	16.89	M. Bol	9.12	A. Robertson	5.02
1987	J. Stockton	17.31	M. Bol	9.34	A. Robertson	4.63
1988	J. Stockton	19.05	M. Eaton	5.34	J. Stockton	4.09
1989	T. Bogues	16.96	M. Bol	9.36	A. Robertson	4.13

MISCELLANEOUS LEADERS

Listed below are the annual leaders in three different categories. The first column represents the annual Most Valuable Player (see Chapter 1 for explanation of formula). Column two represents the most dominant player at his position each year (see Chapter 1 for explanation of formula). Column three shows the top rookie each year by Production Rating.

	MVP		POSITION DOMINANCE		ROOKIE	
1950	D. Schayes	2.219	D. Schayes	1.508	A. Groza	25.13
1951	G. Mikan	2.067	G. Mikan	1.471	P. Arizin	19.66
1952	G. Mikan	1.908	P. Arizin	1.423	M. Hutchins	18.11
1953	B. Cousy	2.012	B. Cousy	1.394	D. Meineke	13.18
1954	H. Gallatin	2.037	H. Gallatin	1.513	R. Felix	20.57
1955	B. Cousy	1.831	N. Johnston	1.366	B. Pettit	24.85
1956	N. Johnston	1.963	B. Cousy	1.353	M. Stokes	25.15
1957	B. Cousy	1.957	N. Johnston	1.313	B. Russell	25.17
1958	B. Russell	1.871	T. Gola	1.289	W. Sauldsberry	12.99
1959	B. Russell	2.259	B. Russell	1.535	E. Baylor	29.27
1960	W. Chamberlain	2.100	W. Chamberlain	1.502	W. Chamberlain	43.83
1961	W. Chamberlain	2.125	W. Chamberlain	1.602	O. Robertson	36.42
1962	E. Baylor	2.159	O. Robertson	1.571	W. Bellamy	37.96
1963	O. Robertson	2.082	W. Chamberlain	1.625	T. Dischinger	25.68
1964	O. Robertson	2.250	O. Robertson	1.641	J. Lucas	30.39
1965	O. Robertson	2.103	O. Robertson	1.549	W. Reed	24.19
1966	W. Chamberlain	2.094	W. Chamberlain	1.483	R. Barry	25.48
1967	W. Chamberlain	2.345	W. Chamberlain	1.543	D. Bing	16.69
1968	W. Chamberlain	2.128	W. Chamberlain	1.442	E. Monroe	21.56
1969	W. Chamberlain	1.876	J. Lucas	1.368	E. Hayes	29.45
1970	K. Abdul-Jabbar	1.925	K. Abdul-Jabbar	1.291	K. Abdul-Jabbar	33.63
1971	K. Abdul-Jabbar	2.153	K. Abdul-Jabbar	1.335	D. Cowens	24.26
1972	K. Abdul-Jabbar	2.098	K. Abdul-Jabbar	1.394	S. Wicks	25.23
1973	K. Abdul-Jabbar	1.965	N. Archibald	1.372	L. Neal	19.98
1974	K. Abdul-Jabbar	1.936	S. Haywood	1.283	E. DiGregorio	13.58
1975	R. Barry	1.950	R. Barry	1.318	J. Drew	19.69
1976	K. Abdul-Jabbar	1.904	K. Abdul-Jabbar	1.416	A. Adams	22.30
1977	K. Abdul-Jabbar	1.916	K. Abdul-Jabbar	1.351	A. Dantley	20.14
1978	G. Gervin	1.811	K. Abdul-Jabbar	1.255	M. Johnson	24.13
1979	G. Gervin	1.873	G. Gervin	1.317	P. Ford	17.32
1980	E. Johnson	2.028	G. Gervin	1.340	L. Bird	25.26
1981	L. Bird	2.034	L. Bird	1.297	J. Carroll	19.37
1982	E. Johnson	2.174	E. Johnson	1.424	B. Williams	21.94
1983	M. Malone	2.080	E. Johnson	1.397	T. Cummings	26.04
1984	E. Johnson	2.059	E. Johnson	1.397	R. Sampson	24.01
1985	L. Bird	2.131	M. Jordan	1.393	M. Jordan	29.24
1986	L. Bird	2.123	E. Johnson	1.346	P. Ewing	20.56
1987	E. Johnson	2.175	M. Jordan	1.416	C. Person	19.63
1988	L. Bird	2.043	M. Jordan	1.426	M. Jackson	20.68
1989	E. Johnson	2.046	M. Jordan	1.483	M. Richmond	19.44

MISCELLANEOUS LEADERS

Listed below are the annual NBA champions and the champions' Total Percentage (TP). In brief, the TP is the ratio of wins versus games played, with three times the emphasis on playoff games. Chapter two explains Total Percentage in more detail. The second column lists the top 40 MVP's ever, regardless of year. MVP = PD + TP. (See chapter one for explanation.)

CHAMPIONS		TP		TOP MVP's		
1950	Minneapolis Lakers	.785	1.	W. Chamberlain	1967	2.345
1951	Rochester Royals	.618	2.	B. Russell	1959	2.259
1952	Minneapolis Lakers	.638	3.	O. Robertson	1964	2.250
1953	Minneapolis Lakers	.708	4.	D. Schayes	1950	2.219
1954	Minneapolis Lakers	.658	5.	E. Johnson	1987	2.175
1955	Syracuse Nationals	.610	6.	E. Johnson	1982	2.174
1956	Philadelphia Warriors	.647	7.	E. Baylor	1962	2.159
1957	Boston Celtics	.637	8.	G. Mikan	1950	2.158
1958	St. Louis Hawks	.619	9.	K. Abdul-Jabbar	1971	2.153
1959	Boston Celtics	.724	10.	L. Bird	1985	2.131
1960	Boston Celtics	.728	11.	W. Chamberlain	1968	2.128
1961	Boston Celtics	.743	12.	W. Chamberlain	1961	2.125
1962	Boston Celtics	.689	13.	L. Bird	1986	2.123
1963	Boston Celtics	.689	14.	O. Robertson	1965	2.103
1964	Boston Celtics	.755	15.	W. Chamberlain	1960	2.100
1965	Boston Celtics	.741	16.	W. Chamberlain	1962	2.100
1966	Boston Celtics	.672	17.	K. Abdul-Jabbar	1972	2.098
1967	Philadelphia 76ers	.802	18.	W. Chamberlain	1966	2.094
1968	Boston Celtics	.647	19.	O. Robertson	1963	2.082
1969	Boston Celtics	.618	20.	M. Malone	1983	2.080
1970	New York Knicks	.691	21.	O. Robertson	1962	2.071
1971	Milwaukee Bucks	.823	22.	G. Mikan	1951	2.067
1972	Los Angeles Lakers	.827	23.	E. Johnson	1984	2.059
1973	New York Knicks	.699	24.	L. Bird	1987	2.052
1974	Boston Celtics	.676	25.	E. Johnson	1985	2.046
1975	Golden State Warriors	.632	26.	E. Johnson	1989	2.046
1976	Boston Celtics	.662	27.	E. Johnson	1983	2.043
1977	Portland Trailblazers	.655	28.	L. Bird	1988	2.043
1978	Washington Bullets	.593	29.	E. Johnson	1986	2.040
1979	Seattle Supersonics	.662	30.	M. Jordan	1989	2.040
1980	Los Angeles Lakers	.738	31.	H. Gallatin	1954	2.037
1981	Boston Celtics	.737	32.	L. Bird	1981	2.034
1982	Los Angeles Lakers	.750	33.	E. Johnson	1980	2.028
1983	Philadelphia 76ers	.835	34.	L. Bird	1982	2.026
1984	Boston Celtics	.709	35.	K. Abdul-Jabbar	1980	2.024
1985	Los Angeles Lakers	.770	36.	W. Chamberlain	1964	2.022
1986	Boston Celtics	.824	37.	J. West	1972	2.015
1987	Los Angeles Lakers	.809	38.	B. Cousy	1953	2.012
1988	Los Angeles Lakers	.695	39.	W. Chamberlain	1963	2.012
1989	Detroit Pistons	.812	40.	O. Robertson	1961	2.008

OFFENSE VS DEFENSE
JAMES WORTHY VS RODMAN/DUMARS

AP/WIDE WORLD PHOTOS

CHAPTER 7

SEASONAL SUMMARIES

SEASONAL SUMMARIES

On the following pages I cite the top players by Production Rating by position every year since 1982 (see chapter one for Production Rating argument). I should point out that the years 1950-1981 can be found in my 1987-88 edition of Basketball Heaven. I would like to have included them in this year's book as well, but was subject to limitations on space (see the last page in the book for address on how to order BBH 1988 or BBH 1989).

Despite not showing the earlier years, I will go ahead and explain some of the distinctions between the years prior to 1982 and those after that date. By doing so, it should help give a feel for some of the variations the game has gone through.

I began making a distinction between small forwards and power forwards as well as point guards and off guards in 1974. For each year I have also recorded the top players by Position Dominance and MVP (see chapter one as well for a discussion of the PD and MVP formulas). Also listed are the top rookies by Production Ratings. All players, including rookies, must qualify to be ranked.

In order to qualify, a player must have played in 61 or more games and averaged at least 19 minutes per game. A player could play less than 61 games and still qualify. He could even play as few as 50 games as long as his minutes-per-game plus games-played equals at least 80. In earlier years when the schedule was shorter, the same principle was applied. But instead of a minimum 50 games, the requirement was 60% of the total games a team played. Nineteen minutes per game has always been a requirement since NBA games have always been 48 minutes long.

I have also shown the leaders in the 6 major performance categories for each year (steals and blocks are listed only since 1974). Each category, with the exception of scoring, is based on 48 minutes per game. There are two reasons for this. The first reason is that one can find the assist-per-game leader for a given year in a variety of places. All sources include the leaders of each category based on so many per game. I wanted to offer a statistic that was different, yet valid. The following pages represent the only available lists that I am aware of based on 48 minutes per game. The second reason is that, although assists per game is a perfectly meaningful statistic, assists per 48 minutes is also meaningful in a different way. Some players are role players. That is, they come into a game when specific situations develop. It may be to provide muscle on the boards or tough defense. Whatever the reason, a player who plays sparingly will not show very much of anything per game. By showing his statistics based on 48 minutes, I believe I offer a truer picture of a particular player's strengths. My statistics do not reflect a player's durability, but that is what the per-game ratings are for. As I mentioned earlier, scoring is on a per-game basis while the other categories are not. The reason I made an exception for scoring is because if I were to show scoring as a 48 minute statistic, it would likely promote a player who shoots constantly when in the game. That may or may not be desirable. On the other hand, when was the last time a rebound or an assist or a steal or a block was not desirable? (Read additional discussion of 48-minute projections on page 12.) Thus the distinction between scoring and the other statistical categories.

The last statistical category is shooting and is broken down into three areas - 3pt FG%, 2pt FG%, and FT%. I devised a relatively simple statistic which evenhandedly evaluates all three. Simply put, if a player hits 50% of his 2pt FGs (average) and 33% of his 3 pt FGs (ideal average) and 75% of his free throws (average), he would have a 1.000 shooting rating. The formula is relatively simple. SHT = (points + one third FTs made) / shots attempted.

It may be difficult to perceive, but each of the three categories is fairly and equally dealt with in the statistic. In 1989, Mark Price led with a 1.157 rating. He shot 54.8% from 2-pt range, 44.1% from 3-pt country, and shot 90.1% from the line. Manute Bol, on the other hand, was last of the 176 qualifiers in shooting. His rating was .798. He shot 2-pt FGs at 42.3%, FTs at 60.6% and 3-pointers at 22%. As I said, 1.000 is average. It makes sense, then, that the best shooter (1.157) would be roughly the same amount over 1.000 as the worst shooter (.798) is below that mark.

I have used abbreviations for team names. These should be clear to the reader. A couple examples would be G.St = Golden State or LA.L = Los Angeles Lakers. Also abbreviated are the categories. See designations below.

PR = Production Rating (see chapter one for explanation)

OR = Overall Rank

PD = Position Dominance (see chapter one for explanation)

MVP = Most Valuable Player (see chapter one for explanation)

SCR = Scoring (points/game)

SHT = Shooting (see previous paragraphs for a brief explanation)

REB = Rebounds per 48 minutes played

AST = Assists per 48 minutes played

BLK = Blocked Shots per 48 minutes played

STL = Steals per 48 minutes played

When looking at a particular year, I thought it might be interesting to know how many total players qualified. This should give a better feel for how a particular player ranked with respect to the total. Listed below are the number of players who qualified during each year.

1950 -- 85	1960 -- 56	1970 -- 97	1980 -- 157
1951 -- 70	1961 -- 56	1971 -- 115	1981 -- 165
1952 -- 70	1962 -- 60	1972 -- 108	1982 -- 160
1953 -- 69	1963 -- 67	1973 -- 108	1983 -- 157
1954 -- 66	1964 -- 57	1974 -- 114	1984 -- 161
1955 -- 55	1965 -- 65	1975 -- 119	1985 -- 158
1956 -- 59	1966 -- 60	1976 -- 123	1986 -- 158
1957 -- 55	1967 -- 67	1977 -- 150	1987 -- 160
1958 -- 54	1968 -- 85	1978 -- 159	1988 -- 159
1959 -- 54	1969 -- 95	1979 -- 154	1989 -- 176

Clearly, since 1980, there has been little to no change in the total numbers of qualifiers. That will rise approximately 15 in 1990 as the two new franchises are added to the league. Of course, it goes without saying, but a player who ranked number 10 in any particular category in 1954, is hardly comparable to a number 10 ranking in 1989. I deal with this dilemma in the next chapter (see page 268).

1988-89
NBA STATISTICS

PRODUCTION RATINGS

OR	PLAYER	TEAM	PR
1.	Michael Jordan	Chic	36.99
2.	Earvin Johnson	LA.L	33.31
3.	Charles Barkley	Phil	32.68
4.	Akeem Olajuwon	Hous	31.02
5.	Karl Malone	Utah	29.53
6.	Clyde Drexler	Port	28.87
7.	Lafayette Lever	Denv	27.48
8.	Pat Ewing	N.Y.	27.46
9.	John Stockton	Utah	27.40
10.	Kevin Johnson	Phoe	27.06
11.	Robert Parish	Bost	26.10
12.	Chris Mullin	G.St	26.01
13.	Tom Chambers	Phoe	24.11
14.	Moses Malone	Atla	23.84
15.	Kevin McHale	Bost	23.68
16.	Dominique Wilkins	Atla	22.84
17.	Larry Nance	Clev	22.66
18.	Terry Porter	Port	22.42
19.	Brad Daugherty	Clev	22.37
20.	Mark Price	Clev	22.33
21.	James Worthy	LA.L	21.80
22.	Terry Cummings	Milw	21.54
23.	Alex English	Denv	21.38
24.	Dale Ellis	Seat	21.13
25.	Benoit Benjamin	LA.C	21.11
26.	Ron Harper	Clev	21.09
27.	Otis Thorpe	Hous	20.62
28.	Mike Gminski	Phil	20.55
29.	Alvin Robertson	S.A.	20.52
30.	Mark Jackson	N.Y.	20.49
31.	Ken Norman	LA.C	20.34
32.	Jerome Kersey	Port	20.24
33.	Bill Laimbeer	Detr	19.70
34.	Michael Adams	Denv	19.60
35.	Mitch Richmond	G.St	19.44
36.	Derek Harper	Dall	19.33
37.	Isiah Thomas	Detr	19.09
38.	Chuck Person	Indi	19.00
39.	Willie Anderson	S.A.	18.99
40.	John S. Williams	Wash	18.74
41.	Glenn Rivers	Atla	18.70
42.	A.C. Green	LA.L	18.61
43.	Sam Perkins	Dall	18.51
44.	Jack Sikma	Milw	18.48
45.	Eric Floyd	Hous	18.46
46.	Charles Oakley	N.Y.	18.44
47.	Wayman Tisdale	Sacr	18.43
48.	LaSalle Thompson	Indi	17.95
49.	Eddie Johnson	Phoe	17.93
50.	Byron Scott	LA.L	17.89
51.	Kurt Rambis	Char	17.80
52.	James Donaldson	Dall	17.70
53.	Danny Ainge	Sacr	17.64
54.	Reggie Lewis	Bost	17.64
55.	Kelly Tripucka	Char	17.61
56.	Horace Grant	Chic	17.52
57.	Vern Fleming	Indi	17.49
58.	Bernard King	Wash	17.35
59.	Derrick McKey	Seat	17.29
60.	Jeff Hornacek	Phoe	17.06
61.	Kenny Smith	Sacr	17.04
62.	Buck Williams	N.J.	16.92
63.	Michael Cage	Seat	16.90
64.	Lester Conner	N.J.	16.87
65.	Thurl Bailey	Utah	16.79
66.	Winston Garland	G.St	16.76
67.	Rolando Blackman	Dall	16.74
68.	Kevin Duckworth	Port	16.72
69.	Charles Smith	LA.C	16.66
70.	Rodney McCray	Sacr	16.65
71.	Nate McMillan	Seat	16.63
72.	Mark Eaton	Utah	16.59
73.	Joe Dumars	Detr	16.59
74.	Paul Pressey	Milw	16.39
75.	Maurice Cheeks	Phil	16.38
76.	Scottie Pippen	Chic	16.38
77.	Dennis Rodman	Detr	16.32
78.	Xavier McDaniel	Seat	16.29
79.	Adrian Dantley	Dall	16.29
80.	Darrell Walker	Wash	16.13
81.	Reggie Miller	Indi	16.12
82.	Armon Gilliam	Phoe	15.74
83.	Mark Aguirre	Detr	15.74
84.	Joe Barry Carroll	N.J.	15.59
85.	Danny Schayes	Denv	15.49
86.	Frank Brickowski	S.A.	15.42
87.	Roy Hinson	N.J.	15.33
88.	Larry Krystkowiak	Milw	15.29
89.	Jeff Malone	Wash	15.26
90.	Greg Anderson	S.A.	15.11
91.	Reggie Theus	Atla	15.06
92.	Ricky Pierce	Milw	14.95
93.	Ron Anderson	Phil	14.93
94.	John Williams	Clev	14.87
95.	Harold Pressley	Sacr	14.60
96.	Wayne Cooper	Denv	14.43
97.	Grant Long	Miam	14.41
98.	Ed Pinckney	Bost	14.28
99.	Jay Humphries	Milw	14.07
100.	Rik Smits	Indi	14.06

POSITION DOMINANCE

OR	PLAYER	TEAM	PD
1.	Michael Jordan	Chic	1.483
2.	Earvin Johnson	LA.L	1.337
3.	Charles Barkley	Phil	1.311
4.	Akeem Olajuwon	Hous	1.289
5.	Karl Malone	Utah	1.184
6.	Chris Mullin	G.St	1.183
7.	Clyde Drexler	Port	1.158
8.	Pat Ewing	N.Y.	1.141
9.	Lafayette Lever	Denv	1.102
10.	John Stockton	Utah	1.100
11.	Tom Chambers	Phoe	1.097
12.	Kevin Johnson	Phoe	1.086
13.	Robert Parish	Bost	1.084
14.	Dominique Wilkins	Atla	1.039
15.	James Worthy	LA.L	.992
16.	Moses Malone	Atla	.990
17.	Terry Cummings	Milw	.979
18.	Alex English	Denv	.972
19.	Kevin McHale	Bost	.950
20.	Brad Daugherty	Clev	.929

MOST VALUABLE PLAYER

OR	PLAYER	TEAM	MVP
1.	Earvin Johnson	LA.L	2.046
2.	Michael Jordan	Chic	2.040
3.	Charles Barkley	Phil	1.816
4.	Akeem Olajuwon	Hous	1.800
5.	Pat Ewing	N.Y.	1.756
6.	Karl Malone	Utah	1.744
7.	Tom Chambers	Phoe	1.741
8.	Kevin Johnson	Phoe	1.730
9.	Chris Mullin	G.St	1.702
10.	James Worthy	LA.L	1.701
11.	John Stockton	Utah	1.660
12.	Dominique Wilkins	Atla	1.637
13.	Bill Laimbeer	Detr	1.631
14.	Robert Parish	Bost	1.590
15.	Moses Malone	Atla	1.588
16.	Clyde Drexler	Port	1.587
17.	Lafayette Lever	Denv	1.586
18.	Brad Daugherty	Clev	1.579
19.	Isiah Thomas	Detr	1.578
20.	Larry Nance	Clev	1.558

1988-89 POSITION RATINGS

POWER FORWARDS

OR	PLAYER	TEAM	PR
1.	Charles Barkley	Phil	32.68
2.	Karl Malone	Utah	29.52
3.	Kevin McHale	Bost	23.68
4.	Larry Nance	Clev	22.66
5.	Otis Thorpe	Hous	20.62
6.	Ken Norman	LA.C	20.34
7.	A.C. Green	LA.L	18.61
8.	Sam Perkins	Dall	18.51
9.	Charles Oakley	N.Y.	18.44
10.	Wayman Tisdale	Sacr	18.43
11.	LaSalle Thompson	Indi	17.95
12.	Kurt Rambis	Char	17.80
13.	Horace Grant	Chic	17.52
14.	Buck Williams	N.J.	16.92
15.	Michael Cage	Seat	16.90
16.	Armon Gilliam	Phoe	15.74
17.	Roy Hinson	N.J.	15.33
18.	Larry Krystkowiak	Milw	15.29
19.	Greg Anderson	S.A.	15.11
20.	John Williams	Clev	14.87

POINT GUARDS

OR	PLAYER	TEAM	PR
1.	Earvin Johnson	LA.L	33.31
2.	John Stockton	Utah	27.40
3.	Kevin Johnson	Phoe	27.06
4.	Terry Porter	Port	22.42
5.	Mark Price	Clev	22.33
6.	Mark Jackson	N.Y.	20.49
7.	Michael Adams	Denv	19.60
8.	Derek Harper	Dall	19.33
9.	Isiah Thomas	Detr	19.09
10.	Glenn Rivers	Atla	18.70
11.	Eric Floyd	Hous	18.46
12.	Vern Fleming	Indi	17.49
13.	Kenny Smith	Sacr	17.04
14.	Lester Conner	N.J.	16.87
15.	Winston Garland	G.St	16.76
16.	Nate McMillan	Seat	16.63
17.	Paul Pressey	Milw	16.39
18.	Maurice Cheeks	Phil	16.38
19.	Darrell Walker	Wash	16.13
20.	Jay Humphries	Milw	14.07

CENTERS

OR	PLAYER	TEAM	PR
1.	Akeem Olajuwon	Hous	31.02
2.	Pat Ewing	N.Y.	27.46
3.	Robert Parish	Bost	26.10
4.	Moses Malone	Atla	23.84
5.	Brad Daugherty	Clev	22.37
6.	Benoit Benjamin	LA.C	21.11
7.	Mike Gminski	Phil	20.55
8.	Bill Laimbeer	Detr	19.70
9.	Jack Sikma	Milw	18.47
10.	James Donaldson	Dall	17.70
11.	Kevin Duckworth	Port	16.72
12.	Mark Eaton	Utah	16.59
13.	Joe Barry Carroll	N.J.	15.59
14.	Danny Schayes	Denv	15.49
15.	Frank Brickowski	S.A.	15.42
16.	Rik Smits	Indi	14.06
17.	Herb Williams	Dall	13.78
18.	Mark West	Phoe	13.17
19.	Bill Cartwright	Chic	12.49
20.	Alton Lister	Seat	12.34

SMALL FORWARDS

OR	PLAYER	TEAM	PR
1.	Chris Mullin	G.St	26.01
2.	Tom Chambers	Phoe	24.11
3.	Dominique Wilkins	Atla	22.84
4.	James Worthy	LA.L	21.80
5.	Terry Cummings	Milw	21.54
6.	Alex English	Denv	21.38
7.	Jerome Kersey	Port	20.24
8.	Chuck Person	Indi	19.00
9.	Willie Anderson	S.A.	18.99
10.	John S. Williams	Wash	18.74
11.	Reggie Lewis	Bost	17.64
12.	Kelly Tripucka	Char	17.61
13.	Bernard King	Wash	17.35
14.	Derrick McKey	Seat	17.29
15.	Thurl Bailey	Utah	16.79
16.	Charles Smith	LA.C	16.66
17.	Rodney McCray	Sacr	16.65
18.	Scottie Pippen	Chic	16.38
19.	Dennis Rodman	Detr	16.32
20.	Xavier McDaniel	Seat	16.29

OFF GUARDS

OR	PLAYER	TEAM	PR
1.	Michael Jordan	Chic	36.99
2.	Clyde Drexler	Port	28.87
3.	Fat Lever	Denv	27.48
4.	Dale Ellis	Seat	21.13
5.	Ron Harper	Clev	21.09
6.	Alvin Robertson	S.A.	20.52
7.	Mitch Richmond	G.St	19.44
8.	Eddie Johnson	Phoe	17.93
9.	Byron Scott	LA.L	17.89
10.	Danny Ainge	Sacr	17.64
11.	Jeff Hornacek	Phoe	17.06
12.	Rolando Blackman	Dall	16.74
13.	Joe Dumars	Detr	16.59
14.	Reggie Miller	Indi	16.12
15.	Jeff Malone	Wash	15.26
16.	Reggie Theus	Atla	15.06
17.	Ricky Pierce	Milw	14.95
18.	Harold Pressley	Sacr	14.60
19.	Hersey Hawkins	Phil	13.68
20.	Dennis Johnson	Bost	12.87

ROOKIES

OR	PLAYER	TEAM	PR
1.	Mitch Richmond	G.St	19.44
2.	Willie Anderson	S.A.	18.99
3.	Charles Smith	LA.C	16.66
4.	Grant Long	Miam	14.41
5.	Rik Smits	Indi	14.06
6.	Gary Grant	LA.C	13.70
7.	Hersey Hawkins	Phil	13.68
8.	Chris Morris	N.J.	13.14
9.	Brian Shaw	Bost	12.88
10.	Kevin Edwards	Miam	11.91
11.	Rex Chapman	Char	11.03
12.	Ron Seikaly	Miam	10.38
13.	Vernon Maxwell	S.A.	10.30
14.	Dan Majerle	Phoe	9.91
15.	Ricky Berry	Sacr	9.58
16.	Tom Garrick	LA.C	8.68
17.	Vinnie Del Negro	Sacr	8.36
18.	Ledell Eackles	Wash	8.13
19.	Derrick Chevious	Hous	7.36

1988-89 PERFORMANCE CATEGORIES

SCORING

OR	PLAYER	TEAM	SCR
1.	Michael Jordan	Chic	32.51
2.	Karl Malone	Utah	29.08
3.	Dale Ellis	Seat	27.48
4.	Clyde Drexler	Port	27.22
5.	Chris Mullin	G.St	26.54
6.	Alex English	Denv	26.52
7.	Dominique Wilkins	Atla	26.24
8.	Charles Barkley	Phil	25.78
9.	Tom Chambers	Phoe	25.74
10.	Akeem Olajuwon	Hous	24.80
11.	Terry Cummings	Milw	22.86
12.	Pat Ewing	N.Y.	22.69
13.	Kelly Tripucka	Char	22.62
14.	Kevin McHale	Bost	22.54
15.	Earvin Johnson	L.A.L	22.47
16.	Mitch Richmond	G.St	22.04
17.	Jeff Malone	Wash	21.72
18.	Chuck Person	Indi	21.60
19.	Eddie Johnson	Phoe	21.49
20.	Bernard King	Wash	20.67

REBOUNDS

OR	PLAYER	TEAM	REB
1.	Akeem Olajuwon	Hous	17.54
2.	Robert Parish	Bost	16.83
3.	Dennis Rodman	Detr	16.78
4.	Larry Smith	G.St	16.50
5.	Wayne Cooper	Denv	15.94
6.	Moses Malone	Atla	15.94
7.	Charles Oakley	Chic	15.87
8.	James Donaldson	Dall	15.67
9.	Charles Barkley	Phil	15.33
10.	Kurt Rambis	Char	15.11
11.	LaSalle Thompson	Indi	14.80
12.	Alton Lister	Seat	14.49
13.	Michael Cage	L.A.C	14.48
14.	Jon Koncak	Atla	14.20
15.	A.C. Green	L.A.L	14.13
16.	Bill Laimbeer	Detr	14.11
17.	Mark Eaton	Utah	13.89
18.	Buck Williams	N.J.	13.66
19.	Greg Anderson	S.A.	13.51
20.	Mike Gminski	Phil	13.48

BLOCKS

OR	PLAYER	TEAM	BLK
1.	Manute Bol	G.St	9.36
2.	Wayne Cooper	Denv	5.43
3.	Mark Eaton	Utah	5.19
4.	Alton Lister	Seat	4.78
5.	Pat Ewing	N.Y.	4.66
6.	Akeem Olajuwon	Hous	4.48
7.	Mark West	Phoe	4.45
8.	Benoit Benjamin	L.A.C	4.10
9.	Larry Nance	Clev	3.91
10.	Rik Smits	Indi	3.55
11.	John Koncak	Atla	3.07
12.	John Williams	Clev	3.03
13.	Herb Williams	Dall	2.60
14.	K. Abdul-Jabbar	L.A.L	2.41
15.	John Salley	Detr	2.37
16.	Ron Seikaly	Miam	2.35
17.	Roy Hinson	N.J.	2.28
18.	James Donaldson	Dall	2.23
19.	Billy Thompson	Miam	2.22
20.	Orlando Woolridge	N.J.	2.09

SHOOTING

OR	PLAYER	TEAM	SHT
1.	Mark Price	Clev	1.157
2.	Dennis Rodman	Detr	1.119
3.	Craig Hodges	Chic	1.119
4.	Earvin Johnson	L.A.L	1.118
5.	Charles Barkley	Phil	1.115
6.	John Stockton	Utah	1.113
7.	James Donaldson	Dall	1.112
8.	Trent Tucker	N.Y.	1.106
9.	Michael Jordan	Chic	1.104
10.	Mark West	Phoe	1.098
11.	Pat Ewing	N.Y.	1.096
12.	Dale Ellis	Seat	1.095
13.	Kevin McHale	Bost	1.091
14.	Reggie Miller	Indi	1.090
15.	Robert Parish	Bost	1.089
16.	James Worthy	L.A.L	1.086
17.	Dave Hoppen	Char	1.085
18.	Larry Nance	Clev	1.075
19.	Chris Mullin	G.St	1.072
20.	Tyrone Corbin	Phoe	1.071

ASSISTS

OR	PLAYER	TEAM	AST
1.	Tyrone Bogues	Char	16.96
2.	John Stockton	Utah	16.92
3.	Earvin Johnson	L.A.L	16.43
4.	Kevin Johnson	Phoe	14.96
5.	Nate McMillan	Seat	14.27
6.	Gary Grant	L.A.C	12.62
7.	Eric Floyd	Hous	12.21
8.	Mark Jackson	N.Y.	12.00
9.	Michael Holton	Char	12.00
10.	Scott Skiles	Indi	11.92
11.	Terry Porter	Port	11.91
12.	Maurice Cheeks	Phil	11.57
13.	Lester Conner	N.J.	11.45
14.	John Bagley	N.J.	11.43
15.	Mark Price	Clev	11.10
16.	Isiah Thomas	Detr	10.88
17.	Glenn Rivers	Atla	10.24
18.	Brian Shaw	Bost	9.83
19.	Dennis Johnson	Bost	9.81
20.	Lafayette Lever	Denv	9.77

STEALS

OR	PLAYER	TEAM	STL
1.	Alvin Robertson	S.A.	4.13
2.	John Stockton	Utah	3.98
3.	Gary Grant	L.A.C	3.59
4.	Glenn Rivers	Atla	3.53
5.	Michael Jordan	Chic	3.45
6.	Lester Conner	N.J.	3.43
7.	Lafayette Lever	Denv	3.41
8.	Akeem Olajuwon	Hous	3.38
9.	Clyde Drexler	Port	3.34
10.	Sedale Threatt	Seat	3.27
11.	Nate McMillan	Seat	3.20
12.	Winston Garland	G.St	3.16
13.	Ron Harper	Clev	3.11
14.	Jay Humphries	Milw	3.07
15.	Tyrone Bogues	Char	3.04
16.	Reggie Williams	L.A.C	2.98
17.	Darrell Walker	Wash	2.90
18.	Michael Adams	Denv	2.86
19.	Kevin Edwards	Miam	2.84
20.	Craig Ehlo	Clev	2.83

1987-88
NBA STATISTICS

PRODUCTION RATINGS

OR	PLAYER	TEAM	PR
1.	Michael Jordan	Chic	35.05
2.	Larry Bird	Bost	34.01
3.	Charles Barkley	Phil	32.51
4.	Akeem Olajuwon	Hous	28.10
5.	Clyde Drexler	Port	27.94
6.	Earvin Johnson	LA.L	27.71
7.	Karl Malone	Utah	27.63
8.	John Stockton	Utah	26.54
9.	Kevin McHale	Bost	26.28
10.	Lafayette Lever	Denv	25.94
11.	Larry Nance	Clev	24.51
12.	Dominique Wilkins	Atla	24.27
13.	Otis Thorpe	Sacr	23.71
14.	Buck Williams	N.J.	22.96
15.	Alvin Robertson	S.A.	22.94
16.	Terry Porter	Port	22.87
17.	Pat Ewing	N.Y.	22.61
18.	Moses Malone	Wash	22.53
19.	Jerome Kersey	Port	21.87
20.	Jack Sikma	Milw	21.77
21.	Byron Scott	LA.L	21.73
22.	Alex English	Denv	21.70
23.	Michael Cage	LA.C	21.24
24.	Mark Aguirre	Dall	21.13
25.	Brad Daugherty	Clev	20.70
26.	Mark Jackson	N.Y.	20.68
27.	Mike Gminski	Phil	20.56
28.	Dale Ellis	Seat	20.55
29.	Charles Oakley	Chic	20.54
30.	Glenn Rivers	Atla	20.36
31.	Roy Tarpley	Dall	20.23
32.	Chris Mullin	G.St	20.17
33.	Bill Laimbeer	Detr	20.17
34.	James Worthy	LA.L	20.09
35.	Isiah Thomas	Detr	19.86
36.	Xavier McDaniel	Seat	19.78
37.	Maurice Cheeks	Phil	19.22
38.	Vern Fleming	Indi	19.19
39.	Derek Harper	Dall	19.17
40.	Terry Cummings	Milw	19.16
41.	Robert Parish	Bost	19.15
42.	Thurl Bailey	Utah	18.94
43.	Frank Brickowski	S.A.	18.71
44.	Paul Pressey	Milw	18.67
45.	Danny Shcayes	Denv	18.63
46.	Reggie Theus	Sacr	18.44
47.	Johnny Dawkins	S.A.	18.37
48.	Danny Ainge	Bost	18.26
49.	Steve Stipanovich	Indi	18.12
50.	Benoit Benjamin	LA.C	17.97
51.	Ralph Sampson	G.St	17.94
52.	Tom Chambers	Seat	17.73
53.	Adrian Dantley	Detr	17.29
54.	Rodney McCray	Hous	17.27
55.	Mark Price	Clev	16.92
56.	Nate McMillan	Seat	16.71
57.	Sam Perkins	Dall	16.71
58.	Chuck Person	Indi	16.65
59.	Rod Higgins	G.St	16.65
60.	Cliff Robinson	Phil	16.61
61.	Roy Hinson	N.J.	16.60
62.	Eric Floyd	Hous	16.58
63.	Michael Adams	Denv	16.57
64.	Rolando Blackman	Dall	16.48
65.	A.C. Green	LA.L	16.44
66.	Walter Berry	S.A.	16.23
67.	Ron Harper	Clev	16.23
68.	Dennis Johnson	Bost	16.13
69.	K. Abdul-Jabbar	LA.L	15.90
70.	Dennis Rodman	Detr	15.84
71.	Wayman Tisdale	Indi	15.82
72.	Rick Mahorn	Detr	15.67
73.	Kevin Duckworth	Port	15.42
74.	Walter Davis	Phoe	15.41
75.	Armon Gilliam	Phoe	15.36
76.	Jeff Malone	Wash	15.24
77.	Kenny Smith	Sacr	15.23
78.	James Donaldson	Dall	14.98
79.	Eddie Johnson	Phoe	14.82
80.	John Williams	Clev	14.79
81.	Jeff Hornacek	Phoe	14.78
82.	Winston Garland	G.St	14.76
83.	Randy Breuer	Milw	14.47
84.	John S. Williams	Wash	14.37
85.	Tim McMormick	N.J.	14.29
86.	Mark Eaton	Utah	14.27
87.	Bernard King	Wash	13.96
88.	Gerald Wilkins	N.Y.	13.86
89.	Mike Woodson	LA.C	13.80
90.	Cliff Levingston	Atla	13.78
91.	Dave Corzine	Chic	13.73
92.	Joe Dumars	Detr	13.59
93.	Jay Humphries	Milw	13.47
94.	John Bagley	N.J.	13.43
95.	Blair Rasmussen	Denv	13.42
96.	Kevin Willis	Atla	13.33
97.	Greg Anderson	S.A.	13.11
98.	J.B. Carroll	Hous	12.92
99.	Jay Vincent	Denv	12.92
100.	Joe Kleine	Sacr	12.88

POSITION DOMINANCE

OR	PLAYER	TEAM	PD
1.	Michael Jordan	Chic	1.426
2.	Larry Bird	Bost	1.411
3.	Charles Barkley	Phil	1.321
4.	Akeem Olajuwon	Hous	1.297
5.	Earvin Johnson	LA.L	1.221
6.	John Stockton	Utah	1.170
7.	Clyde Drexler	Port	1.137
8.	Karl Malone	Utah	1.123
9.	Kevin McHale	Bost	1.068
10.	Lafayette Lever	Denv	1.055
11.	Pat Ewing	N.Y.	1.043
12.	Moses Malone	Wash	1.040
13.	Larry Nance	Clev	1.016
14.	Terry Porter	Port	1.008
15.	Dominique Wilkins	Atla	1.006
16.	Otis Thorpe	Sacr	.963
17.	Brad Daugherty	Clev	.955
18.	Mike Gminski	Phil	.948
19.	Alvin Robertson	S.A.	.933
20.	Buck Williams	N.J.	.933

MOST VALUABLE PLAYER

OR	PLAYER	TEAM	MVP
1.	Larry Bird	Bost	2.043
2.	Michael Jordan	Chic	1.980
3.	Earvin Johnson	LA.L	1.916
4.	Akeem Olajuwon	Hous	1.818
5.	Charles Barkley	Phil	1.760
6.	John Stockton	Utah	1.735
7.	Clyde Drexler	Port	1.733
8.	Kevin McHale	Bost	1.700
9.	Karl Malone	Utah	1.688
10.	Lafayette Lever	Denv	1.655
11.	Terry Porter	Port	1.604
12.	Dominique Wilkins	Atla	1.583
13.	Byron Scott	LA.L	1.579
14.	Bill Laimbeer	Detr	1.566
15.	James Worthy	LA.L	1.528
16.	Robert Parish	Bost	1.516
17.	Isiah Thomas	Detr	1.511
18.	Larry Nance	Clev	1.511
19.	Jerome Kersey	Port	1.503
20.	Mark Aguirre	Dall	1.500

1987-88 POSITION RATINGS

POWER FORWARDS

OR	PLAYER	TEAM	PR
1.	Charles Barkley	Phil	32.51
2.	Karl Malone	Utah	27.63
3.	Kevin McHale	Bost	26.28
4.	Otis Thorpe	Sacr	23.71
5.	Buck Williams	N.J.	22.96
6.	Jack Sikma	Milw	21.77
7.	Michael Cage	LA.C	21.24
8.	Charles Oakley	Chic	20.54
9.	Roy Tarpley	Dall	20.23
10.	Frank Brickowski	S.A.	18.71
11.	Tom Chambers	Seat	17.73
12.	Sam Perkins	Dall	16.71
13.	Roy Hinson	N.J.	16.60
14.	A.C. Green	LA.L	16.44
15.	Wayman Tisdale	Indi	15.82
16.	Rick Mahorn	Detr	15.67
17.	Armon Gilliam	Phoe	15.36
18.	John Williams	Clev	14.79
19.	Cliff Levingston	Atla	13.78
20.	Blair Rasmussen	Denv	13.42

POINT GUARDS

OR	PLAYER	TEAM	PR
1.	Earvin Johnson	LA.L	27.71
2.	John Stockton	Utah	26.54
3.	Terry Porter	Port	22.87
4.	Mark Jackson	N.Y.	20.68
5.	Glenn Rivers	Atla	20.36
6.	Isiah Thomas	Detr	19.86
7.	Maurice Cheeks	Phil	19.22
8.	Vern Fleming	Indi	19.19
9.	Derek Harper	Dall	19.17
10.	Paul Pressey	Milw	18.67
11.	Johnny Dawkins	S.A.	18.37
12.	Mark Price	Clev	16.92
13.	Nate McMillan	Seat	16.71
14.	Eric Floyd	Hous	16.58
15.	Michael Adams	Denv	16.57
16.	Dennis Johnson	Bost	16.13
17.	Kenny Smith	Sacr	15.23
18.	Jeff Hornacek	Phoe	14.78
19.	Winston Garland	G.St	14.76
20.	Jay Humphries	Milw	13.47

CENTERS

OR	PLAYER	TEAM	PR
1.	Akeem Olajuwon	Hous	28.10
2.	Pat Ewing	N.Y.	22.61
3.	Moses Malone	Wash	22.53
4.	Brad Daugherty	Clev	20.70
5.	Mike Gminski	Phil	20.56
6.	Bill Laimbeer	Detr	20.17
7.	Robert Parish	Bost	19.15
8.	Danny Schayes	Denv	18.63
9.	Steve Stipanovich	Indi	18.13
10.	Benoit Benjamin	LA.C	17.97
11.	Ralph Sampson	G.St	17.94
12.	K. Abdul-Jabbar	LA.L	15.90
13.	Kevin Duckworth	Port	15.42
14.	James Donaldson	Dall	14.98
15.	Randy Breuer	Milw	14.47
16.	Mike McCormick	N.J.	14.29
17.	Mark Eaton	Utah	14.27
18.	Dave Corzine	Chic	13.72
19.	Greg Anderson	S.A.	13.11
20.	Joe Kleine	Sacr	12.88

SMALL FORWARDS

OR	PLAYER	TEAM	PR
1.	Larry Bird	Bost	34.01
2.	Larry Nance	Clev	24.51
3.	Dominique Wilkins	Atla	24.27
4.	Jerome Kersey	Port	21.87
5.	Alex English	Denv	21.70
6.	Mark Aguirre	Dall	21.13
7.	James Worthy	LA.L	20.09
8.	Xavier McDaniel	Seat	19.78
9.	Terry Cummings	Milw	19.16
10.	Thurl Bailey	Utah	18.94
11.	Adrian Dantley	Detr	17.29
12.	Rodney McCray	Hous	17.27
13.	Rod Higgins	G.St	16.65
14.	Chuck Person	Indi	16.65
15.	Cliff Robinson	Phil	16.61
16.	Walter Berry	S.A.	16.23
17.	Dennis Rodman	Detr	15.84
18.	Eddie Johnson	Phoe	14.82
19.	John S. Williams	Wash	14.37
20.	Bernard King	Wash	13.96

OFF GUARDS

OR	PLAYER	TEAM	PR
1.	Michael Jordan	Chic	35.05
2.	Clyde Drexler	Port	27.94
3.	Fat Lever	Denv	25.94
4.	Alvin Robertson	S.A.	22.94
5.	Byron Scott	LA.L	21.73
6.	Dale Ellis	Seat	20.55
7.	Chris Mullin	G.St	20.17
8.	Reggie Theus	Sacr	18.44
9.	Danny Ainge	Bost	18.26
10.	Rolando Blackman	Dall	16.48
11.	Ron Harper	Clev	16.23
12.	Walter Davis	Phoe	15.41
13.	Jeff Malone	Wash	15.24
14.	Gerald Wilkins	N.Y.	13.86
15.	Mike Woodson	LA.C	13.80
16.	Joe Dumars	Detr	13.59
17.	Sidney Moncrief	Milw	12.45
18.	Michael Cooper	LA.L	11.98
19.	Purvis Short	Hous	11.74
20.	Harold Pressley	Sacr	11.52

ROOKIES

OR	PLAYER	TEAM	PR
1.	Mark Jackson	N.Y.	20.68
2.	Armon Gilliam	Phoe	15.36
3.	Kenny Smith	Sacr	15.23
4.	Winston Garland	G.St	14.76
5.	Greg Anderson	S.A.	13.11
6.	Kevin Johnson	Phoe	12.33
7.	Horace Grant	Chic	10.56
8.	Derrick McKey	Seat	10.23
9.	Reggie Miller	Indi	9.23
10.	Scottie Pippen	Chic	9.22
11.	Larry Krystkowiak	Milw	8.94
12.	Tyrone Bogues	Wash	8.68
13.	Tellis Frank	G.St	8.49
14.	Ken Norman	LA.C	8.23
15.	Dennis Hopson	N.J.	7.18

1987-88 PERFORMANCE CATEGORIES

SCORING

OR	PLAYER	TEAM	SCR
1.	Michael Jordan	Chic	34.98
2.	Dominique Wilkins	Atla	30.73
3.	Larry Bird	Bost	29.93
4.	Charles Barkley	Phil	28.30
5.	Karl Malone	Utah	27.66
6.	Clyde Drexler	Port	26.98
7.	Dale Ellis	Seat	25.84
8.	Mark Aguirre	Dall	25.09
9.	Alex English	Denv	25.00
10.	Akeem Olajuwon	Hous	22.85
11.	Kevin McHale	Bost	22.59
12.	Byron Scott	L.A.L	21.65
13.	Reggie Theus	Sacr	21.56
14.	Xavier McDaniel	Seat	21.40
15.	Terry Cummings	Milw	21.33
16.	Otis Thorpe	Sacr	20.78
17.	Jeff Malone	Wash	20.51
18.	Tom Chambers	Seat	20.41
19.	Moses Malone	Wash	20.34
20.	Chris Mullin	G.St	20.22

REBOUNDS

OR	PLAYER	TEAM	REB
1.	Roy Tarpley	Dall	19.95
2.	Charles Oakley	Chic	18.17
3.	Michael Cage	L.A.C	16.93
4.	Alton Lister	Seat	16.61
5.	Akeem Olajuwon	Hous	16.29
6.	Dennis Rodman	Detr	15.99
7.	Moses Malone	Wash	15.76
8.	Buck Williams	N.J.	15.18
9.	Sidney Green	N.Y.	15.04
10.	Karl Malone	Utah	14.80
11.	Danny Schayes	Denv	14.67
12.	Charles Barkley	Phil	14.40
13.	James Donaldson	Dall	14.36
14.	Joe Kleine	Sacr	13.90
15.	Rick Mahorn	Detr	13.82
16.	Bill Laimbeer	Detr	13.79
17.	Ralph Sampson	G.St	13.33
18.	Mike Gminski	Phil	13.20
19.	Otis Thorpe	Sacr	13.08
20.	Robert Parish	Bost	13.04

BLOCKS

OR	PLAYER	TEAM	BLK
1.	Mark Eaton	Utah	5.34
2.	Benoit Benjamin	L.A.C	4.97
3.	Pat Ewing	N.Y.	4.62
4.	Charles Jones	Wash	4.13
5.	Alton Lister	Seat	3.71
6.	Akeem Olajuwon	Hous	3.64
7.	Wayne Rollins	Atla	3.59
8.	Herb Williams	Indi	3.56
9.	Mark West	Phoe	3.36
10.	John Williams	Clev	3.30
11.	John Salley	Detr	3.28
12.	Larry Nance	Clev	3.20
13.	Greg Anderson	S.A.	2.95
14.	Caldwell Jones	Port	2.67
15.	Roy Hinson	N.J.	2.59
16.	Joe Barry Carroll	Hous	2.54
17.	Ralph Sampson	G.St	2.54
18.	Randy Breuer	Milw	2.27
19.	Blair Rasmussen	Denv	2.19
20.	Thurl Bailey	Utah	2.14

SHOOTING

OR	PLAYER	TEAM	SHT
1.	John Stockton	Utah	1.161
2.	Kevin McHale	Bost	1.161
3.	Danny Ainge	Bost	1.138
4.	Larry Bird	Bost	1.136
5.	Robert Parish	Bost	1.130
6.	Charles Barkley	Phil	1.120
7.	Byron Scott	L.A.L	1.108
8.	Rick Mahorn	Detr	1.106
9.	Mark Price	Clev	1.103
10.	Danny Schayes	Denv	1.095
11.	Rod Higgins	G.St	1.094
12.	Craig Hodges	Phoe	1.092
13.	James Donaldson	Dall	1.090
14.	Cliff Levingston	Atla	1.089
15.	Michael Jordan	Chic	1.088
16.	Brad Davis	Dall	1.085
17.	Terry Porter	Port	1.082
18.	Chris Mullin	G.St	1.081
19.	Bill Cartwright	N.Y.	1.077
20.	Adrian Dantley	Detr	1.076

ASSISTS

OR	PLAYER	TEAM	AST
1.	John Stockton	Utah	19.05
2.	Earvin Johnson	L.A.L	15.62
3.	Glenn Rivers	Atla	14.33
4.	Nate McMillan	Seat	13.74
5.	Terry Porter	Port	13.34
6.	Mark Jackson	N.Y.	12.82
7.	Sam Vincent	Chic	12.18
8.	Tyrone Bogues	Wash	11.91
9.	Jeff Hornacek	Phoe	11.56
10.	Darnell Valentine	L.A.C	11.21
11.	Isiah Thomas	Detr	11.12
12.	Kevin Johnson	Phoe	10.94
13.	Dennis Johnson	Bost	10.75
14.	John Lucas	Milw	10.65
15.	Maurice Cheeks	Phil	10.62
16.	Johnny Dawkins	S.A.	10.57
17.	Jay Humphries	Milw	10.48
18.	Eric Floyd	Hous	10.39
19.	Paul Pressey	Milw	10.11
20.	Derek Harper	Dall	10.04

STEALS

OR	PLAYER	TEAM	STL
1.	John Stockton	Utah	4.09
2.	Alvin Robertson	S.A.	3.92
3.	Dudley Bradley	N.J.	3.81
4.	Michael Jordan	Chic	3.75
5.	Tyrone Bogues	Wash	3.74
6.	Darnell Valentine	L.A.C	3.58
7.	Lafayette Lever	Denv	3.50
8.	Nate McMillan	Seat	3.31
9.	Ron Harper	Clev	3.20
10.	Clyde Drexler	Port	3.18
11.	Dwayne Washington	N.J.	3.17
12.	Mark Jackson	N.Y.	3.03
13.	Dell Curry	Clev	3.01
14.	Michael Adams	Denv	2.90
15.	Otis Smith	G.St	2.82
16.	Maurice Cheeks	Phil	2.79
17.	Allen Leavell	Hous	2.77
18.	Akeem Olajuwon	Hous	2.75
19.	Glenn Rivers	Atla	2.69
20.	Chris Mullin	G.St	2.67

1986-87
NBA STATISTICS

PRODUCTION RATINGS

OR	PLAYER	TEAM	PR
1.	Larry Bird	Bost	34.28
2.	Charles Barkley	Phil	33.46
3.	Michael Jordan	Chic	31.91
4.	Earvin Johnson	L.A.L	31.79
5.	Kevin McHale	Bost	30.92
6.	Akeem Olajuwon	Hous	28.99
7.	Larry Nance	Phoe	27.25
8.	Lafayette Lever	Denv	26.93
9.	Clyde Drexler	Port	25.29
10.	Moses Malone	Wash	24.86
11.	Dominique Wilkins	Atla	24.15
12.	Alex English	Denv	23.90
13.	Robert Parish	Bost	23.66
14.	Buck Williams	N.J.	23.66
15.	Sleepy Floyd	G.St	23.65
16.	Otis Thorpe	Sacr	22.82
17.	Bill Laimbeer	Detr	22.65
18.	Terry Cummings	Milw	22.56
19.	Xavier McDaniel	Seat	22.41
20.	Karl Malone	Utah	22.05
21.	Isiah Thomas	Detr	22.04
22.	Michael Cage	L.A.C	21.95
23.	Pat Ewing	N.Y.	21.90
24.	Kiki Vandeweghe	Port	21.85
25.	Dale Ellis	Seat	21.77
26.	Mark Aguirre	Dall	21.29
27.	James Donaldson	Dall	21.05
28.	Reggie Theus	Sacr	20.90
29.	Rodney McCray	Hous	20.70
30.	Charles Oakley	Chic	20.59
31.	Maurice Cheeks	Phil	20.56
32.	Tom Chambers	Seat	20.50
33.	J.B. Carroll	G.St	20.36
34.	Glenn Rivers	Atla	20.33
35.	James Worthy	L.A.L	20.20
36.	Kevin Willis	Atla	19.88
37.	Walter Davis	Phoe	19.85
38.	Derek Harper	Dall	19.77
39.	Chuck Person	Indi	19.63
40.	Orlando Woolridge	N.J.	19.59
41.	Terry Porter	Port	19.52
42.	K. Abdul-Jabbar	L.A.L	19.50
43.	Alvin Robertson	S.A.	19.47
44.	Jack Sikma	Milw	19.37
45.	Steve Stipanovich	Indi	19.22
46.	David Greenwood	S.A.	19.13
47.	Brad Daugherty	Clev	19.10
48.	Bill Cartwright	N.Y.	19.09
49.	Ron Harper	Clev	18.90
50.	Paul Pressey	Milw	18.79
51.	Mike Gminski	N.J.	18.46
52.	John Williams	Clev	18.41
53.	Adrian Dantley	Detr	18.21
54.	Sam Perkins	Dall	18.19
55.	Rolando Blackman	Dall	17.98
56.	Alton Lister	Seat	17.36
57.	Ricky Pierce	Milw	17.25
58.	Larry Smith	G.St	17.25
59.	Steve Johnson	Port	17.18
60.	Danny Ainge	Bost	17.15
61.	Herb Williams	Indi	17.12
62.	Byron Scott	L.A.L	16.54
63.	Jeff Malone	Wash	16.39
64.	Dennis Johnson	Bost	16.37
65.	Julius Erving	Phil	16.30
66.	Gerald Wilkins	N.Y.	16.23
67.	Vern Fleming	Indi	16.17
68.	LaSalle Thompson	Sacr	16.05
69.	A.C. Green	L.A.L	16.03
70.	Benoit Benjamin	L.A.C	15.89
71.	Tim McCormick	Phil	15.80
72.	Jay Humphries	Phoe	15.70
73.	Jerome Kersey	Port	15.70
74.	Eddie A. Johnson	Sacr	15.56
75.	Ed Pinckney	Phoe	15.50
76.	Artis Gilmore	S.A.	15.50
77.	Nate McMillan	Seat	15.35
78.	Mark Eaton	Utah	15.29
79.	Roy Hinson	Phil	15.09
80.	John Stockton	Utah	14.80
81.	Wayman Tisdale	Indi	14.36
82.	Jim Petersen	Hous	14.33
83.	Chris Mullin	G.St	14.10
84.	Vinnie Johnson	Detr	14.05
85.	Walter Berry	S.A.	13.97
86.	Cliff Robinson	Phil	13.96
87.	Derek Smith	Sacr	13.90
88.	Alvan Adams	Phoe	13.74
89.	Darrell Walker	Denv	13.46
90.	Robert Reid	Hous	13.41
91.	Rickey Green	Utah	13.40
92.	Dave Corzine	Chic	13.22
93.	Gerald Henderson	N.Y.	13.18
94.	John Paxson	Chic	13.09
95.	Darnell Valentine	L.A.C	13.06
96.	Michael Cooper	L.A.L	13.04
97.	Bill Hanzlik	Denv	12.96
98.	Cedric Maxwell	Hous	12.91
99.	Thurl Bailey	Utah	12.77
100.	Terry Catledge	Wash	12.76

POSITION DOMINANCE

OR	PLAYER	TEAM	PD
1.	Michael Jordan	Chic	1.416
2.	Larry Bird	Bost	1.403
3.	Earvin Johnson	L.A.L	1.366
4.	Charles Barkley	Phil	1.306
5.	Akeem Olajuwon	Hous	1.261
6.	Kevin McHale	Bost	1.206
7.	Lafayette Lever	Denv	1.157
8.	Clyde Drexler	Port	1.122
9.	Larry Nance	Phoe	1.115
10.	Moses Malone	Wash	1.081
11.	Robert Parish	Bost	1.029
12.	Eric Floyd	G.St	1.016
13.	Dominique Wilkins	Atla	.988
14.	Bill Laimbeer	Detr	.985
15.	Alex English	Denv	.978
16.	Dale Ellis	Seat	.966
17.	Pat Ewing	N.Y.	.952
18.	Isiah Thomas	Detr	.947
19.	Buck Williams	N.J.	.923
20.	James Donaldson	Dall	.915

MOST VALUABLE PLAYER

OR	PLAYER	TEAM	MVP
1.	Earvin Johnson	L.A.L	2.175
2.	Larry Bird	Bost	2.052
3.	Michael Jordan	Chic	1.856
4.	Kevin McHale	Bost	1.855
5.	Charles Barkley	Phil	1.832
6.	Akeem Olajuwon	Hous	1.770
7.	Robert Parish	Bost	1.678
8.	Clyde Drexler	Port	1.675
9.	K. Abdul-Jabbar	L.A.L	1.657
10.	James Worthy	L.A.L	1.636
11.	Bill Laimbeer	Detr	1.631
12.	Dominique Wilkins	Atla	1.621
13.	Isiah Thomas	Detr	1.593
14.	Lafayette Lever	Denv	1.564
15.	Larry Nance	Phoe	1.554
16.	Moses Malone	Wash	1.543
17.	Byron Scott	L.A.L	1.536
18.	James Donaldson	Dall	1.532
19.	Glenn Rivers	Atla	1.506
20.	Eric Floyd	G.St	1.498

1986-87 POSITION RATINGS

POWER FORWARDS

OR	PLAYER	TEAM	PR
1.	Charles Barkley	Phil	33.46
2.	Kevin McHale	Bost	30.92
3.	Buck Williams	N.J.	23.66
4.	Otis Thorpe	Sacr	22.82
5.	Terry Cummings	Milw	22.56
6.	Xavier McDaniel	Seat	22.41
7.	Karl Malone	Utah	22.05
8.	Michael Cage	LA.C	21.95
9.	Charles Oakley	Chic	20.59
10.	Kevin Willis	Atla	19.88
11.	David Greenwood	S.A.	19.13
12.	John Williams	Clev	18.41
13.	Sam Perkins	Dall	18.19
14.	Larry Smith	G.St	17.25
15.	Herb Williams	Indi	17.12
16.	A.C. Green	LA.L	16.03
17.	Ed Pinckney	Phoe	15.50
18.	Roy Hinson	Phil	15.09
19.	Wayman Tisdale	Indi	14.36
20.	Jim Petersen	Hous	14.33

POINT GUARD

OR	PLAYER	TEAM	PR
1.	Earvin Johnson	LA.L	31.79
2.	Lafayette Lever	Denv	26.93
3.	Eric Floyd	G.St	23.65
4.	Isiah Thomas	Detr	22.04
5.	Reggie Theus	Sacr	20.90
6.	Maurice Cheeks	Phil	20.56
7.	Glenn Rivers	Atla	20.33
8.	Derek Harper	Dall	19.77
9.	Terry Porter	Port	19.52
10.	Dennis Johnson	Bost	16.37
11.	Vern Fleming	Indi	16.17
12.	Jay Humphries	Phoe	15.70
13.	Nate McMillan	Seat	15.35
14.	John Stockton	Utah	14.80
15.	Rickey Green	Utah	13.40
16.	Gerald Henderson	N.Y.	13.18
17.	John Paxson	Chic	13.09
18.	Darnell Valentine	LA.C	13.06
19.	John Bagley	Clev	12.38
20.	Ennis Whatley	Wash	11.78

CENTER

OR	PLAYER	TEAM	PR
1.	Akeem Olajuwon	Hous	28.99
2.	Moses Malone	Wash	24.86
3.	Robert Parish	Bost	23.66
4.	Bill Laimbeer	Detr	22.65
5.	Pat Ewing	N.Y.	21.90
6.	James Donaldson	Dall	21.05
7.	J.B. Carroll	G.St	20.36
8.	K. Abdul-Jabbar	LA.L	19.50
9.	Jack Sikma	Milw	19.37
10.	Steve Stipanovich	Indi	19.22
11.	Brad Daugherty	Clev	19.10
12.	Bill Cartwright	N.Y.	19.09
13.	Mike Gminski	N.J.	18.46
14.	Alton Lister	Seat	17.36
15.	Steve Johnson	Port	17.18
16.	LaSalle Thompson	Sacr	16.05
17.	Benoit Benjamin	LA.C	15.89
18.	Tim McCormick	Phil	15.80
19.	Artis Gilmore	S.A.	15.50
20.	Mark Eaton	Utah	15.29

SMALL FORWARDS

OR	PLAYER	TEAM	PR
1.	Larry Bird	Bost	34.28
2.	Larry Nance	Phoe	27.25
3.	D. Wilkins	Atla	24.15
4.	Alex English	Denv	23.90
5.	Kiki Vandeweghe	Port	21.85
6.	Mark Aguirre	Dall	21.29
7.	Rodney McCray	Hous	20.70
8.	Tom Chambers	Seat	20.50
9.	James Worthy	LA.L	20.20
10.	Chuck Person	Indi	19.63
11.	Orlando Woolridge	N.J.	19.59
12.	Paul Pressey	Milw	18.79
13.	Adrian Dantley	Detr	18.21
14.	Jerome Kersey	Port	15.70
15.	Eddie A. Johnson	Sacr	15.56
16.	Bill Hanzlik	Denv	12.96
17.	Gene Banks	Chic	12.65
18.	Phil Hubbard	Clev	12.51
19.	Kenny Walker	N.Y.	11.84
20.	John Williams	Wash	11.42

OFF GUARD

OR	PLAYER	TEAM	PR
1.	Michael Jordan	Chic	31.91
2.	Clyde Drexler	Port	25.29
3.	Dale Ellis	Seat	21.77
4.	Walter Davis	Phoe	19.85
5.	Alvin Robertson	S.A.	19.47
6.	Ron Harper	Clev	18.90
7.	R. Blackman	Dall	17.98
8.	Ricky Pierce	Milw	17.25
9.	Danny Ainge	Bost	17.15
10.	Byron Scott	LA.L	16.54
11.	Jeff Malone	Wash	16.39
12.	Julius Erving	Phil	16.30
13.	Gerald Wilkins	N.Y.	16.23
14.	Chris Mullin	G.St	14.10
15.	Vinnie Johnson	Detr	14.05
16.	Derek Smith	Sacr	13.90
17.	Darrell Walker	Denv	13.46
18.	Robert Reid	Hous	13.41
19.	Michael Cooper	LA.L	13.04
20.	Mike Woodson	LA.C	11.92

ROOKIES

OR	PLAYER	TEAM	PR
1.	Chuck Person	Indi	19.63
2.	Brad Daugherty	Clev	19.10
3.	Ron Harper	Clev	18.90
4.	John Williams	Clev	18.41
5.	Nate McMillan	Seat	15.35
6.	Walter Berry	S.A.	13.97
7.	Kenny Walker	N.Y.	11.84
8.	John Williams	Wash	11.42
9.	Brad Sellers	Chic	10.08
10.	Johnny Dawkins	S.A.	9.58
11.	D. Washington	N.J.	9.19
12.	Jeff Hornacek	Phoe	8.41
13.	David Wingate	Phil	7.53

1986-87 PERFORMANCE CATEGORIES

SCORING

OR	PLAYER	TEAM	SCR
1.	Michael Jordan	Chic	37.09
2.	Dominique Wilkins	Atla	29.04
3.	Alex English	Denv	28.60
4.	Larry Bird	Bost	28.05
5.	Kiki Vandeweghe	Port	26.86
6.	Kevin McHale	Bost	26.08
7.	Mark Aguirre	Dall	25.70
8.	Dale Ellis	Seat	24.89
9.	Moses Malone	Wash	24.11
10.	Earvin Johnson	LA.L	23.86
11.	Walter Davis	Phoe	23.63
12.	Akeem Olajuwon	Hous	23.40
13.	Tom Chambers	Seat	23.28
14.	Xavier McDaniel	Seat	23.05
15.	Charles Barkley	Phil	23.00
16.	Ron Harper	Clev	22.85
17.	Larry Nance	Phoe	22.49
18.	Jeff Malone	Wash	21.98
19.	Clyde Drexler	Port	21.73
20.	Karl Malone	Utah	21.70

REBOUNDS

OR	PLAYER	TEAM	REB
1.	Larry Smith	G.St	18.54
2.	Sidney Green	Detr	17.49
3.	Charles Barkley	Phil	17.41
4.	Charles Oakley	Chic	17.30
5.	Buck Williams	N.J.	16.50
6.	Bill Laimbeer	Detr	16.06
7.	Moses Malone	Wash	15.90
8.	Blair Rasmussen	Denv	15.71
9.	Jack Sikma	Milw	15.56
10.	Kevin Willis	Atla	15.52
11.	James Donaldson	Dall	15.42
12.	LaSalle Thompson	Sacr	15.22
13.	Michael Cage	LA.C	15.15
14.	Akeem Olajuwon	Hous	14.92
15.	Alton Lister	Seat	14.79
16.	Wayne Cooper	Denv	14.54
17.	David Greenwood	S.A.	14.53
18.	Karl Malone	Utah	14.36
19.	Kurt Rambis	LA.L	14.36
20.	Rick Mahorn	Detr	14.08

BLOCKS

OR	PLAYER	TEAM	BLK
1.	Manute Bol	Wash	9.34
2.	Mark Eaton	Utah	6.15
3.	Charles Jones	Wash	4.92
4.	Akeem Olajuwon	Hous	4.42
5.	Benoit Benjamin	LA.C	4.03
6.	Wayne Rollins	Atla	3.81
7.	Alton Lister	Seat	3.78
8.	Pat Ewing	N.Y.	3.20
9.	Wayne Cooper	Denv	3.11
10.	Roy Hinson	Phil	3.10
11.	John Williams	Clev	2.95
12.	LaSalle Thompson	Sacr	2.79
13.	Larry Nance	Phoe	2.77
14.	Kevin McHale	Bost	2.70
15.	Julius Erving	Phil	2.35
16.	Caldwell Jones	Port	2.34
17.	Robert Parish	Bost	2.31
18.	Danny Schayes	Denv	2.28
19.	J.B. Carroll	G.St	2.17
20.	Jon Koncak	Atla	2.17

SHOOTING

OR	PLAYER	TEAM	SHT
1.	Kevin McHale	Bost	1.182
2.	Charles Barkley	Phil	1.137
3.	James Donaldson	Dall	1.137
4.	Larry Bird	Bost	1.134
5.	Ricky Pierce	Milw	1.100
6.	Kiki Vandeweghe	Port	1.099
7.	Danny Ainge	Bost	1.092
8.	Ed Pinckney	Phoe	1.092
9.	Artis Gilmore	S.A.	1.084
10.	K. Abdul-Jabbar	LA.L	1.084
11.	Robert Parish	Bost	1.082
12.	Eric Floyd	G.St	1.082
13.	Rodney McCray	Hous	1.082
14.	Dale Ellis	Seat	1.080
15.	Larry Nance	Phoe	1.080
16.	Earvin Johnson	LA.L	1.076
17.	Adrian Dantley	Detr	1.074
18.	Craig Hodges	Milw	1.073
19.	Rod Higgins	G.St	1.070
20.	Wayne Rollins	Atla	1.065

ASSISTS

OR	PLAYER	TEAM	AST
1	John Stockton	Utah	17.31
2.	Earvin Johnson	LA.L	16.15
3.	Glenn Rivers	Atla	15.25
4.	Nate McMillan	Seat	14.19
5.	Eric Floyd	G.St	13.28
6.	Isiah Thomas	Detr	12.95
7.	Terry Porter	Port	12.65
8.	Rickey Green	Utah	12.42
9.	Darnell Valentine	LA.C	12.20
10.	Jay Humphries	Phoe	11.76
11.	Reggie Theus	Sacr	11.57
12.	Derek Harper	Dall	11.44
13.	Danny Young	Seat	11.43
14.	Brad Davis	Dall	11.32
15.	Jeff Hornacek	Phoe	11.10
16.	Gerald Henderson	N.Y.	11.06
17.	Rory Sparrow	N.Y.	10.63
18.	Dirk Minniefield	Hous	10.44
19.	Ennis Whatley	Wash	10.36
20.	Paul Pressey	Milw	10.29

STEALS

OR	PLAYER	TEAM	STL
1.	Alvin Robertson	S.A.	4.63
2.	John Stockton	Utah	4.57
3.	John Williams	Wash	3.47
4.	Michael Jordan	Chic	3.45
5.	Trent Tucker	N.Y.	3.29
6.	Maurice Cheeks	Phil	3.29
7.	Ron Harper	Clev	3.27
8.	Glenn Rivers	Atla	3.17
9.	Michael Adams	Wash	3.17
10.	Darnell Valentine	LA.C	3.17
11.	Lafayette Lever	Denv	3.16
12.	Clyde Drexler	Port	3.14
13.	Derek Harper	Dall	3.14
14.	Nate McMillan	Seat	3.04
15.	Darrell Walker	Denv	2.85
16.	Terry Porter	Port	2.81
17.	Jerome Kersey	Port	2.80
18.	David Wingate	Phil	2.77
19.	D. Washington	N.J.	2.76
20.	Cliff Robinson	Phil	2.60

1985-86
NBA STATISTICS

PRODUCTION RATINGS

OR	PLAYER	TEAM	PR
1.	Larry Bird	Bost	31.30
2.	Earvin Johnson	LA.L	28.50
3.	Akeem Olajuwon	Hous	28.40
4.	Charles Barkley	Phil	28.26
5.	Adrian Dantley	Utah	25.82
6.	Dominique Wilkins	Atla	25.50
7.	Kevin McHale	Bost	24.75
8.	Isiah Thomas	Detr	24.44
9.	Alex English	Denv	24.36
10.	Larry Nance	Phoe	24.23
11.	K. Abdul-Jabbar	LA.L	24.20
12.	Bill Laimbeer	Detr	23.87
13.	Moses Malone	Phil	23.73
14.	Ralph Sampson	Hous	22.85
15.	Alvin Robertson	S.A.	22.48
16.	Clyde Drexler	Port	22.44
17.	Herb Williams	Indi	21.79
18.	Purvis Short	G.St	21.77
19.	Maurice Cheeks	Phil	21.65
20.	Jack Sikma	Seat	21.54
21.	Eric Floyd	G.St	21.33
22.	Buck Williams	N.J.	21.26
23.	Sidney Moncrief	Milw	21.03
24.	Reggie Theus	Sacr	21.02
25.	James Worthy	LA.L	20.92
26.	Robert Parish	Bost	20.84
27.	Paul Pressey	Milw	20.74
28.	Pat Ewing	N.Y.	20.56
29.	Jor Barry Carroll	G.St	20.43
30.	Artis Gilmore	S.A.	20.31
31.	Marques Johnson	LA.C	20.21
32.	Mark Aguirre	Dall	20.08
33.	Roy Hinson	Clev	20.06
34.	Mike Gminski	N.J.	20.01
35.	Kiki Vandeweghe	Port	19.84
36.	Sam Perkins	Dall	19.67
37.	Terry Cummings	Milw	19.50
38.	Cliff Robinson	Wash	19.46
39.	LaSalle Thompson	Sacr	18.76
40.	Rolando Blackman	Dall	18.52
41.	Orlando Woolridge	Chic	18.36
42.	Lafayette Lever	Denv	18.26
43.	Kelly Tripucka	Detr	18.15
44.	Vern Fleming	Indi	17.99
45.	Walter Davis	Phoe	17.99
46.	World B. Free	Clev	17.81
47.	Calvin Natt	Denv	17.81
48.	Mike Mitchell	S.A.	17.62
49.	Cedric Maxwell	LA.C	17.58
50.	Julius Erving	Phil	17.51
51.	John Lucas	Hous	17.43
52.	Xavier McDaniel	Seat	17.41
53.	Steve Stipanovich	Indi	17.23
54.	Wayne Cooper	Denv	17.12
55.	Tom Chambers	Seat	16.97
56.	Jeff Malone	Wash	16.90
57.	James Donaldson	Dall	16.84
58.	Lewis Lloyd	Hous	16.80
59.	Larry Smith	G.St	16.64
60.	Mel Turpin	Clev	16.50
61.	Dennis Johnson	Bost	16.37
62.	Mark Eaton	Utah	16.31
63.	John Bagley	Clev	16.28
64.	Norm Nixon	LA.C	16.16
65.	Glenn Rivers	Atla	16.11
66.	Karl Malone	Utah	16.11
67.	Benoit Benjamin	LA.C	16.04
68.	Steve Johnson	S.A.	15.97
69.	Rodney McCray	Hous	15.79
70.	Eddie A. Johnson	Sacr	15.76
71.	Derek Harper	Dall	15.68
72.	Mychal Thompson	Port	15.66
73.	Alvan Adams	Phoe	15.42
74.	Sidney Green	Chic	15.24
75.	Kenny Carr	Port	15.18
76.	Dan Roundfield	Wash	15.18
77.	Thurl Bailey	Utah	14.79
78.	Kevin Willis	Atla	14.74
79.	Gerald Henderson	Seat	14.71
80.	Jay Humphries	Phoe	14.62
81.	Wayman Tisdale	Indi	14.60
82.	Charles Oakley	Chic	14.40
83.	Alton Lister	Milw	14.25
84.	John Stockton	Utah	13.99
85.	Danny Ainge	Bost	13.83
86.	Ricky Pierce	Milw	13.63
87.	Bill Walton	Bost	13.38
88.	Michael Cooper	LA.L	13.34
89.	Jay Vincent	Dall	13.34
90.	Dave Corzine	Chic	13.31
91.	David Greenwood	S.A.	13.28
92.	Rory Sparrow	N.Y.	13.23
93.	Wes Matthews	S.A.	13.20
94.	Byron Scott	LA.L	13.12
95.	Mike Woodson	Sacr	13.10
96.	Brad Davis	Dall	13.10
97.	Bill Hanzlik	Denv	13.03
98.	Randy Wittman	Atla	13.02
99.	Vinnie Johnson	Detr	13.00
100.	Otis Birdsong	N.J.	12.96

POSITION DOMINANCE

OR	PLAYER	TEAM	PD
1.	Earvin Johnson	LA.L	1.346
2.	Larry Bird	Bost	1.299
3.	Akeem Olajuwon	Hous	1.248
4.	Alvin Robertson	S.A.	1.178
5.	Clyde Drexler	Port	1.176
6.	Charles Barkley	Phil	1.173
7.	Isiah Thomas	Detr	1.155
8.	Adrian Dantley	Utah	1.144
9.	Dominique Wilkins	Atla	1.130
10.	Sidney Moncrief	Milw	1.102
11.	Reggie Theus	Sacr	1.101
12.	Alex English	Denv	1.080
13.	Larry Nance	Phoe	1.074
14.	K. Abdul-Jabbar	LA.L	1.063
15.	Bill Laimbeer	Detr	1.049
16.	Moses Malone	Phil	1.042
17.	Kevin McHale	Bost	1.027
18.	Maurice Cheeks	Phil	1.023
19.	Eric Floyd	G.St	1.008
20.	Rolando Blackman	Dall	.970

MOST VALUABLE PLAYER

OR	PLAYER	TEAM	MVP
1.	Larry Bird	Bost	2.123
2.	Earvin Johnson	LA.L	2.040
3.	Akeem Olajuwon	Hous	1.882
4.	Kevin McHale	Bost	1.851
5.	Charles Barkley	Phil	1.783
6.	K. Abdul-Jabbar	LA.L	1.757
7.	Robert Parish	Bost	1.739
8.	Sidney Moncrief	Milw	1.731
9.	Dominique Wilkins	Atla	1.699
10.	Isiah Thomas	Detr	1.676
11.	Moses Malone	Phil	1.652
12.	Alex English	Denv	1.634
13.	Maurice Cheeks	Phil	1.633
14.	Clyde Drexler	Port	1.633
15.	Adrian Dantley	Utah	1.623
16.	James Worthy	LA.L	1.621
17.	Dennis Johnson	Bost	1.600
18.	Ralph Sampson	Hous	1.582
19.	Bill Laimbeer	Detr	1.570
20.	Alvin Robertson	S.A.	1.563

1985-86 POSITION RATINGS

POWER FORWARD

OR	PLAYER	TEAM	PR
1.	Charles Barkley	Phil	28.26
2.	Kevin McHale	Bost	24.75
3.	Ralph Sampson	Hous	22.85
4.	Herb Williams	Indi	21.79
5.	Buck Williams	N.J.	21.26
6.	Roy Hinson	Clev	20.06
7.	Sam Perkins	Dall	19.67
8.	Terry Cummings	Milw	19.50
9.	Cliff Robinson	Wash	19.46
10.	Cedric Maxwell	L.A.C	17.58
11.	Tom Chambers	Seat	16.97
12.	Larry Smith	G.St	16.64
13.	Karl Malone	Utah	16.11
14.	Steve Johnson	S.A.	15.97
15.	Mychal Thompson	Port	15.66
16.	Alvan Adams	Phoe	15.42
17.	Sidney Green	Chic	15.24
18.	Kenny Carr	Port	15.18
19.	Dan Roundfield	Wash	15.18
20.	Thurl Bailey	Utah	14.79

POINT GUARD

OR	PLAYER	TEAM	PR
1.	Earvin Johnson	L.A.L	28.50
2.	Isiah Thomas	Detr	24.44
3.	Maurice Cheeks	Phil	21.65
4.	Eric Floyd	G.St	21.33
5.	Lafayette Lever	Denv	18.26
6.	John Lucas	Hous	17.43
7.	Dennis Johnson	Bost	16.37
8.	John Bagley	Clev	16.28
9.	Norm Nixon	L.A.C	16.16
10.	Glenn Rivers	Atla	16.11
11.	Derek Harper	Dall	15.68
12.	Gerald Henderson	Seat	14.71
13.	Jay Humphries	Phoe	14.62
14.	John Stockton	Utah	13.99
15.	Rory Sparrow	N.Y.	13.23
16.	Wes Matthews	S.A.	13.20
17.	Brad Davis	Dall	13.10
18.	Rickey Green	Utah	12.75
19.	Gus Williams	Wash	12.69
20.	Kyle Macy	Chic	11.94

CENTER

OR	PLAYER	TEAM	PR
1.	Akeem Olajuwon	Hous	28.40
2.	K. Abdul-Jabbar	L.A.L	24.20
3.	Bill Laimbeer	Detr	23.87
4.	Moses Malone	Phil	23.73
5.	Jack Sikma	Seat	21.54
6.	Robert Parish	Bost	20.84
7.	Pat Ewing	N.Y.	20.56
8.	Joe Barry Carroll	G.St	20.43
9.	Artis Gilmore	S.A.	20.31
10.	Mike Gminski	N.J.	20.01
11.	LaSalle Thompson	Sacr	18.76
12.	Steve Stipanovich	Indi	17.23
13.	Wayne Cooper	Denv	17.12
14.	James Donaldson	Dall	16.84
15.	Mel Turpin	Clev	16.50
16.	Mark Eaton	Utah	16.31
17.	Benoit Benjamin	L.A.C	16.04
18.	Alton Lister	Milw	14.25
19.	Bill Walton	Bost	13.38
20.	Dave Corzine	Chic	13.31

SMALL FORWARD

OR	PLAYER	TEAM	PR
1.	Larry Bird	Bost	31.30
2.	Adrian Dantley	Utah	25.82
3.	Dominique Wilkins	Atla	25.50
4.	Alex English	Denv	24.36
5.	Larry Nance	Phoe	24.23
6.	Purvis Short	G.St	21.77
7.	James Worthy	L.A.L	20.92
8.	Paul Pressey	Milw	20.74
9.	Marques Johnson	L.A.C	20.21
10.	Mark Aguirre	Dall	20.08
11.	Kiki Vandeweghe	Port	19.84
12.	Orlando Woolridge	Chic	18.36
13.	Kelly Tripucka	Detr	18.15
14.	Calvin Natt	Denv	17.81
15.	Mike Mitchell	S.A.	17.62
16.	Xavier McDaniel	Seat	17.41
17.	Rodney McCray	Hous	15.79
18.	Eddie A. Johnson	Sacr	15.76
19.	Jay Vincent	Dall	13.34
20.	Bill Hanzlik	Denv	13.03

OFF GUARD

OR	PLAYER	TEAM	PR
1.	Alvin Robertson	S.A.	22.48
2.	Clyde Drexler	Port	22.44
3.	Sidney Moncrief	Milw	21.03
4.	Reggie Theus	Sacr	21.02
5.	Rolando Blackman	Dall	18.52
6.	Vern Fleming	Indi	17.99
7.	Walter Davis	Phoe	17.99
8.	World B. Free	Clev	17.81
9.	Julius Erving	Phil	17.51
10.	Jeff Malone	Wash	16.90
11.	Lewis Lloyd	Hous	16.80
12.	Danny Ainge	Bost	13.83
13.	Ricky Pierce	Milw	13.63
14.	Michael Cooper	L.A.L	13.34
15.	Byron Scott	L.A.L	13.12
16.	Mike Woodson	Sacr	13.10
17.	Randy Wittman	Atla	13.02
18.	Vinnie Johnson	Detr	13.00
19.	Otis Birdsong	N.J.	12.96
20.	Jim Paxson	Port	12.63

ROOKIES

OR	PLAYER	TEAM	PR
1.	Pat Ewing	N.Y.	20.56
2.	Xavier McDaniel	Seat	17.41
3.	Karl Malone	Utah	16.11
4.	Benoit Benjamin	L.A.C	16.04
5.	Wayman Tisdale	Indi	14.60
6.	Charles Oakley	Chic	14.40
7.	Manute Bol	Wash	12.05
8.	Chris Mullin	G. St	11.84
9.	Jon Koncak	Atla	10.27
10.	Joe Dumars	Detr	10.23
11.	Ed Pinckney	Phoe	9.43
12.	Gerald Wilkins	N.Y.	8.64

1985-86 PERFORMANCE CATEGORIES

SCORING

OR	PLAYER	TEAM	SCR
1.	Dominique Wilkins	Atla	30.33
2.	Adrian Dantley	Utah	29.83
3.	Alex English	Denv	29.80
4.	Larry Bird	Bost	25.79
5.	Purvis Short	G.St	25.50
6.	Kiki Vandeweghe	Port	24.84
7.	Moses Malone	Phil	23.77
8.	Akeem Olajuwon	Hous	23.49
9.	Mike Mitchell	S.A.	23.43
10.	World B. Free	Clev	23.39
11.	K. Abdul-Jabbar	L.A.L	23.37
12.	Mark Aguirre	Dall	22.57
13.	Jeff Malone	Wash	22.44
14.	Walter Davis	Phoe	21.76
15.	Rolando Blackman	Dall	21.49
16.	Kevin McHale	Bost	21.29
17.	Joe Barry Carroll	G.St	21.23
18.	Isiah Thomas	Detr	20.90
19.	Orlando Woolridge	Chic	20.69
20.	Marques Johnson	L.A.C	20.33

REBOUNDS

OR	PLAYER	TEAM	REB
1.	Charles Oakley	Chic	17.99
2.	Bill Laimbeer	Detr	17.85
3.	Bill Walton	Bost	16.89
4.	Larry Smith	G.St	16.83
5.	Charles Barkley	Phil	16.68
6.	Kurt Rambis	L.A.L	15.78
7.	Alton Lister	Milw	15.68
8.	LaSalle Thompson	Sacr	15.55
9.	Maurice Lucas	L.A.L	15.52
10.	Moses Malone	Phil	15.47
11.	Buck Williams	N.J.	15.42
12.	Akeem Olajuwon	Hous	15.20
13.	Kenny Carr	Port	15.17
14.	Ralph Sampson	Hous	14.73
15.	Kevin Willis	Atla	14.69
16.	Robert Parish	Bost	14.40
17.	James Donaldson	Dall	14.23
18.	Karl Malone	Utah	13.92
19.	Wayne Cooper	Denv	13.86
20.	Benoit Benjamin	L.A.C	13.79

BLOCKS

OR	PLAYER	TEAM	BLK
1.	Manute Bol	Wash	9.12
2.	Mark Eaton	Utah	6.94
3.	Wayne Cooper	Denv	5.16
4.	Benoit Benjamin	L.A.C	4.74
5.	Wayne Rollins	Atla	4.50
6.	Akleem Olajuwon	Hous	4.49
7.	Charles Jones	Wash	3.97
8.	Alton Lister	Milw	3.76
9.	Bill Walton	Bost	3.29
10.	Herb Williams	Indi	3.19
11.	Terry Tyler	Sacr	3.14
12.	Randy Breuer	Milw	3.11
13.	Pat Ewing	N.Y.	2.79
14.	Kevin McHale	Bost	2.68
15.	Larry Nance	Phoe	2.51
16.	James Donaldson	Dall	2.49
17.	Joe Barry Carroll	G.St	2.45
18.	K. Abdul-Jabbar	L.A.L	2.37
19.	Thurl Bailey	Utah	2.32
20.	Kurt Nimphius	L.A.C	2.26

SHOOTING

OR	PLAYER	TEAM	SHT
1.	Jerry Sichting	Bost	1.166
2.	Brad Davis	Dall	1.137
3.	Craig Hodges	Milw	1.133
4.	Steve Johnson	S.A.	1.130
5.	James Worthy	L.A.L	1.129
6.	Kurt Rambis	L.A.L	1.118
7.	Kevin McHale	Bost	1.113
8.	Artis Gilmore	S.A.	1.112
9.	Kiki Vandeweghe	Port	1.105
10.	K. Abdul-Jabbar	L.A.L	1.102
11.	Adrian Dantley	Utah	1.101
12.	James Donaldson	Dall	1.100
13.	Bobby Jones	Phil	1.097
14.	Ricky Pierce	Milw	1.097
15.	Earvin Johnson	L.A.L	1.095
16.	Larry Nance	Phoe	1.092
17.	Maurice Cheeks	Phil	1.090
18.	Mel Turpin	Clev	1.087
19.	Mark Olberding	Sacr	1.086
20.	Mike Gminski	N.J.	1.080

ASSISTS

OR	PLAYER	TEAM	AST
1.	Earvin Johnson	L.A.L	16.89
2.	John Stockton	Utah	15.13
3.	Isiah Thomas	Detr	14.28
4.	John Bagley	Clev	14.27
5.	Glenn Rivers	Atla	13.54
6.	Reggie Theus	Sacr	12.96
7.	Eric Floyd	G.St	12.96
8.	Norm Nixon	L.A.C	12.93
9.	John Lucas	Hous	12.93
10.	Wes Matthews	S.A.	12.33
11.	Brad Davis	Dall	11.37
12.	Clyde Drexler	Port	11.18
13.	Paul Pressey	Milw	11.06
14.	Maurice Cheeks	Phil	11.05
15.	Eddie Johnson Jr.	Clev	10.82
16.	Lafayette Lever	Denv	10.72
17.	Michael Cooper	L.A.L	9.86
18.	Rickey Green	Utah	9.81
19.	Darnell Valentine	L.A.C	9.70
20.	Rory Sparrow	N.Y.	9.67

STEALS

OR	PLAYER	TEAM	STL
1.	Alvin Robertson	S.A.	5.02
2.	John Stockton	Utah	3.89
3.	Darwin Cook	N.J.	3.81
4.	Clyde Drexler	Port	3.67
5.	Glenn Rivers	Atla	3.67
6.	Darrell Walker	N.Y.	3.46
7.	Derek Harper	Dall	3.42
8.	Lafayette Lever	Denv	3.27
9.	T.R. Dunn	Denv	3.10
10.	Maurice Cheeks	Phil	3.04
11.	Paul Pressey	Milw	2.98
12.	Isiah Thomas	Detr	2.94
13.	Steve Colter	Port	2.90
14.	Franklin Edwards	L.A.C	2.87
15.	Darnell Valentine	L.A.C	2.84
16.	Charles Barkley	Phil	2.81
17.	Danny Young	Seat	2.78
18.	Eric Floyd	G.St	2.73
19.	Akeem Olajuwon	Hous	2.61
20.	Bill Hanzlik	Denv	2.59

1984-85
NBA STATISTICS

PRODUCTION RATINGS

OR	PLAYER	TEAM	PR
1.	Larry Bird	Bost	34.39
2.	Michael Jordan	Chic	29.24
3.	Earvin Johnson	LA.L	28.77
4.	Isiah Thomas	Detr	27.85
5.	Moses Malone	Phil	27.30
6.	Bernard King	N.Y.	26.80
7.	K. Abdul-Jabbar	LA.L	25.87
8.	Jack Sikma	Seat	25.60
9.	Akeem Olajuwon	Hous	25.22
10.	Larry Nance	Phoe	25.02
11.	Artis Gilmore	S.A.	24.85
12.	Alex English	Denv	24.79
13.	Calvin Natt	Denv	24.31
14.	Terry Cummings	Milw	24.13
15.	Bill Laimbeer	Detr	24.05
16.	Adrian Dantley	Utah	23.75
17.	M. R. Richardson	N.J.	23.63
18.	Ralph Sampson	Hous	23.39
19.	Kevin McHale	Bost	23.29
20.	Buck Williams	N.J.	22.98
21.	Sidney Moncrief	Milw	22.40
22.	Robert Parish	Bost	22.33
23.	Dominique Wilkins	Atla	22.01
24.	Clark Kellogg	Indi	21.25
25.	Mark Aguirre	Dall	21.21
26.	Purvis Short	G.St	21.12
27.	Orlando Woolridge	Chic	20.74
28.	Clyde Drexler	Port	20.71
29.	Johnny Moore	S.A.	20.71
30.	Paul Pressey	Milw	20.56
31.	Mark Eaton	Utah	20.52
32.	Derek Smith	LA.C	20.20
33.	Tom Chambers	Seat	20.06
34.	Jay Vincent	Dall	19.65
35.	James Worthy	LA.L	19.59
36.	Mychal Thompson	Port	19.54
37.	Eddie A. Johnson	K.C.	19.41
38.	Julius Erving	Phil	19.41
39.	Rodney McCray	Hous	19.12
40.	Herb Williams	Indi	19.08
41.	LaSalle Thompson	K.C.	19.01
42.	Cliff Robinson	Wash	18.43
43.	Charles Barkley	Phil	18.40
44.	Maurice Cheeks	Phil	18.38
45.	Alvan Adams	Phoe	18.34
46.	Sam Bowie	Port	18.32
47.	Gus Williams	Wash	18.20
48.	Reggie Theus	K.C.	18.20
49.	Kiki Vandeweghe	Port	18.19
50.	Lafayette Lever	Denv	18.10
51.	Mike Mitchell	S.A.	18.00
52.	Roy Hinson	Clev	17.80
53.	Dennis Johnson	Bost	17.74
54.	World B.Free	Clev	17.72
55.	Rolando Blackman	Dall	17.60
56.	Norm Nixon	LA.C	17.49
57.	Larry Smith	G.St	17.49
58.	Pat Cummings	N.Y.	17.27
59.	Jim Paxson	Port	17.21
60.	Glenn Rivers	Atla	17.16
61.	Bill Walton	LA.C	16.96
62.	Darrell Griffith	Utah	16.92
63.	George Gervin	S.A.	16.81
64.	Rickey Green	Utah	16.78
65.	Otis Birdsong	N.J.	16.75
66.	Steve Stipanovich	Indi	16.73
67.	Thurl Bailey	Utah	16.44
68.	Mike Gminski	N.J.	16.43
69.	Eddie Johnson Jr.	Atla	16.40
70.	Danny Ainge	Bost	16.35
71.	John Bagley	Clev	16.32
72.	Andrew Toney	Phil	16.24
73.	Maurice Lucas	Phoe	16.16
74.	James Donaldson	LA.C	16.11
75.	Kelly Tripucka	Detr	15.98
76.	Larry Drew	K.C.	15.96
77.	Greg Ballard	G.St	15.83
78.	Eric Floyd	G.St	15.72
79.	Phil Hubbard	Clev	15.47
80.	Marques Johnson	LA.C	15.46
81.	Wayne Cooper	Denv	15.45
82.	Darnell Valentine	Port	15.32
83.	Gerald Henderson	Seat	15.30
84.	Brad Davis	Dall	15.28
85.	Byron Scott	LA.L	15.12
86.	Jerome Whitehead	G.St	15.10
87.	Alton Lister	Milw	15.07
88.	Sam Perkins	Dall	15.05
89.	Jeff Malone	Wash	14.91
90.	James Edwards	Phoe	14.63
91.	Dan Roundfield	Detr	14.55
92.	Otis Thorpe	K.C.	14.49
93.	Kyle Macy	Phoe	14.42
94.	Cliff Levingston	Atla	14.39
95.	Al Wood	Seat	14.25
96.	Mark Olberding	K.C.	14.06
97.	Mickey Johnson	G.St	13.89
98.	Rory Sparrow	N.Y.	13.82
99.	Gene Banks	S.A.	13.82
100.	Mike Woodson	K.C.	13.74

POSITION DOMINANCE

OR	PLAYER	TEAM	PD
1.	Larry Bird	Bost	1.428
2.	Michael Jordan	Chic	1.393
3.	Earvin Johnson	LA.L	1.276
4.	Isiah Thomas	Detr	1.235
5.	Moses Malone	Phil	1.159
6.	Bernard King	N.Y.	1.133
7.	K. Abdul-Jabbar	LA.L	1.098
8.	Jack Sikma	Seat	1.087
9.	Akeem Olajuwon	Hous	1.071
10.	Sidney Moncrief	Milw	1.067
11.	Larry Nance	Phoe	1.058
12.	Artis Gilmore	S.A.	1.055
13.	M.R. Richardson	N.J.	1.048
14.	Alex English	Denv	1.048
15.	Calvin Natt	Denv	1.028
16.	Bill Laimbeer	Detr	1.021
17.	Adrian Dantley	Utah	1.004
18.	Terry Cummings	Milw	1.002
19.	Clyde Drexler	Port	.987
20.	Ralph Sampson	Hous	.971

MOST VALUABLE PLAYER

OR	PLAYER	TEAM	MVP
1.	Larry Bird	Bost	2.131
2.	Earvin Johnson	LA.L	2.046
3.	K. Abdul-Jabbar	LA.L	1.868
4.	Moses Malone	Phil	1.837
5.	Michael Jordan	Chic	1.829
6.	Isiah Thomas	Detr	1.795
7.	Sidney Moncrief	Milw	1.709
8.	Kevin McHale	Bost	1.670
9.	Robert Parish	Bost	1.651
10.	Alex English	Denv	1.646
11.	Terry Cummings	Milw	1.644
12.	Akeem Olajuwon	Hous	1.628
13.	Calvin Natt	Denv	1.626
14.	James Worthy	LA.L	1.598
15.	Bill Laimbeer	Detr	1.581
16.	Artis Gilmore	S.A.	1.540
17.	Ralph Sampson	Hous	1.528
18.	Paul Pressey	Milw	1.511
19.	M.R. Richardson	N.J.	1.510
20.	Maurice Cheeks	Phil	1.493

1984-85 POSITION RATINGS

POWER FORWARD

OR	PLAYER	TEAM	PR
1.	Terry Cummings	Milw	24.13
2.	Ralph Sampson	Hous	23.39
3.	Kevin McHale	Bost	23.29
4.	Buck Williams	N.J.	22.98
5.	Clark Kellogg	Indi	21.25
6.	Tom Chambers	Seat	20.06
7.	Mychal Thompson	Port	19.54
8.	Herb Williams	Indi	19.08
9.	Cliff Robinson	Wash	18.43
10.	Charles Barkley	Phil	18.40
11.	Alvan Adams	Phoe	18.34
12.	Roy Hinson	Clev	17.80
13.	Larry Smith	G.St	17.49
14.	Pat Cummings	N.Y.	17.27
15.	Thurl Bailey	Utah	16.44
16.	Maurice Lucas	Phoe	16.16
17.	Greg Ballard	Wash	15.83
18.	Sam Perkins	Dall	15.05
19.	Dan Roundfield	Detr	14.55
20.	Otis Thorpe	K.C.	14.49

POINT GUARD

OR	PLAYER	TEAM	PR
1.	Earvin Johnson	LA.L	28.77
2.	Isiah Thomas	Detr	27.85
3.	M.R. Richardson	N.J.	23.63
4.	Johnny Moore	S.A.	20.71
5.	Maurice Cheeks	Phil	18.38
6.	Gus Williams	Wash	18.20
7.	Lafayette Lever	Denv	18.10
8.	Dennis Johnson	Bost	17.74
9.	Norm Nixon	LA.C	17.49
10.	Glenn Rivers	Atla	17.16
11.	Rickey Green	Utah	16.78
12.	John Bagley	Clev	16.32
13.	Larry Drew	K.C.	15.96
14.	Eric Floyd	G.St	15.72
15.	Darnell Valentine	Port	15.32
16.	Gerald Henderson	Seat	15.30
17.	Brad Davis	Dall	15.28
18.	Kyle Macy	Phoe	14.42
19.	Rory Sparrow	N.Y.	13.83
20.	Derek Harper	Dall	12.93

CENTER

OR	PLAYER	TEAM	PR
1.	Moses Malone	Phil	27.30
2.	K. Abdul-Jabbar	LA.L	25.87
3.	Jack Sikma	Seat	25.60
4.	Akeem Olajuwon	Hous	25.22
5.	Artis Gilmore	S.A.	24.85
6.	Bill Laimbeer	Detr	24.05
7.	Robert Parish	Bost	22.33
8.	Mark Eaton	Utah	20.52
9.	LaSalle Thompson	K.C.	19.01
10.	Sam Bowie	Port	18.32
11.	Bill Walton	LA.C	16.96
12.	Steve Stipanovich	Indi	16.73
13.	Mike Gminski	N.J.	16.43
14.	James Donaldson	LA.C	16.11
15.	Wayne Cooper	Denv	15.45
16.	Jerome Whitehead	G.St	15.10
17.	Alton Lister	Milw	15.07
18.	James Edwards	Phoe	14.63
19.	Dan Issel	Denv	12.53
20.	Wayne Rollins	Atla	12.51

SMALL FORWARD

OR	PLAYER	TEAM	PR
1.	Larry Bird	Bost	34.39
2.	Bernard King	N.Y.	26.80
3.	Larry Nance	Phoe	25.02
4.	Alex English	Denv	24.79
5.	Calvin Natt	Denv	24.31
6.	Adrian Dantley	Utah	23.75
7.	Dominique Wilkins	Atla	22.01
8.	Mark Aguirre	Dall	21.21
9.	Purvis Short	G.St	21.12
10.	Orlando Woolridge	Chic	20.74
11.	Paul Pressey	Milw	20.56
12.	Jay Vincent	Dall	19.65
13.	James Worthy	LA.L	19.59
14.	Eddie A. Johnson	K.C.	19.41
15.	Julius Erving	Phil	19.41
16.	Rodney McCray	Hous	19.12
17.	Kiki Vandeweghe	Port	18.19
18.	Mike Mitchell	S.A.	18.00
19.	Kelly Tripucka	Detr	15.98
20.	Phil Hubbard	Clev	15.47

OFF GUARD

OR	PLAYER	TEAM	PR
1.	Michael Jordan	Chic	29.24
2.	Sidney Moncrief	Milw	22.40
3.	Clyde Drexler	Port	20.71
4.	Derek Smith	LA.C	20.20
5.	Reggie Theus	K.C.	18.20
6.	World B. Free	Clev	17.72
7.	Rolando Blackman	Dall	17.60
8.	Jim Paxson	Port	17.21
9.	Darrell Griffith	Utah	16.92
10.	George Gervin	S.A.	16.81
11.	Otis Birdsong	N.J.	16.75
12.	Eddie Johnson Jr.	Atla	16.40
13.	Danny Ainge	Bost	16.35
14.	Andrew Toney	Phil	16.24
15.	Byron Scott	LA.L	15.12
16.	Jeff Malone	Wash	14.91
17.	Al Wood	Seat	14.25
18.	Mike Woodson	K.C	13.74
19.	Darrell Walker	N.Y.	13.54
20.	Vern Fleming	Indi	12.98

ROOKIES

OR	PLAYER	TEAM	PR
1.	Michael Jordan	Chic	29.24
2.	Akeem Olajuwon	Hous	25.22
3.	Charles Barkley	Phil	18.40
4.	Sam Bowie	Port	18.32
5.	Sam Perkins	Dall	15.05
6.	Otis Thorpe	K.C.	14.49
7.	Vern Fleming	Indi	12.98
8.	Melvin Turpin	Clev	12.05
9.	Alvin Robertson	S.A.	11.44
10.	Tim McCormick	Seat	10.90
11.	Kevin Willis	Atla	10.60
12.	Charles A.Jones	Phoe	10.54
13.	Michael Cage	LA.C	10.00
14.	Jay Humphries	Phoe	9.86
15.	Antoine Carr	Atla	9.77
16.	Tony Brown	Indi	7.80
17.	Jeff Turner	N.J.	6.58

1984-85 PERFORMANCE CATEGORIES

SCORING

OR	PLAYER	TEAM	SCR
1.	Bernard King	N.Y.	32.89
2.	Larry Bird	Bost	28.69
3.	Michael Jordan	Chic	28.21
4.	Purvis Short	G.St	28.03
5.	Alex English	Denv	27.93
6.	Dominique Wilkins	Atla	27.37
7.	Adrian Dantley	Utah	26.58
8.	Mark Aguirre	Dall	25.69
9.	Moses Malone	Phil	24.57
10.	Terry Cummings	Milw	23.56
11.	Calvin Natt	Denv	23.29
12.	Orlando Woolridge	Chic	22.95
13.	Eddie A. Johnson	K.C.	22.88
14.	Darrell Griffith	Utah	22.62
15.	World B. Free	Clev	22.49
16.	Kiki Vandeweghe	Port	22.44
17.	Mike Mitchell	S.A.	22.24
18.	Derek Smith	LA.C	22.09
19.	Ralph Sampson	Hous	22.06
20.	K. Abdul-Jabbar	LA.L	21.96

REBOUNDS

OR	PLAYER	TEAM	REB
1.	Bill Walton	LA.C	17.49
2.	Bill Laimbeer	Detr	16.81
3.	Moses Malone	Phil	16.74
4.	Larry Smith	G.St	16.70
5.	LaSalle Thompson	K.C.	16.68
6.	Akeem Olajuwon	Hous	16.04
7.	Maurice Lucas	Phoe	16.01
8.	Mark Eaton	Utah	15.82
9.	Kurt Rambis	LA.L	15.67
10.	Buck Williams	N.J.	15.16
11.	Wayne Cooper	Denv	14.91
12.	Alton Lister	Milw	14.85
13.	Artis Gilmore	S.A.	14.73
14.	Dan Roundfield	Detr	14.57
15.	Jack Sikma	Seat	14.45
16.	Charles Barkley	Phil	14.38
17.	Sam Bowie	Port	14.21
18.	Clark Kellogg	Indi	14.19
19.	Robert Parish	Bost	14.15
20.	Rick Mahorn	Wash	14.08

BLOCKS

OR	PLAYER	TEAM	BLK
1.	Mark Eaton	Utah	7.78
2.	Wayne Cooper	Denv	4.66
3.	Wayne Rollins	Atla	4.58
4.	Sam Bowie	Port	4.40
5.	Bill Walton	LA.C	4.08
6.	Alton Lister	Milw	3.83
7.	Akeem Olajuwon	Hous	3.62
8.	Roy Hinson	Clev	3.54
9.	Antoine Carr	Atla	3.13
10.	Artis Gilmore	S.A.	3.01
11.	Kurt Nimphius	Dall	3.01
12.	K. Abdul-Jabbar	LA.L	2.96
13.	Ralph Sampson	Hous	2.61
14.	James Donaldson	LA.C	2.61
15.	Herb Williams	Indi	2.52
16.	LaSalle Thompson	K.C.	2.50
17.	Rick Mahorn	Wash	2.41
18.	Larry Nance	Phoe	2.27
19.	Kevin McHale	Bost	2.17
20.	Terry Tyler	Detr	2.16

SHOOTING

OR	PLAYER	TEAM	SHT
1.	James Donaldson	LA.C	1.176
2.	Maurice Cheeks	Phil	1.152
3.	K. Abdul-Jabbar	LA.L	1.143
4.	Artis Gilmore	S.A.	1.140
5.	Earvin Johnson	LA.L	1.127
6.	Gene Banks	S.A.	1.126
7.	James Worthy	LA.L	1.124
8.	Larry Nance	Phoe	1.124
9.	Brad Davis	Dall	1.108
10.	Kiki Vandeweghe	Port	1.108
11.	Byron Scott	LA.L	1.103
12.	Bobby Jones	Phil	1.101
13.	Kevin McHale	Bost	1.101
14.	Larry Bird	Bost	1.096
15.	Orlando Woolridge	Chic	1.090
16.	Danny Ainge	Bost	1.089
17.	Cedric Maxwell	Bost	1.084
18.	Calvin Natt	Denv	1.081
19.	Jerry Sichting	Indi	1.075
20.	Alvan Adams	Phoe	1.073

ASSISTS

OR	PLAYER	TEAM	AST
1.	Isiah Thomas	Detr	17.45
2.	Earvin Johnson	LA.L	16.71
3.	Johnny Moore	S.A.	14.57
4.	John Bagley	Clev	13.93
5.	Ennis Whatley	Chic	13.20
6.	Reggie Theus	K.C.	12.38
7.	Norm Nixon	LA.C	11.79
8.	Rickey Green	Utah	11.79
9.	Rory Sparrow	N.Y.	11.66
10.	Lafayette Lever	Denv	11.50
11.	Eddie Johnson Jr.	Atla	11.48
12.	Wes Matthews	Chic	11.16
13.	Darnell Valentine	Port	11.00
14.	Brad Davis	Dall	10.98
15.	Johnny Davis	Clev	10.65
16.	M.R. Richardson	N.J.	10.27
17.	Lionel Hollins	Hous	10.26
18.	Gerald Henderson	Seat	10.13
19.	Kelvin Ransey	N.J.	10.09
20.	Gus Williams	Wash	9.86

STEALS

OR	PLAYER	TEAM	STL
1.	Johnny Moore	S.A.	4.09
2.	Lafayette Lever	Denv	3.79
3.	M.R. Richardson	N.J.	3.73
4.	Glenn Rivers	Atla	3.68
5.	Alvin Robertson	S.A.	3.62
6.	Lester Conner	G.St	3.42
7.	Clyde Drexler	Port	3.33
8.	Darrell Walker	N.Y.	3.22
9.	Derek Harper	Dall	3.12
10.	Maurice Cheeks	Phil	3.10
11.	Darnell Valentine	Port	3.01
12.	Michael Jordan	Chic	2.99
13.	T.R. Dunn	Denv	2.93
14.	Isiah Thomas	Detr	2.91
15.	Gus Williams	Wash	2.89
16.	Mike Woodson	K.C.	2.81
17.	Rickey Green	Utah	2.61
18.	Alvan Adams	Phoe	2.58
19.	John Bagley	Clev	2.58
20.	Julius Erving	Phil	2.56

1983-84
NBA STATISTICS

PRODUCTION RATINGS

OR	PLAYER	TEAM	PR
1.	Earvin Johnson	LA.L	30.30
2.	Larry Bird	Bost	29.99
3.	Adrian Dantley	Utah	27.96
4.	Jeff Ruland	Wash	27.67
5.	Kiki Vandeweghe	Denv	26.40
6.	Moses Malone	Phil	25.85
7.	Alex English	Denv	25.74
8.	Jack Sikma	Seat	25.66
9.	Mark Aguirre	Dall	25.04
10.	Bill Laimbeer	Detr	24.59
11.	Isiah Thomas	Detr	24.38
12.	Julius Erving	Phil	24.06
13.	Ralph Sampson	Hous	24.01
14.	Robert Parish	Bost	23.65
15.	K. Abdul-Jabbar	LA.L	23.26
16.	Larry Nance	Phoe	22.91
17.	Bernard King	N.Y.	22.86
18.	Sidney Moncrief	Milw	22.76
19.	Terry Cummings	S.D.	22.21
20.	Artis Gilmore	S.A.	22.16
21.	Clark Kellogg	Indi	21.99
22.	Dan Roundfield	Atla	21.48
23.	Buck Williams	N.J.	21.33
24.	Marques Johnson	Milw	21.20
25.	Rolando Blackman	Dall	21.17
26.	Mychal Thompson	Port	20.48
27.	Mike Mitchell	S.A.	20.25
28.	Bill Cartwright	N.Y.	20.18
29.	Kevin McHale	Bost	20.16
30.	Dan Issel	Denv	20.08
31.	George Gervin	S.A.	20.08
32.	Joe Barry Carroll	G.St	20.04
33.	Maurice Lucas	Phoe	19.91
34.	Rickey Green	Utah	19.74
35.	Dominique Wilkins	Atla	19.60
36.	Norm Nixon	S.D.	19.52
37.	Gus Williams	Seat	19.39
38.	Eddie A. Johnson	K.C.	19.11
39.	Cliff Robinson	Clev	18.95
40.	Purvis Short	G.St	18.81
41.	Darryl Dawkins	N.J.	18.70
42.	Walter Davis	Phoe	18.40
43.	Gene Banks	S.A.	18.17
44.	Calvin Natt	Port	18.10
45.	Bill Walton	S.D.	18.04
46.	David Greenwood	Chic	18.03
47.	John Lucas	S.A.	18.02
48.	Kenny Carr	Port	17.76
49.	Herb Williams	Indi	17.71
50.	Jim Paxson	Port	17.64
51.	James Worthy	LA.L	17.27
52.	Johnny Moore	S.A.	17.25
53.	Andrew Toney	Phil	17.22
54.	Tom Chambers	Seat	17.12
55.	James Donaldson	S.D.	17.00
56.	Maurice Cheeks	Phil	16.85
57.	Orlando Woolridge	Chic	16.73
58.	Larry Drew	K.C.	16.62
59.	Greg Ballard	Wash	16.59
60.	Darrell Griffith	Utah	16.57
61.	Bob Lanier	Milw	16.56
62.	Jamaal Wilkes	LA.L	16.52
63.	Kelly Tripucka	Detr	16.39
64.	Lewis Lloyd	Hous	16.34
65.	LaSalle Thompson	K.C.	16.27
66.	Ray Williams	N.Y.	16.22
67.	Pat Cummings	Dall	16.12
68.	Dave Corzine	Chic	15.87
69.	Rick Mahorn	Wash	15.68
70.	Wayne Rollins	Atla	15.65
71.	World B. Free	Clev	15.60
72.	Robert Reid	Hous	15.41
73.	Brad Davis	Dall	15.31
74.	Otis Birdsong	N.J.	15.14
75.	Steve Stipanovich	Indi	14.78
76.	Eric Floyd	G.St	14.77
77.	Michael Cooper	LA.L	14.74
78.	Lester Conner	G.St	14.65
79.	James Edwards	Phoe	14.64
80.	Mickey Johnson	G.St	14.46
81.	Mark Eaton	Utah	14.33
82.	Caldwell Jones	Hous	14.32
83.	Albert King	N.J.	14.28
84.	Jerry Sichting	Indi	14.15
85.	Quintin Dailey	Chic	14.13
86.	T.R. Dunn	Denv	14.11
87.	John Long	Detr	14.07
88.	George L. Johnson	Indi	14.02
89.	Cedric Maxwell	Bost	14.01
90.	John Drew	Utah	13.95
91.	Dennis Johnson	Bost	13.83
92.	Frank Johnson	Wash	13.79
93.	Junior Bridgeman	Milw	13.63
94.	Larry Smith	G.St	13.59
95.	Truck Robinson	N.Y.	13.54
96.	Kurt Nimphius	Dall	13.54
97.	Rodney McCray	Hous	13.44
98.	Ricky Sobers	Wash	13.38
99.	Bobby Jones	Phil	13.15
100.	Rory Sparrow	N.Y.	13.08

POSITION DOMINANCE

OR	PLAYER	TEAM	PD
1.	Earvin Johnson	LA.L	1.397
2.	Larry Bird	Bost	1.291
3.	Sidney Moncrief	Milw	1.207
4.	Jeff Ruland	Wash	1.191
5.	Adrian Dantley	Utah	1.177
6.	Moses Malone	Phil	1.132
7.	Isiah Thomas	Detr	1.124
8.	Jack Sikma	Seat	1.123
9.	Rolando Blackman	Dall	1.123
10.	Kiki Vandeweghe	Denv	1.112
11.	Alex English	Denv	1.112
12.	Bill Laimbeer	Detr	1.077
13.	George Gervin	S.A.	1.065
14.	Mark Aguirre	Dall	1.055
15.	Ralph Sampson	Hous	1.051
16.	Robert Parish	Bost	1.035
17.	K. Abdul-Jabbar	LA.L	1.018
18.	Julius Erving	Phil	1.013
19.	Walter Davis	Phoe	.976
20.	Artis Gilmore	S.A.	.970

MOST VALUABLE PLAYER

OR	PLAYER	TEAM	MVP
1.	Earvin Johnson	LA.L	2.059
2.	Larry Bird	Bost	2.000
3.	Sidney Moncrief	Milw	1.776
4.	Robert Parish	Bost	1.744
5.	Moses Malone	Phil	1.730
6.	Adrian Dantley	Utah	1.699
7.	Isiah Thomas	Detr	1.691
8.	K. Abdul-Jabbar	LA.L	1.680
9.	Bill Laimbeer	Detr	1.644
10.	Jack Sikma	Seat	1.618
11.	Rolando Blackman	Dall	1.614
12.	Julius Erving	Phil	1.611
13.	Jeff Ruland	Wash	1.595
14.	Kevin McHale	Bost	1.577
15.	Kiki Vandeweghe	Denv	1.566
16.	Mark Aguirre	Dall	1.546
17.	Alex English	Denv	1.538
18.	George Gervin	S.A.	1.516
19.	Bernard King	N.Y.	1.514
20.	Andrew Toney	Phil	1.512

1983-84 POSITION RATINGS

POWER FORWARD

OR	PLAYER	TEAM	PR
1.	Jeff Ruland	Wash	27.67
2.	Terry Cummings	S.D.	22.21
3.	Clark Kellogg	Indi	21.99
4.	Dan Roundfield	Atla	21.48
5.	Buck Williams	N.J.	21.33
6.	Kevin McHale	Bost	20.16
7.	Maurice Lucas	Phoe	19.91
8.	Cliff Robinson	Clev	18.95
9.	David Greenwood	Chic	18.03
10.	Kenny Carr	Port	17.76
11.	Herb Williams	Indi	17.71
12.	Tom Chambers	Seat	17.12
13.	Caldwell Jones	Hous	14.32
14.	George L. Johnson	Indi	14.02
15.	Cedric Maxwell	Bost	14.01
16.	Larry Smith	G.St	13.59
17.	Truck Robinson	N.Y.	13.54
18.	Alton Lister	Milw	12.72
19.	Cliff Levingston	Detr	12.68
20.	Thurl Bailey	Utah	12.62

POINT GUARD

OR	PLAYER	TEAM	PR
1.	Earvin Johnson	L.A.L	30.30
2.	Isiah Thomas	Detr	24.38
3.	Rickey Green	Utah	19.74
4.	Norm Nixon	S.D.	19.52
5.	Gus Williams	Seat	19.39
6.	John Lucas	S.A.	18.02
7.	Johnny Moore	S.A.	17.25
8.	Maurice Cheeks	Phil	16.85
9.	Larry Drew	K.C.	16.62
10.	Brad Davis	Dall	15.31
11.	Lester Conner	G.St	14.65
12.	Jerry Sichting	Indi	14.15
13.	Frank Johnson	Wash	13.79
14.	Rory Sparrow	N.Y.	13.08
15.	Ennis Whatley	Chic	13.08
16.	Allen Leavell	Hous	12.54
17.	Rob Williams	Denv	12.43
18.	Kyle Macy	Phoe	12.30
19.	Gerald Henderson	Bost	12.08
20.	Darnell Valentine	Port	12.06

CENTER

OR	PLAYER	TEAM	PR
1.	Moses Malone	Phil	25.85
2.	Jack Sikma	Seat	25.66
3.	Bill Laimbeer	Detr	24.59
4.	Ralph Sampson	Hous	24.01
5.	Robert Parish	Bost	23.65
6.	K. Abdul-Jabbar	L.A.L	23.26
7.	Artis Gilmore	S.A.	22.16
8.	Mychal Thompson	Port	20.48
9.	Bill Cartwright	N.Y.	20.18
10.	Dan Issel	Denv	20.08
11.	Joe Barry Carroll	G.St	20.04
12.	Darryl Dawkins	N.J.	18.70
13.	Bill Walton	S.D.	18.04
14.	James Donaldson	S.D.	17.00
15.	Bob Lanier	Milw	16.56
16.	LaSalle Thompson	K.C.	16.27
17.	Pat Cummings	Dall	16.12
18.	Dave Corzine	Chic	15.87
19.	Rick Mahorn	Wash	15.68
20.	Wayne Rollins	Atla	15.65

SMALL FORWARD

OR	PLAYER	TEAM	PR
1.	Larry Bird	Bost	29.99
2.	Adrian Dantley	Utah	27.96
3.	Kiki Vandeweghe	Denv	26.40
4.	Alex English	Denv	25.74
5	Mark Aguirre	Dall	25.04
6.	Julius Erving	Phil	24.06
7.	Larry Nance	Phoe	22.91
8.	Bernard King	N.Y.	22.86
9.	Marques Johnson	Milw	21.20
10.	Mike Mitchell	S.A.	20.25
11.	Dominique Wilkins	Atla	19.60
12.	Eddie A. Johnson	K.C.	19.11
13.	Purvis Short	G.St	18.81
14.	Gene Banks	S.A.	18.17
15.	Calvin Natt	Port	18.10
16.	James Worthy	L.A.L	17.27
17.	Orlando Woolridge	Chic	16.73
18.	Greg Ballard	Wash	16.59
19.	Jamaal Wilkes	L.A.L	16.52
20.	Kelly Tripucka	Detr	16.39

OFF GUARD

OR	PLAYER	TEAM	PR
1.	Sidney Moncrief	Milw	22.76
2.	Rolando Blackman	Dall	21.17
3.	George Gervin	S.A.	20.08
4.	Walter Davis	Phoe	18.40
5.	Jim Paxson	Port	17.64
6.	Andrew Toney	Phil	17.22
7.	Darrell Griffith	Utah	16.57
8.	Lewis Lloyd	Hous	16.34
9.	Ray Williams	N.Y.	16.22
10.	World B. Free	Clev	15.60
11.	Otis Birdsong	N.J.	15.14
12.	Eric Floyd	G.St	14.77
13.	Michael Cooper	L.A.L	14.74
14.	Quintin Dailey	Chic	14.13
15.	T.R. Dunn	Denv	14.11
16.	John Long	Detr	14.07
17.	Dennis Johnson	Bost	13.83
18.	Ricky Sobers	Wash	13.38
19.	Al Wood	Seat	12.90
20.	Mike Woodson	K.C.	12.55

ROOKIES

OR	PLAYER	TEAM	PR
1.	Ralph Sampson	Hous	24.01
2.	Steve Stipanovich	Indi	14.78
3.	Rodney McCray	Hous	13.44
4.	Ennis Whatley	Chic	13.08
5.	Thurl Bailey	Utah	12.62
6.	Mitchell Wiggins	Chic	11.54
7.	Glenn Rivers	Atla	11.27
8.	Roy Hinson	Clev	10.46
9.	Paul Thompson	Clev	10.04
10.	Byron Scott	L.A.L	9.86
11.	Fred Roberts	S.A.	9.52
12.	Jeff Malone	Wash	8.32
13.	Derek Harper	Dall	7.34

1983-84 PERFORMANCE CATEGORIES

SCORING

OR	PLAYER	TEAM	SCR
1.	Adrian Dantley	Utah	30.61
2.	Mark Aguirre	Dall	29.49
3.	Kiki Vandeweghe	Denv	29.42
4.	Alex English	Denv	26.43
5.	Bernard King	N.Y.	26.32
6.	George Gervin	S.A.	25.88
7.	Larry Bird	Bost	24.15
8.	Mike Mitchell	S.A.	23.28
9.	Terry Cummings	S.D.	22.89
10.	Purvis Short	G.St	22.82
11.	Moses Malone	Phil	22.66
12.	Julius Erving	Phil	22.43
13.	Rolando Blackman	Dall	22.41
14.	World B.Free	Clev	22.25
15.	Jeff Ruland	Wash	22.20
16.	Eddie A. Johnson	K.C.	21.88
17.	Dominique Wilkins	Atla	21.60
18.	K. Abdul-Jabbar	LA.L	21.46
19.	Isiah Thomas	Detr	21.32
20.	Kelly Tripucka	Detr	21.29

REBOUNDS

OR	PLAYER	TEAM	REB
1.	LaSalle Thompson	K.C.	17.77
2.	Moses Malone	Phil	17.45
3.	Bill Laimbeer	Detr	16.81
4.	Ralph Sampson	Hous	16.27
5.	Buck Williams	N.J.	15.98
6.	Artis Gilmore	S.A.	15.62
7.	Bill Walton	S.D.	15.51
8.	Larry Smith	G.St	15.43
9.	Maurice Lucas	Phoe	15.07
10.	Cliff Robinson	Clev	15.05
11.	Cliff Levingston	Detr	14.98
12.	Alton Lister	Milw	14.81
13.	Jack Sikma	Seat	14.61
14.	Jeff Ruland	Wash	14.36
15.	Robert Parish	Bost	14.35
16.	Rich Kelley	Utah	14.05
17.	David Greenwood	Chic	13.88
18.	Wayne Cooper	Port	13.75
19.	Mark Eaton	Utah	13.35
20.	Dan Roundfield	Atla	13.26

BLOCKS

OR	PLAYER	TEAM	BLK
1.	Mark Eaton	Utah	7.88
2.	Wayne Rollins	Atla	5.66
3.	Roy Hinson	Clev	3.75
4.	LaSalle Thompson	K.C.	3.63
5.	Ralph Sampson	Hous	3.51
6.	Alton Lister	Milw	3.44
7.	Artis Gilmore	S.A.	3.12
8.	Wayne Cooper	Port	3.06
9.	Kurt Nimphius	Dall	3.03
10.	Thurl Bailey	Utah	2.91
11.	Edgar Jones	S.A.	2.90
12.	Larry Nance	Phoe	2.86
13.	Bill Walton	S.D.	2.86
14.	Bobby Jones	Phil	2.81
15.	Darryl Dawkins	N.J.	2.70
16.	James Donaldson	S.D.	2.64
17.	K. Abdul-Jabbar	LA.L	2.62
18.	Julius Erving	Phil	2.49
19.	Kevin McHale	Bost	2.35
20.	Joe Barry Carroll	G.St	2.30

SHOOTING

OR	PLAYER	TEAM	SHT
1.	Calvin Natt	Port	1.139
2.	Artis Gilmore	S.A.	1.137
3.	James Donaldson	S.D.	1.130
4.	Adrian Dantley	Utah	1.128
5.	Kiki Vandeweghe	Denv	1.127
6.	Earvin Johnson	LA.L	1.120
7.	Darryl Dawkins	N.J.	1.115
8.	Bernard King	N.Y.	1.113
9.	K. Abdul-Jabbar	LA.L	1.110
10.	Bill Cartwright	N.Y.	1.103
11.	Kent Benson	Detr	1.099
12.	Larry Nance	Phoe	1.099
13.	Gene Banks	S.A.	1.097
14.	Rolando Blackman	Dall	1.091
15.	James Worthy	LA.L	1.090
16.	Jeff Ruland	Wash	1.089
17.	Fred Roberts	S.A.	1.088
18.	Bob Lanier	Milw	1.087
19.	Kevin McHale	Bost	1.086
20.	Jerry Sichting	Indi	1.085

ASSISTS

OR	PLAYER	TEAM	AST
1.	John Lucas	S.A.	17.88
2.	Johnny Moore	S.A.	16.47
3.	Earvin Johnson	LA.L	16.36
4.	Ennis Whatley	Chic	14.72
5.	Isiah Thomas	Detr	14.59
6.	Norm Nixon	S.D.	14.37
7.	Rickey Green	Utah	12.97
8.	Kelvin Ransey	N.J.	11.97
9.	Rob Williams	Denv	11.58
10.	Gus Williams	Seat	11.50
11.	Larry Drew	K.C.	11.33
12.	Reggie Theus	K.C.	11.28
13.	Allen Leavell	Hous	10.97
14.	Rory Sparrow	N.Y.	10.62
15.	Frank Johnson	Wash	10.13
16.	Brad Davis	Dall	10.10
17.	Darnell Valentine	Port	10.02
18.	Phil Ford	Hous	9.74
19.	Michael Cooper	LA.L	9.69
20.	Ray Williams	N.Y.	9.66

STEALS

OR	PLAYER	TEAM	STL
1.	Darwin Cook	N.J.	4.21
2.	Rickey Green	Utah	3.73
3.	Johnny Moore	S.A.	3.58
4.	Ray Williams	N.Y.	3.49
5.	Maurice Cheeks	Phil	3.29
6.	Isiah Thomas	Detr	3.26
7.	Lafayette Lever	Port	3.22
8.	Gus Williams	Seat	3.22
9.	Glenn Rivers	Atla	3.15
10.	T.R. Dunn	Denv	3.07
11.	Lester Conner	G.St	3.02
12.	Butch Carter	Indi	3.00
13.	Bobby Jones	Phil	2.92
14.	Earvin Johnson	LA.L	2.80
15.	Darnell Valentine	Port	2.71
16.	Gerald Henderson	Bost	2.69
17.	Derek Harper	Dall	2.66
18.	Ennis Whatley	Chic	2.65
19.	Allen Leavell	Hous	2.56
20.	Julius Erving	Phil	2.52

1982-83
NBA STATISTICS

PRODUCTION RATINGS

OR	PLAYER	TEAM	PR
1.	Moses Malone	Phil	30.08
2.	Larry Bird	Bost	30.04
3.	Earvin Johnson	LA.L	28.63
4.	Alex English	Denv	28.30
5.	Terry Cummings	S.D.	26.04
6.	Artis Gilmore	S.A.	25.68
7.	K. Abdul-Jabbar	LA.L	24.63
8.	Robert Parish	Bost	24.31
9.	Kiki Vandeweghe	Denv	24.23
10.	Jack Sikma	Seat	23.79
11.	Joe Barry Carroll	G.St	23.62
12.	Buck Williams	N.J.	23.51
13.	Jeff Ruland	Wash	23.48
14.	Julius Erving	Phil	23.24
15.	Sidney Moncrief	Milw	22.80
16.	Dan Roundfield	Atla	22.78
17.	Clark Kellogg	Indi	22.77
18.	Bill Laimbeer	Detr	22.71
19.	Marques Johnson	Milw	22.59
20.	Larry Nance	Phoe	22.29
21.	Dan Issel	Denv	22.29
22.	Kelly Tripucka	Detr	21.97
23.	Isiah Thomas	Detr	21.68
24.	George Gervin	S.A.	21.63
25.	Mark Aguirre	Dall	20.77
26.	Calvin Natt	Port	20.71
27.	Cliff Robinson	Clev	20.16
28.	Gus Williams	Seat	20.12
29.	Reggie Theus	Chic	20.12
30.	Mychal Thompson	Port	20.11
31.	Larry Drew	K.C.	20.05
32.	Maurice Lucas	Phoe	19.96
33.	Rickey Green	Utah	19.38
34.	Herb Williams	Indi	19.33
35.	Johnny Moore	S.A.	19.13
36.	Gene Banks	S.A.	18.88
37.	Purvis Short	G.St	18.81
38.	Jay Vincent	Dall	18.77
39.	Bernard King	N.Y.	18.62
40.	Greg Ballard	Wash	18.62
41.	Mike Mitchell	S.A.	18.54
42.	Alvan Adams	Phoe	18.30
43.	Bill Cartwright	N.Y.	18.29
44.	Eddie A. Johnson	K.C.	18.10
45.	Wayne Rollins	Atla	18.09
46.	Jim Paxson	Port	17.67
47.	Maurice Cheeks	Phil	17.44
48.	Walter Davis	Phoe	17.39
49.	Darrell Griffith	Utah	17.16
50.	Kevin McHale	Bost	17.04
51.	Dave Corzine	Chic	16.98
52.	Jamaal Wilkes	LA.L	16.96
53.	Vinnie Johnson	Detr	16.79
54.	Brad Davis	Dall	16.75
55.	Mike Woodson	K.C.	16.64
56.	World B.Free	Clev	16.58
57.	Rick Mahorn	Wash	16.54
58.	Albert King	N.J.	16.32
59.	Tom Chambers	S.D.	16.32
60.	Terry Tyler	Detr	16.11
61.	Andrew Toney	Phil	16.09
62.	David Greenwood	Chic	15.86
63.	Dennis Johnson	Phoe	15.69
64.	Dominique Wilkins	Atla	15.63
65.	Ben Poquette	Utah	15.61
66.	Pat Cummings	Dall	15.59
67.	Billy Knight	Indi	15.38
68.	Orlando Woolridge	Chic	15.35
69.	Allen Leavell	Hous	15.23
70.	Michael Brooks	S.D.	15.21
71.	Norm Nixon	LA.L	15.19
72.	Rolando Blackman	Dall	15.19
73.	M.R. Richardson	N.J.	15.14
74.	Ray Williams	K.C.	15.14
75.	Elvin Hayes	Hous	14.74
76.	James Worthy	LA.L	14.71
77.	Lonnie Shelton	Seat	14.62
78.	Mickey Johnson	G.St	14.59
79.	Danny Schayes	Denv	14.35
80.	Caldwell Jones	Hous	14.32
81.	T.R. Dunn	Denv	14.30
82.	Darwin Cook	N.J.	14.30
83.	Kenny Carr	Port	13.89
84.	David Thompson	Seat	13.83
85.	Cedric Maxwell	Bost	13.82
86.	Frank Johnson	Wash	13.63
87.	Otis Birdsong	N.J.	13.56
88.	George L. Johnson	Indi	13.52
89.	Johnny Davis	Atla	13.45
90.	Jeff Wilkins	Utah	13.43
91.	Darryl Dawkins	N.J.	13.35
92.	Eddie Johnson Jr.	Atla	13.30
93.	Junior Bridgeman	Milw	13.14
94.	Lionel Hollins	S.D.	13.07
95.	Bobby Jones	Phil	13.04
96.	Alton Lister	Milw	13.00
97.	Wayne Cooper	Port	12.98
98.	Kurt Rambis	LA.L	12.79
99.	James Bailey	Hous	12.79
100.	Clemon Johnson	Phil	12.72

POSITION DOMINANCE

OR	PLAYER	TEAM	PD
1.	Earvin Johnson	LA.L	1.397
2.	Larry Bird	Bost	1.292
3.	Moses Malone	Phil	1.245
4.	Alex English	Denv	1.245
5.	Sidney Moncrief	Milw	1.211
6.	George Gervin	S.A.	1.149
7.	Terry Cummings	S.D.	1.120
8.	Reggie Theus	Chic	1.068
9.	Kiki Vandeweghe	Denv	1.066
10.	Artis Gilmore	S.A.	1.063
11.	Isiah Thomas	Detr	1.058
12.	Julius Erving	Phil	1.023
13.	K. Abdul-Jabbar	LA.L	1.019
14.	Buck Williams	N.J.	1.011
15.	Jeff Ruland	Wash	1.010
16.	Robert Parish	Bost	1.006
17.	Marques Johnson	Milw	.994
18.	Jack Sikma	Seat	.985
19.	Gus Williams	Seat	.982
20.	Larry Nance	Phoe	.981

MOST VALUABLE PLAYER

OR	PLAYER	TEAM	MVP
1.	Moses Malone	Phil	2.080
2.	Earvin Johnson	LA.L	2.043
3.	Larry Bird	Bost	1.897
4.	Julius Erving	Phil	1.858
5.	Sidney Moncrief	Milw	1.817
6.	George Gervin	S.A.	1.766
7.	Alex English	Denv	1.754
8.	Andrew Toney	Phil	1.689
9.	Maurice Cheeks	Phil	1.686
10.	Artis Gilmore	S.A.	1.680
11.	K. Abdul-Jabbar	LA.L	1.665
12.	Robert Parish	Bost	1.608
13.	Marques Johnson	Milw	1.600
14.	Larry Nance	Phoe	1.596
15.	Kiki Vandeweghe	Denv	1.575
16.	Buck Williams	N.J.	1.568
17.	Johnny Moore	S.A.	1.551
18.	Walter Davis	Phoe	1.538
19.	Jack Sikma	Seat	1.530
20.	Larry Drew	K.C.	1.528

1982-83 POSITION RATINGS

POWER FORWARD

OR	PLAYER	TEAM	PR
1.	Larry Bird	Bost	30.04
2.	Terry Cummings	S.D.	26.04
3.	Buck Williams	N.J.	23.51
4.	Jeff Ruland	Wash	23.48
5.	Dan Roundfield	Atla	22.78
6.	Clark Kellogg	Indi	22.77
7.	Cliff Robinson	Clev	20.16
8.	Maurice Lucas	Phoe	19.96
9.	Kevin McHale	Bost	17.04
10.	Tom Chambers	S.D.	16.32
11.	David Greenwood	Chic	15.86
12.	Ben Poquette	Utah	15.61
13.	Elvin Hayes	Hous	14.74
14.	Lonnie Shelton	Seat	14.62
15.	Kenny Carr	Port	13.89
16.	George L.Johnson	Indi	13.52
17.	Jeff Wilkins	Utah	13.43
18.	Alton Lister	Milw	13.00
19.	Kurt Rambis	LA.L	12.79
20.	James Bailey	Hous	12.79

POINT GUARD

OR	PLAYER	TEAM	PR
1.	Earvin Johnson	LA.L	28.63
2.	Isiah Thomas	Detr	21.68
3.	Gus Williams	Seat	20.12
4.	Larry Drew	K.C.	20.05
5.	Rickey Green	Utah	19.38
6.	Johnny Moore	S.A.	19.13
7.	Maurice Cheeks	Phil	17.44
8.	Brad Davis	Dall	16.75
9.	Allen Leavell	Hous	15.23
10.	Norm Nixon	LA.L	15.19
11.	M.R. Richardson	N.J.	15.14
12.	Darwin Cook	N.J.	14.30
13.	Frank Johnson	Wash	13.63
14.	Johnny Davis	Atla	13.45
15.	Lionel Hollins	S.D.	13.07
16.	Rory Sparrow	N.Y.	12.44
17.	Geoff Huston	Clev	12.44
18.	Jerry Sichting	Indi	11.83
19.	Lafayette Lever	Port	11.53
20.	Kyle Macy	Phoe	11.07

CENTER

OR	PLAYER	TEAM	PR
1.	Moses Malone	Phil	30.08
2.	Artis Gilmore	S.A.	25.68
3.	K. Abdul-Jabbar	LA.L	24.63
4.	Robert Parish	Bost	24.31
5.	Jack Sikma	Seat	23.79
6.	Joe Barry Carroll	G.St	23.62
7.	Bill Laimbeer	Detr	22.71
8.	Dan Issel	Denv	22.29
9.	Mychal Thompson	Port	20.11
10.	Herb Williams	Indi	19.33
11.	Alvan Adams	Phoe	18.30
12.	Bill Cartwright	N.Y.	18.29
13.	Wayne Rollins	Atla	18.09
14.	Dave Corzine	Chic	16.98
15.	Rick Mahorn	Wash	16.54
16.	Pat Cummings	Dall	15.59
17.	Danny Schayes	Denv	14.35
18.	Caldwell Jones	Hous	14.32
19.	Darryl Dawkins	N.J.	13.35
20.	Wayne Cooper	Port	12.98

SMALL FORWARD

OR	PLAYER	TEAM	PR
1.	Alex English	Denv	28.30
2.	Kiki Vandeweghe	Denv	24.23
3.	Julius Erving	Phil	23.24
4.	Marques Johnson	Milw	22.59
5.	Larry Nance	Phoe	22.29
6.	Kelly Tripucka	Detr	21.97
7.	Mark Aguirre	Dall	20.77
8.	Calvin Natt	Port	20.71
9.	Gene Banks	S.A.	18.88
10.	Purvis Short	G.St	18.81
11.	Jay Vincent	Dall	18.77
12.	Bernard King	N.Y.	18.62
13.	Greg Ballard	Wash	18.62
14.	Mike Mitchell	S.A.	18.54
15.	Eddie A. Johnson	K.C.	18.10
16.	Jamaal Wilkes	LA.L	16.96
17.	Albert King	N.J.	16.32
18.	Terry Tyler	Detr	16.11
19.	Dominique Wilkins	Atla	15.63
20.	Orlando Woolridge	Chic	15.35

OFF GUARD

OR	PLAYER	TEAM	PR
1.	Sidney Moncrief	Milw	22.80
2.	George Gervin	S.A.	21.63
3.	Reggie Theus	Chic	20.12
4.	Jim Paxson	Port	17.67
5.	Walter Davis	Phoe	17.39
6.	Darrell Griffith	Utah	17.16
7.	Vinnie Johnson	Detr	16.79
8.	Mike Woodson	K.C.	16.64
9.	World B. Free	Clev	16.58
10.	Andrew Toney	Phil	16.09
11.	Dennis Johnson	Phoe	15.69
12.	Billy Knight	Indi	15.38
13.	Rolando Blackman	Dall	15.19
14.	Ray Williams	K.C.	15.14
15.	T.R. Dunn	Denv	14.30
16.	David Thompson	Seat	13.83
17.	Otis Birdsong	N.J.	13.56
18.	Eddie Johnson Jr.	Atla	13.30
19.	Quinton Dailey	Chic	12.55
20.	Michael Cooper	LA.L	12.27

ROOKIES

OR	PLAYER	TEAM	PR
1.	Terry Cummings	S.D.	26.04
2.	Clark Kellogg	Indi	22.77
3.	Dominique Wilkins	Atla	15.63
4.	James Worthy	LA.L	14.71
5.	Quintin Dailey	Chic	12.55
6.	Rod Higgins	Chic	11.62
7.	Lafayette Lever	Port	11.53
8.	Ed Nealy	K.C.	9.71
9.	Ed Sherod	N.Y.	9.11
10.	Trent Tucker	N.Y.	8.83
11.	Paul Pressey	Milw	8.61
12.	Craig Hodges	S.D.	8.55
13.	Rob Williams	Denv	8.22
14.	Jerry Eaves	Utah	7.96
15.	Terry Teagle	Hous	7.63
16.	Marc Iavaroni	Phil	6.68

1982-83 PERFORMANCE CATEGORIES

SCORING

OR	PLAYER	TEAM	SCR
1.	Alex English	Denv	28.37
2.	Kiki Vandeweghe	Denv	26.66
3.	Kelly Tripucka	Detr	26.48
4.	George Gervin	S.A.	26.19
5.	Moses Malone	Phil	24.46
6.	Mark Aguirre	Dall	24.43
7.	Joe Barry Carroll	G.St	24.14
8.	World B.Free	Clev	23.88
9.	Reggie Theus	Chic	23.82
10.	Terry Cummings	S.D.	23.71
11.	Larry Bird	Bost	23.63
12.	Isiah Thomas	Detr	22.89
13.	Sidney Moncrief	Milw	22.53
14.	Darrell Griffith	Utah	22.19
15.	Bernard King	N.Y.	21.85
16.	K. Abdul-Jabbar	L.A.L	21.80
17.	Jim Paxson	Port	21.68
18.	Dan Issel	Denv	21.58
19.	Purvis Short	G.St	21.45
20.	Marques Johnson	Milw	21.42

REBOUNDS

OR	PLAYER	TEAM	REB
1.	Moses Malone	Phil	19.61
2.	Artis Gilmore	S.A.	16.89
3.	Buck Williams	N.J.	16.65
4.	Bill Laimbeer	Detr	16.60
5.	Robert Parish	Bost	16.14
6.	Jack Sikma	Seat	16.06
7.	Cliff Robinson	Clev	15.80
8.	David Greenwood	Chic	15.59
9.	Dan Roundfield	Atla	15.03
10.	Clark Kellogg	Indi	14.95
11.	Maurice Lucas	Phoe	14.83
12.	Jeff Ruland	Wash	14.61
13.	Alton Lister	Milw	14.46
14.	Wayne Rollins	Atla	14.43
15.	Rich Kelley	Utah	14.42
16.	Ed Nealy	K.C.	14.17
17.	Kurt Rambis	L.A.L	14.11
18.	Terry Cummings	S.D.	14.11
19.	Larry Bird	Bost	14.00
20.	Wayne Cooper	Port	13.97

BLOCKS

OR	PLAYER	TEAM	BLK
1.	Wayne Rollins	Atla	6.66
2.	Harvey Catchings	Milw	4.57
3.	Alton Lister	Milw	4.51
4.	Kevin McHale	Bost	3.93
5.	Larry Nance	Phoe	3.57
6.	Darryl Dawkins	N.J.	3.49
7.	Artis Gilmore	S.A.	3.29
8.	Herb Williams	Indi	3.27
9.	K. Abdul-Jabbar	L.A.L	3.19
10.	Edgar Jones	S.A.	3.13
11.	Wayne Cooper	Port	3.11
12.	Terry Tyler	Detr	3.02
13.	Robert Parish	Bost	2.89
14.	Sam Williams	G.St	2.79
15.	James Donaldson	Seat	2.71
16.	Julius Erving	Phil	2.60
17.	Steve Johnson	K.C.	2.58
18.	Moses Malone	Phil	2.58
19.	Caldwell Jones	Hous	2.58
20.	Bobby Jones	Phil	2.50

SHOOTING

OR	PLAYER	TEAM	SHT
1.	Artis Gilmore	S.A.	1.157
2.	Brad Davis	Dall	1.152
3.	K. Abdul-Jabbar	L.A.L	1.135
4.	Kiki Vandeweghe	Denv	1.121
5.	Darryl Dawkins	N.J.	1.105
6.	James Donaldson	Seat	1.090
7.	Kyle Macy	Phoe	1.088
8.	Earvin Johnson	L.A.L	1.087
9.	James Worthy	L.A.L	1.087
10.	Calvin Natt	Port	1.079
11.	Bobby Jones	Phil	1.078
12.	Bill Cartwright	N.Y.	1.077
13.	Steve Johnson	K.C.	1.077
14.	Kurt Rambis	L.A.L	1.074
15.	Michael Cooper	L.A.L	1.073
16.	Ed Nealy	K.C.	1.073
17.	Sidney Moncrief	Milw	1.067
18.	Billy Knight	Indi	1.066
19.	Maurice Cheeks	Phil	1.066
20.	Gene Banks	S.A.	1.062

ASSISTS

OR	PLAYER	TEAM	AST
1.	Johnny Moore	S.A.	14.16
2.	Earvin Johnson	L.A.L	13.69
3.	Mike Dunleavy	S.A.	12.96
4.	Ray Williams	K.C.	12.59
5.	Rickey Green	Utah	12.02
6.	Rob Williams	Denv	12.01
7.	Brad Davis	Dall	11.67
8.	Frank Johnson	Wash	11.34
9.	Gus Williams	Seat	11.18
10.	Ronnie Lester	Chic	11.09
11.	Larry Drew	K.C.	10.88
12.	Nate Archibald	Bost	10.84
13.	Paul Westphal	N.Y.	10.65
14.	Maurice Cheeks	Phil	10.57
15.	Johnny Davis	Atla	10.32
16.	Lorenzo Romar	G.St	10.25
17.	Lafayette Lever	Port	10.12
18.	Norm Nixon	L.A.L	10.02
19.	M.R. Richardson	N.J.	9.99
20.	Isiah Thomas	Detr	9.84

STEALS

OR	PLAYER	TEAM	STL
1.	M.R. Richardson	N.J.	4.21
2.	Rickey Green	Utah	3.79
3.	Johnny Moore	S.A.	3.65
4.	Lafayette Lever	Port	3.64
5.	Maurice Cheeks	Phil	3.58
6.	Darwin Cook	N.J.	3.55
7.	Quinn Buckner	Bost	3.31
8.	Gus Williams	Seat	3.16
9.	Paul Pressey	Milw	3.11
10.	Isiah Thomas	Detr	3.09
11.	Allen Leavell	Hous	3.04
12.	Rob Williams	Denv	2.96
13.	Gerald Henderson	Bost	2.94
14.	Earvin Johnson	L.A.L	2.91
15.	Lionel Hollins	S.D.	2.89
16.	Ed Sherod	N.Y.	2.84
17.	Kurt Rambis	L.A.L	2.79
18.	Mike Woodson	K.C.	2.71
19.	T.R. Dunn	Denv	2.67
20.	Ray Williams	K.C.	2.65

1981-82
NBA STATISTICS

PRODUCTION RATINGS

OR	PLAYER	TEAM	PR
1.	Moses Malone	Hous	33.12
2.	Earvin Johnson	LA.L	29.65
3.	Larry Bird	Bost	29.16
4.	Adrian Dantley	Utah	27.81
5.	Alex English	Denv	27.44
6.	K. Abdul-Jabbar	LA.L	27.16
7.	Jack Sikma	Seat	27.01
8.	Julius Erving	Phil	26.69
9.	Artis Gilmore	Chic	25.76
10.	Mychal Thompson	Port	25.63
11.	George Gervin	S.A.	24.82
12.	Robert Parish	Bost	24.58
13.	Dan Issel	Denv	23.43
14.	Dan Roundfield	Atla	23.20
15.	Sidney Moncrief	Milw	22.96
16.	Buck Williams	N.J.	21.94
17.	Gus Williams	Seat	21.80
18.	Bernard King	G.St	21.57
19.	Maurice Lucas	N.Y.	21.48
20.	M. R. Richardson	N.Y.	21.39
21.	Kiki Vandeweghe	Denv	21.32
22.	Greg Ballard	Wash	21.20
23.	Calvin Natt	Port	20.93
24.	Truck Robinson	Phoe	20.50
25.	David Greenwood	Chic	20.06
26.	Alvan Adams	Phoe	19.78
27.	Ray Williams	N.J.	19.72
28.	Cliff Robinson	Clev	19.31
29.	Jay Vincent	Dall	19.07
30.	Dennis Johnson	Phoe	19.00
31.	Kelly Tripucka	Detr	18.77
32.	Maurice Cheeks	Phil	18.75
33.	Jerome Whitehead	S.D.	18.56
34.	Rickey Green	Utah	18.44
35.	Mike Mitchell	S.A.	18.36
36.	Joe Barry Carroll	G.St	18.34
37.	Jeff Ruland	Wash	18.32
38.	Michael Brooks	S.D.	18.26
39.	Norm Nixon	LA.L	18.05
40.	Marques Johnson	Milw	18.03
41.	Bobby Jones	Phil	17.79
42.	Jamaal Wilkes	LA.L	17.76
43.	Kent Benson	Detr	17.71
44.	James Edwards	Clev	17.65
45.	Elvin Hayes	Hous	17.61
46.	World B. Free	G.St	17.40
47.	Johnny Moore	S.A.	17.22
48.	Rick Mahorn	Wash	17.19
49.	Cedric Maxwell	Bost	17.17
50.	Reggie Theus	Chic	17.10
51.	Jim Paxson	Port	16.87
52.	Robert Reid	Hous	16.77
53.	Kevin McHale	Bost	16.72
54.	John Long	Detr	16.64
55.	Kyle Macy	Phoe	16.57
56.	Lonnie Shelton	Seat	16.27
57.	Tom Chambers	S.D.	16.14
58.	Mark Olberding	S.A.	16.06
59.	Bob Lanier	Milw	15.99
60.	Larry Smith	G.St	15.88
61.	Isiah Thomas	Detr	15.63
62.	Herb Williams	Indi	15.50
63.	Bill Cartwright	N.Y.	15.39
64.	Kelvin Ransey	Port	15.37
65.	Eddie Johnson Jr.	Atla	15.37
66.	Dave Corzine	S.A.	15.18
67.	Brad Davis	Dall	14.99
68.	Mickey Johnson	Milw	14.87
69.	Caldwell Jones	Phil	14.86
70.	Darrell Griffith	Utah	14.85
71.	John Drew	Atla	14.84
72.	Brian Winters	Milw	14.80
73.	Reggie King	K.C.	14.60
74.	Terry Tyler	Detr	14.55
75.	Mike Woodson	K.C.	14.47
76.	Wayne Rollins	Atla	14.42
77.	Steve Johnson	K.C.	14.31
78.	Sly Williams	N.Y.	14.30
79.	Quinn Buckner	Milw	14.24
80.	Nate Archibald	Bost	14.24
81.	Ron Brewer	Clev	14.15
82.	T.R. Dunn	Denv	14.10
83.	Michael Cooper	LA.L	13.76
84.	Johnny Davis	Indi	13.74
85.	Don Buse	Indi	13.74
86.	Bill Laimbeer	Detr	13.73
87.	Clemon Johnson	Indi	13.72
88.	Geoff Huston	Clev	13.62
89.	Kenny Carr	Detr	13.49
90.	Allen Leavell	Hous	13.39
91.	Reggie Johnson	K.C.	13.17
92.	Purvis Short	G.St	13.16
93.	Andrew Toney	Phil	13.13
94.	Rory Sparrow	Atla	13.07
95.	Ronnie Lester	Chic	13.04
96.	Wayne Cooper	Dall	12.80
97.	Scott Wedman	Clev	12.76
98.	Dwight Jones	Chic	12.76
99.	Campy Russell	N.Y.	12.64
100.	Spencer Haywood	Wash	12.61

POSITION DOMINANCE

OR	PLAYER	TEAM	PD
1.	Earvin Johnson	LA.L	1.424
2.	Larry Bird	Bost	1.314
3.	Moses Malone	Hous	1.313
4.	George Gervin	S.A.	1.268
5.	Adrian Dantley	Utah	1.229
6.	Alex English	Denv	1.213
7.	Julius Erving	Phil	1.180
8.	Sidney Moncrief	Milw	1.173
9.	K. Abdul-Jabbar	LA.L	1.077
10.	Jack Sikma	Seat	1.071
11.	Gus Williams	Seat	1.047
12.	Dan Roundfield	Atla	1.046
13.	M.R. Richardson	N.Y.	1.027
14.	Artis Gilmore	Chic	1.021
15.	Mychal Thompson	Port	1.016
16.	Ray Williams	N.J.	1.007
17.	Buck Williams	N.J.	.989
18.	Robert Parish	Bost	.975
19.	Dennis Johnson	Phoe	.971
20.	Maurice Lucas	N.Y.	.968

MOST VALUABLE PLAYER

OR	PLAYER	TEAM	MVP
1.	Earvin Johnson	LA.L	2.174
2.	Larry Bird	Bost	2.026
3.	Moses Malone	Hous	1.851
4.	Julius Erving	Phil	1.828
5.	K. Abdul-Jabbar	LA.L	1.827
6.	George Gervin	S.A.	1.818
7.	Sidney Moncrief	Milw	1.751
8.	Alex English	Denv	1.751
9.	Robert Parish	Bost	1.689
10.	Jack Sikma	Seat	1.646
11.	Gus Williams	Seat	1.622
12.	Norm Nixon	LA.L	1.617
13.	Maurice Cheeks	Phil	1.549
14.	Adrian Dantley	Utah	1.534
15.	Mychal Thompson	Port	1.528
16.	Dan Roundfield	Atla	1.523
17.	Ray Williams	N.J.	1.507
18.	Bernard King	G.St	1.502
19.	Buck Williams	N.J.	1.489
20.	Cedric Maxwell	Bost	1.486

1981-82 POSITION RATINGS

POWER FORWARD

OR	PLAYER	TEAM	PR
1.	Larry Bird	Bost	29.16
2.	Dan Roundfield	Atla	23.20
3.	Buck Williams	N.J.	21.94
4.	Maurice Lucas	N.Y.	21.48
5.	Truck Robinson	Phoe	20.50
6.	David Greenwood	Chic	20.06
7.	Cliff Robinson	Clev	19.31
8.	Jeff Ruland	Wash	18.32
9.	Elvin Hayes	Hous	17.61
10.	Kevin McHale	Bost	16.72
11.	Lonnie Shelton	Seat	16.27
12.	Tom Chambers	S.D.	16.14
13.	Mark Olberding	S.A.	16.06
14.	Larry Smith	G.St	15.88
15.	Herb Williams	Indi	15.50
16.	Reggie King	K.C.	14.60
17.	Kenny Carr	Detr	13.49
18.	Reggie Johnson	K.C.	13.17
19.	Dwight Jones	Chic	12.76
20.	Spencer Haywood	Wash	12.61

POINT GUARD

OR	PLAYER	TEAM	PR
1.	Earvin Johnson	LA.L	29.65
2.	Gus Williams	Seat	21.80
3.	M.R. Richardson	N.Y.	21.39
4.	Maurice Cheeks	Phil	18.75
5.	Rickey Green	Utah	18.44
6.	Norm Nixon	LA.L	18.05
7.	Johnny Moore	S.A.	17.22
8.	Kyle Macy	Phoe	16.57
9.	Isiah Thomas	Detr	15.63
10.	Kelvin Ransey	Port	15.37
11.	Brad Davis	Dall	14.99
12.	Quinn Buckner	Milw	14.24
13.	Nate Archibald	Bost	14.24
14.	Johnny Davis	Indi	13.74
15.	Don Buse	Indi	13.74
16.	Geoff Huston	Clev	13.62
17.	Allen Leavell	Hous	13.39
18.	Rory Sparrow	Atla	13.07
19.	Ronnie Lester	Chic	13.04
20.	Billy McKinney	Denv	11.88

CENTER

OR	PLAYER	TEAM	PR
1.	Moses Malone	Hous	33.12
2.	K. Abdul-Jabbar	LA.L	27.16
3.	Jack Sikma	Seat	27.01
4.	Artis Gilmore	Chic	25.76
5.	Mychal Thompson	Port	25.63
6.	Robert Parish	Bost	24.58
7.	Dan Issel	Denv	23.43
8.	Alvan Adams	Phoe	19.78
9.	Jerome Whitehead	S.D.	18.56
10.	Joe Barry Carroll	G.St	18.34
11.	Kent Benson	Detr	17.71
12.	James Edwards	Clev	17.65
13.	Rick Mahorn	Wash	17.19
14.	Bob Lanier	Milw	15.99
15.	Bill Cartwright	N.Y.	15.39
16.	Dave Corzine	S.A.	15.18
17.	Caldwell Jones	Phil	14.86
18.	Wayne Rollins	Atla	14.42
19.	Steve Johnson	K.C.	14.31
20.	Bill Laimbeer	Detr	13.73

SMALL FORWARD

OR	PLAYER	TEAM	PR
1.	Adrian Dantley	Utah	27.81
2.	Alex English	Denv	27.44
3.	Julius Erving	Phil	26.69
4.	Bernard King	G.St	21.57
5.	Kiki Vandeweghe	Denv	21.32
6	Greg Ballard	Wash	21.20
7.	Calvin Natt	Port	20.93
8.	Jay Vincent	Dall	19.07
9.	Kelly Tripucka	Detr	18.77
10.	Mike Mitchell	S.A.	18.36
11.	Michael Brooks	S.D.	18.26
12.	Marques Johnson	Milw	18.03
13.	Bobby Jones	Phil	17.79
14.	Jamaal Wilkes	LA.L	17.76
15.	Cedric Maxwell	Bost	17.17
16.	Robert Reid	Hous	16.77
17.	Mickey Johnson	Milw	14.87
18.	John Drew	Atla	14.84
19.	Terry Tyler	Detr	14.55
20.	Sly Williams	N.Y.	14.30

OFF GUARD

OR	PLAYER	TEAM	PR
1.	George Gervin	S.A.	24.82
2.	Sidney Moncrief	Milw	22.96
3.	Ray Williams	N.J.	19.72
4.	Dennis Johnson	Phoe	19.00
5.	World B. Free	G.St	17.40
6.	Reggie Theus	Chic	17.10
7.	Jim Paxson	Port	16.87
8.	John Long	Detr	16.64
9.	Eddie Johnson Jr.	Atla	15.37
10.	Darrell Griffith	Utah	14.85
11.	Brian Winters	Milw	14.80
12.	Mike Woodson	K.C.	14.47
13.	Ron Brewer	Clev	14.15
14.	T.R. Dunn	Denv	14.10
15.	Michael Cooper	LA.L	13.76
16.	Andrew Toney	Phil	13.13
17.	Bob Wilkerson	Clev	11.49
18.	David Thompson	Denv	11.44
19.	Rolando Blackman	Dall	11.38
20.	Billy Knight	Indi	10.84

ROOKIES

OR	PLAYER	TEAM	PR
1.	Buck Williams	N.J.	21.94
2.	Jay Vincent	Dall	19.07
3.	Kelly Tripucka	Detr	18.77
4.	Jeff Ruland	Wash	18.32
5.	Tom Chambers	S.D.	16.14
6.	Isiah Thomas	Detr	15.63
7.	Herb Williams	Indi	15.50
8.	Steve Johnson	K.C.	14.31
9.	Rolando Blackman	Dall	11.38
10.	Gene Banks	S.A.	11.04
11.	Albert King	N.J.	10.96
12.	Danny Schayes	Utah	10.57
13.	Frank Johnson	Wash	9.68
14.	Eddie A. Johnson	K.C.	9.32
15.	Elston Turner	Dall	8.93

1981-82 PERFORMANCE CATEGORIES

SCORING

OR	PLAYER	TEAM	SCR
1.	George Gervin	S.A.	32.29
2.	Moses Malone	Hous	31.11
3.	Adrian Dantley	Utah	30.33
4.	Alex English	Denv	25.39
5.	Julius Erving	Phil	24.37
6.	K. Abdul-Jabbar	L.A.L	23.92
7.	Gus Williams	Seat	23.44
8.	Bernard King	G.St	23.20
9.	World B .Free	G.St	22.94
10.	Larry Bird	Bost	22.87
11.	Dan Issel	Denv	22.86
12.	John Long	Detr	21.94
13.	Kelly Tripucka	Detr	21.61
14.	Kiki Vandeweghe	Denv	21.46
15.	Jay Vincent	Dall	21.38
16.	Jamaal Wilkes	L.A.L	21.15
17.	Mychal Thompson	Port	20.78
18.	Mike Mitchell	S.A.	20.55
19.	Ray Williams	N.J.	20.41
20.	Robert Parish	Bost	19.87

REBOUNDS

OR	PLAYER	TEAM	REB
1.	Larry Smith	G.St	17.63
2.	Buck Williams	N.J.	17.08
3.	Moses Malone	Hous	16.78
4.	Jeff Ruland	Wash	16.52
5.	Robert Parish	Bost	16.40
6.	Jack Sikma	Seat	16.34
7.	Maurice Lucas	N.Y.	16.23
8.	Bill Laimbeer	Detr	16.19
9.	Dan Roundfield	Atla	15.61
10.	Wayne Rollins	Atla	14.53
11.	Wayne Cooper	Dall	14.52
12.	Jerome Whitehead	S.D.	14.40
13.	Artis Gilmore	Chic	14.33
14.	Mychal Thompson	Port	14.13
15.	Caldwell Jones	Phil	13.89
16.	Clemon Johnson	Indi	13.85
17.	George Johnson	S.A.	13.81
18.	Dave Corzine	S.A.	13.79
19.	James Donaldson	Seat	13.75
20.	Larry Bird	Bost	13.74

BLOCKS

OR	PLAYER	TEAM	BLK
1.	George Johnson	S.A.	7.12
2.	Wayne Rollins	Atla	5.33
3.	Harvey Catchings	Milw	4.04
4.	James Donaldson	Seat	3.90
5.	Terry Tyler	Detr	3.86
6.	Kevin McHale	Bost	3.81
7.	Artis Gilmore	Chic	3.79
8.	Herb Williams	Indi	3.75
9.	K. Abdul-Jabbar	L.A.L	3.71
10.	Robert Parish	Bost	3.64
11.	Caldwell Jones	Phil	2.87
12.	Wayne Cooper	Dall	2.80
13.	Dave Corzine	S.A.	2.76
14.	Mike Harper	Port	2.75
15.	Clemon Johnson	Indi	2.72
16.	James Bailey	N.J.	2.71
17.	Rick Mahorn	Wash	2.49
18.	Bobby Jones	Phil	2.46
19.	Steve Johnson	K.C.	2.45
20.	Julius Erving	Phil	2.43

SHOOTING

OR	PLAYER	TEAM	SHT
1.	Artis Gilmore	Chic	1.194
2.	Kiki Vandeweghe	Denv	1.127
3.	Adrian Dantley	Utah	1.112
4.	Calvin Natt	Port	1.107
5.	Bobby Jones	Phil	1.105
6.	Alex English	Denv	1.105
7.	K. Abdul-Jabbar	L.A.L	1.103
8.	Steve Johnson	K.C.	1.101
9.	Jerome Whitehead	S.D.	1.093
10.	Sly Williams	N.Y.	1.092
11.	Kyle Macy	Phoe	1.089
12.	Bill Cartwright	N.Y.	1.089
13.	Bob Lanier	Milw	1.088
14.	Bernard King	G.St	1.080
15.	James Donaldson	Seat	1.079
16.	Jeff Ruland	Wash	1.077
17.	Dan Issel	Denv	1.076
18.	Julius Erving	Phil	1.073
19.	Wayne Rollins	Atla	1.072
20.	Bob Gross	Port	1.063

ASSISTS

OR	PLAYER	TEAM	AST
1.	Johnny Moore	S.A.	15.94
2.	John Lucas	Wash	13.63
3.	Mike Bratz	S.A.	13.01
4.	Maurice Cheeks	Phil	12.82
5.	Nate Archibald	Bost	11.98
6.	Earvin Johnson	L.A.L	11.92
7.	Geoff Huston	Clev	11.76
8.	Kenny Higgs	Denv	11.18
9.	Isiah Thomas	Detr	11.15
10.	Phil Ford	K.C.	11.09
11.	Kelvin Ransey	Port	11.02
12.	Rickey Green	Utah	10.72
13.	Allan Bristow	Dall	10.57
14.	Norm Nixon	L.A.L	10.35
15.	Foots Walker	N.J.	10.27
16.	Allen Leavell	Hous	10.20
17.	Larry Drew	K.C.	10.19
18.	Brad Davis	Dall	9.35
19.	Gus Williams	Seat	9.16
20.	M.R. Richardson	N.Y.	9.02

STEALS

OR	PLAYER	TEAM	STL
1.	Maurice Cheeks	Phil	4.02
2.	Quinn Buckner	Milw	3.87
3.	Ray Williams	N.J.	3.50
4.	Johnny Moore	S.A.	3.41
5.	M.R. Richardson	N.Y.	3.36
6.	Darwin Cook	N.J.	3.35
7.	Allen Leavell	Hous	3.35
8.	Earvin Johnson	L.A.L	3.34
9.	Mike Gale	G.St	3.24
10.	Rickey Green	Utah	3.15
11.	Don Buse	Indi	3.11
12.	Foots Walker	N.J.	3.10
13.	Isiah Thomas	Detr	2.96
14.	Mike Woodson	K.C.	2.92
15.	Gus Williams	Seat	2.87
16.	Julius Erving	Phil	2.77
17.	Larry Drew	K.C.	2.68
18.	Don Collins	Wash	2.66
19.	Michael Cooper	L.A.L	2.62
20.	Bob Gross	Port	2.61

WAR ZONE
KAREEM VS MAHORN

CHAPTER 8

CAREER CAPSULES

CAREER CAPSULES

On the following pages I've cited all the present players in the NBA who have qualified at least once in recent years (see page 240 for qualification explanation). DNQ means a player "did not qualify". Following the present players are all the former players who qualified at least six years. Each player is listed alphabetically with several statistical categories listed for each year the player played as well as the university he played at. I have used abbreviations for team names. A couple examples would be S.A. (San Antonio) or LA.C (Los Angeles Clippers).

YR = Year

TM = Team

PR = Production Rating (see chapter one for explanation)

OR = Overall Rank by Production Rating

PS = Position Rank by Production Rating

SC = Scoring Rank (points/games)

SH = Shooting Rank (see page 240 for explanation)

RB = Rebounding Rank based on 48 minutes played

AS = Assists Rank based on 48 minutes played

BL = Blocked Shots Rank based on 48 minutes played

ST = Steals Rank based on 48 minutes played

Blocks and steals were not officially kept as records until 1974. As you can see from Kareem Abdul-Jabbar's register, nothing is listed for those categories prior to 1974. In addition, a dash (-) means the player was not in the top 20% in this category. If the player did place in the top 20% his rank is shown. The reason I did not list a player's rank regardless of his percentile is because I wanted a player's strengths to be evident at a glance. Additionally, a player who ranked 30th in 1955 is nowhere near as impressive as a player who ranked 30th in 1989 when over three times as many players qualified. By my only showing the rank of the top 20% a player's overall dominance can easily be seen. I should mention that Overall Rank and Position Rank are shown on every player for every year. Only the six performance categories reflect the upper 20%.

As I have said before, the NBA did not officially begin keeping statistics on blocks and steals until 1974. Prior to 1974, I only show four performance categories (scoring, shooting, rebounds, and assists), whereas after 1974 that total jumps to six categories.

It will surprise a lot of people, no doubt, but the only NBA player since 1974 to place in the top 20% of all six categories at least once in his career is Alvan Adams. Adams certainly hasn't dominated any one particular category, but he has shown excellence and versatility in all phases of the game (see Adams' register on page 287). Julius Erving also accomplishes this feat if his ABA category rankings are included.

Only two NBA players have placed in the top 20% in five categories in the same year (no player has placed in all six the same year). The two players are Bill Walton - 1978 (Walton failed to place in the top 20% in steals only. His percentile on steals was 75%.) and Charles Barkley - 1986 (Barkley failed to place in the top 20% in assists only. His percentile was 41%.).

On the following two pages you will find several "best" lists. All players who are still playing in the NBA are italicized. ABA rankings are not included.

It is, of course, very possible that some players prior to 1974 would have qualified in five or six categories. Since records were not kept for blocks and steals we'll never know for sure. Listed below are two groups. Group one lists those players who have placed in the top 20% for all four categories (scoring, shooting, rebounds, and assists) sometime in their career. Group two lists those players who have placed in the top 20% for all four categories the same year. Also listed is the percentile for each category. You might note the question mark for Dolph Schayes in group two. Schayes did not rank in the top 20% in rebounds in 1950 because rebounds were not kept until the following year. Doubtless, he would have been in the top 20% since he was #1 in rebounds the following two years.

Group One	**Group Two**		SCR	SHT	REB	AST
Dolph Schayes	Dolph Schayes	1950	7%	11%	?	7%
Ed Macauley	Ed Macauley	1951	4%	3%	13%	13%
Wilt Chamberlain	Wilt Chamberlain	1967	7%	3%	1%	7%
Jerry Lucas	Bill Walton	1978	19%	14%	1%	18%
Bill Walton	*Larry Bird*	1985	1%	9%	19%	20%
Alvan Adams						
Larry Bird						

Listed below are the only 11 players who have placed in the upper 20% of both blocks and steals during the same year.

Charles Barkley	1986
Don Chaney	1975
Julius Erving	1977,78,80, 81,82,84,85
Bob Gross	1976
Garfield Heard	1978,81
Mickey Johnson	1980
Bobby Jones	1978,83,84
Sam Lacey	1978
Akeem Olajuwon	1986,87,88,89
Lonnie Shelton	1977
Michael Jordan	1987,88

Listed below are the players who had the most years qualifying without placing in the top 20% in any category. Shown is the number of years each player came up "empty".

Bill Bradley	8
Keith Erickson	8
Junior Bridgeman	8
Jim Washington	8
Mike Bantom	9
John Johnson	9
Bingo Smith	9
Dave DeBusschere	10
Tom Hawkins	10
Tom Meschery	10
Tom Sanders	10

Only 12 players have placed first in more than one statistical category during their career. Only Kareem Abdul-Jabbar, Oscar Robertson, and John Stockton have placed first in more than two. Shown below are the number of firsts out of the number of categories possible.

Kareem Abdul-Jabbar	4-6	3-4	George Mikan		2-4
Oscar Robertson		3-4	Swen Nater		2-4
John Stockton	3-6	2-4	Jerry West		2-4
Wilt Chamberlain		2-4	Neil Johnston		2-4
Nate Archibald		2-4	Slick Watts	2-6	
Elvin Hayes		2-4	Larry Steele	2-6	

Listed below are the players who have rated over 30 credits per game (Production Rating) the most years. Shown are the number of 30 + seasons out of the total number of years they qualified.

Wilt Chamberlain	13-13	*Larry Bird*	5-9
Kareem Abdul-Jabbar	12-18	*Earvin Johnson*	4-9
Bill Russell	10-13	*Moses Malone*	4-12
Oscar Robertson	9-14	Elgin Baylor	4-12
Jerry Lucas	6-10	Bob Lanier	4-13
Bob Pettit	6-11	*Michael Jordan*	3-5

Listed below are the only twelve players ever to lead in Production Rating during a given year (Overall Rank #1). The number of years each player accomplished this feat is shown.

Kareem Abdul-Jabbar	11	George Mikan	2
Wilt Chamberlain	10	*Michael Jordan*	2
Moses Malone	3	Paul Arizin	1
Neil Johnston	3	Dolph Schayes	1
Larry Bird	3	Bill Russell	1
Bob Pettit	2	*Earvin Johnson*	1

Listed below are the players who won their position (Production Ratings leader) the most years. Shown are the players and the number of years each finished first.

Kareem Abdul-Jabbar	11	George Gervin	6
Wilt Chamberlain	10	George Mikan	6
Oscar Robertson	9	Neil Johnston	5
Larry Bird	9	Bob Pettit	5
Earvin Johnson	9	Dolph Schayes	5
Bob Cousy	7	*Moses Malone*	5

Listed below are the players who finished first in each statistical category. Shown is the category, the player, and the number of years each finished first.

Scoring (pts/games)		**Shooting** (pg. 240)		**Assists** (48 min.)	
Wilt Chamberlain	7	Oscar Robertson	5	Bob Cousy	10
George Gervin	4	Kenny Sears	3	Kevin Porter	6
Neil Johnston	3	K. Abdul-Jabbar	3	Guy Rodgers	3
Bob McAdoo	3	Artis Gilmore	3	Art Williams	2
George Mikan	2	Neil Johnston	2	Slick Watts	2
Adrian Dantley	2	Jerry West	2	Oscar Robertson	2
K. Abdul-Jabbar	2	Jerry Lucas	2	Andy Phillip	2
Michael Jordan	2	Dave Twardzik	2	*John Stockton*	2
Others	15	Others	18	Others	11

Rebounds (48 min.)		**Blocks** (48 min.)		**Steals** (48 min.)	
Bill Russell	7	George Johnson	4	*Alvin Robertson*	3
Wilt Chamberlain	6	*Wayne Rollins*	3	Slick Watts	2
Moses Malone	3	*Mark Eaton*	3	Dudley Bradley	2
Larry Smith	3	*Manute Bol*	3	Johnny Moore	1
Dolph Schayes	2	Elmore Smith	2	*Darwin Cook*	1
Tom Boerwinkle	2	K. Abdul-Jabbar	1	M.R. Richardson	1
Swen Nater	2			*Maurice Cheeks*	1
Charles Oakley	1			Larry Steele	1
LaSalle Thompson	1			Ron Lee	1
Roy Tarpley	1			*John Stockton*	1
Others	12			Others	2

PRESENT PLAYERS

MICHAEL ADAMS — BCU

YR	TM	PR	OR	PS	SC	SH	RB	AS	BL	ST
1986	Sacr	1.94	DNQ							
1987	Wash	9.19	141	27	-	-	-	28	-	9
1988	Denv	16.57	63	15	-	27	-	30	-	14
1989	Denv	19.60	34	7	-	-	-	33	-	18

MARK AGUIRRE — DEPAUL

YR	TM	PR	OR	PS	SC	SH	RB	AS	BL	ST
1982	Dall	15.18	DNQ							
1983	Dall	20.77	25	7	6	-	-	-	-	-
1984	Dall	25.04	9	5	2	-	-	-	-	-
1985	Dall	21.21	25	8	8	-	-	-	-	-
1986	Dall	20.08	32	10	12	-	-	-	-	-
1987	Dall	21.29	26	6	7	-	-	-	-	-
1988	Dall	21.13	24	6	8	-	-	-	-	-
1989	Detr	15.74	83	22	32	-	-	-	-	-

DANNY AINGE — BYU

YR	TM	PR	OR	PS	SC	SH	RB	AS	BL	ST
1982	Bost	3.74	DNQ							
1983	Bost	11.06	117	21	-	-	-	-	-	23
1984	Bost	5.44	DNQ							
1985	Bost	16.35	70	13	-	16	-	-	-	31
1986	Bost	13.83	85	14	-	28	-	-	-	-
1987	Bost	17.15	60	9	-	7	-	-	-	-
1988	Bost	18.26	48	9	-	3	-	-	-	-
1989	Sacr	17.64	53	10	-	-	-	35	-	-

GREG ANDERSON — HOUSTON

YR	TM	PR	OR	PS	SC	SH	RB	AS	BL	ST
1988	S.A.	13.11	97	19	-	-	27	-	13	-
1989	S.A.	15.11	90	19	-	-	19	-	21	-

RON ANDERSON — FRESNO STATE

YR	TM	PR	OR	PS	SC	SH	RB	AS	BL	ST
1985	Clev	5.17	DNQ							
1986	Indi	9.68	138	26	-	-	-	-	-	-
1987	Indi	5.86	DNQ							
1988	Indi	7.54	DNQ							
1989	Phil	14.93	93	23	-	-	-	-	-	-

WILLIE ANDERSON — GEORGIA

YR	TM	PR	OR	PS	SC	SH	RB	AS	BL	ST
1989	S.A.	18.99	39	9	35	-	-	-	-	29

JOHN BAGLEY — BCU

YR	TM	PR	OR	PS	SC	SH	RB	AS	BL	ST
1983	Clev	5.26	DNQ							
1984	Clev	8.99	148	28	-	-	-	22	-	-
1985	Clev	16.32	71	12	-	-	-	4	-	19
1986	Clev	16.28	63	8	-	-	-	4	-	27
1987	Clev	12.38	103	19	-	-	-	-	-	-
1988	N.J.	13.43	94	21	-	-	-	32	-	-
1989	N.J.	9.38	155	28	-	-	-	14	-	-

THURL BAILEY — N.C.STATE

YR	TM	PR	OR	PS	SC	SH	RB	AS	BL	ST
1984	Utah	12.62	105	20	-	-	-	-	10	-
1985	Utah	16.44	67	15	-	-	-	-	23	-
1986	Utah	14.79	77	20	-	-	-	-	19	-
1987	Utah	12.77	99	25	-	-	-	-	24	-
1988	Utah	18.94	42	10	26	-	-	-	20	-
1989	Utah	16.79	65	15	28	-	-	-	-	-

CHARLES BARKLEY — AUBURN

YR	TM	PR	OR	PS	SC	SH	RB	AS	BL	ST
1985	Phil	18.40	43	10	-	31	16	-	-	-
1986	Phil	28.26	4	1	23	27	5	-	26	16
1987	Phil	33.46	2	1	15	2	3	-	-	-
1988	Phil	32.51	3	1	4	6	12	-	-	-
1989	Phil	32.68	3	1	8	5	9	-	-	-

JOHN BATTLE — RUTGERS

YR	TM	PR	OR	PS	SC	SH	RB	AS	BL	ST
1986	Atla	3.73	DNQ							
1987	Atla	5.23	DNQ							
1988	Atla	8.40	DNQ							
1989	Atla	8.27	167	41	-	-	-	-	-	-

BENOIT BENJAMIN — CREIGHTON

YR	TM	PR	OR	PS	SC	SH	RB	AS	BL	ST
1986	L.A.C	16.04	67	17	-	-	20	-	4	-
1987	L.A.C	15.89	70	17	-	-	31	-	5	-
1988	L.A.C	17.97	50	10	-	-	-	-	2	-
1989	L.A.C	21.11	25	6	-	30	27	-	8	-

RICKY BERRY — OREGON ST.

YR	TM	PR	OR	PS	SC	SH	RB	AS	BL	ST
1989	Sacr	9.58	151	33	-	-	-	-	-	-

WALTER BERRY — ST. JOHN'S

YR	TM	PR	OR	PS	SC	SH	RB	AS	BL	ST
1987	S.A.	13.97	85	22	-	-	-	-	-	-
1988	S.A.	16.23	66	16	-	-	-	-	-	-
1989	Hous	9.43	154	35	-	-	-	-	33	-

LARRY BIRD — INDIANA ST.

YR	TM	PR	OR	PS	SC	SH	RB	AS	BL	ST
1980	Bost	25.26	6	1	16	-	15	-	-	-
1981	Bost	26.74	5	1	16	-	22	-	-	31
1982	Bost	29.16	3	1	10	-	20	-	-	28
1983	Bost	30.04	2	1	11	-	19	-	-	29
1984	Bost	29.99	2	1	7	-	26	28	-	31
1985	Bost	34.39	1	1	2	14	30	31	-	-
1986	Bost	31.30	1	1	4	21	-	28	-	22
1987	Bost	34.28	1	1	4	4	-	26	-	-
1988	Bost	34.01	2	1	3	4	-	-	-	-
1989	Bost	21.00	DNQ							

OTIS BIRDSONG — HOUSTON

YR	TM	PR	OR	PS	SC	SH	RB	AS	BL	ST
1978	K.C.	11.88	108	22	-	-	-	-	-	-
1979	K.C.	18.63	40	4	19	-	-	-	-	-
1980	K.C.	18.04	43	6	9	-	-	-	-	-
1981	K.C.	20.31	20	2	6	24	-	-	-	-
1982	N.J.	11.03	DNQ							
1983	N.J.	13.56	87	17	-	-	-	-	-	-
1984	N.J.	15.14	74	11	30	-	-	-	-	-
1985	N.J.	16.75	65	11	26	-	-	-	-	-
1986	N.J.	12.96	100	19	-	-	-	-	-	-
1987	N.J.	5.14	DNQ							
1988	N.J.	9.12	140	28	-	-	-	-	-	-
1989	Bost	2.38	DNQ							

ROLANDO BLACKMAN — KANSAS ST.

YR	TM	PR	OR	PS	SC	SH	RB	AS	BL	ST
1982	Dall	11.38	116	19	-	-	-	-	-	-
1983	Dall	15.19	72	13	-	-	-	-	-	-
1984	Dall	21.17	25	2	13	14	-	-	-	-
1985	Dall	17.60	55	7	-	-	-	-	-	-
1986	Dall	18.52	40	5	15	-	-	-	-	-
1987	Dall	17.98	55	7	24	-	-	-	-	-
1988	Dall	16.48	64	10	-	-	-	-	-	-
1989	Dall	16.74	67	12	26	-	-	-	-	-

TYRONE BOGUES — WAKE FOREST

YR	TM	PR	OR	PS	SC	SH	RB	AS	BL	ST
1988	Wash	8.68	147	30	-	-	-	8	-	5
1989	Char	11.90	127	24	-	-	-	1	-	15

MANUTE BOL — BRIDGEPORT

YR	TM	PR	OR	PS	SC	SH	RB	AS	BL	ST
1986	Wash	12.05	112	22	-	-	-	-	1	-
1987	Wash	8.96	144	31	-	-	-	-	1	-
1988	Wash	6.95	DNQ							
1989	Gost	10.46	140	24	-	-	29	-	1	-

SAM BOWIE — KENTUCKY

YR	TM	PR	OR	PS	SC	SH	RB	AS	BL	ST
1985	Port	18.32	46	10	-	-	17	-	4	-
1986	Port	18.07	DNQ							
1987	Port	14.40	DNQ							
1988	DID NOT PLAY									
1989	Port	10.75	DNQ							

RANDY BREUER — MINNESOTA

YR	TM	PR	OR	PS	SC	SH	RB	AS	BL	ST
1984	Milw	3.25	DNQ							
1985	Milw	6.96	DNQ							
1986	Milw	11.54	118	23	-	-	-	-	12	-
1987	Milw	8.87	145	32	-	-	-	-	23	-
1988	Milw	14.47	83	15	-	-	-	-	18	-
1989	Milw	5.38	DNQ							

FRANK BRICKOWSKI — PENN STATE

YR	TM	PR	OR	PS	SC	SH	RB	AS	BL	ST
1985	Seat	6.50	DNQ							
1986	Seat	2.70	DNQ							
1987	S.A.	4.86	DNQ							
1988	S.A.	18.71	43	10	-	-	-	-	-	-
1989	S.A.	15.42	86	15	-	-	-	-	-	26

MICHAEL CAGE — SAN DIEGO ST.

YR	TM	PR	OR	PS	SC	SH	RB	AS	BL	ST
1985	LA.C	10.00	138	32	-	27	-	-	-	-
1986	LA.C	9.31	142	35	-	-	27	-	-	-
1987	LA.C	21.95	22	8	-	-	13	-	-	-
1988	LA.C	21.24	23	7	-	-	3	-	-	-
1989	Seat	16.90	63	15	-	-	13	-	-	-

ANTOINE CARR — WICHITA STATE

YR	TM	PR	OR	PS	SC	SH	RB	AS	BL	ST
1985	Atla	9.77	142	33	-	28	-	-	9	-
1986	Atla	8.06	DNQ							
1987	Atla	6.05	DNQ							
1988	Atla	10.32	DNQ							
1989	Atla	8.86	159	37	-	-	-	-	23	-

JOE BARRY CARROLL — PURDUE

YR	TM	PR	OR	PS	SC	SH	RB	AS	BL	ST
1981	G.St	19.37	27	11	27	-	-	-	29	-
1982	G.St	18.34	36	10	-	-	-	-	21	-
1983	G.St	23.62	11	6	7	-	-	-	21	-
1984	G.St	20.04	32	11	25	-	-	-	20	-
1985	DID NOT PLAY									
1986	G.St	20.43	29	8	17	-	-	-	17	-
1987	G.St	20.36	33	7	23	-	-	-	19	-
1988	Hous	12.92	98	22	-	-	-	-	17	-
1989	N.J.	15.59	84	13	-	-	-	-	27	-

BILL CARTWRIGHT — USF

YR	TM	PR	OR	PS	SC	SH	RB	AS	BL	ST
1980	N.Y.	23.59	11	5	13	8	-	-	-	-
1981	N.Y.	20.63	17	8	19	11	-	-	-	-
1982	N.Y.	15.39	63	15	-	12	-	-	-	-
1983	N.Y.	18.29	43	12	-	12	-	-	22	-
1984	N.Y.	20.18	28	9	-	10	30	-	32	-
1985	DID NOT PLAY									
1986	N.Y.	9.00	DNQ							
1987	N.Y.	19.09	48	12	-	28	-	-	-	-
1988	N.Y.	12.28	106	23	-	19	-	-	-	-
1989	Chic	12.49	118	19	-	-	-	-	-	-

TERRY CATLEDGE — S. ALABAMA

YR	TM	PR	OR	PS	SC	SH	RB	AS	BL	ST
1986	Phil	7.48	DNQ							
1987	Wash	12.76	100	26	-	-	32	-	-	-
1988	Wash	11.10	119	27	-	-	31	-	-	-
1989	Wash	12.30	122	26	-	-	23	-	-	-

TOM CHAMBERS — UTAH

YR	TM	PR	OR	PS	SC	SH	RB	AS	BL	ST
1982	S.D.	16.14	57	12	-	-	-	-	-	-
1983	S.D.	16.32	58	10	-	-	-	-	-	-
1984	Seat	17.12	54	12	-	-	-	-	-	-
1985	Seat	20.06	33	6	22	-	-	-	-	-
1986	Seat	16.97	55	11	-	-	-	-	-	-
1987	Seat	20.50	32	8	13	-	-	-	-	-
1988	Seat	17.73	52	11	18	-	-	-	-	-
1989	Phoe	24.11	13	2	9	-	-	-	-	-

REX CHAPMAN — KENTUCKY

YR	TM	PR	OR	PS	SC	SH	RB	AS	BL	ST
1989	Char	11.03	133	29	-	-	-	-	-	-

MAURICE CHEEKS — W. TEXAS ST.

YR	TM	PR	OR	PS	SC	SH	RB	AS	BL	ST
1979	Phil	12.73	96	16	-	-	-	15	-	5
1980	Phil	17.37	50	5	-	10	-	8	-	7
1981	Phil	16.26	60	6	-	16	-	7	-	4
1982	Phil	18.75	32	4	-	-	-	4	-	1
1983	Phil	17.44	47	7	-	18	-	14	-	5
1984	Phil	16.85	56	8	-	24	-	23	-	5
1985	Phil	18.38	44	5	-	2	-	24	-	10
1986	Phil	21.65	19	3	-	17	-	14	-	10
1987	Phil	20.56	31	6	-	30	-	24	-	6
1988	Phil	19.22	37	7	-	-	-	15	-	-
1989	Phil	16.38	76	18	-	-	-	12	-	-

DERRICK CHEVIOUS — MISSOURI

YR	TM	PR	OR	PS	SC	SH	RB	AS	BL	ST
1989	Hous	7.36	174	44	-	-	-	-	-	-

STEVE COLTER — NEW MEXICO ST.

YR	TM	PR	OR	PS	SC	SH	RB	AS	BL	ST
1985	Port	7.80		DNQ						
1986	Port	9.80	136	29	-	-	-	-	-	13
1987	Phil	6.96		DNQ						
1988	Wash	9.53	132	27	-	-	-	-	-	-
1989	Wash	8.30	166	32	-	-	-	-	-	-

LESTER CONNER — OREGON ST.

YR	TM	PR	OR	PS	SC	SH	RB	AS	BL	ST
1983	Gost	8.81		DNQ						
1984	Gost	14.65	78	11	-	-	-	-	-	11
1985	Gost	11.94	117	25	-	-	-	-	-	6
1986	Gost	3.94		DNQ						
1987		DID NOT PLAY								
1988	Hous	3.23		DNQ						
1989	N.J.	16.87	64	14	-	-	-	13	-	6

MICHAEL COOPER — NEW MEXICO

YR	TM	PR	OR	PS	SC	SH	RB	AS	BL	ST
1979	L.A.L	1.33		DNQ						
1980	L.A.L	10.33	129	25	-	24	-	-	-	-
1981	L.A.L	13.74	94	17	-	-	-	-	-	29
1982	L.A.L	13.76	83	15	-	-	-	-	-	19
1983	L.A.L	12.27	107	20	-	15	-	-	-	22
1984	L.A.L	14.74	77	13	-	25	-	19	-	32
1985	L.A.L	12.65	107	22	-	-	-	22	-	-
1986	L.A.L	13.34	94	15	-	-	-	-	-	-
1987	L.A.L	13.04	96	19	-	-	-	-	-	-
1988	L.A.L	11.98	111	18	-	-	-	-	-	-
1989	L.A.L	10.11	147	35	-	-	-	-	-	-

WAYNE COOPER — NEW ORLEANS

YR	TM	PR	OR	PS	SC	SH	RB	AS	BL	ST
1979	G.St	6.34		DNQ						
1980	G.St	12.04	109	23	-	-	17	-	22	-
1981	Utah	9.68	144	31	-	-	10	-	-	-
1982	Dall	12.80	96	22	-	-	11	-	12	-
1983	Port	12.98	97	20	-	-	20	-	11	-
1984	Port	11.89	118	25	-	-	18	-	8	-
1985	Denv	15.45	81	15	-	-	11	-	2	-
1986	Denv	17.12	54	13	-	-	19	-	3	-
1987	Denv	11.70	112	24	-	-	16	-	9	-
1988	Denv	10.31		DNQ						
1989	Denv	14.43	96	21	-	-	6	-	2	-

TYRONE CORBIN — DEPAUL

YR	TM	PR	OR	PS	SC	SH	RB	AS	BL	ST
1986	S.A.	3.88		DNQ						
1987	Clev	7.51		DNQ						
1988	Phoe	9.29	135	26	-	-	-	-	-	-
1989	Phoe	11.73	128	29	-	20	-	-	-	-

DAVE CORZINE — DEPAUL

YR	TM	PR	OR	PS	SC	SH	RB	AS	BL	ST
1979	Wash	4.63		DNQ						
1980	Wash	4.99		DNQ						
1981	S.A.	14.50	84	22	-	-	6	-	23	-
1982	S.A.	15.18	66	16	-	-	18	-	13	-
1983	Chic	16.98	51	14	-	-	22	-	27	-
1984	Chic	15.87	68	18	-	-	-	-	23	-
1985	Chic	10.88	126	22	-	-	-	-	-	-
1986	Chic	13.31	90	20	-	-	-	-	-	-
1987	Chic	13.22	92	22	-	-	-	-	32	-
1988	Chic	13.72	91	18	-	-	-	-	23	-
1989	Chic	7.60	172	30	-	-	-	-	-	-

PAT CUMMINGS — DETROIT

YR	TM	PR	OR	PS	SC	SH	RB	AS	BL	ST
1980	Milw	7.21		DNQ						
1981	Milw	8.21		DNQ						
1982	Milw	6.87		DNQ						
1983	Dall	15.59	66	16	-	-	21	-	-	-
1984	Dall	16.12	67	17	-	-	25	-	-	-
1985	N.Y.	17.27	58	14	-	-	-	-	-	-
1986	N.Y.	16.48		DNQ						
1987	N.Y.	9.80		DNQ						
1988	N.Y.	6.26		DNQ						
1989	Miam	9.58		DNQ						

TERRY CUMMINGS — DEPAUL

YR	TM	PR	OR	PS	SC	SH	RB	AS	BL	ST
1983	S.D.	26.04	5	2	10	-	18	-	-	27
1984	S.D.	22.21	19	2	9	-	24	-	-	-
1985	Milw	24.13	14	1	10	-	-	-	-	-
1986	Milw	19.50	37	8	28	-	-	-	-	-
1987	Milw	22.56	18	5	25	-	-	-	-	-
1988	Milw	19.16	40	9	15	-	-	-	-	-
1989	Milw	21.54	22	5	11	-	-	-	-	-

EARL CURETON — DETROIT

YR	TM	PR	OR	PS	SC	SH	RB	AS	BL	ST
1981	Phil	5.19		DNQ						
1982	Phil	7.05		DNQ						
1983	Phil	4.96		DNQ						
1984	Detr	5.37		DNQ						
1985	Detr	8.63	148	35	-	-	-	-	-	-
1986	Detr	11.51	120	30	-	-	-	-	-	-
1987	LA.C	10.44	125	29	-	-	-	-	-	-
1988	LA.C	6.32		DNQ						
1989	Char	10.46	139	23	-	-	-	-	-	-

DELL CURRY — VIRGINIA TECH

YR	TM	PR	OR	PS	SC	SH	RB	AS	BL	ST
1987	Clev	3.78		DNQ						
1988	Clev	8.68	146	29	-	-	-	-	-	13
1989	Char	9.50		DNQ						

QUINTIN DAILEY — SAN FRANCISCO

YR	TM	PR	OR	PS	SC	SH	RB	AS	BL	ST
1983	Chic	12.55	103	19	-	-	-	-	-	-
1984	Chic	14.13	85	14	-	-	-	-	-	-
1985	Chic	12.04	115	21	-	-	-	-	-	-
1986	Chic	9.14		DNQ						
1987	LA.C	6.84		DNQ						
1988	LA.C	9.21		DNQ						
1989	LA.C	12.48	119	24	-	-	-	-	-	30

ADRIAN DANTLEY — NOTRE DAME

YR	TM	PR	OR	PS	SC	SH	RB	AS	BL	ST
1977	Buff	20.14	24	8	21	8	-	-	-	-
1978	LA.L	22.72	14	2	18	16	-	-	-	-
1979	LA.L	17.18	53	16	-	18	-	-	-	-
1980	Utah	27.46	4	2	3	3	-	-	-	-
1981	Utah	28.23	3	1	1	8	-	-	-	-
1982	Utah	27.81	4	1	3	3	-	-	-	-
1983	Utah	29.68	DNQ								
1984	Utah	27.96	3	2	1	4	-	-	-	-
1985	Utah	23.75	16	6	7	24	-	-	-	-
1986	Utah	25.82	5	2	2	11	-	-	-	-
1987	Detr	18.21	53	13	22	17	-	-	-	-
1988	Detr	17.29	53	11	22	20	-	-	-	-
1989	Dall	16.29	79	21	29	-	-	-	-	-

BRAD DAUGHERTY — N CAROLINA

YR	TM	PR	OR	PS	SC	SH	RB	AS	BL	ST
1987	Clev	19.10	47	11	-	-	-	-	-	-
1988	Clev	20.70	25	4	32	-	-	-	-	-
1989	Clev	22.37	19	5	30	-	33	-	-	-

BRAD DAVIS — MARYLAND

YR	TM	PR	OR	PS	SC	SH	RB	AS	BL	ST
1978	LA.L	4.03	DNQ								
1979	Indi	4.33	DNQ								
1980	Utah	6.61	DNQ								
1981	Dall	15.73	65	8	-	6	-	8	-	-
1982	Dall	14.99	67	11	-	26	-	18	-	-
1983	Dall	16.75	54	8	-	2	-	7	-	-
1984	Dall	15.31	73	10	-	22	-	16	-	-
1985	Dall	15.28	84	17	-	9	-	14	-	-
1986	Dall	13.10	96	17	-	2	-	11	-	-
1987	Dall	9.29	137	24	-	-	-	14	-	-
1988	Dall	9.28	136	26	-	16	-	23	-	-
1989	Dall	7.71	DNQ								

WALTER DAVIS — N. CAROLINA

YR	TM	PR	OR	PS	SC	SH	RB	AS	BL	ST
1978	Phoe	21.96	19	6	10	6	-	-	-	-
1979	Phoe	22.70	16	4	10	3	-	-	-	14
1980	Phoe	20.51	27	9	15	4	-	-	-	-
1981	Phoe	15.92	62	12	31	10	-	-	-	-
1982	Phoe	11.95	DNQ								
1983	Phoe	17.39	48	5	-	31	-	-	-	-
1984	Phoe	18.40	42	4	27	31	-	30	-	-
1985	Phoe	11.80	DNQ								
1986	Phoe	17.99	45	7	14	-	-	-	-	-
1987	Phoe	19.85	37	4	11	25	-	-	-	-
1988	Phoe	15.41	74	12	-	-	-	-	-	-
1989	Denv	12.21	123	26	-	-	-	-	-	-

JOHNNY DAWKINS — DUKE

YR	TM	PR	OR	PS	SC	SH	RB	AS	BL	ST
1987	S.A.	9.58	135	28	-	-	-	-	-	-
1988	S.A.	18.37	47	11	-	-	16	-	-	-
1989	S.A.	15.25	DNQ								

VINNY DEL NEGRO — N. CAROLINA ST.

YR	TM	PR	OR	PS	SC	SH	RB	AS	BL	ST
1989	Sacr	8.36	165	31	-	-	-	-	-	-

JAMES DONALDSON — WASH. ST.

YR	TM	PR	OR	PS	SC	SH	RB	AS	BL	ST
1981	Seat	8.03	DNQ								
1982	Seat	12.20	103	24	-	15	19	-	4	-
1983	Seat	12.67	102	23	-	6	23	-	15	-
1984	S.D.	17.00	55	14	-	3	32	-	16	-
1985	LA.C	16.11	74	14	-	1	26	-	14	-
1986	Dall	16.84	57	14	-	12	17	-	16	-
1987	Dall	21.05	27	6	-	3	11	-	21	-
1988	Dall	14.98	78	14	-	13	13	-	22	-
1989	Dall	17.70	52	10	-	7	8	-	18	-

LARRY DREW — MISSOURI

YR	TM	PR	OR	PS	SC	SH	RB	AS	BL	ST
1981	Detr	6.42	165	31	-	-	-	-	-	16
1982	K.C.	11.62	109	22	-	-	-	17	-	17
1983	K.C.	20.05	31	4	23	-	-	11	-	-
1984	K.C.	16.62	58	9	-	-	-	11	-	23
1985	K.C.	15.96	76	13	-	-	-	21	-	-
1986	Sacr	11.40	123	22	-	-	-	-	-	-
1987	LA.C	11.10	118	21	-	-	-	23	-	-
1988	LA.C	10.31	127	26	-	-	-	26	-	-
1989		DID NOT PLAY									

CLYDE DREXLER — HOUSTON

YR	TM	PR	OR	PS	SC	SH	RB	AS	BL	ST
1984	Port	8.24	DNQ								
1985	Port	20.71	28	3	-	-	-	28	-	7
1986	Port	22.44	16	2	-	-	-	12	-	4
1987	Port	25.29	9	2	19	-	-	30	-	12
1988	Port	27.94	5	2	6	-	-	-	-	10
1989	Port	28.87	6	2	4	-	-	-	-	9

KEVIN DUCKWORTH — E. ILLINOIS

YR	TM	PR	OR	PS	SC	SH	RB	AS	BL	ST
1987	Port	5.89	DNQ								
1988	Port	15.42	73	13	-	-	26	-	-	-
1989	Port	16.72	68	11	-	-	-	-	-	-

JOE DUMARS — MCNEESE ST.

YR	TM	PR	OR	PS	SC	SH	RB	AS	BL	ST
1986	Detr	10.23	134	27	-	-	-	21	-	-
1987	Detr	11.71	111	22	-	-	-	-	-	-
1988	Detr	13.59	92	16	-	-	-	-	-	-
1989	Detr	16.59	72	13	-	31	-	-	-	-

T.R. DUNN — ALABAMA

YR	TM	PR	OR	PS	SC	SH	RB	AS	BL	ST
1978	Port	4.59	DNQ								
1979	Port	9.23	141	25	-	-	-	-	-	-
1980	Port	9.01	142	28	-	-	-	-	-	20
1981	Denv	6.61	DNQ								
1982	Denv	14.10	82	14	-	-	-	-	-	22
1983	Denv	14.30	81	15	-	-	-	-	-	19
1984	Denv	14.11	86	15	-	-	-	-	-	10
1985	Denv	10.44	133	28	-	-	-	-	-	13
1986	Denv	10.40	132	26	-	-	-	-	-	9
1987	Denv	7.35	158	34	-	-	-	-	-	24
1988	Denv	6.04	DNQ								
1989	Phoe	2.91	DNQ								

LEDELL EACKLES — NEW ORLEANS

YR	TM	PR	OR	PS	SC	SH	RB	AS	BL	ST
1989	Wash	8.13	168	42	-	-	-	-	-	-

MARK EATON — UCLA

YR	TM	PR	OR	PS	SC	SH	RB	AS	BL	ST
1983	Utah	10.44	DNQ							
1984	Utah	14.33	81	23	-	-	19	-	1	-
1985	Utah	20.52	31	8	-	-	8	-	1	-
1986	Utah	16.31	62	16	-	-	30	-	2	-
1987	Utah	15.29	78	20	-	-	26	-	2	-
1988	Utah	14.27	86	17	-	-	23	-	1	-
1989	Utah	16.59	73	12	-	-	17	-	3	-

JAMES EDWARDS — WASHINGTON

YR	TM	PR	OR	PS	SC	SH	RB	AS	BL	ST
1978	Indi	14.18	75	23	-	-	-	-	-	-
1979	Indi	18.10	44	14	-	-	-	21	-	-
1980	Indi	17.17	53	17	-	-	-	21	-	-
1981	Indi	17.89	39	12	-	-	-	17	-	-
1982	Clev	17.65	44	12	-	-	-	24	-	-
1983	Phoe	10.58	DNQ							
1984	Phoe	14.64	79	22	-	-	-	-	-	-
1985	Phoe	14.63	90	18	-	-	-	-	-	-
1986	Phoe	15.15	DNQ							
1987	Phoe	12.57	DNQ							
1988	Detr	11.23	117	25	-	-	-	-	-	-
1989	Detr	7.01	DNQ							

KEVIN EDWARDS — DEPAUL

YR	TM	PR	OR	PS	SC	SH	RB	AS	BL	ST
1989	Miam	11.91	125	27	-	-	-	-	-	19

CRAIG EHLO — WASHINGTON ST.

YR	TM	PR	OR	PS	SC	SH	RB	AS	BL	ST
1984	Hous	3.00	DNQ							
1985	Hous	2.09	DNQ							
1986	Hous	3.36	DNQ							
1987	Clev	8.57	DNQ							
1988	Clev	9.44	133	25	-	-	-	-	-	31
1989	Clev	10.50	137	30	-	-	-	-	-	20

DALE ELLIS — TENNESSEE

YR	TM	PR	OR	PS	SC	SH	RB	AS	BL	ST
1984	Dall	7.84	DNQ							
1985	Dall	7.68	DNQ							
1986	Dall	5.89	DNQ							
1987	Seat	21.77	25	3	8	14	-	-	-	-
1988	Seat	20.55	28	6	7	-	-	-	-	-
1989	Seat	21.13	24	4	3	12	-	-	-	-

ALEX ENGLISH — S. CAROLINA

YR	TM	PR	OR	PS	SC	SH	RB	AS	BL	ST
1977	Milw	5.45	DNQ							
1978	Milw	11.51	DNQ							
1979	Indi	19.52	35	9	-	-	-	-	-	-
1980	Denv	18.62	38	12	-	-	-	-	-	-
1981	Denv	24.37	7	4	10	-	-	-	-	-
1982	Denv	27.44	5	2	4	6	-	-	30	-
1983	Denv	28.30	4	1	1	27	-	-	29	-
1984	Denv	25.74	7	3	4	28	-	-	-	-
1985	Denv	24.79	12	4	5	-	-	-	-	-
1986	Denv	24.36	9	4	3	-	-	-	-	-
1987	Denv	23.90	12	4	3	-	-	-	-	-
1988	Denv	21.70	22	5	9	-	-	-	-	-
1989	Denv	21.38	23	6	5	-	-	-	-	-

PATRICK EWING — GEORGETOWN

YR	TM	PR	OR	PS	SC	SH	RB	AS	BL	ST
1986	N.Y.	20.56	28	7	26	-	-	-	13	-
1987	N.Y.	21.90	23	5	21	-	-	-	8	-
1988	N.Y.	22.61	17	2	21	24	22	-	3	-
1989	N.Y.	27.46	8	2	12	11	31	-	5	-

VERN FLEMING — GEORGIA

YR	TM	PR	OR	PS	SC	SH	RB	AS	BL	ST
1985	Indi	12.98	104	20	-	-	-	-	-	-
1986	Indi	17.99	44	6	-	-	-	29	-	-
1987	Indi	16.17	67	11	-	-	-	29	-	-
1988	Indi	19.19	38	8	-	32	-	22	-	-
1989	Indi	17.49	57	12	-	-	-	26	-	-

ERIC FLOYD — GEORGETOWN

YR	TM	PR	OR	PS	SC	SH	RB	AS	BL	ST
1983	G.St	6.91	DNQ							
1984	G.St	14.77	76	12	-	-	-	-	-	-
1985	G.St	15.72	78	14	-	-	-	-	-	-
1986	G.St	21.33	21	4	-	-	-	7	-	18
1987	G.St	23.65	15	3	-	12	-	5	-	-
1988	Hous	16.58	62	14	-	-	-	18	-	-
1989	Hous	18.46	45	11	-	-	-	7	-	-

WINSTON GARLAND — SW MISSOURI ST.

YR	TM	PR	OR	PS	SC	SH	RB	AS	BL	ST
1988	G.St	14.76	82	19	-	-	-	24	-	23
1989	G.St	16.76	66	15	-	-	-	29	-	12

TOM GARRICK — RHODE ISLAND

YR	TM	PR	OR	PS	SC	SH	RB	AS	BL	ST
1989	LA.C	8.68	163	39	-	-	-	-	-	31

ARMON GILLIAM — UNLV

YR	TM	PR	OR	PS	SC	SH	RB	AS	BL	ST
1988	Phoe	15.36	75	17	-	-	-	-	-	-
1989	Phoe	15.74	82	16	-	-	32	-	-	-

MIKE GMINSKI — DUKE

YR	TM	PR	OR	PS	SC	SH	RB	AS	BL	ST
1981	N.J.	14.46	85	23	-	-	29	-	9	-
1982	N.J.	6.23	DNQ							
1983	N.J.	10.08	DNQ							
1984	N.J.	10.62	135	29	-	-	28	-	26	-
1985	N.J.	16.43	68	13	-	-	-	28	-	-
1986	N.J.	20.01	34	10	-	20	31	-	-	-
1987	N.J.	18.46	51	13	-	-	-	27	-	-
1988	Phil	20.56	27	5	-	-	-	18	-	25
1989	Phil	20.55	28	7	-	-	-	20	-	30

GARY GRANT — MICHIGAN

YR	TM	PR	OR	PS	SC	SH	RB	AS	BL	ST
1989	LA.C	13.70	104	21	-	-	-	6	-	3

HORACE GRANT — AUBURN

YR	TM	PR	OR	PS	SC	SH	RB	AS	BL	ST
1988	Chic	10.56	124	29	-	-	-	-	-	-
1989	Chic	17.52	56	13	-	-	-	-	-	-

SYLVESTER GRAY   MEMPHIS ST.

YR	TM	PR	OR	PS	SC	SH	RB	AS	BL	ST
1989	Maim	9.45			DNQ					

A.C. GREEN   OREGON ST.

YR	TM	PR	OR	PS	SC	SH	RB	AS	BL	ST
1986	LA.L	8.67			DNQ					
1987	LA.L	16.03	69	16	-	21	30	-	-	-
1988	LA.L	16.44	65	14	-	-	21	-	-	-
1989	LA.L	18.61	42	7	-	29	15	-	-	-

RICKEY GREEN   MICHIGAN

YR	TM	PR	OR	PS	SC	SH	RB	AS	BL	ST
1978	G.St	4.17			DNQ					
1979	Detr	4.89			DNQ					
1980		DID NOT PLAY								
1981	Utah	11.68			DNQ					
1982	Utah	18.44	34	5	-	-	12	-	10	
1983	Utah	19.38	33	5	-	-	5	-	2	
1984	Utah	19.74	34	3	-	-	7	-	2	
1985	Utah	16.78	64	11	-	-	8	-	17	
1986	Utah	12.75	104	18	-	-	18	-	24	
1987	Utah	13.40	91	15	-	-	8	-	22	
1988	Utah	6.37			DNQ					
1989	Milw	6.19			DNQ					

SIDNEY GREEN   UNLV

YR	TM	PR	OR	PS	SC	SH	RB	AS	BL	ST
1984	Chic	5.69			DNQ					
1985	Chic	7.75			DNQ					
1986	Chic	15.24	74	17	-	21	-	-	-	
1987	Detr	12.08	104	27	-	2	-	-	-	
1988	N.Y.	11.40	116	26	-	9	-	-	-	
1989	N.Y.	8.02			DNQ					

DAVID GREENWOOD   UCLA

YR	TM	PR	OR	PS	SC	SH	RB	AS	BL	ST
1980	Chic	19.95	33	6	-	-	26	-	19	-
1981	Chic	18.89	31	6	-	-	26	-	26	-
1982	Chic	20.06	25	6	-	-	23	-	-	
1983	Chic	15.86	62	11	-	-	8	-	-	
1984	Chic	18.03	46	9	-	-	17	-	-	
1985	Chic	10.15	135	31	-	-	-	-	-	
1986	S.A.	13.28	91	24	-	-	22	-	-	
1987	S.A.	19.13	46	11	-	-	17	-	-	
1988	S.A.	12.40			DNQ					
1989	Denv	3.49			DNQ					

DARRELL GRIFFITH   LOUISVILLE

YR	TM	PR	OR	PS	SC	SH	RB	AS	BL	ST
1981	Utah	14.31	87	16	17	-	-	-	-	-
1982	Utah	14.85	70	10	21	-	-	-	-	-
1983	Utah	17.16	49	6	14	-	-	-	-	30
1984	Utah	16.57	60	7	28	-	-	-	-	-
1985	Utah	16.92	62	9	14	-	-	-	-	29
1986		DID NOT PLAY								
1987	Utah	11.20	117	23	-	-	-	-	-	22
1988	Utah	8.27			DNQ					
1989	Utah	11.50	130	28	-	-	-	-	-	-

BOB HANSEN   IOWA

YR	TM	PR	OR	PS	SC	SH	RB	AS	BL	ST
1984	Utah	2.44			DNQ					
1985	Utah	4.32			DNQ					
1986	Utah	9.00	145	33	-	-	-	-	-	-
1987	Utah	8.36	151	26	-	-	-	-	-	-
1988	Utah	9.68	131	24	-	22	-	-	-	-
1989	Utah	7.09			DNQ					

BILL HANZLIK   NOTRE DAME

YR	TM	PR	OR	PS	SC	SH	RB	AS	BL	ST
1981	Seat	6.38			DNQ					
1982	Seat	8.62	155	38	-	-	-	-	-	-
1983	Denv	8.11			DNQ					
1984	Denv	8.19			DNQ					
1985	Denv	8.41	149	29	-	-	-	-	-	27
1986	Denv	13.03	97	20	-	-	-	-	-	20
1987	Denv	12.96	97	16	-	-	-	-	-	-
1988	Denv	5.99			DNQ					
1989	Denv	6.17			DNQ					

DEREK HARPER   ILLINOIS

YR	TM	PR	OR	PS	SC	SH	RB	AS	BL	ST
1984	Dall	7.34	158	30	-	-	-	-	-	17
1985	Dall	12.93	105	20	-	-	-	-	-	9
1986	Dall	15.68	71	11	-	-	24	-	7	
1987	Dall	19.77	38	8	-	-	12	-	13	
1988	Dall	19.17	39	9	-	-	20	-	21	
1989	Dall	19.33	36	8	-	34	-	28	-	22

RON HARPER   MIAMI OF OHIO

YR	TM	PR	OR	PS	SC	SH	RB	AS	BL	ST
1987	Clev	18.90	49	6	16	-	-	-	-	7
1988	Clev	16.23	67	11	-	-	-	-	-	9
1989	Clev	21.09	26	5	34	-	-	-	-	13

HERSEY HAWKINS   BRADLEY

YR	TM	PR	OR	PS	SC	SH	RB	AS	BL	ST
1989	Phil	13.68	105	19	-	-	-	-	-	-

GERALD HENDERSON   VCU

YR	TM	PR	OR	PS	SC	SH	RB	AS	BL	ST
1980	Bost	5.57			DNQ					
1981	Bost	6.71	163	34	-	-	-	-	-	33
1982	Bost	9.52	146	25	-	-	-	-	-	-
1983	Bost	7.21			DNQ					
1984	Bost	12.08	113	19	-	29	-	-	-	16
1985	Seat	15.30	83	16	-	-	-	18	-	21
1986	Seat	14.71	79	12	-	-	-	26	-	21
1987	N.Y.	13.18	93	16	-	-	-	16	-	31
1988	Phil	7.77	155	32	-	-	-	-	-	-
1989	Phil	5.82			DNQ					

ROD HIGGINS   FRESNO ST.

YR	TM	PR	OR	PS	SC	SH	RB	AS	BL	ST
1983	Chic	11.62	109	27	-	-	-	-	-	-
1984	Chic	6.95	160	35	-	-	-	-	-	-
1985	Chic	4.63			DNQ					
1986	Chic	3.50			DNQ					
1987	G.St	9.74	133	25	-	19	-	-	-	-
1988	G.St	16.65	58	13	-	11	-	-	-	-
1989	G.St	12.64	115	28	-	26	-	-	-	-

ROY HINSON — RUTGERS

YR	TM	PR	OR	PS	SC	SH	RB	AS	BL	ST
1984	Clev	10.46	139	30	-	-	23	-	3	-
1985	Clev	17.80	52	12	-	-	-	-	8	-
1986	Clev	20.06	33	6	29	-	-	-	28	-
1987	Phil	15.09	79	18	-	-	-	-	10	-
1988	N.J.	16.60	61	13	-	-	-	-	15	-
1989	N.J.	15.33	87	17	-	-	-	-	17	-

CRAIG HODGES — CAL ST.-L.B.

YR	TM	PR	OR	PS	SC	SH	RB	AS	BL	ST
1983	S.D.	8.55	142	31	-	-	-	-	-	-
1984	S.D.	5.67	161	31	-	-	-	-	-	-
1985	Milw	11.84	118	22	-	-	-	-	-	-
1986	Milw	11.42	122	21	-	3	-	-	-	-
1987	Milw	10.28	127	23	-	18	-	-	-	-
1988	Phoe	8.15	153	30	-	12	-	-	-	-
1989	Chic	8.78	162	38	-	2	-	-	-	-

MICHAEL HOLTON — UCLA

YR	TM	PR	OR	PS	SC	SH	RB	AS	BL	ST
1985	Phoe	7.50	156	34	-	-	-	-	-	-
1986	Chic	5.04	DNQ								
1987	Port	2.88	DNQ								
1988	Port	6.70	DNQ								
1989	Char	10.88	134	26	-	-	-	8	-	-

DAVE HOPPEN — NEBRASKA

YR	TM	PR	OR	PS	SC	SH	RB	AS	BL	ST
1988	Gost	8.69	DNQ								
1989	Char	9.32	156	28	-	17	26	-	-	-

DENNIS HOPSON — OHIO STATE

YR	TM	PR	OR	PS	SC	SH	RB	AS	BL	ST
1988	N.J.	7.18	157	31	-	-	-	-	-	-
1989	N.J.	10.37	143	33	-	-	-	-	-	-

JEFF HORNACEK — IOWA ST.

YR	TM	PR	OR	PS	SC	SH	RB	AS	BL	ST
1987	Phoe	8.41	150	30	-	-	-	15	-	-
1988	Phoe	14.78	81	18	-	30	-	9	-	32
1989	Phoe	17.06	60	11	-	-	-	30	-	32

PHIL HUBBARD — MICHIGAN

YR	TM	PR	OR	PS	SC	SH	RB	AS	BL	ST
1980	Detr	9.64	DNQ								
1981	Detr	14.86	79	18	-	-	-	-	-	-
1982	Clev	10.87	125	33	-	-	-	-	-	-
1983	Clev	10.68	118	30	-	-	-	-	-	-
1984	Clev	11.33	127	28	-	-	-	-	-	-
1985	Clev	15.47	79	20	-	-	-	-	-	-
1986	Clev	9.87	DNQ								
1987	Clev	12.51	102	18	-	-	-	-	-	-
1988	Clev	8.31	149	30	-	-	-	-	-	-
1989	Clev	2.52	DNQ								

JAY HUMPHRIES — COLORADO

YR	TM	PR	OR	PS	SC	SH	RB	AS	BL	ST
1985	Phoe	9.86	140	28	-	-	-	29	-	23
1986	Phoe	14.62	80	13	-	-	-	25	-	29
1987	Phoe	15.70	72	12	-	-	-	10	-	-
1988	Milw	13.47	93	20	-	-	-	17	-	-
1989	Milw	14.07	100	20	-	-	-	31	-	14

MARK JACKSON — ST. JOHN'S

YR	TM	PR	OR	PS	SC	SH	RB	AS	BL	ST
1988	N.Y.	20.68	26	4	-	-	-	6	-	12
1989	N.Y.	20.49	30	6	-	-	-	9	-	25

BUCK JOHNSON — ALABAMA

YR	TM	PR	OR	PS	SC	SH	RB	AS	BL	ST
1987	Hous	3.77	DNQ								
1988	Hous	6.14	DNQ								
1989	Hous	11.42	131	30	-	-	-	-	-	-

DENNIS JOHNSON — PEPPERDINE

YR	TM	PR	OR	PS	SC	SH	RB	AS	BL	ST
1977	Seat	10.09	116	25	-	-	-	-	-	9
1978	Seat	11.57	111	23	-	-	-	-	-	-
1979	Seat	15.20	74	10	-	-	-	-	30	-
1980	Seat	17.17	52	8	30	-	-	-	-	-
1981	Phoe	17.10	48	4	29	-	-	-	-	24
1982	Phoe	19.00	30	4	24	-	-	-	-	-
1983	Phoe	15.69	63	11	-	-	-	-	-	-
1984	Bost	13.83	91	17	-	-	-	-	-	-
1985	Bost	17.74	53	8	-	-	-	27	-	-
1986	Bost	16.37	61	7	-	-	-	-	-	-
1987	Bost	16.37	64	10	-	-	-	25	-	-
1988	Bost	16.13	68	16	-	-	-	13	-	-
1989	Bost	12.87	111	20	-	-	-	19	-	-

EARVIN JOHNSON — MICHIGAN ST.

YR	TM	PR	OR	PS	SC	SH	RB	AS	BL	ST
1980	L.A.L	25.13	7	1	-	13	-	13	-	9
1981	L.A.L	30.19	DNQ								
1982	L.A.L	29.65	2	1	30	23	-	6	-	8
1983	L.A.L	28.63	3	1	-	8	-	2	-	14
1984	L.A.L	30.30	1	1	-	6	-	3	-	14
1985	L.A.L	28.77	3	1	-	5	-	2	-	-
1986	L.A.L	28.50	2	1	31	15	-	1	-	-
1987	L.A.L	31.79	4	1	10	16	-	2	-	-
1988	L.A.L	27.71	6	1	24	-	-	2	-	-
1989	L.A.L	33.31	2	1	15	4	-	3	-	-

EDDIE A. JOHNSON — ILLINOIS

YR	TM	PR	OR	PS	SC	SH	RB	AS	BL	ST
1982	K.C.	9.32	151	36	-	-	-	-	-	-
1983	K.C.	18.10	44	15	27	-	-	-	-	-
1984	K.C.	19.11	38	12	16	-	-	-	-	-
1985	K.C.	19.41	37	14	13	-	-	-	-	-
1986	Sacr	15.76	70	18	-	-	-	-	-	-
1987	Sacr	15.56	74	15	-	-	-	-	-	-
1988	Phoe	14.82	79	18	-	-	-	-	-	-
1989	Phoe	17.93	49	8	19	22	-	-	-	-

KEVIN JOHNSON — CALIFORNIA

YR	TM	PR	OR	PS	SC	SH	RB	AS	BL	ST
1988	Phoe	12.32	105	22	-	-	-	12	-	24
1989	Phoe	27.06	10	3	23	23	-	4	-	-

STEVE JOHNSON — OREGON ST.

YR	TM	PR	OR	PS	SC	SH	RB	AS	BL	ST
1982	K.C.	14.31	77	19	-	8	29	-	19	-
1983	K.C.	12.68	101	22	-	13	-	-	17	-
1984	Chic	11.05	DNQ								
1985	Chic	11.97	116	25	-	-	-	-	30	-
1986	S.A.	15.97	68	14	-	4	-	-	30	-
1987	Port	17.18	59	15	-	-	-	-	-	-
1988	Port	12.91	DNQ								
1989	Port	10.04	148	27	-	-	-	-	-	-

VINNIE JOHNSON — BAYLOR

YR	TM	PR	OR	PS	SC	SH	RB	AS	BL	ST
1980	Seat	3.50	DNQ							
1981	Seat	15.06	76	10	-	17	-	-	-	-
1982	Detr	8.07	DNQ							
1983	Detr	16.79	53	7	-	-	-	-	-	-
1984	Detr	11.66	120	22	-	-	-	-	-	-
1985	Detr	12.35	112	23	-	-	-	-	-	-
1986	Detr	13.00	99	18	-	-	-	-	-	-
1987	Detr	14.05	84	15	-	-	-	-	-	-
1988	Detr	10.00	129	23	-	-	-	-	-	-
1989	Detr	12.30	121	25	-	-	-	-	-	-

CALDWELL JONES — ALBANY ST.

YR	TM	PR	OR	PS	SC	SH	RB	AS	BL	ST
1974	ABA	22.57	7	3	-	-	3	-	1	-
1975	ABA	26.56	5	2	-	-	6	-	1	-
1976	ABA	19.25	15	5	-	-	6	-	1	-
1977	Phil	12.66	86	22	-	-	11	-	2	-
1978	Phil	10.79	120	30	-	-	11	-	6	-
1979	Phil	16.50	62	19	-	-	7	-	7	-
1980	Phil	16.69	60	11	-	-	7	-	9	-
1981	Phil	15.14	75	21	-	-	11	-	22	-
1982	Phil	14.86	69	17	-	-	15	-	11	-
1983	Hous	14.32	80	18	-	-	26	-	19	-
1984	Hous	14.32	82	13	-	-	-	-	-	-
1985	Chic	7.03	DNQ							
1986	Port	8.10	DNQ							
1987	Port	9.12	142	30	-	-	24	-	16	-
1988	Port	8.94	144	32	-	-	-	-	14	-
1989	Port	6.50	DNQ							

CHARLES JONES — ALBANY ST.

YR	TM	PR	OR	PS	SC	SH	RB	AS	BL	ST
1984	Phil	1.00	DNQ							
1985	Wash	11.41	DNQ							
1986	Wash	8.28	153	37	-	-	-	-	7	-
1987	Wash	9.06	143	32	-	-	-	-	3	-
1988	Wash	8.16	152	35	-	-	30	-	4	-
1989	Wash	8.25	DNQ							

MICHAEL JORDAN — N. CAROLINA

YR	TM	PR	OR	PS	SC	SH	RB	AS	BL	ST
1985	Chic	29.24	2	1	3	25	-	-	-	12
1986	Chic	18.89	DNQ							
1987	Chic	31.91	3	1	1	-	-	31	4	
1988	Chic	35.05	1	1	1	15	-	26	4	
1989	Chic	36.99	1	1	1	9	-	22	-	5

JEROME KERSEY — LONGWOOD

YR	TM	PR	OR	PS	SC	SH	RB	AS	BL	ST
1985	Port	6.43	DNQ							
1986	Port	9.71	DNQ							
1987	Port	15.70	72	14	-	-	-	-	-	17
1988	Port	21.87	19	4	28	-	-	-	-	34
1989	Port	20.24	32	7	-	-	-	-	-	34

BERNARD KING — TENNESSEE

YR	TM	PR	OR	PS	SC	SH	RB	AS	BL	ST
1978	N.J.	21.32	23	8	11	-	-	-	-	-
1979	N.J.	20.10	32	8	20	-	-	-	-	-
1980	Utah	9..58	DNQ							
1981	G.St	22.31	13	5	12	4	-	-	-	-
1982	G.St	21.57	18	4	8	14	-	-	-	-
1983	N.Y.	18.62	39	12	15	-	-	-	-	-
1984	N.Y.	22.86	17	8	5	8	-	-	-	-
1985	N.Y.	26.80	6	2	1	-	-	-	-	-
1986		DID NOT PLAY								
1987	N.Y.	18.33	DNQ							
1988	Wash	13.96	87	20	-	-	-	-	-	-
1989	Wash	17.35	58	13	20	-	-	-	-	-

ALBERT KING — MARYLAND

YR	TM	PR	OR	PS	SC	SH	RB	AS	BL	ST
1982	N.J.	10.96	124	32	-	-	-	-	-	-
1983	N.J.	16.32	58	17	-	-	-	-	-	-
1984	N.J.	14.28	83	23	-	-	-	-	-	-
1985	N.J.	11.48	DNQ							
1986	N.J.	12.82	102	22	-	-	-	-	-	-
1987	N.J.	8.36	152	27	-	-	-	-	-	-
1988	Phil	6.28	158	32	-	-	-	-	-	-
1989	S.A.	6.72	DNQ							

JOE KLEINE — ARKANSAS

YR	TM	PR	OR	PS	SC	SH	RB	AS	BL	ST
1986	Sacr	7.05	DNQ							
1987	Sacr	10.56	123	28	-	-	22	-	-	-
1988	Sacr	12.88	100	20	-	-	14	-	-	-
1989	Bost	8.08	170	29	-	-	28	-	-	-

JON KONCAK — SMU

YR	TM	PR	OR	PS	SC	SH	RB	AS	BL	ST
1986	Atla	10.27	133	26	-	-	24	-	27	-
1987	Atla	9.44	136	29	-	-	21	-	20	-
1988	Atla	10.45	DNQ							
1989	Atla	10.36	144	26	-	-	14	-	11	-

LARRY KRYSTKOWIAK — MONTANA

YR	TM	PR	OR	PS	SC	SH	RB	AS	BL	ST
1988	Milw	8.94	143	31	-	-	-	-	-	-
1989	Milw	15.29	88	18	-	-	-	-	-	-

BILL LAIMBEER — NOTRE DAME

YR	TM	PR	OR	PS	SC	SH	RB	AS	BL	ST
1981	Clev	16.46	59	18	-	-	21	-	-	-
1982	Detr	13.73	86	20	-	-	8	-	-	-
1983	Detr	22.71	18	7	-	-	4	-	30	-
1984	Detr	24.59	10	3	-	21	3	-	-	-
1985	Detr	24.05	15	6	-	-	2	-	-	-
1986	Detr	23.87	12	3	-	-	2	-	-	-
1987	Detr	22.65	17	4	-	32	6	-	-	-
1988	Detr	20.17	32	6	-	-	16	-	-	-
1989	Detr	19.70	33	8	-	36	16	-	31	-

ALLEN LEAVELL   OKLAHOMA CITY

YR	TM	PR	OR	PS	SC	SH	RB	AS	BL	ST
1980	Hous	13.34	94	16	-	-	-	16	-	15
1981	Hous	9.72	143	26	-	-	-	10	-	14
1982	Hous	13.39	90	17	-	-	-	16	-	7
1983	Hous	15.23	69	9	-	-	-	21	-	11
1984	Hous	12.54	108	16	-	-	-	13	-	19
1985	Hous	4.90	DNQ							
1986	Hous	8.01	DNQ							
1987	Hous	8.79	DNQ							
1988	Hous	12.09	109	23	-	-	-	27	-	17
1989	Hous	3.42	DNQ							

LAFAYETTE LEVER   ARIZONA ST.

YR	TM	PR	OR	PS	SC	SH	RB	AS	BL	ST
1983	Port	11.53	111	19	-	-	-	17	-	4
1984	Port	12.05	115	21	-	-	-	25	-	7
1985	Denv	18.10	50	7	-	-	-	10	-	2
1986	Denv	18.26	42	5	-	-	-	16	-	8
1987	Denv	26.93	8	2	32	-	-	21	-	11
1988	Denv	25.94	10	3	31	-	-	21	-	7
1989	Denv	27.48	7	3	25	-	-	20	-	7

REGGIE LEWIS   NORTHEASTERN

YR	TM	PR	OR	PS	SC	SH	RB	AS	BL	ST
1988	Bost	3.88	DNQ							
1989	Bost	17.84	54	11	36	-	-	-	-	-

CLIFF LEVINGSTON   WICHITA ST.

YR	TM	PR	OR	PS	SC	SH	RB	AS	BL	ST
1983	Detr	6.68	DNQ							
1984	Detr	12.68	104	19	-	-	11	-	24	-
1985	Atla	14.39	94	21	-	-	25	-	-	-
1986	Atla	12.65	107	26	-	-	25	-	-	-
1987	Atla	11.85	106	28	-	-	23	-	-	-
1988	Atla	13.78	90	19	-	14	-	-	28	-
1989	Atla	13.04	109	24	-	-	-	-	-	-

ALTON LISTER   ARIZONA ST.

YR	TM	PR	OR	PS	SC	SH	RB	AS	BL	ST
1982	Milw	8.04	DNQ							
1983	Milw	13.00	96	18	-	-	13	-	3	-
1984	Milw	12.72	103	18	-	-	12	-	6	-
1985	Milw	15.07	87	17	-	-	12	-	6	-
1986	Milw	14.25	83	18	-	-	7	-	8	-
1987	Seat	17.36	56	14	-	-	15	-	7	-
1988	Seat	11.94	112	24	-	-	4	-	5	-
1989	Seat	12.34	120	20	-	-	12	-	4	-

GRANT LONG   E. MICHIGAN

YR	TM	PR	OR	PS	SC	SH	RB	AS	BL	ST
1989	Miam	14.41	98	22	-	-	-	-	-	36

JOHN LONG   DETROIT

YR	TM	PR	OR	PS	SC	SH	RB	AS	BL	ST
1979	Detr	12.17	100	18	-	-	-	-	-	-
1980	Detr	17.67	47	7	26	-	-	-	-	22
1981	Detr	13.10	99	19	-	-	-	-	-	20
1982	Detr	16.64	54	8	12	-	-	-	-	-
1983	Detr	7.41	153	31	-	-	-	-	-	-
1984	Detr	14.07	87	16	-	-	-	-	-	-
1985	Detr	12.26	113	24	-	-	-	-	-	-
1986	Detr	8.00	DNQ							
1987	Indi	11.71	110	21	-	-	-	-	-	-
1988	Indi	11.42	115	24	-	-	-	-	-	-
1989	Detr	4.21	DNQ							

JOHN LUCAS   MARYLAND

YR	TM	PR	OR	PS	SC	SH	RB	AS	BL	ST
1977	Hous	13.32	75	12	-	-	-	10	-	-
1978	Hous	17.12	49	5	-	-	-	2	-	30
1979	G.St	19.10	38	4	-	-	-	4	-	29
1980	G.St	16.00	66	10	-	-	-	7	-	30
1981	G.St	11.38	123	20	-	-	-	3	-	-
1982	Wash	11.84	107	21	-	-	-	2	-	27
1983	Wash	4.71	DNQ							
1984	S.A.	18.02	47	6	-	-	-	1	-	24
1985	Hous	13.22	DNQ							
1986	Hous	17.43	51	6	-	-	-	9	-	-
1987	Milw	18.14	DNQ							
1988	Milw	10.84	120	24	-	-	-	14	-	27
1989	Seat	5.96	DNQ							

RICK MAHORN   HAMPTON INST.

YR	TM	PR	OR	PS	SC	SH	RB	AS	BL	ST
1981	Wash	7.60	DNQ							
1982	Wash	17.19	48	13	-	-	28	-	17	-
1983	Wash	16.54	57	15	-	-	-	25	-	-
1984	Wash	15.68	69	19	-	-	21	-	22	-
1985	Wash	13.01	103	23	-	-	20	-	17	-
1986	Detr	7.96	DNQ							
1987	Detr	9.63	134	31	-	-	20	-	29	-
1988	Detr	15.67	72	16	-	8	15	-	-	-
1989	Detr	11.90	126	27	-	-	22	-	32	-

DAN MAJERLE   C. MICHIGAN

YR	TM	PR	OR	PS	SC	SH	RB	AS	BL	ST
1989	Phoe	9.91	149	32	-	-	-	-	-	-

JEFF MALONE   MISSISSIPPI ST.

YR	TM	PR	OR	PS	SC	SH	RB	AS	BL	ST
1984	Wash	8.32	154	31	-	-	-	-	-	-
1985	Wash	14.91	89	16	-	-	-	-	-	-
1986	Wash	16.90	56	10	13	-	-	-	-	-
1987	Wash	16.39	63	11	18	-	-	-	-	-
1988	Wash	15.24	76	13	17	-	-	-	-	-
1989	Wash	15.26	89	15	17	-	-	-	-	-

KARL MALONE   LOUISIANA TECH

YR	TM	PR	OR	PS	SC	SH	RB	AS	BL	ST
1986	Utah	16.11	66	13	-	-	18	-	-	-
1987	Utah	22.05	20	7	20	-	18	-	-	-
1988	Utah	27.63	7	2	5	-	10	-	-	-
1989	Utah	29.52	5	2	2	-	25	-	-	-

MOSES MALONE   NONE

YR	TM	PR	OR	PS	SC	SH	RB	AS	BL	ST
1975	ABA	26.36	7	4	-	-	5	-	-	-
1976	ABA	18.02	DNQ							
1977	Hous	20.40	22	9	-	-	2	-	7	-
1978	Hous	24.15	11	8	29	-	1	-	-	-
1979	Hous	32.60	2	2	5	25	1	-	-	-
1980	Hous	28.68	2	2	5	-	3	-	30	-
1981	Hous	31.67	1	1	2	-	2	-	24	-
1982	Hous	33.12	1	1	2	-	3	-	-	-
1983	Phil	30.08	1	1	5	-	1	-	18	-
1984	Phil	25.85	6	1	11	-	2	-	27	-
1985	Phil	27.30	5	1	9	-	3	-	25	-
1986	Phil	23.73	13	4	7	-	10	-	-	-
1987	Wash	24.86	10	2	9	-	7	-	-	-
1988	Wash	22.53	18	3	19	-	7	-	-	-
1989	Atla	23.84	14	4	24	-	5	-	34	-

DANNY MANNING — KANSAS

YR	TM	PR	OR	PS	SC	SH	RB	AS	BL	ST
1989	LA.C	17.58	DNQ							

VERNON MAXWELL — FLORIDA

YR	TM	PR	OR	PS	SC	SH	RB	AS	BL	ST
1989	S.A.	10.30	145	27	-	-	-	-	-	

TIM MCCORMICK — MICHIGAN

YR	TM	PR	OR	PS	SC	SH	RB	AS	BL	ST
1985	Seat	10.90	125	27	-	30	-	-	-	-
1986	Seat	10.95	128	32	-	25	-	-	-	-
1987	Phil	15.80	71	18						
1988	Phil	14.29	85	16						
1989	Hous	6.05	DNQ							

RODNEY MCCRAY — LOUISVILLE

YR	TM	PR	OR	PS	SC	SH	RB	AS	BL	ST
1984	Hous	13.44	97	26	-	-	-	-	-	
1985	Hous	19.12	39	16						
1986	Hous	15.79	69	17						
1987	Hous	20.70	29	7	-	13				
1988	Hous	17.27	54	12						
1989	Sacr	16.65	70	17						

XAVIER MCDANIEL — WICHITA ST.

YR	TM	PR	OR	PS	SC	SH	RB	AS	BL	ST
1986	Seat	17.41	52	16						
1987	Seat	22.41	19	6	14					
1988	Seat	19.78	36	8	14					
1989	Seat	16.29	78	20	22					

MIKE MCGEE — MICHIGAN

YR	TM	PR	OR	PS	SC	SH	RB	AS	BL	ST
1982	LA.L	3.46	DNQ							
1983	LA.L	3.09	DNQ							
1984	LA.L	8.87	DNQ							
1985	LA.L	8.07	DNQ							
1986	LA.L	6.46	DNQ							
1987	Atla	8.32	DNQ							
1988	Sacr	9.04	DNQ							
1989	N.J.	9.51	153	36	-	-	-	-	-	

KEVIN MCHALE — MINNESOTA

YR	TM	PR	OR	PS	SC	SH	RB	AS	BL	ST
1981	Bost	11.44	120	26	-	-	-	-	4	-
1982	Bost	16.72	53	10	-	31	-	-	6	-
1983	Bost	17.04	50	9	-	24	-	-	4	-
1984	Bost	20.16	29	6	-	19	-	-	19	-
1985	Bost	23.29	19	3	31	13	29	-	19	-
1986	Bost	24.75	7	2	16	7	-	-	14	-
1987	Bost	30.92	5	2	6	1	-	-	14	-
1988	Bost	26.28	9	3	11	2	-	-	29	-
1989	Bost	23.68	15	3	14	13	-	-	36	-

DERRICK MCKEY — ALABAMA

YR	TM	PR	OR	PS	SC	SH	RB	AS	BL	ST
1988	Seat	10.23	128	25	-	-	-	-	31	-
1989	Seat	17.29	59	14	-	-	-	-	-	-

NATE MCMILLAN — N.C.STATE

YR	TM	PR	OR	PS	SC	SH	RB	AS	BL	ST
1987	Seat	15.35	77	13	-	-	-	4	-	14
1988	Seat	16.71	56	13	-	-	-	4	-	8
1989	Seat	16.63	71	16	-	-	-	5	-	11

REGGIE MILLER — UCLA

YR	TM	PR	OR	PS	SC	SH	RB	AS	BL	ST
1988	Indi	9.23	137	27	-	21	-	-	-	-
1989	Indi	16.12	81	14	-	14	-	-	-	-

SIDNEY MONCRIEF — ARKANSAS

YR	TM	PR	OR	PS	SC	SH	RB	AS	BL	ST
1980	Milw	10.34	128	24	-	-	-	-	-	-
1981	Milw	16.96	50	9	-	12	-	-	-	-
1982	Milw	22.96	15	2	22	22	-	-	-	32
1983	Milw	22.80	15	1	13	17	-	-	-	-
1984	Milw	22.76	18	1	23	-	-	-	-	-
1985	Milw	22.40	21	2	21	-	-	-	-	-
1986	Milw	21.03	23	3	22	-	-	-	-	-
1987	Milw	12.56	DNQ							
1988	Milw	12.45	103	17	-	-	-	-	-	-
1989	Milw	12.79	113	22	-	24	-	-	-	-

CHRIS MORRIS — AUBURN

YR	TM	PR	OR	PS	SC	SH	RB	AS	BL	ST
1989	N.J.	13.14	108	27	-	-	-	-	-	-

CHRIS MULLIN — ST. JOHN'S

YR	TM	PR	OR	PS	SC	SH	RB	AS	BL	ST
1986	G.St	11.84	115	23	-	-	-	-	-	26
1987	G.St	14.10	83	14	-	24	-	-	-	-
1988	G.St	20.17	33	7	20	18	-	-	-	20
1989	G.St	26.01	12	1	6	19	-	-	-	24

LARRY NANCE — CLEMSON

YR	TM	PR	OR	PS	SC	SH	RB	AS	BL	ST
1982	Phoe	7.81	DNQ							
1983	Phoe	22.29	20	5	-	22	-	-	5	-
1984	Phoe	22.91	16	7	-	12	-	-	12	-
1985	Phoe	25.02	10	3	30	8	-	-	18	-
1986	Phoe	24.23	10	5	21	16	-	-	15	-
1987	Phoe	27.25	7	2	17	15	-	-	13	-
1988	Clev	24.51	11	2	29	29	28	-	12	-
1989	Clev	22.66	17	4	-	18	-	-	9	-

CALVIN NATT — NE LOUISIANA

YR	TM	PR	OR	PS	SC	SH	RB	AS	BL	ST
1980	Port	20.03	32	10	24	-	-	-	-	-
1981	Port	13.92	91	23	-	-	-	-	-	-
1982	Port	20.93	23	7	-	4	-	-	-	-
1983	Port	20.71	26	8	22	10	-	-	-	-
1984	Port	18.10	44	15	-	1	-	-	-	-
1985	Denv	24.31	13	5	11	18	-	-	-	-
1986	Denv	17.81	47	14	-	-	-	-	-	-
1987	Denv	11.00	DNQ							
1988	Denv	9.70	DNQ							
1989	S.A.	5.71	DNQ							

JOHNNY NEWMAN — RICHMOND

YR	TM	PR	OR	PS	SC	SH	RB	AS	BL	ST
1987	Clev	3.37	DNQ							
1988	N.Y.	7.60	156	33	-	-	-	-	-	-
1989	N.Y.	13.27	106	26	-	28	-	-	-	-

KEN NORMAN — ILLINOIS

YR	TM	PR	OR	PS	SC	SH	RB	AS	BL	ST
1988	LA.C	8.23	151	32	-	-	-	-	-	-
1989	LA.C	20.34	31	6	-	-	-	-	-	-

CHARLES OAKLEY — VIRGINIA UNION

YR	TM	PR	OR	PS	SC	SH	RB	AS	BL	ST
1986	Chic	14.40	82	23	-	-	1	-	-	-
1987	Chic	20.59	30	9	-	-	4	-	-	-
1988	Chic	20.54	29	8	-	-	2	-	-	-
1989	N.Y.	18.44	46	9	-	-	7	-	-	-

AKEEM OLAJUWON — HOUSTON

YR	TM	PR	OR	PS	SC	SH	RB	AS	BL	ST
1985	Hous	25.22	9	4	25	-	6	-	7	-
1986	Hous	28.40	3	1	8	-	12	-	6	19
1987	Hous	28.99	6	1	12	-	14	-	4	27
1988	Hous	28.10	4	1	10	-	5	-	6	18
1989	Hous	31.02	4	1	10	-	1	-	6	8

ROBERT PARISH — CENTENARY

YR	TM	PR	OR	PS	SC	SH	RB	AS	BL	ST
1977	G.St	13.21	DNQ								
1978	G.St	14.89	66	22	-	-	12	-	10	-
1979	G.St	23.39	12	6	-	-	2	-	4	-
1980	G.St	20.82	24	9	-	-	4	-	13	-
1981	Bost	23.55	8	4	25	22	4	-	3	-
1982	Bost	24.58	12	6	20	27	5	-	10	-
1983	Bost	24.31	8	4	31	23	5	-	13	-
1984	Bost	23.65	14	5	-	27	15	-	31	-
1985	Bost	22.33	22	7	-	29	19	-	-	-
1986	Bost	20.84	26	6	-	31	16	-	23	-
1987	Bost	23.66	13	3	-	11	25	-	17	-
1988	Bost	19.15	41	7	-	5	20	-	32	-
1989	Bost	26.10	11	3	33	15	2	-	26	-

JIM PAXSON — DAYTON

YR	TM	PR	OR	PS	SC	SH	RB	AS	BL	ST
1980	Port	4.99	DNQ								
1981	Port	16.57	58	11	-	20	-	-	-	25
1982	Port	16.87	51	7	26	28	-	-	-	30
1983	Port	17.67	46	4	17	30	-	-	-	25
1984	Port	17.64	50	5	21	30	-	-	-	-
1985	Port	17.21	59	8	-	-	-	-	-	-
1986	Port	12.63	108	20	-	-	-	-	-	28
1987	Port	11.00	119	24	-	-	-	-	-	-
1988	Bost	6.49	DNQ								
1989	Bost	7.02	DNQ								

JOHN PAXSON — NOTRE DAME

YR	TM	PR	OR	PS	SC	SH	RB	AS	BL	ST
1984	S.A.	4.45	DNQ								
1985	S.A.	6.23	DNQ								
1986	Chic	7.52	156	28	-	-	-	30	-	-
1987	Chic	13.09	94	17	-	-	-	-	-	-
1988	Chic	8.96	142	29	-	-	-	-	-	-
1989	Chic	8.78	161	30	-	33	-	32	-	-

SAM PERKINS — N. CAROLINA

YR	TM	PR	OR	PS	SC	SH	RB	AS	BL	ST
1985	Dall	15.05	88	18	-	-	-	-	-	-
1986	Dall	19.67	36	7	-	-	-	-	31	-
1987	Dall	18.19	54	13	-	-	-	-	-	-
1988	Dall	16.71	57	12	-	-	-	-	-	-
1989	Dall	18.51	43	8	-	-	-	-	-	-

CHUCK PERSON — AUBURN

YR	TM	PR	OR	PS	SC	SH	RB	AS	BL	ST
1987	Indi	19.63	39	10	-	-	-	-	-	-
1988	Indi	16.65	59	14	-	-	-	-	-	-
1989	Indi	19.00	38	8	18	-	-	-	-	-

JIM PETERSEN — MINNESOTA

YR	TM	PR	OR	PS	SC	SH	RB	AS	BL	ST
1985	Hous	4.42	DNQ								
1986	Hous	8.93	146	36	-	-	-	-	-	-
1987	Hous	14.33	82	20	-	-	-	22	-	-
1988	Hous	12.09	110	25	-	-	-	-	-	-
1989	Sacr	11.61	129	28	-	-	34	-	24	-

RICKY PIERCE — DETROIT

YR	TM	PR	OR	PS	SC	SH	RB	AS	BL	ST
1983	Detr	1.51	DNQ								
1984	S.D.	7.43	DNQ								
1985	Milw	10.19	DNQ								
1986	Milw	13.63	86	13	-	14	-	-	-	-
1987	Milw	17.25	57	8	29	5	-	-	-	-
1988	Milw	12.97	DNQ								
1989	Milw	14.95	92	17	-	25	-	-	-	-

ED PINCKNEY — VILLANOVA

YR	TM	PR	OR	PS	SC	SH	RB	AS	BL	ST
1986	Phoe	9.43	141	34	-	-	-	-	-	-
1987	Phoe	15.50	75	17	-	8	-	-	-	-
1988	Sacr	7.24	DNQ								
1989	Bost	14.27	99	23	-	-	-	-	-	-

SCOTTIE PIPPEN — CENTRAL ARKANSAS

YR	TM	PR	OR	PS	SC	SH	RB	AS	BL	ST
1988	Chic	9.22	139	28	-	-	-	-	-	22
1989	Chic	16.38	75	18	-	-	-	-	-	23

TERRY PORTER — WISC.-ST.POINT.

YR	TM	PR	OR	PS	SC	SH	RB	AS	BL	ST
1986	Port	7.44	DNQ								
1987	Port	19.52	41	9	-	-	-	7	-	16
1988	Port	22.87	16	3	-	17	-	5	-	26
1989	Port	22.42	18	4	-	-	-	11	-	-

PAUL PRESSEY — TULSA

YR	TM	PR	OR	PS	SC	SH	RB	AS	BL	ST
1983	Milw	8.61	141	35	-	-	-	-	-	9
1984	Milw	10.56	138	31	-	-	-	-	-	27
1985	Milw	20.56	30	11	-	-	-	25	-	-
1986	Milw	20.74	27	8	-	-	-	13	-	11
1987	Milw	18.79	50	12	-	-	-	20	-	21
1988	Milw	18.67	44	10	-	-	-	20	-	21
1989	Milw	16.39	74	17	-	-	-	21	-	28

HAROLD PRESSLEY — VILLINOVA

YR	TM	PR	OR	PS	SC	SH	RB	AS	BL	ST
1987	Sacr	6.09	DNQ								
1988	Sacr	11.52	114	20	-	-	-	-	-	-
1989	Sacr	14.60	95	18	-	-	-	-	-	-

MARK PRICE — GEORGIA TECH

YR	TM	PR	OR	PS	SC	SH	RB	AS	BL	ST
1987	Clev	6.79	DNQ								
1988	Clev	16.92	55	12	-	9	-	29	-	-
1989	Clev	22.33	20	5	31	1	-	15	-	-

KURT RAMBIS — SANTA CLARA

YR	TM	PR	OR	PS	SC	SH	RB	AS	BL	ST
1982	LA.L	9.22	DNQ							
1983	LA.L	12.79	98	19	-	14	17	-	-	17
1984	LA.L	8.13	DNQ							
1985	LA.L	10.71	129	28	-	-	9	-	-	26
1986	LA.L	11.53	119	29	-	6	6	-	-	
1987	LA.L	10.08	130	30	-	-	19	-	-	32
1988	LA.L	6.97	DNQ							
1989	Char	17.80	51	12	-	-	10	-	-	-

BLAIR RASMUSSEN — OREGON

YR	TM	PR	OR	PS	SC	SH	RB	AS	BL	ST
1986	Denv	2.96	DNQ							
1987	Denv	11.74	109	23	-	-	8	-	25	-
1988	Denv	13.42	95	20	-	-	33	-	19	-
1989	Denv	7.90	DNQ							

ROBERT REID — ST. MARY'S

YR	TM	PR	OR	PS	SC	SH	RB	AS	BL	ST
1978	Hous	9.45	139	26	-	-	-	-	-	-
1979	Hous	14.02	83	21	-	-	-	-	-	-
1980	Hous	15.84	67	18	-	-	-	-	-	18
1981	Hous	19.61	23	7	-	-	-	-	-	18
1982	Hous	16.77	52	16	-	-	-	-	-	-
1983	DID NOT PLAY									
1984	Hous	15.41	72	21	-	-	-	-	-	-
1985	Hous	9.17	144	30	-	-	-	-	-	-
1986	Hous	12.15	110	21	-	-	-	-	-	-
1987	Hous	13.41	90	18	-	-	-	-	-	-
1988	Hous	6.00	DNQ							
1989	Char	10.85	135	31	-	-	-	-	-	-

MITCH RICHMOND — KANSAS ST.

YR	TM	PR	OR	PS	SC	SH	RB	AS	BL	ST
1989	G.St	19.44	35	7	16	-	-	-	-	-

GLENN RIVERS — MARQUETTE

YR	TM	PR	OR	PS	SC	SH	RB	AS	BL	ST
1984	Atla	11.27	128	22	-	-	-	31	-	9
1985	Atla	17.16	60	10	-	-	-	23	-	4
1986	Atla	16.11	65	10	-	-	-	5	-	5
1987	Atla	20.33	34	7	-	-	-	3	-	8
1988	Atla	20.36	30	5	-	-	-	3	-	19
1989	Atla	18.70	41	10	-	-	-	17	-	4

FRED ROBERTS — BYU

YR	TM	PR	OR	PS	SC	SH	RB	AS	BL	ST
1984	S.A.	9.52	DNQ							
1985	Utah	7.95	DNQ							
1986	Utah	5.07	DNQ							
1987	Bost	6.12	DNQ							
1988	Bost	6.08	DNQ							
1989	Milw	6.79	DNQ							

ALVIN ROBERTSON — ARKANSAS

YR	TM	PR	OR	PS	SC	SH	RB	AS	BL	ST
1985	S.A.	11.44	120	26	-	-	-	-	-	5
1986	S.A.	22.48	15	1	-	-	-	-	-	1
1987	S.A.	19.47	43	5	-	-	-	-	-	1
1988	S.A.	22.94	15	4	25	-	-	28	-	2
1989	S.A.	20.52	29	6	-	-	-	34	-	1

CLIFF ROBINSON — USC

YR	TM	PR	OR	PS	SC	SH	RB	AS	BL	ST
1980	N.J.	14.24	82	15	-	-	13	-	-	-
1981	N.J.	17.90	38	9	21	-	31	-	-	-
1982	Clev	19.31	28	7	32	-	21	-	23	-
1983	Clev	20.16	27	7	-	-	7	-	-	-
1984	Clev	18.95	39	8	-	-	10	-	-	-
1985	Wash	18.43	42	9	-	-	22	-	-	-
1986	Wash	19.46	38	9	-	-	29	-	-	-
1987	Phil	13.96	86	23	-	-	-	-	-	20
1988	Phil	16.61	60	15	30	-	-	-	-	-
1989	Phil	13.93	DNQ							

DENNIS RODMAN — SE OKLAHOMA

YR	TM	PR	OR	PS	SC	SH	RB	AS	BL	ST
1987	Detr	8.45	DNQ							
1988	Detr	15.84	70	17	-	-	6	-	-	-
1989	Detr	16.32	77	19	-	3	3	-	35	-

WAYNE ROLLINS — CLEMSON

YR	TM	PR	OR	PS	SC	SH	RB	AS	BL	ST
1978	Atla	13.55	83	25	-	-	30	-	1	-
1979	Atla	15.10	75	23	-	-	19	-	1	-
1980	Atla	18.17	42	13	-	16	6	-	2	-
1981	Atla	14.56	DNQ							
1982	Atla	14.42	76	18	-	19	10	-	2	-
1983	Atla	18.09	45	13	-	-	14	-	1	-
1984	Atla	15.65	70	20	-	-	-	-	2	-
1985	Atla	12.51	109	20	-	23	-	-	3	-
1986	Atla	11.26	124	24	-	-	-	-	5	-
1987	Atla	11.61	113	25	-	20	29	-	6	-
1988	Atla	10.39	125	26	-	28	25	-	7	-
1989	Clev	3.97	DNQ							

JOHN SALLEY — GEORGIA TECH

YR	TM	PR	OR	PS	SC	SH	RB	AS	BL	ST
1987	Detr	8.34	DNQ							
1988	Detr	12.34	104	23	-	26	-	-	11	-
1989	Detr	9.88	150	29	-	-	-	-	15	-

RALPH SAMPSON — VIRGINIA

YR	TM	PR	OR	PS	SC	SH	RB	AS	BL	ST
1984	Hous	24.01	13	4	22	-	4	-	5	-
1985	Hous	23.39	18	2	19	-	28	-	13	-
1986	Hous	22.85	14	3	30	-	14	-	25	-
1987	Hous	18.05	DNQ							
1988	G.St	17.94	51	11	-	-	17	-	16	-
1989	G.St	9.00	DNQ							

MICHAEL SANDERS — UCLA

YR	TM	PR	OR	PS	SC	SH	RB	AS	BL	ST
1983	S.A.	7.65	DNQ							
1984	Phoe	4.84	DNQ							
1985	Phoe	10.60	DNQ							
1986	Phoe	11.15	127	24	-	-	-	-	-	31
1987	Phoe	10.12	129	22	-	-	-	-	-	-
1988	Clev	5.98	DNQ							
1989	Clev	9.54	152	34	-	-	-	-	-	-

DANNY SCHAYES — SYRACUSE

YR	TM	PR	OR	PS	SC	SH	RB	AS	BL	ST
1982	Utah	10.57	132	29	-	-	30	-	25	-
1983	Denv	14.35	79	17	-	-	24	-	28	-
1984	Denv	10.16	DNQ							
1985	Denv	5.28	DNQ							
1986	Denv	11.19	126	25	-	-	28	-	29	-
1987	Denv	11.22	116	27	-	-	-	-	18	-
1988	Denv	18.63	45	8	-	10	11	-	21	-
1989	Denv	15.49	85	14	-	21	30	-	22	-

DETLEF SCHREMPF — WASHINGTON

YR	TM	PR	OR	PS	SC	SH	RB	AS	BL	ST
1986	Dall	7.83	DNQ							
1987	Dall	10.04	132	24	-	-	-	-	-	-
1988	Dall	9.07	141	29	-	-	-	-	-	-
1989	Indi	13.91	102	25	-	-	-	-	-	-

BYRON SCOTT — ARIZONA ST.

YR	TM	PR	OR	PS	SC	SH	RB	AS	BL	ST
1984	LA.L	9.86	142	28	-	-	-	-	-	28
1985	LA.L	15.12	85	15	-	11	-	-	-	-
1986	LA.L	13.12	94	15	-	-	-	-	-	-
1987	LA.L	16.54	62	10	-	23	-	-	-	-
1988	LA.L	21.73	21	5	12	7	-	-	-	25
1989	LA.L	17.89	50	9	27	27	-	-	-	-

RON SEIKALY — SYRACUSE

YR	TM	PR	OR	PS	SC	SH	RB	AS	BL	ST
1989	Miam	10.38	141	25	-	-	21	-	16	-

BRAD SELLERS — OHIO ST.

YR	TM	PR	OR	PS	SC	SH	RB	AS	BL	ST
1987	Chic	10.08	131	23	-	-	-	-	30	-
1988	Chic	9.22	138	27	-	-	-	-	-	-
1989	Chic	8.11	169	38	-	-	-	-	29	-

BRIAN SHAW — SANTA BARBARA

YR	TM	PR	OR	PS	SC	SH	RB	AS	BL	ST
1989	Gost	12.88	110	22	-	-	-	18	-	-

PURVIS SHORT — JACKSON ST.

YR	TM	PR	OR	PS	SC	SH	RB	AS	BL	ST
1979	G.St	10.19	129	32	-	-	-	-	-	-
1980	G.St	15.47	69	19	-	-	-	-	-	-
1981	G.St	15.42	68	13	-	-	-	-	-	-
1982	G.St	13.16	92	21	-	-	-	-	-	-
1983	G.St	18.81	37	10	19	-	-	-	-	-
1984	G.St	18.81	40	13	10	-	-	-	-	-
1985	G.St	21.12	26	9	4	-	-	-	-	-
1986	G.St	21.77	18	6	5	-	-	-	-	-
1987	G.St	16.00	DNQ							
1988	Hous	11.74	113	19	-	-	-	-	-	-
1989	Hous	7.09	DNQ							

JERRY SICHTING — PURDUE

YR	TM	PR	OR	PS	SC	SH	RB	AS	BL	ST
1981	Indi	2.85	DNQ							
1982	Indi	5.16	DNQ							
1983	Indi	11.83	108	18	-	-	-	27	-	-
1984	Indi	14.15	84	12	-	20	-	26	-	-
1985	Indi	11.19	123	25	-	19	-	-	-	-
1986	Bost	7.61	155	27	-	1	-	-	-	-
1987	Bost	6.47	159	31	-	-	-	-	-	-
1988	Port	4.92	DNQ							
1989	Port	4.84	DNQ							

JACK SIKMA — ILL. WESLEYAN

YR	TM	PR	OR	PS	SC	SH	RB	AS	BL	ST
1978	Seat	13.96	78	15	-	-	-	-	-	-
1979	Seat	22.17	20	9	-	-	8	-	-	-
1980	Seat	21.09	23	8	-	-	8	-	-	-
1981	Seat	22.09	15	7	30	-	15	-	-	-
1982	Seat	27.01	7	3	23	-	6	-	-	-
1983	Seat	23.79	10	5	-	-	6	-	-	-
1984	Seat	25.66	8	2	-	-	13	-	-	-
1985	Seat	25.60	8	3	-	-	15	-	29	-
1986	Seat	21.54	20	5	-	-	26	-	-	-
1987	Milw	19.37	44	9	-	-	9	-	-	-
1988	Milw	21.77	20	6	-	-	-	-	-	-
1989	Milw	18.47	44	9	-	-	-	-	-	-

SCOTT SKILES — MICHIGAN ST.

YR	TM	PR	OR	PS	SC	SH	RB	AS	BL	ST
1987	Milw	4.54	DNQ							
1988	Indi	5.61	DNQ							
1989	Indi	8.95	158	29	-	-	-	10	-	-

CHARLES SMITH — PITTSBURG

YR	TM	PR	OR	PS	SC	SH	RB	AS	BL	ST
1989	LA.C	16.66	69	16	-	-	-	-	25	-

DEREK SMITH — LOUISVILLE

YR	TM	PR	OR	PS	SC	SH	RB	AS	BL	ST
1983	G.St	2.00	DNQ							
1984	S.D.	9.69	144	29	-	26	-	-	-	-
1985	LA.C	20.20	32	4	18	21	-	-	-	-
1986	LA.C	19.36	DNQ							
1987	Sacr	13.90	87	16	-	-	-	-	-	-
1988	Sacr	11.69	DNQ							
1989	Phil	7.72	171	39	-	-	-	-	-	-

KENNY SMITH — NORTH CAROLINA

YR	TM	PR	OR	PS	SC	SH	RB	AS	BL	ST
1988	Sacr	15.23	77	17	-	-	-	25	-	-
1989	Sacr	17.04	61	13	-	-	-	23	-	-

LARRY SMITH — ALCORN ST.

YR	TM	PR	OR	PS	SC	SH	RB	AS	BL	ST
1981	G.St	17.62	40	10	-	-	1	-	-	-
1982	G.St	15.88	60	14	-	-	1	-	-	-
1983	G.St	15.20	DNQ							
1984	G.St	13.59	94	16	-	-	8	-	-	-
1985	G.St	17.49	57	13	-	-	4	-	-	-
1986	G.St	16.64	59	12	-	-	4	-	-	-
1987	G.St	17.25	58	14	-	-	1	-	-	-
1988	G.St	12.00	DNQ							
1989	G.St	12.66	114	25	-	-	4	-	-	-

OTIS SMITH — JACKSONVILLE

YR	TM	PR	OR	PS	SC	SH	RB	AS	BL	ST
1987	Denv	2.18	DNQ							
1988	G.St	12.24	107	22	-	-	-	-	-	15
1989	G.St	10.30	146	34	-	-	-	-	-	27

RIK SMITS — MARIST

YR	TM	PR	OR	PS	SC	SH	RB	AS	BL	ST
1989	Indi	14.06	101	16	-	-	-	-	10	-

RORY SPARROW — VILLANOVA

YR	TM	PR	OR	PS	SC	SH	RB	AS	BL	ST
1981	N.J.	3.93	DNQ							
1982	Atla	13.07	94	18	-	-	-	26	-	-
1983	N.Y.	12.44	104	16	-	-	-	-	-	-
1984	N.Y.	13.08	100	14	-	-	-	14	-	-
1985	N.Y.	13.82	98	19	-	-	-	9	-	-
1986	N.Y.	13.23	92	15	-	-	-	20	-	-
1987	N.Y.	9.29	138	25	-	-	-	17	-	-
1988	Chic	5.17	DNQ							
1989	Miam	12.62	117	23	-	-	-	36	-	-

STEVE STIPANOVICH — MISSOURI

YR	TM	PR	OR	PS	SC	SH	RB	AS	BL	ST
1984	Indi	14.78	75	21	-	-	-	-	-	-
1985	Indi	16.73	66	12	-	-	31	-	-	-
1986	Indi	17.23	53	12	-	-	-	-	-	-
1987	Indi	19.22	45	10	-	-	-	-	-	-
1988	Indi	18.13	49	9	-	-	32	-	-	-
1989	Indi	DID NOT PLAY								

JOHN STOCKTON — GONZAGA

YR	TM	PR	OR	PS	SC	SH	RB	AS	BL	ST
1985	Utah	8.66	DNQ							
1986	Utah	13.99	84	14	-	-	-	2	-	2
1987	Utah	14.80	80	14	-	-	-	1	-	2
1988	Utah	26.54	8	2	-	1	-	1	-	1
1989	Utah	27.40	9	2	-	6	-	2	-	2

JOHN SUNDVOLD — MISSOURI

YR	TM	PR	OR	PS	SC	SH	RB	AS	BL	ST
1984	Seat	5.57	DNQ							
1985	Seat	5.10	DNQ							
1986	S.A.	7.50	DNQ							
1987	S.A.	10.54	124	22	-	-	-	32	-	-
1988	S.A.	8.00	DNQ							
1989	Miam	7.29	175	33	-	-	-	-	-	-

ROY TARPLEY — MICHIGAN

YR	TM	PR	OR	PS	SC	SH	RB	AS	BL	ST
1987	Dall	11.59	DNQ							
1988	Dall	20.23	31	9	-	-	1	-	30	-
1989	Dall	22.89	DNQ							

TERRY TEAGLE — BAYLOR

YR	TM	PR	OR	PS	SC	SH	RB	AS	BL	ST
1983	Hous	7.63	151	30	-	-	-	-	-	-
1984	Hous	3.85	DNQ							
1985	G.St	7.10	DNQ							
1986	G.St	11.55	117	24	-	-	-	-	-	-
1987	G.St	8.24	154	32	-	-	-	-	-	-
1988	G.St	7.87	DNQ							
1989	G.St	12.85	112	21	-	-	-	-	-	35

REGGIE THEUS — UNLV

YR	TM	PR	OR	PS	SC	SH	RB	AS	BL	ST
1979	Chic	13.88	85	14	-	-	-	28	-	-
1980	Chic	19.35	35	5	20	-	-	21	-	-
1981	Chic	18.12	37	6	26	-	-	-	-	-
1982	Chic	17.10	50	6	-	-	-	25	-	-
1983	Chic	20.12	29	3	9	-	-	-	-	28
1984	K.C.	11.51	124	26	-	-	-	12	-	-
1985	K.C.	18.20	48	5	-	-	-	6	-	-
1986	Sacr	21.02	24	4	-	-	-	6	-	-
1987	Sacr	20.90	28	5	28	-	-	11	-	-
1988	Sacr	18.44	46	8	13	-	-	31	-	-
1989	Atla	15.06	91	16	-	-	-	-	-	-

ISIAH THOMAS — INDIANA

YR	TM	PR	OR	PS	SC	SH	RB	AS	BL	ST
1982	Detr	15.63	61	9	-	-	-	9	-	13
1983	Detr	21.68	23	2	12	-	-	20	-	10
1984	Detr	24.38	11	2	19	-	-	5	-	6
1985	Detr	27.85	4	2	23	-	-	1	-	14
1986	Detr	24.44	8	2	18	-	-	3	-	12
1987	Detr	22.04	21	4	27	-	-	6	-	26
1988	Detr	19.86	35	6	27	-	-	11	-	30
1989	Detr	19.09	37	9	-	-	-	16	-	-

BILLY THOMPSON — LOUISVILLE

YR	TM	PR	OR	PS	SC	SH	RB	AS	BL	ST
1987	LA.L	6.81	DNQ							
1988	LA.L	.78	DNQ							
1989	Miam	14.42	97	24	-	-	35	-	19	-

LA SALLE THOMPSON — TEXAS

YR	TM	PR	OR	PS	SC	SH	RB	AS	BL	ST
1983	K.C.	8.56	DNQ							
1984	K.C.	16.27	65	16	-	-	1	-	4	-
1985	K.C.	19.01	41	9	-	-	5	-	16	-
1986	Sacr	18.76	39	11	-	-	8	-	22	-
1987	Sacr	16.05	68	16	-	-	12	-	12	-
1988	Sacr	11.25	DNQ							
1989	Indi	17.95	48	11	-	-	11	-	28	-

MYCHAL THOMPSON — MINNESOTA

YR	TM	PR	OR	PS	SC	SH	RB	AS	BL	ST
1979	Port	17.22	52	17	-	-	-	-	11	-
1980		DID NOT PLAY								
1981	Port	20.35	19	9	-	-	-	-	12	-
1982	Port	25.63	10	5	17	-	14	-	-	-
1983	Port	20.11	30	9	-	-	-	-	-	-
1984	Port	20.48	26	8	-	31	-	29	-	-
1985	Port	19.54	36	7	-	-	-	26	-	-
1986	Port	15.66	72	15	-	-	-	-	-	-
1987	LA.L	11.35	115	26	-	-	-	-	-	-
1988	LA.L	12.81	101	21	-	-	-	-	27	-
1989	LA.L	12.11	124	21	-	32	-	-	-	-

OTIS THORPE — PROVIDENCE

YR	TM	PR	OR	PS	SC	SH	RB	AS	BL	ST
1985	K.C.	14.49	92	20	-	22	23	-	-	-
1986	Sacr	12.07	111	28	-	23	-	-	-	-
1987	Sacr	22.82	16	4	-	29	28	-	-	-
1988	Sacr	23.71	13	4	16	-	19	-	-	-
1989	Hous	20.62	27	5	-	35	36	-	-	-

SEDALE THREATT — W. VIRG.TECH

YR	TM	PR	OR	PS	SC	SH	RB	AS	BL	ST
1984	Phil	2.67	DNQ							
1985	Phil	5.41	DNQ							
1986	Phil	8.81	147	34	-	-	-	-	-	23
1987	Chic	9.21	139	29	-	-	-	31	-	25
1988	Seat	7.35	DNQ							
1989	Seat	10.38	142	32	-	-	-	25	-	10

WAYMAN TISDALE — OKLAHOMA

YR	TM	PR	OR	PS	SC	SH	RB	AS	BL	ST
1986	Indi	14.60	81	22	-	-	-	-	-	-
1987	Indi	14.36	81	19	-	-	-	-	-	-
1988	Indi	15.82	71	15	-	-	-	-	-	-
1989	Sacr	18.43	47	10	-	-	-	-	-	-

KELLY TRIPUCKA — NOTRE DAME

YR	TM	PR	OR	PS	SC	SH	RB	AS	BL	ST
1982	Detr	18.77	31	9	13	-	-	-	-	-
1983	Detr	21.97	22	6	3	-	-	-	-	-
1984	Detr	16.39	63	20	20	-	-	-	-	-
1985	Detr	15.98	75	19	-	-	-	-	-	-
1986	Detr	18.15	43	13	24	-	-	-	-	-
1987	Utah	10.80	122	20	-	-	-	-	-	-
1988	Utah	7.90	DNQ								
1989	Char	17.61	55	12	13	-	-	-	-	-

TRENT TUCKER — MINNESOTA

YR	TM	PR	OR	PS	SC	SH	RB	AS	BL	ST
1983	N.Y.	8.83	138	24	-	-	-	-	-	-
1984	N.Y.	8.46	153	30	-	-	-	-	-	21
1985	N.Y.	9.65	143	29	-	-	-	-	-	-
1986	N.Y.	10.00	135	28	-	-	-	-	-	-
1987	N.Y.	10.81	121	26	-	-	-	-	-	5
1988	N.Y.	6.65	DNQ								
1989	N.Y.	8.67	164	40	-	8	-	-	-	-

ELSTON TURNER — MISSISSIPPI

YR	TM	PR	OR	PS	SC	SH	RB	AS	BL	ST
1982	Dall	8.93	154	28	-	-	-	-	-	-
1983	Dall	9.81	DNQ								
1984	Dall	3.62	DNQ								
1985	Denv	6.80	DNQ								
1986	Denv	6.53	DNQ								
1987	Chic	4.57	DNQ								
1988	Chic	.65	DNQ								
1989	Denv	7.45	173	43	-	-	-	-	-	33

TERRY TYLER — DETROIT

YR	TM	PR	OR	PS	SC	SH	RB	AS	BL	ST
1979	Detr	16.98	55	17	-	-	-	-	5	-
1980	Detr	16.76	58	16	-	-	-	-	4	-
1981	Detr	17.21	47	11	-	-	-	-	7	-
1982	Detr	14.55	74	19	-	-	-	-	5	-
1983	Detr	16.11	60	18	-	-	-	-	12	-
1984	Detr	8.67	151	33	-	-	-	-	-	-
1985	Detr	12.49	110	25	-	-	-	-	20	-
1986	Sacr	10.94	129	25	-	-	-	-	11	-
1987	Sacr	10.27	121	21	-	-	-	-	26	-
1988	Sacr	6.88	DNQ								
1989	Dall	6.30	DNQ								

DARNELL VALENTINE — KANSAS

YR	TM	PR	OR	PS	SC	SH	RB	AS	BL	ST
1982	Port	7.33	DNQ								
1983	Port	14.40	DNQ								
1984	Port	12.06	114	20	-	-		17	-	15
1985	Port	15.32	82	15	-	-		13	-	11
1986	LA.C	8.29	152	26	-	-		19	-	15
1987	LA.C	13.06	95	18	-	-		9	-	10
1988	LA.C	9.33	134	28	-	-		10	-	6
1989	Clev	5.45	DNQ								

KIKI VANDEWEGHE — UCLA

YR	TM	PR	OR	PS	SC	SH	RB	AS	BL	ST
1981	Denv	11.41	DNQ								
1982	Denv	21.32	21	5	14	2	-	-	-	-
1983	Denv	24.23	9	2	2	4	-	-	-	-
1984	Denv	26.40	5	3	3	5	-	-	-	-
1985	Port	18.19	49	17	16	10	-	-	-	-
1986	Port	19.84	35	11	6	9	-	-	-	-
1987	Port	21.85	24	5	5	6	-	-	-	-
1988	Port	16.51	DNQ								
1989	N.Y.	8.73	DNQ								

SAM VINCENT — MICHIGAN ST.

YR	TM	PR	OR	PS	SC	SH	RB	AS	BL	ST
1986	Bost	3.14	DNQ								
1987	Bost	3.43	DNQ								
1988	Chic	10.67	122	25	-	-	-	7	-	-
1989	Chic	11.24	132	25	-	-	-	24	-	-

JAY VINCENT — MICHIGAN ST.

YR	TM	PR	OR	PS	SC	SH	RB	AS	BL	ST
1982	Dall	19.07	29	8	15	-	-	-	-	-
1983	Dall	18.77	38	11	-	-	-	-	-	-
1984	Dall	9.61	145	32	-	-	-	-	-	-
1985	Dall	19.65	34	1	-	-	27	-	-	-
1986	Dall	13.34	89	19	-	-	-	-	-	-
1987	Wash	11.27	DNQ								
1988	Denv	12.92	99	21	-	-	-	-	-	-
1989	S.A.	6.24	DNQ								

DARRELL WALKER — ARKANSAS

YR	TM	PR	OR	PS	SC	SH	RB	AS	BL	ST
1984	N.Y.	8.37	DNQ								
1985	N.Y.	13.54	101	19	-	-	-	-	-	8
1986	N.Y.	10.73	131	25	-	-	-	-	-	6
1987	Denv	13.46	89	17	-	-	-	-	-	15
1988	Wash	6.54	DNQ								
1989	Wash	16.13	80	19	-	-	-	27	-	17

KENNY WALKER — KENTUCKY

YR	TM	PR	OR	PS	SC	SH	RB	AS	BL	ST
1987	N.Y.	11.84	107	19	-	-	-	-	-	-
1988	N.Y.	11.17	118	23	-	-	-	-	-	-
1989	N.Y.	6.66	DNQ								

DWAYNE WASHINGTON — SYRACUSE

YR	TM	PR	OR	PS	SC	SH	RB	AS	BL	ST
1987	N.J.	9.19	140	26	-	-	-	27	-	19
1988	N.J.	8.12	154	31	-	-	-	-	-	11
1989	Miam	8.70	DNQ								

MARK WEST — OLD DOMINION

YR	TM	PR	OR	PS	SC	SH	RB	AS	BL	ST
1984	Dall	1.59	DNQ								
1985	Clev	5.59	DNQ								
1986	Clev	7.09	DNQ								
1987	Clev	8.00	DNQ								
1988	Phoe	12.63	102	22	-	-	29	-	9	-
1989	Phoe	13.17	107	18	-	10	24	-	7	-

DOMINIQUE WILKINS — GEORGIA

YR	TM	PR	OR	PS	SC	SH	RB	AS	BL	ST
1983	Atla	15.63	64	19	-	-	-	-	-	-
1984	Atla	19.60	35	11	17	-	-	-	-	-
1985	Atla	22.01	23	7	6	-	-	-	-	-
1986	Atla	25.50	6	3	1	-	-	-	-	-
1987	Atla	24.15	11	3	2	-	-	-	-	-
1988	Atla	24.27	12	3	2	-	-	-	-	-
1989	Atla	22.84	16	3	7	-	-	-	-	-

GERALD WILKINS — TENN-CHAT

YR	TM	PR	OR	PS	SC	SH	RB	AS	BL	ST
1986	N.Y.	8.64	149	35	-	-	-	-	-	-
1987	N.Y.	16.23	66	13	31	-	-	-	-	-
1988	N.Y.	13.86	88	14	-	-	-	-	-	-
1989	N.Y.	12.64	116	23	-	-	-	-	-	-

BUCK WILLIAMS — MARYLAND

YR	TM	PR	OR	PS	SC	SH	RB	AS	BL	ST
1982	N.J.	21.94	16	3	-	21	2	-	-	-
1983	N.J.	23.51	12	3	-	28	3	-	-	-
1984	N.J.	21.33	23	5	-	-	5	-	28	-
1985	N.J.	22.98	20	4	-	-	10	-	-	-
1986	N.J.	21.26	22	5	-	-	11	-	-	-
1987	N.J.	23.66	14	3	-	26	5	-	-	-
1988	N.J.	22.96	14	5	-	-	8	-	-	-
1989	N.J.	16.92	62	14	-	-	18	-	-	-

HERB WILLIAMS — OHIO ST.

YR	TM	PR	OR	PS	SC	SH	RB	AS	BL	ST
1982	Indi	15.50	62	15	-	-	26	-	8	-
1983	Indi	19.33	34	10	-	-	-	-	8	-
1984	Indi	17.71	49	11	-	-	21	-	-	-
1985	Indi	19.08	40	8	-	-	15	-	-	-
1986	Indi	21.79	17	4	27	-	-	-	10	-
1987	Indi	17.12	61	15	-	-	-	-	-	-
1988	Indi	12.17	108	24	-	-	8	-	-	-
1989	Dall	13.78	103	17	-	-	13	-	-	-

JOHN WILLIAMS — TULANE

YR	TM	PR	OR	PS	SC	SH	RB	AS	BL	ST
1987	Clev	18.41	52	12	-	-	-	11	-	-
1988	Clev	14.79	80	18	-	-	-	10	-	-
1989	Clev	14.87	94	20	-	-	-	12	-	-

JOHN S. WILLIAMS — LSU

YR	TM	PR	OR	PS	SC	SH	RB	AS	BL	ST
1987	Wash	11.42	114	20	-	-	-	-	-	3
1988	Wash	14.37	84	19	-	-	-	-	-	29
1989	Wash	18.74	40	10	-	-	-	-	-	21

REGGIE WILLIAMS — GEORGETOWN

YR	TM	PR	OR	PS	SC	SH	RB	AS	BL	ST
1988	LA.C	6.71	DNQ							
1989	LA.C	8.83	160	37	-	-	-	-	-	16

KEVIN WILLIS — MICHIGAN STATE

YR	TM	PR	OR	PS	SC	SH	RB	AS	BL	ST
1985	Atla	10.60	131	24	-	-	21	-	-	-
1986	Atla	14.74	78	21	-	-	15	-	-	-
1987	Atla	19.88	36	10	-	-	10	-	-	-
1988	Atla	13.33	96	21	-	-	24	-	-	-
1989	Atla	DID NOT PLAY								

DAVID WINGATE — GEORGETOWN

YR	TM	PR	OR	PS	SC	SH	RB	AS	BL	ST
1987	Phil	7.53	157	33	-	-	-	-	-	18
1988	Phil	6.07	159	33	-	-	-	-	-	-
1989	Phil	4.70	DNQ							

RANDY WITTMAN — INDIANA

YR	TM	PR	OR	PS	SC	SH	RB	AS	BL	ST
1984	Atla	3.86	DNQ							
1985	Atla	9.01	DNQ							
1986	Atla	13.02	98	17	-	-	-	-	-	-
1987	Atla	11.00	119	24	-	-	-	-	-	-
1988	Atla	10.39	126	22	-	-	-	-	-	-
1989	Indi	4.78	DNQ							

JOE WOLF — N. CAROLINA

YR	TM	PR	OR	PS	SC	SH	RB	AS	BL	ST
1988	LA.C	8.95	DNQ							
1989	LA.C	7.15	176	40	-	-	-	-	-	-

MIKE WOODSON — INDIANA

YR	TM	PR	OR	PS	SC	SH	RB	AS	BL	ST
1981	N.Y.	3.99	DNQ							
1982	K.C.	14.47	75	12	-	-	-	-	-	14
1983	K.C.	16.64	55	8	-	-	-	-	-	18
1984	K.C.	12.55	107	20	-	-	-	-	-	-
1985	K.C.	13.74	100	18	-	-	-	-	-	16
1986	Sacr	13.10	95	16	-	-	-	-	-	-
1987	LA.C	11.92	105	20	-	-	-	-	-	-
1988	LA.C	13.80	89	15	-	-	-	-	-	-
1989	Hous	10.48	138	31	-	-	-	-	-	-

ORLANDO WOOLRIDGE — N. DAME

YR	TM	PR	OR	PS	SC	SH	RB	AS	BL	ST
1982	Chic	7.23	DNQ							
1983	Chic	15.35	68	20	-	26	-	-	-	-
1984	Chic	16.73	57	17	31	-	-	-	-	-
1985	Chic	20.74	27	10	12	15	-	-	-	-
1986	Chic	18.36	41	12	19	-	-	-	-	-
1987	N.J.	19.59	40	11	26	-	-	-	-	-
1988	N.J.	14.95	DNQ							
1989	LA.L	9.22	157	36	-	-	-	-	20	-

JAMES WORTHY — N. CAROLINA

YR	TM	PR	OR	PS	SC	SH	RB	AS	BL	ST
1983	LA.L	14.71	76	22	-	9	-	-	-	-
1984	LA.L	17.27	51	16	-	15	-	-	-	-
1985	LA.L	19.59	35	13	-	7	-	-	-	-
1986	LA.L	20.92	25	7	25	5	-	-	-	-
1987	LA.L	20.20	35	9	30	27	-	-	-	-
1988	LA.L	20.09	34	7	23	25	-	-	-	-
1989	LA.L	21.80	21	4	21	16	-	-	-	-

DANNY YOUNG — WAKE FOREST

YR	TM	PR	OR	PS	SC	SH	RB	AS	BL	ST
1985	Seat	2.00	DNQ							
1986	Seat	9.51	139	30	-	22	-	-	-	17
1987	Seat	8.79	146	30	-	-	-	13	-	30
1988	Seat	5.38	DNQ							
1989	Port	7.46	DNQ							

FORMER PLAYERS

Kareem Abdul-Jabbar played 20 years in the NBA. He also played until the age of 42. Both are milestones accomplished by no other NBA player.

KAREEM ABDUL-JABBAR — UCLA

YR	TM	PR	OR	PS	SC	SH	RB	AS	BL	ST
1970	Milw	33.63	1	1	2	-	15	-		
1971	Milw	38.88	1	1	1	6	-			
1972	Milw	42.63	1	1	1	9	-			
1973	Milw	39.12	1	1	2	3	10	-		
1974	Milw	35.91	1	1	3	4	15	-	4	-
1975	Milw	35.62	1	1	3	11	13	-	3	-
1976	LA.L	39.65	1	1	2	10	1	-	1	-
1977	LA.L	35.16	1	1	3	2	9	-	5	-
1978	LA.L	34.39	1	1	5	4	9	-	4	-
1979	LA.L	34.68	1	1	8	4	12	-	3	-
1980	LA.L	32.87	1	1	6	1	20	-	3	-
1981	LA.L	30.95	2	2	4	5	23	-	5	-
1982	LA.L	27.16	6	2	6	7	-	9	-	
1983	LA.L	24.63	7	3	16	3	-	-	9	-
1984	LA.L	23.26	15	6	18	9	-	17	-	
1985	LA.L	25.87	7	2	20	3	-	12	-	
1986	LA.L	24.20	11	2	11	10	-	18	-	
1987	LA.L	19.50	42	8	-	10	-	27	-	
1988	LA.L	15.90	69	12	-	31	-	24	-	
1989	LA.L	10.74	136	22	-	14	-			

ALVAN ADAMS — OKLAHOMA

YR	TM	PR	OR	PS	SC	SH	RB	AS	BL	ST
1976	Phoe	22.30	9	8	24	-	-	5	14	-
1977	Phoe	20.83	19	8	-	-	-	30	29	-
1978	Phoe	17.81	41	14	-	-	-	-	-	
1979	Phoe	22.94	14	7	-	16	22	-	-	
1980	Phoe	20.48	28	10	-	18	23	-	-	31
1981	Phoe	19.76	21	10	-	28	28	22	-	26
1982	Phoe	19.78	26	8	-	-	-	-	-	29
1983	Phoe	18.30	42	11	-	-	-	-	-	
1984	Phoe	12.21	112	23	-	-	-	-	-	25
1985	Phoe	18.34	45	11	-	20	-	-	-	18
1986	Phoe	15.42	73	16	-	-	-	-	-	25
1987	Phoe	13.74	88	21						

LUCIUS ALLEN — UCLA

YR	TM	PR	OR	PS	SC	SH	RB	AS	BL	ST
1970	Seat	11.04	81	29	-	-	-	7		
1971	Milw	8.08	113	44	-	-	-	21		
1972	Milw	14.66	63	22	-	15	-	19		
1973	Milw	16.27	59	21	-	-	-	17		
1974	Milw	17.65	31	5	-	16	-	17	-	13
1975	LA.L	16.89	34	6	-	-	-	10	-	11
1976	LA.L	13.11	65	13	-	-	-	16	-	
1977	LA.L	14.04	64	9	-	-	-	17	-	
1978	K.C.	11.61	110	17	-	-	-	18	-	
1979	K.C.	4.03	DNQ							

NATE ARCHIBALD — UTEP

YR	TM	PR	OR	PS	SC	SH	RB	AS	BL	ST
1971	Cinc	15.65	59	24	-	-	-	14		
1972	Cinc	28.21	6	1	2	12	-	4		
1973	K.C.	33.18	2	1	1	9	-	1		
1974	K.C.	20.66	DNQ							
1975	K.C.	20.74	13	2	4	-	-	8	-	-
1976	K.C.	19.71	20	4	4	-	-	4	-	-
1977	NY.N	17.92	DNQ							
1978	DID NOT PLAY									
1979	Bost	9.74	135	28	-	-	-	11	-	
1980	Bost	17.35	51	6	-	-	-	4	-	
1981	Bost	15.84	63	7	-	-	-	11	-	
1982	Bost	14.24	80	13	-	-	-	5	-	
1983	Bost	10.30	122	24	-	-	-	12	-	
1984	Milw	7.63	DNQ							

PAUL ARIZIN — VILLANOVA

YR	TM	PR	OR	PS	SC	SH	RB	AS	BL	ST
1951	Phil	19.66	7	3	5	5	8	-		
1952	Phil	27.06	1	1	1	2	-	-		
1953	DID NOT PLAY									
1954	DID NOT PLAY									
1955	Phil	20.42	8	4	3	-	-	-		
1956	Phil	21.94	7	4	2	2	-	-		
1957	Phil	22.08	7	4	1	2	-	-		
1958	Phil	17.56	16	8	6	-	-	-		
1959	Phil	23.40	8	6	2	4	-	-		
1960	Phil	20.54	14	9	8	-	-	-		
1961	Phil	21.71	13	8	9	10	-	-		
1962	Phil	18.44	20	9	-	-	-	-		

AL ATTLES — N.C. A&T

YR	TM	PR	OR	PS	SC	SH	RB	AS	BL	ST
1961	Phil	7.05	56	23	-	-	-	-		
1962	Phil	13.89	36	13	-	-	-	-		
1963	S.F.	10.17	50	17	-	-	-	-		
1964	S.F.	10.79	46	17	-	-	-	-		
1965	S.F.	8.38	61	23	-	-	-	13		
1966	S.F.	12.29	45	17	-	10	-	-		
1967	S.F.	11.36	54	22	-	-	-	9		
1968	S.F.	14.42	52	17	-	-	-	6		
1969	S.F.	12.84	68	24	-	-	-	5		
1970	S.F.	6.33	DNQ							
1971	S.F.	3.44	DNQ							

GREG BALLARD — OREGON

YR	TM	PR	OR	PS	SC	SH	RB	AS	BL	ST
1978	Wash	6.07	DNQ							
1979	Wash	10.29	DNQ							
1980	Wash	17.74	45	14	-	-	-	-		
1981	Wash	17.30	44	10	-	-	-	-		
1982	Wash	21.20	22	6	28	-	-	-	31	
1983	Wash	18.62	40	13	-	-	-	-		
1984	Wash	16.59	59	18	-	-	-	-		
1985	Wash	15.83	77	17	-	-	-	-		
1986	G.St	11.44	121	31	-	-	-	-		
1987	G.St	8.33	153	33	-	-	-	-		
1989	Seat	0.00	DNQ							

GENE BANKS — DUKE

YR	TM	PR	OR	PS	SC	SH	RB	AS	BL	ST
1982	S.A.	11.04	122	31	-	-	-	-	-	-
1983	S.A.	18.88	36	9	-	20	-	-	-	-
1984	S.A.	18.17	43	14	-	13	-	-	-	-
1985	S.A.	13.82	99	23	-	6	-	-	-	-
1986	Chic	12.85	101	21	-	-	-	-	-	-
1987	Chic	12.65	101	17	-	22	-	-	-	-

MIKE BANTOM — ST. JOE

YR	TM	PR	OR	PS	SC	SH	RB	AS	BL	ST
1974	Phoe	10.59	88	17	-	-	-	-	-	-
1975	Phoe	13.17	65	11	-	-	-	-	-	-
1976	Seat	9.32	103	22	-	-	-	-	-	-
1977	NY.N	12.91	83	12	-	-	-	-	-	-
1978	Indi	17.13	48	9	-	-	-	-	-	-
1979	Indi	16.88	57	10	-	-	-	-	-	-
1980	Indi	14.83	76	13	-	-	-	-	-	-
1981	Indi	15.30	73	15	-	-	-	-	-	-
1982	Phil	10.85	126	23	-	-	-	-	-	-

DICK BARNETT — TENN. ST

YR	TM	PR	OR	PS	SC	SH	RB	AS	BL	ST
1960	Syra	9.77	43	19	-	-	-	-	-	-
1961	Syra	13.72	32	12	-	-	-	-	-	-
1962		DID NOT PLAY								
1963	LA.L	15.13	26	7	-	9	-	-	-	-
1964	LA.L	14.90	25	6	-	-	-	-	-	-
1965	LA.L	10.51	49	17	-	-	-	-	-	-
1966	N.Y.	19.29	19	7	6	6	-	-	-	-
1967	N.Y.	14.43	36	12	-	9	-	-	-	-
1968	N.Y.	15.36	47	14	-	10	-	-	-	-
1969	N.Y.	15.10	52	16	-	18	-	-	-	-
1970	N.Y.	13.43	66	25	-	-	-	-	-	-
1971	N.Y.	12.28	84	33	-	-	-	-	-	-
1972	N.Y.	9.43	100	38	-	-	-	-	-	-
1973	N.Y.	2.57		DNQ						
1974	N.Y.	2.20		DNQ						

JIM BARNETT — OREGON

YR	TM	PR	OR	PS	SC	SH	RB	AS	BL	ST
1967	Bost	2.90		DNQ						
1968	S.D.	8.94		DNQ						
1969	S.D.	14.49	58	18	-	-	-	14		
1970	S.D.	14.45	61	22	-	-	-	-		
1971	Port	17.22	49	17	-	-	-	22		
1972	G.St	12.03	79	28	-	-	-	-		
1973	G.St	12.72	75	28	-	-	-	-		
1974	G.St	10.30	92	16	-	-	-	-		
1975	N.Y.	9.01	101	20	-	-	-	-	-	-
1976	N.Y.	5.52		DNQ						
1977	Phil	2.81		DNQ						

RICK BARRY — MIAMI OF FLORIDA

YR	TM	PR	OR	PS	SC	SH	RB	AS	BL	ST
1966	S.F.	25.48	8	2	4	11	-	-		
1967	S.F.	31.32	4	1	8	-	-			
1968		DID NOT PLAY								
1969	ABA	35.11		DNQ						
1970	ABA	26.94	3	2	3	1	-	-		
1971	ABA	28.08	4	1	2	12	-	-		
1972	ABA	28.64	7	3	2	14	-	-		
1973	G.St	24.72	14	5	15	-	-	-		
1974	G.St	24.49	8	2	7	-	-	12	-	12
1975	G.St	26.26	5	1	2	-	-	15	-	3
1976	G.St	20.75	16	3	12	-	-	11	-	8
1977	G.St	21.94	15	5	13	-	-	16	-	20
1978	G.St	22.13	17	4	14	-	-	-		
1979	Hous	15.60	72	19	-	-	-	10	-	-
1980	Hous	12.08	107	25	-	-	-	-	-	-

ELGIN BAYLOR — SEATTLE

YR	TM	PR	OR	PS	SC	SH	RB	AS	BL	ST
1959	Minn	29.27	3	2	4	-	8	-		
1960	Minn	31.93	4	2	3	-	8	-		
1961	LA.L	40.19	2	1	2	-	6	-		
1962	LA.L	39.31	3	1	2	-	7	-		
1963	LA.L	35.98	3	1	2	-	11	-		
1964	LA.L	27.29	8	3	6	-	-	-		
1965	LA.L	26.65	7	2	4	-	-	-		
1966	LA.L	18.72	20	8	-	-	-	-		
1967	LA.L	27.53	8	3	4	-	12	-		
1968	LA.L	28.74	5	2	4	-	-	-		
1969	LA.L	26.92	7	2	5	-	-	-		
1970	LA.L	28.30	8	3	10	-	-	-		
1971	LA.L	10.00		DNQ						
1972	LA.L	14.56		DNQ						

BUTCH BEARD — LOUISVILLE

YR	TM	PR	OR	PS	SC	SH	RB	AS	BL	ST
1970	Atla	7.29		DNQ						
1971		DID NOT PLAY								
1972	Clev	18.28	45	13	-	-	-	6		
1973	Seat	8.48	103	42	-	-	-	9		
1974	G.St	13.51	67	16	-	14	-	-	-	21
1975	G.St	14.89	51	12	-	3	-	-	-	19
1976	N.Y.	10.40	88	15	-	-	-	-	-	-
1977	N.Y.	2.30		DNQ						
1978	N.Y.	12.37	100	19	-	27	-	16	-	13
1979	N.Y.	5.14		DNQ						

ZELMO BEATY — PRAIRIE VIEW

YR	TM	PR	OR	PS	SC	SH	RB	AS	BL	ST
1963	St.L	13.71	35	7	-	-	10	-		
1964	St.L	17.90	19	6	-	-	-	-		
1965	St.L	21.88	13	6	-	10	-	-		
1966	St.L	25.59	7	4	10	7	10	-		
1967	St.L	20.81		DNQ						
1968	St.L	25.33	9	4	13	5	-	-		
1969	Atla	23.28	15	8	18	-	-	-		
1970		DID NOT PLAY								
1971	ABA	32.11	1	1	11	1	3	-		
1972	ABA	29.56	5	3	13	2	9	-		
1973	ABA	20.95	13	7	-	7	-	-		
1974	ABA	17.43	19	10	-	3	-	-	-	-
1975	LA.L	8.25		DNQ						

WALT BELLAMY — INDIANA

YR	TM	PR	OR	PS	SC	SH	RB	AS	BL	ST
1962	Chic	37.96	4	2	3	3	3	-		
1963	Chic	34.40	4	2	5	4	4	-		
1964	Balt	32.34	5	3	5	7	5	-		
1965	Balt	29.91	5	3	6	7	9	-		
1966	N.Y.	29.65	6	3	7	12	7	-		
1967	N.Y.	25.81	10	4	-	10	10	-		
1968	N.Y.	22.99	13	5	-	4	12	-		
1969	Detr	23.26	16	9	-	14	15	-		
1970	Atla	16.32	50	10	-	-	13	-		
1971	Atla	22.27	24	11	-	-	13	-		
1972	Atla	25.61	15	9	-	-	21	-		
1973	Atla	22.26	23	9	-	-	14	-		
1974	Atla	16.29	42	15	-	-	-	-	-	-
1975	N.O.	10.00		DNQ						

KENT BENSON — INDIANA

YR	TM	PR	OR	PS	SC	SH	RB	AS	BL	ST
1978	Milw	9.10		DNQ						
1979	Milw	16.56	61	18	-	-	-	27	-	
1980	Detr	13.37	93	21	-	-	-	18	-	
1981	Detr	16.63	55	16	-	-	-	-	-	
1982	Detr	17.71	43	11	-	27	-	31	-	
1983	Detr	13.91		DNQ						
1984	Detr	11.49	125	26	-	11	-	-	-	-
1985	Detr	9.86	141	25	-	-	-	-	-	-
1986	Detr	9.53		DNQ						
1987	Utah	5.95		DNQ						

DAVE BING — SYRACUSE

YR	TM	PR	OR	PS	SC	SH	RB	AS	BL	ST
1967	Detr	16.69	28	8	12	-	-	-		
1968	Detr	22.41	16	4	2	-	-	11		
1969	Detr	21.21	23	7	9	-	-	8		
1970	Detr	21.07	23	9	12	-	-	10		
1971	Detr	23.38	19	5	4	17	-	-		
1972	Detr	20.46		DNQ						
1973	Detr	22.17	24	6	14	-	-	6		
1974	Detr	16.27	43	9	-	-	-	8	-	-
1975	Detr	17.66	26	4	-	-	-	4	-	-
1976	Wash	15.12	50	8	-	-	-	7	-	-
1977	Wash	10.42	112	19	-	-	-	12	-	-
1978	Bost	11.39	115	19	-	-	-	-	-	-

JOHN BLOCK — USC

YR	TM	PR	OR	PS	SC	SH	RB	AS	BL	ST
1967	L.A.L	3.27		DNQ						
1968	S.D.	21.40	21	6	17	-	-	-		
1969	S.D.	16.99	43	9	-	-	-	-		
1970	S.D.	15.70	54	23	-	-	-	-		
1971	S.D.	11.58	93	36	-	-	-	-		
1972	Milw	10.27	95	40	-	-	-	-		
1973	K.C.	16.22	60	23	-	-	-	-		
1974	K.C.	8.99	99	21	-	-	-	-		
1975	Chic	9.20		DNQ						
1976	Chic	1.50		DNQ						

BUCKY BOCKHORN — DAYTON

YR	TM	PR	OR	PS	SC	SH	RB	AS	BL	ST
1959	Cinc	12.07	34	12	-	-	-	-		
1960	Cinc	11.88	35	12	-	-	-	-		
1961	Cinc	13.53	33	13	-	-	-	-		
1962	Cinc	15.58	29	11	-	-	-	-		
1963	Cinc	10.98	46	15	-	-	-	-		
1964	Cinc	8.33	53	21	-	-	-	-		
1965	Cinc	7.37		DNQ						

RON BOONE — IDAHO ST.

YR	TM	PR	OR	PS	SC	SH	RB	AS	BL	ST
1969	ABA	17.60	24	8	-	-	-	14		
1970	ABA	13.83	47	15	-	-	-	11		
1971	ABA	17.48	36	11	-	-	-	-		
1972	ABA	12.98	52	20	-	-	-	-		
1973	ABA	20.25	15	2	-	6	-	-		
1974	ABA	20.10	12	2	-	7	-	-	-	-
1975	ABA	23.09	9	1	5	-	-	-	-	-
1976	ABA	20.90	12	3	8	10	-	9	-	-
1977	K.C.	16.83	41	7	11	-	-	-	-	-
1978	K.C.	13.15	91	17	-	-	-	-	-	-
1979	L.A.L	6.26	154	32	-	-	-	-	-	-
1980	Utah	11.26	120	22	-	-	-	-	-	-
1981	Utah	6.75		DNQ						

BOB BOOZER — KANSAS ST.

YR	TM	PR	OR	PS	SR	SH	RB	AS	BL	ST
1961	Cinc	10.49	46	19	-	-	-	-		
1962	Cinc	17.49	23	10	-	-	-	-		
1963	Cinc	18.47	17	7	-	9	-	-		
1964	N.Y.	14.42	29	16	-	-	-	-		
1965	N.Y.	15.28	26	12	-	-	-	-		
1966	L.A.L	14.58	35	18	-	3	-	-		
1967	Chic	19.23	21	11	-	5	-	-		
1968	Chic	22.92	14	6	10	7	-	-		
1969	Chic	21.23	22	7	16	10	-	-		
1970	Seat	18.38	41	17	-	18	-	-		
1971	Milw	11.29	96	38	-	-	-	-		

BILL BRADLEY — PRINCETON

YR	TM	PR	OR	PS	SC	SH	RB	AS	BL	ST
1968	N.Y.	6.96		DNQ						
1969	N.Y.	13.22	65	29	-	-	-	-		
1970	N.Y.	14.37	62	27	-	-	-	-		
1971	N.Y.	12.56	82	29	-	-	-	-		
1972	N.Y.	14.50	65	26	-	-	-	-		
1973	N.Y.	15.67	63	25	-	-	-	-		
1974	N.Y.	10.60	87	19	-	-	-	-		
1975	N.Y.	10.65	88	18	-	-	-	-		
1976	N.Y.	9.23	104	21	-	-	-	-		
1977	N.Y.	4.70		DNQ						

CARL BRAUN — COLGATE

YR	TM	PR	OR	PS	SC	SH	RB	AS	BL	ST
1948	N.Y.	14.30			6			9		
1949	N.Y.	14.20			9			-		
1950	N.Y.	13.25	17	2	7	-		9		
1951		DID NOT PLAY								
1952		DID NOT PLAY								
1953	N.Y.	12.84	27	7	13	7	-	-		
1954	N.Y.	12.67	21	7	9	5	-	-		
1955	N.Y.	13.28	28	8	-	-	-	-		
1956	N.Y.	13.04	28	7	-	-	-	-		
1957	N.Y.	11.71	31	7	-	-	-	10		
1958	N.Y.	17.56	15	2	-	9	-	4		
1959	N.Y.	12.76	30	9	-	-	-	3		
1960	N.Y.	13.67	31	8	-	-	-	7		
1961	N.Y.	7.93	DNQ							
1962	Bost	3.35	DNQ							

JIM BREWER — MINNESOTA

YR	TM	PR	OR	PS	SC	SH	RB	AS	BL	ST
1974	Clev	8.88	102	23	-	-	-	-	-	-
1975	Clev	10.87	87	19	-	-	-	-	-	-
1976	Clev	18.05	31	7	-	-	20	-	21	-
1977	Clev	14.78	56	9	-	-	-	-	-	-
1978	Clev	9.06	145	29	-	-	-	-	-	-
1979	Detr	8.56	149	25	-	-	24	-	24	-
1980	Port	6.28	DNQ							
1981	LA.L	5.77	DNQ							

JUNIOR BRIDGEMAN — LOUISVILLE

YR	TM	PR	OR	PS	SC	SH	RB	AS	BL	ST
1976	Milw	7.64	114	26	-	-	-	-	-	-
1977	Milw	13.09	79	19	-	-	-	-	-	-
1978	Milw	12.18	103	20	-	26	-	-	-	-
1979	Milw	14.07	82	20	-	-	-	-	-	-
1980	Milw	15.04	73	21	-	-	-	-	-	-
1981	Milw	15.40	70	16	-	-	-	-	-	-
1982	Milw	11.56	DNQ							
1983	Milw	13.14	93	25	-	-	-	-	-	-
1984	Milw	13.63	93	25	-	-	-	-	-	-
1985	LA.C	11.38	121	27	-	-	-	-	-	-
1986	LA.C	7.48	DNQ							
1987	Milw	4.79	DNQ							

BILL BRIDGES — KANSAS

YR	TM	PR	OR	PS	SC	SH	RB	AS	BL	ST
1963	St.L	8.07	DNQ							
1964	St.L	13.23	39	19	-	-	11	-		
1965	St.L	16.27	25	11	-	-	7	-		
1966	St.L	19.40	18	7	-	-	8	-		
1967	St.L	25.65	11	5	-	-	8	-		
1968	St.L	23.83	11	5	-	-	14	-		
1969	Atla	22.91	17	4	-	-	10	-		
1970	Atla	26.02	12	4	-	-	10	-		
1971	Atla	22.89	21	7	-	-	8	-		
1972	Phil	22.24	25	8	-	-	6	-		
1973	LA.L	18.33	42	17	-	-	-	-		
1974	LA.L	11.74	78	15	-	-	-	-	-	
1975	G.St	5.12	DNQ							

FREDDY BROWN — IOWA

YR	TM	PR	OR	PS	SC	SH	RB	AS	BL	ST
1972	Seat	3.30	DNQ							
1973	Seat	15.54	65	23	-	-	-	7		
1974	Seat	17.51	33	2	-	-	-	13	-	16
1975	Seat	18.10	22	2	16	-	-	-	-	4
1976	Seat	18.62	26	3	5	19	-	-	-	14
1977	Seat	13.86	67	14	-	-	-	-		21
1978	Seat	14.40	73	11	-	-	-	-		24
1979	Seat	12.43	99	17	-	-	-	-		13
1980	Seat	10.06	134	26	-	-	-	-		-
1981	Seat	13.06	100	20	-	-	-	-		-
1982	Seat	9.62	144	24	-	-	-	-		-
1983	Seat	9.48	DNQ							
1984	Seat	8.20	DNQ							

QUINN BUCKNER — INDIANA

YR	TM	PR	OR	PS	SC	SH	RB	AS	BL	ST
1977	Milw	10.68	109	18	-	-	-	13	-	2
1978	Milw	12.34	102	15	-	-	-	5	-	2
1979	Milw	10.81	120	25	-	-	-	2	-	2
1980	Milw	14.07	84	14	-	-	-	6	-	6
1981	Milw	14.62	82	12	-	-	-	31	-	3
1982	Milw	14.24	79	12	-	-	-	-	-	2
1983	Bost	8.75	139	30	-	-	-	28	-	7
1984	Bost	5.71	DNQ							
1985	Bost	6.72	DNQ							
1986	Indi	5.59	DNQ							

DON BUSE — EVANSVILLE

YR	TM	PR	OR	PS	SC	SH	RB	AS	BL	ST
1973	ABA	8.08	71	31	-	-	-	10		
1974	ABA	8.53	66	26	-	-	-	11	-	2
1975	ABA	10.35	60	21	-	-	-	-	-	3
1976	ABA	18.26	20	5	-	-	-	1	-	4
1977	Indi	16.26	46	5	-	-	-	3	-	1
1978	Phoe	12.66	95	14	-	-	-	24	-	4
1979	Phoe	11.94	105	17	-	-	-	-	-	11
1980	Phoe	10.60	124	18	-	-	-	-		25
1981	Indi	5.57	DNQ							
1982	Indi	13.74	84	14	-	-	-	27	-	11
1983	Port	5.91	DNQ							
1984	K.C.	7.39	DNQ							
1985	K.C.	4.89	DNQ							

JOE CALDWELL — ARIZONA ST.

YR	TM	PR	OR	PS	SC	SH	RB	AS	BL	ST
1965	Detr	10.62	48	22	-	-	-	-		
1966	St.L	12.16	46	22	-	-	-	-		
1967	St.L	12.32	51	21	-	-	-	-		
1968	St.L	13.81	56	26	-	-	-	-		
1969	Atla	15.09	53	17	-	19	-	-		
1970	Atla	19.44	35	13	-	-	-	-		
1971	ABA	19.25	29	15	9	-	-	-		
1972	ABA	16.18	38	16	-	-	-	15		
1973	ABA	16.03	28	9	-	-	-	-		
1974	ABA	15.72	28	11	-	-	-	-		5
1975	ABA	15.60	DNQ							

BILL CALHOUN

YR	TM	PR	OR	PS	SC	SH	RB	AS	BL	ST
1948	Roch	1.90	DNQ							
1949	Roch	6.60		-				.		
1950	Roch	7.47	70	30	-			.		
1951	Roch	6.23	63	28	-	-		.		
1952	Balt	7.53	58	27	-	-		.		
1953	Milw	9.18	48	16	-	-		.		
1954	Milw	8.67	43	16	-	-		.		
1955	Milw	8.30	47	14	-	-		.		

AUSTIN CARR   NOTRE DAME

YR	TM	PR	OR	PS	SC	SH	RB	AS	BL	ST
1972	Clev	15.09	DNQ							
1973	Clev	17.06	56	19	18					
1974	Clev	15.65	49	7	14	-	-	-	-	
1975	Clev	12.55	DNQ							
1976	Clev	7.51	117	24	-	-	-	-		
1977	Clev	11.87	94	21	-	-	-	-		
1978	Clev	9.65	134	27	-	-	-	-		
1979	Clev	13.91	84	13	-	-	-	-		
1980	Clev	8.62	145	30	-	-	-	-		
1981	Wash	2.65	DNQ							

KENNY CARR   N.C.STATE

YR	TM	PR	OR	PS	SC	SH	RB	AS	BL	ST
1978	LA.L	5.81	DNQ							
1979	LA.L	7.76	DNQ							
1980	Clev	13.65	89	16	-		10	-	-	-
1981	Clev	19.48	25	4	-		8	-	-	-
1982	Detr	13.49	89	17	-		22	-	-	-
1983	Port	13.89	83	15	-		-	-	-	
1984	Port	17.76	48	10	-	32	29	-	-	-
1985	Port	12.38	DNQ							
1986	Port	15.18	75	18	-		13	-	-	-
1987	Port	16.50	DNQ							

FRED CARTER   MT. ST. MARY'S

YR	TM	PR	OR	PS	SC	SH	RB	AS	BL	ST
1970	Balt	5.12	DNQ							
1971	Balt	8.78	111	42	-	-	-	-		
1972	Phil	11.75	81	29	-	-	-			
1973	Phil	17.37	52	18	-	-	-			
1974	Phil	16.94	35	8	17	-	-	19	-	-
1975	Phil	16.18	39	10	11	-	-	-	-	
1976	Phil	13.27	64	12	-	-	-	-		
1977	Milw	5.94	DNQ							

WILT CHAMBERLAIN   KANSAS

YR	TM	PR	OR	PS	SC	SH	RB	AS	BL	ST
1960	Phil	43.83	1	1	1	-	1	-		
1961	Phil	45.58	1	1	1	-	1	-		
1962	Phil	52.29	1	1	1	8	1	-		
1963	S.F.	50.59	1	1	1	8	2	-		
1964	S.F.	44.60	1	1	1	10	2	-		
1965	Phil	40.62	1	1	1	-	2	-		
1966	Phil	45.76	1	1	1	-	2	-		
1967	Phil	45.54	1	1	5	2	1	5		
1968	Phil	42.80	1	1	5	-	1	9		
1969	LA.L	34.68	1	1	-	-	2	-		
1970	LA.L	34.42	DNQ							
1971	LA.L	32.61	2	2	21	-	5	-		
1972	LA.L	31.01	2	2	-	18	2	-		
1973	LA.L	31.61	3	2	-	2	1	-		

DON CHANEY   HOUSTON

YR	TM	PR	OR	PS	SC	SH	RB	AS	BL	ST
1969	Bost	1.85	DNQ							
1970	Bost	4.83	DNQ							
1971	Bost	13.96	68	28	-	-	-	-		
1972	Bost	13.53	70	23	-	-	-	-		
1973	Bost	15.27	67	24	-	-	-	-		
1974	Bost	11.19	81	14	-	-	-	-	-	
1975	Bost	10.63	89	14	-	-	-		17	15
1976	ABA	9.81	DNQ							
1977	LA.L	9.72	124	27	-	-	-	-	-	24
1978	Bost	4.83	DNQ							
1979	Bost	5.40	DNQ							
1980	Bost	2.44	DNQ							

PHIL CHENIER   CALIFORNIA

YR	TM	PR	OR	PS	SC	SH	RB	AS	BL	ST
1972	Balt	10.25	96	36	-	-	-	-		
1973	Balt	17.00	57	20	-	-	-	-		
1974	Capt	16.65	41	3	18	-	-	-		18
1975	Wash	17.09	32	5	12	-	-	-		7
1976	Wash	16.96	38	7	17	24	-	-		18
1977	Wash	15.64	50	12	23	-	-	-		-
1978	Wash	10.39	DNQ							
1979	Wash	3.19	DNQ							
1980	Indi	5.63	DNQ							
1981	G.St	1.67	DNQ							

JIM CHONES   MARQUETTE

YR	TM	PR	OR	PS	SC	SH	RB	AS	BL	ST
1973	ABA	13.91	43	12	-	-	-	\		
1974	ABA	16.98	23	11	-	12	-	-	8	-
1975	Clev	18.06	23	8	-	-	-	-	10	-
1976	Clev	16.68	42	13	-	-	-	-	20	-
1977	Clev	14.80	55	15	-	-	-	-	-	
1978	Clev	17.96	38	13	-	-	-	-	-	
1979	Clev	17.43	48	16	-	-	23	-	29	-
1980	LA.L	13.39	91	17	-	-	-	-	-	
1981	LA.L	14.98	77	16	-	-	-	-	32	-
1982	Wash	5.15	DNQ							

ARCHIE CLARK   MINNESOTA

YR	TM	PR	OR	PS	SC	SH	RB	AS	BL	ST
1967	LA.L	10.05	62	28	-	-	-	-		
1968	LA.L	18.76	32	9	-	15	-	-		
1969	Phil	13.28	64	21	-	-	-	17		
1970	Phil	19.62	33	15	-	-	-	-		
1971	Phil	21.84	26	7	17	8	-	-		
1972	Balt	24.18	19	4	9	-	-	7		
1973	Balt	20.49	DNQ							
1974	Capt	11.96	76	18	-	-	-	15	-	
1975	Seat	14.57	55	13	-	18	-	7	-	
1976	Detr	6.94	118	21	-	-	-	-	-	

JIM CLEAMONS — OHIO ST.

YR	TM	PR	OR	PS	SC	SH	RB	AS	BL	ST
1972	L.A.L	2.61	DNQ							
1973	Clev	7.18	DNQ							
1974	Clev	7.69	110	22	-	-	-	-	-	
1975	Clev	14.35	57	14	-	-	-	22	-	-
1976	Clev	14.85	52	9	-	-	-	15	-	-
1977	Clev	13.33	74	11	-	-	-	22	-	-
1978	N.Y.	9.15	143	28	-	-	-	-	-	-
1979	N.Y.	11.49	114	21	-	-	-	27	-	-
1980	Wash	8.27	146	26	-	-	-	24	-	-

NAT CLIFTON — XAVIER (LA.)

YR	TM	PR	OR	PS	SC	SH	RB	AS	BL	ST
1951	N.Y.	9.95	38	9	-	-	-	-		
1952	N.Y.	16.56	14	5	-	-	3	-		
1953	N.Y.	15.30	13	6	-	-	8	-		
1954	N.Y.	11.76	26	9	-	-	-	-		
1955	N.Y.	14.97	21	10	-	-	-	-		
1956	N.Y.	11.16	35	16	-	-	-	-		
1957	N.Y.	12.70	30	10	-	-	-	-		
1958	Detr	8.37	46	19	-	-	-	-		

JACK COLEMAN — LOUISVILLE

YR	TM	PR	OR	PS	SC	SH	RB	AS	BL	ST
1950	Roch	13.12	18	8	-	-	-	-		
1951	Roch	16.01	11	5	-	10	11	-		
1952	Roch	17.47	12	6	-	14	-	-		
1953	Roch	18.01	8	4	-	-	9	-		
1954	Roch	13.17	19	7	-	-	-	-		
1955	Roch	18.89	12	7	-	5	-	-		
1956	St.L	17.48	15	8	-	-	-	-		
1957	St.L	14.75	19	11	-	-	-	-		
1958	St.L	10.72	38	15	-	-	-	-		

LARRY COSTELLO — NIAGARA

YR	TM	PR	OR	PS	SC	SH	RB	AS	BL	ST
1955	Phil	7.68	DNQ							
1956	DID NOT PLAY									
1957	Phil	10.39	35	10	-	-	-	9		
1958	Syra	16.71	22	6	-	4	-	-		
1959	Syra	17.84	14	4	-	6	-	6		
1960	Syra	18.87	21	5	-	4	-	6		
1961	Syra	17.12	25	9	-	2	-	4		
1962	Syra	15.98	27	9	-	-	-	5		
1963	Syra	13.01	39	13	-	12	-	5		
1964	Phil	12.47	DNQ							
1965	Phil	13.83	32	10	-	9	-	7		
1966	DID NOT PLAY									
1967	Phil	9.12	DNQ							
1968	Phil	8.04	DNQ							

BOB COUSY — HOLY CROSS

YR	TM	PR	OR	PS	SC	SH	RB	AS	BL	ST
1951	Bost	15.46	12	2	10	-	-	4		
1952	Bost	20.03	7	1	3	-	-	3		
1953	Bost	20.27	6	1	4	-	-	1		
1954	Bost	19.56	8	1	2	12	-	1		
1955	Bost	22.27	5	1	2	-	-	3		
1956	Bost	22.49	6	1	7	-	-	1		
1957	Bost	19.39	9	1	8	-	-	1		
1958	Bost	16.71	23	7	-	-	-	1		
1959	Bost	21.25	10	1	9	-	-	1		
1960	Bost	20.33	15	3	-	-	-	1		
1961	Bost	17.46	24	8	-	-	-	1		
1962	Bost	16.25	26	8	-	-	-	1		
1963	Bost	13.63	36	11	-	-	-	1		
1970	Cinc	2.57	DNQ							

DAVE COWENS — FLORIDA ST.

YR	TM	PR	OR	PS	SC	SH	RB	AS	BL	ST
1971	Bost	24.26	15	8	-	-	7	-		
1972	Bost	27.46	11	6	-	-	8	-		
1973	Bost	29.16	6	4	19	-	7	-		
1974	Bost	26.80	6	5	-	-	5	-	19	-
1975	Bost	28.37	4	4	19	-	5	-	19	-
1976	Bost	28.04	3	3	-	-	3	-		
1977	Bost	24.68	7	5	-	-	7	-		
1978	Bost	27.91	6	6	-	-	14	-		
1979	Bost	20.82	29	11	-	-	-	-		
1980	Bost	17.65	48	16	-	-	-	-		
1981	DID NOT PLAY									
1982	DID NOT PLAY									
1983	Milw	12.50	DNQ							

BILLY CUNNINGHAM — N.CAROLINA

YR	TM	PR	OR	PS	SC	SH	RB	AS	BL	ST
1966	Phil	15.09	31	15	-	-	-	-		
1967	Phil	18.01	25	12	-	-	-	-		
1968	Phil	18.19	36	15	-	-	-	-		
1969	Phil	26.54	10	3	4	-	-	-		
1970	Phil	30.48	3	1	4	-	14	-		
1971	Phil	27.38	9	4	10	-	-	-		
1972	Phil	28.83	5	2	13	-	-	17		
1973	ABA	31.33	3	2	4	-	7	7		
1974	ABA	25.47	DNQ							
1975	Phil	21.44	12	4	21	-	-	13	-	-	-
1976	Phil	19.70	DNQ							

LOU DAMPIER — KENTUCKY

YR	TM	PR	OR	PS	SC	SH	RB	AS	BL	ST
1968	ABA	16.36	29	8	-	-	-	-		
1969	ABA	20.94	11	5	5	11	-	5		
1970	ABA	20.44	23	6	5	-	-	7		
1971	ABA	17.49	35	10	-	-	-	9		
1972	ABA	17.31	33	11	-	-	-	7		
1973	ABA	17.25	25	8	-	-	-	5		
1974	ABA	16.96	24	5	-	-	-	5		
1975	ABA	17.11	28	8	-	-	-	10		
1976	ABA	14.28	31	11	-	-	-	3		
1977	S.A.	6.38	149	29	-	-	-	26		
1978	S.A.	9.89	131	26	-	29	-	-	-	
1979	S.A.	5.24	DNQ							

BOB DANDRIDGE — NORFOLK ST.

YR	TM	PR	OR	PS	SC	SH	RB	AS	BL	ST
1970	Milw	18.00	42	18	-	-	-	-		
1971	Milw	21.22	28	10	-	11	-	-		
1972	Milw	20.34	35	14	-	-	-	-		
1973	Milw	20.73	27	11	21	-	-			
1974	Milw	18.90	26	6	-	12	-	-		
1975	Milw	18.76	19	5	20	-	-	-		
1976	Milw	21.07	15	2	9	12	-	-	-	
1977	Milw	18.90	28	10	19	-	-	-		
1978	Wash	18.19	36	11	30	-	-	-		
1979	Wash	20.59	31	7	25	-	-	-		
1980	Wash	16.00	DNQ							
1981	Wash	9.91	DNQ							
1982	Milw	3.36	DNQ							

MEL DANIELS — NEW MEXICO

YR	TM	PR	OR	PS	SC	SH	RB	AS	BL	ST
1968	ABA	22.97	4	2	9	-	2	-		
1969	ABA	28.29	1	1	7	-	1	-		
1970	ABA	27.81	2	1	-	-	1	-		
1971	ABA	31.26	2	2	-	13	1	-		
1972	ABA	28.68	6	4	-	-	1	-		
1973	ABA	26.75	6	2	-	-	2	-		
1974	ABA	19.67	14	6	-	-	5	-		
1975	ABA	14.62	38	12	-	-	4	-	4	-
1976	DID NOT PLAY									
1977	NY.N	4.64	DNQ							

BOB DAVIES — SETON HALL

YR	TM	PR	OR	PS	SC	SH	RB	AS	BL	ST
1946	Roch	9.00	DNQ							
1947	Roch	14.40			2					
1948	Roch	9.80			-					
1949	Roch	15.10			10			1		
1950	Roch	11.45	29	8	-	-		3		
1951	Roch	12.86	23	6	12	-	-	6		
1952	Roch	14.38	21	5	5	-	-	4		
1953	Roch	12.85	26	6	8	-	-	6		
1954	Roch	11.01	30	10	-	-	-	4		
1955	Roch	12.50	32	10	-	-	-	4		

JOHNNY DAVIS — DAYTON

YR	TM	PR	OR	PS	SC	SH	RB	AS	BL	ST
1977	Port	6.38	DNQ							
1978	Port	9.22	141	27	-	-	-	-	-	
1979	Indi	15.62	71	10	-	-	-	29	-	-
1980	Indi	14.46	79	12	-	-	-	29	-	-
1981	Indi	14.92	78	11	-	-	-	17	-	-
1982	Indi	13.74	84	14	-	-	-	-	-	
1983	Atla	13.45	89	14	-	-	-	15	-	-
1984	Atla	11.19	129	23	-	-	-	32	-	-
1985	Clev	11.61	119	23	-	-	-	15	-	-
1986	Atla	6.61	DNQ							

DARRYL DAWKINS — NONE

YR	TM	PR	OR	PS	SC	SH	RB	AS	BL	ST
1976	Phil	2.24	DNQ							
1977	Phil	7.65	DNQ							
1978	Phil	16.96	50	17	-	3	19	-	8	-
1979	Phil	16.37	65	20	-	-	18	-	8	-
1980	Phil	17.85	44	14	-	-	-	-	10	-
1981	Phil	16.97	49	15	-	2	-	-	19	-
1982	Phil	13.67	DNQ							
1983	N.J.	13.35	91	19	-	5	-	-	6	-
1984	N.J.	18.70	41	12	-	7	-	-	15	-
1985	N.J.	15.72	DNQ							
1986	N.J.	15.94	DNQ							
1987	N.J.	8.17	DNQ							
1988	Detr	0.00	DNQ							
1989	Detr	0.93	DNQ							

DAVE DEBUSSCHERE — DETROIT

YR	TM	PR	OR	PS	SC	SH	RB	AS	BL	ST
1963	Detr	16.25	24	13	-	-	-	-		
1964	Detr	10.53	DNQ							
1965	Detr	20.63	14	6	-	-	-	-		
1966	Detr	19.41	17	6	-	-	-	-		
1967	Detr	21.35	14	7	-	-	-	-		
1968	Detr	22.86	15	7	-	-	13	-		
1969	N.Y.	20.88	24	8	-	-	-	-		
1970	N.Y.	18.51	38	16	-	-	-	-		
1971	N.Y.	19.37	36	14	-	-	-	-		
1972	N.Y.	20.69	33	13	-	-	-	-		
1973	N.Y.	20.08	31	13	-	-	-	-		
1974	N.Y.	21.01	18	5	-	-	-	-		

COBY DIETRICK — SAN JOSE ST.

YR	TM	PR	OR	PS	SC	SH	RB	AS	BL	ST
1971	ABA	4.81	DNQ							
1972	ABA	7.00	DNQ							
1973	ABA	8.99	DNQ							
1974	ABA	12.11	47	13	-	-	-	-		
1975	ABA	11.82	48	15	-	-	12	-	-	-
1976	ABA	9.38	DNQ							
1977	S.A.	9.91	120	28	-	-	-	-		
1978	S.A.	10.61	122	24	-	-	-	-		
1979	S.A.	10.75	121	30	-	23	-	-	-	
1980	Chic	10.77	123	29	-	-	-	-		
1981	Chic	6.68	DNQ							
1982	Chic	5.03	DNQ							
1983	S.A.	1.00	DNQ							

TERRY DISCHINGER — PURDUE

YR	TM	PR	OR	PS	SC	SH	RB	AS	BL	ST
1963	Chic	25.68	9	4	7	3	-	-		
1964	Balt	21.78	13	7	9	5	-	-		
1965	Detr	18.05	19	5	-	6	-	-		
1966	DID NOT PLAY									
1967	DID NOT PLAY									
1968	Detr	14.68	50	24	-	6	-	-		
1969	Detr	10.36	80	34	-	4	-	-		
1970	Detr	12.77	71	30	-	7	-	-		
1971	Detr	13.95	69	23	-	5	-	-		
1972	Detr	10.80	90	37	-	6	-	-		
1973	Port	7.46	DNQ							

JOHN DREW — GARDNER-WEBB

YR	TM	PR	OR	PS	SC	SH	RB	AS	BL	ST
1975	Atla	19.69	16	3	-	-	4	-	-	20
1976	Atla	22.14	11	1	8	20	-	-	-	12
1977	Atla	21.55	17	6	7	-	-	-	-	
1978	Atla	20.43	27	9	13	-	-	-	-	
1979	Atla	18.51	41	12	13	-	-	-	-	20
1980	Atla	15.01	74	22	25	-	-	-	-	
1981	Atla	16.66	54	14	14	-	-	-	-	
1982	Atla	14.84	71	18	31	-	-	-	-	
1983	Utah	16.41	DNQ							
1984	Utah	13.95	90	24	-	-	-	-	-	29
1985	Utah	12.16	DNQ							

WALTER DUKES — SETON HALL

YR	TM	PR	OR	PS	SC	SH	RB	AS	BL	ST
1956	N.Y.	10.95	36	10	-	-	9	-		
1957	Minn	14.80	18	6	-	-	3	-		
1958	Detr	16.28	25	8	-	-	5	-		
1959	Detr	16.86	16	3	-	-	3	-		
1960	Detr	19.36	19	4	-	-	6	-		
1961	Detr	20.29	15	4	-	-	4	-		
1962	Detr	15.25	33	7	-	-	6	-		
1963	Detr	7.65	DNQ							

JOHN EGAN — PROVIDENCE

YR	TM	PR	OR	PS	SC	SH	RB	AS	BL	ST
1962	Detr	5.43	DNQ							
1963	Detr	5.30	DNQ							
1964	N.Y.	14.18	30	7	-	-	-	4		
1965	N.Y.	10.34	50	18	-	5	-	5		
1966	Balt	10.24	52	19	-	-	-	5		
1967	Balt	11.03	56	24	-	-	-	8		
1968	Balt	6.28	DNQ							
1969	LA.L	8.18	90	35	-	-	-	-		
1970	LA.L	7.65	95	36	-	-	-	-		
1971	S.D.	3.73	DNQ							
1972	Hous	3.13	DNQ							

LEROY ELLIS — ST. JOHN'S

YR	TM	PR	OR	PS	SC	SH	RB	AS	BL	ST
1963	LA.L	9.55	53	26	-	-	13	-		
1964	LA.L	9.23	DNQ							
1965	LA.L	13.08	36	16	-	-	-	-		
1966	LA.L	14.71	34	17	-	-	-	-		
1967	Balt	19.73	19	6	-	-	13	-		
1968	Balt	19.08	31	10	-	-	-	-		
1969	Balt	10.28	83	35	-	-	-	-		
1970	Balt	8.99	DNQ							
1971	Port	22.42	23	10	-	-	16	-		
1972	LA.L	6.85	DNQ							
1973	Phil	16.54	58	22	-	-	-	-		
1974	Phil	16.89	38	13	-	-	21	-	17	-
1975	Phil	11.05	84	20	-	-	-	-	22	-
1976	Phil	6.41	DNQ							

WAYNE EMBRY — MIAMI OF OHIO

YR	TM	PR	OR	PS	SC	SH	RB	AS	BL	ST
1959	Cinc	13.71	29	7	-	-	7	-		
1960	Cinc	13.74	30	9	-	-	3	-		
1961	Cinc	18.49	21	6	-	-	7	-		
1962	Cinc	24.49	12	6	-	-	11	-		
1963	Cinc	22.66	11	5	-	-	7	-		
1964	Cinc	20.23	15	5	-	-	-	-		
1965	Cinc	16.54	23	8	-	-	-	-		
1966	Cinc	9.83	53	8	-	-	-	-		
1967	Bost	6.08	DNQ							
1968	Bost	6.44	DNQ							
1969	Milw	15.40	49	14	-	-	-	-		

KEITH ERICKSON — UCLA

YR	TM	PR	OR	PS	SC	SH	RB	AS	BL	ST
1966	S.F.	3.73	DNQ							
1967	Chic	7.86	67	27	-	-	-			
1968	Chic	12.97	61	21	-	-	-			
1969	LA.L	9.48	86	33	-	-	-			
1970	LA.L	11.53	79	35	-	-	-			
1971	LA.L	13.82	70	24	-	-	-			
1972	LA.L	7.73	DNQ							
1973	LA.L	11.16	85	32	-	-	-			
1974	Phoe	15.44	51	9	-	-	-			
1975	Phoe	12.56	DNQ							
1976	Phoe	10.88	86	18	-	-	-			
1977	Phoe	7.30	DNQ							

JULIUS ERVING — MASSACHUSETTS

YR	TM	PR	OR	PS	SC	SH	RB	AS	BL	ST
1972	ABA	34.14	2	1	4	-	5	-		
1973	ABA	33.61	1	1	2	-	11	-		
1974	ABA	31.21	2	1	3	-	-	-	5	7
1975	ABA	32.20	3	2	4	-	-	-	9	12
1976	ABA	32.79	1	1	1	3	-	10	-	-
1977	Phil	23.84	9	2	15	30	-	-	28	29
1978	Phil	21.89	20	7	20	17	-	-	27	28
1979	Phil	22.74	15	3	12	-	-	-	-	-
1980	Phil	27.78	3	1	4	29	-	-	16	13
1981	Phil	27.38	4	2	7	29	-	-	21	11
1982	Phil	26.69	8	3	5	18	-	-	20	16
1983	Phil	23.24	14	3	21	-	-	-	16	-
1984	Phil	24.06	12	6	12	-	-	-	18	20
1985	Phil	19.41	38	15	28	-	-	-	22	20
1986	Phil	17.51	50	9	-	-	-	-	-	-
1987	Phil	16.30	65	12	-	-	-	-	15	-

RAY FELIX — LONG ISLAND

YR	TM	PR	OR	PS	SC	SH	RB	AS	BL	ST
1954	Balt	20.57	7	6	5	-	4	-		
1955	N.Y.	17.60	13	5	-	-	2	-		
1956	N.Y.	14.25	23	6	-	-	6	-		
1957	N.Y.	13.64	25	8	-	-	10	-		
1958	N.Y.	16.33	24	7	-	-	4	-		
1959	N.Y.	11.60	37	10	-	-	10	-		
1960	Minn	9.40	DNQ							
1961	LA.L	9.13	51	11	-	-	9	-		
1962	LA.L	8.66	DNQ							

CHRIS FORD — VILLANOVA

YR	TM	PR	OR	PS	SC	SH	RB	AS	BL	ST
1973	Detr	9.15	100	39	-	-	-	-	-	-
1974	Detr	9.71	95	17	-	-	-	-	-	4
1975	Detr	8.71	103	22	-	-	-	-	-	12
1976	Detr	10.15	90	16	-	-	-	-	-	3
1977	Detr	13.12	78	15	-	-	-	-	-	11
1978	Detr	12.40	99	18	-	-	-	31	-	10
1979	Bost	14.41	80	12	-	-	-	-	-	-
1980	Bost	11.48	118	20	-	-	-	-	-	26
1981	Bost	9.34	150	32	-	-	-	-	-	-
1982	Bost	5.34	160	30	-	-	-	-	-	-

WALT FRAZIER — S. ILLINOIS

YR	TM	PR	OR	PS	SC	SH	RB	AS	BL	ST
1968	N.Y.	12.04	66	24	-	-	-	-	-	7
1969	N.Y.	23.75	14	4	-	5	-	-	-	4
1970	N.Y.	26.06	11	4	-	9	-	-	-	3
1971	N.Y.	25.34	12	2	14	10	-	-	-	15
1972	N.Y.	26.00	14	3	14	5	-	-	-	20
1973	N.Y.	24.45	16	3	17	11	-	-	-	-
1974	N.Y.	23.46	10	1	19	-	-	14	-	22
1975	N.Y.	23.56	9	1	15	23	-	19	-	9
1976	N.Y.	22.15	10	1	21	23	-	20	-	-
1977	N.Y.	17.68	36	2	-	-	-	23	-	-
1978	Clev	15.98	58	9	-	-	-	-	-	-
1979	Clev	8.33	DNQ							
1980	Clev	5.33	DNQ							

PHIL FORD — N. CAROLINA

YR	TM	PR	OR	PS	SC	SH	RB	AS	BL	ST
1979	K.C.	17.32	50	6	-	-	-	3	-	9
1980	K.C.	16.12	63	8	-	-	-	5	-	27
1981	K.C.	18.21	36	3	-	-	-	2	-	-
1982	K.C.	10.35	135	25	-	-	-	10	-	-
1983	Milw	7.53	152	33	-	-	-	25	-	-
1984	Hous	9.85	143	27	-	-	-	18	-	-
1985	Hous	3.00	DNQ							

WORLD FREE — GUILFORD COLLEGE

YR	TM	PR	OR	PS	SC	SH	RB	AS	BL	ST
1976	Phil	5.69	DNQ							
1977	Phil	12.26	92	20	-	-	-	-	-	-
1978	Phil	13.16	90	16	-	-	-	30	-	-
1979	S.D.	21.35	23	2	2	-	-	-	-	-
1980	S.D.	21.38	20	3	2	-	-	-	-	-
1981	G.St	18.83	32	5	9	-	-	-	-	-
1982	G.St	17.40	46	5	9	-	-	-	-	-
1983	Clev	16.58	56	9	8	-	-	-	-	-
1984	Clev	15.60	71	10	14	-	-	-	-	-
1985	Clev	17.72	54	6	15	-	-	-	-	-
1986	Clev	17.81	46	8	10	-	-	-	-	-
1987	Phil	3.05	DNQ							
1988	Hous	3.88	DNQ							

LARRY FOUST — LASALLE

YR	TM	PR	OR	PS	SC	SH	RB	AS	BL	ST
1951	Ft.W	13.74	17	6	-	-	7	-		
1952	Ft.W	21.23	3	2	7	-	6	-		
1953	Ft.W	17.84	9	4	11	-	4	-		
1954	Ft.W	21.36	6	5	8	9	3	-		
1955	Ft.W	20.96	6	2	-	1	10	-		
1956	Ft.W	18.94	9	3	11	3	11	-		
1957	Ft.W	14.82	17	5	-	-	9	-		
1958	Minn	20.35	12	5	-	-	8	-		
1959	Minn	14.50	24	6	-	-	-			
1960	St.L	14.90	26	7	-	-	-	-		
1961	St.L	9.99	DNQ							
1962	St.L	12.23	DNQ							

JOE FULKS — MURRAY ST.

YR	TM	PR	OR	PS	SC	SH	RB	AS	BL	ST
1947	Phil	23.20		1						
1948	Phil	22.10		2						
1949	Phil	26.00		2						
1950	Phil	8.22	59	24	11	-	-			
1951	Phil	13.38	21	11	4	-	14	-		
1952	Phil	10.13	40	18	12	-	-	-		
1953	Phil	9.51	45	20	-	-	-	-		
1954	Phil	1.48	DNQ							

JIM FOX — S. CAROLINA

YR	TM	PR	OR	PS	SC	SH	RB	AS	BL	ST
1968	Detr	5.82	DNQ							
1969	Phoe	18.11	36	11	-	-	16	-		
1970	Phoe	15.64	55	12	-	4	-	-		
1971	Chic	14.39	65	17	-	-	11	-		
1972	Cinc	15.19	62	17	-	-	-	-		
1973	Seat	20.28	29	11	-	-	4	15		
1974	Seat	16.94	35	12	-	17	19	-	-	
1975	Seat	11.96	75	19	-	-	-	-		
1976	Milw	5.77	DNQ							
1977	NY.N	7.89	DNQ							

MIKE GALE — ELIZABETH CITY

YR	TM	PR	OR	PS	SC	SH	RB	AS	BL	ST
1972	ABA	8.68	71	31	-	-	-	-		
1973	ABA	9.11	69	30	-	-	-	-		
1974	ABA	12.33	44	15	-	8	-	-	-	4
1975	ABA	9.07	66	26	-	-	-	-	-	13
1976	ABA	8.79	49	19	-	-	8	-	-	-
1977	S.A.	14.39	61	8	-	-	11	-	-	10
1978	S.A.	13.21	89	12	-	-	12	-	-	3
1979	S.A.	11.13	116	23	-	-	16	-	-	6
1980	S.A.	10.40	127	19	-	-	9	-	-	5
1981	Port	6.96	DNQ							
1982	G.St	9.23	152	32	-	-	-	-	-	9

HARRY GALLATIN — N.E MISSOURI.

YR	TM	PR	OR	PS	SC	SH	RB	AS	BL	ST
1949	N.Y.	8.30					-			
1950	N.Y.	17.54	5	2	-		5			-
1951	N.Y.	19.97	6	2	-		9	3		-
1952	N.Y.	17.53	11	5	-		3	4		-
1953	N.Y.	20.36	5	2	-		6	1		-
1954	N.Y.	23.61	2	1	13		4	2		-
1955	N.Y.	22.29	4	3	-		11	3		-
1956	N.Y.	18.07	13	7	-		-	-		-
1957	N.Y.	18.06	10	6	-		7	7		-
1958	Detr	17.26	19	10	-		-	9		-

JACK GEORGE — LASALLE

YR	TM	PR	OR	PS	SC	SH	RB	AS	BL	ST
1954	Phil	11.08	29	9	-	-	-	10		
1955	Phil	12.81	30	9	-	-	-	8		
1956	Phil	15.10	20	4	-	-	-	6		
1957	Phil	11.06	33	8	-	-	-	5		
1958	Phil	9.79	43	16	-	-	-	9		
1959	N.Y.	9.04	47	16	-	-	-	-		
1960	N.Y.	9.35	46	20	-	-	-	9		
1961	N.Y.	5.06	DNQ							

GEORGE GERVIN — E. MICHIGAN

YR	TM	PR	OR	PS	SC	SH	RB	AS	BL	ST
1973	ABA	12.80	DNQ							
1974	ABA	22.38	8	5	11	-	-	9		-
1975	ABA	22.86	10	6	7	-	-	10		-
1976	ABA	21.60	11	6	9	5	-	9		-
1977	S.A.	21.68	16	1	9	3	-	27		-
1978	S.A.	24.93	7	1	1	5	-	-		-
1979	S.A.	25.31	6	1	1	7	-	-		-
1980	S.A.	27.19	5	1	1	7	-	-		-
1981	S.A.	22.10	14	1	3	-	-	-		-
1982	S.A.	24.82	11	1	1	-	-	-		-
1983	S.A.	21.63	24	2	4	-	-	-		-
1984	S.A.	20.08	30	3	6	-	-	-		-
1985	S.A.	16.81	63	10	24	-	-	-		-
1986	Chic	11.89	114	22	-	-	-	-		-

JOHN GIANELLI — PACIFIC

YR	TM	PR	OR	PS	SC	SH	RB	AS	BL	ST
1973	N.Y.	4.81	DNQ							
1974	N.Y.	9.04	98	21	-	-	-	-	22	-
1975	N.Y.	14.91	50	13	-	-	-	-	15	-
1976	N.Y.	11.51	78	19	-	-	-	-	-	-
1977	Buff	10.18	115	27	-	-	-	-	18	-
1978	Milw	12.52	97	28	-	-	-	-	31	-
1979	Milw	10.44	124	31	-	-	-	-	-	-
1980	Utah	4.29	DNQ							

HERM GILLIAM — PURDUE

YR	TM	PR	OR	PS	SC	SH	RB	AS	BL	ST
1970	Cinc	9.37	DNQ							
1971	Buff	11.98	89	36	-	-	-	19		
1972	Atla	13.29	73	25	-	-	-	13		
1973	Atla	18.20	43	13	-	-	-	10		
1974	Atla	15.71	47	11	-	-	-	10		6
1975	Atla	10.60	91	15	-	-	-	-		14
1976	Seat	8.22	110	22	-	-	-	-		21
1977	Port	7.54	145	31	-	-	-	-		-

ARTIS GILMORE — JACKSONVILLE

YR	TM	PR	OR	PS	SC	SH	RB	AS	BL	ST
1972	ABA	35.33	1	1	13	1	2	-		
1973	ABA	32.96	2	1	-	10	1	-		
1974	ABA	31.35	1	1	-	-	1	-	2	-
1975	ABA	33.37	2	1	7	4	3	-	2	-
1976	ABA	32.26	2	1	4	6	2	-	2	-
1977	Chic	24.15	8	6	30	-	5	-	8	-
1978	Chic	28.24	5	5	16	10	10	-	13	-
1979	Chic	29.79	3	3	9	6	15	-	18	-
1980	Chic	22.25	DNQ							
1981	Chic	25.02	6	3	32	1	14	-	8	-
1982	Chic	25.76	9	4	32	1	13	-	7	-
1983	S.A.	25.68	6	2	-	1	2	-	7	-
1984	S.A.	22.16	20	7	-	2	6	-	7	-
1985	S.A.	24.85	11	5	-	4	13	-	10	-
1986	S.A.	20.31	30	9	-	8	-	-	24	-
1987	S.A.	15.50	75	19	-	9	-	-	28	-
1988	Bost	4.68	DNQ							

TOM GOLA — LASALLE

YR	TM	PR	OR	PS	SC	SH	RB	AS	BL	ST
1956	Phil	19.34	8	2	-	-	-	5		
1957		DID NOT PLAY								
1958	Phil	21.81	9	1	-	-	-	5		
1959	Phil	20.95	11	2	-	-	-	-		
1960	Phil	22.44	11	1	-	-	-	11		
1961	Phil	19.50	16	4	-	-	-	-		
1962	Phil	20.08	19	5	-	-	-	-		
1963	N.Y.	16.90	23	12	-	-	-	-		
1964	N.Y.	13.43	36	12	-	-	-	11		
1965	N.Y.	10.16	51	19	-	-	-	8		
1966	N.Y.	8.57	DNQ							

GAIL GOODRICH — UCLA

YR	TM	PR	OR	PS	SC	SH	RB	AS	BL	ST
1966	LA.L	6.09	DNQ							
1967	LA.L	11.82	52	21	-	-	-	-		
1968	LA.L	12.52	65	23	-	8	-	-		
1969	Phoe	20.86	25	8	8	-	-	11		
1970	Phoe	21.85	20	7	-	-	-	8		
1971	LA.L	16.77	53	20	-	22	-	-		
1972	LA.L	22.37	24	7	5	13	-	-		
1973	LA.L	19.53	36	10	8	-	-	-		
1974	LA.L	18.60	28	4	6	-	-	-		-
1975	LA.L	18.11	21	1	8	-	-	11		-
1976	LA.L	16.39	45	8	20	-	-	10		-
1977	N.O.	9.79	DNQ							
1978	N.O.	14.44	72	10	-	-	-	27		-
1979	N.O.	12.14	102	19	-	-	-	18		-

JOE GRABOSKI

YR	TM	PR	OR	PS	SC	SH	RB	AS	BL	ST
1949	Chic	6.84	DNQ							
1950	Chic	11.86	DNQ							
1951		DID NOT PLAY								
1952	Indi	15.91	16	6	-	-	-	-		
1953	Indi	15.17	14	7	-	-	-	-		
1954	Phil	14.32	12	3	11	-	-	-		
1955	Phil	13.63	25	11	-	-	-	-		
1956	Phil	15.11	19	11	-	-	-	-		
1957	Phil	13.72	24	13	-	-	-	-		
1958	Phil	11.83	36	10	-	-	-	-		
1959	Phil	15.90	19	4	-	-	-	-		
1960	Phil	8.56	DNQ							
1961	Phil	5.99	DNQ							
1962	Syra	5.39	DNQ							

JOHNNY GREEN — MICHIGAN ST.

YR	TM	PR	OR	PS	SC	SH	RB	AS	BL	ST
1960	N.Y.	10.45	DNQ							
1961	N.Y.	14.96	26	11	-	-	5	-		
1962	N.Y.	21.28	16	6	-	-	9	-		
1963	N.Y.	21.53	12	5	-	-	6	-		
1964	N.Y.	17.17	20	11	-	-	6	-		
1965	N.Y.	12.87	38	18	-	-	-	-		
1966	Balt	14.86	33	16	-	-	5	-		
1967	Balt	9.97	DNQ							
1968	Phil	11.19	DNQ							
1969	Phil	7.05	DNQ							
1970	Cinc	20.71	26	10	-	17	7	-		
1971	Cinc	19.87	32	13	-	4	-	-		
1972	Cinc	13.70	68	28	-	11	-	-		
1973	KC-O	10.91	DNQ							

MIKE GREEN — LOUISIANA. TECH

YR	TM	PR	OR	PS	SC	SH	RB	AS	BL	ST
1974	ABA	13.46	37	15	-	-	6	-	3	-
1975	ABA	20.73	17	5	-	9	13	-	3	-
1976	ABA	19.15	16	6	-	-	9	-	4	-
1977	Seat	12.29	90	24	-	-	-	-	10	-
1978	S.A.	10.17	129	31	-	-	-	-	9	-
1979	S.A.	10.87	119	29	-	-	-	-	6	-
1980	K.C.	9.38	DNQ							

HAL GREER — MARSHALL

YR	TM	PR	OR	PS	SC	SH	RB	AS	BL	ST
1959	Syra	9.41	45	15	-	5	-	-	-	
1960	Syra	13.53	32	9	-	3	-	-		
1961	Syra	18.49	20	6	-	8	-	-		
1962	Syra	22.32	15	4	11	11	-	-		
1963	Syra	19.11	15	4	12	10	-	-		
1964	Phil	21.71	14	3	7	11	-	-		
1965	Phil	18.53	18	4	9	-	-	10		
1966	Phil	21.23	11	3	8	-	-	-		
1967	Phil	19.58	20	4	7	-	-	-		
1968	Phil	22.15	18	5	7	13	-	-		
1969	Phil	21.60	20	5	10	17	-	-		
1970	Phil	20.21	27	12	15	-	-	-		
1971	Phil	17.06	50	18	-	-	-	-		
1972	Phil	12.54	76	26	-	-	-	-		
1973	Phil	7.45	DNQ							

BOB GROSS — LONG BEACH ST.

YR	TM	PR	OR	PS	SC	SH	RB	AS	BL	ST
1976	Port	9.79	95	19	-	16	-	-	22	10
1977	Port	14.27	62	15	-	5	-	-	-	-
1978	Port	16.17	56	14	-	8	-	-	-	-
1979	Port	12.96	93	24	-	-	-	-	-	-
1980	Port	11.06	121	29	-	-	-	-	-	-
1981	Port	11.90	114	24	-	15	-	-	-	-
1982	Port	11.25	119	30	-	20	-	-	-	20
1983	S.D.	4.74	DNQ							

RICHIE GUERIN — IONA

YR	TM	PR	OR	PS	SC	SH	RB	AS	BL	ST
1957	N.Y.	9.14	41	11	-	-	-	-	-	
1958	N.Y.	16.83	21	5	-	-	-	-	8	
1959	N.Y.	20.70	12	3	-	8	-	-	5	
1960	N.Y.	22.35	12	2	9	-	-	-	4	
1961	N.Y.	22.63	12	2	-	-	-	-	7	
1962	N.Y.	27.54	8	3	7	9	-	-	7	
1963	N.Y.	19.05	16	5	9	-	-	-	12	
1964	St.L	13.85	32	8	-	-	-	-	6	
1965	St.L	14.11	30	9	-	-	-	-	4	
1966	St.L	15.30	29	10	-	-	-	-	6	
1967	St.L	12.59	49	20	-	-	-	-	10	
1968	DID NOT PLAY									
1969	Atla	8.44	DNQ							
1970	Atla	1.63	DNQ							

MATT GUOKAS — ST.JOE

YR	TM	PR	OR	PS	SC	SH	RB	AS	BL	ST
1967	Phil	3.46	DNQ							
1968	Phil	7.77	82	36	-	9	-	-		
1969	Phil	3.96	DNQ							
1970	Phil	8.15	94	41	-	-	-	-		
1971	Chic	9.67	103	40	-	15	-	16		
1972	Cinc	11.41	85	32	-	19	-	12		
1973	KC-O	14.01	71	27	-	1	-	-		
1974	Buff	6.25	114	23	-	-	-	-		
1975	Chic	6.59	115	27	-	14	-	-		
1976	K.C.	1.41	DNQ							

CLIFF HAGAN — KENTUCKY

YR	TM	PR	OR	PS	SC	SH	RB	AS	BL	ST
1957	St.L	6.25								
1958	St.L	21.79	10	5	7	6	-	-		
1959	St.L	25.60	4	3	5	3	-	-		
1960	St.L	27.04	5	3	5	5	-	-		
1961	St.L	24.52	9	6	11	7	-	11		
1962	St.L	24.69	10	3	9	4	-	-		
1963	St.L	14.37	30	16	-	-	-	-		
1964	St.L	15.75	22	12	-	-	-	-		
1965	St.L	11.04	47	21	-	-	-	-		
1966	St.L	11.61	48	24	-	-	-	-		
1967	DID NOT PLAY									
1968	ABA	20.84	9	5	-	4	-	2		
1969	ABA	13.23	DNQ							
1970	ABA	6.67	DNQ							

HAROLD HAIRSTON — N.Y.U.

YR	TM	PR	OR	PS	SC	SH	RB	AS	BL	ST
1965	Cinc	6.84	DNQ							
1966	Cinc	15.13	30	14	-	8	-	-		
1967	Cinc	15.65	30	14	-	-	-	-		
1968	Detr	18.59	33	14	-	-	-	-		
1969	Detr	22.00	18	5	-	19	-	-		
1970	LA.L	23.01	17	7	-	15	-	-		
1971	LA.L	21.21	29	11	-	-	-	-		
1972	LA.L	22.09	26	9	-	7	-	-		
1973	LA.L	24.50	DNQ							
1974	LA.L	22.22	13	3	-	13	3	-	-	
1975	LA.L	19.15	17	6	-	7	1	-	-	

ALEX HANNUM　　　　USC

YR	TM	PR	OR	PS	SC	SH	RB	AS	BL	ST
1949	Oshk	5.70		-						
1950	Syra	8.56	55	22	-	-	-			
1951	Syra	7.76	49	21	-	-	-			
1952	Roch	8.73	50	23	-	-	-			
1953	Roch	6.32	DNQ							
1954	Roch	7.18	56	24	-	-	-			
1955	Milw	7.26	55	25	-	-	-			
1956	St.L	7.30	53	21	-	-	-			
1957	St.L	3.59	DNQ							

BOB HARRISON　　　　MICHIGAN

YR	TM	PR	OR	PS	SC	SH	RB	AS	BL	ST
1950	Minn	5.82	DNQ							
1951	Minn	6.75	58	18	-	-	-			
1952	Minn	5.89	66	25	-	-	-	12		
1953	Minn	6.13	62	25	-	-	-			
1954	Milw	4.41	66	29	-	-	-			
1955	Milw	7.88	49	15	-	-	-			
1956	St.L	7.99	51	18	-	-	-			
1957	Syra	7.17	51	20	-	-	-			
1958	Syra	6.01	53	22	-	-	-			

CLEM HASKINS　　　　W. KENTUCKY

YR	TM	PR	OR	PS	SC	SH	RB	AS	BL	ST
1968	Chic	8.22	79	33	-	-	-			
1969	Chic	15.24	51	15	-	-	-			
1970	Chic	21.46	22	8	-	-	-			
1971	Phoe	16.60	55	21	-	-	-	20		
1972	Phoe	15.38	60	21	-	17	-			
1973	Phoe	9.95	91	34	-	-	-			
1974	Phoe	10.67	85	15	-	-	-	21	-	-
1975	Wash	3.29	DNQ							
1976	Wash	5.82	DNQ							

JOHN HAVLICEK　　　　OHIO ST.

YR	TM	PR	OR	PS	SC	SH	RB	AS	BL	ST
1963	Bost	14.83	28	15	-	-	-			
1964	Bost	15.74	23	5	10	-	-			
1965	Bost	13.52	33	11	-	-	-			
1966	Bost	15.41	27	13	-	-	-			
1967	Bost	19.89	18	10	8	-	-			
1968	Bost	20.24	25	8	15	-	-			
1969	Bost	20.20	29	9	17	-	-	6		
1970	Bost	27.23	10	3	9	-	-	14		
1971	Bost	30.40	3	1	2	-	-	10		
1972	Bost	29.11	4	1	3	-	-	11		
1973	Bost	24.99	12	4	11	-	-	18		
1974	Bost	21.17	16	4	11	-	-	20		
1975	Bost	18.85	18	4	23	-	-	23	-	-
1976	Bost	14.84	53	10	-	-	-			
1977	Bost	16.16	47	10	-	-	-			
1978	Bost	14.39	74	12	-	-	-			

CONNIE HAWKINS　　　　IOWA

YR	TM	PR	OR	PS	SC	SH	RB	AS	BL	ST
1968	ABA	33.80	1	1	3	2	-	9		
1969	ABA	32.64	DNQ							
1970	Phoe	28.77	6	2	7	-	-			
1971	Phoe	23.58	18	5	19	-	-			
1972	Phoe	22.96	21	7	-	-	-			
1973	Phoe	21.17	26	10	-	20	-	-		
1974	L.A.L	18.15	29	7	-	15	-	18	-	-
1975	L.A.L	10.23	DNQ							
1976	Atla	12.11	72	16	-	-	-			

TOM HAWKINS　　　　NOTRE DAME

YR	TM	PR	OR	PS	SC	SH	RB	AS	BL	ST
1960	Minn	8.86	49	19	-	-	-			
1961	L.A.L	10.55	45	18	-	-	-			
1962	L.A.L	10.58	50	22	-	-	-			
1963	Cinc	12.13	41	21	-	-	-			
1964	Cinc	10.07	49	23	-	-	-			
1965	Cinc	8.92	59	25	-	-	-			
1966	Cinc	11.54	50	25	-	-	-			
1967	L.A.L	10.01	63	24	-	-	-			
1968	L.A.L	12.62	63	30	-	-	-			
1969	L.A.L	7.42	93	41	-	-	-			

ELVIN HAYES　　　　HOUSTON

YR	TM	PR	OR	PS	SC	SH	RB	AS	BL	ST
1969	S.D.	29.45	5	3	1	-	12	-		
1970	S.D.	30.54	2	2	3	-	5	-		
1971	S.D.	29.38	6	3	3	-	10	-		
1972	Hous	27.17	12	7	10	-	16	-		
1973	Balt	24.49	15	6	16	-	13	-		
1974	Capt	28.72	4	4	16	-	1	-	8	-
1975	Wash	25.70	6	1	7	-	-	7	-	
1976	Wash	21.69	13	2	19	-	24	-	5	-
1977	Wash	26.87	5	1	8	-	21	-	11	-
1978	Wash	23.30	13	2	24	-	16	-	20	-
1979	Wash	24.56	8	1	18	-	14	-	13	-
1980	Wash	22.96	14	2	8	-	21	-	8	-
1981	Wash	18.47	34	7	33	-	25	-	13	-
1982	Hous	17.61	45	9	-	-	-			
1983	Hous	14.74	75	13	-	-	30	-	-	-
1984	Hous	5.16	DNQ							

SPENCER HAYWOOD　　　　DETROIT

YR	TM	PR	OR	PS	SC	SH	RB	AS	BL	ST
1970	ABA	37.81	1	1	2	10	2	-		
1971	Seat	22.64	DNQ							
1972	Seat	27.97	8	3	4	-	-	-		
1973	Seat	30.81	4	1	3	21	-	-		
1974	Seat	26.92	5	1	10	-	16	-	15	-
1975	Seat	21.47	11	3	9	-	-	14	-	
1976	N.Y.	20.29	19	3	18	-	21	-	24	-
1977	NY.K	17.27	DNQ							
1978	N.Y.	14.60	69	14	-	-	-	25	-	
1979	N.O.	19.59	33	8	22	-	-	-		
1980	L.A.L	10.30	130	27	-	-	26	-		
1981	DID NOT PLAY									
1982	Wash	12.61	100	20	-	-	-	-		
1983	Wash	7.55	DNQ							

WALT HAZZARD — UCLA

YR	TM	PR	OR	PS	SC	SH	RB	AS	BL	ST
1965	LA.L	4.80	DNQ							
1966	LA.L	13.63	40	14	-	-	-	4		
1967	LA.L	10.53	59	26	-	-	-	3		
1968	Seat	21.08	24	7	8	-	-	8		
1969	Atla	12.85	67	23	-	-	-	6		
1970	Atla	18.50	39	16	-	-	-	4		
1971	Atla	17.73	45	16	-	-	-	6		
1972	Buff	15.86	58	20	-	-	-	9		
1973	G.St	5.80	DNQ							
1974	Seat	4.78	DNQ							

GARFIELD HEARD — OKLAHOMA

YR	TM	PR	OR	PS	SC	SH	RB	AS	BL	ST
1971	Seat	7.22	DNQ							
1972	Seat	10.74	91	38	-	-	-			
1973	Chic	9.79	93	39	-	-	-			
1974	Buff	21.69	15	4	-	-	18	-	5	-
1975	Buff	16.60	36	8	-	-	17	-	6	-
1976	Phoe	16.86	41	10	-	-	17	-	18	-
1977	Phoe	14.41	DNQ							
1978	Phoe	13.71	81	17	-	-	27	-	22	11
1979	Phoe	9.83	134	20	-	-	-	-	19	-
1980	Phoe	8.13	DNQ							
1981	S.D.	8.63	153	35	-	-	-	-	27	10

TOM HEINSOHN — HOLY CROSS

YR	TM	PR	OR	PS	SC	SH	RB	AS	BL	ST
1957	Bost	17.17	12	7	-	-	-	-		
1958	Bost	17.42	17	9	-	-	-	-		
1959	Bost	18.76	13	8	-	-	-	-		
1960	Bost	20.99	13	8	10	-	-	-		
1961	Bost	19.11	17	9	-	-	-	-		
1962	Bost	20.94	18	8	12	-	-	-		
1963	Bost	16.93	22	11	-	-	-	-		
1964	Bost	14.54	28	15	-	-	-	-		
1965	Bost	12.42	40	20	-	-	-	-		

TOM HENDERSON — HAWAII

YR	TM	PR	OR	PS	SC	SH	RB	AS	BL	ST
1975	Atla	9.67	97	19	-	-	-	20	-	-
1976	Atla	11.64	75	15	-	-	-	-	-	-
1977	Wash	13.57	70	10	-	-	-	5	-	-
1978	Wash	11.51	112	18	-	-	-	15	-	-
1979	Wash	12.91	94	15	-	-	-	8	-	-
1980	Hous	7.82	149	27	-	-	-	19	-	-
1981	Hous	7.80	160	29	-	-	-	12	-	-
1982	Hous	8.09	156	33	-	-	-	23	-	-
1983	Hous	5.63	DNQ							

WAYNE HIGHTOWER — KANSAS

YR	TM	PR	OR	PS	SC	SH	RB	AS	BL	ST
1963	S.F.	7.44	65	31	-	-	-			
1964	S.F.	13.25	38	18	-	-	-			
1965	Balt	8.37	62	27	-	-	-			
1966	Balt	9.76	DNQ							
1967	Detr	8.10	DNQ							
1968	ABA	15.45	32	15	-	-	-			
1969	ABA	18.07	22	11	-	-	-			
1970	ABA	20.41	DNQ							
1971	ABA	16.96	40	10	-	-	-			
1972	ABA	5.69	DNQ							

DARNELL HILLMAN — SAN JOSE ST.

YR	TM	PR	OR	PS	SC	SH	RB	AS	BL	ST
1972	ABA	10.53	DNQ							
1973	ABA	13.76	44	18	-	-	12	-	-	-
1974	ABA	13.35	41	17	-	-	14	-	4	-
1975	ABA	18.70	24	8	-	13	14	-	6	-
1976	ABA	15.74	27	8	-	-	7	-	8	-
1977	Indi	14.84	54	8	-	-	26	-	22	-
1978	Denv	12.90	92	19	-	-	-	-	24	-
1979	K.C.	9.42	139	22	-	-	-	-	26	-
1980	G.St	5.71	DNQ							

LIONELL HOLLINS — ARIZONA ST.

YR	TM	PR	OR	PS	SC	SH	RB	AS	BL	ST
1976	Port	10.35	89	17	-	-	-	9	-	6
1977	Port	12.92	82	17	-	-	-	-	-	8
1978	Port	14.06	76	13	-	-	-	-	-	17
1979	Port	13.00	92	14	-	-	-	21	-	15
1980	Phil	8.17	DNQ							
1981	Phil	10.05	136	28	-	-	-	27	-	-
1982	Phil	11.12	120	23	-	-	-	-	-	-
1983	S.D.	13.07	94	15	-	-	-	22	-	15
1984	Detr	2.88	DNQ							
1985	Hous	9.98	139	27	-	-	-	17	-	-

BAILEY HOWELL — MISSISSIPPI ST.

YR	TM	PR	OR	PS	SC	SH	RB	AS	BL	ST
1960	Detr	19.55	17	11	-	9	-	-		
1961	Detr	29.08	6	3	7	4	8	-		
1962	Detr	25.01	9	2	-	5	-	-		
1963	Detr	27.92	7	3	8	2	-	-		
1964	Detr	24.25	9	4	8	6	-	-		
1965	Balt	24.51	10	4	11	2	-	-		
1966	Balt	21.00	12	4	-	4	-	-		
1967	Bost	20.65	17	9	13	3	-	-		
1968	Bost	21.22	23	11	-	16	-	-		
1969	Bost	20.53	28	11	-	12	-	-		
1970	Bost	13.39	68	29	-	-	-	-		
1971	Phil	12.04	88	32	-	-	-	-		

LOU HUDSON — MINNESOTA

YR	TM	PR	OR	PS	SC	SH	RB	AS	BL	ST
1967	St.L	14.96	34	16	-	-	-	-	-	
1968	St.L	11.20	DNQ							
1969	Atla	20.78	26	9	15	8	-	-	-	
1970	Atla	23.34	15	5	5	2	-	-	-	
1971	Atla	22.07	25	8	6	16	-	-	-	
1972	Atla	22.69	23	6	11	9	-	-	-	
1973	Atla	23.68	17	7	4	-	-	-	-	
1974	Atla	21.98	14	3	5	10	-	-	-	-
1975	Atla	16.05	DNQ							
1976	Atla	14.07	60	11	-	-	-	-	-	23
1977	Atla	11.41	101	23	-	-	-	-	-	-
1978	LA.L	11.26	116	25	-	-	-	-	-	-
1979	LA.L	9.03	144	27	-	17	-	-	-	-

MEL HUTCHINS BYU

YR	TM	PR	OR	PS	SC	SH	RB	AS	BL	ST
1952	Milw	18.11	10	4	-	-	7	-		
1953	Milw	17.27	10	5	-	-	11	-		
1954	Ft.W	15.74	9	2	-	-	-	-		
1955	Ft.W	15.82	16	8	-	-	-	-		
1956	Ft.W	14.39	21	12	-	-	-	-		
1957	Ft.W	14.35	21	12	-	-	-	-		
1958	N.Y.	8.17			DNQ						

DARRALL IMHOFF CALIFORNIA

YR	TM	PR	OR	PS	SC	SH	RB	AS	BL	ST
1961	N.Y.	6.53			DNQ						
1962	N.Y.	8.54	58	11	-	-	-			
1963	Detr	3.82			DNQ						
1964	Detr	7.31			DNQ						
1965	LA.L	9.64	54	11	-	-	-			
1966	LA.L	9.82			DNQ						
1967	LA.L	20.73	16	5	-	-	7	-		
1968	LA.L	17.48	38	11	-	-	7	-		
1969	Phil	16.06	45	12	-	-	17	-		
1970	Phil	19.72	30	6	-	11	-	-		
1971	Cinc	12.41			DNQ						
1972	Port	4.39			DNQ						

DAN ISSEL KENTUCKY

YR	TM	PR	OR	PS	SC	SH	RB	AS	BL	ST
1971	ABA	30.54	3	3	2	-	14	-		
1972	ABA	29.80	4	2	2	-	-	-		
1973	ABA	28.92	4	3	4	-	-	-		
1974	ABA	25.07	4	3	4	-	-	-	-	
1975	ABA	19.16	23	11	-	-	-	-	-	
1976	ABA	26.64	4	3	7	-	5	-	-	
1977	Denv	22.38	13	7	10	14	-	-	-	
1978	Denv	24.57	9	7	19	19	-	-	-	
1979	Denv	21.09	27	10	-	-	-	-	-	
1980	Denv	24.34	8	3	7	-	-	-	-	
1981	Denv	22.73	12	6	13	-	-	-	-	
1982	Denv	23.43	13	7	11	17	-	-	-	
1983	Denv	22.29	21	8	18	29	-	-	-	
1984	Denv	20.08	30	10	29	-	-	-	-	
1985	Denv	12.53	108	19	-	-	-	-	-	

EDDIE JOHNSON JR. AUBURN

YR	TM	PR	OR	PS	SC	SH	RB	AS	BL	ST
1978	Atla	9.63	135	28	-	-	-	-	-	
1979	Atla	14.92	76	11	-	26	-	-	25	
1980	Atla	16.58	61	11	-	-	-	-	-	
1981	Atla	17.56	41	7	23	-	-	-	-	
1982	Atla	15.37	65	9	-	-	31	-	-	
1983	Atla	13.30	92	18	-	-	29	-	-	
1984	Atla	12.00	116	21	-	-	21	-	-	
1985	Atla	16.40	69	12	-	-	11	-	-	
1986	Clev	9.20	143	31	-	-	15	-	-	
1987	Seat	9.83			DNQ						

GEORGE T. JOHNSON DILLARD

YR	TM	PR	OR	PS	SC	SH	RB	AS	BL	ST
1973	G.St	2.96			DNQ						
1974	G.St	12.39	75	17	-	-	2	-	2	
1975	G.St	10.67			DNQ						
1976	G.St	11.96	74	18	-	-	6	-	2	-
1977	Buff	12.77	85	21	-	-	6	-	1	-
1978	N.J.	15.26	64	21	-	-	18	-	2	-
1979	N.J.	13.51	88	26	-	-	21	-	2	-
1980	N.J.	14.07	85	19	-	-	19	-	1	-
1981	S.A.	13.48	96	24	-	-	9	-	1	-
1982	S.A.	10.60	130	28	-	-	17	-	1	-
1983	Atla	5.70			DNQ						

GUS JOHNSON IDAHO

YR	TM	PR	OR	PS	SC	SH	RB	AS	BL	ST
1964	Balt	22.03	12	6	-	-	7	-		
1965	Balt	22.97	12	5	12	-	11	-		
1966	Balt	22.00			DNQ						
1967	Balt	23.16	12	6	10	-	-	-		
1968	Balt	24.07	10	4	-	-	15	-		
1969	Balt	21.57			DNQ						
1970	Balt	24.67	14	6	-	-	6	-		
1971	Balt	28.03	7	3	-	-	2	-		
1972	Balt	8.72			DNQ						
1973	Phoe	9.86			DNQ						

JOHN JOHNSON IOWA

YR	TM	PR	OR	PS	SC	SH	RB	AS	BL	ST
1971	Clev	18.37	43	17	-	-	-	18		
1972	Clev	19.90	36	15	-	-	-	-		
1973	Clev	16.11	61	24	-	-	-	-		
1974	Port	17.93	30	7	-	-	-	-	-	
1975	Port	16.08	41	8	-	-	-	-	-	
1976	Hous	10.99	85	17	-	-	-	-	-	
1977	Hous	8.56	137	30	-	-	-	-	-	
1978	Seat	9.16	142	27	-	-	-	-	-	
1979	Seat	11.91	106	26	-	-	-	-	-	
1980	Seat	14.74	78	23	-	-	-	22	-	
1981	Seat	11.39	122	25	-	-	-	-	-	
1982	Seat	5.00			DNQ						

MARQUES JOHNSON UCLA

YR	TM	PR	OR	PS	SC	SH	RB	AS	BL	ST
1978	Milw	24.13	12	1	27	20	-	-	-	
1979	Milw	26.64	4	1	3	10	-	-	-	
1980	Milw	23.90	3	14	9	-	-	-	-	
1981	Milw	22.92	10	4	18	18	-	-	-	
1982	Milw	18.03	40	12	-	-	-	-	-	
1983	Milw	22.59	19	4	20	-	-	-	-	
1984	Milw	21.20	24	9	24	-	-	-	-	
1985	LA.C	15.46	80	21	-	-	-	-	-	
1986	LA.C	20.21	31	9	20	-	-	-	-	
1987	LA.C	12.80			DNQ						

MICKEY JOHNSON — AURORA

YR	TM	PR	OR	PS	SC	SH	RB	AS	BL	ST
1975	Chic	4.44	DNQ							
1976	Chic	18.31	28	5	-	16	-	-	-	
1977	Chic	19.95	26	9	-	-	-	-	-	
1978	Chic	20.26	29	10	-	-	-	-	-	
1979	Chic	17.59	47	14	-	-	-	-	-	
1980	Indi	21.83	18	6	29	-	-	-	23	17
1981	Milw	15.27	74	17	-	-	-	-	-	
1982	Milw	14.87	68	17	-	-	-	-	-	
1983	G.St	14.59	78	23	-	-	-	-	-	
1984	G.St	14.46	80	22	-	-	-	-	-	30
1985	G.St	13.89	97	22	-	-	-	-	-	
1986	N.J.	9.48	140	27	-	-	-	-	-	

OLLIE JOHNSON — TEMPLE

YR	TM	PR	OR	PS	SC	SH	RB	AS	BL	ST
1973	Port	13.17	72	28	-	14	-	-		
1974	Port	8.67	104	21	-	21	-	-		
1975	K.C.	7.93	107	21	-	-	-	-		
1976	K.C.	11.46	79	14	-	5	-	-		
1977	K.C.	7.11	DNQ							
1978	Atla	9.00	146	28	-	-	-	-		
1979	Chic	10.31	127	31	-	24	-	-		
1980	Chic	8.13	147	31	-	-	-	-		
1981	Phil	5.23	DNQ							
1982	Phil	2.69	DNQ							

NEIL JOHNSTON — OHIO ST.

YR	TM	PR	OR	PS	SC	SH	RB	AS	BL	ST
1952	Phil	8.66	DNQ							
1953	Phil	26.99	1	1	1	3	7	-		
1954	Phil	25.53	1	1	1	3	-	-		
1955	Phil	29.00	1	1	1	3	5	-		
1956	Phil	27.36	2	1	3	1	10	-		
1957	Phil	27.20	2	1	3	1	-	-		
1958	Phil	22.77	7	4	8	3	-	-		
1959	Phil	7.43	DNQ							

BOBBY JONES — N. CAROLINA

YR	TM	PR	OR	PS	SC	SH	RB	AS	BL	ST
1975	ABA	21.56	14	8	-	1	-	5	6	
1976	ABA	22.84	8	4	-	1	-	7	9	
1977	Denv	22.09	14	4	-	4	-	9	7	
1978	Denv	22.07	18	5	-	2	-	17	23	
1979	Phil	16.76	59	18	-	19	-	23	-	
1980	Phil	16.06	64	17	-	22	-	11	-	
1981	Phil	16.79	52	13	-	14	-	-	-	
1982	Phil	17.79	41	13	-	5	-	18	-	
1983	Phil	13.04	95	26	-	11	-	20	31	
1984	Phil	13.15	99	27	-	-	-	14	13	
1985	Phil	10.75	128	26	-	12	-	-	25	
1986	Phil	8.77	148	28	-	13	-	-	-	

DWIGHT JONES — HOUSTON

YR	TM	PR	OR	PS	SC	SH	RB	AS	BL	ST
1974	Atla	10.86	84	19	-	-	22	-	11	-
1975	Atla	14.79	52	14	-	-	12	-	23	-
1976	Atla	13.94	62	16	-	-	23	-	19	-
1977	Hous	7.14	DNQ							
1978	Hous	13.30	88	18	-	-	-	-	-	-
1979	Hous	6.80	DNQ							
1980	Chic	10.45	126	26	-	-	-	-	-	-
1981	Chic	9.47	148	33	-	-	-	-	-	-
1982	Chic	12.76	98	19	-	-	-	-	-	-
1983	LA.L	5.90	DNQ							

K.C. JONES — USF

YR	TM	PR	OR	PS	SC	SH	RB	AS	BL	ST
1959	Bost	4.37	DNQ							
1960	Bost	7.66	DNQ							
1961	Bost	8.10	53	21	-	-	-	10		
1962	Bost	10.76	48	14	-	-	-	6		
1963	Bost	9.19	57	20	-	-	-	4		
1964	Bost	11.43	43	15	-	-	-	3		
1965	Bost	11.97	42	14	-	-	-	3		
1966	Bost	12.79	43	15	-	-	-	3		
1967	Bost	9.79	65	29	-	-	-	7		

SAM JONES — N. CARO. COLL.

YR	TM	PR	OR	PS	SC	SH	RB	AS	BL	ST
1958	Bost	5.36	DNQ							
1959	Bost	11.93	35	13	-	-	-	-		
1960	Bost	12.15	34	11	-	8	-	-	-	
1961	Bost	14.91	27	10	-	9	-	-	-	
1962	Bost	17.73	22	7	-	6	-	-	-	
1963	Bost	18.22	19	6	11	11	-	-	-	
1964	Bost	15.89	21	4	11	-	-	-	-	
1965	Bost	20.16	15	3	5	-	-	-	-	
1966	Bost	20.13	14	5	5	5	-	-	-	
1967	Bost	18.44	24	7	6	12	-	-	-	
1968	Bost	18.27	34	10	12	-	-	-	-	
1969	Bost	13.41	62	20	-	-	-	-		

RICH KELLEY — STANFORD

YR	TM	PR	OR	PS	SC	SH	RB	AS	BL	ST
1976	N.O.	13.05	DNQ							
1977	N.O.	13.47	72	20	-	-	4	-	23	-
1978	N.O.	17.76	42	15	-	25	6	-	12	-
1979	N.O.	25.66	5	4	-	28	3	-	12	-
1980	Phoe	13.13	96	22	-	-	24	-	15	-
1981	Phoe	12.05	111	26	-	-	-	23	33	
1982	Phoe	12.28	102	23	-	-	31	30		
1983	Utah	10.33	121	25	-	-	15	-		
1984	Utah	10.68	134	28	-	-	16	-		
1985	Utah	7.55	DNQ							
1986	Sacr	4.43	DNQ							

LARRY KENON MEMPHIS ST.

YR	TM	PR	OR	PS	SC	SH	RB	AS	BL	ST
1974	ABA	19.73	13	6	-	-	8	-	-	-
1975	ABA	22.33	12	7	-	-	-	-	-	-
1976	ABA	22.27	9	5	-	-	8	-	-	-
1977	S.A.	25.17	6	1	12	-	30	-	-	27
1978	S.A.	22.20	16	3	21	-	-	-	-	-
1979	S.A.	24.68	7	2	16	-	-	-	-	21
1980	S.A.	21.88	16	4	21	-	25	-	-	-
1981	Chic	12.74	105	22	-	-	-	-	-	-
1982	Chic	6.23		DNQ						
1983	Clev	6.21		DNQ						

JOHN KERR ILLINOIS

YR	TM	PR	OR	PS	SC	SH	RB	AS	BL	ST
1955	Syra	11.39	36	9	-	-	9	-		
1956	Syra	13.68	25	7	-	-	-	-		
1957	Syra	16.75	13	4	-	-	8	-		
1958	Syra	19.31	14	6	-	-	7	-		
1959	Syra	23.78	7	2	-	9	6	-		
1960	Syra	19.11	20	5	-	-	9	-		
1961	Syra	18.84	18	5	-	-	10	-		
1962	Syra	24.55	11	5	-	-	5	-		
1963	Syra	23.34	10	4	-	13	3	-		
1964	Phil	22.86	11	4	-	-	-	-		
1965	Phil	11.21	45	10	-	-	-	-		
1966	Balt	15.82	25	6	-	-	12			

BILLY KNIGHT PITTSBURGH

YR	TM	PR	OR	PS	SC	SH	RB	AS	BL	ST
1975	ABA	20.15	20	9	-	6	-	-	-	-
1976	ABA	29.39	3	2	2	-	-	-	-	-
1977	Indi	23.72	10	3	2	29	-	-	-	-
1978	Buff	21.64	22	3	15	31	-	-	-	-
1979	Indi	13.10	90	23	-	12	-	-	-	-
1980	Indi	14.32	80	14	-	11	-	-	-	-
1981	Indi	16.79	51	10	-	13	-	-	-	-
1982	Indi	10.84	127	20	-	-	-	-	-	-
1983	Indi	15.38	67	12	-	18	-	-	-	-
1984	K.C.	11.63	121	23	-	-	-	-	-	-
1985	S.A.	4.88		DNQ						

DON KOJIS MARQUETTE

YR	TM	PR	OR	PS	SC	SH	RB	AS	BL	ST
1964	Balt	6.53		DNQ						
1965	Detr	7.02		DNQ						
1966	Detr	7.00		DNQ						
1967	Chic	10.37	61	23	-	-	-			
1968	S.D.	21.36	22	10	-	-	-			
1969	S.D.	21.79	19	6	13	-	-			
1970	S.D.	15.09	58	25	-	-	-			
1971	Seat	13.76	71	25	-	-	-			
1972	Seat	11.44	84	34	-	-	-			
1973	K.C.	7.87		DNQ						
1974	K.C.	11.78	77	15	-	-	-			
1975	K.C.	4.48		DNQ						

BUTCH KOMIVES BOWLING GRN

YR	TM	PR	OR	PS	SC	SH	RB	AS	BL	ST
1965	N.Y.	9.41	56	21	-	-	-	-		
1966	N.Y.	13.75	39	13	-	-	-	7		
1967	N.Y.	15.02	33	11	-	-	-	4		
1968	N.Y.	7.50	84	38	-	-	-	14		
1969	Detr	12.04	75	28	-	-	-	12		
1970	Detr	10.51	86	33	-	-	-	-		
1971	Detr	7.50	114	45	-	-	-	23		
1972	Detr	8.51	105	42	-	-	-	-		
1973	Buff	7.30	107	45	-	-	-	12		
1974	K.C.	4.11		DNQ						

SAM LACEY NEW MEXICO ST.

YR	TM	PR	OR	PS	SC	SH	RB	AS	BL	ST
1971	Cinc	17.27	48	13	-	-	19	-		
1972	Cinc	18.12	46	13	-	-	19	-		
1973	K.C.	20.44	28	10	-	-	20	-		
1974	K.C.	24.34	9	6	-	-	14	-	10	-
1975	K.C.	24.41	7	5	-	-	10	-	9	-
1976	K.C.	22.42	8	7	-	-	11	-	15	-
1977	K.C.	18.54	31	11	-	-	-	24	17	-
1978	K.C.	16.49	54	19	-	-	-	-	18	21
1979	K.C.	19.45	36	13	-	-	-	22	17	-
1980	K.C.	17.72	48	15	-	-	-	17	20	-
1981	K.C.	15.35	72	20	-	-	32	19	18	-
1982	N.J.	4.50		DNQ						
1983	Clev	6.62	157	27	-	-	-	-	-	-

BOB LANIER ST. BONAVENTURE

YR	TM	PR	OR	PS	SC	SH	RB	AS	BL	ST
1971	Detr	16.89	51	14	-	-	23	-		
1972	Detr	30.79	3	3	8	20	13	-		
1973	Detr	30.35	5	3	10	-	8	-		
1974	Detr	30.95	3	3	12	11	9	-	3	-
1975	Detr	30.36	3	3	6	6	19	-	5	-
1976	Detr	27.16	4	4	10	3	19	-	17	-
1977	Detr	29.83	2	2	6	6	25	-	16	-
1978	Detr	28.54	4	4	9	7	28	-	26	-
1979	Detr	24.23	10	5	11	-	-	25	-	
1980	Milw	23.32	12	6	27	17	-	24	-	
1981	Milw	17.30	45	14	-	33	-	25	-	
1982	Milw	15.99	59	14	-	13	-	-	-	-
1983	Milw	12.49		DNQ						
1984	Milw	16.56	61	15	-	18	-	-	-	-

RUDY LARUSSO DARTMOUTH

YR	TM	PR	OR	PS	SC	SH	RB	AS	BL	ST
1960	Minn	15.31	24	12	-	-	-	-		
1961	LA.L	17.84	23	10	-	-	-	-		
1962	LA.L	21.04	17	7	-	7	-	-		
1963	LA.L	17.43	21	10	-	-	-	-		
1964	LA.L	18.03	18	10	-	-	-	-		
1965	LA.L	19.04	17	8	-	13	-	-		
1966	LA.L	18.59	21	9	-	9	-	-		
1967	LA.L	14.24		DNQ						
1968	S.F.	21.81	19	9	9	-	-	-		
1969	S.F.	18.96	32	13	-	-	-	-		

CLYDE LEE — VANDERBILT

YR	TM	PR	OR	PS	SC	SH	RB	AS	BL	ST
1967	S.F.	10.59			DNQ					
1968	S.F.	19.80	26	7	-	-	5	-		
1969	S.F.	18.05	39	16	-	-	7	-		
1970	S.F.	16.21	51	11	-	-	12	-		
1971	S.F.	9.88			DNQ					
1972	G.St	18.71	41	19	-	-	4	-		
1973	G.St	12.03	81	33	-	-	3	-		
1974	G.St	12.81	70	13	-	-	7	-	-	-
1975	Phil	10.98	85	21	-	-	18	-	-	-
1976	Phil	6.08			DNQ					

EARL LLOYD — W. VIRGINIA ST.

YR	TM	PR	OR	PS	SC	SH	RB	AS	BL	ST
1951	Wash	11.43			DNQ					
1952		DID NOT PLAY								
1953	Syra	9.56	43	19	-	-	-			
1954	Syra	11.50	28	11	-	-	-			
1955	Syra	12.28	34	16	-	-	-			
1956	Syra	10.31	41	18	-	-	-			
1957	Syra	9.99	37	16	-	-	-			
1958	Syra	6.51			DNQ					
1959	Detr	9.92	43	17	-	-	-			
1960	Detr	8.13	52	21	-	-	-			

LEWIS LLOYD — DRAKE

YR	TM	PR	OR	PS	SC	SH	RB	AS	BL	ST
1982	G.St	2.94			DNQ					
1983	G.St	8.75			DNQ					
1984	Hous	16.34	64	8	-	-	-	-	-	-
1985	Hous	12.70	106	21	-	-	-	-	-	-
1986	Hous	16.80	58	11	-	26	-	-	-	-

KEVIN LOUGHERY — ST. JOHN'S

YR	TM	PR	OR	PS	SC	SH	RB	AS	BL	ST
1963	Detr	5.19			DNQ					
1964	Balt	7.15	57	25	-	-	-			
1965	Balt	11.69	44	15	-	-	-	9		
1966	Balt	15.31	28	9	-	-	-	11		
1967	Balt	15.25	32	10	-	-	-			
1968	Balt	12.57	64	22	-	-	-			
1969	Balt	18.08	37	15	12	-	-			
1970	Balt	18.49	40	17	16	-	-	18		
1971	Balt	12.06	87	35	-	-	-			
1972	Phil	10.51	92	35	-	-	-			

BOB LOVE — SOUTHERN

YR	TM	PR	OR	PS	SC	SH	RB	AS	BL	ST
1967	Cinc	6.98			DNQ					
1968	Cinc	5.97			DNQ					
1969	Chic	5.41			DNQ					
1970	Chic	21.54	21	9	-	-	-			
1971	Chic	23.05	20	6	7	-	-			
1972	Chic	19.43	37	16	6	-	-			
1973	Chic	17.71	48	19	12	-	-			
1974	Chic	13.98	62	11	15	-	-			
1975	Chic	15.62	42	9	10	-	-	-		
1976	Chic	13.59	63	12	22	-	-	-		

CLYDE LOVELLETTE — KANSAS

YR	TM	PR	OR	PS	SC	SH	RB	AS	BL	ST
1954	Minn	9.51			DNQ					
1955	Minn	20.21	9	4	6	-	8	-		
1956	Minn	25.00	4	2	4	-	3	-		
1957	Minn	23.45	6	3	7	-	6	-		
1958	Cinc	23.80	6	3	4	-	-			
1959	St.L	16.81	17	10	-	2	5	-		
1960	St.L	23.10	10	3	-	2	10	-		
1961	St.L	23.01	11	3	-	5	-	-		
1962	St.L	21.00			DNQ					
1963	Bost	7.00			DNQ					
1964	Bost	5.82			DNQ					

JERRY LUCAS — OHIO ST.

YR	TM	PR	OR	PS	SC	SH	RB	AS	BL	ST
1964	Cinc	30.39	6	2	-	1	3	-		
1965	Cinc	34.26	3	1	8	3	3	-		
1966	Cinc	33.66	3	1	9	-	3	-		
1967	Cinc	30.84	5	2	-	-	4	-		
1968	Cinc	34.37	2	1	11	3	4	-		
1969	Cinc	33.66	2	1	-	1	4	-		
1970	S.F.	25.15	13	5	-	10	3	-		
1971	S.F.	29.85	4	2	-	9	9	-		
1972	N.Y.	26.53	13	8	-	7	17	-		
1973	N.Y.	17.11	54	16	-	5	-	16		

MAURICE LUCAS — MARQUETTE

YR	TM	PR	OR	PS	SC	SH	RB	AS	BL	ST
1975	ABA	20.16	19	6	-	-	10	-	-	-
1976	ABA	18.02	10	3	-	-	3	-	-	-
1977	Port	22.57	12	3	22	-	16	-		
1978	Port	18.13	37	6	-	-	-	-		
1979	Port	22.26	18	5	24	-	29	-		
1980	N.J.	16.70	59	10	-	-	16	-		
1981	N.J.	17.54	43	11	-	-	27	-		
1982	N.Y.	21.48	19	4	-	-	7	-		
1983	Phoe	19.96	32	8	-	-	11	-		
1984	Phoe	19.91	33	7	-	-	9	-		
1985	Phoe	16.16	73	16	-	-	7	-		
1986	L.A.L	12.75	103	25	-	-	9	-		
1987	Seat	9.56			DNQ					
1988	Port	7.95			DNQ					

ED MACAULEY — ST. LOUIS

YR	TM	PR	OR	PS	SC	SH	RB	AS	BL	ST
1950	St.L	18.03	4	3	5	12	-			
1951	Bost	23.21	4	3	3	2	9	11		
1952	Bost	21.15	4	3	4	5	-			
1953	Bost	23.16	4	3	3	2	-			
1954	Bost	22.03	5	4	3	1	-			
1955	Bost	20.55	7	3	10	4	-			
1956	Bost	16.82	16	5	8	6	-			
1957	St.L	15.78	15	9	9	-	-			
1958	St.L	14.38	29	13	-	-	-			
1959	St.L	3.64			DNQ					

PETE MARAVICH — LSU

YR	TM	PR	OR	PS	SC	SH	RB	AS	BL	ST
1971	Atla	19.22	39	13	9	-	-	-		
1972	Atla	18.55	43	11	-	-	-	8		
1973	Atla	23.23	18	4	5	-	-	8		
1974	Atla	20.62	19	1	2	-	-	-	-	
1975	N.O.	17.67	25	3	14	-	9	-	-	
1976	N.O.	20.39	18	1	3	-	-	21	-	
1977	N.O.	20.82	20	3	1	-	-	-	-	
1978	N.O.	19.86	31	4	3	-	-	20	-	
1979	N.O.	14.37	DNQ							
1980	Bost	5.23	DNQ							

JACK MARIN — DUKE

YR	TM	PR	OR	PS	SC	SH	RB	AS	BL	ST
1967	Balt	9.57	DNQ							
1968	Balt	13.71	57	27	-	-	-	-		
1969	Balt	18.01	40	17	-	16	-	-		
1970	Balt	19.78	29	11	-	-	-	-		
1971	Balt	18.12	44	18	-	-	-	-		
1972	Balt	20.99	30	11	16	16	-	-		
1973	Hous	18.91	38	16	-	-	-	-		
1974	Buff	10.62	86	18	-	7	-	-		
1975	Buff	10.44	93	20	-	-	-	-		
1976	Chic	8.41	108	23	-	-	-	-		
1977	Chic	4.95	DNQ							

SLATER MARTIN — TEXAS

YR	TM	PR	OR	PS	SC	SH	RB	AS	BL	ST
1950	Minn	4.66	DNQ							
1951	Minn	8.82	42	13	-	-	-	12		
1952	Minn	9.85	43	13	-	-	-	-		
1953	Minn	10.61	37	11	-	9	-	-		
1954	Minn	9.22	38	12	-	-	-	-		
1955	Minn	14.04	23	6	-	-	-	7		
1956	Minn	14.33	22	5	-	-	-	7		
1957	St.L	10.94	34	9	-	-	-	8		
1958	St.L	9.80	42	15	-	-	-	-		
1959	St.L	10.68	39	14	-	-	-	7		
1960	St.L	9.86	41	17	-	-	-	5		

CEDRIC MAXWELL — UNCC

YR	TM	PR	OR	PS	SC	SH	RB	AS	BL	ST
1978	Bost	10.36	DNQ							
1979	Bost	24.48	9	2	-	2	-	-	-	
1980	Bost	21.85	17	5	-	2	-	-	-	
1981	Bost	18.99	30	9	-	3	-	-	-	
1982	Bost	17.17	49	15	-	25	-	-	-	
1983	Bost	13.82	85	24	-	-	-	-	-	
1984	Bost	14.01	89	15	-	-	-	-	-	
1985	Bost	12.40	111	24	-	17	-	-	-	
1986	LA.C	17.58	49	10	-	-	-	-	-	
1987	Hous	12.91	98	24	-	31	-	-	-	
1988	Hous	5.14	DNQ							

BOB MCADOO — N. CAROLINA

YR	TM	PR	OR	PS	SC	SH	RB	AS	BL	ST
1973	Buff	19.01	37	15	-	-	-	-		
1974	Buff	35.68	2	2	1	2	11	-	6	-
1975	Buff	34.59	2	2	1	5	15	-	11	-
1976	Buff	31.13	2	2	1	-	-	-	11	-
1977	N.Y.	28.11	4	4	5	28	10	-	30	-
1978	N.Y.	29.92	2	2	4	23	23	-	29	-
1979	Bost	23.55	11	3	4	-	-	-	-	
1980	Detr	20.16	31	5	17	-	-	-	-	
1981	N.J.	5.38	DNQ							
1982	LA.L	9.15	DNQ							
1983	LA.L	14.62	DNQ							
1984	LA.L	11.37	126	26	-	-	-	-		
1985	LA.L	11.00	124	26	-	-	-	24	-	
1986	Phil	8.86	DNQ							

GEORGE MCGINNIS — INDIANA

YR	TM	PR	OR	PS	SC	SH	RB	AS	BL	ST
1972	ABA	18.96	23	9	-	-	15	-		
1973	ABA	28.54	5	4	4	-	8	-		
1974	ABA	30.14	3	2	4	-	4	-	-	9
1975	ABA	34.24	1	1	4	-	8	11	-	5
1976	Phil	25.05	5	1	6	-	13	-	-	7
1977	Phil	22.89	11	2	16	-	12	-	-	22
1978	Phil	21.77	21	3	22	-	21	-	-	31
1979	Denv	23.30	13	4	14	-	10	-	-	24
1980	Indi	17.03	55	9	-	-	12	31	-	-
1981	Indi	13.75	93	17	-	-	19	-	-	21
1982	Indi	8.22	DNQ							

JON MCGLOCKLIN — INDIANA

YR	TM	PR	OR	PS	SC	SH	RB	AS	BL	ST
1966	Cinc	5.03	DNQ							
1967	Cinc	7.65	DNQ							
1968	S.D.	10.77	71	27	-	-	-	-		
1969	Milw	18.54	35	11	-	6	-	-		
1970	Milw	17.15	45	18	-	1	-	-		
1971	Milw	15.83	57	22	-	2	-	-		
1972	Milw	11.16	88	33	-	4	-	-		
1973	Milw	10.01	90	33	-	7	-	-		
1974	Milw	7.90	109	22	-	-	-	-		
1975	Milw	8.33	104	23	-	19	-	-		
1976	Milw	2.58	DNQ							

DICK MCGUIRE — DARTMOUTH

YR	TM	PR	OR	PS	SC	SH	RB	AS	BL	ST
1950	N.Y.	12.40	22	3	-	-	1			
1951	N.Y.	13.61	18	3	-	-	2			
1952	N.Y.	14.59	20	4	-	13	-	1		
1953	N.Y.	10.92	36	10	-	-	2			
1954	N.Y.	12.78	20	6	-	-	5			
1955	N.Y.	14.76	22	5	-	-	1			
1956	N.Y.	10.47	39	11	-	-	2			
1957	N.Y.	6.51	DNQ							
1958	Detr	12.83	33	10	-	-	2			
1959	Detr	14.15	27	7	-	-	2			
1960	Detr	11.82	36	13	-	-	2			

JACK MCMAHON — ST. JOHN'S

YR	TM	PR	OR	PS	SC	SH	RB	AS	BL	ST
1953	Roch	6.24	61	24	-	-	-	11		
1954	Roch	8.83	41	14	-	-	-	9		
1955	Roch	7.64	51	17	-	-	-	10		
1956	St.L	6.11	59	24	-	-	-	-		
1957	St.L	8.89	43	13	-	-	-	2		
1958	St.L	7.00	50	19	-	-	-	6		
1959	St.L	7.64	52	19	-	-	-	8		
1960	St.L	3.28	DNQ							

TOM MCMILLEN — MARYLAND

YR	TM	PR	OR	PS	SC	SH	RB	AS	BL	ST
1976	Buff	16.38	DNQ							
1977	N.Y.	8.87	134	22	-	-	-	-	-	-
1978	Atla	11.75	109	21	-	-	-	-	-	-
1979	Atla	7.95	DNQ							
1980	Atla	9.70	DNQ							
1981	Atla	7.94	158	36	-	-	-	-	-	-
1982	Atla	10.99	123	22	-	-	-	-	-	-
1983	Atla	8.31	144	26	-	-	-	-	-	-
1984	Wash	8.89	149	29	-	-	-	-	-	-
1985	Wash	8.03	152	36	-	-	-	-	-	-
1986	Wash	5.18	DNQ							

JIM MCMILLIAN — COLUMBIA

YR	TM	PR	OR	PS	SC	SH	RB	AS	BL	ST
1971	LA.L	9.52	105	43	-	-	-	-		
1972	LA.L	18.59	42	20	-	-	-	-		
1973	LA.L	17.09	55	21	-	-	-	-		
1974	Buff	20.27	20	5	-	8	-	-	-	-
1975	Buff	16.16	40	7	-	8	-	-	-	-
1976	Buff	16.93	39	7	-	1	-	-	-	-
1977	N.Y.	10.28	114	24	-	-	-	-		
1978	N.Y.	10.12	130	25	-	-	-	-		
1979	Port	4.61	DNQ							

JOE MERIWEATHER — S. ILLINOIS

YR	TM	PR	OR	PS	SC	SH	RB	AS	BL	ST
1976	Hous	12.11	71	17	-	-	-	-	6	-
1977	Atla	14.51	58	16	-	-	22	-	26	-
1978	N.O.	12.67	DNQ							
1979	N.Y.	10.17	130	32	-	-	-	-	15	-
1980	N.Y.	11.92	111	28	-	-	-	-	6	-
1981	K.C.	9.97	140	29	-	-	-	-	20	-
1982	K.C.	10.33	DNQ							
1983	K.C.	11.09	115	24	-	-	21	-	23	-
1984	K.C.	9.56	146	31	-	-	-	-	30	-
1985	K.C.	6.11	DNQ							

TOM MESCHERY — ST. MARY'S

YR	TM	PR	OR	PS	SC	SH	RB	AS	BL	ST
1962	Phil	15.50	30	13	-	-	-	-		
1963	S.F.	17.61	20	9	-	-	-	-		
1964	S.F.	15.46	24	13	-	-	-	-		
1965	S.F.	14.09	31	14	-	-	-	-		
1966	S.F.	15.75	26	12	-	-	-	-		
1967	S.F.	12.81	46	19	-	-	-	-		
1968	Seat	19.35	29	13	-	-	-	-		
1969	Seat	18.59	34	14	-	-	-	-		
1970	Seat	16.64	49	21	-	-	-	-		
1971	Seat	11.91	90	33	-	-	-	-		

GEORGE MIKAN — DEPAUL

YR	TM	PR	OR	PS	SC	SH	RB	AS	BL	ST
1947	Chic	16.50			1					
1948	Minn	21.30			1					
1949	Minn	28.30			1					
1950	Minn	28.13	1	1	1	3	-			
1951	Minn	30.16	1	1	1	4	2	-		
1952	Minn	24.88	2	1	2	-	5	-		
1953	Minn	25.33	2	2	2	12	2	-		
1954	Minn	23.15	3	2	4	-	1	-		
1955		DID NOT PLAY								
1956	Minn	13.41	DNQ							

VERN MIKKELSEN — HAMLINE

YR	TM	PR	OR	PS	SC	SH	RB	AS	BL	ST
1950	Minn	16.25	7	3	-	13				
1951	Minn	17.45	8	4	-	-	6			
1952	Minn	19.36	8	3	11	8	12			
1953	Minn	18.04	7	3	9	5	13			
1954	Minn	13.49	15	4	-	-	12			
1955	Minn	20.00	10	5	8	6				
1956	Minn	16.10	18	10						
1957	Minn	15.60	16	10						
1958	Minn	20.65	11	6						
1959	Minn	15.29	20	12						

EDDIE MILES — SEATTLE

YR	TM	PR	OR	PS	SC	SH	RB	AS	BL	ST
1964	Detr	3.53	DNQ							
1965	Detr	11.14	46	16	-	-	-	-		
1966	Detr	15.01	32	11	-	-	-	-		
1967	Detr	12.91	43	17	-	-	-	-		
1968	Detr	15.49	46	13	-	14	-	-		
1969	Detr	11.18	78	30	-	-	-	-		
1970	Balt	11.21	DNQ							
1971	Balt	8.43	112	43	-	-	-	-		
1972	N.Y.	1.24	DNQ							

MIKE MITCHELL — AUBURN

YR	TM	PR	OR	PS	SC	SH	RB	AS	BL	ST
1979	Clev	10.39	125	29	-	-	-	-		
1980	Clev	20.72	25	8	10	27	-	-	-	-
1981	Clev	19.17	28	8	8	-	-	-		
1982	S.A.	18.36	35	10	18	-	-	-		
1983	S.A.	18.54	41	14	26	-	-	-		
1984	S.A.	20.25	27	10	8	-	-	-		
1985	S.A.	18.00	51	18	17	-	-	-		
1986	S.A.	17.62	48	15	9	-	-	-		
1987	S.A.	8.43	DNQ							
1988	S.A.	10.84	121	24	-	-	-	-	-	

EARL MONROE — WINSTON-SALEM

YR	TM	PR	OR	PS	SC	SH	RB	AS	BL	ST
1968	Balt	21.56	20	6	6	-	-			
1969	Balt	19.67	30	10	3	-	-			
1970	Balt	19.63	32	14	11	-	-			
1971	Balt	16.80	52	19	15	-	-			
1972	N.Y.	9.00	102	39	-	-				
1973	N.Y.	15.19	68	25	-	16	-	-		
1974	N.Y.	11.43	DNQ							
1975	N.Y.	17.21	30	4	17	-	-			
1976	N.Y.	17.39	36	5	14	-	-			
1977	N.Y.	18.23	34	5	24	10	-	-		
1978	N.Y.	15.54	62	7	-	30	-	26	-	
1979	N.Y.	9.55	138	24	-	-				
1980	N.Y.	5.45	DNQ							

OTTO MOORE — PAN AMERICAN

YR	TM	PR	OR	PS	SC	SH	RB	AS	BL	ST
1969	Detr	10.53	79	16	-	-	-	-	-
1970	Detr	17.67	44	8	-	11	-
1971	Detr	12.74	81	21	-	14	-
1972	Phoe	10.41	94	20	-	20	-
1973	Hous	17.96	44	14	-	19	-
1974	K.C.	6.37	DNQ
1975	N.O.	12.26	DNQ
1976	N.O.	16.01	47	14	-	-	12	-	8	-
1977	N.O.	11.83	96	25	-	-	23	-	15	-

JEFF MULLINS — DUKE

YR	TM	PR	OR	PS	SC	SH	RB	AS	BL	ST
1965	St.L	4.98	DNQ
1966	St.L	4.55	DNQ
1967	S.F.	13.56	41	15	-	-	-	-
1968	S.F.	18.22	35	11	-	-	-	-
1969	S.F.	21.58	21	6	11	13	-	-
1970	S.F.	20.89	25	11	14	-	-	-
1971	S.F.	20.01	31	8	20	12	-	-
1972	G.St	22.04	27	8	18	-	-	18
1973	G.St	17.85	46	14	-	12	-	-
1974	G.St	14.09	58	9	-	-	-	-
1975	G.St	7.56	DNQ
1976	G.St	4.56	DNQ

CALVIN MURPHY — NIAGARA

YR	TM	PR	OR	PS	SC	SH	RB	AS	BL	ST
1971	S.D.	15.07	63	26	-	21	-	13
1972	Hous	17.26	51	16	-	-	-	15
1973	Hous	12.25	79	30	-	18	-	19
1974	Hous	20.02	22	2	21	3	-	4	-	17
1975	Hous	16.38	37	8	-	13	-	16	-	22
1976	Hous	20.73	17	3	11	6	-	2	-	20
1977	Hous	15.79	49	11	-	23	-	-	-
1978	Hous	18.51	33	5	6	-	-	-	-
1979	Hous	16.88	56	6	26	30	-	-	-
1980	Hous	16.91	57	10	23	-	-	-	23
1981	Hous	13.26	98	18	-	-	-	-	17
1982	Hous	7.19	DNQ
1983	Hous	9.27	134	23	-	-	-	-	-

SWEN NATER — UCLA

YR	TM	PR	OR	PS	SC	SH	RB	AS	BL	ST
1974	ABA	22.63	6	2	-	2	2	-	-
1975	ABA	26.55	6	3	-	8	1	-	-
1976	ABA	15.67	28	9	-	1	-	-
1977	Milw	20.21	23	10	-	12	1	-	-
1978	Buff	22.56	15	9	-	4	-	-
1979	S.D.	16.22	67	21	-	1	5	-	-
1980	S.D.	23.74	10	4	-	14	1	-	-
1981	S.D.	23.13	9	5	-	9	3	-	-
1982	S.D.	17.00	DNQ
1983	S.D.	2.14	DNQ
1984	LA.L	5.93	DNQ

WILLIE NAULLS — UCLA

YR	TM	PR	OR	PS	SC	SH	RB	AS	BL	ST
1957	N.Y.	11.68	32	15	-	-	-	-
1958	N.Y.	19.81	13	7	10	-	-	-
1959	N.Y.	17.25	15	9	-	-	-
1960	N.Y.	25.48	8	6	11	-	7	-
1961	N.Y.	25.59	7	4	8	-	11	-
1962	N.Y.	24.17	13	4	8	-	-	-
1963	S.F.	13.79	34	18	-	-	-	-
1964	Bost	9.06	DNQ
1965	Bost	8.99	57	24	-	-	-	-
1966	Bost	8.97	56	27	-	-	-	-

DON NELSON — IOWA

YR	TM	PR	OR	PS	SC	SH	RB	AS	BL	ST
1963	Chic	8.81	DNQ
1964	LA.L	7.23	DNQ
1965	LA.L	3.44	DNQ
1966	Bost	10.63	51	26	-	-	-	-
1967	Bost	7.90	DNQ
1968	Bost	11.70	DNQ
1969	Bost	12.73	71	31	-	11	-	-
1970	Bost	17.70	43	19	-	14	-	-
1971	Bost	15.62	60	21	-	-	-	-
1972	Bost	15.38	61	24	-	-	-	-
1973	Bost	11.46	84	35	-	19	-	-
1974	Bost	11.12	82	17	-	9	-	-	-
1975	Bost	15.46	44	10	-	2	-	-	-
1976	Bost	6.11	DNQ

MIKE NEWLIN — UTAH

YR	TM	PR	OR	PS	SC	SH	RB	AS	BL	ST
1972	Hous	7.13	DNQ
1973	Hous	17.44	51	17	-	-	-	20
1974	Hous	15.89	44	4	-	-	-	-	-
1975	Hous	14.78	53	7	-	17	-	17	-
1976	Hous	18.98	23	2	-	2	-	17	-
1977	Hous	11.71	98	22	-	-	21	-	-
1978	Hous	12.44	DNQ
1979	Hous	10.46	123	22	-	-	-	26	-
1980	N.J.	17.10	54	9	18	-	-	-	-
1981	N.J.	17.24	46	8	15	25	-	-	-
1982	N.Y.	7.21	158	29	-	-	-	-	-

JACK NICHOLS — WASHINGTON

YR	TM	PR	OR	PS	SC	SH	RB	AS	BL	ST
1949	Wash	10.65	DNQ
1950	T.C.	13.40	16	8	15	-	-	-
1951	T.C.	15.80	DNQ
1952		DID NOT PLAY
1953	Milw	14.13	17	8	7	-	-	-
1954	Bost	6.69	57	11	-	-	-	-
1955	Bost	13.55	27	13	-	-	-	-
1956	Bost	18.72	10	5	-	-	-	-
1957	Bost	9.62	39	13	-	-	-	-
1958	Bost	6.22	DNQ

NORM NIXON — DUQUESNE

YR	TM	PR	OR	PS	SC	SH	RB	AS	BL	ST
1978	LA.L	15.37	63	8	-	-	-	7	-	-
1979	LA.L	21.79	22	2	-	11	-	5	-	8
1980	LA.L	18.89	37	4	-	-	-	14	-	-
1981	LA.L	18.48	33	2	-	-	-	6	-	32
1982	LA.L	18.05	39	6	-	-	-	14	-	-
1983	LA.L	15.19	71	10	-	-	-	18	-	-
1984	S.D.	19.52	36	4	-	-	-	6	-	-
1985	LA.C	17.49	56	9	-	-	-	7	-	-
1986	LA.C	16.16	64	9	-	-	-	8	-	-
1987		DID NOT PLAY								
1988		DID NOT PLAY								
1989	LA.C.	8.92		DNQ						

DON OHL — ILLINOIS

YR	TM	PR	OR	PS	SC	SH	RB	AS	BL	ST
1961	Detr	10.62	43	18	-	-	-			
1962	Detr	13.61	41	15	-	-	-			
1963	Detr	14.90	27	8	13	-	-			
1964	Detr	11.27	45	16	-	-	-			
1965	Balt	15.23	27	7	13	-	-			
1966	Balt	16.67	23	8	11	-	-			
1967	Balt	15.67	29	9	11	-	-			
1968	St.L	10.86	70	26	-	-	-			
1969	Atla	9.62	85	32	-	-	-			
1970	Atla	3.62		DNQ						

MARK OLBERDING — MINNESOTA

YR	TM	PR	OR	PS	SC	SH	RB	AS	BL	ST
1976	ABA	13.65	34	17	-	-	-	-	-	-
1977	S.A.	11.85	95	14	-	20	-	-	-	-
1978	S.A.	10.27	127	27	-	-	-	-	-	-
1979	S.A.	11.95	104	17	-	-	-	-	-	-
1980	S.A.	14.32	80	14	-	-	-	27	-	-
1981	S.A.	15.39	71	14	-	26	-	-	-	-
1982	S.A.	16.06	58	13	-	-	-	-	-	-
1983	Chic	9.61	133	25	-	-	-	-	-	-
1984	K.C.	12.30	111	22	-	-	-	-	-	-
1985	K.C.	14.06	96	22	-	-	-	-	-	-
1986	Sacr	12.26	109	27	-	19	-	-	-	-
1987	Sacr	5.13		DNQ						

LOUIS ORR — SYRACUSE

YR	TM	PR	OR	PS	SC	SH	RB	AS	BL	ST
1981	Indi	11.09	127	26	-	-	-	-	-	-
1982	Indi	11.44	114	27	-	-	-	-	-	-
1983	N.Y.	7.94	148	36	-	-	-	-	-	-
1984	N.Y.	8.03	156	34	-	-	-	-	-	-
1985	N.Y.	13.35	102	24	-	-	-	-	-	-
1986	N.Y.	11.72	116	23	-	-	-	-	-	-
1987	N.Y.	8.08	156	28	-	-	-	-	-	-
1988	N.Y.	1.14		DNQ						

TOM OWENS — S. CAROLINA

YR	TM	PR	OR	PS	SC	SH	RB	AS	BL	ST
1972	ABA	9.77		DNQ						
1973	ABA	15.59	31	11	-	12	10	-		
1974	ABA	18.43	17	8	-	4	-	-		
1975	ABA	22.22	13	4	-	14	9	-		
1976	ABA	8.19		DNQ						
1977	Hous	5.30		DNQ						
1978	Port	12.84	94	26	-	-	26	-	-	-
1979	Port	22.60	17	8	-	8	-	-	-	-
1980	Port	18.17	41	12	-	-	-	-	-	-
1981	Port	12.87	102	25	-	-	-	-	-	-
1982	Indi	11.32	118	27	-	-	-	-	-	-
1983	Detr	5.78		DNQ						

BILLY PAULTZ — ST. JOHN'S

YR	TM	PR	OR	PS	SC	SH	RB	AS	BL	ST
1971	ABA	21.57	15	5	-	4	13	-		
1972	ABA	21.10	14	6	-	-	7	-		
1973	ABA	23.98	7	3	-	-	4	-		
1974	ABA	20.66	10	5	-	-	-	-		
1975	ABA	19.81	21	7	-	-	-	-		
1976	ABA	23.23	7	2	-	-	-	-		
1977	S.A.	18.46	32	12	-	-	-	13	-	
1978	S.A.	21.08	25	11	-	12	-	5	-	
1979	S.A.	16.19	68	22	-	-	25	-	14	-
1980	Hous	13.77	87	20	-	-	-	25	-	
1981	Hous	9.54	146	32	-	-	-	28	-	
1982	Hous	3.95		DNQ						
1983	S.A.	3.44		DNQ						
1984	Atla	3.63		DNQ						
1985	Utah	2.03		DNQ						

GEOFF PETRIE — PRINCETON

YR	TM	PR	OR	PS	SC	SH	RB	AS	BL	ST
1971	Port	19.24	38	12	8	-	-	-		
1972	Port	13.48	71	24	-	-	-	-		
1973	Port	19.53	35	9	7	-	-	-		
1974	Port	17.42	34	7	9	19	-	-	-	
1975	Port	13.93	62	15	-	-	-	-		
1976	Port	14.13	58	10	-	-	-	-		

BOB PETTIT — LSU

YR	TM	PR	OR	PS	SC	SH	RB	AS	BL	ST
1955	Milw	24.85	2	1	4	-	4	-		
1956	St.L	29.74	1	1	1	11	2	-		
1957	St.L	26.85	3	2	2	10	4	-		
1958	St.L	29.54	2	2	3	-	2	-		
1959	St.L	32.99	1	1	1	7	2	-		
1960	St.L	32.29	3	1	4	10	4	-		
1961	St.L	36.17	4	2	4	-	3	-		
1962	St.L	37.31	5	3	4	10	4	-		
1963	St.L	31.76	6	2	3	-	5	-		
1964	St.L	32.41	4	1	4	9	8	-		
1965	St.L	25.46	9	3	7	-	8	-		

ANDY PHILLIP — ILLINOIS

YR	TM	PR	OR	PS	SC	SH	RB	AS	BL	ST
1948	Chic	10.80			-				6		
1949	Chic	12.00			17				2		
1950	Chic	14.83	11	1	-	-		2			
1951	Phil	17.00	9	1	-	-		1			
1952	Phil	18.24	9	2	-	-		2			
1953	Ft.W	14.64	16	3	-	-		4			
1954	Ft.W	13.39	16	5	-	-		3			
1955	Ft.W	15.00	20	4	-	-		2			
1956	Ft.W	10.44	40	12	-	-		3			
1957	Bost	6.36	53	22	-	-		7			
1958	Bost	4.43		DNQ						

JIM POLLARD — STANFORD

YR	TM	PR	OR	PS	SC	SH	RB	AS	BL	ST
1948	Minn	12.90			7			-			
1949	Minn	14.80			11			-			
1950	Minn	15.36	9	4	9	-		7			
1951	Minn	14.56	14	7	-	-	10	-			
1952	Minn	15.55	17	8	10	-	-				
1953	Minn	13.39	21	8	-	-	-				
1954	Minn	13.21	17	5	-	-	-				
1955	Minn	12.38	15	-	-	-	-				

KEVIN PORTER — ST. FRANCIS

YR	TM	PR	OR	PS	SC	SH	RB	AS	BL	ST
1973	Balt	6.99	DNQ							
1974	Capt	12.54	74	17	-	-	-	5	-	-
1975	Wash	13.78	63	16	-	-	-	1	-	10
1976	Detr	15.59	DNQ							
1977	Detr	11.12	106	16	-	27	-	1	-	-
1978	N.J.	17.40	46	4	-	-	-	1	-	-
1979	Detr	21.27	24	3	-	-	-	1	-	23
1980	Wash	9.90	136	21	-	-	-	1	-	-
1981	Wash	16.59	56	5	-	31	-	1	-	-
1982		DID NOT PLAY								
1983	Wash	6.09	DNQ							

FRANK RAMSEY — KENTUCKY

YR	TM	PR	OR	PS	SC	SH	RB	AS	BL	ST
1955	Bost	13.55	26	12	-	-	-	-		
1956		DID NOT PLAY								
1957	Bost	11.80	DNQ							
1958	Bost	17.33	18	3	-	7	-	-		
1959	Bost	14.17	26	14	-	-	-	-		
1960	Bost	14.33	27	13	-	-	-	-		
1961	Bost	13.38	34	14	-	-	-	-		
1962	Bost	13.27	44	19	-	-	-	-		
1963	Bost	9.12	58	29	-	-	-	-		
1964	Bost	7.16	DNQ							

KELVIN RANSEY — OHIO ST.

YR	TM	PR	OR	PS	SC	SH	RB	AS	BL	ST
1981	Port	14.25	88	13	-	-	-	9	-	-
1982	Port	15.37	64	10	-	-	-	11	-	-
1983	Dall	9.87	126	27	-	-	-	30	-	-
1984	N.J.	11.15	130	24	-	-	-	8	-	-
1985	N.J.	10.07	137	26	-	-	-	19	-	24
1986	N.J.	7.52	157	29	-	-	-	-	-	-

CLIFFORD RAY — OKLAHOMA

YR	TM	PR	OR	PS	SC	SH	RB	AS	BL	ST
1972	Chic	17.00	53	16	-	-	1	-		
1973	Chic	18.62	40	13	-	-	5	-		
1974	Chic	20.00	23	10	-	-	6	-	9	
1975	G.St	17.34	28	9	-	-	9	-	13	-
1976	G.St	14.50	57	15	-	-	7	-	16	-
1977	G.St	13.84	68	19	-	17	24	-	24	-
1978	G.St	16.61	52	18	-	18	15	-	28	-
1979	G.St	11.76	110	27	-	-	16	-	-	-
1980	G.St	10.15	132	31	-	-	27	-	-	-
1981	G.St	4.06	DNQ							

WILLIS REED — GRAMBLING

YR	TM	PR	OR	PS	SC	SH	RB	AS	BL	ST
1965	N.Y.	24.19	11	5	10	-	5	-		
1966	N.Y.	19.53	15	5	-	11	-			
1967	N.Y.	26.90	9	4	9	7	6	-		
1968	N.Y.	25.78	8	3	14	12	10	-		
1969	N.Y.	28.74	6	4	-	2	11	-		
1970	N.Y.	27.73	9	4	18	13	9	-		
1971	N.Y.	25.75	10	5	18	-	17	-		
1972	N.Y.	16.00	DNQ							
1973	N.Y.	15.55	64	17	-	-	-	-		
1974	N.Y.	13.84	DNQ							

M. R. RICHARDSON — MONTANA

YR	TM	PR	OR	PS	SC	SH	RB	AS	BL	ST
1979	N.Y.	7.64	DNQ							
1980	N.Y.	23.05	13	2	-	-	-	2	-	2
1981	N.Y.	21.81	16	1	-	-	-	14	-	7
1982	N.Y.	21.39	20	3	-	-	-	20	-	5
1983	N.J.	15.14	73	11	-	-	-	19	-	1
1984	N.J.	13.54	DNQ							
1985	N.J.	23.63	17	3	27	-	-	16	-	3
1986	N.J.	19.36	DNQ							

ARNOLD RISEN — OHIO ST.

YR	TM	PR	OR	PS	SC	SH	RB	AS	BL	ST
1946	Indi	12.20			6					
1947	Indi	13.20			5					
1948	Roch	13.23			5					
1949	Roch	16.60			4			-		
1950	Roch	15.55	8	5	-	-				
1951	Roch	20.45	5	4	9	14	4	-		
1952	Roch	20.20	5	4	9	-	2	-		
1953	Roch	16.50	11	5	-	-	6	-		
1954	Roch	15.60	10	7	12	-	8	-		
1955	Roch	15.59	17	7	-	-	6	-		
1956	Bost	11.99	29	9	-	-	8	-		
1957	Bost	10.35	DNQ							
1958	Bost	4.52	DNQ							

OSCAR ROBERTSON — CINCINNATI

YR	TM	PR	OR	PS	SC	SH	RB	AS	BL	ST
1961	Cinc	36.42	3	1	3	1	-	3		
1962	Cinc	40.51	2	1	6	1	-	2		
1963	Cinc	36.81	2	1	4	1	-	3		
1964	Cinc	39.15	2	1	2	2	-	1		
1965	Cinc	37.49	2	1	3	4	-	1		
1966	Cinc	36.41	2	1	3	2	-	2		
1967	Cinc	35.13	2	1	2	1	-	2		
1968	Cinc	33.46	3	1	1	1	-	2		
1969	Cinc	30.51	3	1	6	3	-	3		
1970	Cinc	29.00	5	2	6	5	-	5		
1971	Milw	25.06	14	3	-	6	-	4		
1972	Milw	21.97	28	9	-	-	-	5		
1973	Milw	20.01	32	8	-	-	-	4		
1974	Milw	14.04	60	11	-	-	-	7	-	-

LEN ROBINSON — TENNESSEE ST.

YR	TM	PR	OR	PS	SC	SH	RB	AS	BL	ST
1975	Wash	6.77	DNQ							
1976	Wash	12.62	66	14	-	-	-	9	-	
1977	Atla	20.05	25	4	29	-	-	-	-	
1978	N.O.	24.77	8	1	17	-	8	-	-	
1979	Phoe	22.25	19	6	21	-	17	-	-	
1980	Phoe	18.44	40	7	-	-	18	-	-	
1981	Phoe	19.68	22	3	28	-	-	-	-	
1982	Phoe	20.50	24	5	25	-	32	-	-	
1983	N.Y.	12.35	106	21	-	-	27	-	-	
1984	N.Y.	13.54	95	17	-	-	-	-	-	
1985	N.Y.	6.50	DNQ							

DAVE ROBISCH — KANSAS

YR	TM	PR	OR	PS	SC	SH	RB	AS	BL	ST
1972	ABA	18.41	25	7	-	-	14	-		
1973	ABA	20.19	16	8	-	-	-			
1974	ABA	17.64	18	9	-	-	-			
1975	ABA	15.65	35	11	-	10	-	-	-	
1976	ABA	17.26	23	7	-	-	-	-		
1977	Indi	13.94	66	18	-	-	-	-		
1978	LA.L	7.81	DNQ							
1979	LA.L	6.81	DNQ							
1980	Clev	19.15	36	11	-	19	-	-	-	
1981	Denv	12.65	106	23	-	-	-	-		
1982	Denv	14.00	DNQ							
1983	Denv	4.61	DNQ							
1984	K.C.	3.16	DNQ							

RED ROCHA — OREGON ST.

YR	TM	PR	OR	PS	SC	SH	RB	AS	BL	ST
1948	St.L	12.80			9			-		
1949	St.L	10.50						-		
1950	St.L	14.57	14	6	-	14	-			
1951	Balt	13.92	15	8	-	-	-			
1952	Syra	15.24	18	7	-	11	-	-		
1953	Syra	13.32	22	9	-	-	-			
1954	DID NOT PLAY									
1955	Syra	12.65	31	8	-	-	-			
1956	Syra	10.61	38	11	-	-	-	-		
1957	Ft.W	6.18	DNQ							

GUY RODGERS — TEMPLE

YR	TM	PR	OR	PS	SC	SH	RB	AS	BL	ST
1959	Phil	14.44	25	6	-	-	4			
1960	Phil	15.56	22	6	-	-	3			
1961	Phil	18.72	19	5	-	-	2			
1962	Phil	13.79	37	14	-	-	3			
1963	S.F.	19.42	14	3	-	-	2			
1964	S.F.	13.77	33	9	-	-	2			
1965	S.F.	14.92	28	8	-	-	2			
1966	S.F.	20.75	13	4	-	-	1			
1967	Chic	22.00	13	3	-	-	1			
1968	Cinc	7.96	81	35	-	-	1			
1969	Milw	12.79	69	25	-	-	2			
1970	Milw	5.38	DNQ							

DAN ROUNDFIELD — C. MICHIGAN

YR	TM	PR	OR	PS	SC	SH	RB	AS	BL	ST
1976	ABA	5.51	DNQ							
1977	Indi	16.82	42	14	-	-	15	-	6	-
1978	Indi	19.90	30	4	-	-	17	-	11	-
1979	Atla	21.25	25	7	-	-	9	-	10	-
1980	Atla	21.26	21	3	-	-	9	-	14	-
1981	Atla	22.84	11	2	-	-	12	-	16	-
1982	Atla	23.20	14	2	29	-	9	-	27	-
1983	Atla	22.78	16	5	-	-	9	-	31	-
1984	Atla	21.48	22	4	-	-	20	-	-	-
1985	Detr	14.55	91	19	-	-	14	-	31	-
1986	Wash	15.18	76	19	-	-	23	-	-	-
1987	Wash	7.78	DNQ							

CURTIS ROWE — UCLA

YR	TM	PR	OR	PS	SC	SH	RB	AS	BL	ST
1972	Detr	14.63	64	25	-	-	-			
1973	Detr	19.91	34	14	-	17	-			
1974	Detr	11.61	80	16	-	-	-			
1975	Detr	13.26	64	14	-	-	-			
1976	Detr	16.65	43	8	-	-	-			
1977	Bost	12.27	91	21	-	-	-			
1978	Bost	4.07	DNQ							
1979	Bost	7.30	DNQ							

BILL RUSSELL — USF

YR	TM	PR	OR	PS	SC	SH	RB	AS	BL	ST
1957	Bost	25.17	4	3	-	-	1	-		
1958	Bost	30.71	1	1	-	-	1	-		
1959	Bost	32.70	2	1	-	-	1	-		
1960	Bost	35.39	2	2	-	-	2	-		
1961	Bost	32.42	5	2	-	-	2	-		
1962	Bost	35.38	6	4	-	-	2	-		
1963	Bost	33.32	5	3	-	-	1	-		
1964	Bost	34.15	3	2	-	-	1	-		
1965	Bost	34.06	4	2	-	-	1	12		
1966	Bost	31.04	5	2	-	-	1	-		
1967	Bost	31.98	3	2	-	-	2	13		
1968	Bost	26.65	7	3	-	-	3	-		
1969	Bost	26.88	8	5	-	-	3	-		

CAMPY RUSSELL — MICHIGAN

YR	TM	PR	OR	PS	SC	SH	RB	AS	BL	ST
1975	Clev	4.76	DNQ							
1976	Clev	12.61	67	13	-	-	-			
1977	Clev	15.21	52	14	-	-	-			
1978	Clev	17.58	43	13	28	-	-	-		
1979	Clev	21.18	26	5	17	-	-	-		
1980	Clev	16.88	DNQ							
1981	N.Y.	14.37	86	20	-	-	-			
1982	N.Y.	12.64	99	23	-	-	-			

CAZZIE RUSSELL — MICHIGAN

YR	TM	PR	OR	PS	SC	SH	RB	AS	BL	ST
1967	N.Y.	10.53	58	25	-	-	-			
1968	N.Y.	15.18	48	23	-	-	-			
1969	N.Y.	14.96	55	24	-	-	-			
1970	N.Y.	10.78	83	37	-	-	-			
1971	N.Y.	8.39	DNQ							
1972	G.St	18.75	39	18	20	-	-	-		
1973	G.St	14.04	70	27	-	-	-			
1974	G.St	15.24	55	10	20	22	-	-	-	
1975	LA.L	11.10	DNQ							
1976	LA.L	8.86	106	22	-	-	-			
1977	LA.L	13.51	71	17	-	-	-			
1978	Chic	7.44	DNQ							

SATCH SANDERS — NYU

YR	TM	PR	OR	PS	SC	SH	RB	AS	BL	ST
1961	Bost	14.04	DNQ							
1962	Bost	15.16	35	16	-	-	-	-		
1963	Bost	13.30	38	19	-	-	-	-		
1964	Bost	14.08	31	17	-	-	-	-		
1965	Bost	14.14	29	13	-	-	-	-		
1966	Bost	13.54	41	20	-	-	-	-		
1967	Bost	10.89	57	22	-	-	-	-		
1968	Bost	11.49	69	31	-	-	-	-		
1969	Bost	12.78	70	30	-	-	-	-		
1970	Bost	12.77	72	31	-	-	-	-		
1971	Bost	2.24	DNQ							
1972	Bost	8.02	107	43	-	-	-	-		
1973	Bost	2.00	DNQ							

WOODY SAULDSBERRY — TEX. SOU.

YR	TM	PR	OR	PS	SC	SH	RB	AS	BL	ST
1958	Phil	12.99	32	14	-	-	-	-		
1959	Phil	14.78	23	13	-	-	-	-		
1960	Phil	7.99	53	22	-	-	-	-		
1961	St.L	7.23	54	22	-	-	-	-		
1962	Chic	10.89	47	20	-	-	-	-		
1963	St.L	9.19	56	28	-	-	-	-		
1966	Bost	3.79	DNQ							

DOLPH SCHAYES — NYU

YR	TM	PR	OR	PS	SC	SH	RB	AS	BL	ST
1949	Syra	12.80				6				
1950	Syra	25.20	2	1	6	9	-	6		
1951	Syra	25.80	2	1	6	-	1	10		
1952	Syra	20.06	6	2	-	-	1	-		
1953	Syra	23.31	3	1	5	13	3	-		
1954	Syra	22.32	4	3	6	6	6	-		
1955	Syra	22.97	3	2	7	10	7	-		
1956	Syra	24.11	5	3	5	10	7	-		
1957	Syra	27.44	1	1	4	6	11	-		
1958	Syra	29.07	3	1	2	5	10	-		
1959	Syra	24.88	5	4	6	-	9	-		
1960	Syra	26.37	6	4	7	11	11	-		
1961	Syra	25.57	8	5	6	-	-	-		
1962	Syra	15.45	31	14	-	-	-	-		
1963	Syra	12.12	42	22	-	-	-	13		
1964	Phil	7.58	DNQ							

CHARLIE SCOTT — N. CAROLINA

YR	TM	PR	OR	PS	SC	SH	RB	AS	BL	ST
1971	ABA	23.64	10	2	4	-	-	8		
1972	ABA	26.15	9	1	2	-	-	-		
1973	Phoe	21.75	25	7	6	-	14			
1974	Phoe	19.88	24	3	4	-	-	-		20
1975	Phoe	16.80	35	7	5	-	-	-		
1976	Bost	14.60	55	10	-	-	-	-		
1977	Bost	15.30	DNQ							
1978	L.A.L	12.09	105	21	-	-	-	25	-	
1979	Denv	11.68	111	20	-	-	-	23	-	
1980	Denv	7.49	153	31	-	-	-	-		

RAY SCOTT — PORTLAND

YR	TM	PR	OR	PS	SC	SH	RB	AS	BL	ST
1962	Detr	16.97	24	11	-	-	8	-		
1963	Detr	18.32	18	8	-	-	-	-		
1964	Detr	22.90	10	5	-	9	-	-		
1965	Detr	16.86	22	9	-	-	-	-		
1966	Detr	21.81	10	3	12	-	-	-		
1967	Balt	18.00	26	7	-	-	-	-		
1968	Balt	22.32	17	8	-	-	8	-		
1969	Balt	14.84	57	26	-	18	-			
1970	Balt	11.53	DNQ							
1971	ABA	16.14	41	11	-	-	7	-		
1972	ABA	8.25	DNQ							

KENNY SEARS — SANTA CLARA

YR	TM	PR	OR	PS	SR	SH	RB	AS	BL	ST
1956	N.Y.	16.44	17	9	-	5	-	-		
1957	N.Y.	16.72	14	8	-	4	-	-		
1958	N.Y.	22.03	8	4	9	1	-	-		
1959	N.Y.	23.79	6	5	7	1	-	-		
1960	N.Y.	26.31	7	5	-	1	5	-		
1961	N.Y.	14.63	28	12	-	6	-	-		
1962		DID NOT PLAY								
1963	S.F.	7.45	DNQ							
1964	S.F.	4.39	DNQ							

FRANK SELVY — FURMAN

YR	TM	PR	OR	PS	SC	SH	RB	AS	BL	ST
1955	Milw	15.18	19	9	5	-	-	-		
1956	St.L	8.35	DNQ							
1957		DID NOT PLAY								
1958	Minn	2.76	DNQ							
1959	N.Y.	8.50	50	20	-	-	-	-		
1960	Minn	7.71	54	23	-	-	-	-		
1961	LA.L	11.06	40	16	-	-	-	-		
1962	LA.L	15.85	28	10	-	-	12			
1963	LA.L	11.11	44	14	-	-	-	-		
1964	LA.L	5.19	DNQ							

PAUL SEYMOUR — TOLEDO

YR	TM	PR	OR	PS	SC	SH	RB	AS	BL	ST
1947	Tole	3.17	DNQ							
1948	Balt	6.90								
1949	Syra	4.90								
1950	Syra	8.13	DNQ							
1951	Syra	8.75	DNQ							
1952	Syra	8.71	51	17	-	-	-	-		
1953	Syra	13.79	20	5	12	11	-	-		
1954	Syra	14.01	13	3	-	11	-	7		
1955	Syra	15.43	18	3	-	-	-	6		
1956	Syra	10.21	43	14	-	-	-	8		
1957	Syra	5.98	55	24	-	-	-	3		
1958	Syra	3.89	DNQ							
1959	Syra	4.57	DNQ							
1960	Syra	0.00	DNQ							

CHARLIE SHARE — BOWLING GREEN

YR	TM	PR	OR	PS	SC	SH	RB	AS	BL	ST
1952	Ft.W	6.76	DNQ							
1953	Ft.W	8.60	DNQ							
1954	Milw	11.87	25	8	-	-	5	-		
1955	Milw	16.03	15	6	-	-	1	-		
1956	St.L	18.21	12	4	-	-	5	-		
1957	St.L	14.39	20	7	-	11	5	-		
1958	St.L	14.85	27	9	-	-	6	-		
1959	St.L	12.69	31	8	-	-	4	-		

BILL SHARMAN — USC

YR	TM	PR	OR	PS	SC	SH	RB	AS	BL	ST
1951	Wash	9.06	DNQ							
1952	Bost	9.98	41	12	-	10	-	-		
1953	Bost	14.70	15	2	6	1	-	-		
1954	Bost	14.93	11	2	7	2	-	-		
1955	Bost	17.44	14	2	9	2	-	-		
1956	Bost	17.86	14	3	6	4	-	-		
1957	Bost	17.46	11	2	6	3	-	-		
1958	Bost	17.16	20	4	5	8	-	-		
1959	Bost	15.24	21	5	8	-	-	-		
1960	Bost	15.08	25	7	-	6	-	-		
1961	Bost	13.15	35	14	-	-	-	-		

LONNIE SHELTON — OREGON ST.

YR	TM	PR	OR	PS	SC	SH	RB	AS	BL	ST
1977	N.Y.	15.32	51	7	-	28	-	21	-	9
1978	N.Y.	17.49	44	8	-	28	-	21	-	-
1979	Seat	14.38	81	15	-	-	-	-	-	
1980	Seat	17.50	49	8	-	25	-	27	-	
1981	Seat	11.36	DNQ							
1982	Seat	16.27	56	11	-	-	-	-	-	
1983	Seat	14.62	77	14	-	-	-	-	-	
1984	Clev	11.84	119	25	-	-	-	-	-	
1985	Clev	7.74	DNQ							
1986	Clev	6.39	DNQ							

GENE SHUE — MARYLAND

YR	TM	PR	OR	PS	SC	SH	RB	AS	BL	ST
1955	N.Y.	4.74	DNQ							
1956	N.Y.	8.49	50	17	-	-	-	-		
1957	Ft.W	12.97	29	6	-	-	-	-		
1958	Detr	13.81	31	9	-	-	-	-		
1959	Detr	14.11	28	8	-	-	-	-		
1960	Detr	19.55	18	4	6	-	-	-		
1961	Detr	21.23	14	3	10	-	-	9		
1962	Detr	17.90	21	6	-	-	-	10		
1963	N.Y.	9.38	55	19	-	-	-			
1964	Balt	4.72	DNQ							

LARRY SIEGFRIED — OHIO ST.

YR	TM	PR	OR	PS	SC	SH	RB	AS	BL	ST
1964	Bost	3.52	DNQ							
1965	Bost	6.01	DNQ							
1966	Bost	11.55	49	18	-	-	-	-		
1967	Bost	13.56	40	14	-	13	-	-		
1968	Bost	13.84	55	19	-	-	-	13		
1969	Bost	13.67	60	19	-	-	-	13		
1970	Bost	12.03	74	27	-	-	-	-		
1971	S.D.	13.58	72	29	-	-	-	5		
1972	Atla	4.74	DNQ							

JAMES SILAS — S.F. AUSTIN

YR	TM	PR	OR	PS	SC	SH	RB	AS	BL	ST
1973	ABA	15.83	29	10	-	8	-	-	-	-
1974	ABA	16.44	26	6						
1975	ABA	20.49	18	5	-	7	-			
1976	ABA	24.26	6	2	6	2	-	7	-	
1977	S.A.	7.77	DNQ							
1978	S.A.	2.68	DNQ							
1979	S.A.	13.86	86	12	-	27	-			
1980	S.A.	16.01	65	9	-	15	-	28	-	
1981	S.A.	15.45	67	9	-					
1982	Clev	9.79	139	27	-	-	-	32		

PAUL SILAS — CREIGHTON

YR	TM	PR	OR	PS	SC	SH	RB	AS	BL	ST
1965	St.L	8.49	DNQ							
1966	St.L	6.83	DNQ							
1967	St.L	11.62	53	11	-	-	5	-		
1968	St.L	19.76	27	12	-	-	11	-		
1969	Atla	14.03	59	27	-	-	6	-		
1970	Phoe	19.65	31	12	-	-	-	-		
1971	Phoe	20.26	30	12	-	-	20	-		
1972	Phoe	25.35	16	4	-	-	-	-		
1973	Bost	22.39	22	9	-	-	4	-		
1974	Bost	16.90	37	8	-	-	10	-		
1975	Bost	17.61	27	7	-	-	2	-		
1976	Bost	17.84	34	8	-	-	5	-		
1977	Denv	9.27	131	21	-	-	18	-		
1978	Seat	10.49	123	25	-	-	31	-		
1979	Seat	9.61	137	21	-	-	26	-		
1980	Seat	6.48	156	31	-	-	31	-		

JERRY SLOAN — EVANSVILLE

YR	TM	PR	OR	PS	SC	SH	RB	AS	BL	ST
1966	Balt	7.93	DNQ							
1967	Chic	18.87	23	6	-	-	-	-		
1968	Chic	15.06	49	15	-	-	-	-		
1969	Chic	18.05	38	12	-	-	-	-		
1970	Chic	15.58	56	24	-	-	-	-		
1971	Chic	19.79	33	9	-	-	-	-		
1972	Chic	17.39	49	15	-	-	-	-		
1973	Chic	12.33	78	29	-	-	-	-		
1974	Chic	14.09	58	9	-	-	-	-	-	7
1975	Chic	14.06	60	8	-	-	-	-	-	5
1976	Chic	9.27	DNQ							

ADRIAN SMITH — KENTUCKY

YR	TM	PR	OR	PS	SC	SH	RB	AS	BL	ST
1962	Cinc	6.84	DNQ							
1963	Cinc	8.42	61	23	-	-	-	-		
1964	Cinc	8.02	54	22	-	-	-	-		
1965	Cinc	13.24	34	12	-	11	-	-		
1966	Cinc	14.53	36	12	-	-	-	-		
1967	Cinc	13.05	42	16	-	11	-	-		
1968	Cinc	13.61	60	20	-	11	-	-		
1969	Cinc	7.73	DNQ							
1970	S.F.	2.49	DNQ							
1971	S.F.	5.14	DNQ							
1972	ABA	4.47	DNQ							

BINGO SMITH
TULSA

YR	TM	PR	OR	PS	SC	SH	RB	AS	BL	ST
1970	S.D.	7.97		DNQ						
1971	Clev	15.43	62	25	-	-	-	-		
1972	Clev	15.51	59	23	-	-	-	-		
1973	Clev	7.66		DNQ						
1974	Clev	13.82	63	12	-	-	-	-	-	-
1975	Clev	15.13	47	11	-	-	-	-		-
1976	Clev	11.42	80	15	-	-	-	-		-
1977	Clev	11.80	97	23	-	-	-	-		-
1978	Clev	7.61	155	29	-	-	-	-		-
1979	Clev	9.18	142	34	-	-	-	-		-
1980	S.D.	9.35	140	30	-	-	-	-		-

ELMORE SMITH
KENTUCKY ST.

YR	TM	PR	OR	PS	SC	SH	RB	AS	BL	ST
1972	Buff	22.85	22	10	-	-	11	-		
1973	Buff	22.80	21	8	-	-	16	-		
1974	LA.L	20.19	21	9	-	-	-	-	1	-
1975	LA.L	18.55	20	7	-	-	8	-	1	-
1976	Milw	21.81	12	9	-	-	15	-	4	-
1977	Clev	11.40	102	26	-	-	29	-	3	-
1978	Clev	16.27	55	20	-	-	13	-	3	-
1979	Clev	7.79		DNQ						

PHIL SMITH
USF

YR	TM	PR	OR	PS	SC	SH	RB	AS	BL	ST
1975	G.St	7.19		DNQ						
1976	G.St	17.87	33	4	16	-	-	-	-	-
1977	G.St	16.33	44	9	28	-	-	-	-	-
1978	G.St	16.78	51	7	25	-	-	-	-	-
1979	G.St	17.80	45	5	27	-	-	-	-	-
1980	G.St	13.43	90	15	-	-	-	-	-	-
1981	S.D.	14.72	80	14	-	-	-	-	-	-
1982	Seat	10.80	128	21	-	-	-	-	-	-
1983	Seat	7.51		DNQ						

RANDY SMITH
BUFFALO ST.

YR	TM	PR	OR	PS	SC	SH	RB	AS	BL	ST
1972	Buff	13.41	72	29	-	-	-	-		-
1973	Buff	16.00	62	22	-	-	-	13		
1974	Buff	15.44	52	13	-	-	-	-	-	3
1975	Buff	18.00	24	3	-	-	6	-	-	-
1976	Buff	21.46	14	2	7	15	-	14	-	24
1977	Buff	19.76	27	4	20	-	-	28	-	26
1978	Buff	20.33	28	2	8	-	-	-	-	-
1979	S.D.	17.05	54	7	23	-	-	-	-	16
1980	Clev	14.82	77	13	-	-	-	-	-	-
1981	Clev	13.04	101	21	-	-	-	28	-	27
1982	N.Y.	9.39	149	27	-	-	-	-	-	-
1983	Atla	7.33		DNQ						

DICK SNYDER
DAVIDSON

YR	TM	PR	OR	PS	SC	SH	RB	AS	BL	ST
1967	St.L	5.09		DNQ						
1968	St.L	8.09	80	34	-	-	-	-		
1969	Phoe	12.41	72	26	-	-	-	-		
1970	Seat	15.85	52	20	-	3	-	-		
1971	Seat	19.17	40	14	-	3	-	-		
1972	Seat	16.97	54	18	-	2	-	-		
1973	Seat	14.48	69	26	-	-	-	-		
1974	Seat	15.66	48	6	-	20	-	-		
1975	Clev	13.17	66	9	-	9	-	-		
1976	Clev	11.24	82	14	-	13	-	-		
1977	Clev	7.66	143	30	-	-	-	-	-	-
1978	Clev	3.98		DNQ						
1979	Seat	3.32		DNQ						

RICKY SOBERS
UNLV

YR	TM	PR	OR	PS	SC	SH	RB	AS	BL	ST
1976	Phoe	9.46	100	20	-	-	-	-	-	16
1977	Phoe	12.46	88	18	-	18	-	-	-	-
1978	Indi	18.35	34	3	-	-	-	8	-	22
1979	Indi	16.43	63	7	-	-	-	25	-	30
1980	Chic	13.77	88	15	-	-	-	25	-	29
1981	Chic	12.18	108	23	-	-	-	33	-	19
1982	Chic	9.50	147	26	-	-	-	29	-	-
1983	Wash	13.71		DNQ						
1984	Wash	13.38	98	18	-	-	-	-	-	-
1985	Seat	8.13	151	32	-	-	-	30	-	-
1986	Seat	6.76		DNQ						

MARION SPEARS
W. KENTUCKY

YR	TM	PR	OR	PS	SC	SH	RB	AS	BL	ST
1949	Chic	9.30				-		-			
1950	Chic	8.47	56	23	-	-	-	-		
1951		DID NOT PLAY									
1952	Roch	9.86	42	19	-	-	-	-		
1953	Roch	9.98	42	18	-	8	-	-		
1954	Roch	8.25	48	20	-	-	-	-		
1955	Roch	9.99	42	20	-	-	-	-		
1956	Ft.W	6.93	55	22	-	-	-	-		
1957	St.L	3.27		DNQ						

LARRY STEELE
KENTUCKY

YR	TM	PR	OR	PS	SC	SH	RB	AS	BL	ST
1972	Port	2.64		DNQ						
1973	Port	7.74	106	44	-	-	-	-		
1974	Port	12.74	71	13	-	-	-	-	-	1
1975	Port	11.79	78	13	-	1	-	-	-	2
1976	Port	12.36	69	12	-	22	-	-	-	4
1977	Port	9.96	118	26	-	24	-	-	-	12
1978	Port	7.06		DNQ						
1979	Port	7.15	153	31	-	-	-	-	-	27
1980	Port	10.13		DNQ						

BRIAN TAYLOR — PRINCETON

YR	TM	PR	OR	PS	SC	SH	RB	AS	BL	ST
1973	ABA	14.44	41	14	-	-				
1974	ABA	12.63	43	14	-	-	-	12	-	6
1975	ABA	14.23	40	10	-	-	-	-	-	2
1976	ABA	15.87	26	8	-	8	-	-	-	3
1977	K.C.	17.47	38	4	-	19	-	-	-	6
1978	Denv	11.21	DNQ							
1979	S.D.	3.70	DNQ							
1980	S.D.	14.12	83	13	-	31	-	-	-	24
1981	S.D.	13.89	92	14	-	7	-	16	-	28
1982	S.D.	13.63	DNQ							

DAVID THOMPSON — N.C. STATE

YR	TM	PR	OR	PS	SC	SH	RB	AS	BL	SL
1976	ABA	25.19	5	1	3	4	-	-	-	
1977	Denv	20.85	18	2	4	26	-	-	-	
1978	Denv	24.55	10	2	2	15	-	-	-	
1979	Denv	19.55	34	3	6	-	-	-	-	
1980	Denv	17.67	DNQ							
1981	Denv	19.55	24	3	5	-	-	-	-	
1982	Denv	11.44	112	18	-	-	-	-	-	
1983	Seat	13.83	84	16	-	-	-	-	-	
1984	Seat	10.84	DNQ							

NATE THURMOND — BOWLING GREEN

YR	TM	PR	OR	PS	SC	SH	RB	AS	BL	ST
1964	S.F.	13.11	40	20	-	-	4	-		
1965	S.F.	25.74	8	4	-	4	-			
1966	S.F.	24.63	9	5	-	4	-			
1967	S.F.	30.71	6	3	-	3	-			
1968	S.F.	32.92	4	2	16	-	2	-		
1969	S.F.	29.82	4	2	19	-	5	-		
1970	S.F.	29.93	DNQ							
1971	S.F.	25.63	11	6	-	21	-			
1972	G.St	28.01	7	4	19	-	10	-		
1973	G.St	28.00	7	5	-	6	-			
1974	G.St	22.27	12	7	-	8	-	7	-	
1975	Chic	17.12	31	10	-	14	-	4	-	
1976	Clev	7.79	DNQ							
1977	Clev	11.39	DNQ							

RUDY TOMJANOVICH — MICHIGAN

YR	TM	PR	OR	PS	SC	SH	RB	AS	BL	ST
1971	S.D.	7.18	DNQ							
1972	Hous	20.97	31	12	-	18	-			
1973	Hous	23.15	19	8	-	21	-			
1974	Hous	25.73	7	1	8	1	-	-	-	
1975	Hous	20.26	14	2	18	4	-	-	-	
1976	Hous	18.84	25	4	-	8	-	-	-	
1977	Hous	20.75	21	7	14	15	-	-	-	
1978	Hous	17.26	DNQ							
1979	Hous	19.03	39	11	30	-	-	-	-	
1980	Hous	13.77	86	24	-	-	-	-		
1981	Hous	10.42	DNQ							

DAVE TWARDZIK — OLD DOMINION

YR	TM	PR	OR	PS	SC	SH	RB	AS	BL	ST
1973	ABA	7.56	DNQ							
1974	ABA	10.91	53	19	-	-	-	-	-	
1975	ABA	17.39	27	7	-	2	-	13	-	
1976	ABA	9.02	DNQ							
1977	Port	13.15	77	14	-	1	-	-	-	16
1978	Port	10.40	126	22	-	1	-	-	-	15
1979	Port	11.05	118	24	-	5	-	-	-	19
1980	Port	10.10	133	20	-	-	-	20	-	

JACK TWYMAN — CINCINNATI

YR	TM	PR	OR	PS	SC	SH	RB	AS	BL	ST
1956	Roch	14.04	24	13	-	-	-	-		
1957	Roch	13.75	23	4	11	5	-	-		
1958	Cinc	16.10	26	11	-	2	-	-		
1959	Cinc	22.46	9	7	3	-	-	-		
1960	Cinc	25.40	9	7	2	-	-	-		
1961	Cinc	24.16	10	7	5	3	-	-		
1962	Cinc	22.49	14	5	10	2	-	-		
1963	Cinc	20.41	13	6	10	6	-	-		
1964	Cinc	14.69	27	14	-	-	-	-		
1965	Cinc	12.91	37	17	-	-	-	-		
1966	Cinc	6.51	DNQ							

WES UNSELD — LOUISVILLE

YR	TM	PR	OR	PS	SC	SH	RB	AS	BL	ST
1969	Balt	26.63	9	6	-	-	1	-		
1970	Balt	28.56	7	3	-	-	2	-		
1971	Balt	27.93	8	4	-	20	4	-		
1972	Balt	27.49	10	5	-	-	5	-		
1973	Balt	26.61	9	6	-	-	2	-		
1974	Capt	13.11	69	12	-	-	-	-		
1975	Wash	22.81	10	6	-	-	3	-		
1976	Wash	23.23	7	6	-	7	8	24	-	
1977	Wash	18.02	35	13	-	-	20	-		
1978	Wash	19.30	32	12	-	-	5	-		
1979	Wash	20.81	30	12	-	13	6	-		
1980	Wash	22.52	15	5	-	-	5	-		
1981	Wash	17.56	42	13	-	-	5	-		

DICK VAN ARSDALE — INDIANA

YR	TM	PR	OR	PS	SC	SH	RB	AS	BL	ST
1966	N.Y.	12.03	47	23	-	-	-	-		
1967	N.Y.	17.11	27	13	-	-	-	-		
1968	N.Y.	12.72	62	29	-	-	-	-		
1969	Phoe	20.59	27	10	-	-	-	-		
1970	Phoe	20.19	28	13	-	6	-	-		
1971	Phoe	19.14	41	15	13	-	-	-		
1972	Phoe	18.54	44	12	-	21	-	-		
1973	Phoe	17.63	49	16	-	10	-	-		
1974	Phoe	15.81	45	5	-	5	-	-	-	
1975	Phoe	12.20	73	11	-	-	-	-		
1976	Phoe	9.95	93	17	-	17	-	-	-	
1977	Phoe	5.65	150	32	-	-	-	-	-	

TOM VAN ARSDALE — INDIANA

YR	TM	PR	OR	PS	SC	SH	RB	AS	BL	ST
1966	Detr	9.42	55	20	-	-	-	-		
1967	Detr	11.20	55	23	-	-	-	-		
1968	Cinc	7.69	83	37						
1969	Cinc	16.04	46	14						
1970	Cinc	19.32	36	14	13	-	-	-		
1971	Cinc	18.49	42	16	11	-	-	-		
1972	Cinc	16.37	56	21						
1973	Phil	12.58	76	30	-	-	-	-		
1974	Phil	13.59	65	14	22	-	-	-	-	
1975	Atla	12.04	74	12	-	-	-	-	-	
1976	Atla	7.69	113	25	-	-	-	-	-	
1977	Phoe	4.38	DNQ							

JAN VAN BREDA KOLFF — VAND.

YR	TM	PR	OR	PS	SC	SH	RB	AS	BL	ST
1975	ABA	9.58	65	25	-	-	-	-	-	
1976	ABA	11.66	43	19	-	-	-	-	-	
1977	NY.N	13.07	80	20	-	-	-	-	-	
1978	N.J.	6.68	157	30	-	-	-	-	-	
1979	N.J.	10.75	121	28	-	-	-	28	-	
1980	N.J.	12.00	110	26	-	-	-	-	-	
1981	N.J.	5.73	DNQ							
1982	N.J.	4.02	DNQ							
1983	N.J.	1.85	DNQ							

NORM VAN LIER — ST. FRANCIS

YR	TM	PR	OR	PS	SC	SH	RB	AS	BL	ST
1970	Cinc	14.49	60	21	-	-	-	13		
1971	Cinc	24.26	16	4	-	-	-	1		
1972	Chic	16.63	55	19	-	-	-	3		
1973	Chic	18.55	41	12	-	-	-	5		
1974	Chic	15.55	50	12	-	-	-	6	-	14
1975	Chic	15.37	45	11	-	-	-	12	-	17
1976	Chic	14.12	59	11	-	-	-	8	-	22
1977	Chic	14.66	57	7	-	-	-	8	-	-
1978	Chic	12.85	93	13	-	-	-	6	-	18
1979	Milw	6.68	DNQ							

CHET WALKER — BRADLEY

YR	TM	PR	OR	PS	SC	SH	RB	AS	BL	ST
1963	Syra	14.01	32	17	-	-	-	-		
1964	Phil	19.24	16	8	-	-	-	-		
1965	Phil	13.20	35	15	-	-	-	-		
1966	Phil	17.33	22	10	-	-	-	-		
1967	Phil	20.86	15	8	-	6	-	-		
1968	Phil	17.68	37	16	-	-	-	-		
1969	Phil	19.27	31	12	-	7	-	-		
1970	Chic	22.22	18	8	19	16	-	-		
1971	Chic	21.23	27	9	12	14	-	-		
1972	Chic	21.50	29	10	17	3	-	-		
1973	Chic	17.94	45	18	-	15	-	-		
1974	Chic	16.66	40	8	-	6	-	-		
1975	Chic	17.29	29	6	22	10	-	-	-	-

JIMMY WALKER — PROVIDENCE

YR	TM	PR	OR	PS	SC	SH	RB	AS	BL	ST
1968	Detr	7.26	85	39	-	-	-	15		
1969	Detr	11.29	77	29	-	15	-	18		
1970	Detr	16.84	47	19	-	-	-	-		
1971	Detr	14.18	66	27	-	-	-	-		
1972	Detr	17.64	48	14	21	-	-	-		
1973	Hous	17.73	47	15	-	-	-	-		
1974	K.C.	14.01	61	14	-	-	-	-		
1975	K.C.	12.58	71	10	-	-	-	-		
1976	K.C.	11.97	73	13	-	18	-	-		

BILL WALTON — UCLA

YR	TM	PR	OR	PS	SC	SH	RB	AS	BL	ST
1975	Port	25.02	DNQ							
1976	Port	23.31	6	5	-	-	2	-	10	-
1977	Port	29.11	3	3	-	21	3	-	4	-
1978	Port	28.67	3	3	31	22	2	29	7	-
1979		DID NOT PLAY								
1980	S.D.	18.93	DNQ							
1981		DID NOT PLAY								
1982		DID NOT PLAY								
1983	S.D.	21.97	DNQ							
1984	S.D.	18.04	45	13	-	-	7	-	13	-
1985	LA.C	16.96	61	11	-	-	1	-	5	-
1986	Bost	13.38	87	19	-	29	3	-	9	-
1987	Bost	4.10	DNQ							

BOBBY WANZER — SETON HALL

YR	TM	PR	OR	PS	SC	SH	RB	AS	BL	ST
1948	Roch	4.20	DNQ							
1949	Roch	10.20			-			10		
1950	Roch	12.03	24	4	-	2		-		
1951	Roch	10.76	32	9	-	6		-		
1952	Roch	17.33	13	3	8	1		-		
1953	Roch	14.09	18	4	10					
1954	Roch	13.57	14	4	10					
1955	Roch	13.71	24	7	-					
1956	Roch	10.26	42	13	-					
1957	Roch	3.81	DNQ							

CORNELL WARNER — JACKSON ST.

YR	TM	PR	OR	PS	SC	SH	RB	AS	BL	ST
1971	Buff	9.42	109	46	-	-	-	-		
1972	Buff	9.53	99	41	-	-	-	-		
1973	Clev	10.04	88	38	-	-	9	-		
1974	Milw	8.96	100	22	-	18	-	-	20	-
1975	Milw	14.00	61	10	-	-	16	-	-	-
1976	LA.L	12.41	68	15	-	-	-	-		
1977	LA.L	6.57	DNQ							

JIM WASHINGTON — VILLANOVA

YR	TM	PR	OR	PS	SC	SH	RB	AS	BL	ST
1966	St.L	7.58	DNQ							
1967	Chic	9.00	66	26	-	-	-	-		
1968	Chic	16.79	41	19	-	-	-	-		
1969	Chic	17.17	42	18	-	-	-	-		
1970	Phil	16.89	46	20	-	-	-	-		
1971	Phil	17.67	46	19	-	18	-	-		
1972	Atla	16.25	57	22	-	-	-	-		
1973	Atla	17.17	53	20	-	-	-	-		
1974	Atla	15.25	54	10	-	-	-	-		
1975	Buff	7.60	110	23	-	-	-	-		

SCOTT WEDMAN — COLORADO

YR	TM	PR	OR	PS	SC	SH	RB	AS	BL	ST
1975	K.C.	12.51	72	16	-	-	-	-	-	
1976	K.C.	16.26	46	9	-	-	-	-	-	
1977	K.C.	15.95	48	13	-	-	-	-	-	
1978	K.C.	17.83	40	12	-	14	-	-	-	-
1979	K.C.	18.14	43	13	-	15	-	-	-	-
1980	K.C.	18.51	39	13	31	-	-	-	-	-
1981	K.C.	16.79	52	12	24	-	-	-	-	-
1982	Clev	12.76	97	22	-	-	-	-	-	-
1983	Bost	9.87	127	32	-	-	-	-	-	-
1984	Bost	4.47		DNQ						
1985	Bost	5.81		DNQ						
1986	Bost	6.54		DNQ						
1987	Bost	2.83		DNQ						

BOB WEISS — PENN STATE

YR	TM	PR	OR	PS	SC	SH	RB	AS	BL	ST
1966	Phil	1.57		DNQ						
1967	Phil	2.83		DNQ						
1968	Seat	10.52	72	28	-	-	-	5		
1969	Chic	6.82	95	37	-	-	-	19		
1970	Chic	13.59	64	24	-	-	-	9		
1971	Chic	11.39	95	37	-	-	-	7		
1972	Chic	11.70	82	30	-	-	-	16		
1973	Chic	9.20	99	38	-	-	-	-		
1974	Chic	8.95	101	20	-	-	-	9	-	9
1975	Buff	5.50		DNQ						
1976	Buff	5.82		DNQ						
1977	Wash	4.85		DNQ						

JERRY WEST — WEST VIRGINIA

YR	TM	PR	OR	PS	SC	SH	RB	AS	BL	ST
1961	L.A.L	18.13	22	7	-	-	-	-		
1962	L.A.L	27.91	7	2	5	12	-	-		
1963	L.A.L	25.82	8	2	6	-	-	10		
1964	L.A.L	27.68	7	2	3	3	-	8		
1965	L.A.L	28.77	6	2	2	1	-	11		
1966	L.A.L	31.24	4	2	2	1	-	9		
1967	L.A.L	28.83	7	2	3	4	-	6		
1968	L.A.L	27.57	6	2	3	2	-	10		
1969	L.A.L	25.36	11	2	2	9	-	9		
1970	L.A.L	30.01	4	1	1	8	-	11		
1971	L.A.L	29.62	5	1	5	7	-	3		
1972	L.A.L	27.74	9	2	7	-	-	2		
1973	L.A.L	24.87	13	2	13	-	-	2		

PAUL WESTPHAL — USC

YR	TM	PR	OR	PS	SC	SH	RB	AS	BL	ST
1973	Bost	3.98		DNQ						
1974	Bost	7.09		DNQ						
1975	Bost	9.60	98	20	-	12	-	18	-	-
1976	Phoe	18.84	24	5	15	14	-	19	-	5
1977	Phoe	18.86	29	1	17	11	-	14	-	-
1978	Phoe	20.67	26	1	7	13	-	14	-	27
1979	Phoe	21.89	21	1	7	9	-	9	-	-
1980	Phoe	20.20	30	4	12	6	-	26	-	-
1981	Seat	13.58		DNQ						
1982	N.Y.	10.72		DNQ						
1983	N.Y.	10.60	119	22	-	-	-	13	-	-
1984	Phoe	6.42		DNQ						

JO JO WHITE — KANSAS

YR	TM	PR	OR	PS	SC	SH	RB	AS	BL	ST
1970	Bost	10.73	84	31	-	-	-	-		
1971	Bost	19.77	34	10	16	-	-	-		
1972	Bost	20.39	34	10	15	-	-	-		
1973	Bost	18.73	39	11	-	-	-	21		
1974	Bost	15.72	46	10	-	-	-	-		
1975	Bost	16.26	38	9	-	-	-	21		
1976	Bost	15.98	48	7	-	-	-	-		
1977	Bost	17.59	37	3	25	-	-	25		
1978	Bost	12.85		DNQ						
1979	G.St	11.11	117	21	-	-	-	-		
1980	G.St	9.58	138	23	-	-	-	-		
1981	K.C.	6.31		DNQ						

SIDNEY WICKS — UCLA

YR	TM	PR	OR	PS	SC	SH	RB	AS	BL	ST
1972	Port	25.23	17	5	12	-	-	-		
1973	Port	26.83	8	2	9	-	-	-		
1974	Port	22.40	11	2	13	-	-	-		
1975	Port	24.02	8	2	13	-	-	21	-	
1976	Port	19.20	22	4	23	-	-	-		
1977	Bost	17.44	39	6	-	-	17	-	-	-
1978	Bost	14.91	65	12	-	-	-	-		
1979	S.D.	9.94	132	19	-	-	-	-		
1980	S.D.	10.30	131	28	-	-	-	-		
1981	S.D.	8.39		DNQ						

MITCHELL WIGGINS — FLORIDA ST.

YR	TM	PR	OR	PS	SC	SH	RB	AS	BL	ST
1984	Chic	11.54	123	25	-	-	-	-	-	26
1985	Hous	8.83	147	31	-	-	-	-	-	22
1986	Hous	6.33		DNQ						

LENNY WILKENS — PROVIDENCE

YR	TM	PR	OR	PS	SC	SH	RB	AS	BL	ST
1961	St.L	11.88	38	15	-	-	-	-		
1962	St.L	18.05		DNQ						
1963	St.L	14.32	31	10	-	-	-	7		
1964	St.L	13.63	34	10	-	-	-	7		
1965	St.L	16.97	21	6	-	-	-	6		
1966	St.L	19.45	16	6	-	-	-	8		
1967	St.L	19.19	22	5	-	-	-	11		
1968	St.L	23.05	12	3	-	-	-	4		
1969	Seat	24.87	12	3	14	-	-	7		
1970	Seat	22.12	19	6	-	-	-	2		
1971	Seat	22.66	22	6	-	-	-	2		
1972	Seat	23.17	20	5	-	-	-	1		
1973	Clev	23.03	20	5	20	-	-	3		
1974	Clev	17.55	32	6	-	-	-	3	-	
1975	Port	8.12		DNQ						

BOB WILKERSON — INDIANA

YR	TM	PR	OR	PS	SC	SH	RB	AS	BL	ST
1977	Seat	6.47	148	33	-	-	-	-		
1978	Denv	13.33	86	18	-	-	-	23	-	-
1979	Denv	12.81	95	25	-	-	-	-		
1980	Denv	11.51	117	28	-	-	-	-		
1981	Chic	11.14	126	21	-	-	-	-		
1982	Clev	11.49	111	17	-	-	-	-	-	23
1983	Clev	7.08	155	33	-	-	-	-		

JAMAAL WILKES — UCLA

YR	TM	PR	OR	PS	SC	SH	RB	AS	BL	ST
1975	G.St	15.09	48	12	-	-	-	-	-	
1976	G.St	17.98	32	6	-	-	-	-	-	
1977	G.St	18.43	33	11	-	-	-	-	-	
1978	LA.L	16.06	57	15	-	-	-	-	-	
1979	LA.L	19.40	37	10	-	-	-	-	-	
1980	LA.L	21.24	22	7	22	12	-	-	-	
1981	LA.L	20.37	18	6	11	30	-	-	-	
1982	LA.L	17.76	42	14	16	-	-	-	-	
1983	LA.L	16.96	52	16	29	25	-	-	-	
1984	LA.L	16.52	62	19	-	-	-	.	-	
1985	LA.L	6.50	DNQ							
1986	LA.C	5.23	DNQ							

GUS WILLIAMS — USC

YR	TM	PR	OR	PS	SC	SH	RB	AS	BL	ST
1976	G.St	10.10	91	18	-	-	-	22	-	2
1977	G.St	10.41	113	20	-	-	-	20	-	17
1978	Seat	15.62	59	6	-	-	-	-	-	5
1979	Seat	17.33	49	5	29	-	-	-	-	7
1980	Seat	20.26	29	3	11	-	-	-	-	8
1981	DID NOT PLAY									
1982	Seat	21.80	17	2	7	-	-	19	-	15
1983	Seat	20.12	28	3	25	-	-	9	-	8
1984	Seat	19.39	37	5	-	-	-	10	-	8
1985	Wash	18.20	47	6	29	-	-	20	-	15
1986	Wash	12.69	106	19	-	-	-	23	-	
1987	Atla	5.42	DNQ							

NATE WILLIAMS — UTAH STATE

YR	TM	PR	OR	PS	SC	SH	RB	AS	BL	ST
1972	Cinc	11.28	86	35	-	-	-	-	-	
1973	K.C.	11.54	83	31	-	-	-	-		
1974	K.C.	13.16	68	12	-	-	-	-	-	11
1975	N.O.	11.86	77	17	-	-	-	-	-	23
1976	N.O.	11.11	84	16	-	-	-	-	-	15
1977	N.O.	9.62	125	25	-	-	-	-	-	
1978	G.St	7.93	DNQ							
1979	G.St	7.49	DNQ							

RAY WILLIAMS — MINNESOTA

YR	TM	PR	OR	PS	SC	SH	RB	AS	BL	ST
1978	N.Y.	9.43	140	26	-	-	-	4	-	7
1979	N.Y.	16.42	64	9	-	-	-	7	-	18
1980	N.Y.	21.78	19	2	19	-	-	15	-	10
1981	N.Y.	19.13	29	4	20	-	-	32	-	9
1982	N.J.	19.72	27	3	19	-	-	22	-	3
1983	K.C.	15.14	74	14	-	-	-	4	-	20
1984	N.Y.	16.22	66	9	-	-	-	20	-	4
1985	Bost	7.88	DNQ							
1986	N.J.	8.34		DNQ						
1987	N.J.	11.28		DNQ						

JOHN WILLIAMSON — N. MEX. ST.

YR	TM	PR	OR	PS	SC	SH	RB	AS	BL	ST
1974	ABA	13.40	39	15	-	-	-	-	-	
1975	ABA	10.53	58	20	-	-	-	-	-	
1976	ABA	12.26	39	14	-	-	-	-	-	
1977	Indi	14.00	65	13	18	-	-	-	-	
1978	N.J.	14.77	67	10	2	-	-	-	-	
1979	N.J.	15.76	70	9	15	-	-	-	-	
1980	Wash	9.53	139	27	-	-	-	-	-	
1981	Wash	2.22	DNQ							

BRIAN WINTERS — S. CAROLINA

YR	TM	PR	OR	PS	SC	SH	RB	AS	BL	ST
1975	LA.L	9.06	100	19	-	-	-	-	-	
1976	Milw	15.37	49	9	-	-	-	-	-	
1977	Milw	16.67	43	8	26	25	-	-	-	
1978	Milw	16.52	53	8	23	-	-	-	-	--
1979	Milw	16.03	69	8	28	-	-	-	-	
1980	Milw	15.11	71	12	-	-	-	-	-	
1981	Milw	10.55	130	26	-	-	-	-	-	
1982	Milw	14.80	72	11	-	32	-	-	-	
1983	Milw	8.68	140	25	-	-	-	-	-	

GEORGE YARDLEY — STANFORD

YR	TM	PR	OR	PS	SC	SH	RB	AS	BL	ST
1954	Ft.W	11.56	27	10	-	7	13	-		
1955	Ft.W	19.07	11	6	11	8	-	-		
1956	Ft.W	18.56	11	6	9	-	-	-		
1957	Ft.W	21.69	8	5	5	8	-	-		
1958	Detr	24.47	5	3	1	10	-	-		
1959	Syra	16.70	18	11	10	10	-	-		
1960	Syra	19.58	16	10	-	7	-	-		

MAX ZASLOFSKY — ST. JOHN'S

YR	TM	PR	OR	PS	SC	SH	RB	AS	BL	ST
1947	Chic	20.60			3						
1948	Chic	21.00			2						
1949	Chic	14.40			5						
1950	Chic	11.18	32	9	4	-					
1951	N.Y.	8.80	44	14	-	-	-				
1952	N.Y.	8.36	54	18	14	-	-				
1953	N.Y.	8.03	DNQ								
1954	Ft.W	8.38	45	18	-	-	-	-			
1955	Ft.W	7.46	54	20	-	-	-				
1956	Ft.W	7.00	DNQ								

INDEX

On the following 7 pages are all the players, coaches, general managers, and owners listed in the book. References in Chapter 7 (Seasonal Summaries) are not shown. Any player who is listed in Chapter 7 can be found by checking his career capsule (Chapter 8).

TO ORDER ANY OF THE FOLLOWING, SEND CHECK OR MONEY ORDER OR VISA OR MC NUMBER TO:

FACTS PUBLISHING CO.
P.O. Box 47025
Topeka, KS 66647

1987-88 Martin Manley's Basketball Heaven

$9.95 + $2.00 Shipping & Handling

- What publications have the best record for predicting finishes?
- What universities and conferences produce the most NBA players?
- What player breaks the 10 second free throw rule 93.3% of the time?
- What players have the most affect on their team's chances of winning?
- Statistical stategies for game ending situations.

1988-89 Martin Manley's Basketball Heaven

$12.95 + $3.00 Shipping & Handling

- The most amazing coincidences in NBA history.
- Settling the argument whether the officials give the best players the breaks.
- What teams have the best home court advantage and why?
- Who are the most overpaid and underpaid NBA players?
- What effect does luck of schedule have on total wins?

1990 NBA MIDSEASON REPORT

$4.25 + .50 Shipping & Handling

- Examining the top players by all categories in the 1st half.
- Look at who got snubbed in the all-star voting.
- Power ratings of all NBA teams
- Projected second half finishes
- Interesting facts and figures

Allow 2 weeks for delivery.